The Government and Politics of the Middle East and North Africa

Other Titles of Interest

About the Book and Editors

The Government and Politics
of the Middle East
and North Africa
edited by David E. Long and Bernard Reich

Up-to-date, and unique in its scope, this textbook meets the increasing need for a comprehensive introduction to the politics—and especially the political dynamics—of the states of the Middle East and North Africa. Written by specialists from both academic and policy circles, the book reflects the latest developments in the Middle East; yet, by focusing on the inherent features of each political system and the factors that influence them—e.g., political and cultural heritage, social attitudes, and economic constraints—the authors ensure that the progression of events will not quickly date the book. Multiple authorship has the advantage of great depth and expertise for each of the countries, and, while each chapter follows a common outline, its approach reflects the individuality of the particular political system covered.

David E. Long is a senior analyst in the Office of Research for the Near East and South Asia, U.S. Department of State. He was formerly executive director of the Center for Contemporary Arab Studies at Georgetown University. Bernard Reich is professor of political science and international affairs and chairman of the Department of Political Science at George Washington University.

Northern Africa and the Middle East

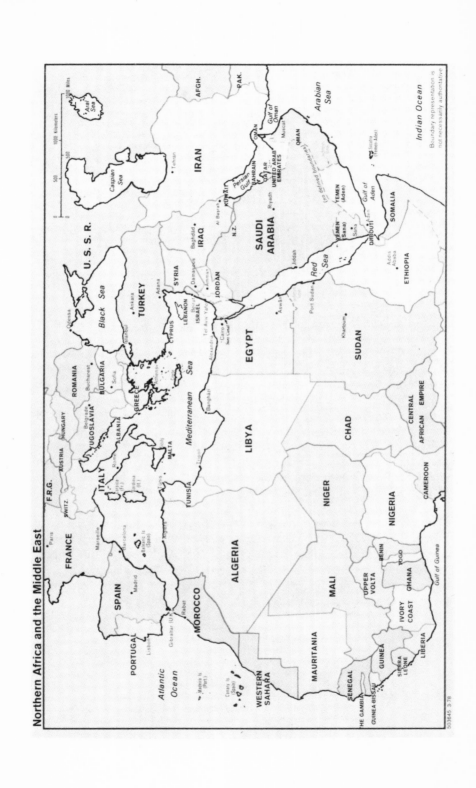

503645 3-78

The Government
and Politics
of the
Middle East
and North Africa

**edited by David E. Long
and Bernard Reich**

Westview Press • Boulder, Colorado

All rights reserved. No part of this publication may be reproduced or transmitted in any form or by any means, electronic or mechanical, including photocopy, recording, or any information storage and retrieval system, without permission in writing from the publisher.

Copyright © 1980 by Westview Press, Inc.

Published in 1980 in the United States of America by
  Westview Press, Inc.
  5500 Central Avenue
  Boulder, Colorado 80301
  Frederick A. Praeger, Publisher

Library of Congress Cataloging in Publication Data
Main entry under title:
The government and politics of the Middle East and North Africa.
  Bibliography: p.
  Includes index.
  1. Near East—Politics and government. 2. Africa, North—Politics and government.
  I. Long, David E. II. Reich, Bernard.
DS62.8.G68   320.956   79-25373
ISBN 0-89158-593-1
ISBN 0-89158-871-X pbk.

Printed and bound in the United States of America

Contents

Illustrations

Preface

In recent years considerable attention has been devoted to the Middle East by people in all walks of life, from the layman to the student to the policymaker. Writing about the region has continued to grow in quantum leaps. Books and articles by serious scholars exist in large number and cover many aspects of the region, especially its history, politics, and economics. Many have been fascinated by what they see as a newly discovered region of the world. Student interest has also increased. Despite this interest and the large number of specialized works on the area, no introductory work on the politics of the states of the region that is both comprehensive and up-to-date exists for the general student. It was with this in mind that the editors sought the assistance of a diverse group of Middle East specialists with academic and policy-oriented experience to produce a current, comprehensive, and general book that focuses on the politics (and especially political dynamics) of the region known as the Middle East. To ensure its comprehensiveness, we have included the states of Arab North Africa. Multiple authorship has the advantage of providing greater depth of expertise on the individual countries and political systems than can be provided by a single author. Although all authors have followed a common outline, each chapter differs according to the peculiarities of the particular political system being examined and the approach of the author.

The preparation of a book of this type requires the cooperation and assistance of many people, including, of course, each of the authors listed. In addition, the editors wish to acknowledge the assistance of all those without whom the work would not have been seen in print. Brian Flora, Callie Gass, and Sally Ann Baynard have been particularly helpful. Our wives, Barbara and Madelyn, ensured completion of the work.

Washington, D.C.

David E. Long
Bernard Reich

Contributors

John Duke Anthony is associate professor of Middle East Studies at the Johns Hopkins University School of Advanced International Studies. His publications include *The Middle East: Oil, Politics and Development; The Sultanate of Oman and the Emirates of Eastern Arabia;* and *Arab States of the Lower Gulf: People, Politics, and Petroleum.*

M. Graeme Bannerman is a professional staff member of the U.S. Senate Foreign Relations Committee with responsibility for the Near East. He has taught at the American University of Beirut, Georgetown University, and George Washington University.

John P. Entelis is professor of political science and director of the graduate program in international political economy and development at Fordham University. His publications include *Pluralism and Party Transformation in Lebanon* (1974) and *Comparative Politics of North Africa: Algeria, Morocco and Tunisia* (1980).

George S. Harris is director of the Office of Research and Analysis for the Near East and South Asia in the Bureau of Intelligence and Research in the Department of State. He has taught at the School of Advanced International Studies of Johns Hopkins University and at George Washington University. Among his publications are *The Origins of Communism in Turkey* (1967) and *Troubled Alliance: Turkish-American Problems in Historical Perspective, 1945–1971* (1972).

John A. Hearty is a Ph.D. candidate in the Department of Political Science at George Washington University, where he specializes in the politics of the Middle East. He was a Peace Corps volunteer in Tunisia.

David E. Long is a senior analyst in the Office of Research for the Near East and South Asia, U.S. Department of State. Among his publications are *Saudi Arabia* (1976) and *The Hajj Today: A Survey of the Contemporary Makkah Pilgrimage* (1979).

David McClintock is a career Foreign Service officer presently serving as food and agriculture adviser in the Bureau of Oceans and International Environmental and Scientific Affairs. He has served in Yemen and Jordan and was director of political training at the Foreign Service Institute. He is author of *U.S. Food: Making the Most of a Global Resource* (1978).

Bernard Reich is professor of political science and international affairs and chairman of the Department of Political Science at George Washington University in Washington, D.C., and a consultant to the Department of State on Middle Eastern affairs. Among his publications is *Quest For Peace: United States–Israel Relations and the Arab-Israeli Conflict (1977)*.

1

Introduction

David E. Long
Bernard Reich

For centuries the Middle East has fascinated scholars and observers and has been the focal point of great-power attention. The region's strategic significance and the variety and importance of its political, social, and cultural heritage have generated this concern. Through the years the Middle East has had intense religious meaning for the peoples of the Western world. Judaism, Christianity, and Islam all originated in the area and the most sacred holy places of these three monotheistic faiths are located there. In the mid-twentieth century occasional wars and superpower rivalry have added to the region's strategic dimension. The overall importance of the region, however, is broader and is tied to its location and to its primary resource—oil.

Situated at the hub of Europe, Asia, and Africa, the Middle East is a crossroads and a bridge. Historically it linked the trade routes connecting Europe with Asia and Africa. Today its location makes the Middle East a critical link in the communications network joining Western and Eastern Europe with Eastern Africa, the Indian subcontinent, Southeast Asia, the Far East, and Australasia. The Middle East's military importance is a direct result of its location and has long fascinated the powers interested in greater control of that portion of the world and the adjacent areas.

Oil is the major resource of the Middle East. Middle Eastern oil is abundant, is of unusually high quality, and is exported in huge quantity. It is an essential energy source for the industrialized West and for many of the developing states. The export and sale of Middle Eastern oil, at high prices, has generated a surplus of "petro-dollars" in many of the oil-producing states, has contributed to area-wide economic growth, and has provided the leading producers with increased potential in the international financial community. The importance of Middle Eastern oil and the oil-producing countries' economic potential have combined to in-

crease the concern shown for the Middle East by outside commercial and
strategic-political interests.

This interest in the Middle East seems unlikely to abate. The ongoing
and intensified efforts to achieve a settlement of the Arab-Israeli conflict
continue to involve the superpowers in the Middle East. Further, it seems
likely that the dependence of both the industrializing and the industrialized world on Middle Eastern oil will persist for the foreseeable future.

The states of the Middle East have a variety of political systems that
reflect their differing historical backgrounds, colonial experiences, social
and economic conditions, religions, geographical settings, climate, and
population pressures. There is no single category that can include all of
these systems. They run the gamut of alternative political structures and
dynamics. Personalized one-man authoritarian regimes coexist with
Marxist regimes, monarchies, and democratic regimes. However, the
Middle Eastern governments perform the various functions of the standard political system, albeit with varying degrees of ability or success
and in numerous and diverse ways. These differences in background and
in existing conditions provide for variations in political life, structure,
and style.

The very real differences that exist among the states of the Middle East
should not obscure the similarities, such as the heritage of Islam, the
presence of foreign influences, and the concentration of leadership in the
urban upper and middle classes and the rise of new elites of technocrats
and military officers that link them. Throughout the Middle East,
political life in the past few decades has been characterized by the shift
from traditional to modern activity. The traditional elite of kings and
landowners is either declining in power or has already been replaced in
most of the political units in the area. A new salaried middle class is
emerging as the most active political, social, and economic force, and
leadership is increasingly passing into their hands. This group of salaried
civilian politicians, organizers, administrators, and experts is supplemented by growing numbers of secondary and university students and
by the military. In many of the states the military forms the core of this
new politically conscious middle class striving to modernize the state.
They have assumed this role as a result of their training, skills, and moti-
vation. The great majority of the population—the peasants and the
workers—are only now beginning to enter the realm of politics.

Pan-Arabism and the Islamic revival are integral parts of contemporary activity in the Middle East. In a sense they are complementary
movements that have rekindled an Arab and Muslim identity among the
diverse peoples of the area. This in turn has affected both the foreign and
domestic policies of the Middle Eastern states. In the postwar era, for in-

stance, pan-Arabism has helped to determine the Arab response to Israel and it has led to attempts at federation and economic cooperation among several of the Arab states. The Islamic heritage and revival have acted simultaneously as a revolutionary and a conservative force. In such countries as Saudi Arabia it has helped to shape the response to modernization and Westernization by advocating an Islamic way of life in the face of change. At the same time, Islam has been a divisive force as differences between and among the various sects and traditions surface and intrude into politics.

This book has been planned in keeping with this general view of the Middle East. The authors intend to provide not only a comprehensive discussion of the politics of each of the states, within the context of each system's unique characteristics, but also to provide a view of the basic factors affecting politics so that comparisons across national boundaries can be made. The book reflects our view that certain commonalities exist in Middle Eastern political systems that can provide a basis for the comparison of their politics.

Understanding the politics of the Middle East requires more than an examination of the institutions of government. It is particularly important that the student of the Middle East understand the context in which politics is played. Accordingly, this book examines the political systems in terms of their approach to the problems confronting them. The machinery of government is examined not only in terms of what it is, but also in terms of why it is the way it is; why and how it works; and what it has done, or attempted to do, in confronting the state's problems.

Consideration of the legislative, executive, and judicial machinery of politics is thus complemented by study of the elements that affect the actual translation of goals and policy into action. To convey the full flavor of each individual system and its operation the authors have examined several components of each system, such as its historical setting, its available resources, its economic and social structure, and its ideologies, as well as the more traditional topics such as political parties, and/or other instruments of mobilization elites, and leadership. While these elements operate in each of the systems, they do so with differing results. Thus the factors are considered differently in each of the studies in this book. This, in itself, provides a useful means of comparison of systems and can be illuminating.

Obviously, detailed investigation of all of the influences on the politics of any country requires more space than can be allotted in one volume. Therefore, the authors have isolated the most important elements for examination and discussion. This system concept is reflected in the structure of each of the studies. Each country is examined in terms of its

- historical background
- political environment
- political structure
- political dynamics
- foreign policy

Historical Background

The Middle Eastern sense of history is strong and comprehension of the political systems of the region is almost impossible without an understanding of the historical background of each of the states. Tangible evidence of ancient systems can be found not only in archaeological ruins, but also in functioning political systems. The origins of contemporary problems often can be traced back to the ancient civilizations that developed in the region. Throughout the region, history tends to be of such importance that there is little attempt to divorce contemporary developments from historical events and there is little sense of time to suggest that they should be separated. Thus the origins of Judaism, Christianity, and Islam provide a working context for twentieth-century politics. Specific historic events, such as the Jewish exodus from Egypt and the subsequent establishment of a Jewish state, the Ottoman Turkish conquests, and European colonization and domination continue to affect the political systems of the Middle East in profound ways.

The style of politics often emulates or responds to ancient methods and conflicts. In many of the countries, centuries of history have helped to determine the roles of the elites and the masses and the present-day interaction between them. The form and style of decision making is also the result of historical development as well as of the modern demands placed upon the system. Nowhere is this more apparent than in the continued importance of the kinship group in the decision-making process. Ancient rivalries and boundary disputes still affect the relations among the states of the region. In the Middle East the past tends to provide the parameters for the systems operating today.

Political Environment

Despite its crucial role in developing an understanding of the modern Middle East, history alone cannot completely explain modern politics. Geography, demography, climate, and economics have all contributed to the emergence of the Middle East as we know it. The individual environment of each state provides a further understanding of the special and unique forces operating in it. Environment can help to explain the diversity of politics that exists in the face of shared historical background. The geopolitical uniqueness of the region and of its component states is essential in any explanation of political behavior. Geography partially determines the wealth or poverty of a nation and indicates its potential for development. It can point to a nation's strategic value and to the problems it may face. Such problems, and the means and the methods used to deal with them, provide much of the substance of modern politics and policy.

Demography too must be considered. Wars, famines, and religious and national upheaval have led to large-scale immigration and migration throughout the region. These migrations have left many of the states with substantial ethnic minorities as well as with chronic problems of overpopulation or underpopulation. Regional, national, and religious minorities abound. In most areas these minorities have been relegated to second-class status, but in some they have become the ruling elite. In either case, the social structure that determines the weight and merit of minority groups as well as the problems that result from over- or underpopulation can tell us much about the nature of politics.

Economics also plays a key role in determining the political environment of the Middle East. All of the states are undergoing some form of economic and social development and the governments are very much involved in the process by which such development will be achieved. Here too, however, there is diversity, for the states of the Middle East range from some of the wealthiest in the world to some of the poorest. Oil is a prime factor in explaining this disparity, but other conditions are involved. The population size, education, the human resource endowment, and the state's ability to mobilize modernization all affect the context in which policy is made. The different states have adopted different methods to meet the challenge presented by economic and social development. These methods reflect their own economic needs, resources, and capabilities.

Political Structure

The description and analysis of the formal governmental institutions, their powers, and their decision-making processes traditionally have been the initial step in the study of a state's politics. The Middle East is characterized by a wide range of diverse political institutions—some of which have no match anywhere in the world.

The systems of the Middle East can be examined in terms of the presence, or absence, of such political institutions as constitutions, political parties, judicial systems, and modern bureaucracies. Examination of these institutions helps to provide some insight into the decision-making process and to identify both the decision makers themselves and the locus of power within the system. This, in turn, provides a framework for making comparisons between and among the states of the region. It should also provide the ability to assess the differences and similarities between the systems and to understand the nature, extent, and direction of political development and modernization.

Political Dynamics

Identifying the institutions of politics and the constitutional methods, if any, by which they are supposed to work provides only a partial picture of a political system. In any state there is a dichotomy between theory and practice. The methods by which a state really operates and the interaction between and among its institutions can only be appreciated through an assessment of its political dynamics. Essentially this is an attempt to view the government in action. To the Western student (especially the American) who resides in a country where political systems operate relatively openly and in an orderly and systematic fashion, the complexities of the more closed systems and the Byzantine methods of the Middle Eastern systems may seem unduly complicated. These Middle Eastern systems have their own dynamic conditioned by history and environment. To know only the institutions of government, without understanding the political dynamics involved, is to know only how the system ought to work—not how the system works. The examination of the dynamics of Middle Eastern politics must be undertaken with the particular viewpoint of the Middle East in mind, if the student is to understand Middle Eastern politics.

Foreign Policy

To help the reader understand the interaction of the history, environment, structure, and dynamics in the states, each study concludes with an examination of the foreign policy of that state. Examination of the totality of international relationships for each state is impossible, but the main directions of that policy are looked at in order to develop a picture of both the concept of politics at work in each system and of the methods of operation. These overviews of foreign policy provide insight into the decision-making process and into the views of the decision makers. Foreign policy thus acts as something of a summary of state concerns, capabilities, and actions, as well as of the processes by which politics is played within the political system.

Ultimately, this multifaceted examination of the more than twenty independent states of the Middle East and North Africa reveals a good deal not only about the politics of the individual states but also about the region as a whole and about Third World developing states in general. Because of their diversity and the wide range of patterns and approaches they represent, the states of the Middle East provide a useful case study of the examination of politics in Third World states. By examining the basic factors affecting politics, the organization of the political system, and its dynamics and foreign policy, we will ultimately come to understand more about the complex and important part of the world known as the **Middle East.**

2

The Land and People
of the Middle East

David E. Long

The Land

One of the most difficult tasks in studying the Middle East is to agree upon the lands that it comprises. In some respects, it is like defining a mirage. From a distance, the region appears as a coherent whole, but the closer one approaches, the faster it disappears. One difficulty is that no single demographic factor is uniformly applicable throughout the area. For example, the single most unifying factor is the cultural heritage of Islam. Yet the Islamic world extends far beyond the Middle East, from the Far East to sub-Saharan Africa; and there are also a number of very important non-Muslim groups in the Middle East.

The Middle East is often equated with the Arab world, but to do so excludes other important ethnic groups, such as the Turks, Persians, Jews, Kurds, Berbers, Nubians, and Armenians. On the other hand, Arabic-speaking Mauritanians are more often included in studies of sub-Saharan Africa than in those of the Arab states to the north.

Even history is not always the best guide. The term Middle East was coined at the turn of the century to refer to the Persian Gulf area lying between the Near East and the Far East.[1] Since then, it has come to incorporate the older term, Near East, and North Africa as well. Politics have led to the inclusion and exclusion of various countries over time. For example, in the nineteenth century, the Balkan countries were regarded as a part of what is now known as the Middle East, whereas today they are studied as a part of Eastern Europe. Few people unfamiliar with Middle Eastern history realize that the founder of the Egyptian monarchy overthrown by Colonel Nasser was an Albanian, and that Albania as well as other Balkan states have significant Muslim populations.

One way to define the Middle East is to begin with those countries that are virtually always considered to be within the region, and then move outward to those on the periphery. Egypt, Israel, the Arab states of the Fertile Crescent, the Arabian peninsula, and Turkey thus comprise the core area. The rest of North Africa, particularly the Maghrib (Tunisia, Algeria, and Morocco), is sometimes considered separately, and the Sudan is often grouped with sub-Saharan Africa. Because of their close Arab ties, however, we have chosen to include them in this study. Likewise, Iran is also sometimes grouped with Afghanistan and Pakistan as an extension of South Asia, but its location on the Persian Gulf and its identity as a major Middle East oil producer dictate its inclusion.

Several countries that could have been included were not. Mauritania, which has been accepted into the Arab League, is one. With Arab politics overlapping into the Horn of Africa, Somalia (which was also accepted into the Arab League) and Ethiopia have some claim to inclusion. By the same token, Greece, because of its relations with Turkey, could have been considered, as could Afghanistan (which came under the original Middle East designation) and Pakistan. While realizing that our choice of countries is somewhat arbitrary, we feel that it best represents the broadest group of countries that still contain sufficient commonality to comprise a single region.

Topography

The topography of such a vast area is diverse and complex. Physically, the Middle East can be described as a large, generally arid area dissected by several large inland seas that radiate from the center like spokes in a wheel: the Mediterranean, Red, Black, and Caspian seas and the Persian (Arabian) Gulf. The northern reaches of the Indian Ocean, including the Arabian Sea, the Gulf of Oman, and the Gulf of Aden may also be added.

The land itself is further divided by large sand "seas" and mountain ranges. The mountains of the Middle East are geologically young and tend to be rocky, jagged, and difficult to traverse. In the Maghrib countries, the Atlas Mountains, reaching 4,000 m (13,000 ft.), form a barrier between fertile coastal areas and the Sahara to the south. Further east, the Sahara extends all the way to the coast except in eastern Libya where the highlands of Jabal al-Akhdar, which jut out into the Mediterranean at the tip of Cyrenaica, bring some moisture into the area.

The Sahara, which in Arabic means desert, stretches from the Red Sea Hills to the Atlantic in a belt that extends nearly 2,500 km (1,500 mi.) south into Africa. This expanse is broken up into great sand "seas" such as the Nubian desert of Egypt and Sudan, the Libyan desert, and the Great Eastern and Western Ergs of Algeria. Interspersed through the area are high massifs such as Jabal Marra in the Sudan (3,000 m or 9,800 ft.),

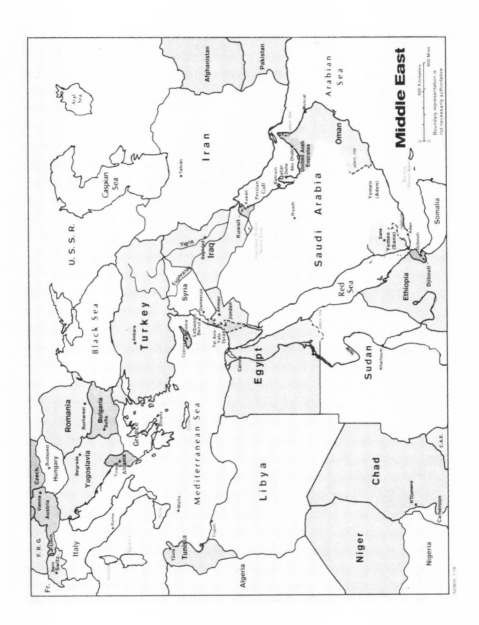

Middle East

the Tibesti-Toda region of Chad and Libya (2,500 m or 8,200 ft.), and the Ahaggar (Hoggar) massif in Algeria (2,300 m or 7,500 ft.).

In the north, mountain ranges stretch in a line eastward to the Himalayas. In Turkey, the Pontus Mountains, which rise along the Black Sea in the north, and the Tarus Mountains, which begin on the Mediterranean coast in the south, join near Mt. Ararat (5,165 m or 16,945 ft.) close to the Iranian border. From there the Elburz Mountains continue eastward across northern Iran, reaching their highest point at Mt. Demavand (el. 5600 m or 18,400 ft.) near Tehran.

Running roughly perpendicular to these mountains are several less imposing highland areas. Two of them flank both sides of the Great Rift Valley, a geological fault system that runs from Turkey through the Jordan Valley and the Red Sea before branching into the Indian Ocean and East Africa. In the north the Great Rift Valley divides the Lebanon Mountains from the Anti-Lebanon range, which rises to 3,000 m (9,800 ft.) at Mt. Hermon (Jabal al-Shaykh) on the Syrian-Lebanese border.

Further south on the African side of the Red Sea, the Red Sea Hills stretch southward from Egypt, rising abruptly as they reach the Ethiopian highlands to peaks over 4,000 m (13,000 ft.). On the Arabian side, the Hijaz Mountains also gain in altitude as they extend southward to the Asir Mountains and finally to the Yemen highlands where altitudes reach 3,700 m (12,000 ft.). From the Yemen the mountains curve back to the northeast along the south Arabian coast. They gradually lose altitude except for the Qara Mountains of western Oman, which reach 1,500 m (5,000 ft.). In easternmost Arabia the Hajar Mountains separate the coastal area of Oman from the interior. The highest elevation, Jabal al-Akhdar (Green Mountain), exceeds 3,000 m (9,800 ft.).

Across the narrow Straits of Hormuz, the broad Zagros Mountains of Iran extend southeast from the Tarus and Elburz ranges, down the eastern shore of the Persian Gulf and eastward along the Gulf of Oman. The highest peak, Zard Khuh, is 4,500 m (14,800 ft.). Finally, on the eastern frontier of Iran, the less imposing eastern Iranian highlands branch southward from the Elburz to the Arabian Sea, where they connect with the Zagros.

Juxtaposed between these mountain ranges are a number of high plateaus and two major river systems. The high, arid central plateau of Iran is totally enclosed by the Zagros, the Elburz, and the eastern Iranian highlands. In its center are two huge, shallow saucerlike salt deserts that serve as drainage basins for the plateau. They are the Dasht-e-Kavir in the north and the Dasht-e-Lut in the south. In Turkey, the Tarus and Pontus mountains ring the high Anatolian plateau. Central Anatolia is less arid and better drained than Iran. While salt flats and dry lake beds do exist, several river systems cut through the northern mountains to the Black Sea. In a sense, nearly the entire continent of Africa can be considered a relatively high plateau area that drops abruptly as it nears the coast. Along the Mediterranean, this drop is much more gradual than elsewhere in the continent, particularly in the east where the Nile River gradually descends some 6,500 km (4,000 mi.) from the East African and Ethiopian highlands.

The Nile is one of the Middle East's two great river systems. As it leaves the swamps and grasslands of the Sudan, its banks are confined to a narrow valley that winds like a great serpent through the brown expanses of the Sahara. The second great river system is formed by the Tigris and Euphrates rivers, which meet about 150 km (95 mi.) north of the Persian Gulf to form the Shatt-al-Arab River. Their watershed extends southward from the Tarus Mountains of Turkey. The Tigris and Euphrates provided water for the development of ancient civilizations in the otherwise flat, arid Iraqi plain just as the Nile in Egypt.

Further south, central Arabia drops gradually toward the Persian Gulf from the western Arabian highlands. The area is bisected by occasional westward-facing escarpments such as Jabal Tuwaiq, which extends for some 1,000 km (620 mi.) in a shallow arc. Although arid, central Arabia contains several large, dry, river-drainage systems. Riyadh, the Saudi capital, is located along one of them, the Wadi Hanifa. There are also two great sand "seas" in Arabia, the Great Nafud in the north and the Rub'al-Khali in the south. They are connected by a narrow strip of sand dunes east of Riyadh known as the Dahna. Passing through the Dahna between Riyadh and the gulf coast, the traveler can envision the Rub'al-Khali where some of the great dunes reach over 2,000 m (6,600 ft.) in height.

Geology

For the layman, geology is a subject so technical that it generally seems best left alone. In the Middle East, the problem is compounded by the fact that the geology is particularly complex. At the same time, however, its geology is the primary source of interest in the contemporary Middle East and has made it a region of major political and economic importance to the rest of the world. For the same quirk of fate that produced vast deserts and steep barren mountain ranges also produced the world's richest oil reserves.

In the last dozen or so years, geologists have developed new theories of continental drift. Continental landmasses, according to these theories, rest on huge plates that slide over the denser material beneath the earth's crust. As the plates separate, they cause the seafloor to spread and create new seas. When plates collide, they create crush zones that cause mountain ranges to push up. The surface of one plate can also be dragged beneath that of another.[2]

During the Mesozoic period, the Afro-Arabian landmass began to drift northward. As it came in contact with a similar northern landmass, probably in the Tertiary period, a crush zone was created. This gave birth to a line of mountains that extends from the Alps to the Himalayas.

Along the leading edge of this Afro-Arabian landmass, a number of smaller plates were created. Three of these, the Aegean plate, an adjacent Turkish plate, and a central Iranian plate, have been the source of considerable earthquake activity in recent years. The three major plates in the Middle East are the African plate, the Eurasian plate, and the Arabian plate. Once part of the African landmass, the Arabian plate moved northeast and is now separated from Africa by the Red Sea. As the Arabian plate moved, it collided with the Iranian plate and created a crush zone. The leading edge of the Arabian plate was pushed downward under the Persian Gulf and the Zagros Mountains were thrust up on the other side. As a result of this collision, the rock strata in Arabia tilt downward from west to east. The pre-Cambrian or basement complex rock that is found on the surface in western Arabia is buried deep underground in the Persian Gulf. In eastern Arabia, the basement complex is covered over with younger sedimentary rock formed by the broad ancient sea that used to separate Arabia and Iran and of which only the Persian Gulf remains. As the Arabian plate was pushed down, marine matter from this ancient sea collected in pockets called domes or anticlines. These domes now constitute the gulf's oil and gas fields. Similarly in North Africa, older pre-Cambrian formations are found on the surface only on the Red Sea coast. Further west, newer sedimentary rock was formed by marine deposits in the large prehistoric sea between Africa and Europe. These deposits have become the source of African oil and gas.

Climate

One hears much about the Middle East as the crossroads of three continents: Africa, Europe, and Asia. It is no less a climatic crossroads, falling almost entirely into a transitional or subtropical zone between the tropics of sub-Saharan Africa and the temperate zone of Europe and Asia. One common characteristic of subtropical zones centering around 30 degrees latitude is aridity, whether on land or at sea.[3] Although the reasons for this are not entirely clear, aridity appears to be related to the prevailing wind systems.

The wind systems of the Middle East are characterized by prevailing westerly winds called cyclones, which are generated along the front of polar air, separating it from tropical air masses. These cyclone winds are the primary determinants of the weather conditions throughout the Middle East. In the summer they blow across the northern portions of the region so that scarcely any air movement occurs further south, and the hot, dry air masses of North Africa and Arabia prevail. The low pressure systems that develop during the summer months generate strong, hot local winds that scourge the entire region. For example, in southern Iraq, they are called the *shamal* ("north wind"), and in southeast Iran, the *sadou-bist* ("120-day wind"). Maximum temperatures can average 40°C in some places with absolute temperatures approaching 50°C. After sunset, temperatures can drop 30°C since the dry air does not retain heat. The effect on the body, however, is even more pronounced. I once saw a man shivering in an overcoat in Saudi Arabia at a mild 20°C. The temperature, however, had dropped from 45°C in less than three hours.

In the winter the cyclones move south, creating prevailing westerly winds from the Atlantic Ocean to Pakistan. Moist air from the North Atlantic is drawn into the region, bringing most of the rain that falls in the Middle East. Extremely cold, dry, polar air can also be drawn from Siberia into Anatolia and central Iran, causing temperatures to plummet below zero in mountain areas. Warm air from the Red Sea, the gulf, and the Indian Ocean can also be drawn northward, and as frontal systems pass eastward, strong, hot, desert winds are occasionally funnelled northwards. They are known as the *khamsin* ("50-day wind") in Egypt, the *ghibli* in Libya, the *shlur* in Syria and Lebanon, the *sharqi* in Iraq, and the *simun* in Iran.

As the winter westerlies travel eastward, they lose more and more moisture so that by the time they reach Arabia, Iraq, and Iran, the rains can be extremely fickle. Indeed, if the mountains of Iran were not high enough to capture the remaining moisture, most of Iran would be virtually uninhabitable. Average annual rainfall figures for this area can be deceiving as an indication of climate since torrential downpours do occur in the deserts, only to be followed by droughts of perhaps several years' duration.

This weather system does not reach the southernmost regions of Sudan eastward to southern Arabia. There the monsoons of the Indian Ocean govern the weather. The Qara Mountains of Dhufar province in Oman, and the Yemeni and Ethiopian highlands all receive rains in the summer from moisture-laden winds blowing up from the Indian Ocean. In Dhufar, the traveler is struck by the sight of coconut palms growing in place of the more common date palms of the Middle East since there is too much rain. In the Sudan, which also experiences cool winters, the summer monsoon winds bring moisture to the southern part of the country. By the time the monsoon winds reach Khartoum, however, most of the moisture is expended. Occasionally in the summer, these now-dry winds blow across central Sudan driving huge clouds of dust called *habubs* thousands of meters high.

In the winter the monsoons shift direction, blowing steadily southward. The cause of this semiannual cycle is not precisely known. It seems to be related to seasonal shifts in a westerly jet stream in the upper atmosphere that flows north of the Himalayas in summer and to the south of them in winter. Although as a weather determinant the monsoons are only peripherally important to the Middle East, they have had a major impact on society in the Persian Gulf and southern Arabia. For centuries Arab mariners have sailed their dhows southward to India and Africa on the winter monsoons and back home again on the summer monsoons. Thus, until recent politics intervened, people in this part of the world looked south and east as much as westward toward the more traditionally accepted "centers" of the Middle East.

The Peoples

The peoples of the Middle East are extremely heterogeneous, and, as a result of massive, oil-funded economic and social development, their societies are changing practically overnight. Yet despite heterogeneity and social change, Middle Eastern peoples are still predominantly traditional in outlook. Among the uneducated, this is fairly obvious. Among the sophisticated classes, however, traditional attitudes are often obscured behind a facade of Westernization and reappear only in times of great stress or crisis.

Social Organization

Race and Language. Contrary to popular belief, racial distinctions mean relatively little in the Middle East. In fact, what are often taken by outsiders to be major racial distinctions—as between Jews and Arabs, Turks and Persians—are not racial at all, but linguistic and cultural. Nevertheless, major racial differences do exist.

A number of racial types can be identified, none of which coincide exactly with any one country or subregion and all of which are found outside the Middle East as well. The most prevalent by far is the Mediterranean race, which originated within the region. Mediterranean types are found from the Atlantic to Afghanistan, and, as a darker-skinned and finer-boned variation, are the major racial element in the Indian subcontinent as well.

Mediterranean types vary in size and color. Though generally white, their skin color ranges from cream colored to olive. They are usually medium in height and build, but can also be quite tall. The hair is usually dark brown or black but can be red or even blond. Blondism is noted more frequently in the form of blue or green eyes than in skin or hair color, although brown eyes are more usual. Among the Berbers of North Africa, one can find blond, blue-eyed Nordic-looking types, while Circassians who emigrated south to Syria and Jordan could double for red-haired Scotsmen.

Mediterranean faces are generally long and their noses prominent, the stereotype being an Arab bedouin or a Jewish merchant. Arabs and Jews together possess the highest concentration of Mediterranean racial characteristics.

In Turkey and the Levant, people of a different racial stock can be observed. Dark, short and stocky with large chests and round heads, they have a tendency to baldness. These are Alpine types. A similar group, the Armenoids, are found in northern Iran and eastern Turkey. They generally have heavier body hair, very prominent wide or aquiline noses, and high foreheads.

Along the southern reaches of the Middle East, Negroid strains from sub-Saharan Africa are found. Finally, in eastern Iran, western Afghanistan and the adjacent Soviet Union, Mongoloid types can be observed—small, round-headed, and possessing folds of skin over their eyes that make them appear slanted. Ironically they no longer speak a Mongolian language but speak Persian. The Turks were originally Mongoloid but centuries of mixing with the larger indigenous population of Anatolia have all but obliterated these traits.

Language is far more important than race as a distinguishing characteristic. There are two major language groups in the Middle East, Semitic and Indo-European. Semites are those who now speak or who spoke in ancient times a Semitic language. Arabic and Hebrew both belong to this group.

Semitic languages are characterized by a triconsonantal root system. Typically, each word is identified by the placement of three consonants that form a root. Words with the same root tend to have similar or related meanings and different words are formed by adding vowels, suffixes, and prefixes around these root sounds. For example, the Arabic root, K-T-B, is found in *kitab* ("book"), *maktab* ("office"), *maktaba* ("library"), and *kaatib* ("secretary"). Over time, of course, many non-Semitic words have entered the vocabulary. Consider the consternation of a beginning Arabic student trying to find the triconsonantal root in "shurshyl" only to discover that it is the Arabic transliteration of "Churchill." In Israel, many three-letter acronyms have been transformed into Hebrew verbs and nouns, leaving the uninitiated with no idea of the meaning or the origin of the word.

Akkadian is the earliest known Semitic language. From it developed Babylonian and ancient Assyrian. (Assyrian is not to be confused with the language of contemporary Assyrians in Syria and Iraq who speak a dialect of Syriac.) These ancient languages, all dead, comprise the "eastern Semitic group."

The "western Semitic group" is more pertinent to the modern Middle East. It is generally divided into northern and southern subgroups. The northern subgroup includes ancient Canaanite, from which developed Phoenician, Aramaean, and Hebrew. Phoenician speakers, who may have originally come from the Persian Gulf, brought their maritime skills to present-day Lebanon. They also perfected the alphabet, begun earlier by the Canaanites who borrowed the idea of writing consonantal signs from the ancient Egyptians. As masters of the sea, the Phoenicians spread the concept throughout the ancient Middle East. Semitic script has usually been written right to left.

From Aramaean have come Aramaic and Syriac. The former was the prevalent language of the Levant during the time of Christ and is still spoken in a few isolated villages in Syria. Another derivative, Syriac, has been preserved as the liturgical language of several eastern churches and as so-called Assyrian, mentioned above.

Hebrew also survived as a ritual language of the Jewish faith. In recent years it has been revived as a modern living language in the state of Israel. Ironically, many a Jewish tourist in Israel has become frustrated when he cannot communicate in Yiddish, a Germanic language, to Sabras (native-born Israelis) who speak Hebrew.

The southern subgroup of western Semitic languages includes Arabic, ancient south Arabian and the closely related dialects of Ethiopia, just across the Red Sea. South Arabian dialects were spoken by ancient city states that reached their zenith during the Roman empire, growing rich in their monopoly over the supply of frankincense and myrrh. These spices, found only on the coasts of south Arabia and Somalia across the Gulf of Aden, were used to sweeten the smoke of Roman funeral pyres. The south Arabian languages are collectively called Sabean after one of the city states, Saba, thought to be the ancient Sheba of King Solomon's day. With Christianization and the decline of pagan Rome, demand for the spices declined, undercutting the economies of the city states. The final collapse of south Arabian civilization is generally dated at 450 B.C. when the famous dam at Ma'rib, in what is now the Yemen Arab Republic, broke for the second and last time, rendering irrigated agriculture no longer possible.

South Arabian languages survive on the Arabian side of the Red Sea only in isolated pockets, such as Socotra Island off South Yemen, and among the Qara and Mahra tribesmen in eastern South Yemen and western Oman. In Ethiopia, however, descendants of Sabean languages survive as Amharic, Tigre, and Tigrina. The historic link between Ethiopians and south Arabians via Sheba and the ancient Jewish kingdoms of the Yemen was the origin of the late Emperor Haile Selassie's title, "Lion of Judah."

The latest Semitic language and probably the most influential of all languages in the Middle East is Arabic. At the time of Muhammad, it was spoken in central Arabia between the Aramaic areas in the north and Sabean areas in the south. Arabic's principal political importance originated during the Muslim conquests when it was spread throughout the Middle East. Moreover, neighboring languages such as Turkish and Persian have borrowed heavily from Arabic vocabulary. In East Africa, Swahili originated as a trade or contact language using a largely Arabic-derived vocabulary on a Bantu grammatical base.

The importance of Arabic transcends politics. Even before the time of Muhammad, Arab tribes, while speaking different but mutually intelligible dialects, used a single literary language. The Arabic of the Quran, because of its holy inspiration, represents to this day the highest form of the literary language. Though understood by few, it is the holy language of hundreds of millions throughout the Muslim world.

Many changes have occurred to Arabic over the years since Muhammad. Spoken dialects have changed so greatly that Maghribi dialects and eastern Arabic dialects are no longer even mutually comprehensible. Pride of dialect is so great, however, that one can virtually guarantee a vociferous argument over which dialect is closest to classical Quranic Arabic. Since nearly all dialects have some elements closer to and others farther from the classical, there is no winning of this argument on literary merits alone.

Between classical Quranic and spoken dialects, a modern literary language that is universal to the entire Arab world has developed. Actually a simplified form of classical Arabic, it is not mutually intelligible with spoken dialects and is therefore known only to the educated classes. This is generally the language of the media as well as literature, since spoken dialects are considered too inferior to be used on such occasions. As a result the uneducated masses often do not understand what is being spoken or written in the media.

Arabic is also the major art form throughout much of the Middle East. For the nomadic people who originally developed the language, the spoken word was logically the primary means of artistic expression. Even the graphic arts were largely devoted to calligraphy—the Arabesque. Oratory and singing are also highly regarded. One of the highest compliments ever paid to Christian missionaries in the Arab world in the last century was for the Muslim community to attend services in order to rapture over the beauty of a gifted preacher's command of Arabic. When the Arab world's premier singer, an elderly grandmother named Umm Kalthum, died a few years ago, more people wept for her than for any Middle Eastern political figure in modern times.

Next to Semitic, Indo-European languages are probably the most important in the Middle East. This same group includes English and most of the European languages. The largest group of Indo-European speakers in the Middle East speak various dialects of Iranian. These include Persian and the closely related dialects of the Bakhhari and Lurs tribes of Iran; Kurdish, which is spoken by tribes living in the area where Iran, Iraq and Turkey meet; and Baluchi, the language of southeastern Iran and neighboring Afghanistan and Pakistan. Another Indo-European language of note in the Middle East is Armenian. Although the Armenians, originally situated along the Iranian–Soviet–Turkish frontier, have been scattered all over the world by political upheavals in their former homeland, they have striven to preserve their language and culture.

Two other language groups are also found in the Middle East. The Ural-Altaic group, which includes Mongolian, Siberian, and the Turkic or Altaic languages, as well as Finnish and Magyar (Uralic), is represented by several Turkic languages. By the seventh century, Turkic speakers had moved westward to the lands east of the Caspian Sea and soon thereafter were converted to Islam. One group, the Seljuk Turks, moved west into Anatolia and established the sultanate of Rum. The Mongol invasions of the thirteenth century put an end to this sultanate and it was superseded by a new sultanate of Ottoman Turks. Neither Seljuks nor Ottomans were ever in the majority in Anatolia, as evidenced by the virtual disappearance of Mongoloid racial features, but Turkish became the language of the entire area.

Farther east, there are also Turkic speaking tribes in Iran: the Azeris of Azerbaijan in the northwest, the Qashqa'is in the eastern Zagros, and Turkomen tribes in northeastern Iran who have kinship ties across the border in the Soviet Union.

Hamitic, another group of languages in the Middle East, is apparently of African origin. Within this group are ancient Egyptian, the Berber dialects of North Africa, and the Kushitic dialects of the Horn of Africa, including Somali Beja and others. Modern Coptic, the last surviving descendant of ancient Egyptian, is the liturgical language of the Coptic Christian church in Egypt and Ethiopia.

The Role of Religion: The Impact of Islam. Throughout history, religion has played an important, often crucial, role in politics. Yet nowhere has religious force had a stronger impact on the politics of an area than Islam has had on the Middle East. More than just a religion, Islam is an entire way of life, with no distinction made between the secular and the sacred.

The theological aspects of Islam are quite simple. They are embodied in the *shahada* ("profession of faith"): *la ilaha illa llah wa muhammadun rasula llah*, "there is no god but God and Muhammad is the messenger [prophet] of God." The word *Islam* itself refers to the total submission of the believer to God. The requirements of Islam are also simple, the five pillars of Islam. In addition to the profession of faith, they are prayer, alms giving, fasting during the Muslim lunar month of Ramadan, and the *hajj* or great pilgrimage to Mecca, to be made once in the lifetime of all believers physically and financially able to do so. *Jihad*, or "holy war," to defend the faith is sometimes considered a sixth pillar.

The many writings and treatises of Islamic scholars are more juridical than theological in nature, for Islam is in essence a system of jurisprudence. Muslims believe that God revealed himself to man in Judaism and Christianity as well as Islam. The followers of these faiths are called "people of the book." It may be noted that because Judaism is respected as a revealed religion, Arab Muslims invariably characterize Zionism, which they oppose, as a political rather than a religious doctrine.

For Muslims, God's final revelation of himself to man is embodied in Islam. The revelation was brought by God's messenger, Muhammad, in the form of holy law, called the *Shari'a*. The law is based on the Quran and the Sunna. The Quran is the revealed word of God expressed in the recorded preachings of Muhammad. The Sunna is a compendium of the "Traditions" (teachings and sayings) attributed to the Prophet. Each tradition is contained in a *hadith* ("short narrative"). Collectively they are called "the Hadith."

The Quran and the Hadith do not comprise a codified system of law, but are the sources of the law. These sources are applied to everyday problems through an elaborate system of analogy developed by early Muslim scholars and accepted by the consensus of the Muslim community. Where there was no consensus, individual interpretation was allowed. As consensus over the interpretation of the law increased through the years, however, individual interpretation was restricted and finally disallowed altogether by orthodox or Sunni Muslims. To this day, orthodox Islamic law is applied on the basis of interpretations and consensus formed prior to the ninth century.

Four major orthodox schools of jurisprudence were established, each generally recognized by the others. They are the Hanafi school, named after Abu Hanifa (d. 767); the Maliki school, founded by Malik ibn Anas (d. 795); the Shafi'i school, founded by al-Shafi'i (d. 820); and the Hanbali school, founded by Ahmad ibn Hanbal (d. 855). The Hanafi school was used in the courts of the Ottoman Empire and is prevalent in lower Egypt, India, and most orthodox Muslim areas in Asia outside Arabia. Malikis are found in North Africa, upper Egypt, and the Sudan. The Shafi'is are found in the lowland areas of the Yemen, South Yemen, and Indonesia; and the Hanbalis are found in Saudi Arabia and Qatar.

In addition to orthodox or Sunni Muslims, there are several groups of heterodox, or Shi'a Muslims. Most of the inhabitants of Iran as well as large numbers of Iraqis, Bahrainis, and Yemenis are Shi'ites. The Sunni-Shi'a schism first arose in a dispute over who would succeed the fourth caliph, Ali, and juridically there is little difference between the two. Over time, however, other differences developed. For example, a relatively greater element of mysticism crept into Shi'ism than into Sunni Islam. Shi'as believe that the views of an *imam* ("leader of the faithful") should predominate over the consensus of the Islamic community as a whole. A Shi'a imam, therefore, was the absolute authority on doctrine, unlike the Sunni caliph, who, while being the absolute political and religious leader, could not interpret or define dogma. Because Shi'as were not prohibited from individual interpretation of Islamic law, Shi'a scholars have continued to reinterpret the law in light of social and political changes over the years.

Three main groups of Shi'as have survived. The Imami sect, which is the state religion of Iran, is the largest and generally the most liberal. It is also found in Iraq, where it originated in the oases of the Persian Gulf, in Syria, and in southern Lebanon, where a branch, the Matawila, live. Imamis trace the line of imams from Ali, whom they consider the first, through twelve imams. The last, Muhammad al-Mahdi, disappeared around A.D. 873 and is expected to return at a propitious moment.

The Ismailis, a more radical sect, believe that the eldest rather than the second son of the sixth imam succeeded him, and that this son was the last "visible" imam. Ismailis under the leadership of the Agha Khan are found mainly in Pakistan, India, and Iran. There are a few Ismaili remnants of a once terrifying branch, the Assassins, who are now farmers in the hills of central Syria.

The third major group of Shi'as is comprised of the Zaydis of the highlands of the Yemen. They trace a separate line of succession from the fifth imam but do not believe that any successors are concealed or have supernatural powers. The last Zaydi imam to rule in the Yemen was the Imam Ahmad. Soon after his death, his son Badr was overthrown in a revolution in 1962.

An even earlier schism in Islam involved the Kharijites, who broke with the orthodox Muslim consensus that the leader (caliph) should be a descendant of the Prophet. They insisted that he be popularly elected by the community. The movement all but disappeared, but still survives in Oman, where a majority of the people are Ibadi Muslims, and also in southern Algeria.

In the twentieth century most Muslim states have incorporated Western legal codes. In order to maintain that they have not broken with the Shari'a, or Islamic law, they accomplished this transition through the use of legal distinctions within Islamic law itself. The Shari'a goes farther than distinguishing between right and wrong, employing instead a five-stage system. There are acts that are mandatory, recommended but not mandatory, forbidden, discouraged but not forbidden, and a last category concerning which the law is indifferent. It has been by placing Western legal codes in this last category that their adoption has been justified in legal reform throughout the Muslim world. Rather than calling them laws, however, since only God can make a law, they are generally called regulations.

In sum, Islam is essentially a system of legal norms for human behavior. Because Muslims believe that the law is of God, it is theoretically unchangeable. Moreover, since the prohibition of independent interpretation in the ninth century, orthodox Islam has become a closed system in which conformity with the teachings of the great classical jurists is required. Later scholars have been able merely to comment on the work of their predecessors.

Within this system, God's will as revealed in God's law inevitably determines whatever happens. This doctrine has enhanced if not created a highly developed sense of the inevitable, which is often referred to as Islamic fatalism. It is expressed in the widely heard Arabic phrase, *insha'allah*, or "God willing." Against God's will no man can prevail. This sense of the inevitability of life beyond man's will to change it pervades Middle Eastern culture in general, is shared by Muslim and non-Muslim alike, and is experienced even by those who no longer practice any religion.

The fixation on the omnipresence of divine will has enabled Middle Easterners to view events as separate exercises of God's will or fate, having little or no association with related events. This has made it relatively easy for them to hold more than one position on the same issue that Westerners might find too contradictory. It has also tended to keep problems over conflicting loyalties or interests to a minimum. For example, hostile political relations in the Middle East need not rule out good commercial relations, for the two are viewed quite separately.

There is also a tendency to view political and economic relationships in highly concrete, personalized terms rather than abstract or ideological terms. A conspiratorial explanation of events involving specific people, for example, is quite common, and the conduct of business or government is viewed more in terms of specific persons or interest groups than as a system or a process. Thus political parties and organizations, even those with highly developed ideologies, are usually little more than confederations of personal followings. Each contender for power within the party or organization tends to be in competition for leadership, and each party in competition with other parties for national leadership, winner take all. A classical example of personalized politics in the Middle East is the rapidity with which "Nasserism" died after the death of Nasser, for Nasserism amounted to little more than the ideological trappings of Arab nationalism.

There are other religions in the Middle East. In fact, probably every major schism of Christendom still extant is present there. Christianity, however, has not had the cultural impact that Islam has. So it was also with Judaism until the rise of Zionism and creation of Israel. Because Judaism as a cultural-political force is almost exclusively linked to Israel, discussions of Judaism will be deferred to the chapter on Israel itself.

Group Identification and Social Stratification. Middle Easterners, like peoples everywhere, profess multiple loyalties. Among their principal loyalties are the nuclear and extended family, clan and tribal affiliation, the professional group, the hometown or region, ethnic origin, religious confession, state nationalism, pan-Arabism, pan-Islam, identification with the developing countries, and, for some, the Organization of Petroleum Exporting Countries (OPEC). Of these, primary loyalty is to the extended family. Traditionally, it includes the father and mother, the sons and their families, and unmarried daughters. This unit is the glue that holds together Middle Eastern society.

Strife and tensions are often rife within the extended family but to outsiders it presents a unified front. Although its cohesion has been under assault by the forces of modernity, the extended family still has major influence on such basic decisions as choosing a spouse, a residence, or a career. On the other hand, certain benefits also accrue from membership in an extended family. For example, the strategic location of relatives can be vital to the success of a young businessman or bureaucrat.

The existence of compartmentalized multiple loyalties and intense personalization of behavior has tended to limit the degree of social and political institutional cohesion. Most of the major decision making in the Middle East takes place in small, informal groups. Membership in such a group, whether a revolutionary command council, a palace clique, or a group of businessmen, bureaucrats, or junior army officers, is usually based on similarity of interests. Called *shilla* in Egypt, *jama'* ("group") in Saudi Arabia, and *dowrah* ("circle") in Iran, these groups are quasi-social and totally unstructured. Typically, members of the group gather in the evenings to talk, play cards, and discuss the business of the day. A reflection of the favor-oriented Middle Eastern society, each member is expected to aid and support each other member as the need arises.

The impact of these perceptions, loyalties, and social attitudes on Middle East politics cannot be underestimated. At the same time, they are seldom consciously considered by the decision makers. Like politicians everywhere, Middle East political leaders are primarily searching for solutions to day-to-day operational problems. Their cultural heritage, however, serves as the filter through which all problems are viewed.

Notes

1. See Roderic H. Davison, "Where Is the Middle East," *Foreign Affairs*, vol. 38 (July 1960), pp. 665–675.
2. See Peter Beaumont, Gerald Blake, and J. Malcolm Wagstaff, *The Middle East: A Geographical Study* (New York: John Wiley and Sons, 1976), pp. 19ff.
3. Ibid., pp. 49ff.

Bibliography

Two articles have attempted to capture the elusive confines of the Middle East: Roderic H. Davison, "Where Is the Middle East," (*Foreign Affairs*, vol. 38, July 1960, pp. 665–675), and Nikki R. Keddie, "Is There a Middle East," (*International Journal of Middle East Studies*, vol. 4, 1973, pp. 255–271). For a longer work, Peter Beaumont, Gerald Blake, and J. Malcolm Wagstaff, *The Middle East: A Geographical Study* (New York: John Wiley and Sons, 1976), offer an excellent and comprehensive overview of the region's geography.

A number of social scientists have endeavored in recent years to identify the common traits and values of Middle Eastern peoples. Raphael Patai, *The Arab Mind* (New York: Charles Scribner and Sons, 1973); Sania Hamady, *Temperament and Character of the Arab* (New York: Twayne Publishers, 1960); and Morroe Berger, *The Arab World Today* (Garden City, New York: Doubleday and

Company, 1962), present interesting descriptions on how Arabs live, work, and think. Though dated, Carleton Coon's *Caravan: The Story of the Middle East* (New York: Henry Holt, 1951) is still a classic and is recommended to every beginning student.

Louise E. Sweet, ed., *Peoples and Cultures of the Middle East: An Anthropological Reader* (Garden City, New York: Natural History Press, 1970), focuses on urbanization, status of women, development of Islam, and the family. David Lerner, *The Passing of Traditional Society: Modernizing the Middle East* (London: Free Press, 1958), discusses the universal modernizing role of literacy and media, its development, and its relationship to the emergence of modern institutions.

3

Republic of Turkey

George S. Harris

Historical Background

Modern Turkey differs profoundly from most of the nations that have emerged in the past century. Its distinctive quality stems directly from the fact that it had long and deep roots in an imperial past as an independent state. Of cardinal significance, it inherited from its Ottoman forebears a highly developed system of institutions and traditions. To be sure, Turkey was only one of a number of countries that came into being in the lands once ruled by the Ottomans. But while all betrayed influences of the six centuries of Ottoman rule, Turkey alone embodied the continuation of both the empire's institutions and the ruling class that had run one of the most successful multiethnic and multireligious states in world history.

The Ottoman structure offered the fledgling state an experienced, functioning, and strong central administration. A flair for bureaucratic organization distinguished the Ottomans from the earliest days of their existence; this talent may have provided the critical edge over the other Turkish principalities that were vying to displace the Byzantine Empire in the fourteenth and fifteenth centuries. Organizational ability remained characteristic of the Ottomans, even though the state suffered from periods of misrule and insurrection. Indeed, the reorganizations of the nineteenth century (the so-called Tanzimat reforms) played a significant part in keeping the empire from collapsing during increasingly difficult days.

Initially, the government apparatus was dominated by the armed forces; construction and expansion of the state were first of all military ventures. But once the era of conquest was over, the problems of administering the huge Ottoman territories demanded increased attention. In response, the civilian hierarchy, already impressive in the earliest Ottoman period, expanded in prestige, size, and complexity. By the time the empire neared its end, the Ottomans had evolved machinery of government capable of handling far-flung domains in such areas as taxation, justice, and, to a lesser degree, education. Thus, while the army always played an important role, the Ottoman Empire was far more than a praetorian state run by a dominant military caste.

The lengthy Ottoman experience with state-directed reform left a valuable legacy for the Turkish nation. The impetus for persistent efforts at self-improvement was defensive. By the end of the eighteenth century the Ottoman leaders recognized that Europe was clearly outstripping the empire in power. Hence, the tradition of reform did not grow out of efforts to satisfy popular pressures within the Ottoman state, but instead represented a conscious policy of the top leadership to galvanize the populace in ways that even violated popular will and custom on occasion. This elitist approach, predicated on the notion that the rulers know best, has remained an enduring hallmark of Turkish reform through the centuries.

At the same time, the effort to keep the Ottoman state competitive triggered an important conflict within the ruling group. Secular modernizers, who came into ascendance by the nineteenth century, saw the adaptation of European technology as the sole means of coping with the intrusions of the West. On the other hand, traditionalists looked toward a return to religious purity and a rejection of Western materialism as the recipe for staving off the European challenge.

By the end of the empire, however, the religious branch of the governing class had lost the battle and the argument had shifted significantly. The idea of utilizing European technology was accepted and the nub of dispute centered on whether wholesale cultural borrowings from the West were essential to complement technology or whether science and hardware from Europe could be implanted in Turkish society without disturbing traditional patterns. This debate has not yet been resolved.

The Ottoman Empire embraced peoples of sharply differing languages and religions. In the era before national consciousness had been awakened among its subject peoples, the Ottoman system of working through existing religious communities was a cost-effective method of rule. But the persistence of communal identity, which the Ottoman way fostered, provided a fertile ground for separatist movements once the seed of nationalism had been planted. These ethnic separatists threatened to dismember the empire from within, while the European powers were pressing from without.

Turkish nationalism did not emerge full-blown until the fall of the Ottoman Empire. But as early as the Young Turk period, powerful protagonists of Turkism were in evidence. After the 1908 revolution, Com-

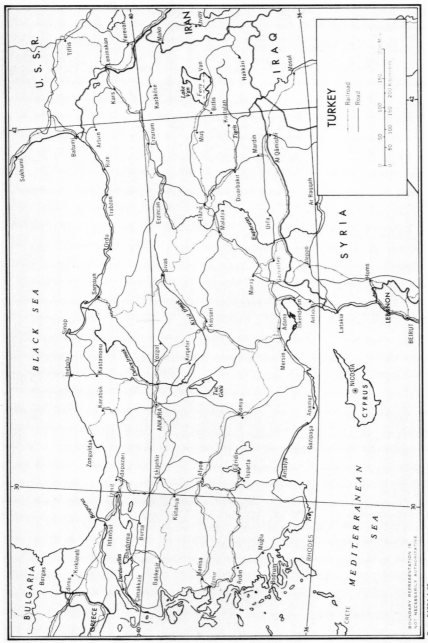

TURKEY

Railroad
Road

0   50   100   150   200 Miles
0 50 100 150 200 Kilometers

BLACK SEA

U. S. S. R.

Sukhumi
Batumi
Tiflis
Leninakan
Yerevan
Mako
Khvoy
Kars
Artvin
Rize
Karaköse
Van
Trabzon
Erzurum
Lake Van
Ferry
Bitlis
Ordu
Erzincan
Muş
Kuţalan
Hakkâri
Giresun
Sivas
Elazığ
Diyarbakır
Mardin
Samsun
Malatya
Urfa
Al Qāmishli
Sinop
Yozgat
Kayseri
Maraş
Gaziantep
At Raqqah
İnebolu
Kırşehir
Aleppo
Kastamonu
Karabük
Tuz Gölü
Adana
İskenderun
Antioch
Homs
Zonguldak
ANKARA
Konya
Mersin
Latakia
Adapazarı
Eskişehir
Afyon
Anamur
İzmit
Kütahya
Eğridir
Isparta
Antalya
Gazipaşa
İstanbul
Bursa
Gördes
Manisa
Bandırma
Balıkesir
Muğla
İzmir
Bodrum
Edirne
Kırklareli
Çanakkale
Aydın
Burgas
Bosporus
Dardanelles

BULGARIA
GREECE
IRAN
IRAQ
SYRIA
LEBANON
BEIRUT
CYPRUS
NICOSIA
RHODES
CRETE
Mosul

MEDITERRANEAN
SEA

Kızıl Irmak
Delice Irmak
Euphrates
Tigris

40
42
30
36

BOUNDARY REPRESENTATION IS
NOT NECESSARILY AUTHORITATIVE

Base 54754 1-69

mittee of Union and Progress Central Committee member Ziya Gok Alp spearheaded an effort to celebrate Turkish achievements and to turn the Ottoman Empire into a Turkish state. In reaction to the financial controls imposed on the Ottomans by European creditors through the Public Debt Administration, the Turkists also espoused economic nationalism. Yet, although Turkey's World War I political leader Enver Pasha was a convinced exponent of assembling the world's Turks in a single state, neither he nor his fellow Young Turks ever abandoned their hopes of maintaining the empire, especially its Arab Islamic elements.

The political structure erected by the Young Turks also set the shape for modern Turkey. The parliamentary mode instituted after 1908 led to the war-time assembly in Ankara and the facade of parliamentary process that ensued. The Committee of Union and Progress, which was the dominant political party during much of the Young Turk period, served, in addition, as a model and precursor of Mustafa Kemal Ataturk's own political organization. Likewise some of the patterns of political controversy carried over into the modern Turkish state.

The Turkish Republic

Ataturk is generally credited with establishing the new Turkey out of the ruins of the Ottoman state. His resistance movement in 1919 was not, however, the first revolt against the European plan to dismember the empire and carve up the Turkish heartland after the First World War. In fact, local organizations for the "defense of rights" of Turks had arisen spontaneously in Anatolia and Thrace before Ataturk's move was actively under way. A "National Congress" of over fifty organizations to coordinate resistance quite independently of Ataturk was even held in Istanbul in November 1918 under the leadership of Esat Pasha.

Kemal Ataturk, however, did play a critical role in creating modern Turkey. Of all the prominent generals he was the least tainted by the military fiasco of the First World War and he was able to provide a firm rallying point for the resistance effort. With his pragmatic approach and clear perception of power realities, he was uniquely fit to unite the disparate nationalist currents, lead the difficult military struggle against the invading Greeks and their allies, and head the ensuing Republican regime. His authority and charisma were essential in focusing the elite on an all-encompassing effort to modernize Turkish society. Thanks to his determined leadership, modernization was secured as Turkey's overriding national goal and has remained the goal ever since. As a result, the direction of modern Turkey has been identified with Ataturk; Ataturkism *(Ataturkculuk)*, a loosely defined pragmatic approach to modernizing reform, remains the touchstone for legitimacy today.

Ataturk built his movement directly on Turkish foundations. His chief original contribution was to recognize the folly of striving to retain a multiethnic state (the only significant exception being the retention of the Kurds, who shared a segment of the Anatolian core area Ataturk saw essential for modern Turkey). Abandoning from the start all the outlying territories, he relentlessly pursued the goal of creating a Turkish national identity. To boost pride in being a Turk, a term of derision for rude peasants in Ottoman usage, he sought to translate attachment to religion into patriotic fervor for the new state.

For all its revolutionary aspects, the Ataturk movement was essentially an evolutionary process. By no means a rapid social revolution, it was based on the Ottoman elite. At first Ataturk did not challenge the right of the monarchy to reign, although the realities of power and Ataturk's own ambition doomed any such possibility over the longer run. It was only after the republic was established that the sultan-caliph was stripped of his final title and the Ottoman house was formally disestablished. The governing elite of the new republic, however, represented an expansion of the Ottoman ruling class through the slow process of education. Social change was thus gradual; no sizable group was expelled from the elite to create a nucleus thirsting to return the old regime to power.

The new Turkish state was a parliamentary republic in form, though an autocracy in practice. Even if Ataturk had had the passing fancy of crowning himself sultan, the need to derive legitimacy from the people for his revolt against the established monarchical government would have scuttled this idea. Thus Turkey became a republic under the slogan "Sovereignty Belongs to the People"; and this sovereignty was formally exercised by a single-house parliament.

Yet Ataturk was not entirely a democrat in approach. A master of the rough-and-tumble of partisan political maneuver in winning support from a divided wartime parliament, he bridled at opposition to his desires from unruly politicians. By organizing a political party that he controlled absolutely and through a system with heavy overtones of "democratic centralism," he became "permanent" (later "eternal") president of the Republican Peoples party. With this political tool firmly in hand, Ataturk was free to rule without hindrance despite the symbolic nature of his position as president of the republic. He eliminated rival political organizations, starting with supporters of the caliph in the 1923 elections, the Progressive Republican party in 1925. Later he dissolved his own tame creation—the "opposition" Free party—when it threatened to get out of hand in 1930. Thereafter, he sponsored a corporate state system, identifying party and government positions, that left no possibility for political opposition to manifest itself legally. Fortunately for Turkey, however, the fusion of party and government led to the atrophy of the former and the clear dominance of the latter. Thus, Turkey did not follow the example of Hitler's Germany or Mussolini's Italy.

Ataturk's autocratic practices behind the facade of a one-party parliament could not long survive his death. In fact, his long-time second-in-command, Ismet Inonu, gave notice almost immediately on taking office that he intended to liberalize the regime. And as soon as the dangers of the Second World War had passed, Turkey moved resolutely toward a multiparty system. To be sure, foreign imperatives assisted in this course—principally the desire to assure Western support against Soviet encroachments. But Inonu's conscious design to complete what he understood as the Ataturk revolution cannot be ignored. Nor indeed would domestic pressures have permitted further delay in instituting competitive party politics.

The Democrat party was established in 1946 by four prominent defectors from the Republican Peoples party. Headed by Celal Bayar, who had been Ataturk's last prime minister, this organization scored creditably in the general elections, which had been advanced to July 1946 to catch the new party before it could fully organize. Profiting from the widespread discontent generated by decades of Republican Peoples party rule, the Democrats handily won the 1950 elections. Inonu thereupon gracefully surrendered power to the opposition he had permitted to organize.

The first stage of Turkey's postwar democratic experiment was deeply flawed, however. There was no tradition of tolerance of dissenting views. The Democrat administration thus wasted little time in retaliating against its opposition. In 1953 it sequestered the assets of the Republican Peoples party on the grounds that the party had benefited from state assistance during the one-party period. The Democrats also closed the splinter Nation party in 1954 for engaging in the exploitation of religion. In 1957, as opposition to these high-handed acts mounted, the Democrats banned electoral coalitions in order to head off a combined challenge from the Republican Peoples party and the small Freedom party, which had split from the Democrats in protest against their intolerance of criticism.

A climate of oppressive political tension developed in Turkey. The emerging socioeconomic competition that reinforced the personal rivalry between the leaders of the two major parties endowed the political contest with an especially bitter edge. The persistent efforts of the Democrat party to enlist those upset by the Ataturkist zeal in religious and social reform also increased the fervor of the combat. Further, the constant attempts of the Democrats, after reaching power, to manipulate foreign assistance for partisan advantage added insult to injury. The final blow was the growing suspicion among the Ataturkist elite—especially the military establishment—that the Democrat party was about to use the concentration of power in the one-house parliament to squash all opposition and return to an anti-Ataturkist single-party system.

The Second Republic

In this situation, the middle levels of the officer corps led a revolt in 1960 to relieve the intolerable political pressure of the bitter conflict between the ins and outs. The legality of this move was not seriously questioned, but the military rulers never felt truly legitimate in office. They had imbibed deeply the tradition of parliamentary rule. Moreover, they had not been able to agree among themselves on a long-range program before they came to power. An important faction within the junta, aided by the senior generals who quickly perceived the dangers of politicizing the armed forces, viewed their proper role as merely that of putting the political process "back on the tracks" and returning power to responsible politicians. The presence of Inonu (Ataturk's closest collaborator and a former general) as head of the party that had been in opposition during the decade before the military revolt, also offered the reluctant officers an attractive way to surrender the reins of government.

Thus, after dissolving the Democrat party and after presiding over popular ratification of a set of constitutional checks and balances designed to prevent the excesses of the earlier concentration of power, the junta held elections. The military leadership, however, did not immediately fade into the background. Revanchist sentiment animated substantial numbers of the voters who backed parties that campaigned more or less openly as continuations of the former ruling Democrat party. As a result, Inonu's Republican Peoples party received merely a plurality. With the military ostentatiously looking over his shoulder, he formed a series of coalitions that served as transitional regimes to reassure the officers that there would be no retaliation for the 1960 intervention.

Inonu's three years in office were a period of dextrous maneuver. On the one hand, the supporters of the former regime among his government partners constantly agitated for immediate amnesty. At the same time, two abortive coups by restive military elements signaled the distress of the armed forces at the possibility of pardon for political prisoners. Torn between these opposing tendencies, the Inonu governments of the early 1960s were weak, unstable, and short-lived. They could not provide a sure sense of direction for the country. And by early 1965 Inonu's last cabinet was brought down during the budget debate. It was succeeded by a caretaker government that did not include the Republican Peoples party, but was backed by the former Democrat party constituency.

In the ensuing election, the Justice party, whose very name reflected the demand for fairer treatment of the old regime, managed to win a decisive majority. Suleyman Demirel, representing the moderate, progressive wing of the party, took over as prime minister. On the political front, his administration passed legislation granting amnesty for the Democrat party politicians sentenced after the military takeover. The Justice party also made a number of changes among senior civil servants to bring more sympathetic personnel to the top posts. Although Demirel's government enjoyed a clear majority in parliament, he seemed loath to insist on controversial measures. Much of the routine work of the government was carried on by decree rather than through legislation. While Demirel seemed relatively cautious in initiating economic departures, he did encourage foreign industrial investment during these years. Moreover, he was fortunate that Turkey's long-standing balance-of-payments pinch was alleviated by a rapidly rising tide of remittances from Turkish workers in Europe. Thanks to this essentially unplanned and unforeseen development, Turkey entered an era of unaccustomed prosperity. In this atmosphere, the Justice party scored a second victory at the polls in 1969, increasing its majority in parliament, although dropping somewhat in its proportion of popular vote.

At the same time, trends were developing in Turkey that would confront Demirel with his most serious challenge. The liberalization introduced in the Second Republic permitted a testing and exploration that led to a flowering of the extremes of both the left and right. This growth of extremism was manifested in growing student restiveness accompanied by political violence. Right-wing youths disrupted meetings of the small but active Turkish Labor party; left-wing students used strong-arm tactics in raiding dormitories of conservative opponents. Perhaps recalling the solidarity between students and the armed forces that had been so much in evidence during the 1960 military move, Demirel appeared undecided at first on how to deal with this turmoil. By 1971, an anarchist movement was fomenting terrorist incidents and kidnapping that seriously embarrassed the government.

This mounting violence, which spread well beyond the campuses, aroused not sympathy but great anxiety among the senior military commanders. In March 1971, they therefore issued an extraordinary public demand for more effective government to cope with the threat to law and order. They warned that "if this is not promptly undertaken, the Turkish Armed Forces will use their legal rights and seize power directly to accomplish the duty of protecting and supervising the Turkish Republic."

Wasting no time arguing legal niceties with his generals, Demirel immediately resigned. Parliament responded to this challenge by voting a series of cabinets under nonpartisan prime ministers. In an effort to assuage military fears, Parliament composed these cabinets primarily of technocrats drawn from outside the assembly. These governments curbed political debate by placing important sections of the country, including all the provinces where universities were located, under martial law. The Turkish Labor party, Turkey's only legal Marxist party, was banned and stern repression succeeded in putting down the terrorist movement, but only after the Israeli consul general was assassinated in Istanbul. Political prisoners, some charged with offenses as nebulous as encouraging sedition through scholarly textbooks, filled the jails.

In this atmosphere, the 1973 elections produced a standoff among the major parties. The right-of-center, which had been the constituency behind the Justice party, had fragmented badly: a religious party (the National Salvation party) successfully wooed the so-called prayer rug vote; a group of conservatives also left the Justice party in a factional dispute largely over cabinet representation. On the other hand, the Republican Peoples party was able to solidify its grip on the left-of-center constituency, especially with the closing of the more extreme Turkish Labor party, which had previously siphoned off left-wing votes. When the returns were tallied in October 1973, the smaller centrist parties thus ended up in the swing position between the Justice party and Republican Peoples party, now led by Bulent Ecevit, who had replaced the aging Inonu in a final showdown.

The next four years were difficult ones of coalition government. First, a combination of Ecevit's party and the National Salvation party was assembled after a three-month interregnum of partisan maneuver. Effective coordination of domestic policy proved troublesome for the Ecevit coalition. It did take the widely popular move of ending the ban on poppy cultivation imposed by the previous military-backed regimes. The main accomplishment of Ecevit's government in its nine months in office, however, was to carry out military intervention on the island of Cyprus following a Greek-inspired putsch against President Makarios.

When political maneuvering led to the demise of Ecevit's coalition in September 1974, the Justice party finally succeeded in putting together a government of the center right, but again, only after months of political bargaining. The survival of this alignment for two and one-half difficult years demonstrated that Demirel had regained the confidence of the military leadership. Yet it was unquestionably hard for this center-right coalition to concert policy in both domestic and foreign affairs. The National Salvation party used its position to extract important concessions, which limited maneuver on foreign issues. Indeed, the problems of managing this uneasy coalition finally led Demirel to agree with the Republican Peoples party and to advance the date of the general elections from October to June 1977.

The 1977 vote produced another parliamentary standoff. Ecevit and his Republican Peoples party emerged with a plurality. His 213 seats were tantalizingly close to the majority of 226 needed to seat a government; he thus tried to form a minority government, counting on abstentions and crossover votes to install his cabinet. This gamble failed. The parties of the center and right used their absolute majority of 229 seats in the lower house to install a new Demirel coalition. But this alignment was brought down in December 1977 by the defection of nearly a dozen Justice party deputies. These dissidents and a three-man contingent from the centrist Republican Reliance party then joined Ecevit in an enlarged cabinet based on the Republican Peoples party. While this combination had a very narrow majority in parliament, Ecevit appeared to enjoy considerable support in the press and public opinion as a leader who might be able to supply the leadership that the electorate plainly desired.

Political Environment

Turkey is a land of pronounced physical contrasts. Stretching over 780,576 square kilometers (301,380 square miles or over 40 percent larger than France), it ranges from sea level to the 5,165-meter (16,945-foot) peak of Mt. Ararat, higher than any European mountain. The western part of the country, bordering on the Aegean and Marmara seas, is a region of developed communication and easy access to the inland plateau. Well-watered farming areas produce cash crops, such as cotton, tobacco, and raisins. Eastern Turkey, abutting on the USSR, Iran, and Iraq, is mountainous, cut by rivers into more or less isolated valleys. The thinly covered lava terrain, which produces sparse vegetation except in the river corridors, and the relatively severe climate encourage pastoral pursuits rather than settled farming in much of the area. The central Anatolian region, though more arid, supports wheat and fruit trees as well as sheep and cattle raising. From the Mediterranean coast on the south and the Black Sea littoral on the north, the land rises sharply to the rim of the Anatolian plateau. In the narrow coastal strips, tea and hazelnuts are grown in the north and citrus fruits and early market vegetables in the south.

A country of about 43 million people in 1979, Turkey's inhabitants are increasing at a rate of slightly over 2.5 percent a year. Population density generally declines from west to east and from the coast to the interior. Istanbul, the former Ottoman capital on the Bosporus, remains Turkey's largest city, with a metropolitan population of some 2.5 million. Thanks to its governmental status, Ankara, the capital in west-central Anatolia is a magnet second only to Istanbul in drawing power; it now boasts about 1.5 million inhabitants. Izmir, on the Aegean coast, and Adana, on the Mediterranean, complete the roster of major urban foci. On the other hand, the southeast has the sparsest population; moreover, its inhabitants lead in migration to other parts of the country or abroad.

It is often said that by giving up empire, modern Turkey achieved a remarkably homogeneous population. While this characterization may be valid when comparing the present state with the extreme diversity of the Ottoman multinational imperial past, there remain notable religious and ethnic differences among the population today.

The census records that Turkey is presently about 99 percent Muslim. The Sunni version of Islam clearly predominates in the country as a whole, but impressionistic data suggest that, particularly in a number of central and east Anatolian provinces, Shi'ite Muslims form a significant proportion of the population. Unfortunately the census sheds no light on the proportion of Shi'ites in Turkey, though some experts allege that their numbers may run to 20 percent or more. The Shi'ites are supposed generally to favor the Republican Peoples party in recognition of its non-discriminatory secular stance; in the 1969 election, however, some Shi'ites apparently backed the Turkish Unity party, a tiny left-leaning organization. Yet in subsequent voting, the Republican Peoples party swept the Shi'ite region in impressive fashion, while the Turkish Unity party has all but disappeared.

Another important minority are the Kurds. Earlier censuses (when such data were published) show that people of Kurdish linguistic background comprised some 10 percent of the population. Speakers of this Indo-European language form the overwhelming majority in Turkey's southeast provinces. Indeed, Diyarbakir remains a largely Kurdish-speaking city and has the largest urban concentration of Kurds—though Istanbul's squatter communities are becoming increasingly a mecca for this minority.

Most of the Kurds in Turkey, while no longer migratory nomads, lead a pastoral, transhumant life organized in tribes led by traditional chiefs. The latter are frequently also leaders of the various dervish orders (Nakshibandi and Kadiri) or belong to religious sects (such as the Nurcular) to which Kurds seem particularly drawn. This tight social organization serves on the one hand to perpetuate an identity quite separate from that of the mass of the Turkish population, but at the same

time divides the various tribes and clans into sharply rival units
nourishing ancient feuds over grazing rights and marriage partners.
Thus, overarching Kurdish nationalism has not been evident in Turkey.
The three revolts of Kurdish leaders in the 1920s and 1930s failed to unite
the bulk of the tribal entities. Some loyalists even cooperated with
Ankara in suppressing these insurrections. Men of Kurdish origin have
indeed risen as high as chief-of-staff of the Turkish armed forces during
the Republican era.

Today, Kurdish ethnic distinctiveness is fed by economic grievances.
Eastern Turkey remains comparatively underdeveloped. Kurdish students at universities in the western part of the country and at Erzurum
have joined in demanding a faster rate of development for their native
areas. Some Kurdish elements have backed the small socialist parties that
in recent years took up the cry for greater economic opportunity for
these provinces.

In the Kurdish areas, tribal leaders have used their social and religious
status as bases of political power within the multiparty democratic
system. As a result, they dominate politics in southeastern Turkey. Confident of their blocs of voters, they have bargained for top positions on
the major party tickets or have shifted to minor parties or run as independents as they deemed fit. The price they pay for freedom to represent their social and religious constituencies in this way in parliament is
to eschew all overt appeals to ethnicity. Kurdish nationalist propaganda
is rigorously banned by the government; those few intellectuals who
have refused to abide by this ban have been jailed by the regime.

Another important cleavage with significant political implications is
the sharp rural-urban divide. In effect, there are two quite distinct
Turkeys. About 60 percent of the population still lives in small towns
and villages, many of which lack the rudimentary accoutrements of
modern life. The village remains steeped in tradition, is primarily agricultural, and is moving only slowly into the twentieth century. Peasant
demands for roads and water form the grist for political campaigns.
Many of the more modern peasants have voted for parties that promise
material improvement without challenging time-honored social patterns.
The more developed regions of the country have formed the main bas-
tions of support for first the Democrat party in the 1950s and then the
Justice party since 1961.

If the village is slow to change its ways, peasants are not. They have
been moving off the farm at a steadily increasing rate in recent decades,
especially from the poorer, less-developed regions of the country.
Typically they head for Istanbul as first choice, but rapidly growing
squatter communities of rural migrants now surround all of Turkey's

larger cities. Indeed, well over half of Ankara's population now consists of these transplanted villagers. Their sprawling mushroom housing, usually grouping people from the same geographic locality or region, forms a transitional state facing both the traditional life of the village and the more modern style of the city. Unemployment is high and living conditions relatively primitive in these ghettos. But despite the problems, these migrants see the city as offering more amenities and hope than the villages that they have left.

Until recently, the Justice party had a majority among these squatters, who tended to vote according to the customary patterns of their original homes. In the past two elections, however, the majority has gone to the Republican Peoples party, perhaps in part because of the influx of peasants from the central and eastern regions who were always more disposed to support the party of Ataturk. Perhaps as well, the inhabitants of these slums are protesting the inability of governments dominated or led by the Justice party to alleviate their plight.

The cities proper are the home of the elite and represent the modern, richer sector of the economy. They are the loci of education and for the most part are oriented toward the West. City dwellers provide the national leadership for political parties, run the bureaucracy, and manage the economy. In short, they are the leaders of national life and culture, setting the goals for the rest of society.

Turkish culture is highly status conscious. Age and position elicit respect among the elite as among the masses. Traditionally, government and the military have been the most honored careers, with education and the free professions ranking next. In recent years, business has increased in esteem, as the top ranks of industry have expanded and have come to command far better salaries and perquisites than the traditional occupations. University education is more than ever the dividing line between the elite and the rest of the population. But the expanding numbers of educated urban dwellers are fragmented in political allegiance. The elite no longer proceeds in lock step along a commonly agreed path.

Unlike many of its neighbors, Turkey has brought its urban women into the mainstream of political, professional, and cultural life. Women's educational level is rising steadily, and women have not faced legal discrimination in their activities since the 1930s. In the villages, however, custom has maintained the traditional male-dominated pattern of life.

The government is the pacesetter in employing women. More than token numbers serve as senior officials. While women are well represented in the free professions as well, in politics their role has declined somewhat in recent years. During the one-party era, Ataturk used parliament as a showcase of women's progress, securing the election of sixteen women to the then 339-seat parliament in 1935. But with the advent of competitive politics, the ranks of women deputies thinned. Despite the activities of women's organizations in all of the parties, only six women were elected to the 450-place lower house in 1973. Half of these were from the Republican Peoples party, and all represented urban areas. In 1977, only four women won deputyships, divided equally between the two major parties. Of the two successful Republican Peoples party candidates, one was named by the party national headquarters to a safe Istanbul seat, the other won on her own from the same constituency.

Economic development is one of the major engines of the transformation that all aspects of Turkish life are undergoing. The state has led the way in fostering economic advance; indeed, the responsibility for national planning is explicitly assigned by the 1961 constitution to the State Planning Organization, a body set up in 1960 by the junta to give coherence to what had been a particularly chaotic effort. Nonetheless, Turkey has always had a mixed economy, although the largest enterprises have been government-run or quasi-public.

In the period immediately following the Second World War, foreign—mostly American—assistance fueled a great expansion of Turkey's infrastructure. The spread of the transistor radio brought modern influences and the knowledge of the outside world to the most isolated and remote villages. Even more important, the construction of a ramified road net, well beyond the limited main railway lines built before the Second World War, added a dimension of communications flexibility that has revolutionized the daily lives of the populace. Over the years, the new mobility has fed a large-scale internal migration of labor in quest of work, of the untutored in search of education, and of the ambitious seeking advancement. In the 1960s, this migration branched outside of Turkey as well; at present there are about one million Turks in Europe, mostly in West Germany. Of course, roads also have let the outside world in. The village in Turkey is becoming less isolated and culturally retrograde than in earlier decades. As a result many communities are now part of the national market economy.

The second major factor in Turkey's economic progress has been the continuing course toward creating an industrial base. Using foreign assistance in the first instance, then private foreign capital, and more recently the earnings of workers from abroad, increasingly sophisticated industry has been set up. Economists may question whether the proliferating steel and aluminum mills as well as other major facilities will be able to compete with Europe once Turkey joins the European communities. Yet for the Turks such industries not only cater to national pride but provide experience with modern production installations that augurs well for the future. Nonetheless, the growing industrial sector cannot now, nor for the foreseeable future, soak up the substantial unemployment—or reduce significantly the high level of underemployment. Nor can domestic industry come close to meeting Turkey's needs for continuing development and fulfill consumer expectations at the same time.

Consumption patterns have also changed markedly over the years. Consumer goods, mainly imported, have customarily been scarce in Turkey. But the flow of remittances in the later 1960s permitted a level of imports that went a long way toward satisfying pent-up demand. Turkey is now experiencing traffic jams, pressure to subsidize cheap energy, and monumental pollution. This enlarged appetite for consumption not only offers scope for politicians to compete for favor, but poses taxing problems for future government economic policy as Turkey experiences an energy crunch and is caught up in worldwide inflationary trends. The resulting balance-of-payments deficits are rising rapidly and threaten continuing imports of consumer and investment goods.

Economic development is also increasing the disparities between the very rich and those who virtually have been left out of the process of economic advance. On the one hand, with the mounting prestige of business, the spirit of entrepreneurship is spreading through acquaintanceship with more modern life and the availability of money in larger quantities. In response, the perception of the need for social justice is becoming more acute among some circles of the elite. A Marxist party, the Turkish Labor party, has been the spokesman for a general redistribution of wealth in society. While less radical in its approach, the Republican Peoples party has made appeals for social justice a prominent part of its rhetoric. Just how Turkey will proceed to balance these conflicting interests is not yet clear. The voters in Turkey have not been willing to give an unmistakable mandate to any party to set its stamp on economic development.

Political Structure

As the preceding discussion has made evident, Turkey possesses a rich variety of political mechanisms that endow the multiparty structure with vitality unusual in this part of the world. Unlike some of its neighbors, Turkey follows constitutional precepts with considerable precision. Laws and statutes cannot lightly be ignored in the Turkish context. As a result, it boasts a smoothly functioning procedure for the transfer of power and for rendering the votes of citizens meaningful. Despite the recurrent fears of some, both inside and outside the system, the military establishment clearly accepts the legitimacy and primacy of civilian politics. And the

political gamut is broad enough—although formally excluding the anar-
chists and communists on the left and overt pan-Turanists on the
right—to offer significant choice in philosophy and program.

The heart of the Turkish system lies in the bicameral legislature introduced in 1961 in an effort to impose some checks and balances on the
powers of the elected deputies. The lower house (National Assembly) is
composed of 450 members elected for four-year terms, although elections
may be held earlier by consent of the assembly. It can pass legislation
over the veto of both the upper house and of the president; the prime
minister is responsible to this body. The Senate of the republic has 150
members elected for staggered six-year terms and an additional 15
presidential appointees serving similar terms. The 18 remaining members
of the military junta and all ex-presidents (one is currently seated) are ex-
officio senators. Through the appointment prerogative of the president,
potential presidential or prime ministerial candidates can be brought into
the legislature (membership in which is essential for qualification for
these posts) as needed.

Executive authority is clearly subordinated to the legislative in the
Turkish system of parliamentary rule. But the cabinet can issue decrees
with the force of law unless directly countermanded by the lower house.
The presidency, by contrast, is an almost totally symbolic post. The
president is free to exercise his discretion in naming the prime minister,
but strong tradition dictates that the head of the largest party be given
the first chance to form a cabinet. Otherwise the position of president is
largely ceremonial.

As for the cabinet ministers, they are "jointly and equally responsible"
for the actions of the government as well as personally responsible for
the acts of their ministries. This corporate responsibility, requiring the
signature of all cabinet ministers to validate administrative actions, has
been used as a lever by the smaller coalition partners to extract concessions on government personnel assignments and to block legislation
that contravened their partisan interests.

The State Planning Organization mandated by the 1961 constitution
fulfilled an earlier demand by the Republican Peoples party for centralized planning. But the means for meshing this body of technocrats with
the politicians heading the government was not clearly specified. It took
a wholesale purge of the State Planning Organization in 1963 and several
near crises, once the Justice party took over in 1965, for this mechanism
to evolve a harmonious working relationship with the elected politicians.
Today the State Planning Organization is firmly under the control of the
political leaders; its findings require parliamentary approval to go into
force. Its plans, once approved, are prescriptive for the government sec-

tor, but only descriptive for the private sector.

In 1961, the role of the judiciary was greatly strengthened in the effort to forestall legislative abuses. The Constitutional Court gained the unfettered right to annul any law it found in violation of the constitution. It also was accorded the authority to try top-ranking elected and appointed officials, including the president, for high crimes and misdemeanors. While the court has not yet used its impeachment function it has ruled a number of laws and provisions of laws unconstitutional over the past fifteen years.

A final innovation introduced in 1961 is the National Security Council. This body, mandated by the constitution to assist "in making decisions related to national security and coordination," was designed as a safety valve. It permits the senior military commanders to be able to communicate legally their views and concerns to the top civilian leaders. The aim of such an institution was to obviate the impasse that had stymied the military establishment during the decade of the 1950s when there was no way short of revolution for the officer corps to put its point across. The National Security Council frequently has been used for public expressions of military desires; the force commanders who issued the declaration in March 1971 that brought down the Demirel government pointedly signed their ultimatum as members of the National Security Council.

Integral to the success of Turkey's parliamentary system is the panoply of well-organized political parties. Ataturk's original single party spawned its major rival, the Democrat party, by splitting in 1945. Current parties are derived principally from these two major groupings. While the Justice party (successor to the Democrat party) and the Republican Peoples party can be distinguished in approach, neither is doctrinaire and both compete for the allegiance of the center, whose votes are necessary for victory at the polls. The Republican Peoples party now considers itself akin to a European social democratic party in outlook; while the Justice party is more favorable to private enterprise.

In the shadow of these two large organizations are six minor entities that also ran in the 1977 elections. The largest of these, the National Salvation party, appeals to Islamic conservatives and is staunchly opposed to big business, particularly that which is linked to foreign capital. It is supported by provincial business interests and professionals from the less-developed areas of Turkey. Next in size comes the National Action party, a utopian right-wing organization, intensely anticommunist and militant. It has found its main response from youth in provincial centers and from artisans and tradesmen. Neither the Republican Reliance party, a right-of-center splinter from the Republican Peoples party, nor the

Democratic party, a conservative offshoot of the Justice party, now have constituencies beyond the immediate followers of their top leaders. The Turkish Unity party courts the Shi'ites of south-central Turkey on a platform of socialist secular reform. Finally, the Turkish Labor party, which had been banned in 1971, but resumed legal existence in 1975, is today a tiny, avowedly Marxist organization drawing its chief backing from socialist intellectuals and Kurdish traditional leaders.

Statistics on the formal membership of these parties are not published, but political organizations do make a ritual of registering prominent adherents at public ceremonies. In theory, members are obliged to pay dues to their parties; this was to provide the main funding for political activities. In practice, however, no party insists on financial support from its supporters as the criterion of membership. Since the late 1960s legislation has provided that parties with ten deputies in the lower house (or that receive 5 percent of the national vote) would be eligible to receive a government subvention; this subsidy has become the major source of funds for those parties that qualify, since the law specifies that the total government aid each year will be 1/5,000 of the total state revenue for the previous year. Government support payments are distributed in proportion to the votes received in the latest election. The small left-wing parties are particularly disadvantaged by this system because they have little prospect of qualifying for state aid, while at the same time there is a legal prohibition against receiving political contributions from labor unions, the most obvious natural source of funds for these parties.

The electoral system in Turkey operates to the advantage of organized parties. Provinces form Turkey's electoral constituencies; the number of deputies to be elected ranges from one in sparsely populated Hakkari to forty-four in Istanbul. Anyone not constitutionally barred from being a candidate may run for election either on a party ticket or as an independent. But in provinces that elect more than one deputy (the overwhelming majority), those who vote for an independent lose the right to mark their ballots for other candidates. On the other hand, voters are entitled to cast ballots for a party's entire slate in a province, thus making party affiliation a distinct advantage, especially in populous parts of the country. It is, however, necessary for a party to have completed its formal organization at all levels in fifteen out of the sixty-seven provinces in order to be permitted to field candidates in national elections.

Starting with the Second Republic, Turkey's election law mandated proportional representation. The d'Hondt system currently in use favors the larger parties at the expense of the others. Votes of a party or independent that do not exceed the quotient of the number of registered voters in the province divided by the number of seats in contest are ignored. In consequence, the proportion of deputies due the largest party in a province increases significantly if there are parties or independents that do not cross this threshold. For example, in the 1973 elections the Republican Peoples party won 41 percent of the seats with only 33 percent of the vote; in 1977 this party won 47 percent of the seats with but 41 percent of the vote.

Under the system of proportional representation, position on the party slate becomes a paramount determinant of electoral success. Candidates are placed on the list through primary contests in which voting is confined to the segment of formal party membership authorized by the various party statutes. In many provinces, the number of primary electors is thus very small, consisting almost exclusively of professional politicians representing local interests. While the right of the national headquarters to place its nominees on the list is limited to 5 percent of the candidates nationwide, the leadership can place these nominees at the head of the ticket. In the case of the major parties, this virtually assures their election. Further, the national leaders have a veto right over all candidates of the party, and this mechanism has been used to block local figures in disfavor with Ankara. Necmettin Erbakan, for one, was vetoed in this way by Justice party headquarters in 1969 after winning the primary. Although he subsequently won election as an independent, this veto experience spurred his interest in forming the National Salvation party.

In theory, the voters in the general elections can use a highly complicated mechanism to indicate individual preference among a party's nominees, thus directly selecting the candidates irrespective of their position on the slate. Such a substantial proportion of a party's supporters must give their endorsement in this way that in practice it is all but impossible to change the rank order of a party's ticket. In fact, efforts to use this cumbersome procedure—or to vote for independents—often lead only to invalidated ballots. Thus, in Corum in 1977 the Republican Peoples party lost an additional deputyship solely because nine thousand votes were invalidated through misuse of the preference system. Four hundred more ballots were thrown out because party members tried to vote for a mixed slate including independents who had previously belonged to the party.

While parties dominate the political scene, interest groups also have gained some political role. Among the most important are labor organizations, although unions remain formally prohibited from political affiliation. Nonetheless, parties have sought to gain the informal support of the two main labor confederations, whose membership of about one million represents a quarter of all workers outside of agriculture. The Confederation of Turkish Trade Unions, Turk-Is, by far the largest labor organization, has almost always taken a stand above party positions. The Confederation of Reformist Workers' Unions (DISK), on the other hand, has supported first the Turkish Labor party and more recently the Republican Peoples party. Employers' unions also exist. They, along with chambers of commerce and craft associations, work closely with the government in recommending broad economic policies.

Student and youth groups have been active in Turkey in the political realm as well. Two organizations, the rightist Turkish National Students Union, founded in 1916, and the centrist Turkish National Student Federation, established in 1948, dominated the movement until the late 1960s. Both of these became increasingly politicized as the multiparty period went on, while their membership declined. They held meetings, demonstrated, made speeches, issued declarations, and mounted academic boycotts. Until the 1960s, their activities focused on anti-communism, defense of Kemalist reforms, and Cyprus. In the Second Republic they emphasized social justice, economic development, and Turkey's international orientation. The moderation of their approach and the reaction against the efforts of the Justice party governments to dominate both organizations led to a proliferation of leftist Idea Clubs (Fikir Klubu) that were strongly opposed to the regime.

Out of these radical organizations grew the Revolutionary Youth Federation (Dev Genc) in 1969; it espoused guerrilla tactics and sought to intimidate its student opponents and to challenge the government by force. At the same time, on the far right the National Action party organized youthful "Commandos" who actively engaged the left-wing organizations. The disruptions and violence fomented by the clashes between these extreme groups triggered the military intervention in 1971. Dev Genc was outlawed and has been largely suppressed by the government. "Commandos," on the other hand, remain in operation.

Following the lifting of martial law restrictions in 1973, a resurgence of anarchist and left-wing radical organizations took place. These splinter groups maintained more or less direct connection with the mushrooming extreme socialist parties that sprang up in the mid-1970s. And conflict between student extremists on the campuses again became commonplace.

Political Dynamics

Turkey's impressive array of political institutions clearly has much to do with the country's success in multiparty politics. The parliamentary system that was grafted onto the Ottoman structure with little background or preparation finally "took," if only in the past few decades. Today, the expectation of the civilian elite to share in the governing process is broad and deep. It is paralleled by the general expectation of the masses of the opportunity for a meaningful vote. If there was vote fraud in some localities in the hastily held 1946 elections and if in 1957 the mysterious burning of the records of the Gaziantep election forestalled full investigation into charges of irregularities in that province, these are the only black marks on Turkey's election slate in the period since the Second World War. While the military establishment has intervened on the political stage in ways that will be discussed in a subsequent section, it is nonetheless evident that, although democracy was not a native product at the start, it has by now been thoroughly assimilated and adapted to Turkey's own conditions.

In part, this accomplishment has been due to the quality of leadership in the political arena. Perhaps the Turks were fortunate that the high status and prestige of government service meant that virtually the entire personnel resources of the country were at the disposal of politics. Until recently, business or private careers did not beguile the "best and the brightest." Ataturk, to be sure, may have delayed the advent of multiparty politics by his autocratic behavior, but Inonu's consistent dedication to building democracy as his monument made his steady hand and cool eye available even in his 80s to help over the rough spots. Beyond the top leaders, the second and middle echelon politicians were often also of uncommon ability. There were always many qualified candidates to lead the government and phalanxes of choices for the cabinet. "Musical chairs" between a limited pool of ministerial talent has not been common in Turkey. Nor has it been difficult to secure competent administrators or judges to man the bureaucracy and judiciary.

The political parties have operated relatively efficiently to mobilize the voters. Participation in the electoral process has generally been high (ranging between 89 and 64 percent of the eligible voters). Starting from the tradition of universal voting as the duty of citizenry in the one-party era, however, the percentage of those actually going to the polls declined until 1973. Turkey's experience thus was contrary to the expectation of those who theorize that increasing education, involvement in the political process, and development should be accompanied by rising interest in using the ballot. The prevailing explanation of the Turkish performance ascribes the falling rate of participation to the decline in bloc voting as Turkey became more modern. It seemed reasonable to assume that as individuals became increasingly responsible for their own voting decisions, there would be a natural fall in the number using their vote.

The generally higher rate of voter participation in eastern Turkey, where bloc voting remains prevalent, has been taken as additional substantiation for this hypothesis.

The rebound in the proportion of those voting in 1973 and especially 1977 calls this explanation somewhat into question and suggests that additional nuances are required at the very least. By way of special circumstances, it could be argued that reaction to the military intervention of 1971 may have spurred participation in 1973. Moreover, particularly in 1977, the parties ran spirited campaigns that may well have piqued voter interest more than in previous elections. Bulent Ecevit, campaigning at the head of the Republican Peoples party, has proved something of a charismatic figure since his role in the Cyprus intervention. His appearance in Istanbul on the heels of unprecedented government warnings that he might be assassinated attracted an enthusiastic crowd of several hundred thousand sympathizers in the closing days of the campaign. On this occasion, his party's well-disciplined cadre proved that it could maintain order at the same time. Its performance indicates that the party's emphasis on directing its appeal toward the masses may be influencing the participation rates, which are increasing faster in areas where the Republican Peoples party is especially successful than elsewhere in the country. The lower voter participation rate in 1965 and 1969, by contrast, may, to some extent, reflect the fears of the traditional rural notables whose long-term marriage of convenience with the Republican Peoples party was sundered by the party's "left of center" campaign stance introduced in 1965 and the bitter internal dispute in the party at that time. In this situation, these voters may simply have stayed home on election day.

For most of the period since the Second World War, the political contest in Turkey has been a "two-party affair." In the First Republic, with a majority vote system, the victorious party usually (though not always) swept the entire slate in a province. Under these circumstances, the larger parties ended up with the lion's share of the seats; a minor party had to have a strong base of power in one locality or region in order to be able to elect any deputies at all. The Republican Nation party of Osman Bolukbasi drew its main strength from his home province of Kirsehir. Efforts by defectors from the Democrat party to establish the Freedom party in 1955 foundered after the insurgents failed to win a single seat except in the tiny province of Burdur, the stronghold of their leader. Recognizing the impossibility of making a major impact on their own, the leaders of the Freedom party decided to join the Republican Peoples party in 1958. In such an atmosphere, clearly the future of minor parties was unpromising.

The dominance of the two major parties has not been as marked in the Second Republic. The introduction of proportional representation in 1961 facilitated the survival of splinter parties. In the freer political climate of the past two decades, personality conflicts, coupled with disputes over philosophy and course by rival aspirants to the top leadership positions, have contributed to the defection of important parliamentary factions from both major parties. For example, Turhan Feyzioglu led his more conservative wing out of the Republican Peoples party in 1967 to found the Reliance party; Saadettin Bilgic and a group of traditionalists, who were dropped from the cabinet, left the Justice party to form the Democratic party in 1970 (not to be confused with the earlier Democrat party). Differences in political outlook also spurred the formation of the National Salvation party, established in 1972 by lower-level defectors from the Justice party to appeal to the conservative religious segment of the latter's constituency. These fissiparous tendencies went so far that in 1973 neither of the major parties could muster a majority in parliament, and Turkey entered on its second period of precarious coalition politics. Indeed, on the strength of this development, some investigators have expressed doubts that the basically two-party nature of Turkish politics continues to exist.

The 1977 election results, however, indicate that there are strong underlying tendencies toward a two-party system in Turkey. In fact, despite the mushrooming of small entities to compete in the 1973 elections, the overall record of survival of minor parties in the Second Republic is not impressive. With one still insignificant exception, these splinter groups have all lost support, often dramatically, in every election after their first appearance on the electoral stage. The New Turkey party, formed in 1961 in an effort to channel supporters of the old regime, faded out entirely after falling from sixty-five seats to six in its third general election. The Turkish Labor party fell from fifteen seats to two in successive elections; it won no seats at all in 1977. The National Salvation party declined from forty-eight seats in 1973 to twenty-four in 1977, while the Democratic party and the Republican Reliance party were nearly wiped out in 1977. Only the extreme right-wing National Action party has managed to buck this trend, rising from one seat in 1969 to sixteen in 1977. Thus, although since 1973 the minor parties have occupied and continued to occupy the swing position between the relatively evenly matched majors, their total bulk is now receding.

Why these splinter groups have fared so poorly relates to a number of factors. Turks, like most peoples, value strong national leadership. Indeed, given the depth of emotional attachment of most Turks to patriotism and the welfare of their country, the yearning for a decisive

TABLE 3.1

Election Results in the Second Republic: 1961–1977

The Lower House

	1961	1965	1969	1973	1977
PERCENT OF ELIGIBLE VOTERS VOTING	81.0	71.3	64.3	66.8	72.5
REPUBLICAN PEOPLES PARTY founded 1922: Kemal Atatürk successor: İsmet İnönü present leader: Bülent Ecevit	173 seats 36.7%	134 seats 28.7%	143 seats 27.4%	185 seats 33.2%	213 seats 41.4%
JUSTICE PARTY founded Jan. 1961: Gen. Ragip Gümüspala present leader: Süleyman Demirel	158 seats 34.8%	240 seats 52.9%	256 seats 46.5%	149 seats 29.8%	189 seats 36.9%
NATIONAL SALVATION PARTY founded: Oct. 1972: Süleyman Emre present leader: Necmettin Erbakan				48 seats 11.9%	24 seats 8.6%
NATIONAL ACTION PARTY (previously Republican Peasants Nation Party) founded Feb. 1954: Osman Bölükbasi present leader: Alparslan Türkes	54 seats 14.0%	11 seats 2.2%	1 seat 3.0%	3 seats 3.4%	16 seats 6.4%
REPUBLICAN RELIANCE PARTY founded May 1967: Turhan Feyzioğlu present leader: Turhan Feyzioğlu			15 seats 6.6%	13 seats 5.3%	3 seats 1.9%
DEMOCRATIC PARTY founded Dec. 1970: Saadettin Bilgic present leader: Ferruh Bozbeyli				45 seats 11.8%	1 seat 1.8%
TURKISH UNITY PARTY founded Oct. 1966: General Hasan Berkman present leader: Mustafa Timisi			8 seats 2.9%	1 seat 1.1%	0 seat .4%
TURKISH LABOR PARTY founded March 1961: Avni Erkalin present leader: Behice Boran		15 seats 3.0%	2 seats 2.7%	closed by courts	0 seat .1%
INDEPENDENTS	0 seat .8%	0 seat 3.2%	13 seats 5.6%	6 seats 2.8%	4 seats 2.5%
NEW TURKEY PARTY founded Feb. 1961: Ekrem Alican no longer in operation	65 seats 13.7%	19 seats 3.7%	6 seats 2.2%	dissolved of its own initiative	
NATION PARTY founded June 1962: Osman Bölükbasi present leader: Mehmet Tarik Yakova		31 seats 6.3%	6 seats 3.2%	0 seat .6%	not eligible to run

TABLE 3.1 (continued)

The Senate

	1961	1964	1966	1968	1973	1975	1977
Participation	*81.4%	60.2%	56.2%	66.3%	*65.3%	58.4%	*73.8%
REPUBLICAN PEOPLES PARTY							
Seats won	36	19	13	13	25	25	28
% of vote cast	37.2%	40.8%	30.0%	27.1%	33.6%	43.8%	42.4%
cumulative seat total	36	45	50	34	41	60	75
JUSTICE PARTY							
Seats won	71	31	35	38	22	27	21
% of vote cast	35.5%	50.3%	56.3%	49.9%	31.0%	40.8%	38.3%
cumulative seat total	71	77	92	101	80	78	64
NATIONAL SALVATION PARTY							
Seats won					3	2	1
% of vote cast					12.3%	8.8%	8.5%
cumulative seat total					3	5	6
NATIONAL ACTION PARTY							
Seats won	16	0	1	0	0	0	0
% of vote cast	13.5%	3.0%	1.9%	2.0%	2.7%	3.2%	6.6%
cumulative seat total	16	3	1	1	0	1	1
REPUBLICAN RELIANCE PARTY							
Seats won				1	1	0	0
% of vote cast				8.6%	5.9%		1.9%
cumulative seat total				11	10	4	3
DEMOCRATIC PARTY							
Seats won					0	0	0
% of vote cast					10.4%	3.1%	2.2%
cumulative seat total					6	0	0
TURKISH UNITY PARTY							
Seats won					0	0	0
% of vote cast					2.1%	.5%	
cumulative seat total					0	0	0
TURKISH LABOR PARTY							
Seats won			1	0	0	0	0
% of vote cast			3.9%	4.7%			
cumulative seat total		1	1	0	0	0	0
INDEPENDENTS							
Seats won		1	0	0	1	0	0
% of vote cast		2.3%	.5%	1.7%	2.0%	.1%	.1%
cumulative seat total		11	4	0	10	2	1
NEW TURKEY PARTY							
Seats won	27	0	1	0			
%of vote cast	14.0%	3.5%	2.3%				
cumulative seat total	27	9	1	1			
NATION PARTY							
Seats won		0	1	1			
% of vote cast			5.9%	6.0%			
cumulative seat total		3	1	1			

*coincided with general elections to the lower house

hand on the tiller is quite understandable. Especially in these days when
Turkey faces difficult economic and social problems, the value of a commanding personality at the head of an effective government is readily apparent. There is a general desire to avoid drift in Turkey. In this situation,
where coalition politics have produced less efficient rule, it is quite clear to
most Turkish voters that only by backing one of the major parties can the
requisite leadership be found. The electorate seems by and large convinced
that a ballot for a minor party can be merely a means of protest, but that for
effective action one must opt for one of the serious contenders for power.
This bandwagon effect strongly favors the larger entities. It is the two major
parties, moreover, that have the reservoir of impressive talent; the splinter
groups generally have only one or two well-known figures.

Turkish parties also reflect a successful blend of national and local interests. Voters, whether in developed or in less advanced polities, seem
to prefer to be represented by fellow natives rather than by outsiders—at
least unless the latter are of uncommon national or international stature.
In Turkey, reformist politics have always been national; local interests,
on the other hand, have continually been in the van of opposition to far-
reaching social and cultural reform. The accommodation of these conflicting points of view, while preserving the essence of Ataturk's pragmatic modernizing thrust, has been one of the major achievements of
Turkey's political life.

In the one-party era, little moment was attached to local desires in
respect to representatives in the assembly. Indeed, the top leadership of
the Republican Peoples party has to this day been singularly uncon-
cerned with identification with a particular locality of origin. Ataturk,
after all, was born in Salonika, a place not even within the bounds of
modern Turkey. Though originally from Izmir and brought up in Sivas,
Inonu did have family associations with Malatya that eventually became
his electoral constituency; he maintained his home in Ankara and Istanbul, however, not in Malatya. Despite the fact that Bulent Ecevit was a
native of Istanbul, he never represented this constituency; he ran from
Ankara before shifting to Zonguldak in 1965 to emphasize his solidarity
with workers in the mines and mills of this labor center.

The multiparty era brought new concern with selecting popular candidates, although party, not personality, still remains the key to politics in
the more developed regions of Turkey. The Democrat party sought to
emphasize its democratic nature as early as 1949 by prohibiting the national headquarters from putting nominees in more than 20 percent of
the places on local provincial slates. The Republican Peoples party also
moved in this direction, even though its leadership retained the right to
name 30 percent of the party's candidates in the 1950s. Legal restrictions

on the ability of the party headquarters to place candidates on the local lists were imposed in the new election law enacted by the Second Republic. But while this statute limits the national leadership to controlling only 5 percent of the party's slate, candidate selection occasions continuing controversy. Analysis of the 1977 elections, for example, shows that placing of figures not native to the province at the head of the local tickets perceptibly affected a party's performance in a number of smaller provinces. In other cases, especially in eastern Turkey, the failure of aspirants with strong local bases to win the desired place on the lists led them to abandon the party altogether after the primaries and to run on their own. In fact, the four successfully elected independents in 1977 all had quit major parties when denied choice spots on the party tickets.

In this situation, politics in Turkey assumed a character increasingly responsive to local issues and interests. One of the principal ways in which localism has modified Turkey's course has been in the realm of policy toward Islam. Ataturk was personally irreligious and, like many reformers of his generation, saw attachment to religion as the main impediment to Westernizing Turkey. He, therefore, disestablished Islam as the state religion and imposed rigorous discrimination on its practice. He closed the dervish lay religious orders which formed a separate hierarchy outside the control or guidance of the orthodox religious establishment, which itself had been a wing of the government. The formal orthodoxy was also restricted. Religious schools of all sorts were closed, and clerics were prohibited from circulating in religious garb outside of places of worship. Turkish was imposed in place of Arabic as the language of worship. In short, the full weight of the government was directed at discouraging religious practices.

Multiparty competition itself worked to relax these restrictions. Optional courses on religion were added to the curriculum in the 1940s; a faculty of divinity was reopened; Arabic was restored in religious services; and a proliferation of local training schools for worship leaders was eventually permitted. Moreover, as local interests grew stronger relative to the reformist leadership of the major parties, the public observance of religious festivals increased. A binge of mosque building began, capped by a huge and prominent structure dominating the skyline of new Ankara—a development inconceivable in Ataturk's lifetime. It became fashionable for government officials to fast during Ramadan and many educated people could be seen at Friday noon prayers, even before the rise of the National Salvation party, which frankly catered to and encouraged this development.

Localism has also fostered changes in the socioeconomic interests represented in parliament. Ataturk's one-party regime ran heavily to

military and civilian officials in his hand-picked single chamber
assembly. Once the transition to multiparty experience was underway,
the character of the assembly began to alter. Professionals, especially
lawyers, became deputies in increasing numbers. They were joined by
businessmen, who had been scarce in the reformist era. At the same time,
the official contingent declined. This transformation, reflecting the
emergence of a middle class in Turkey, came slowly. At first it affected
the lowest levels of power, but gradually new elements infiltrated the
higher ranks.

The entry of these new men had its effect on deliberations concerning
domestic policy above all. The question of economic approach, the role
of central planning, and the proper place for private enterprise were debated with growing intensity as the new arrivals challenged the older notion of state-directed reform. Clustered around first the Democrat party
and later the Justice party, these elements with their nongovernmental
focus have thus been attacked as seeking to dismantle the Ataturk reforms. In fact, the dispute has been more a question of nuance than principle. Even the new men accept a heavy state involvement and have not,
for example, sought to turn over to private ownership the state economic
enterprises, which still account for perhaps a third of Turkey's industrial
capacity.

While the rise of the center-right constituency was associated with the
burgeoning of the middle class, more recent socioeconomic developments may be favoring the Republican Peoples party. The latter has seen
its fortunes improve significantly in the 1970s. From a low point of just
over 27 percent of the votes cast, it managed to attract over 41 percent in
the 1977 elections. Historically the Republican Peoples party has been
the party of the educated elite in Turkey. A bias toward it as the party of
modernizing reform and the organization created by Ataturk is built into
the education system. As Turkey develops, therefore, and as migration
to the cities brings more youth within easy reach of at least primary
educational institutions, the Republican Peoples party seems likely to
benefit.

Some investigators have held the hypothesis, although it remains quite
unproven, that Turkish development has proceeded to the point of producing a "critical realignment" of voter support—a revolution in attitude
away from "territorial and cultural cleavages" and toward voting along
class lines. In this view, such a realignment would account for the gains
in the last two elections scored by the Republican Peoples party, whose
socialist approach gave it claims to represent the interests of the workers
and fast-growing urban areas. While this theory is intriguing, it seems
clear that sectional, ethnic, linguistic, religious, and cultural factors per-

sist in their saliency in affecting voting patterns of all developed pluralistic societies. There is little evidence that the Turks are more prone to functional solidarity than peoples elsewhere.

There are, to be sure, psychological factors not related to development or social change that have been at work on behalf of the Republican Peoples party in recent years. First is the shock that the Justice party suffered from the military ultimatum in 1971. Demirel in the ensuing election was at a distinct disadvantage in projecting the image of a man who could govern effectively. His campaign thus lacked the spirit and fire characteristic of his performances in the 1960s. This loss of confidence clearly discouraged his normal constituency, which was badly fractured by the defections of the Democratic party and the National Salvation party in any event.

In 1977, although Demirel ran a considerably more confident campaign, having returned to office as prime minister, he faced Ecevit who had emerged in the interval as something of a popular hero. Ecevit's appeal was based on his oratorical ability to project a populist aura as a modern-day Robin Hood (*Karaoglan* in Turkish), coupled with the remnants of the national exultation he had earned from ordering the intervention in Cyprus in 1974. Fears among his party's normal constituency that his "left of center" slogan was synonymous with communism had by this time long since died out, as had the memories of his party's high-handedness during the one-party era. In this more favorable atmosphere, his campaign style unquestionably impressed the voters, who turned out in large crowds to hear him.

Thus, rather than a critical realignment on a class basis, the growing trend in favor of the Republican Peoples party may reflect the fact that Turkish politics is in essence a struggle between the ins and the outs. The desire to change the party in office seems to grow in Turkey after two terms in power. The Democrat party would have lost the 1957 elections had it not changed the election rules on the eve of the contests. Similarly, the Justice party suffered a sharp reverse in the 1970s after winning with impressive margins in the 1960s.

The Role of the Military

The armed forces have occupied a special position in Turkey. They have political weight that enters into all party and government calculations involving military interests. In part, this influence comes from their monopoly of legal force and their status as the de facto organ of last recourse in domestic conflict. In part, their political role derives from the peculiar history of the military establishment in the Turkish reform movement and its centrality in the creation of the republic.

Ataturk and his chief lieutenants were all career officers when they launched the struggle for independence. The armed forces had possessed the major secularist educational institutions at the university level in this era. They were, therefore, the main window on the West at the end of the Ottoman Empire. As a result, officers were the reformists par excellence in Turkey. The officer corps was, in fact, the leading wing of the intellectual elite and did not represent a conservative point of view in the Turkish context. Indeed, Ataturk was archetypical of the outlook of the military establishment, something that stood him in good stead in rallying support for his cause.

The difficult days of the struggle for independence and of the founding of the republic were not times to observe the niceties of separating military and political careers. In accord with the needs of the moment, senior commanders served in parliament, on diplomatic missions abroad, and as government administrators without resigning their commissions. Ataturk depended on the loyalty of the military command structure as an essential prop for his move to abolish the Ottoman royal house.

It was not until the political scene began to clarify in the early years of the republic that the problem of mixing politicians and military officers became manifest. When some of his closest collaborators defected to the mounting civilian opposition in 1924, the threat of military disloyalty imparted urgency to the matter of separating the military and political tracks. In 1927, when the dissident generals requested to be returned to active army commands, Ataturk retired his opponents. At the same time, he and his closest associates gave up their active-duty status as well.

Ataturk and Inonu maintained close ties with the armed forces, even after retirement. Marshal Fevzi Cakmak ran the military establishment on their behalf. He took good care to keep the forces out of day-to-day politics: it was apparently even forbidden for the cadets to read daily newspapers in order to make sure that they were not stirred up by political events. At the same time, Ataturk continually cited the armed forces as the ultimate guardians of the republic, making clear that they were to defend the reform effort as well as protect the shores from foreign foes.

As part of Inonu's move toward meaningful democracy, the special position of the officer corps was changed significantly. In 1944 the armed forces were removed from the purview of the president and brought directly under the control of the prime minister; five years later the general staff was finally placed under the Ministry of National Defense in an effort to enhance civilian control. The loyalty of the top generals to Inonu, however, was not impaired. There are credible reports that the senior commanders sounded him out on the course to be followed toward the Democrat party when that body won the 1950 elections. In keeping with his mission to bring democracy to Turkey, Inonu was categoric in opposing any extralegal acts to prevent the new administration from taking office.

It took a complex of pressures to bring the military establishment to overturn the Democrats in 1960. The ground was prepared by the loss of status and prestige inflicted on the officers by the Democrat party administration during its decade in power. The civilian leaders appeared to be deliberately denying the military its position as the ultimate guarantor of the state at the same time that NATO was reequipping and revitalizing the Turkish forces. But for all the economic hardships and slights to their honor that they suffered, the officer corps might have remained loyal if the Democrats had not threatened the sanctity of the parliamentary system. Under these circumstances, even the Republican Peoples party wished the military to make clear that it would not obey partisan commands by the Democrat party. Of course, the line of disobedience was hard to draw; a group of colonels and younger officers took the bit in their mouths and led a revolt that brought the entire military apparatus along.

The military move was readily accepted in Turkey as necessary to prevent perversion of the political process. The trials of the Democrat leaders did serve to discredit Prime Minister Adnan Menderes. The execution of the three main defendants and the incarceration of many others, however, were harder for the body politic to swallow. Yet, while civilian politicians worked for amnesty of the political prisoners—a goal that was successfully reached in 1964—there was no serious effort to deny the legality of the Second Republic or to seek punishment for the members of the military junta who were guaranteed life membership in the Senate.

It was thanks to the general acceptance of the legitimacy of the military move that the junta could arrange to surrender the reins of government to a civilian regime after only sixteen months. But the process of seizing power and ruling had disrupted the chain of command, damaged discipline, and deeply politicized the officer corps. It took two abortive coups in 1962 and 1963 to teach officers that plotting carried such severe risks and penalties as to be all but out of the question. Indeed, Talat Aydemir's execution for leading the 1963 putsch virtually ended efforts among officers below the level of the senior commanders to overturn the civilian government.

In the 1960s, therefore, it was the National Security Council, presided over by the president of the republic, that spoke in the name of the armed services to convey political messages. The role of the military had become institutionalized in the formal mechanisms erected for this purpose by the constitution of 1961. And while the senior commanders and the president (who was himself a former top general) did make known their views on a number of occasions—for example, objecting in 1969 to the restoration of parliamentary rights to former President Celal Bayar—their actions were accepted as well within the bounds of constitutionality.

The "coup by memorandum" that brought down the Demirel government in March 1971 resulted from the rising tide of lawlessness that engulfed Turkey after 1968. Security of life and limb became of general concern to residents of Turkey's largest cities. It was not surprising, therefore, that the top commanders found the government's efforts to restore tranquillity unsatisfying. Perhaps what equally set the senior generals in motion was concern lest others were readying their own move. A few days after the ultimatum, a group of officers was purged on grounds that they had wanted to take over the government outright.

Demirel's downfall made the military seem overwhelmingly powerful and lent the armed forces an aura threatening to the normal operation of the political process. Parliament continued to function, but most deputies were clearly concerned to form governments that would not offend the generals. This civilian deference evidently whetted the appetite of the chief of the general staff, General Gurler, for further political power.

A battle of wills was joined on this issue in connection with the election of a new president in the spring of 1973. Inasmuch as the incumbent, General Sunay, was legally barred from reelection, Gurler sought to present himself as the military's candidate for the office. Demirel, recognizing that the new president would have the right to name the prime minister after the elections later that year, wished to make sure that a neutral figure, not associated with the 1971 ultimatum, would be chief of state. The Republican Peoples party, under Ecevit's leadership, also wished to break the precedent that would automatically make the chief of staff president of the republic when a vacancy occurred. Military backing for Gurler also seems to have been wavering, perhaps out of interservice rivalries and certainly out of reluctance to resurrect the problems that had troubled the earlier period of military rule. As a result, the otherwise badly divided parliament agreed to reject Gurler and settled instead on retired Admiral Fahri Koruturk, who had left active service thirteen years earlier to serve as an ambassador.

This outcome marked a significant turning point in the relations between the military and civilians. It showed the politicians that the ultimatum was not an ineluctable prelude to a military takeover. Moreover, it demonstrated that the civilians could face down the officers without triggering a move by the armed forces. Thus it changed the specter of military intervention, reemphasizing the supremacy of the civilian sector. For the officer corps, especially when no longer led by General Gurler, the experience with presidential election also encouraged a less activist course. Koruturk himself was, in addition, a staunch supporter of civilian rule and thus a dampening influence on military activism.

The relative withdrawal of the armed forces from the political arena was confirmed by the patience displayed by the commanders in the face of the months of parliamentary wrangling to form the Ecevit coalition after the 1973 elections and the even longer time needed for Demirel to fashion his government after the fall of Ecevit's regime in 1974. Increasing civilian control was also indicated by Demirel's dismissal of General Namik Kemal Ersun on the eve of the 1977 elections, allegedly for partisanship toward the Republican Peoples party. And the wholesale shift of service commanders in August 1977, though arousing strong criticism from Ecevit's party for injecting politics into the army, demonstrated the civilian government's impressive grip on the military assignment process.

Nonetheless, tensions and uncertainties remain in the military role in Turkey. The armed forces no doubt have interests that they consider vital: law and order, assured military supply, and defense of Turkey's national honor obviously being high on the list. If these should be placed in jeopardy, reaction from the military chain of command would appear inevitable. Yet clearly the officers have no interest in day-to-day supervision of the political process. They would be tempted to intervene directly in this realm only if there were widespread consensus that the most weighty causes required such action.

Foreign Policy

Ataturk set the basic Turkish goals for international relations. The corollary of his determination that Turkey be accepted as a powerful modern state was Western orientation. To the Kemalists, and soon to virtually all Turks, therefore, the foremost design of republican Turkey was to become identified as European. This, in turn, implied close ties with England and France in the interwar years and with the United States in the era after the Second World War. There were deep roots in Turkish thinking that ordered membership in NATO as confirmation of the Kemalist dream. Although joining the Common Market occasioned debate over the proper timing, it was not a goal to be easily rejected in principle. In short, Turkey's Western alliance is solidly based on the well-springs of the modern Turkish state.

The yearning for independence, the other principal Kemalist legacy in foreign affairs, is more ambiguous, hence harder to apply in practice. Ataturk himself spoke against entangling alliances such as those that pulled Turkey into the First World War. Yet he concluded two regional pacts—one in the Balkans and one in the Middle East—that were designed to reinforce Turkey's security. Even in the realm of economic independence, about which the Turks have long been judged to be most sensitive, Ataturk's performance was open to conflicting interpretation. He backed the Chester Convention in the mid-1920s, an arrangement that would have given an American group of investors extensive economic rights if they had succeeded in raising the requisite capital to extend Turkey's railroad net. After this scheme fell through, he applauded Turkey's ability to finance its own development, rather than follow the disastrous Ottoman model of extensive foreign borrowings. Yet in the 1930s he accepted Soviet loans to back Turkey's first Five-Year Plan and sought economic assistance from the United Kingdom as well.

Ataturk's goal in international economic relations, therefore, was diversity and balance. Yet, during his era Turkey became disproportionately entangled with Nazi Germany. By the mid-1930s, Hitler's regime had become Turkey's main trading partner in both imports and exports. The dependence of Turkey on spares from Germany had reached such a level that the Kemalist regime had to weigh carefully the competing pressures for and against breaking economic ties with Berlin during the Second World War. Indeed, so enmeshed were the Turks with Germany that the final decision to declare war on Hitler's regime was a wrenching one, even though it came only after the war was effectively over.

To Ankara there was little alternative to grasping the West as tightly as possible after the war's end. Defense against Russia was a deeply ingrained response in Turkey, despite the era of revolutionary cooperation between the new Turkey and the Soviet state in the 1920s and 1930s. It was a cardinal tenet of the Kemalist regime not to be caught in a position that would give Moscow either the opportunity or provocation to confront Turkey. Turkish neutrality during the Second World War spared Turkey the burdens of active military operations or military destruction. It also seemed to offer a way to prevent being forced into the embrace of the Soviet Union. Yet with the defeat of the Nazis, Turkey was left highly exposed to pressure from Moscow.

While the issue of whether or not the Soviets would attack Turkey militarily had already been settled by 1947 as a result of the Turks' stout resistance and Stalin's concern lest he provoke U.S. retaliation, Ankara was enthusiastic about the prospect of military aid from the United States. Once NATO came into being, first a Republican Peoples party and then a Democrat party government worked earnestly to gain admission. In those days of Cold War intensity, foreign policy was bipartisan in Turkey and the American connection was welcomed by virtually everyone.

The Turks thus entered the Atlantic alliance without reservations or afterthoughts. The Democrat party regime was willing to take whatever diplomatic moves (such as setting up the Baghdad Pact) it felt would be pleasing to Washington. Military cooperation between the United States and Turkey consequently was by and large highly successful. Ankara's creaky military apparatus was revitalized and upgraded. American strategic interests were well served by a number of bilateral operations conducted with the Turks under the NATO umbrella. Only in the economic field were problems readily apparent. Washington sought to structure its assistance program at least partly on the basis of economic criteria and objected to the use of aid for partisan political purposes. Prime Minister Menderes interpreted the American program as one of general support to his administration and wished no questioning of the suitability of his policies. By 1958, however, financial stringencies brought him to agree on a far-reaching stabilization program that curbed some of his economic license in return for relief from his most acute financial pressures.

The overthrow of the Democrat party regime in 1960 did not immediately usher in changes in Turkey's foreign relations. During their year and one-half in power, the military rulers were too preoccupied with remaking the domestic political scene to be able to devote sustained attention to devising major foreign initiatives. Moreover, coming out of Turkey's military tradition, they were reasonably satisfied with the American performance, although they did aspire to regulate U.S. personnel more rigorously than in the past in order to prevent abuses of extraterritoriality and to assure the application of Turkish laws.

More important over the long run for Turkey's foreign orientation were the repercussions of the broader political debate triggered by the military's entry into politics. A mood of questioning of traditional institutions swept over the political elite. At first, this probing and testing focused on domestic matters. But the rise of the socialist movement in the early 1960s was accompanied by a changing spirit in Turkish foreign policy as well. Symptomatic in this connection was Turkey's move to show sympathy for the Algerians in their independence struggle against France.

The domestic and foreign trends unleashed by the period of military rule and its aftermath came into focus on Cyprus. In December 1963, violence between the small Turkish and much larger Greek Cypriot communities led Ankara to send planes over the island to demonstrate Turkey's commitment to defend the Turkish minority. Continuing communal troubles brought the Turkish Cypriots to group themselves in enclaves and the Turkish government to consider landing troops, using the authority provided in the Treaty of Guarantee that established the Cypriot state in 1960. Before the Turks could send an expeditionary force to the island, however, U.S. President Lyndon Johnson in June 1964 sent Prime Minister Inonu a harsh letter warning him that NATO might not protect Turkey if Ankara proceeded with military action in Cyprus. The Turks desisted under this pressure, but public resentment against this American intervention was strong and bitter throughout the country. Indeed, this incident marked a turning point in Turkey's foreign policy: the era of unquestioned diplomatic cooperation with the United States was over.

Under pressure from leftist extremists—who took up the cry of moving Turkey out of NATO—the Turkish authorities began to reinspect the alliance. A new agreement restricting the scope of American privileges and freedom of action was hammered out in 1969 after several years of negotiation. As a result, in the early 1970s relations between the United States and Turkey settled into a new pattern of close cooperation within more limited bounds, reflecting the now somewhat divergent interests of the two allies.

Coincidentally, Turkey's position in the East-West confrontation had changed. In the aftermath of the Cuban missile crisis of 1962, medium range surface-to-surface missiles had been removed from Turkish soil. This move reduced Turkey's strategic importance and significantly diminished the likelihood that Moscow would feel the need to attack in the event of broader NATO hostilities. At the same time, the Turks became drawn into the process of East-West détente, with a noticeable quickening and deepening of the pace of diplomatic exchanges with the USSR.

Against this backdrop, the disillusionment with the Western allies resulting from their failure to support Turkey on Cyprus only spurred normalization of Ankara's relations with the Soviet Union. In the mid-1960s, Moscow sent an economic aid mission to Turkey. The Soviets concluded with the Turks a program of major economic projects, including an aluminum plant and a steel mill. But Ankara refrained from seeking arms from the USSR in order not to risk disrupting NATO ties.

The third major effect of the Cyprus controversy was to induce Ankara to broaden its contacts with the Third World in general and with the Arab states in particular. Turkey suffered numerous adverse votes in the United Nations in connection with Cyprus. Turkish policymakers thus both dispatched missions to Africa and the Middle East to explain the Turkish position and sought to appeal to common religious ties of solidarity with other Muslim states. But except for Central Treaty Organization (CENTO) ally Pakistan, the Turks were not notably successful in getting the diplomatic support they were seeking.

Turkey's foreign position faced an even greater challenge from events on Cyprus in July 1974. After some years of gradually improving communal relations on the island, an initially successful coup against Archbishop Makarios was mounted by the military rulers in Athens. Although this action was not directed against the Turkish community in the first instance, the man who seized power in Nicosia, Nicos Sampson, was known as a long-time protagonist of joining Cyprus with Greece and as a dedicated foe of the Turks. In view of this clear violation of the Cypriot constitution, Ankara landed troops on the island, claiming that it was exercising its treaty rights to restore the status quo ante. Under strong international pressure, however, the Turks halted their military action after two days, having secured a foothold in the Kyrenia region, north of Nicosia. Peace talks were held in Geneva. But when the new regime in Athens asked for a delay in negotiations in August, Turkey resumed military operations and speedily secured control over slightly more than one-third of the northern part of the island.

While Ankara insisted that its actions were sanctioned by the Treaty of Guarantee with Cyprus, Turkey found itself largely isolated in the international community. The U.S. Congress imposed a complete embargo on all deliveries of arms to Turkey in February 1975; this ban lasted until September, but was then only partially lifted after the Turks in the meantime had closed all American installations and abrogated the 1969 Defense Cooperation Agreement. The embargo also prevented deliveries of American weapons by all NATO countries, thus impeding the ability of other allies to supply Turkey's military requirements. Moreover, the European powers lent their combined influence to urging Turkey to offer concessions to the Greek side in respect to Cyprus.

In this context, Turkey's relations with Greece took a decided turn for the worse. Suspicions already fanned by the course of events on Cyprus were further inflamed by an emerging dispute over the continental shelf and air rights in the Aegean Sea. The geography of this body of water, with numerous Greek islands hugging the Turkish coast, presents complex problems in apportioning the seabed. Following discovery of oil in commercial quantities in Greek waters in 1973, the Turks issued licenses for exploration in international waters on the Turkish side of the median line in the Aegean Sea, but in areas that Athens claimed were above the continental shelf of its islands.

Neither Turkey nor Greece, however, wished to see their dispute escalate to war. After Turkish seismic exploration in these disputed areas in the summer of 1976 raised tensions to the boiling point, the foreign ministers of both sides agreed to avoid inflammatory tactics and to pursue active negotiations. While no final solution has yet been reached, tempers have cooled and talks continue.

The Carter administration sought to promote resolution of the issues troubling U.S. relations with Turkey by sending Clark Clifford on a fact-finding mission to the area in February 1977. His trip was followed by some tangible progress in the talks between the two communities in Cyprus that had proceeded by fits and starts since late in 1974. But the campaigning for the June elections in Turkey was not a propitious time for diplomatic action by Ankara. The death of Makarios in August 1977 added a further note of uncertainty, as did the elections in Greece in November of that year.

The advent of the Ecevit government in January 1978 imparted new momentum to Turkey's foreign policy. The new prime minister accorded high priority to progress toward resolving the Cyprus issue and to easing tensions with Greece. He met with U.S. Secretary of State Cyrus Vance and with Greek Prime Minister Constantine Caramanlis in short order after taking office. In April 1978, after Secretary Vance had asked the U.S. Congress to lift the remaining restrictions on arms assistance to Turkey, the Turkish side offered more elaborate constitutional proposals and more specific areas for territorial negotiations than ever before in regard to Cyprus. The U.S. congressional process of removing the arms limitations finally succeeded in September 1978. By mid-1979, the leaders of the Turkish and Greek communities were again in negotiation. Yet, as of this writing, it is still too early to tell whether or not the Turks will soon resolve their chief external problems. And the burden of these foreign difficulties overhangs the domestic political scene.

Political Prospects

Coalition politics continues to be the dominant feature of political life in Turkey. The bargaining process, which has deep roots in Turkish culture in the commercial field, is now becoming the norm in politics. In determining Turkey's political prognosis, therefore, the paramount factor is the question of whether or not coalition government can provide effective rule over the longer run.

On the one hand, many Turks are disconcerted at the months of caretaker regimes while party combinations that can get a vote of confidence are assembled. Even after coalitions come into being, disharmony among the constituent parts over more-or-less serious issues raises doubts that such governments are sufficiently responsive to fulfill the country's needs. And the hairline majorities in parliament enjoyed by coalitions have made them vulnerable both to defections of even a handful of supporters and to obstructive tactics by the nearly equal-sized opposition. In these circumstances, there is an undercurrent of desire for a majority government that would have a mandate to carry out programs without the need for extensive compromise.

The strains of coalition politics place a premium on the effective operation of the other institutions that undergird the government. Fortunately for Turkey, the strong bureaucratic structure and tradition provide an underpinning that can cushion the impact of difficulties at the political level of government. Even though private enterprise is luring growing numbers of able civil servants, the economic ministries and the State Planning Organization in particular have developed expertise and sophistication in coping with Turkey's problems. These technocrats are capable of doing much on their own to manage the economy and to deal with international financial institutions, such as the World Bank and the International Monetary Fund. This sort of bureaucratic strength, therefore, is a major asset in offsetting any deleterious effects of coalition regimes.

While prescriptions for radical change do not have much appeal as long as the mechanisms of government function without outright crisis, there is continuing interest in modifying the present political structure. Many in Turkey feel that the checks and balances of the Second Republic work only too well, making it excessively difficult to get strong government leadership. These critics frequently zero in on proportional representation in particular as the root cause of the difficulty. Consequently, there is perennial talk of amending the election law with a view toward encouraging a return to the two-party system.

A number of possible remedies are proposed. Some Turkish politicians have favored single-member constituencies, a solution that would increase the weight of localism. Devotees of reform, on the other hand, are already concerned about resistance from local interests and thus would oppose such a change. There are also those in Turkey who would like to return to the simple majority system on a province-wide basis along the lines of the electoral procedures of the First Republic. They argue that with a two-house parliament and a constitutional court, the problems of the earlier era could not recur. Yet attachment to the principle of proportional representation remains strong within the Republican Peoples party, and no serious effort to abandon this method has yet been made.

Dissatisfaction with the election law would diminish if one of the major parties were to gain a majority in the elections due in 1981. Such an outcome is by no means out of the question. Continuation of present trends would give the Republican Peoples party a good chance to dominate the parliament at that time. Even a gain of a few more percent of the popular vote by this party would probably produce a majority for it in the lower house under the d'Hondt system. The Republican Peoples party has a strong national base, which is distributed more evenly across the country than that of the Justice party. Indeed, some Turkish observers have claimed that Ecevit's party would have achieved a majority in the 1977 elections if it had given its provincial organization in eastern Turkey more scope to select popular candidates and had not assigned nonnatives to head several slates in this region.

The Justice party also has a reasonable possibility of securing a working majority in the next elections. The center-right constituency still holds the key to electoral success. If Demirel could reassemble under his banner even a few more of those who backed his party in the 1960s, he might be able to edge out the Republican Peoples party by a small margin. In this event, his party would benefit from the advantage accorded the largest vote-getter under the electoral law. A showing of about 45 percent of the popular vote might well be enough to return a Justice party majority in parliament.

The desire for strong government is reinforced by the continuing problem of political violence. The universities and even lycées have been the scenes of clashes between rightist and leftist students with dismaying frequency. Much less often, terrorism has been directed at political figures as well—usually local or provincial politicians, however, rather than national personalities. Nonetheless, the attention recent governments have given this problem has thus far prevented political disorder from posing a serious threat to the regime. At bottom, respect for authority is deeply ingrained in Turkey. Those who foment violence do not find ready support among the populace.

Whatever changes take place, therefore, are likely to be gradual, because the political process in Turkey has impressive strengths. The Turks have shown themselves flexible and imaginative in skirting the threats to orderly political development. While it seems certain that Turkey will continue, as in the past, to be faced with challenge in keeping its democratic system operating effectively, the country's substantial resources of talent and strong traditions of successfully finding its own solutions give grounds for optimism.

Bibliography

The standard work, Bernard Lewis, *The Emergence of Modern Turkey* (New York: Oxford University Press, 1961) is by now thoroughly out of date for coverage of contemporary Turkey. It is still the best general treatment of the historical introduction and the First Republic. For the Second Republic, C. H. Dodd, *Politics and Government in Turkey* (Berkeley and Los Angeles: University of California Press, 1969) covers the early years; Ergun Ozbudun, *Social Change and Political Participation in Turkey* (Princeton: Princeton University Press, 1976) brings the picture closer to date. Feroz Ahmad also surveys both republics in his *The Turkish Experiment in Democracy 1950–75* (London: Hurst, 1977). A more detailed study of Turkey's modern ruling class is given in Frederick W. Frey, "Patterns of Elite Politics in Turkey," in George Lenczowski, ed., *Political Elites in the Middle East* (Washington, D.C.: American Enterprise Institute, 1975). The standard account of the First Republic politicians is Frederick W. Frey, *The Turkish Political Elite* (Cambridge, Mass.: MIT Press, 1965). Of a more specialized nature are Kemal H. Karpat, *The Gecekondu: Rural Migration and Urbanization* (London: Cambridge University Press, 1976); and Leslie L. Roos, Jr. and Noralou P. Roos, *Managers of Modernization: Organizations and Elites in Turkey (1950–1969)* (Cambridge: Harvard University Press, 1971). Economic development is analyzed in the standard treatment by Z. Y. Hershlag, *Turkey, The Challenge of Growth* (Leiden: E. J. Brill, 1968). Also useful is Edwin J. Cohn, *Turkish Economic, Social, and Political Change* (New York: Praeger Publishers, 1970). The role of the military is discussed in many works, but the subtleties and complexities appear to elude most analysts. George S. Harris, "The Cause of the 1960 Revolution in Turkey," (*Middle East Journal*, Autumn 1970), sets the stage for the Second Republic. Roger P. Nye gives an exhaustive description of General Gurler's defeat in his "Civil-Military Confrontation in Turkey: The 1973 Presidential Election," (*International Journal of Middle East Studies*, April 1977). Turkey's postwar foreign policy trends are brought together in George S. Harris, *Troubled Alliance: Turkish-American Problems in Historical Perspective: 1945–1971* (Washington, D.C.: American Enterprise Institute, 1972). Also informative is Ferenc A. Vali, *Bridge Across the Bosporus* (Baltimore and London: Johns Hopkins University Press, 1971). The Cyprus crisis of 1974 and its aftermath have yet to receive scholarly treatment. For contemporary domestic issues, see Jacob M. Landau, *Radical Politics in Modern Turkey* (Leiden: E. J. Brill, 1974) and Joseph S. Szyliovicz, *A Political Analysis of Student Activism: The Turkish Case* (Beverly Hills and London: Sage, 1972). The religious question is inspected in Nur Yalman, "Some Observations on Secularism in Islam: The Cultural Revolution in Turkey," (*Daedalus*, Winter 1973).

4

Iran

David E. Long

In October 1971, amid much fanfare, the great and near-great of the world gathered at Persepolis to help celebrate the twenty-five hundredth anniversary of the founding of the Persian monarchy, the oldest then existent in the world. It was a birthday party to end all birthday parties in its lavish hospitality and entertainment, and the government's logistical capabilities were strained to the utmost to stage such a grandiose affair. In many respects, the commemoration symbolized the unique combination of past glory, present reality, and future aspirations that is modern Iran. The country's ruler, Shah Muhammad Reza, while seeking to transform his country into a major twentieth-century power, did not hesitate to evoke the heritage of its past and the dreams of its future as integral parts of Iran's development. It was difficult, therefore, to separate past glory and future hopes from the reality of modern Iran. In January 1979, however, reality overtook the shah. After a year of growing turmoil, his regime collapsed. At this writing, it is still too early to predict what type of governmental system will ultimately take its place.

Historical Background

In the first half of the sixth century B.C., Cyrus the Great united the Medes and the Persians into the first great Persian Empire. Cyrus and successive rulers of the Achaemenid dynasty ushered in a golden age of Persian civilization. Persian culture, its Zoroastrian religion, its statecraft and military science all left an indelible imprint on the course of ancient history. The carved stone wall friezes at Persepolis attest to the magnificence of the Persian Empire, which stretched from present-day Afghanistan to Egypt and Anatolia.

The Achaemenids were beset with wars against the Greeks. In 490 B.C., they suffered a major defeat at Marathon and ten years later were defeated again at Salamis. Finally, the dynasty was overthrown by Alexander the Great, who defeated the Persian army at Arbelia in 331 B.C.and burned the capital at Persepolis. Alexander, who regarded himself as the head of the Persian Empire, began the first period of alien imperial rule that was to alternate with native Persian rule down to modern times.

After the death of Alexander, his empire was divided among his generals. Seleucus became heir to Persia, founding the Seleucid dynasty. This dynasty ruled until 247 B.C., when it gave way to the Parthian Empire of the Arsacids, who ruled for nearly 500 years.

In A.D. 22, another Persian dynasty, the Sassanids, came to power. Although never reaching the glory and power of the Achaemenids, the Sassanids (who were also from the region of Fars) restored Zoroastrianism and made great strides in civil administration. As with past dynasties, its chief military threat was from the west, in this case, Byzantium. So exhausted were the Sassanids by their numerous wars with Byzantines that when the Arab hordes came surging out of the desert, propagating the new religion, Islam, Persia was like a ripe plum free for the taking. In A.D. 642, the Arabs defeated the Persian army at the battle of Nehavend. The empire was dismembered and ruled from Damascus and later Baghdad by various Arab and Persian provincial governors. Zoroastrianism was banished and Islam introduced as the state religion.

In some respects, the Persians conquered the Arabs as much as they themselves were conquered. With the transfer of the caliphate from Damascus to Baghdad in A.D. 750, Persian culture became a major influence on Arab-Muslim civilization, which was then reaching its zenith. With the decline of the Abbasid Empire, Seljuk Turks made their appearance in the north, introducing a system of feudal land tenure and civil administration to Persia. The Arab period came to an end in the thirteenth century with the Mongol invasions under Hulagu Khan who sacked Baghdad in 1258. For the next 250 years, Persia was again under foreign rule.

Modern Persia originated with the rise of the Safavids in the sixteenth century. Under Ismail Safavi (r. 1502–1524), the country reemerged with the same general boundaries that exist today, although some territories were lost to Russian conquests in the eighteenth and nineteenth centuries. Ismail made Shi'a Islam the state religion. The Safavid dynasty also introduced a new golden age that reached its apogee under Shah Abbas I the Great (r. 1558–1629). Isfahan, the Safavid capital, became one of the most beautiful cities in the Middle East.

The Safavids remained in power until 1750. Following an interregnum under Karim Khan Zand (r. 1750–1779), the Qajar dynasty came to power at the end of the century. It remained in power until it was replaced by the

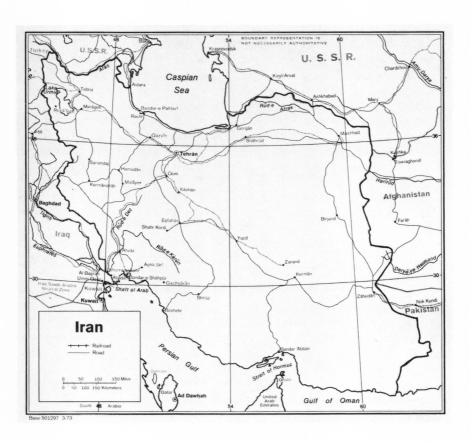

BOUNDARY REPRESENTATION IS
NOT NECESSARILY AUTHORITATIVE

U.S.S.R.

Turkey

Aras

Lake
Urmia

Tabriz

Astara

Caspian
Sea

Krasnovodsk

Kizyl-Arvat

U.S.S.R.

Chardzhou

Amu Darya

Rezaiyeh

Marageh

Bandar-e Pahlavi

Rud-e Atrak

Ashkhabad

Mary

Erbil

Rasht

Gorgan

Mashhad

Kushka

Towraghondi

Sanandaj

Qazvin

Shahrud

Tehran

Hamadan

Qom

Harirud

Afghanistan

Kermanshah

Malayer

Kashan

Baghdad

Rud-e Dez

Esfahan

Shahr Kord

Birjand

Farah

Iraq

Tigris

Yazd

Euphrates

Rud-e Karun

Ahvaz

Zarand

Darya-ye Helmand

Al Basrah

Khorramshahr

Agha Jari

Kerman

Umm Qasr

Abadan

Bandar-e Shahpur

Gachsaran

Iraq Saudi Arabia
Neutral Zone

Kuwait

Shatt al Arab

Shiraz

Zahedan

Nok Kundi

Kuwait

Pakistan

Bushehr

Iran

┼┼┼┼ Railroad
──── Road

Persian Gulf

Bahrain

Bandar Abbas

Strait of Hormuz

Oman

0   50   100   150 Miles
0   50   100 150 Kilometers

Qatar

Ad Dawhah

Saudi   Arabia

United
Arab
Emirates

Gulf of Oman

Base 501297 3-73

recent shah's father in 1925. The Qajars, however, were weak, and their reign was characterized by intrigue and foreign domination.

During the nineteenth and first half of the twentieth centuries, Persia became a pawn of great-power rivalries. For most of this period, Russia and Britain were the two main antagonists. Since the time of Peter the Great, the Russians had desired a warm-water port on the Persian Gulf. The British interest in Persia stemmed from its desire to protect its imperial lines of communication with India. The British desired a relatively strong and independent Persia as a buffer against Russian southern expansionism but did not, however, wish to add Iran to their imperial domain.

In the early nineteenth century, Napoleonic France threatened British hegemony in the area by seeking political and economic concessions from the shah. There ensued a four-way series of intrigues involving Britain, Russia, France, and Persia. The Congress of Vienna ended the French threat, but soon thereafter Russia extracted from Persia territories to and beyond the Aras River. For the next several decades, Russia expanded southward down the east side of the Caspian Sea, touching off several crises involving Britain, Persia, and Afghanistan. In the meantime, the British sought commercial advantages. In 1872, a naturalized British businessman-adventurer, Baron de Reuter, obtained a sweeping concession from Nasir ed-Din Shah. Under Russian pressure it was cancelled, but a British-owned Imperial Bank of Persia was chartered with exclusive rights to issue bank notes. The Russians, however, from whom Persian rulers had borrowed heavily for their personal extravagances, obtained in return the right to collect customs duties over much of Persia.

The most important concession of all, however, was obtained by an Australian. On 28 May 1901, Alfred M. Marriot signed an agreement with Shah Muzafaar ed-Din on behalf of an Australian financier, William Knox D'Arcy, which granted D'Arcy the first Middle Eastern oil concession. In January 1908 oil was discovered, and in the following April D'Arcy's interests were reorganized as the Anglo-Persian Oil Company (APOC). The strategic importance of oil was just being felt. When Winston Churchill became first lord of the admiralty in 1911, the Royal Navy was rapidly converting from coal to oil. Churchill, aware that Britain had no oil resources anywhere in the empire, set about to acquire some. On 14 June 1914, barely two months before World War I broke out, Churchill passed an act through Parliament authorizing the British government to purchase a 51-percent controlling interest in APOC. In 1935, APOC was renamed the Anglo-Iranian Oil Company (AIOC). When Iran subsequently nationalized its oil in 1951, the name was changed to British Petroleum (BP).

Domestic Persian politics during the first decade of the twentieth century were exceptionally turbulent. Not only were the Qajar shahs weak
and despotic, but a movement of political liberalism gained a hold on the
intelligentsia and growing middle class. In 1906, the newly formed
Democratic party organized riots in Tehran, the capital, that ultimately
forced Muhammad Ali Shah to grant a Western-styled constitution and a
parliament (Majlis). Muhammad Ali Shah repudiated the constitution in
1908, but the following year he was forced to abdicate in favor of his
minor son, Ahmad, who restored the constitution.

By that time the clouds of war were already gathering over Europe.
Britain and Russia, long rivals in Persia, found themselves allied against
Imperial Germany. When World War I broke out, the young and in-
effectual Shah Ahmad could not maintain Persia's declared neutrality.
Turkish, British, and Russian troops were active inside Persia, and Ger-
man agents were successful in stirring up tribal unrest.

By the war's end, Persia's internal affairs were in chaos. The Russian
menace, however, had receded at least temporarily as a result of the Russian revolution. Soviet troops on the Caspian did back a Persian rebel
leader, Kuchik Khan, in proclaiming a republic of Gilan, but the troops
were withdrawn following a Soviet-Iranian treaty of friendship in
February 1921. The British also made a bid for primacy in Persia, but,
after failing in 1919 to obtain a treaty guaranteeing them that position,
they began to withdraw their troops that had been stationed there during
the war.

In February 1921 the commander of the Persian Cossack Division,
Reza Shah Pahlevi, and a young nationalist intellectual, Zia ed-Din
Tabatabai, engineered a coup. Reza Shah became minister of war and
commander-in-chief and Zia became prime minister. By 1923, however,
Reza Shah split with Zia and forced him into exile, assuming the premiership himself. Soon after, he forced Shah Ahmad to take a "long
vacation" in Europe, and in 1925 was himself proclaimed "shah-in-shah"
(king of kings).

Reza Shah was a very astute and farsighted politician. Working his
way up through the ranks of the Cossack Division, he engineered the
dismissal of its Russian officers corps in 1920, temporarily used British
officers to fill the gap, then converted the force to an all-Persian unit.
From this base, he rapidly moved up, ultimately becoming the shah.

Having first set out to pacify the country, Reza Shah then turned to
internal reform. In this endeavor, he wished to emulate his contemporary Kemal Ataturk, the great reformer and creator of modern
Turkey. Although Reza Shah's reforms never reached the scope of
Ataturk's, they were impressive in their own right. He began to link the

country through modern communications and was particularly proud of the entirely locally financed trans-Iranian railroad, which was completed in 1939. In education, he laid the groundwork for a modern school system and set up the Iranian Academy of Literature to purge the language of foreign, and particularly Arabic, influences. To reflect this new mood, he changed the Hellenistic name of Persia to Iran (meaning Aryan) in 1935.

In the field of law, Reza Shah introduced the French judicial system, challenging the reactionary religious establishment's hold on the legal system through Islamic law. He did not provoke an open confrontation, however, and explicitly championed Islam as the state religion. In fact, reformer though he was, Reza Shah was no democrat. He did not believe democratic institutions could work in Iranian society and admired efficient, benevolent government administered from the top, as he thought was the case in Nazi Germany. His affinity with the Germans (who before World War I had provided Iranian nationalists with a great-power alternative to the British and the Russians) ultimately led to his downfall. For the Allies, Iran was the only practical route of resupply to the Soviets. Thus, when he refused to accede to Allied demands to expel German expatriates in 1941, the British and Soviets forced him to abdicate in favor of his son, Muhammad Reza. For Iran, the abdication required a total reassessment of its foreign relations. At the war's end, Iran turned to the United States as its major great-power ally. For the rest of Muhammad Reza Shah's reign, the United States remained his foremost ally.

Muhammad Reza Shah's reign began inauspiciously with his father's abdication. In 1953 he weathered a severe threat from Prime Minister Muhammad Mossadeq, who attempted to seize control of the country. In May 1951 Mossadeq, backed by Iranian nationalists, had nationalized the country's oil resources. AIOC immediately threatened to sue any company that bought Iranian oil. Lacking the technical expertise to operate the oil fields, and with world marketing in the hand of the oil companies, Iran witnessed an abrupt reduction in oil production. As government oil revenues dried up, Mossadeq soon began to encounter discontent. He became increasingly more dictatorial as prime minister. In July 1953 he dissolved the Majlis (the lower house of Parliament) and in August tried but failed to seize all powers of the government.

During the 1960s the shah launched his own reform program, known as the White Revolution. The program was originally announced in late 1961 with land reform as the central focus. In January 1962, after ceding all his own personally held land to the nation through the Pahlevi Foundation, the shah decreed the Land Reform Act, which was to give land tenure to the largely landless peasants. A year later, the shah's reform program was submitted to public referendum as the first six Points for Progress of the Revolution of the Shah and the People: land reform, nationalizing forest lands, sale of equity in state-owned factories to the private sector to raise revenues for land reform, provision for sharing with the workers 20 percent of the net profits of industrial establishments, emancipation of women, and the creation of a literacy corps. By 1978 thirteen additional points had been added, including the creation of the Health Corps, the Development and Agricultural Extension Corps, and an equity corps for legal aid. Other points called for nationalization and development of water resources, urban and rural reconstruction, and reform of the civil service.

In 1967 the shah's long-awaited and often-delayed coronation took place. After crowning himself, he crowned Queen Farah, the first time in Iranian-Persian history that a woman had been so honored. This event, however, marked the pinnacle of the shah's power. By 1977, economic and social conditions had begun seriously to deteriorate, and opposition to the regime began to mount. Religious sentiment, led by the exiled Shi'ite religious leader Ayatollah Khomeini, spurred large-scale political unrest. In an attempt to counter discontent the shah relaxed somewhat the tight grip of the government over the people and intensified a campaign against corruption in high places that had become a major issue.

These moves, however, did not satisfy growing discontent with the shah. Antigovernment demonstrations broke out in Qom on 9 January 1978, setting the stage for the growing political turmoil that was to bring down the shah a year later. Demonstrations marking the end of a forty-day period of mourning for those killed in the previous riots provided the impetus for continued strife.

As the situation deteriorated, the shah's efforts to placate the people became more desperate. In June, he dismissed General Nemetollah Nassiri, head of the dreaded SAVAK, the secret police. His efforts, however, were too little and too late. On 19 August, at least 377 people perished in Abadan when an arsonist, suspected of being a part of the Muslim opposition, set fire to the Rex theater. Unrest followed, and on 27 August Prime Minister Amouzegar was replaced by Jafar Sharif Emami. Finally, after massive demonstrations on 7 and 8 September, martial law was proclaimed.

A semblance of order was restored with martial law but proved to be only the calm before the storm. In November Sharif Emami was replaced as prime minister by General Gholam Reza Azhari, but the latter's government survived only into December. The month of December 1978 roughly coincided with the Islamic lunar month of Muharram, held particularly holy by Shi'a Muslims. Popular emotions rose to a fever pitch.

Last-minute efforts by the shah to meet with opposition leaders failed. Rioting again broke out that virtually shut down the oil industry by 27 December.

As the year ended, Shahpur Bakhtiar, a leader in the opposition National Front (a descendant of Mossadeq's political organization), was asked to form a cabinet. The Bakhtiar cabinet, sworn in on 6 January, 1979, was destined to be the last one under the monarchy. The shah left the country on 16 January, and on 1 February Ayatollah Khomeini returned triumphantly from Paris where he had been in exile. On 5 February Khomeini announced the creation of a new provisional government under Mehdi Bazargan, who was sworn in the following week.

The demise of the monarchy was completed six weeks later. Following a plebiscite on 30 March, Khomeini announced the creation of an Islamic republic on 1 April.

Political Environment

The People

Population Structure. The population of Iran in 1977 was estimated to be approximately thirty-eight million. The annual population growth rate has increased from roughly 1.5 percent in the 1920s to around 3 percent today. The Iranian National Family Planning Program has been established to stabilize annual population growth at about 1 percent by the year 2000, but that goal is probably unrealistic. Nevertheless, Iran is still trying to lay a solid groundwork to control excessive population growth in the future.

The growth rate is primarily attributable to the declining death rate resulting from considerable investment in health care over the years. Iran has one of the highest per capita public health expenditures in the developing world. The life expectancy of the average Iranian has greatly increased since the turn of the century and is now fifty-three years.

Although still roughly half the population is rural, the trend toward urbanization is increasing. For example, at the turn of the century, the rural population accounted for roughly 80 percent of the total. Tehran, which had an estimated population in 1977 of around 4.6 million, has been doubling in size about every dozen years since World War II. Without new sources of water and other services, the upward limit on population growth in Tehran is probably around six million. Tehran's phenomenal growth has taken place despite efforts to divert development projects to regional cities and towns. The latter have also grown, however. Isfahan, for example, is the site of major new industrial development and has grown rapidly in the last few years. Most future urban growth is expected to cluster outward from the major cities along the main north-south and east-west transportation routes.

Social Structure. Iranian society is extremely heterogeneous, being divided both by class structure, occupation, and income, and by ethnic identification. Slightly less than half of the population is comprised of native Persian speakers, although Persian is the official language. With the emphasis on Persian language, history and culture in the schools, public media, and government operations, Persian cultural predominance is gaining ground. Nevertheless, the hold of non-Persian ethnic identification remains strong and has been given added impetus by the overthrow of the monarchy.

In the northwest, Turkic-speaking Azeris of Azerbaijan still cling to their old cultural patterns, and in the regional capital, Tabriz, Azeri is heard even in government offices, where anything but Persian would be normally frowned upon. The Azeris are kinsmen of those in neighboring Soviet Azerbaijan, and in 1946 the Soviets tried unsuccessfully to gain control of the Iranian Azeris through the creation of a so-called Azerbaijan Republic with Tabriz as the capital. On the east side of the Caspian Sea live Turkomen tribes who also have blood ties to the north in the Soviet Union. The Qashqa'is comprise the other major Turkic-speaking ethnic group. Their tribal homeland is located in the southern Zagros Mountains.

Two important ethnic tribal groups actually speak dialects of Persian. The Bakhtiaris inhabit the central Zagros near Isfahan, and their cousins the Lurs are located immediately to the west along the Iraqi border. To the north of the Lurs are the Kurds, whose homeland spills over into Iraq, Turkey, and the Soviet Union. The Kurds have a long, proud ethnic heritage, and, unlike most Iranians, they are Sunni Muslims. The Soviets also tried to promote a Kurdish "republic" after World War II. Prior to 1975, the shah's support of Iraqi Kurds in their demands for political autonomy had been a major irritant in Iraqi-Iranian relations. Although this support was withdrawn, the potential for both countries to become involved in Kurdish irredentist movements across the border remains. Within Iran, the collapse of the monarchy also rekindled irridentist Kurdish aspirations, leading to several incidents of violence.

In the oil-rich province of Khuzistan, at the head of the Persian Gulf, and in the region southward along the Iranian coast, most of the population is Arabic speaking and generally Sunni Muslim. When Reza Shah first came to power, one of his first tasks was to curb the semi-independent powers of Shaykh Khazal of Muhammara, whose feudal domain included Khuzistan. There remain today occasional cries of irridentism by Iraqi-supported local dissidents who call the area Arabistan. Though a potential cause of concern in Tehran, their political significance is virtually nil.

A final major ethnic area is located in the far southeast where Baluchistan spills over into neighboring Pakistan and Afghanistan. The Baluchis, who inhabit this barren, hard-bitten land, are known for their warlike qualities and are often contracted as mercenaries by neighboring armies. For centuries, Baluchis have crossed the Gulf of Oman to settle along Oman's Batinah coast. More recently, they have been attracted by relatively good wages as manual laborers in the oil-rich but labor-short Arab shaykhdoms of the lower gulf. The Baluchis are also Sunnis.

There are some smaller groups to be noted. The Jewish community, which dates from the fifth century B.C., is mostly urban and comparatively prosperous. There are small communities of Armenian Christians and Assyrians that date from the beginning of the Christian era. Zoroastrians, who still follow the pre-Islamic religion of Persia, are also found in small numbers.

Social class structure in Iran is complex. At the top of the social order is the elite class. Family ties continue to be a major source of Iran's social order, headed by the so-called first forty families. The actual number is much larger and is augmented by perhaps 150 to 200 prominent provincial families. Although changes in family fortunes have both added and removed families from the political elite over the years, there has been an impressive continuity among the group. As Iranian development programs have taken hold in the last ten to fifteen years, however, the need for top-level skilled technocrats and the rapidly expanding educational system have made membership in the elite more competitive. It is increasingly possible for the most humbly born Iranians with sufficient skill and ability to aspire to positions of major influence.

The middle and working classes are for the most part traditionalist, religious, and conservative in outlook. There is also a growing modern class of new middle-level technocrats who, though playing an increasingly important role in the country's economic development, have not yet become a major political factor. Those young professionals who do show an interest in politics generally aspire to join the elite.

Among the traditional middle class are the bazaar shopkeepers, the middle and lower level bureaucrats, and the Shi'a Islamic clergy, or ulama. A great majority of the population is Shi'ite and it is the established religion of Iran. Broadening the educational system has introduced modern concepts and ideas to this group but old ideas die very slowly. In fact, Shi'ism has undergone a renaissance that became a primary contributing factor to the overthrow of the shah. By the mid-1970s the Shi'a leadership, called ayatollahs, began rapidly to expand the number of their followers while preaching a return to the fundamentals of Islam. Their often violent opposition to the social development programs of the shah helped undermine the stability of the regime. Ayatollah Khomeini, exiled in 1963, was considered by many to be the spiritual leader of the Shi'ite community and was venerated by the mass of Shi'ite faithful. It was under the aegis of Khomeini that the new Islamic republic was created.

The working classes in Iran include peasant farmers, tribesmen, artisans, servants, and a small but growing industrial labor force. Farmers still comprise a major element in Iranian society, with 40 percent of the population engaged in agriculture. In recent years, however, thousands of peasant farmers have swelled the populations of the cities, particularly Tehran, further exacerbating social and urban problems. Living conditions in the cities can be harsh for the working class, particularly for those flocking in from the countryside, but, like the middle class, the peasants are basically conservative in outlook and, in more tranquil times, are generally apolitical.

One other group that has a great influence on politics is comprised of the university students, teachers, and other intellectuals. Though not directly participating in the political process, they are an articulate indicator of political and economic conditions generally. Historically, those with a higher education (in earlier times, the monopoly of the elite) could expect prestigious jobs on the completion of their studies. As the number of graduates increases each year, however, competition for jobs is becoming more intense. In fact, one of the greatest challenges confronting the government in the coming years will be to assimilate effectively the graduating students and highly skilled and educated professional classes into the political process.

A large part of social intercourse in Iran centers around highly unstructured and informal groups of men of roughly the same age, background, and social status. These groups, called *dowrahs* (circles), are essentially social in nature. However, many of the day-to-day decisions of business and government both in high places and low are made under the aegis of a *dowrah*. The institution of *dowrahs*, therefore, tends further to reinforce the high degree of personalization in Iranian society.

Economic Conditions

With an area of 1,648,000 square kilometers (636,296 square miles), and a population approaching forty million, Iran has the potential for a modern, productive economy. Much of the land is arid, but agricultural productivity could be greatly increased.

Iran still has a free market economy, but due to the traditional reluctance of the private sector to risk venture capital, and because the great bulk of foreign currency earnings is derived from oil, the public sector predominates. Government planning has been a major factor in economic development since the First Development Plan was drawn up in 1948. Put into operation the following year, it and the Second Development Plan (1955–1962) both emphasized basic economic infrastructure and dams. Owing largely to the political upheavals and loss of oil revenues during the Mossadeq period and also because of the lack of managerial expertise, these two plans were only partially successful. They did, however, set the stage for more impressive economic gains that were to follow.

The Third Development Plan (1962–1968) ushered in a period of rapid economic growth throughout the 1960s and 1970s. It also encouraged private sector investment, which actually exceeded public sector development during this period. At the heart of the plan was land reform, which was given its political expression in the White Revolution. The plan also called for extension of irrigated land and water resources and improvement of agricultural productivity. The Fourth Development Plan (1968–1973) emphasized industrial growth. During this period, rapid growth (13 percent in 1972) was sustained, but bottlenecks in manpower and infrastructure began to appear.

The Fifth Development Plan was inaugurated in March 1973, but with the quadrupling of oil prices the following fall and winter, the plan was revised to produce an expenditure of $70 billion (with $29 billion allocated for defense expenditures). Because of vastly increased expenditures, the bottlenecks that began to appear earlier became worse, and shortages became more chronic. Both domestic and import inflation also began to affect the economy, and softening of oil demand in 1975–1976 reduced revenues below the level that had been anticipated.

The fifth plan stressed agriculture. Farmers were organized into cooperatives in an attempt to increase productivity, and emphasis was placed on increased mechanization, availability of more agricultural credits, and public sector agri-industrial projects including joint ventures with foreign firms. Despite the focus on the agricultural sector, however, domestic agricultural productivity did not keep pace with demand, and Iran has become a net importer of a number of staples. Subsidizing food prices in the face of rising inflation further undermined the agricultural sector. Poor farmers flocked to the cities for higher pay, creating serious social and infrastructure problems as well. In the years ahead, the agricultural sector will demand major attention if Iran is to regain a balanced economy.

During the last years of the monarchy Iran also attempted to develop a fishing and forestry industry. Prior to nationalization of forest lands in 1963, many forests had been denuded by indiscriminate logging and overgrazing by livestock. A major conservation and reforestation effort now under way is supervised by the Forestry Commission. Fishing was also underdeveloped, with the exception of the caviar industry in the Caspian Sea. Iran is now trying to build up a fishing fleet, particularly for the Persian Gulf and Indian Ocean.

The shah focused his primary interest and investment on the industrial sector. Early industrial development concentrated on import reduction. For example, the first auto assembly plant was built in 1957, with parts imported from abroad. Iranian-assembled vehicles now meet nearly all domestic demand. The largest automotive producer, Iranian National, makes the Peykan, an Iranian version of the Hillman produced under license from Chrysler (U.K.). Iranian National launched an expansion program to build its own engines and hoped ultimately to develop an entirely domestically produced car.

Iran also has tried to develop a steel industry. The first rolling mill, Arya Mehr, was built with Soviet credits in 1965 at Isfahan and is now the second largest employer in the country after the oil industry. Expansion plans call for capacity to increase from 700,000 tons in 1975 to over 10 million in 1985. Also, by acquiring 25 percent interest in the steel works of Germany's Krupp, Iran has tried to assure itself access to the markets and expertise needed to develop further its own steel industry.

The shah's emphasis on rapid industrial development was predicated on the projection that within twenty years, oil production would be insufficient to sustain development expenditures adequately. He saw it as a race against time. Unfortunately, he lost the race. The capital invested in the industrial sector could not be adequately absorbed. The growing labor force it created was not sufficiently productive to compete with Western competitors. The high inflation created by this massive level of investment in the industrial sector produced demands for higher wages which, when granted, made the work force even less competitive. In this connection, it is interesting to speculate how much worse conditions might have been if the shah had dumped the massive funds spent on military arms into the already overheated economy.

The economic structure that the shah attempted to create was funded for the most part by oil revenues. When oil revenues began to decline in real terms due to softening world market conditions in 1976–1978, the shah was forced to cut back on development spending. The resulting contraction of economic activity in Iran was a major factor in the rapid rise of discontent with the regime, which led to the shah's downfall.

Despite declining reserves, oil was and continued to be the basic underpinning of the Iranian economy. When oil was nationalized in 1951, it was placed under the control of the National Iranian Oil Company (NIOC). Lacking the expertise to operate the oil fields, however, NIOC turned in 1954 to a consortium of international oil companies. Participants in the consortium included British Petroleum, 50 percent; Royal Dutch Shell, 14 percent; Gulf, Exxon, Mobil, SOCAL, and TEXACO, each 7 percent; CFP, 6 percent; and IRICON, a group of small American companies, 5 percent. The consortium first operated the oil industry on a leasing agreement. After 1973 it operated as a service company called Iranian Oil Services under contract to NIOC. With the fall of the shah, Iran informed the consortium that its services would no longer be needed and that Western oil technologists would be retained on a direct basis.

As oil reserves have been depleted, Iran has had to invest in programs to maintain production levels. A multibillion-dollar gas injection program to restore and maintain oil field pressure was under way but was interrupted in the political upheaval leading to the ouster of the shah. Iran had sought to develop its large gas reserves through its National Iranian Gas Company (NIGC), a subsidiary of NIOC. The gas industry was already the second largest foreign exchange earner after oil, and Iran hoped to become a major supplier of natural gas to Europe. Under an agreement with the Soviet Union and Ruhrgas of West Germany, the Iranians planned to be exporting 1.3 billion cubic feet of gas per day by pipeline to the Soviet Union for transshipment to Germany by the early 1980s.

Political Structure

Under the shah, Iran was a constitutional monarchy. It had a cabinet form of government with a prime minister appointed by the shah, and a two-house legislature. The lower house, the Majlis, was comprised of 220 members elected by universal suffrage. The upper house, the Senate, played a lesser role in government than the Majlis. Half of the sixty members were elected and the other half were selected by the shah. Senators had to be at least forty years of age.

Shi'a Islam is the official state religion. Under the shah, however, two Majlis deputies were elected by the Armenian Christian community and one each by the Zoroastrian and Jewish communities. In 1963, women gained the right to become deputies and in 1967 four were seated.

Until 1978 Iran had a single political party, the Rastakhiz (Resurgence) party. Its creation was announced by the shah in a press conference in

March 1975. Prior to that, there were two rather moribund parties, the government-sponsored Iran Novin (New Iran) party and the loyal opposition, Mardom, both created by the shah in 1963. The shah had apparently hoped that the new Rastakhiz party could serve as an avenue for public participation in the political process, but by 1978, it became evident that it would not. As a part of his broader liberalization program first announced a year earlier, the shah announced that other parties could be formed. By the fall of 1978, Rastakhiz had almost withered away as many supporters and opponents of the shah alike rushed to form independent parties.

Under the shah Iran also had an independent judiciary. The legal code was based on the French system. The new regime, however, has expressed its intention to reinstitute Islamic law.

Several dissident groups operated outside the law during the monarchy. The oldest was the communist Tudeh ("Masses") party, which was formed in 1941 and outlawed in 1949 after an attempt on the life of the shah. It was also active during the Mossadeq period. The Tudeh party of today has degenerated into little more than a discussion group and plays virtually no role in Iranian politics.

The political structure of the Islamic republic has yet to emerge. In the interim period between the overthrow of the shah's regime and the establishment of new political institutions, a dual system evolved. The religious leadership under Ayatollah Khomeini exercised political control through the Revolutionary Council and subordinate committees. At the same time, a provisional government was created under a prime minister that controlled government administration.

In the meantime, work was begun on a new constitution that the regime claimed would restore constitutionalism to Iran for the first time since the 1906 constitution. The draft of the new constitution was made public 18 June 1979, and called for an "Islamic revolutionary republic." It provided for a strong presidency somewhat along U.S. lines and a legislative assembly (the Majlis). An independent judicial system was based on Islamic or Shari'a law, and Shi'a Islam was to be the state religion. However, Christianity, Judaism, and Zoroastrianism, all recognized as revealed religions by Islam, were also recognized and included in the apportionment of seats in the Majlis.

With the overthrow of the shah, many ethnic groups, such as the Kurds, Azeris, and Khuzistan Arabs, pressed for more local autonomy. The constitution recognized the cultural identity of such groups including the right to use their own languages in schools and newspapers. It did not, however, dilute the essentially unitary nature of the state. Political parties were to be tolerated, and freedom of the press was guaranteed so long as there was no criticism of Islam.

The feature that links the 1979 constitution most closely with the 1906 constitution is the creation of a council of guardians of the constitution, which was empowered to nullify any legislative acts at variance with Islamic law. This was the kind of vehicle through which the religious establishment had hoped to control the Qajar monarchy under the 1906 constitution, and through which Ayatollah Khomeini apparently hoped to control the government without the necessity of assuming a direct governing role.

Political Dynamics

Shah Muhammad Reza, by force of his own personality as well as through an elaborate system for controlling the sources of power, dominated the political process in Iran. It was a form of technocratic absolutism that, while breaking with the traditional distribution of power, was still based on the traditional norms of behavior.

Despite the concentration of power in the shah's hands, his style of governing was much the same as earlier shahs: maintaining control through a complex network of informal, personal relationships. Within this system, a man's personal ties could count for much more than his title. In fact, the shah and his immediate circle—old comrades, ranking military officers, senior technocrats, and key members of the royal family—operated in many ways like a traditional Iranian *dowrah*. The same held true for lesser ranking officials.

The armed forces and security forces were also important elements in Iran's political dynamics under the shah. They held the monopoly on physical force. As professionals, they saw their role as guarantors of stability. In maintaining internal security, the shah depended to a great extent on his secret police, SAVAK.

Having survived the challenge of Mossadeq on the left, the shah next attempted to dominate the tribal, religious, commercial, and other elites that had traditionally shared power. One of the aims of the White Revolution was to break the power of these traditional elites. By 1970 the shah had succeeded in consolidating power in his own hands. Political and economic power was wielded through the bureaucracy with the military and security establishments maintaining internal security. By 1978, however, this consolidation of power began to backfire. As social and economic dislocations grew, the shah, as the personification of the political system, became the focal point of opposition in Iranians from every part of the political spectrum.

Political dynamics under the republic are still developing. It is probably safe to assume, however, that many of the traditional behavioral characteristics of Iranian society will continue to be a major influence on how politics are conducted: a high degree of personalization in addressing political problems, the importance of family, tribal, and ethnic affiliations, and the centralization of political power.

A notable result of the revolution that overthrew the shah was the disintegration of the armed services and dismantling of SAVAK, the secret police. In the process, weapons found their way into many hands, some organized politically and some not. The widespread possession of weapons will thus make the process of rebuilding defense and police forces for national defense and public safety more difficult. As these forces are rebuilt, they will almost certainly play a major role in political decision making. At the time of this writing, however, it is virtually impossible to define that role since it is not certain what the composition and organization of the forces will ultimately look like.

One other presently unknown factor will have a major bearing on the political dynamics of Iran. This is the degree to which the largely Western-educated nationalists—heirs of Mossadeq—and the religious leadership will continue to cooperate, now that the most unifying goal, the ouster of the shah, has been attained. The former are most prominent in the government whereas the latter dominate the Revolutionary Council and revolutionary committees. Perhaps the most crucial test will come when the regime begins the very painful task of economic reconstruction and retrenchment following the overspending of the last years of the shah and the economic disruptions of the revolution.

Foreign Policy

Iran has for centuries found itself subjected to the power politics of two major, competing powers. In the nineteenth and first part of the twentieth centuries, Britain and Russia competed for influence in Iran. Since World War II, the United States and the Soviet Union have been rivals. Iran has generally considered the greater threat to be the Soviet Union, with which it shares a common border. Much of the central USSR was at one time under Persian rule, and three times within living memory Russian troops occupied Iranian territory: in 1906 during the constitutional revolution, again during World War I and the Gilan affair, and during and after World War II when the Soviets again tried to annex Iranian territories.

The U.S. intervention to force the Soviet removal from Azerbaijan in 1946 and U.S. aid and support to the shah during the challenge to his power by Mossadeq in 1953 began an era of cordial U.S.-Iranian relations. The shah believed that the United States harbored no imperialistic designs on Iran, and he preferred U.S. technology and managerial skills to that of the Soviets. He also looked primarily to the United States to contain the Soviet threat both to Iran and to neighboring conservative states. The shah felt that many of his neighbors were particularly vulnerable to Soviet machinations. Thus, Soviet activities in Africa beginning in 1977, the Marxist coup in Afghanistan in April 1978, and the pro-Soviet coup in Aden in June 1978 all caused the shah great concern for regional stability. He also turned to the United States as the major (though not exclusive) supplier of technology for his military and civilian development programs.

The shah never placed Iran's interests second to those of the United States. Rather, he saw the relationship as the best vehicle for enhancing those interests. Moreover, with new confidence born of the success of domestic development plans and consolidation of power, the shah embarked on an active foreign policy particularly in regional affairs. When the British announced in 1968 their intention to withdraw from the lower Persian Gulf by 1971, the shah saw Iran as Britain's natural successor. Iranian hegemony in the gulf, albeit in concert with Saudi Arabia, therefore became a major foreign policy aim. As the shah's confidence and resources continued to develop, a greater role in the entire Indian Ocean region was also envisioned. For example, he began to lay plans for a "blue water" navy that could not be justified in terms of gulf waters alone.

In one respect, Iran under the shah also achieved a global political role. With the shift from a buyer's to a seller's market in the early 1970s, Iran became a major voice in international oil affairs, second only to Saudi Arabia. In the Organization of Petroleum Exporting Countries (OPEC), Iran played a leading role in raising prices to a level more in line with what the shah thought was the real value of its most valuable and diminishing resource, oil.

The general foreign policy direction of Iran under the republic will be more difficult to determine. Historic Persian fear and distrust of the Russians is not only still present but is compounded by the ideological antipathy of Islam toward atheistic Marxism. The new regime, therefore, has been highly critical of the Soviet-supported Marxist regime in Afghanistan.

At the same time, there is a highly socialistic content in the pronouncements of the new Iranian regime that expresses common cause with other regional radical movements such as the Palestine Liberation Organization and that tends to associate the shah's former Western allies with colonialism, exploitation, and moral degeneracy. This anti-Western feeling was reinforced by the more xenophobic strains of Persian nationalism that were manifested in the tumultuous last days of the shah's regime. At least in the short run, therefore, these conflicting tendencies could produce a high degree of ambivalence in Iranian foreign policy as the government sorts out its priorities—the need for Western technology and protection against communism, the rejection of Western imperialism and Western cultural values, and the distrust of the Soviets and rejection of Marxism.

Bibliography

It is too soon for a scholarly study of republican Iran to be written. However, there is an abundance of scholarly research on Iran under the shah, treating in depth its politics, economics, society, and culture. It is somewhat uneven in quality, however. The most comprehensive studies of the Iranian political system are Marvin Zonis, *The Political Elite of Iran* (Princeton: Princeton University Press, 1971), and James Bill, *The Politics of Iran: Groups, Classes and Modernization* (Columbus, Ohio: Charles A. Merrill, 1972). Additionally, James Bill has written a shorter piece, "The Patterns of Elite Politics in Iran," in George Lenczowski, ed., *The Political Elites in the Middle East* (Washington, D.C.: American Enterprise Institute, 1975). For insight into the shah's own views on the development of his country there is Mohammad Reza Shah Pahlavi, *Mission For My Country* (New York: McGraw-Hill Book Co., 1961).

Sepehr Zabih, *The Communist Movement in Iran* (Berkeley: University of California Press, 1966), Nikkie R. Keddie, *Religion and Rebellion in Iran* (London: Frank Cass, 1966) and Ann K. A. Lambton, *The Persian Land Reform, 1962-1966* (New York: Oxford University Press, 1969), provide accounts of three interest groups that could adversely affect the political stability of the country. Zabih presents Iran as a case study of the application of communist doctrine to a developing country; Keddie discusses religion and the constitutional revolution of 1905-1911. In her noted classic, Lambton describes the implementation of land reform and effects it had on the different social economic classes.

Rouhollah Ramazani has written a number of authoritative books and articles dealing with the foreign policy of Iran, including: *The Foreign Policy of Iran, 1500-1941* (Charlottesville: University of Virginia Press, 1966); *Iran's Foreign Policy, 1941-1973: A Study of Foreign Policy in a Modernizing Nation* (Charlottesville: University of Virginia Press, 1975); and *The Persian Gulf: Iran's Role* (Charlottesville: University of Virginia Press, 1972). Two Iranians, Shahram Chubin and Sepehr Zabih, have also written a comprehensive study of Iranian foreign relations, *The Foreign Relations of Iran: A Developing State in a Zone of Great Power Conflict* (Berkeley: University of California Press, 1975). This book gives an excellent analysis of Iran's relations with the Soviet Union.

For an account of Iran's development policy and economics, one should refer to either Fereidun Fesharaki, *The Development of the Iranian Oil Industry* (New York: Praeger Publishers, 1976), or Jahangir Amuzegar, *Iran: An Economic Profile* (Washington, D.C.: Middle East Institute, 1977). Amuzegar discusses the economic forces that are important in Iran today. The author was Iran's principal resident representative to the International Monetary Fund and World Bank. For an overview of Iran's social, economic, or political structures and dynamics, American University's *Area Handbook for Iran* (1971), although outdated, still offers a quick survey.

5

Kingdom of Saudi Arabia

David E. Long

Few countries encompass so many anomalies as Saudi Arabia. A major power in international oil affairs, Arab politics and Islamic world affairs, it has only recently begun to build a modern army commensurate with its economic power. Its rulers have spent billions of dollars on the material and social welfare of their people, yet strive to maintain a spiritually-based society reflecting the earliest years of Islam. It is a country with a strong free-market philosophy, but because of its vast oil reserves and paucity of other resources, the Saudi economy's public sector overwhelms the private sector. It is a country dominated by the royal family but technocrats have a major influence on policymaking. While the leading princes are very visible, the royal family as a whole is highly secretive and avoids publicity. An indication of the complexity of the Saudi political system is that despite Saudi Arabia's prominence in world and regional affairs, a definitive book on Saudi politics by a Western scholar has yet to be written.

Historical Background

Early History

Saudi Arabia has the rare distinction of being named after a family. It was created in 1932 by the ruler, King Abd al-Aziz bin Abd al-Rahman Al Saud, who united the kingdoms of Najd and the Hijaz to form the kingdom of Saudi Arabia. The history of the country is basically the history of the Al Saud (House of Saud), which has ruled from the desert fastness of Najd, as central Arabia is called, for over 200 years. The founder of the dynasty was Amir Muhammad bin Saud (c. 1703–1704 to 1792), the amir (ruler) of Dir'iyyah, a small oasis town located on the Wadi Hanifah, a usually dry streambed in central Najd.

In 1744–1745, the Amir Muhammad came under the influence of a zealous religious revivalist, Muhammad bin Abd al-Wahhab, from the neighboring town of Uyainah. When Shaykh Muhammad bin Abd al-Wahhab was driven from his own town because of his religious beliefs, Amir Muhammad bin Saud became his patron.

The revival movement of Abd al-Wahhab was drawn from the writings of an early Islamic jurist, Ibn Taymiyyah, (c. A.D. 1262–1328). It was based on the Hanbali school of Islamic jurisprudence, the most conservative of the four schools in Sunni Islam. Abd al-Wahhab stressed a return to the fundamentals of Islam and condemned many of the religious practices that had cropped up since the time of Muhammad. Calling for adherence to strict monotheism, he condemned the followers of these practices as idolators and polytheists. Abd al-Wahhab particularly condemned the practice, then in vogue, of making pilgrimages to the tombs of holy men. To this day, the followers of the revival bury their dead in unmarked graves lest their tombs become revered as religious shrines. These followers call themselves "Muwahhidin" (Unitarians), denoting their strict monotheism. To outsiders they have become known as Wahhabis, after the name of the founder, Muhammad bin Abd al-Wahhab, although his followers rejected this name because it could possibly imply worship of Abd al-Wahhab rather than God.

Muhammad bin Abd al-Wahhab was known as the teacher or shaykh (shaykh has many meanings in Arabic, including teacher, leader, ruler, and elder statesman). His descendants are still called Al al-Shaykh (House of the Shaykh), and as they still provide the religious leadership of the country, they are second in prestige in Saudi Arabia only to the Al Sauds. The spiritual fervor of the Wahhabi revival and the temporal power and statecraft of the Al Sauds proved to be a powerful combination, and by the end of the eighteenth century, the Al Sauds had subdued nearly all of Najd and were preparing to expand even further.

Saudi expansion in Najd was carried out almost unnoticed by the outside world. In 1801, however, the Al Sauds and their Wahhabi warriors forced themselves into world consciousness, particularly Islamic world consciousness, when they sacked the Shi'a holy city of Karbala in southern Iraq. They destroyed the tombs of a number of holy men including the tomb of Husayn, the grandson of the Prophet Muhammad. Husayn's large domed tomb was venerated by the Shi'as as a destination of religious pilgrimage second in importance only to Mecca and al-Madinah.

In 1806 Wahhabi forces defeated the Ottoman garrisons in the Hijaz and seized Mecca and al-Madinah. In the east, another army pushed into Oman, forcing the sultan at Muscat to pay annual tribute to the Al Sauds. Persian Gulf sailors, newly converted to the revival, sent

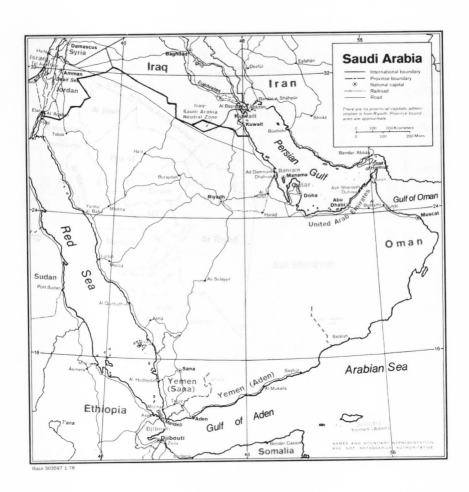

privateers against British and local merchant vessels, deeming the former to be nonbelievers and the latter to be heretics. Thus, in a few short years, Saudi domains had expanded from little more than an oasis to most of the Arabian peninsula.

It is interesting to speculate how far the armies of the Al Sauds would have marched had they not run into superior military technology, for it was just this kind of holy army sweeping out of Arabia that first flung the banners of Islam from Spain to Indonesia a thousand years before. The Wahhabis soon met their match, however. With the fall of the Muslim holy places of Mecca and al-Madinah, the Ottoman sultan in Constantinople was roused into action. He bid his viceroy in Egypt, Muhammad Ali, to send an army against the Wahhabis. Muhammad Ali appointed his son, Ibrahim Pasha, to lead an army dispatched to invade Najd. It took Ibrahim seven years to march through the inhospitable sands of Najd and attack the Al Saud capital of Dir'iyyah. But finally, in 1818, Dir'iyyah fell. Ibrahim laid waste to the city, whose ruins can still be seen today, cut down the palm groves, and took the amir, Abdallah bin Saud Al Saud, fourth in the line, in exile back to Cairo along with many other Al Sauds and Al al-Shaykhs. Abdallah was later sent to Constantinople where he was ultimately beheaded. During the next four years the Ottoman-Egyptian occupiers set out to destroy the Al Sauds' base of power so that they could no longer threaten the holy cities of the Hijaz. In 1822 the Ottomans withdrew to the Hijaz after concluding that Mecca and al-Madinah were no longer under the threat of renewed Wahhabi attack. Najd was again free of foreign influence.

As the Ottoman-Egyptian garrisons in central Arabia were drawn down, several local leaders moved to fill the vacuum. One was Mishari, a brother of the last Saudi amir, who ruled briefly and unsuccessfully in 1820. In 1823–1824 a cousin, Turki bin Abdallah, consolidated power and reestablished Saudi rule. He moved the capital about twenty kilometers south of Dir'iyyah to the town of Riyadh, where it has remained the seat of the Al Sauds ever since. By the time of Turki's assassination in 1834, he had reasserted Saudi rule throughout Najd and eastward to the Persian Gulf.

Turki was succeeded by his son, Faysal. In 1837, however, Faysal was ousted by Khalid, brother of Amir Abdallah and Amir Mishari. With the help of the Egyptians, Khalid had Faysal exiled to Cairo. Khalid was himself overthrown in 1841 by yet another cousin, Abdallah bin Thunayan; but in 1843 Faysal escaped from Cairo and returned once again to become the undisputed ruler of Najd. During his second reign (1843–1865), Saudi leadership reached the zenith of its powers in the nineteenth century. Faysal restored peace in Najd, extended his rule to

Jabal Shammar in the north and laid claim to Buraymi Oasis in Oman. This claim was the basis of a territorial dispute with Oman and Abu Dhabi that extended to the 1970s.

Faysal's death in 1865 signaled another eclipse in the fortunes of the Al Sauds. He was succeeded by his son Abdallah, but Abdallah's leadership was almost immediately challenged by a second son, Saud, who became amir in 1871. After Saud's death in 1875, Abdallah again became amir, but by this time, the Al Sauds' hold over the countryside was slipping. The eastern province (al-Hasa) was reconquered by the Ottomans in 1871, Buraymi Oasis was lost, and the Jabal Shammar tribes rose in revolt. In 1887 the Saudi state again collapsed. This time, Muhammad Ibn Rashid, amir of the Shammar, seized Najd and ruled it from the Jabal Shammar capital at al-Hayil.

A younger brother of Abdallah and Saud, Abd al-Rahman, served briefly as Rashidi governor of his family's capital at Riyadh; but failing in an abortive revolt, he was forced to flee with his family to Kuwait in 1891 where he lived off the hospitality of the ruler, Mubarak the Great.

The rise of the Al Sauds from humiliating exile to leadership of the world's foremost oil state was due primarily to the accomplishments of Abd al-Rahman's son, Abd al-Aziz bin Abd al-Rahman Al Saud, who became known in the West as "Ibn Saud." Abd al-Aziz struck an imposing figure. Well over six feet tall and handsome, he had the natural grace and poise of a true desert aristocrat, which enabled him to deal effectively with tribal shaykh and oil executive alike. From his mother's family, the Al al-Shaykhs, he was well grounded in Islam. His prowess with the opposite sex was also legendary in the best Arabian tradition. Abd al-Aziz's true measure of greatness, however, was in his breadth of vision. Even though he did not fully comprehend the revolutionary changes that his acts would ultimately produce, he brought his country out of the desert confines of Najd to take its place in regional and world political and economic councils.

The first step on the way to recovery of the lost patrimony was to recapture Riyadh in 1902. The nearly legendary tale of how Abd al-Aziz retook Riyadh sounds like the plot for a Hollywood thriller. Having left Kuwait the previous year, the young prince and a band of forty followers stole over the city walls. Once inside the city, they lay alternately sleeping and praying all night long while waiting for the Rashidi governor, Ajlan, to emerge from his stronghold, the Mismak fortress. He slept there as a security precaution. The next morning, as Ajlan left the fortress for home, he was set upon by Abd al-Aziz and his men. Ajlan ran with his retinue back to the fortress, where there was a brief tussle as both sides tried to pull him through the postern gate. During the retreat,

Abd al-Aziz's cousin Abdallah bin Jaluwi threw a spear that landed in the
gate where the broken spear tip remains to this day. Ajlan was finally
pulled through the gate, but before it could be closed, Abdallah bin
Jaluwi forced his way in and slew the governor. All resistance then
ended.

It took two decades from the January morning that Abd al-Aziz retook
Riyadh to accomplish the conquest of the Ibn Rashids. His success was
greatly facilitated by the fratricidal jealousies that split his rivals much
as the Al Sauds had been split a generation earlier. By the time Abd al-
Aziz finally captured al-Hayil in 1922, he had also recovered eastern
Arabia from the Ottomans. He named Abdallah bin Jaluwi the governor
of the Eastern Province, and upon Abdallah's death his son Saud bin
Jaluwi became governor. At the latter's death, a second son, Abd al
Muhsin, became governor, a position he still held in 1978.

Abd al-Aziz might have defeated the Ibn Rashids sooner with his
bedouin force, the Ikhwan (the Brethren), which was composed of
tribesmen newly converted to the Wahhabi revival. World War I, however, temporarily brought the Arabian peninsula into the arena of great-
power politics, with the British and the Turks competing for the support
of the peninsula's three major rulers, Abd al-Aziz of Najd, Saud Ibn
Rashid of the Jabal Shammar, and Sharif Husayn of Mecca. Ibn Rashid
chose the Turks and the Germans; the other two chose the British. It was
during this period that two Britons came to fame in Arabia. Colonel
T. E. Lawrence (Lawrence of Arabia) was sent to the Hijaz to encourage
Sharif Husayn to revolt against the Ottoman sultan and to lead raiding
parties to disrupt Turkish supply routes along the Hijaz railway. In 1917
the British also sent a mission to Abd al-Aziz to persuade him to side
with Sharif Husayn and the Allies and to attack the Ibn Rashids. One
member of the British mission was H. St. John B. Philby, who stayed on
in Arabia as an explorer, writer, and confidant of Abd al-Aziz.

With the war's end, Abd al-Aziz finally conquered the Ibn Rashids. In
the meantime, relations with the Hijaz had begun to deteriorate. After re-
volting against the Ottomans, Sharif Husayn had proclaimed himself
"King of the Arabs," and claimed precedence over the Al Sauds, whom
he regarded as mere desert chieftains. In 1912 Husayn seized Abd
al-Aziz's brother Sa'd, and released him only after he forced Abd al-Aziz
to accept humiliating terms. In 1919 Abd al-Aziz's son (and later king),
Faysal, traveling through Paris on his return from an official visit to London, was snubbed by Husayn's son Faysal, who was there for the Ver-
sailles peace convention. In the same year Abdallah, another of Husayn's
sons, set out east of al-Taif to claim the oasis of Kurmah. While camped
at nearby Turabah, his army was virtually wiped out by the fierce Saudi

Ikhwan. Only those with horses escaped, including Abdallah.

Abd al-Aziz did not press his advantage. However, in 1924 the Ottoman caliphate was dissolved, and King Husayn proclaimed himself the new caliph. This was more than Abd al-Aziz could accept, and he set out to invade the Hijaz. Al-Taif was taken without resistance, but for a still-unexplained reason, a shot rang out and the zealous Ikhwan sacked the city. The Hijazis panicked when they heard of al-Taif's fate and forced Husayn to abdicate in favor of his son Ali. Ali's fortunes were no better, however, and in January 1926 he, too, set sail from Jidda to follow his father into exile.

In a quarter century, Abd al-Aziz, starting with forty men, had regained the Saudi patrimony. In 1934, after a brief war with the Yemens, the Saudis acquired the Wadi Najran, rounding out the present frontiers save for some subsequent boundary settlements. When Abd al-Aziz first captured Najd, he chose the title amir, and later sultan of Najd. After the conquest of the Hijaz, he took the title king of Najd and the Hijaz. Finally, in 1932, he consolidated the two kingdoms into the kingdom of Saudi Arabia.

With the restoration and consolidation of Saudi domains, peace came to Saudi Arabia as it seldom had throughout recorded history. Abd al-Aziz's tribally organized military force, the religiously zealous Ikhwan, became restless. In 1929, the king was forced to put down an uprising of the Ikhwan at al-Sibliah. This became the last great bedouin battle ever fought. Abd al-Aziz disbanded the Ikhwan, and with the exception of the brief campaign in the Yemen in 1934, Saudi Arabia was one of the very few countries to have no regular standing army during the turbulent 1930s and 1940s. The king did, however, declare war on Germany during World War II, and Saudi Arabia became a charter member of the United Nations.

The Postwar Era

The history of Saudi Arabia since World War II has been one of unprecedented economic and social development. The enabling factor has been oil, first found in commercial quantities in 1938 but not exported in commercial quantities until after the war. By the time of his death in 1953, King Abd al-Aziz had constructed a firm foundation on which subsequent leaders could build the modern oil kingdom that is Saudi Arabia today.

King Abd al-Aziz was succeeded by his eldest surviving son, Saud. (His eldest son had died in the influenza pandemic of 1919.) Saud had been groomed for rulership as viceroy of the Najd under his father. More at home among the tribes, however, he lacked the breadth of vision required to propel Saudi Arabia from a desert kingdom to a major oil power. His reign was characterized by intrigue and lavish spending. Despite oil income, the treasury was often virtually empty. In 1964 the royal family withdrew its support from King Saud in favor of his brother Faysal. Saud departed Saudi Arabia, choosing to remain in exile until his death in Athens in 1969.

King Faysal came to the throne with nearly a half-century's experience in public affairs. In 1919, at the age of fourteen, he represented his father on an official visit to England. After his father conquered the Hijaz, Faysal was made viceroy in 1926, and when the Ministry of Foreign Affairs was created in 1930, he became foreign minister, a post he held for the rest of his life with the exception of a short period during the reign of Saud.

King Faysal was dedicated to the preservation of a conservative Islamic way of life both in Saudi Arabia and the Muslim world, while at the same time introducing material and technological progress. His domestic development policies proceeded from a ten-point reform program, which he designed in 1962 while still crown prince and prime minister, and were built upon the foundations already laid by his father. The measure of his success can be explained in large part by his capacity to be ahead of his people, introducing economic and social development programs, but never so far out in front that the essentially conservative Saudi public would not follow. By proceeding carefully and with deliberation, for example, he was able to win over even the most conservative segments of the population to such innovations as public radio and television and education for women. In order to dispel religious opposition to radio and television, for example, Faysal ordered that large portions of programming time be devoted to religious instructions and readings from the Quran.

Foreign affairs, however, held Faysal's greatest interest. As foreign minister, he became one of the most widely traveled Saudi officials of his time. For example, he attended the 1945 San Francisco conference that established the United Nations. Faysal's primary focus was on the Muslim world and the preservation of its values. Because of Saudi Arabia's key position as an oil exporter, Faysal's ability to act as a force for moderation both in the Arab world and the world at large was greatly enhanced by the shift in the control of oil prices from the oil companies to the producing countries in the early 1970s and from the dramatic oil price rises in 1973.

King Faysal was assassinated by a nephew on 25 March, 1975, and was succeeded by his half-brother, King Khalid. Another brother, Fahd, was made crown prince and attends to much of the day-to-day administration of the Saudi government. Under Khalid and Fahd, Saudi domestic and foreign policies have generally followed the lead of Faysal and Abd al-Aziz in their emphasis on economic development and social welfare within the framework of Islamic values.

Political Environment

The People

Population Structure. Saudi Arabia has an estimated population of between four and five million, probably one-fifth of whom are expatriates. The population is scattered throughout the country in cities and towns, oases, mountain villages, and nomadic tribal concentrations. Saudi Arabia has no predominant metropolis such as Cairo, Baghdad, or Tehran. The major cities, Riyadh, Jidda, and Mecca, still have populations of less than one-half million. At the same time, the process of urbanization is accelerating rapidly, particularly since the oil boom in 1974. City skylines are changing overnight, and in one instance, a new city with a projected population of 250,000 is being planned at the Persian Gulf port of Jubail, little more than a fishing village a few years ago.

Oasis and mountain villagers, however, still constitute a major portion of the population. The yeoman farmers of central Arabian oases were the traditional backbone of political support for the Saudi monarchy in the nineteenth century and are beneficiaries of considerable agricultural development. The nomads, still an important segment of the population, are nevertheless no longer a potent political force; their influence has been steadily undercut through the process of modernization. Tribal ties and extended family loyalties, however, are still of primary social importance.

Social Structure. Saudi Arabia is one of the more homogeneous states of the Middle East. Virtually all of the native population is Arab and Muslim. There are, however, significant regional differences. Najd, as central Arabia is called, is not only the geographical center of the country but the political heartland as well. The harsh environment of Najd has had a major impact on the Najdis' perceptions of the world around them. Isolated by vast stretches of desert and never dominated by Western colonial powers, these peoples have developed a strong sense of self-reliance and, ironically, an equally strong fear of encirclement by enemies. They also have a strong sense of pride in their lineage, believing themselves to be the only racially pure Arabs. Their belief in the superiority of their blood lines is so secure that they seldom feel the need to prove it with the regal trappings more common elsewhere in the Middle East. Thus, despite their aristocratic demeanor, Najdis display an easy desert egalitarianism, for even the meanest nomadic tribesman can claim that his lineage is every bit as good as that of the house of Saud.

In contrast to the insular character of Najd, the Hijaz has a highly cosmopolitan society. For centuries, the Muslim pilgrimage (the *hajj*) to its two holy cities, Mecca and al-Madinah, have annually drawn peoples from all over the Muslim world. In earlier years many stayed on in the Hijaz for extended periods, often permanently, making Hijazi society an ethnic melting pot. Though thoroughly Arabized, the Hijazis reflect origins from western Africa to Indonesia. With the pilgrims came commerce and the development of great, old mercantile families that are now mainly located in Jidda. In recent years Riyadh has become the banking and financial center of the kingdom, with the concentration of national income in the form of government-held oil revenues. The Jidda merchants, however, having created nationwide operations, still dominate commerce. Other Hijazis have entered public service as technocrats, administrators, soldiers, and diplomats. Because of the more cosmopolitan background of the Hijazis and the political predominance of the Najdis, a rivalry has developed between the two regions, exacerbated by the fact that the Hijaz was once an independent kingdom. With great advances in social and economic development, however, this rivalry has abated to a great degree in recent years.

South of the Hijaz is Asir, a semimountainous region that has the highest population density in the country. Asiris are hardworking people who till terraced hillside farms and live in villages constructed of stone. Less conservative than Najdis, the women seldom wear veils. The region is also one of the most isolated and least developed in the kingdom. The new road system being constructed by the government, however, will bring change, introducing the positive as well as negative influences associated with rapid development.

The other major region in Saudi Arabia is the Eastern Province, located along the Persian (Arabian) Gulf coast. It is here that the oil deposits are located. Formerly known as al-Hasa (or al-Ahsa), it consists of two major oases, al-Hasa somewhat inland and al-Qatif along the coast; and a number of coastal towns. The largest, Dammam, is the provincial capital. Just south is al-Khubar. Inland a few kilometers from al-Khubar is Dhahran. Not a city at all, Dhahran is the location of the Dhahran air field, the American Consulate General, the Petroleum and Minerals University, and the major headquarters of the Saudi oil-producing company built by ARAMCO (the Arabian American Oil Company). The oil terminal at Ras Tanura is some distance north of Dammam, and further still are the new city and naval base being built at Jubail.

The Eastern Province was traditionally an area of oasis farmers, fishermen, and mariners. With the discovery of oil and the influx of workers from all corners of the kingdom and indeed the world, the Eastern Province lost much of its homogeneity and cohesion. Yet, close by the oil facilities at Ras Tanura, one can still picture an earlier age at the quiet village among the date palms of Tarut Island. However, with much of the Saudi economic-development expenditures being made in the Eastern Province, such serenity may soon be a thing of the past.

Nearly all Saudis are Sunni Muslims and most follow the teachings of the great revivalist, Muhammad bin Abd al-Wahhab. In the Eastern Province there are some groups of Shi'a Muslims, notably at al-Qatif Oasis, who are akin to Shi'a communities in nearby Bahrain and northward to Iraq. The impact of Islam on the society can be seen everywhere. The Muslim lunar calendar is still used because it marks the Muslim holy days, particularly the annual *hajj* or pilgrimage to Mecca that absorbs the energies of virtually everyone in the kingdom for about two months a year. Since the lunar calendar is eleven days shorter than the solar calendar, holidays fall nearly two weeks earlier each year. Strict compliance with Islamic social norms is required in Saudi Arabia and enforced by a religious police force. Shops close five times a day for prayers; women still go veiled in public, and alcohol and public cinemas are illegal.

It is difficult to overestimate the influence of Islam on Saudi society. Old patterns are extremely hard to break, and what are often taken for changes in social values are in reality changes in the social environment to which the society is merely reacting. In Saudi Arabia, the environment is changing almost before one's eyes. As late as the 1940s, Westerners were required to wear Saudi garb in Riyadh to call on the king, and as late as 1967, there were fewer than 100 Westerners in Riyadh, compared to about 15,000 today—an indication of the rapidity of change in the social environment. Traditional values and perceptions, however, are changing much more slowly.

Wahhabism, moreover, has for the past two centuries given the society purpose and moral strength and created a sense of homogeneity among the people. One of the interesting aspects of the revival has been the ability of its adherents to adapt to social change and still maintain their conservative principles. The psychological strains and identity crises often associated with the introduction of Western-style education into a traditional society do not appear to be prevalent among Saudis. This is probably a reflection of strong Islamic-oriented values and extremely strong family ties. Thus, while modernization will undoubtedly create increasing social strains, traditional Saudi social values should on balance remain a stabilizing force in the country.

Economic Conditions

Saudi Arabia has one of the most laissez-faire economies in the world. The same Hanbali school of Islamic law that is so strict on social behavior is ironically the most liberal on business and economic matters. Likewise, there are few political restrictions on commerce. While diplomatic relations with communist countries are prohibited, goods from China and Eastern Europe are plentiful throughout the country.

The freewheeling laissez-faire philosophy based on Islam has in turn created a business ethic that is quite different from that known in the West. Stealing is considered a very serious crime and is harshly dealt with. The traditional Islamic punishment is to cut off a hand. In business dealings, a man's word is his bond regardless of what formal legal commitments he may have acquired. At the same time, it is considered permissible to charge for a service rendered, even in circumstances that might be considered a conflict of interest by Western business ethics. This ethic, which is endemic to the entire Middle East, is best typified by the phrase "buyer beware."

Looking at Saudi Arabia's huge oil wealth today, it is difficult to visualize just how poverty-stricken the country was fifty years ago. When still confined to Najd, the Saudi realm required few financial resources, but seldom possessed enough even then. Ottoman and British subsidies provided a major prop for its meager economy. When the Saudis conquered the Hijaz, government expenses increased greatly. But by taking the Hijaz, the Saudis also gained what was to become the major foreign-exchange earner for the kingdom prior to oil, the annual *hajj*. When the world economic depression and political disorders that preceded World War II combined to reduce greatly the number of pilgrims in the 1930s, the Saudi economy was badly hit. Economic necessity forced the Saudi government to seek to maximize *hajj* revenues despite its commitment to lowering expenses and halting the economic exploitation of the *hajjis* (pilgrims) that had so long been the norm.

The coming of oil has changed all of that. The psychological impact of the years of poverty, however, is still felt on economic policymaking. Most of the present leadership reached manhood before oil had made an impact on the kingdom's economy and society. Thus, despite the billions of dollars in foreign exchange, the laissez-faire capitalism, and the freewheeling traditional business ethic, Saudis tend to be tenacious in negotiating contracts with foreign firms for their many economic development plans.

The first Saudi oil concession was sold to Major Frank Holms, an entrepreneur from New Zealand, in the 1920s, but it was subsequently allowed to lapse. In 1933 Standard Oil of California (SOCAL) obtained a new concession with the good offices of Karl Twitchell, an American geologist who had explored for water in the kingdom, and H. St. John B. Philby, the British explorer and writer who had become a confidant of King Abd al-Aziz. Oil was first discovered in 1935; in 1938, when "Dammam No. 7" was spudded in, Saudi Arabia's future as a major oil-producing country was secured.

To produce the oil, SOCAL created a subsidiary, CASOC (California Arabian Standard Oil Company). In 1936, TEXACO became a joint owner when the two companies combined their overseas operations as CALTEX. In early 1944, CASOC was changed to ARAMCO (Arabian American Oil Company) and in 1948, Exxon and Mobil also bought into ARAMCO.

For almost three decades ARAMCO was the major owner and producer of Saudi oil (Getty and the Arabian Oil Company [Japan] had concessions in the Saudi-Kuwaiti neutral zone). By 1970, however, the market was changing to the advantage of the oil-producing countries, which were by then organized into the Organization of Petroleum Exporting Countries (OPEC). Several years earlier Saudi Petroleum Minister Ahmad Zaki Yamani had announced a scheme for the eventual Saudi control and ownership of its own oil production. He called the scheme "participation." By 1974 the Saudis had bought 60 percent equity in ARAMCO and had begun negotiations to acquire full ownership of the oil-producing company.

With its huge oil revenues accruing directly to the government, Saudi Arabia's economy is dominated by the public sector despite its laissez-faire economic philosophy. Over 90 percent of the Saudi gross national product is oil-related. Government development schemes are ambitious. The first five-year plan (1970–1975) concentrated on diversification of the country's single-commodity (oil) economy. In 1975, the second plan was announced with a budget expenditure of $149 billion. Continuing along the lines of the first plan, it has emphasized agriculture; industrialization, particularly petrochemical industries; and social and economic infrastructure.

The second plan was ambitious, providing general guidelines more than a fixed policy. Moreover, the very successes of the development plan have created a serious manpower bottleneck. With rapidly expanded responsibilities involved in implementing the many projects, the bureaucracy's decision-making ability has been greatly strained, and sustained public spending has created inflationary pressures. Thus, in 1977 the government began to reduce the pace of development in order to allow the economy to consolidate the gains already made. The third plan, to begin in 1980, was designed to continue consolidation and insure the maintenance of Islamic values in Saudi society.

Despite government efforts to diversify the Saudi economy, the oil sector is likely to continue to be dominant for the foreseeable future. Therefore, the government will continue to be the prime mover in economic development. With its strong traditional business ethic and Islamic concept of the social good, Saudi Arabia appears to be developing a unique form of Islamic state capitalism.

Political Structure

Saudi Arabia is an Islamic monarchy. Indeed, Islamic law, according to the Hanbali school, serves as the constitution. Islamic law is considered divinely inspired, and there is no room in classical Islamic political theory for man-made laws or a legislature. There has, however, long been on the books a consultative assembly for the Hijaz, and in recent years there has been talk of reviving it on a nationwide basis.

Operational regulations can be distinguished from holy Islamic law: the former are called *nizams* ("royal decrees"). Disputes involving administrative regulations are heard by administrative tribunals such as the labor and commercial courts and by a special tribunal called the *diwan al-mazalim* ("board of grievances"), which hears cases brought against the government. All other cases are heard in the *quda* (Islamic courts). The chief legal official is the minister of justice, traditionally a member of the Al al-Shaykh. The highest legal official is the king, who serves as imam ("leader of the faithful"). Since the law is higher than the king, he can theoretically be sued in his own courts.

Under the king are a council of ministers and various independent agencies. He is not an absolute monarch, however, for in addition to Islamic law, the royal family also serves as a constraint on his actions.

Political Dynamics

Saudi politics revolves around two distinct though closely related sets of dynamics: royal-family politics and national politics. The country is one of the few in the area in which the military does not play a decisive role.

Royal-Family Politics

The royal family serves as the constituency of the kingdom in that, in order to rule, the king must secure and maintain a consensus of support from the family. No one outside the family is quite sure how it creates such a consensus or even how large the family is, probably several thousand. Very secretive in family dealings, the Al Saud always tries to maintain the image of unity and harmony.

The choice (or, as in 1964, the ouster) of a king is made by an ancient Islamic institution, "the people who bind and loose," *(ahl al-aqd walhall)*, which is dominated by the royal family. The decision is given legal sanction by a *fatwa*, or formal Islamic legal opinion. In practice, however, the process of reaching a consensus on the choice of a king or any other matter is much more complicated.

The locus of power in the family centers around the sons of the late King Abd al-Aziz. Kings Saud, Faysal, and Khalid, and Crown Prince Fahd are all sons of the old king. Since Abd al-Aziz had many wives, the sons are of different mothers, and full brothers tend to work together. The king and his older brother, Muhammad (disqualified by poor health from taking the throne), form such a sibling group. As senior living son and a full brother of the king, Muhammad is very influential in royal-family affairs although he holds no government position. Crown Prince Fahd and his six brothers, including Defense Minister Sultan and Interior Minister Nayif, are another influential group. They are sometimes called "the Sudayri Seven" from the maiden name of their mother. There are also two surviving brothers of King Abd al-Aziz (uncles of the king). Belonging to an older generation, they are quite influential in the family. Several collateral branches also have a voice in family affairs. Muhammad, the head of the Saud al-Kabir branch, actually ranks second behind the king in royal-family protocol because the founder of the branch was an older brother of the founder of the ruling branch. Because of his rank, Muhammad and other older and senior princes comprise an informal senior statesman grouping, sometimes called the "Council of Elders."

National Politics

At the head of the government is the king, who is also prime minister. Royal princes hold all the major national-security-related positions. This does not mean that royal-family politics dominate national politics, however, for there are very powerful members of the family not in government and at least one powerful member of the cabinet, Saud al-Faysal, who is still a junior member of the family.

Despite the high representation of the royal family in government, the leadership has insisted on qualified technocrats being placed in all key public service- and development-oriented ministries. Government decision making, therefore, reflects a combination of royal-family and developmental concerns.

Equal in importance to the makeup of the government leadership in the decision-making process is the structure of the bureaucracy. Historically, the Saudi regime relied on personalities rather than institutions, and the rulers drew from the advice of trusted advisors to create a consensus in policymaking. These advisors came from many walks of life, including a number of influential foreigners. When the Hijaz was conquered in 1926, King Abd al-Aziz inherited a cabinet government and consultative assembly that he maintained in Jidda, but in Riyadh he continued his personalized system of rule. Gradually, however, as the need was perceived, national ministries were created, the Hijazi ministries disappeared, and by the time of Abd al-Aziz's death in 1953, the first Saudi Council of Ministers had been formed. Since many of the ministries predate the cabinet, considerable power remains at the ministerial level, and prerogatives are guarded like feudal fiefdoms. Major decisions affecting the kingdom as a whole are taken at the cabinet level.

The creation of a government bureaucracy has not greatly diminished the personalization of government decision making however. Rather, it has rechanneled the traditional personalized system through more modern bureaucratic institutions. Delegation of authority through a chain of command is still highly limited. Many seemingly minor decisions must still be made at the ministerial level, and high-level decisions are still made by only a handful of men. Though measures are being made to upgrade the efficiency of the bureaucracy, the burden of Saudi Arabia's ambitious development programs has continued to strain the country's bureaucratic resources.

Foreign Policy

The Saudi perception of the world draws heavily on the classical Islamic world view. The central position, according to this concept, is occupied by the Muslim community. The Christian and Jewish communities—the other revealed monotheistic religions recognized by Islam as "peoples of the book"—are allied to the Muslim community, and all of them are surrounded by unbelievers. In its more modern setting, this translates into the Muslim community allied with the United States and the rest of the free world against atheistic and antireligious states espousing communism and kindred radical ideologies. The Saudis, as guardians of the Muslim holy places, Mecca and al-Madinah, feel a special responsibility to protect the Muslim community and the Islamic way of life. Reinforced by the tenets of the Wahhabi revival, this commitment has become the primary determinant of Saudi priorities in foreign affairs.

A second determinant is pan-Arabism. Unlike most of the Arab world, which rediscovered its Arabness only in the last century, the Saudis derive a great degree of their sense of identity from the purity of their ancient Arabian bloodlines. Saudi pan-Arabism, however, is closely associated with pan-Islamism, and the two serve to reinforce each other.

The late King Faysal was convinced that communism and political Zionism were the two greatest threats to the Muslim way of life. The current leaders, while no longer emphasizing Faysal's formulation of a communist-Zionist conspiracy, essentially share his world view. Communism is antireligious and therefore a threat to Muslim society. Political Zionism (as distinct from religious Judaism) is also perceived as a threat. Israel, which is the embodiment of Zionism, has in the Saudi view not only denied access of Jerusalem's Aqsa Mosque to millions of Muslims but, by displacing the Palestinian population, has created frustrations among Arabs that have served to radicalize them. In policy terms, the Saudis view the United States as both the ultimate defender of the free world against communism and the ultimate defender of Zionism. To overcome this anomaly, the Saudis have made a major effort to persuade the United States to use its influence to bring about a fair solution to the Arab-Israeli problem and to be diligent in protecting the free world from communist expansion.

Saudi Arabia's role in world affairs is derived from its position as the world's key oil-exporting country. Thus, its foreign economic and oil policies will make the greatest impact on regional and world affairs. Saudi foreign economic and oil policies are also greatly influenced by the Saudis' world view. The Saudis view a strong United States and free world as the underpinning of the West's will and ability to contain communist and other radical forces. Moreover, with foreign exchange holdings of $60 billion, the Saudis realize that whatever adversely affects the world economy will hurt them also. At the same time, the Saudis have shown themselves willing to use oil as a political weapon. It was King Faysal who led the Arab oil embargo in 1973–1974 after feeling betrayed by the announcement that the United States was committing $2.2 billion in military aid to Israel.

The Saudis have also been concerned about the adverse effect of rising oil prices on the Third World and, as a result, have greatly increased their development aid programs. Their aid programs show a clear distinction between God-fearing and godless states. In order of priority, the recipients of Saudi aid have been the non-oil-producing Arab states, the non-Arab Islamic states, and finally the other less-developed countries.

Bibliography

Considering the importance of Saudi Arabia in world and regional politics, there is a dearth of literature about it. A short introductory overview is presented in the author's *Saudi Arabia*, The Washington Papers, vol. 4. (Washington, D.C.: Georgetown University, Center for Strategic and International Studies, 1976). After a brief description of the people and land, it discusses Saudi political dynamics within the royal family; the government, and the bureaucracy, and also discusses Saudi oil and economic issues. An abbreviated chart of the royal family and a more comprehensive chart of the surviving sons of King Abd al-Aziz delineating male bloodlines are also included.

There are a number of older books about Saudi Arabia that are considered classics. T. E. Lawrence's *The Seven Pillars of Wisdom* (Garden City, New York: Doubleday, 1935); and H. St. John B. Philby's many works, two of which are: *Arabian Jubilee* (London: Robert Hale, 1952); and *Saudi Arabia* (London: Benn, 1955). All of these works offer fascinating personal accounts of the twentieth-century history of the country by men who helped shape it.

The American Enterprise Institute, Washington, D.C., has published a number of monographs that discuss the foreign policy and developmental strategies of Saudi Arabia, including Emile Nakhleh's *The United States and Saudi Arabia: A Policy Analysis* (1976) and Donald Wells's *Saudi Arabia's Developmental Strategy* (1976). The authors and editors have made a reasonably successful effort to delineate a number of possible scenarios of future Saudi policy.

Three recent works on the Saudi economy are Sheikh Rustum Ali, *Saudi Arabia and Oil Diplomacy* (New York: Praeger Publishers, 1976); Ramon Knauerhase, *The Saudi Arabian Economy* (New York: Praeger Publishers, 1976); and Fouad al-Farsy, *Saudi Arabia: A Case Study in Development* (London: Stacey International, 1978). Finally, the American University has updated its *Area Handbook for Saudi Arabia* (1978). Its detailed treatment of the country's economy, politics, and society and an excellent bibliography provide a valuable secondary source for the student of Saudi Arabia.

Four magazine articles are also noteworthy. "A Tale of Two Houses," by William A. Rugh; "Foreign Policy: The View from Riyadh," by John D. Anthony; and "Saudi Oil Policy," by this author all appear in *The Wilson Quarterly* (vol. 3, no. 1, Winter 1979). Peter A. Iseman, "The Arabian Ethos," (*Harper's*, vol. 256, no. 1533, February 1978), is also well worth reading.

6

Republic of Iraq

David E. Long
John A. Hearty

Historical Background

Between the Tigris and Euphrates rivers lies a land with an exceptionally turbulent history. Known as Mesopotamia ("land between the rivers") until the Arab conquests in the seventh century A.D., Iraq has been a battleground of strategic importance and a land of internal strife from ancient times to the present. The geography of the region has been a significant feature in the history of Iraq. Bordered by deserts in the south and a multitude of passes in the north, Iraq is virtually without natural defenses against any invasion. Indeed, the country has been occupied by the Persians, Greeks, Romans, Arabs, Mongols, Ottomans, and the British. Each of these incursions has left its mark on the people and culture, thus fashioning a very complex and heterogeneous society.

Arab Conquests

The Arab conquest of Iraq began in A.D. 634 under the successor to Muhammad, Abu Bakr, who was the first caliph (632–634). A few years later, the fourth caliph, Ali, was assassinated. His rival, Muawiya, declared himself caliph and established the Umayyad Empire in Damascus. In the meantime, Ali's son Husayn, who had fled to Iraq, led a revolt in Karbala, Iraq, and was killed there by the Umayyads in 680. Those events initiated a rivalry that has become an important theme in present-day relations between Iraq and Syria and also initiated a religious schism in Islam that led to two main contending branches, the Shi'as and Sunnis, who disagreed on the succession of the caliphate.

During the sixth and seventh centuries, the Moslem Empire under the Damascus-based Umayyad dynasty expanded politically, economically, and socially, extending from southern France to China. Nonetheless, the seeds of discontent had been sown. The Shi'ites, primarily located in Iraq and Persia, continually challenged the legitimacy of the Umayyads. In 747, Abu al-Abbas embarked from Iraq upon a military campaign that resulted in the collapse of the Umayyad dynasty and the rise of the Abbasid dynasty. The Abbasids moved the capital of the Islamic world from Damascus to Baghdad. The era that followed, from 750 to 1258, was known as the "Golden Age of Islam" and brought tremendous advances in the sciences, literature, and art.

The decline of the Abbasid period was gradual, generated by internal strife. The ultimate destruction and collapse of the Abbasid Empire, however, came at the hand of a foreign invader. In 1258, Hulagu, the grandson of Genghis Khan, unleashed his forces on Baghdad and destroyed, in a relatively short period of time, what had taken five centuries to build. To this day, Iraq has been unable completely to recover or to rebuild what the Mongols destroyed.

However violent the downfall of the Abbasid rule, the Arab conquest of Mesopotamia altered the consciousness and character of the inhabitants of the land between the rivers. Politically and socially, the indigenous population was Arabized to the extent that, many centuries later, a strong Iraqi pan-Arab movement would attempt to join into a series of unions with Jordan, Syria, and Egypt.

Ottoman Rule

From 1258 to 1534 when it was captured from Persia by the Ottomans, Iraq existed in a political vacuum. There was constant turmoil between Sunni tribes of northern Iraq, Kurdistan, and parts of Baghdad on one hand, and Shi'ite-dominated southern Iraq and Baghdad on the other. In 1623 the Safavid dynasty of Persia under Shah Abbas was able to seize Baghdad from the Ottomans. The Ottomans regained control thirteen years later and were able to hold Iraq from that time until after World War I.

The Ottoman rule of Iraq was both inefficient and corrupt. What little was left of the splendor of the Abbasid period was allowed to fall into ruin. The Ottomans were able to exercise little political control over Iraq until Sultan Mahmud II asserted direct rule in 1831. Prior to this, Iraq was divided into three *vilayets* (districts)—Baghdad, Basrah, and Mosul—each directly linked to Istanbul. The central government was concerned only with the collection of taxes and some form of political control. This was accomplished by appointing the strongest tribal chiefs as governors of the provinces. Instead of politically and economically integrating the country, this form of political institutionalization fragmented Iraq, perpetuating constant local uprisings from less powerful tribes in the south and the Kurdish tribes in the north.

Mahmud II was partially successful in extending more direct Ottoman control over Kurdistan and the Persian frontiers, but his gains were soon lost by inept successors. Most Ottoman attempts at administrative and social reforms were failures and, as the people were mercilessly exploited by their Ottoman overlords, the Ottomans came to be generally hated.

During the later stages of the Ottoman rule, Iraq was drawn into international politics, culminating with World War I. Because of its strategic location astride British routes to the latter's Asian empire, Iraq attracted increasing British concern. Britain's interest in Iraq was threefold. First, the Turkish-German alliance and the approach of World War I threatened Britain's Middle Eastern colonies and protectorates. Second, the British perceived a potential strategic threat to their oil interests in Iran. Third, India, the gem of the British Empire, was thought to be endangered by the possible German occupation of either Iraq or Iran. Thus, when war broke out, British troops invaded Iraq and occupied the city of Basrah. Later they captured Baghdad and northern Iraq.

In summary, the Ottoman rule of Iraq was more significant for what it did not accomplish than for what it did accomplish. By not developing unified political institutions or a central administration, Iraq became fragmented. This facilitated a domestic situation that created cleavages among the Sunni and Shi'ite Muslims, the urban and rural populations, the Arabs and the Kurds. Although these feuds were not initiated by the Ottoman occupation of Iraq, the Ottoman administration was a decisive factor in their remaining a feature of Iraqi politics to the present day.

The British Mandate

As early as the Sykes-Picot Agreement of 1916, Great Britain obtained tacit Western consent to the occupation of Iraq. British control was formalized at the San Remo Conference in April 1920. This conference, in effect, granted the British mandatory powers over the region they had already militarily occupied. There were, however, several considerations that placed serious constraints on the role the British could play in effectively ruling Iraq. First of all, there were conflicting demands made upon the British by a myriad of groups and associations within the mandate. For example, the tribal shaykhs wanted grants of new land, while the villagers wanted the tribal incursions stopped. At the same time, there was within Great Britain a growing demand to cut back the financing of any commitment to Iraq. This current of opinion became more pronounced after the anti-British revolt in 1920, which cost nearly forty million pounds sterling to quell. There was growing evidence, especially after the 1920 revolt, that Britain would incur domestically unacceptable costs to maintain any significant military force in Iraq. Another constraint concerned the mandate itself. It was formally designed to prepare the country for independence rather than colonization. Thus, at the very least, the British were under some legal constraints.

The British understood that there could be no colonial status for Iraq. They were faced with finding someone to rule Iraq who would allow them to preserve a predominant role in both the internal and external affairs of the country. They finally chose Prince Faysal of the Hashimite house of Mecca, the son of the former sharif and newly named King Husayn of Hijaz. The Hashimites were loyal supporters of the British during World War I. In 1921 Faysal became the first of three kings from the Hashimite family to sit on the throne of Iraq. The British and Iraqis subsequently signed, in 1922, the first of three treaties that were to govern their relations with each other until 1968. The treaty of 1922 allowed for indirect rather than direct control and was the first sign that the mandate would soon end.

The British structured the political system so that they could maximize their position and influence. Modeled on the British constitutional system, Iraq's government had an independent parliament and judiciary. However, to assure a friendly government, the constitution reserved for the monarch considerable powers, including the right to appoint the prime minister and the right to dismiss parliament. The king was commander-in-chief of the armed forces and had considerable veto power over legislation. These powers enabled the king to wield virtual dictatorial authority.

The problem for Faysal and his successors was to manage a balance between British interests and those of the strong Iraqi nationalists. A significant gain for the nationalists came in 1929, when the British negotiated a treaty with Iraq to end the mandate upon Iraq's acceptance into the League of Nations. Finally, in October 1932, the league admitted Iraq. The Anglo-Iraqi treaty went into effect, the mandate was ended, and Iraq became an independent state under the protection of the British.

Constitutional Monarchy

The internal stability of the newly independent state continued to be plagued by traditional Sunni-Shi'a religious conflicts. Additionally, its borders, created at San Remo, contained a number of separate ethnic groups with little or no loyalty to the new state. The most important of these groups were the Kurds. Comprising about one-fifth of the population of Iraq and located in the northeast, with kin in Turkey, Persia and the Soviet Union, the Kurds had fought a losing battle with Persia and Turkey and now Iraq for an independent state of their own.

Another source of instability was the untimely death of King Faysal I in September 1933. Respected by almost everyone, Faysal had the capabilities and personality to control the internal cleavages, as well as to carry out a delicate balancing act between the British and the nationalists. Faysal was succeeded by his son Ghazi, a well-liked but inexperienced nationalist.

Great Britain itself proved to be a source of instability. Although the British were originally interested in Iraq's strategic location, the discovery of oil in 1923 and the commercial exploitation of oil in 1930 greatly intensified their interests. With the approach of World War II, the significance of Iraq to the British became even more apparent. As the British stake in maintaining control in Iraq grew, anti-British groups sprang up throughout the country, and more portentously, within the army.

It was during Ghazi's reign (1933–1939) that a distinctive pattern for future Iraqi politics became evident. In 1936 a successful coup d'etat was executed by the army. The first of five coups in as many years, it was aimed at the cabinet, not at the king.

Two important consequences ensued: institutionalization of the coup as a method of changing governments, and the splintering of Iraqi politics into two blocs, a pro-British group headed by Nuri al-Said and an anti-British group whose leading spokesman was Rashid Ali al-Gaylani. Because it was anti-British, this group was supported by the Germans.

In 1939, with war on the horizon, the accidental death of King Ghazi placed the prime minister, General Nuri al-Said, in a very tenuous situation. Ghazi was succeeded by King Faysal II, his four-year-old son, and a brother, Abdul Illah, became regent. Two years later, Rashid Ali led a successful coup and ousted Nuri. As the new prime minister was pro-Axis and attempted to alter the Anglo-Iraqi treaty in order to make Iraq neutral in the war, the British reciprocated by invading Iraq, suppressing Rashid Ali and placing Nuri and the monarchy in power again. From 1941 to 1958, the power structure of Iraqi politics remained relatively stable, with King Faysal II assuming full powers from Abdul Illah in 1953. Nuri al-Said was thirteen times prime minister during this period, but even when not occupying a formal position, he maintained his strong influence on decision making. Nuri developed a framework for policymaking early in his career that remained consistent until he was assassinated in 1958. A military man, he placed great emphasis on discipline, loyalty, and integrity. He was also firmly convinced that foreign powers had a role to play in the development and security of Iraq and, thus, he favored close cooperation with the West, relying heavily on Great Britain to provide assistance in the security of his country.

In Nuri's view, pan-Arabism encompassed economic and political cooperation, but not necessarily federation or unity. Nevertheless, in 1946 he was influential in the creation of the Arab League, and in 1958 he reacted to the Egyptian-Syrian union by proclaiming a federal state between Iraq and Jordan. The union never had much of a chance for development because of a coup that overthrew the monarchy five months later.

Nuri and the monarchy were overthrown for a number of interrelated reasons. While Nuri concentrated on such internal long-term development programs as flood control, the majority of the population remained destitute, especially those in the rural regions. Although the programs would have ultimately benefited them, these people were convinced that they were being exploited for the benefit of the wealthy merchant and land-owning classes.

The political institutions of Iraq offered little public participation in the political process. The legislative process, although electoral laws were reformed numerous times, was controlled by the executive. The Parliament, moreover, did not represent the varied economic, religious, or social classes nor was it a check on the executive's power. Although Nuri had allowed five political parties to organize after World War II, he effectively restricted party activity and finally outlawed parties in 1954. The suppression of the parties left little room for opposition. Any individual who voiced concern over the government's decrees was jailed. It was estimated that at one time Nuri had jailed ten thousand political prisoners.

Nuri himself also contributed to the collapse of the Hashimite kingdom. His penchant for public order justified in his mind the need for coercion. His methods of terrorizing all opposition made him one of the most hated men in the country. Even his friends were frustrated by his intransigence and his forceful personality.

Nuri and the monarchy were also vulnerable to the charge of being tools of imperialism. With nationalism strong, the population had been consistently anti-British. The cordial relationships between Iraq and Great Britain widened the rift between Nuri and the people he ruled. Moreover, when the Baghdad Pact was signed in 1955 by Iraq, Pakistan, Turkey, Iran, and Great Britain, with the United States as an observer, Nuri was attacked by the leaders of a great many other Arab nations. President Gamal Nasser of Egypt was so outraged that he called for the Iraqi people to overthrow the prime minister. Relations with the more radical Arab states were further strained when France and Great Britain sided with Israel and invaded Egypt in 1956.

Disaffection with the regime came to a head in 1958. On 14 July, troops under General Abd al-Karim Qasim and Colonel Abd al-Salam Arif moved on Baghdad, and a bloody revolution ensued that did not cease until the entire royal family and Nuri al-Said had been killed.

Republican Iraq

Following the overthrow of the monarchy, Iraq became a republic and the ruling Council of Sovereignty was established. Qasim became acting prime minister and minister of defense. Arif was given the positions of deputy prime minister and minister of interior. Within two weeks after the revolution, a provisional constitution was enacted, placing all executive and some legislative authority in the Council of Ministers, subject to the approval of the Council of Sovereignty. In addition, Qasim released all political prisoners and granted amnesty to all exiled opponents of the old regime. This included the release and return of the communists and other dissidents, including Mustafa Barzani, the leader of the Kurdish rebellion.

In September 1958, an agrarian reform law was enacted that transferred large tracts of land owned by the upper class to the landless *fellahin* (peasant farmers). The new regime also abrogated the Baghdad Pact and recognized the Soviet Union and the People's Republic of China. Finally, differences between Nasser and the Iraqi government were reconciled to the extent that there was even talk of union between Egypt, Syria and Iraq.

The tremendous amount of enthusiasm and support generated for the new regime could not cover up the power struggle that surfaced as early as September 1958. Four major political factions quickly appeared. At one pole were the communists, who tended to follow the Soviet line. At the other were the Arab nationalists, including the currently ruling Baath party, who supported either union or at least very close ties with Egypt. The Kurds constituted a third group. For tactical reasons, they sided with the communists and were thus also considered pro-Soviet. Finally, the more moderate National Democrats and the Istiqlal (Independence) party upheld Iraqi independence but were inclined toward closer relations with Egypt.

Qasim erroneously believed he could play each faction off against the others and thus maintain power. In September 1958 he dismissed Arif as deputy prime minister and assigned him as ambassador to West Germany. Arif never arrived at his new post, however, for he was arrested on charges of conspiracy and imprisoned. Arif's dismissal provoked a rift between Qasim and Nasser, with whom Qasim had just signed a protocol pledging closer cooperation. In March 1959 a rebellion broke out in Mosul. The leaders called upon all Arabs to help overthrow the Qasim regime and to form a union with Egypt. With the assistance of the Kurds and the communists, the rebellion was suppressed, thus crushing the Arab nationalist movement and at the same time providing a greater role for the communists. Qasim then proceeded to reduce the communists' influence by restricting their political activities. Because of his use of terror, however, Qasim's victory over the nationalists resulted in a considerable loss of public support for the regime.

The Kurdish revolt of 1961 further undermined the stability of the Qasim regime. The Kurds felt that Qasim had not fulfilled his promises for some form of regional autonomy. Having revolted in 1919, 1937, and 1946, they again rebelled; with military aid from the Soviets, they effectively engaged a large segment of the Iraqi army, greatly intensifying the divisions within the country.

Another problem facing Qasim was the Iraqi claim to Kuwait, which he renewed in 1961 when Kuwait became independent. His position alienated virtually every Arab country and left Iraq hopelessly isolated. It also cost him domestic support that he could ill afford to lose.

On 8 February 1963, Qasim was ousted in a coup led by the Iraqi Baath ("renaissance") party together with sympathetic army officers and pan-Arab groups. Colonel Arif was appointed president but the real power was exercised by a Baathist general, Ahmad Hasan al-Bakr. The Supreme Revolutionary Council was formed, with the Baathists in control of all important positions, and the first action it took was the execution of Qasim, followed by a purge of the army and government of all communists and their sympathizers. Although the new regime was devoted to Arab unity, a split occurred between moderate Baathists and Nasserites who wanted unity with Egypt, and more radical Baathists who favored closer ties to Baathist Syria. The Nasserites appeared to win out in November 1963. President Arif wrested full powers from the Baathists and established the Revolutionary Command Council.

Arif, who was an admirer of Nasser, had already taken steps toward union with Egypt beginning with integration of military, economic, political, and information policies. In May 1964 Arif and Nasser issued a number of joint statements. They provided that over the next three years a provisional government headed by a joint Presidency Council would begin to merge the two countries. In July 1964 Arif decreed that all political parties would join one organization, the Iraqi Arab Socialist Union. In effect, Iraq was attempting to emulate the Egyptian Arab Socialist Union, thus facilitating movement toward total union.

Although President Arif desired union with Egypt, he differed with elements in his cabinet who thought he was moving too slowly, and six members of his cabinet subsequently resigned. One of Arif's reasons for slowness was his conviction that Iraq's internal problems should be resolved before the union could be consummated. As time went on, however, plans for the union began to recede. After an unsuccessful coup attempt in September 1965 by the pro-Nasser premier, General Arif Abd al-Razzak, all thoughts of union disappeared. Al-Razzak and his supporters fled to Cairo.

Despite his differences with the Baathists, Arif was firmly committed to a socialist program for economic development. At the same time that he announced the formation of the Arab Socialist Union, he also nationalized many of Iraq's leading business firms as well as all Iraqi privately-owned banks and insurance companies. The one noticeable exception was the oil industry. Arif realized that he needed the oil companies to ensure revenues for his development plans.

Like his predecessors, Arif continued to have problems with the Kurds. They remained in a continuous state of rebellion over demands for autonomy from 1962 to 1964, despite an offer of limited autonomy made in 1963. In February Arif obtained a cease-fire from the Kurds, but it lasted less than a year.

Arif's accidental death in a helicopter crash on 3 April 1966, led to a power struggle between the civilians, led by Premier Abd al-Rahman al-Bazzaz, and the military. The cabinet and the National Defense Council were charged with selecting a suitable replacement. In a compromise solution Arif's brother, Major General Abd al-Rahman Arif, became president, and Dr. Bazzaz remained as prime minister. Following an attempted coup by pro-Nasser military officers, the new President Arif consolidated his position and forced Bazzaz to resign in August, 1966.

Prior to his ouster, Bazzaz had negotiated yet another settlement with the Kurds. It was based on a twelve-point declaration that allowed the Kurds a limited degree of autonomy and equal representation in the government. But many key provisions had not been honored and by 1968 war had broken out again. After two years the government again negotiated a settlement. The 1970 Kurdish agreement was more comprehensive than any previous agreement and, it was hoped, would be permanent. After a few years, however, when it became obvious that the Kurds would not receive the degree of autonomy they sought, Kurdish leader Mustafa Barzani again raised the standard of revolt, this time with military aid from Iran. The rebellion was crushed in 1975 after Iran agreed to refrain from aiding the Kurds in return for Iraqi recognition of Iranian sovereignty over half of the Shatt al-Arab River where it forms the border between the two countries. Another result of the agreement was to force Barzani, now an old man, into exile.

On 17 July 1968, the second Arif regime was overthrown in a bloodless coup by General Hasan al-Bakr. The Kurdish rebellion, the humiliating Arab defeat in the 1967 Arab-Israeli War, and Arif's inability to get the country's domestic development moving all contributed to his overthrow. The coup brought the Iraqi Baath party back to power.

In the years since the Baath returned to power, Iraq has known a greater measure of stability than at any time since the overthrow of the monarchy. In July 1973 an abortive coup was attempted by the security chief, Nazim Kazzar, which resulted in the creation of the National Front to broaden the regime's political base. Although the National Front also included the Communist party of Iraq, relations between the Baathists and the communists were never good and in recent years have actually become worse. It was originally hoped that Barzani's Kurdish Democratic party would also join, but that quickly proved illusory. During the second half of the 1970s Saddam Husayn al-Takriti rose to the position of strongman behind President al-Bakr. For several years Saddam maintained a low profile as vice-chairman of the party regional (i.e., Iraqi) command and vice-chairman of the Revolutionary Command Council. On 17 July 1979, the eleventh anniversary of the current Baath regime, Saddam succeeded to the presidency as al-Bakr, stating reasons of ill health, handed over to him the full reins of power.

Political Environment

The present borders of Iraq only date back to 1920 and were created with more of a mind to great-power interests than to ethnic unity. This fact explains, in great part, the chronic lack of political cohesion that has plagued all Iraqi governments since that time. Thus, despite oil wealth and other natural resources, a potentially productive agricultural sector, and a population that is not out of proportion to its resource base, Iraq has been an extremely difficult country to govern regardless of the ideological professions of the regime in power.

The People

The population of Iraq is estimated to be eleven million, with an annual growth rate of 3.3 percent. The capital and largest city is Baghdad with a population of 3.5 million. It is followed by Basrah with a population of around five hundred thousand, and Mosul with four hundred thousand. The population of Iraq is divided into several ethnic groups; the two largest are the Arabs, who make up 75 percent, and the Kurds, who comprise 15 to 20 percent. Iraq is predominantly an Arab country, but in no way should this fact be equated with homogeneity. Differences among the Arabs and between them and the non-Arabs are pronounced.

The Arab population is split along religious confessional lines. Almost three-fourths of the Arabs are Shi'ites. This fact stands out all the more when one considers that the Iraqi government has traditionally been dominated by Arab Sunnis. Most Shi'ite Arabs are farmers, shepherds, or unskilled laborers who live in central and southern Iraq. Because of their religious heritage and their traditional way of life, they tend to be conservative in outlook and resistant to change. This explains in great part their ambivalent attitude toward Arab nationalism. Many Iraqi Shi'ites have a closer affinity with their coreligionists in Iran than with Sunni Arabs in Iraq.

The Sunni Arabs are found in all strata of Iraqi society. In the larger cities like Baghdad they dominate the professional classes. Because of their generally higher level of education than the rural and village-dwelling Shi'ites, they have been better able to assimilate modern secular political concepts and ideologies. Arab Sunnis are also found in agrarian villages, particularly in northern and central Iraq, and in the deserts of the southwest. The desert Arabs, proud of their pure Arabian lineage, consider farming and manual labor subservient ways of life. They prefer to live today in much the same fashion as they lived two thousand years ago. The government, however, contends that they are disruptive and unproductive, and has established programs designed to settle them.

One fascinating though politically insignificant group of Arabs inhabits the marshes and deltas in the south between the Tigris and Euphrates rivers. The so-called "marsh Arabs" are a seminomadic people who have adapted to life in the marshes. They are for the most part Shi'ites although some are Sunnis. The marsh Arabs are tribally organized, and engage in fishing and agriculture. Their population is estimated to be between three and four hundred thousand.

The Kurds are the largest non-Arab minority group in Iraq. They occupy the mountainous regions of the northeast and are also found in contiguous areas of Iran, Turkey, and Syria. Because of their separate cultural heritage and language, the Kurds persist in the dream of self-determination. Thus they continue to be a destabilizing element to Iraq's Arab dominated political system. Predominantly nationalists, they have been willing to side with the Soviets or with Iran to further their aim of autonomy. By no means, however, are the Kurds united on what form autonomy should take.

The Kurds are generally Sunni Moslems and primarily seminomadic, but they are increasingly moving to such urban areas as Mosul and Kirkuk. Nonetheless, the Kurds still maintain a traditional life-style, which includes patterns of seasonal migration and tribal animosities, the latter tending to divide them.

Iraq has a number of other smaller minority groups, many of which

have bonds with neighboring states. Turkomens inhabit parts of northern Iraq bordering Turkey. They compose about 2.5 percent of the
population and are about two-thirds Sunni and one-third Shi'ite. Persians and Lurs (who speak a Persian dialect) are found in eastern Iraq
along the Iranian border. They are generally Shi'ite Muslims. Finally,
about 6 to 8 percent of the population are non-Muslims. Among them
are Christians, Yazidis (the so-called devil-worshippers), Mandeans (a
pre-Christian religion), and a small community of Jews. Although the
Jewish population of Iraq numbered close to one hundred and fifty thousand in 1950, most living in Baghdad, today there are less than seven
thousand. The rest have immigrated, mostly to Israel.

Social Structure. The highly diverse nature of Iraqi society and the
primary loyalty of the individual to his extended family and ethnic group
has inhibited the growth of a purely Iraqi nationalism. This is especially
the case in the rural areas, where resistance against change is most
prevalent. In fact, the gap between attitudes in the cities and the outlying
areas is immense and is further exacerbated by the overwhelming concentration of political power in the capital city, Baghdad. Although the
distribution of income has improved since the prerevolutionary days of
city-dwelling absentee landlords and landless peasants, there is still a
disparity between the rural areas and the more affluent urban areas. The
government has been trying to redress this difference through land
reform and expanded education.

Since 1958, there has been a sixfold increase in the total number of new
graduates from both secondary and higher educational institutions. So
rapid has the expansion of educational programs in Iraq been, in fact,
that increases in employment opportunities have not been sufficient to
keep pace with the new graduates. Since the Baathist regime is committed to a socialist economic structure and has limited the size of the
private sector, the burden of placing the growing number of graduates
has fallen mainly on the government. The problem was aggravated by
sluggish economic growth in the 1960s.

The scarcity of employment opportunities within Iraq led many skilled
persons to seek more financially rewarding jobs abroad. The resulting
"brain drain" was compounded by political instability during the first
decade of the republic. With four regimes coming to power between 1958
and 1968, some of Iraq's intellectuals left Iraq for predominantly political
reasons. In 1974 it was estimated that ten thousand educated Iraqis were
living abroad. In order to combat this problem, the current regime has
offered incentives and rewards to those who return. Although this policy
has been successful to some extent, there remains a very large Iraqi community living in self-imposed exile.

Economic Conditions

The political constraints placed on private enterprise by Iraq's socialist government and the predominating position of the oil sector in the economy place upon the government the main responsibility for the management of the economy. Despite the oil-based economy, agriculture is the largest employer, taking up over half the labor force. Mesopotamia was the bread basket of the ancient world, with an elaborate network of canals for irrigated farming. The Mongol invasions of the thirteenth through the sixteenth centuries utterly destroyed the system and it has never been fully restored.

Modern Iraq has expended a great deal of energy on improving agriculture but it still suffers from inefficient land tenure practices, resistance of the farmers to more modern techniques, and under-capitalization. Republican regimes since 1958 have endeavored to solve the land-tenure problem by stripping the absentee landowning class of their large holdings. Over four hundred thousand farmers have received title to their land. These measures, more politically than economically in-spired, actually lowered agricultural productivity. Moreover, they did not address the system of freeholds, religious endowment (*waqf*) land, and three kinds of government land, which further complicate land tenure. For both political and practical reasons, the government has been attempting to consolidate small holdings into agricultural cooperatives, and particularly in newly reclaimed land, collective farms.

Roughly half of Iraq's 443,000 square kilometers (ca. 171,000 sq. mi.) is arable and of this, only about one-fourth is under cultivation. If the agricultural sector were fully capitalized, it could feed twice the present population. Thus Iraq is one of the few Middle Eastern countries with the potential for a balanced economy. During the 1960s, the country was not only undergoing political upheavals but, due to a dispute with the largely British-owned Iraq Petroleum Company (IPC), oil revenues were down and the government was having a difficult time economically as well. Much of the external financing of Iraq's economic development during that period came from the Soviet Union. During the 1970s, Iraq's fi-nancial position greatly improved, and the government has increased much-needed capital investment in the agricultural sector, including con-struction of dams, canals, and adequate drainage facilities to prevent salinization.

One additional agricultural problem still to be addressed is the control of the Euphrates River waters. Owing in part to bad relations between Syria and Iraq, there is no Euphrates water agreement, and in 1975 Iraq accused Syria of cutting the flow of the river behind its new dam, causing

Iraq severe crop damage. Although control of the Euphrates waters will probably never lead to an open confrontation between the two countries, it remains a potentially threatening problem.

The oil industry is capital-intensive, employing relatively few Iraqis, but it nevertheless dominates the economy. Oil has long been known to exist in Iraq. For centuries the residue of oil seeps was used to fuel lamps, and natural gas was ignited to create the "everlasting sacred fires of Kirkuk." The original modern oil concessionaire was an Armenian from Constantinople named Calouste Gulbenkian who organized German, Dutch, and British interests in the Turkish Petroleum Company in 1912. After World War I, the French took over the German shares and the company was renamed the Iraq Petroleum Company.

The dispute with IPC that had so adversely affected oil revenues in the 1960s was never resolved, and in June 1972 IPC was nationalized. The owners agreed to an arbitrated settlement over compensation in January 1973 that also included the transfer of assets to Iraq of a small sister company, the Mosul Petroleum Company. Two years later, another sister company, the Basrah Petroleum Company, was also nationalized. All of Iraq's oil is now in the hands of the state-owned Iraq National Oil Company (INOC). Brazilian and French companies are currently employed by INOC on service contracts and are conducting major exploration and expansion programs. Iraq hopes to increase production from roughly 3 million barrels a day in 1978 to 4 million by the mid-1980s.

Nonoil industry has never played a major factor in Iraq's economy. The government is concentrating on industrialization utilizing its strongest economic sectors, oil and agriculture. Ultimately it hopes to develop both agri-industry and petrochemicals, and to reduce its dependence on crude oil exports.

Economic development is closely monitored through economic planning, which is based on socialist models. The earliest planning, however, occurred under the monarchy. The main accomplishment of that period was the progress made in controlling the flood-prone Tigris and Euphrates rivers. Succeeding plans followed Soviet planning philosophy, having been designed with the help of Soviet technicians. Prior to 1970, economic planning concentrated primarily on agriculture, with mixed results. In the 1970s, emphasis has been placed on investment in the industrial sector. Although the government refuses to allow foreign private investment, much of the work on Iraq's development programs is actually performed by Western private firms through turnkey projects that are turned over to the government upon completion. With increased revenues to fund these projects after the quantum jump in oil prices in 1973, and with excellent agricultural potential and less population pressure than many of its neighbors, Iraq's economic prospects are fairly bright if it can maintain political stability.

Political Structure

Iraq is a republic dominated by the Socialist Arab Baath party. Technically, the Iraqi Baath party is a branch of the same party that rules Syria, but due to strong ideological and political differences, the two regimes are on bad terms. The titular head of the party's "National Command" ("National" here refers to the Arab nation as a whole) is Michel Aflaq, who helped found the Baath in Syria in 1943. At the state level, the Iraqi "Regional Command," theoretically under the National Command, is headed by President Saddam Husayn. In actuality, Iraqis dominate both the National Command and the Regional Command since Syria does not recognize the authority of either.

The Baath party maintains a separate identity from the government. In this way, there is less conflict of loyalty among party workers who maintain an extensive party organization. Below the Regional Command level are provincially based unit commands that are further subdivided into branches (*far*); sections (*shu'bah*); divisions (*firqah*); and circles or cells (*halaqah*).

In November 1971, the National Action Charter was promulgated in an effort to broaden the Baath's political base by integrating other parties into the party structure. Following negotiations and in the wake of the Kazzar coup attempt in 1973, the Progressive National Front was created to include the Communist party of Iraq, Barzani's Kurdish Democratic party, and two smaller leftist groups, the Independent Democrats and the Progressive Nationalists. As relations with the Kurds deteriorated, Kurdish participation never materialized, and, at any rate, the Baath never intended to give the National Front any real participation in the political process. Non-Baath political views, however, are represented in the council of ministers.

Since the 1958 coup, Iraq has been ruled under several constitutions. The most recent to date, promulgated in July 1970 as a provisional constitution, delineated legislative, executive, and judicial branches of government. The constitution called for a National Assembly, to be initially appointed by the Iraqi Revolutionary Command Council (RCC) and representing all political, economic, and social groups in the country. The National Assembly's powers were fairly limited. It was given the responsibility of considering draft legislation proposed by the RCC, which retains the final legislative powers. Even thus restricted, however, the assembly has never been convened.

Executive powers are shared by the RCC and the national government. The RCC possesses ultimate control. It not only enacts legislation but also oversees all foreign and domestic policies and chooses (by two-thirds vote) the president and vice-president of the republic. The RCC is composed of twenty-two members elected by simple majority from the Regional Command and, in turn, chooses its own chairman and vice-chairman. It is also empowered to relieve any of its members or members of the government, and, if need be, to prosecute him. It is by far, therefore, the most powerful governmental institution in Iraq.

The national government consists of the president, the vice-president, and the cabinet ministers. According to the constitution, the president is the chief executive and commander-in-chief of the armed forces. He is empowered to nominate the vice-president, and chooses his own council of ministers. He is also responsible for choosing and dismissing judges. Under his direction, the government prepares the annual budget for presentation to the RCC.

The 1970 constitution also provided for an independent judiciary. Above the courts of first instance are five courts of appeal and, at the top, a court of cassation. The judiciary also includes religious courts and revolutionary courts. The latter are convened to hear political cases. The legal system of Iraq is based primarily on the French code.

At the local level, Iraq has sixteen provinces administered by governors who are appointed by the president and are responsible to the minister of interior. Because Iraq is a unitary system with all powers reserved at the national level, the governors' powers are relatively limited.

The four Kurdish provinces are theoretically an exception. The 1970 Kurdish settlement (the so-called March Manifesto approved by the RCC on 11 March 1970) granted a degree of autonomy to the Kurds. Though it has never been fully implemented, it does grant proportional Kurdish representation in the RCC and the government and a degree of cultural as well as political autonomy.

Political Dynamics

Baathism professes to be socialist and pan-Arab and takes a revolutionary approach to foreign policy. Baathist ideology, however, is difficult to define in theoretical terms. It is basically an amalgam of antiimperialistic xenophobia, nostalgia for the ancient glory of the Arab empires, and a commitment to redistribution of wealth to benefit the poorer clases. The 1970 constitution, which serves as a statement of Baathist principles and goals, upholds socialism but appears to reject the socialist concept of the collective good in favor of the individual, who should be able "to develop his personality, cultivate the Arab heritage and live in freedom unfettered by social and economic differentials."[1]

Baath ideology has appealed mainly to Sunni Arab urban classes (though many have originally come from villages) at the lowest and least secure levels of the middle class. Since party membership is almost a necessity for career advancement, party roles are probably larger and more representative of all segments of Iraqi society than is the number of ideologically committed. By any standards, the latter group represents a small minority of the population. Despite the urban and revolutionary character of the party, traditional family and village ties can still be important. For example, both al-Bakr and Saddam Husayn al-Tikriti, as well as a number of lesser political figures, come from the same hometown, Tikrit, a small village on the northern Tigris. Saara', a town near Tikrit, and Anah, near the Syrian border, have also supplied a disproportionate number of men to the leadership structure.

The party dominates the political process in Iraq, all the more so because of the traditional weakness of formal political institutions. The government, likewise dominated by the Baath, serves more of an administrative role, formulating operational policies based on guidelines set down by the party. The distinction between the party and the government, however, can be overdrawn since all Iraqi politics are personality-oriented and the party and the government are dominated by the same personalities.

The party is divided into two major factions, civilian and military. Through the military wing, the party dominates the military establishment, which is charged with defending the regime but is at the same time kept under close surveillance to guard against coup plotting among the officer corps. As an additional check on the armed forces, the party has organized its own paramilitary units, the popular militia.

President al-Bakr was the head of the military wing, which was predominant when the Baathists seized power in 1968. In recent years, the civilian wing of the party under Saddam Husayn has gained ascendency in Iraqi politics. Saddam ruthlessly outmaneuvered his political rivals (many of whom are now deceased), but would not have been able to do so without the full support of al-Bakr. He also developed a reputation as a pragmatist. He has never allowed his Baathist principles to be interpreted in so doctrinaire a fashion as to interfere with the needs of his country. Thus, despite the internal Kurdish problem, the endemic lack of legitimacy facing the regime, and the many foreign-policy problems he must deal with, Saddam has brought a considerable degree of political stability to Iraq. With the departure of al-Bakr from active

FIGURE 6.1 The Iraqi Baath Party

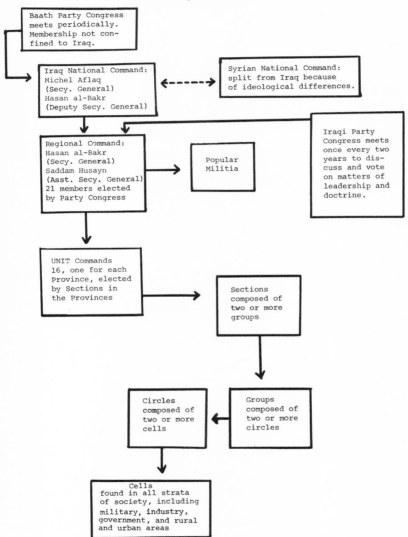

politics, however, one cannot totally rule out the possibility that members of the military wing, perhaps with civilian support, will attempt to reassert their political power by plotting the overthrow of Saddam.

Foreign Policy

Iraqi foreign policy is based on three basic pillars: Iraqi nationalism, pan-Arabism, and Baathist political and economic ideology. In many instances, the three are mutually reinforcing, but not always. Where they conflict, the pull of Iraqi nationalism is generally the strongest.

The overriding concern with national over international interests has been manifested until recently in the relative isolation of Iraq in Middle Eastern, and particularly Arab, world politics. Preoccupation with domestic affairs, however, has not precluded Iraq's playing a growing role in meetings of the Organization of Petroleum Exporting Countries (OPEC). Iraq has become an influential "hawk" in pushing for higher prices. The Baghdad regime also continues to be one of the most stridently anti-Israel states in the Arab world. It sent a significant contingent of its armed forces to fight beside Syrian forces in the October 1973 Arab-Israeli War, despite its bad relations with the Baathist regime in Damascus. The Iraqis have also adamantly opposed any kind of peaceful settlement with Israel, joining the radical Palestinian groups, Libya and Algeria, in the so-called Arab Rejectionist Front. On 2–5 November 1978, the Baghdad summit conference was held to consider sanctions against Egypt for negotiating a treaty with Israel at Camp David. A second conference was convened in Baghdad the spring following the ratification of the treaty in order to implement the sanctions. By persuading Arab moderates and radicals alike to make common cause against Egypt, Iraq's stature in the Arab world was greatly enhanced.

For the most part, Iraq's perception of pan-Arabism is compatible with its radical Baathist ideology. The greatest threat to pan-Arabism in the Iraqi view is Western capitalistic imperialism, both directly and through its "agent," Israel. On the other hand, the socialist states, particularly the Soviet Union, are enemies of both capitalism and imperialism. Iraq, therefore, has developed close relations with the Soviet Union, which has become its principal source of military arms and training. Iraqi-Soviet relations reached their apex with the signing of a Treaty of Friendship in 1972.

There are definite constraints on Iraqi-Soviet relations, however, mainly arising out of Iraq's fierce sense of nationalism. The Baathists, as they see it, did not witness the demise of British colonialism with the monarchy just to exchange it for Soviet imperialism. Thus, in 1978, they began to express concern at the expansion of Soviet influence in

Afghanistan and the Horn of Africa, and actually split with Moscow over the latter's support of the radical regime in Ethiopia against its Eritrean rebels. Iraq had supported the Eritrean dissidents since the early 1960s. Moreover, as if to underscore their displeasure, the Iraqis arrested a number of Iraqi communists on charges of subversive activities against the regime.

Iraq's relations with its immediate neighbors are also motivated to a large degree by ideological considerations. Baghdad considers the Syrian Baath regime to be heretical, a condition possibly even worse than not being Baathist at all. Syrian-Iraqi relations improved after the Baghdad conferences but the basic underlying animosities still appear to be present. Relations with Iran under the shah were equally bad. Before the Soviet-encouraged rapproachement between the two countries in Algiers in 1975, there were real concerns that hostilities would break out. Again, however, national interest in preventing war outweighed nationalistic and ideological antipathy toward Iran and the crisis was averted, another example of Saddam Husayn's pragmatism. Since the overthrow of the shah, Iraq has taken a more ambivalent posture with Iran. While welcoming Iran's new revolutionary policies Baghdad has been highly suspicious of its religious fervor.

Pragmatism also has been manifested in relations with the West. For example, Iraq is the last major Arab state not to restore diplomatic relations with the United States after they were broken in the wake of the June 1967 Arab-Israeli War, and has bitterly attacked the Camp David agreement. Nevertheless, Iraqi leaders admire American technology and are willing to purchase it over East European and friendly West European competitors. The largest single contract let by the Baath regime was to the U.S. firm of Brown and Root to build Iraq's deep-water oil terminal at Fau, in the gulf. In the area of technology, ideology generally takes a back seat.

Notes

1. Majid Khadduri, *Socialist Iraq: A Study in Iraqi Politics Since 1968* (Washington D.C.: The Middle East Institute, 1978), p. 32.

Bibliography

The three studies written over a period of years by Majid Khadduri are among the best studies of modern Iraq in English: *Independent Iraq: A Study in Iraqi Politics from 1932 to 1958* (New York: Oxford University Press, 1961); *Republic*

Iraq: A Study in Iraqi Politics Since the Revolution of 1958 (New York: Oxford University Press, 1969), and *Socialist Iraq: A Study in Iraqi Politics Since 1968* (Washington, D.C.: Middle East Institute, 1978). Khadduri's approach is historical and much of his material is based on personal interviews with leading Iraqi politicians such as Saddam Husayn. A comprehensive book also appearing in 1978 is Edith Penrose and E. F. Penrose, *Iraqi International Relations and National Development* (London: Ernest Benn, and Boulder, Colo.: Westview Press).

An interesting shorter study on Iraqi politics is Phebe A. Marr's "The Political Elite of Iraq," in George Lenczouski, ed., *Political Elites in the Middle East* (Washington, D.C.: American Enterprise Institute, 1975). Marr is concerned with locating factors in the formations of political attitudes by the Iraqi leadership. Two other interesting and informative books that primarily deal with domestic politics are Lorenzo Kent Kimball's *The Changing Pattern of Political Power in Iraq, 1958–1971* (New York: Robert Spiller and Sons, 1973), and Edgar O'Ballance's *The Kurdish Revolt, 1961–1970* (Hamden, Conn.: Archon Books, 1973).

David Long also presents a brief discussion of Iraq's domestic and foreign policies in *The Persian Gulf: An Introduction to Its People, Politics, and Economics*, rev. ed, (Boulder, Colo.: Westview Press, 1978). Finally, American University's *Area Handbook for Iraq* (1970) offers a valuable overview of the political, social, and economic institutions and dynamics of Iraq.

7

Eastern Arabian States:
Kuwait, Bahrain, Qatar, the
United Arab Emirates, and Oman

John Duke Anthony
John A. Hearty

In December 1976, representatives of the member states of the Organization of Petroleum Exporting Countries (OPEC) convened in Doha, capital of Qatar, to set the world price of oil. A great deal of world attention was focused on the meeting at the time. The members failed to reach an agreement and for six months there were two world oil prices. Very little attention, however, was given to the country that played host to the meeting. Its relative anonymity, despite its growing importance as a major oil exporter, is symbolic of all the states of eastern Arabia.

Before the discovery of oil, the eastern Arabian states eked out a subsistence-level existence from pearling, fishing, seaborne commerce, and, among the nomads, animal husbandry. The sudden and dramatic change from relative austerity to oil-generated affluence characterizes nearly all of these states and lends a fairy-tale atmosphere to their capitals, each with its own new international airport and luxury hotels. Beneath the glitter, however, each state remains locked in an ongoing struggle with the awesome tasks of social, economic, and political transformation.

Historical Background

Little is known of eastern Arabia during prehistoric times. In the north, the ancient civilization of Mesopotamia extended along the shores of the Persian (Arabian) Gulf as far south as contemporary Saudi Arabia. From around 4000 to 2000 B.C., much of eastern Arabia was controlled by the ancient civilization of Dilmun, centered in the Bahrain archipelago. A later civilization, called Magan, arose in Oman.

Because most of the hinterland of eastern Arabia has always been ecologically inhospitable, the ancient inhabitants turned primarily to the sea for their livelihoods. The ancestors of the Phoenicians are believed by some to have first learned their maritime skills in the gulf. Inland, nomads began to develop animal husbandry, and at the large oases, irrigated farming was also developed. In Oman there was also farming in the Hajar Mountains. Moreover, despite the isolation of communities in the gulf, fairly regular intercourse has existed between the interior and the coastal towns since ancient times.

Indigenous gulf maritime trade reached its zenith during the reign of the Abbasid caliphs in Baghdad (A.D. 750–1258). Like spokes from the hub of the Abbasid Empire, routes followed by the gulf seafarers extended to India and Africa, supplying goods from the east and the south to the center of the Islamic world. With the fall of the Abbasid capital of Baghdad to the Mongols in 1258, the region's trade declined and politics became increasingly chaotic, producing a situation that changed very little until the first European penetration of the gulf two and one-half centuries later.

The first significant European incursion into the Persian (Arabian) Gulf was made by Vasco da Gama of Portugal in 1497. The Portuguese objectives and administrative practices in the gulf area were subsequently adopted by the Dutch and English who followed Portugal's prime objective—paramountcy in the trading of eastern luxury goods to which Europe had grown accustomed during the time of the Abbasid and Umayyad empires. Another concern was the security of the maritime routes to and from India.

As the Portuguese Empire faded so did its control over the gulf. A successful English-Persian attack on Portuguese-held Hormuz signaled the decline of Portuguese hegemony and the advent of the Dutch, who had begun to establish trade links to the east. By the middle of the eighteenth century, however, the Dutch began to yield to the British. With the abandonment of Kharg Island (offshore contemporary Iran) in 1765, the Dutch presence in the gulf was effectively ended.

The British, like the Portuguese and Dutch before them, became interested in the gulf for both strategic and commercial reasons and, like their predecessors, adopted an administrative policy based on indirect rule, with a minimum of interference in local affairs. British trade with the Orient was obstructed by piracy and civil war in the gulf and was threatened from outside the area by the French.

These impediments to British interests motivated the British government to enter into a number of special treaties with the littoral states. The first such treaty was concluded with Oman and coincided with the

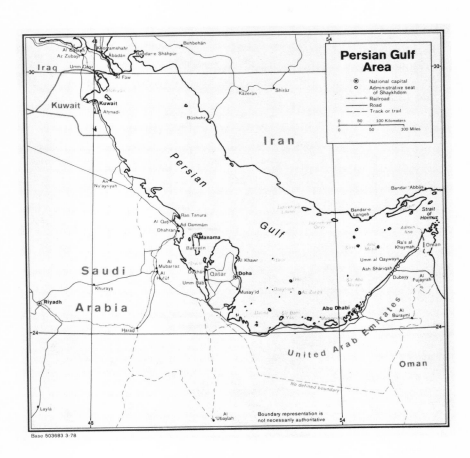

Persian Gulf Area

⊛ National capital
○ Administrative seat of Shaykhdom
┼┼┼ Railroad
─── Road
- - - Track or trail

| 0 | 50 | 100 Kilometers |
| 0 | 50 | 100 Miles |

Iraq
Kuwait
Kuwait
Ahmadi
Al Basrah
Az Zubayr
Khorramshahr
Ābādān
Bandar-e Shāhpur
Umm Qasr
Al Fāw
Behbehān
Kāzerūn
Shīrāz
Būshehr
Iran
Persian
Gulf
An Nu'ayriyah
Ras Tanura
Al Qatif
Ad Dammām
Dhahran
Manama
Bahrain
Al Mubarraz
Al Hufūf
Dukhān
Umm Bāb
Qatar
Doha
Al Khawr
Musay'id
Bandar-e Langeh
Bandar 'Abbās
Strait of Hormuz
Admin. line
Ra's al Khaymah
Oman
Umm al Qaywayn
Ash Shāriqah
Dubayy
Al Fujayrah
Abu Dhabi
Al Buraymi
Saudi
Arabia
Khurays
Riyadh
Harad
United Arab Emirates
Oman
Layla
Al 'Ubaylah
No defined boundary
Boundary representation is not necessarily authoritative

Base 503683 3-78

French invasion of Egypt in 1798. The pact was designed to deny the gulf to the French and to improve the system for protecting Britain's lines of communication with its increasingly important Indian Empire.

As the French Revolution caused the challenge that France had represented to recede, another challenge presented itself in the form of Arab privateers. Sailing from such shaykhdoms as Sharjah and Ras al-Khaymah, gulf mariners would strike at European shipping. Even though a number of military expeditions were dispatched to the gulf from England's Indian dominions, the British were unable to halt such attacks until 1819 when, after heavy fighting, they successfully defeated the Arab fleet based in Ras al-Khaymah. A treaty signed the following year with the local shaykhs became the cornerstone of Britain's political, strategic, military, diplomatic, economic, commercial, and administrative presence in the gulf area for the next 150 years.

Although Arab harassment of British shipping in the gulf and Indian Ocean ceased thereafter, a major problem remained in the sense that the shaykhdoms had not been prohibited from engaging in war with one another on land. Hence, in 1835, the British prevailed upon all the ruling shaykhs to sign a second agreement. The latter treaty prohibited the tribes under the ruler's jurisdiction from raiding each other during the fishing and pearling seasons, which in time came to be called the "trucial period." Taken together, the two pacts marked the beginning of a long series of treaties between the British and what became known as the Trucial States, and were the principal means by which Britain legitimized its administration of the latter's defense and foreign affairs.

From the beginning, British authority in the gulf was exercised indirectly through the local rulers in the area. In fact, control of domestic affairs remained largely in the hands of indigenous, albeit traditional, leaders throughout the long period of British protection. By 1916 Britain was able to assume direct control over the shaykhdoms' external relations and indirect control over domestic affairs. Most rulers acceded to official British "advice"; those who refused or resisted risked almost certain exile, ouster, or British naval bombardment of their principalities. In this manner, Britain introduced an unprecedented degree of stability to the region.

After World War II, and especially following the independence of India and Pakistan in the late 1940s, British interests in the gulf area changed significantly. Although the strategic need to protect the Indian Empire had ceased, oil interests in Iran, Iraq, Kuwait, and other states had not only continued but increased. In the minds of U.K. policymakers, the extent of British involvement in the gulf's petroleum resources was sufficient to warrant the continued stationing of military forces in Oman, Sharjah, and Bahrain. In time, however, the costs to British taxpayers of maintaining a military presence in the gulf became an issue of increasing controversy in British domestic politics. As but one indication of growing disenchantment at home with the country's imperial policies, the British decided three years after the 1958 coup in Iraq to grant full independence to Kuwait, a decision that would be repeated ten years hence when the last of the protected-state treaties with the nine remaining gulf shaykhdoms was terminated.

Britain's greatest impact on the gulf was to introduce and develop modern administrative and legal practices into the region, as exemplified by the establishment of municipal governments and the application of Western-style legal codes. A more pervasive consequence of British influence was the promotion of English as the area's language of international trade, defense, and diplomacy. Rooted in more than a century and a half of cooperation between individual British officials and the indigenous inhabitants, Great Britain's legacy in the gulf is deeply imbedded in the emirates and gives every indication of remaining a prominent feature of life in the area for some time to come.

Modern Gulf States

There are ten gulf emirates and one sultanate comprising five states: Kuwait, Bahrain, Qatar, the seven-member United Arab Emirates (UAE), and Oman, respectively. The governments of these states are all conservative politically and each, save the UAE, which is a federation headed by a president, has a dynastic form of rule. Even in the UAE, the local administrations of the various dynastic emirates have a greater impact on the daily lives of the citizens than that of the federal government. The relatively stable political conditions that prevailed in the gulf throughout most of the 1970s stood in marked contrast to the previous, often violent histories of a number of these states. Their political and social institutions, if not always their economic and military institutions, have exhibited a remarkable degree of resiliency that few would have thought possible a decade earlier when the special treaty relationship with Great Britain was being terminated.

KUWAIT

Historical Background

The Kuwaitis trace their history back to the late seventeenth and early eighteenth centuries when several tribes of the great Unayzah tribal confederation emigrated from their famine-torn homeland in central Arabia.

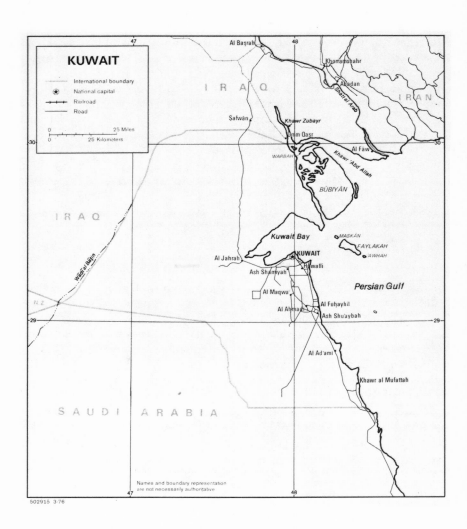

Calling themselves the Bani Utub ("the people who wandered"), roughly half of the the emigrés settled in Bahrain. In 1716, the remainder founded present-day Kuwait.

Over the years, several leading clans of the original wave of emigrés—the Al Sabahs, the Al Ghanims, the Al Khalids, the Janaats and the Al Salihs among others—combined to create an oligarchical merchant principality presided over by the Al Sabahs.

In 1899, Mubarak Al Sabah, subsequently referred to as "Mubarak the Great" (r. 1896–1915), who had expanded Kuwaiti influence along with Al Sabah preeminence, allowed the principality over which he reigned to enter into a protected-state relationship with the British. Shaykh Mubarak's reason was his fear that the Ottomans, who claimed nominal suzerainty over the shaykhdom, might try to implement political control. At his death Mubarak had succeeded in expanding Kuwaiti rule to about twice its present size. In 1922, Kuwait's British protectors negotiated half of the principality's enlarged territory back to the Saudis and to Iraq in the Treaty of Uqayr. The treaty also created the Saudi-Kuwaiti Neutral Zone, the landward side of which was split equally between the two parties in 1970.

The British allowed the bulk of domestic administration to remain in Kuwaiti hands although in time they would provide advisors to help create and staff the beginnings of a modern bureaucracy. As would occur elsewhere in the gulf and especially throughout eastern Arabia, British interests in Kuwait underwent a dramatic transformation following the discovery of oil. The Kuwait Oil Company, jointly owned by Gulf Oil Company and British Petroleum (formerly the Anglo-Iranian Oil Company), received a concession in 1934 and discovered oil in 1938. The first commercial quantities, however, were not exported until after World War II.

In 1961, Kuwait regained full independence from the British. At the time, Iraq made threatening gestures, claiming sovereignty over the emirate based on old Ottoman claims. Britain, under treaty provisions, sent troops to Kuwait and the crisis subsided. In 1963, Kuwait became a member of the United Nations and later the same year Iraq recognized Kuwait's independence.

Even so, in 1973, Iraq laid claim to the Kuwaiti islands of Warbah and Bubiyan, which command the approaches to the Iraqi naval base at Umm Qasr. In May 1973, Iraq occupied the Kuwaiti border post of Samitah on the mainland and a military clash ensued. Although the Iraqis withdrew late in 1974, additional incidents subsequently occurred. Notwithstanding Iraqi overtures to improve relations in the late 1970s, relations between the two states remain uneasy on territorial as well as ideological grounds.

Political Environment

Population and Social Conditions

Kuwait lies at the northeast end of the gulf and contains some 16,000 square kilometers (ca. 6,200 sq. mi.). The emirate's land borders Iraq to the north and Saudi Arabia to the south. In addition, Kuwait shares a de facto maritime boundary (as do all the emirates) with Iran. The terrain is mostly flat, sandy desert with occasional ridges and rock outcroppings, particularly to the west.

The population of Kuwait is roughly one million, most of whom live in the capital city which, as in most of the other gulf emirates, carries the same name as the state itself. Approximately 85 percent of the inhabitants are Arabs, the remaining 15 percent is comprised mainly of Iranians, Indians, Pakistanis, and Europeans. More than 90 percent of the native Kuwaiti population is Sunni Muslim, the remainder are Shi'ite. It is significant, however, that more than half the total population is comprised of aliens. This expatriate and immigrant population is almost entirely the result of requirements by the oil industry and ancillary enterprises for technical skills and services in excess of that which, despite its modernity, can be produced by the Kuwaiti educational system.

The largest nonindigenous group is the Palestinian community, which comprises approximately a quarter of the total population, or, according to unofficial estimates in the late 1970s, about 270,000. The Palestinians began arriving in Kuwait after the first Arab-Israeli War in 1948. Although many of them are well-educated and have lived and worked in Kuwait long enough to attain high positions in business and government, relatively few have attained full Kuwaiti citizenship. Like their compatriots in other countries, they have maintained strong ties to their homeland.

Other foreign groups have come to Kuwait to make their fortunes and then return to their native lands, a phenomenon that accounts for the disproportionate ratio of males to females. Except for Palestinians and Europeans, many workers leave their families behind while sending a high percentage of their earnings back home.

Kuwait's "cradle-to-grave" welfare system, supported by oil revenues, is one of the most unique in the world. In the day-to-day administration of the system there is little distinction made between resident aliens and native Kuwaitis. The government provides medical, educational, and welfare services, and even domestic telephone calls are free. Kuwait's educational establishment is comprehensive, compulsory for all children, and modern. It includes a tuition-free university and numerous vocational schools, all of which are subsidized by the state. The generous welfare program has been credited with reducing substantially the basis for social and economic unrest in the emirates. Nonetheless, owing to the limited opportunities for Kuwaitis and non-Kuwaitis alike to participate in the governing process and, in the case of the latter to obtain citizenship, various forms of political dissatisfaction have been a recurring phenomenon.

Economic Conditions

Prior to the production of oil, most Kuwaitis were engaged in economic activities typical of many other areas in the gulf, such as pearling and fishing along the coast and pastoral nomadism in the interior. Before development of cultured pearls by the Japanese, Kuwait had a fleet of over eight hundred pearl boats and some thirty thousand divers. Kuwaiti trading dhows also sailed annually to Africa and India carrying cargoes laden with limes, dates, and other items exported from Iraq, and returning with timber, textiles, and many other essential items not readily available locally. Since World War II, however, Kuwait has become the world's sixth-largest oil producer. Oil revenues have allowed Kuwait to evolve an advanced welfare system and have provided job opportunities for well over a half-million expatriates. Under the "participation" policies first enunciated by Saudi Arabian Petroleum Minister Shaykh Ahmad Zaki Yamani in the late 1960s, Kuwait has bought 60 percent equity in the Kuwait Oil Company (KOC) and ultimately plans to acquire total equity in both that company and in other foreign oil concessionaire operations. Like all gulf Arabs, the Kuwaitis are greatly concerned about the future of their emirate's economy "after the oil runs out." As but one expression of this widespread anxiety, conservation measures were adopted in 1972, which restricted maximum production to 3 million barrels per day. Subsequently, the Kuwaitis have increasingly adhered to the view that oil left in the ground is worth more than money in the bank, especially in view of inflation and, in the late 1970s, the rather bleak prospects for the discovery of alternate energy resources elsewhere in the world. In the positions they have adopted vis à vis these and other issues for which conventional economic wisdom has posed few answers, the Kuwaitis are not that much different in their thinking than many other gulf Arabs.

Concern about the depletion of oil reserves has resulted in accelerated attempts to modernize and diversify the economy, particularly in the fields of petrochemicals, fertilizer production, and shrimping. Agriculture remains practically nonexistent because of a lack of suitable soil and sufficient quantities of potable water. Indeed, Kuwait's chronic water shortage was only resolved in the 1950s by the installation of costly desalinization plants. Before that, Kuwaiti divers used to collect fresh water in earthen jugs from various springs that bubbled up from the floor of the gulf.

The emirate's success to date in diversifying its economy has been limited owing to the paucity of nonpetroleum resources, the small size of the domestic market, and duplication of industries and projects by other gulf states. Thus far, most industrial enterprise is in state-owned corporations, with the private sector active mainly in retail marketing and investment banking. There is a privately owned fishing company, founded in 1972, and also an oil tanker company that has been in operation since 1958.

By the late 1970s an estimated one billion dollars annually was being accrued as a result of astute public and private investments made over the years since oil production began. The Kuwaitis, considering their experience in this area thus far, foresee returns from capital investments, handled through their own banks and investment firms, as a major source of their national income when oil runs out. Although they have been generous to most developing countries, most of their investments are in Europe and the United States. Much more than any of the other emirates Kuwait has exhibited a willingness to invest a proportion of its assets in foreign real estate holdings, as evidenced by its investment in a major resort island in South Carolina.

Political Structure

The constitution, inaugurated in 1962 under Amir Abdallah al-Salim Al Sabah, provides for the establishment of a legislature, an executive branch, and an independent judicial system.

The legislature, called the National Assembly, was granted significant powers including the right to petition the amir (ruler) concerning cabinet appointees and the prime minister. The electoral base has remained narrow and is limited to citizens of Kuwait who are male, literate, and over twenty-one years old. Although political parties have yet to become legal in the emirate, the National Assembly had become an increasingly vocal force in Kuwaiti politics by the time of its dissolution in August 1976 amidst government concern over the prospects for regional and domestic instability owing, at least in part, to tensions generated by the Lebanese civil war and an inability of the parties concerned to address the Palestinian dimension of the Arab-Israeli conflict.

The executive branch is headed by the amir, who is usually designated by the preceding amir with the consent of the ruling Al Sabah family. The only formal constraints on the selection process are that the prospective ruler be of age and a descendant of Mubarak the Great. The amir rules through a prime minister, who usually holds the post of heir apparent simultaneously, and a council of ministers. In the absence of the National Assembly, the amir has added powers that he shares with the council of ministers. He also serves as commander-in-chief of the armed forces and, in addition, is empowered to select and remove cabinet ministers, members of the judiciary, and other government officials.

According to the constitution, the council of ministers, or cabinet, is responsible to the legislature. In the absence of the National Assembly, the cabinet, which numbered just under twenty portfolios in the late 1970s, carries out many of the legislative functions that would ordinarily be performed by the assembly.

The judiciary is based on the Egyptian model and is an amalgam of Islamic law, English common law, and the Ottoman civil code. The highest court is the Supreme Court of Appeal, although the amir himself can act as the final court of appeal. There are also permanent courts of appeal and a number of courts of first instance that hear such cases as those involving divorce or inheritance. More recently, a State Security Court was established in 1975, to handle political cases deemed to be in violation of specific Kuwaiti laws.

Kuwait is divided administratively into three districts (Kuwait City, Al Ahmadi, and Hawalli), each of which is headed by a governor, appointed by the amir. The governor (*wali*) is charged with maintaining and supervising the work of the municipalities, and he himself is responsible to the ministry of interior.

Members of the military have been prohibited from participating in the governing process per se and, for the most part, have remained depoliticized. The Kuwaiti army is relatively small, consisting of some ten thousand men, but is relatively well trained, equipped, and paid. There is also a National Guard and a National Security Force under the direction of the ministries of defense and interior, respectively.

Political Dynamics

Kuwait is a constitutional monarchy whose rulers have traditionally been chosen from the Al Sabah family. In recent years, the rulership has alternated between two branches of the dynasty that include the descendants of two sons of Mubarak the Great; "the Salims" and "the Jabirs."

This sequence was broken by Shaykh Sabah al-Salim Al Sabah, a Salim who became amir in 1965, succeeding a Salim.

The sequence was restored on January 1, 1978, when Shaykh Sabah, in turn, was succeeded by Shaykh Jabir al-Ahmad Al Sabah, a Jabir. The new ruler maintained the tradition by choosing a Salim, Shaykh Sa'd bin Abdallah, as heir apparent.

Despite the monarchical structure of government, Kuwait is actually an oligarchy. The power of the amirs is shared both with the rest of the Al Sabah family and with the other old, established families of the Bani Utub tribe. With such a small population base, Kuwait, like all other emirates, has had to rely heavily on the services of expatriates to aid in the administration of government. Many key positions have been filled by able Palestinians who have been resident in Kuwait for decades. In some instances, they and other long-time residents have been granted citizenship. Even so, the number involved is very limited, and assimilation of long-time resident aliens remains a major problem confronting the regime.

Foreign Policy

Because of insufficient military and population capabilities to defend itself against such countries as Iraq, Kuwait has long used its oil revenues as its principal foreign-policy instrument. Kuwait has attempted to utilize systematic foreign-assistance programs to neutralize potential opposition. With this and other purposes in mind, the Kuwait Fund for Arab Economic Development was established in 1967. In the aftermath of the June 1967 war, moreover, Kuwait, along with Saudi Arabia and Libya, became a major contributor of financial aid to Jordan and Egypt. The emirate has also significantly aided the Palestinians through financial contributions. In addition, when Jordan expelled the Palestine Liberation Organization (PLO) from its territory in September 1970, Kuwait briefly cut off all economic aid to Jordan. Although it subsequently resumed such assistance, this pragmatic policy won Kuwait a great deal of support among various Palestinian groups and helped to mollify the resentment toward Jordan then expressed by many Palestinians living in Kuwait.

BAHRAIN

The state of Bahrain consists of an archipelago of some thirty islands, located between Saudi Arabia and the Qatar peninsula. The largest island, Bahrain (al-Bahrayn), is 48 kilometers (30 mi.) long and 15.5 kilometers (9.6 mi.) wide, and contains the capital, Manamah (population 90,000). The second largest island is Muharraq, which is nearby and accessible by a four-mile causeway. It contains the state's second largest town, also called Muharraq, and the international airport. The total land area of the emirate is about 662 square kilometers (ca. 256 sq. mi.) and the population is about 250,000.

Historical Background

In the mid-eighteenth century a branch of the Bani Utub tribe, which had settled Kuwait, moved to the northern tip of the Qatar peninsula and established a fishing and pearling ministate at Subarah. In 1782, the Al Khalifah and other families crossed over from Qatar to the nearby Bahrain archipelago, where they formed a ruling merchant oligarchy over the local oasis farmers, fishermen, pearl divers, and seafarers. The Al Khalifahs have remained the ruling family to this day. Initially, Persians contested Al Khalifah rule but had little choice but to acquiesce to the de facto state of affairs when Bahrain came under British protection in the early nineteenth century. The claim was reviewed periodically in the nineteenth and twentieth centuries, and especially during the reign of the Pahlevi dynasty in Iran, which used the occasion to advance the claim once more in 1968 when the British announced their intention to withdraw by the end of 1971. In 1970, however, Iran acceded to the findings of a special UN fact-providing mission sent to Bahrain and formally recognized Bahrain's right to independence. This was granted in August of the following year.

The British exercised indirect control in Bahrain and the lower gulf shaykhdoms (the terms *shaykhdom* and *emirate* are synonymous) through political agents serving under a single British "Resident." From 1763 to 1946 these Residents had their headquarters in Bushire (Iran), after which the Residency was moved to Bahrain. Until they received independence in 1971, Bahrain, Qatar, and the seven Trucial States (now the UAE) all came under the purview of the Resident.

Political Environment

Population and Social Conditions

The population of Bahrain is primarily Arab, although a great many of the local inhabitants are of Persian descent. The proportion of natives to resident aliens is much greater than in the other gulf states like Kuwait or the UAE. The vast majority of the population is Muslim—half Shi'ite and half Sunni. The Al Khalifahs and other Bani Utub families are Sunnis, whereas the older indigenous population has a large proportion of Shi'ites, many of whom have centuries-old ties to Iran. Persian is often spoken alongside other tongues in the markets, although Arabic is the official language.

Some Bahrainis with Iranian ties hail from the south Iranian coastal town of Lingeh, and are called Lingawis. Others, claiming to be the descendants of Arabian migrants to Persia who later returned to the southwest side of the gulf, are called *muhawwalahs*. Still others are Persians from the north, sometimes called Red Iranians.

By gulf standards, Bahrain has a sophisticated society, with one of the oldest oil industries in the gulf. Bahrain has an articulate labor force and in the past has experienced labor unrest, although no unions are permitted. The country is also noted for its intellectual tradition and boasts some of the region's leading poets, artists, and authors.

The Bahraini school system is over fifty years old, the oldest in the gulf. School attendance is compulsory for children between the ages of six and sixteen. This has made possible a highly technical work force of native Bahrainis. There are also free health and social services.

Economic Conditions

Once the center of the pearling industry in the gulf, Bahrain's pearl industry, like that of all the other emirates, suffered heavily from the introduction of Japanese cultured pearls several decades ago. The emirate's agricultural and fishing sectors have fared better; but future prospects for farming are bleak owing to heavy Bahraini and Saudi industrial use of the underground water (Bahrain and Saudi Arabia's Qatif Oasis are connected) that has lowered the water table. Excessive and unregulated exploitation of the region's marine biology resources, especially by the gulf's lucrative shrimping industry, could also threaten fishing.

Bahrain's present economy is oil-based. Petroleum production began in 1932—the operating company, Bahrain Petroleum Company (BAPCO) was originally owned by Standard Oil of California (SOCAL) and the Texas Company (TEXACO)—and has been declining for some years. Nowadays 85 percent of the production at BAPCO's refinery on Bahrain is based on Saudi crude, which arrives through an underwater pipeline.

The emirate has also been and remains a leading entrepôt center. The overall volume of trade passing through the archipelago has been enhanced by the new port, Mina Salman, and the new Bahrain International Airport, which is heavily used because of its central location in the gulf and on the route from Europe to the Far East and Australia. There is also a successful aluminum smelter, Aluminum Bahrain, Ltd. (ALBA), which uses natural gas resources, and a large drydock under the Organization of Arab Oil Producing Countries (OAPEC) sponsorship known as the Arab Shipping and Repair Yard (ASRY). The emirate is also the headquarters of Gulf Air, the flag carrier of the Arab states of the lower gulf. Finally, the emirate has become the nucleus of a burgeoning offshore banking system that hosted more than forty foreign banks in the early 1980s.

Political Structure

Bahrain has developed a constitutional form of government that administers the emirate under the amir, a member of the Al Khalifah family. The constitution provides for separate executive, legislative, and judicial branches of government.

The first parliamentary elections were held in December 1973, shortly after the constitution had been ratified by popular referendum. The national assembly was composed of thirty elected and fourteen appointed cabinet members. Although the assembly had fewer powers than Kuwait's, its electorate was more widely based. The cabinet resigned in 1975 over the issue of alleged assembly interference in the administrative affairs of the government. The ruler, in response to the resignations, issued a decree that dissolved the legislature for an indeterminate time.

The executive branch of government has been headed by the prime minister. As of 1980, the prime minister was Shaykh Khalifah bin Salman Al Khalifah, the brother of the ruler. Shaykh Khalifah, who has held that position since 1973, is charged with managing the fifteen-member cabinet. Since the adjournment of the legislature, the cabinet has performed both legislative as well as executive functions. The ruler, Shaykh Isa bin Salman Al Khalifah, is advised by the cabinet but has long been personally active in tending to the day-to-day affairs of state. He is also assisted by other members of the ruling family, who hold most of the eight important cabinet portfolios. The heir apparent, Shaykh Hamad bin Isa Al Khalifah, Shaykh Isa's son, holds the post of minister of defense.

The Bahraini legal system is based on Western civil law and Islamic (Shari'a) law. The Shari'a court system accommodates the religious divisions within Bahraini society by establishing separate courts for Sunni and Shi'a sects. The amir has final power of review and pardon. The civil court system is organized much the same as the Shari'a system, i.e., there are courts of first instance, courts of appeal, and a supreme court (high court of appeal). The supreme court not only hears appeals from lower courts but also rules on the constitutionality of laws and decrees.

Political parties are not permitted in Bahrain, although the loosely organized "Popular Bloc" of the left won ten seats in the first elections to the national assembly. In addition, there is a radical subversive group of long standing known as the Bahrain National Liberation Front, but it has never been recognized by the government.

Political Dynamics

The ruling family wields the preponderance of influence within the Bahraini power structure despite the constitutional form of government. This pattern has at times enhanced and on occasion endangered the political stability of a country in which relatively sophisticated labor and leftist intellectual groups exist. Such groups have provided an impetus for a great many of the political and social reforms implemented by the government but have also spearheaded much of the emirate's labor unrest over the years. The leftist reform movement, now more than three decades old, suffered a serious setback when the national assembly was dissolved. As a consequence, the ruling family has relied increasingly on the security forces to maintain its internal security.

The merchant community has generally been content to adopt a position of political neutrality so long as their commercial interests did not appear to be threatened. For example, despite the fairly large electoral base at the time of the 1973 elections, the merchants were not widely represented nor did they apparently care to be.

The Bahraini armed forces, consisting of about fifteen hundred men, and a public security force of roughly the same size, are headed by the amir. Both contingents have been loyal to the government. The public security forces are charged with maintaining internal order, a problem that periodically has plagued Bahrain more than any other emirate in the gulf. These forces are primarily responsible for controlling demonstrations and collecting intelligence on radical individuals and groups within Bahrain.

Foreign Policy

In keeping with its status as a small, militarily weak state, Bahrain has taken care to remain on good terms with its immediate neighbors. In general, the nature and orientation of the emirate's external policies are conservative, pro-Arab and, though not without reservations on specific issues, pro-Western. In regional matters, it generally follows the lead of Saudi Arabia. Like the latter country, and indeed like all the emirates of eastern Arabia, it also has close ties with the West. Until independence in 1971, the British maintained a naval base at Jufair (near Manamah). The

United States, which since 1949 had rented space from the British to establish a headquarters for its Middle East Force (MIDEASTFOR), leased much of the former British facility directly from Bahrain from 1971 to 1977.

The Bahraini government was generally pleased to have the U.S. facility as an overt, official symbol of U.S. support for the regime. At the same time, a growing number of Bahraini officials began to view the U.S. presence as potential liability in terms of the opposition it could engender from local and regional radical groups. Primarily for this reason, Bahrain decided to terminate the lease. Since 1977, MIDEASTFOR has ceased to use Jufair as its home port, although the U.S. admiral who commands MIDEASTFOR's flagship still makes his residence there when he is not at sea, and MIDEASTFOR ships continue to make frequent use of the local facilities.

QATAR

The state of Qatar is situated on a peninsula that extends for about 170 kilometers (ca. 106 mi.) north from Arabia into the Persian Gulf. The emirate's territory encompasses approximately 10,360 square kilometers (ca. 4,000 sq. mi.), and of its population of 170,000 more than 130,000 live in the capital at Doha on the eastern coast. The peninsula is low lying and consists largely of sandy or stony desert.

Historical Background

Like Bahrain and the United Arab Emirates, Qatar was under British protection until independence in 1971. The protective status was based on treaties signed in 1869, 1913, and 1916. Apart from its having been admitted into the Arab League, OAPEC, OPEC, and the United Nations, the principal political development since independence was a nonviolent palace coup in 1972. On that occasion, Shaykh Khalifah ibn Hamad al-Thani, long known as one of the most forceful and development-oriented personalities in the gulf, ousted his cousin, Shaykh Ahmad.

Political Environment

Population and Social Conditions

Prior to the production of oil in 1949, the population of Qatar was one of the poorest of any in eastern Arabia. The great majority of the inhabitants lived at subsistence level with most of their income derived from fishing and pearling. Most of the indigenous population is Arab, and a large percentage of this group are *muhawwalah* Arabs with ties of varying strength and duration to their kinfolk along the south Iranian coast. The Arabs of Qatar are largely Sunni Muslims and generally subscribe to the fundamentalist teachings of the same Hanbali school of Islamic jurisprudence as practiced in Saudi Arabia.

There is also a large foreign population of Iranians, Pakistanis, Indians, and Palestinians. The Iranians comprise the majority of the small merchant class while many Indians and Pakistanis are employed as manual laborers, artisans, and clerical staff in local banks and businesses. The Palestinian population occupies the lower and middle levels of the bureaucracy and equivalent white-collar positions in the private sector.

Prior to the discovery and export of petroleum three decades ago, Qatar was devoid of even the remotest semblance of a modern school system, hospitals, clinics, piped water, electricity, and many other government services. Nowadays, however, all of the emirate's primary school teachers are Qataris and the first of what will ultimately be several faculties of the new Gulf University has been opened in Doha. Moreover, whereas in the past most of the local population was bedouin or nomadic, the majority for some years now has been urban and settled.

Economic Conditions

Petroleum production and export, together with the leadership of reform-oriented members within the ruling family, have been responsible for much of the dramatic transformation that has taken place in the country's social and economic life. In 1975, both major oil producers, Qatar Petroleum Company and Shell Oil of Qatar, were nationalized by the government. The emirate's extensive reserves of natural gas have much potential, and a plant has been built at Umm Sa'id (south of Doha) to utilize this resource, with a pipeline paralleling the oil pipeline from the fields at Dukhan on the opposite side of the peninsula. With petroleum providing the emirate's principal export, and nearly everything required beyond basic foodstuffs being imported, the government has been the source of considerable investment in economic infrastructure. The capital city is serviced by paved roads linking Qatar to its neighbors; a new international airport has been built as well as a modern port that is to be expanded.

Qatar is attempting to modernize and diversify its economy as rapidly and efficiently as possible in order to lessen its dependence on oil production. In 1973, it began to manufacture fertilizer. The country has also built a cement plant and flour mills and has expanded its shrimping industry.

Political Structure

In 1970, a year before it achieved independence, Qatar became the first of the lower gulf states to promulgate a written constitution. The constitution provided for a council of ministers and an advisory council, and stipulated that the former be appointed by the ruler and the majority of the latter were to be elected by the general population. A decade later, elections had not been held and there was little indication when the event itself might occur. The council of ministers (or cabinet) is led by the prime minister, who is theoretically appointed by the ruler, although in practice, the ruler himself has served in the post. The cabinet is responsible for proposing laws that must be submitted to the ruler for ratification and is also technically accountable for supervising the state bureaucracy and the financial affairs of the emirate.

The advisory council, finally established in 1972 after the coup, consisted exclusively of members appointed by the ruler. The council, although designed to represent major social and economic interest groups in Qatar, has little more than recommendatory authority and, by itself, is not empowered to initiate legislation.

In keeping with the time-honored practice of legitimizing leadership in eastern Arabia, the ruler is selected by a careful process of consensus within the family dynasty and, like his predecessors since time immemorial, may and indeed can be expected to be replaced by the same process. He is charged with ratifying all laws, commanding the armed forces, appointing governmental officials, and conducting foreign affairs. The constitution also calls upon the amir to select a deputy ruler, who, depending on the consensus of the family at the time the choice is made, may or may not be also designated as heir apparent.

The judicial system includes five secular courts and religious courts. A court of appeals exists, but the function of a supreme court is vested in the ruler, who has the power to reduce or waive penalties.

Finally, although Qatar is a unitary state, progress has been made toward decentralizing the administration. Nevertheless, because the majority of the population lives in Doha, the government has met with only limited success in its efforts to expand the allocation of political authority among the emirate's component political units.

Political Dynamics

The al-Thanis constitute the largest ruling family in the region, numbering in the thousands. To a considerably greater extent than any of its counterparts elsewhere in the region, it has traditionally dominated most of the important functions of government. The primary constraints on the ruler are Islamic law and the influence of what is undoubtedly the most conservative religious establishment of any of the emirates. The al-Thanis, although close-knit and secretive like all the other dynasties in the area, harbor within their midst a great many factions and rivalries based on different personalities and genuine disagreements over what, among various options, should be the most efficacious approach to the emirate's development.

The family holds ten of the fifteen cabinet portfolios including all of the vital ones, such as interior, defense, finance, and foreign affairs. Shaykh Khalifah ibn Hamad al-Thani has maintained close control over the country's affairs while granting to select members of the family a sufficient number of governmental positions to assuage their political ambitions. In much the same way as his counterpart in the ruling family of Saudi Arabia, Shaykh Khalifah is strongly anticommunist and maintains an ongoing vigilance on potential subversion within his borders.

The merchant class has traditionally exerted less influence on government affairs than its larger and older counterparts in Kuwait, Bahrain, Dubai, or Oman. The power of the merchants is primarily exerted on the commercial aspects of the emirate's developmental projects. However, as oil revenues accumulate and as many members of the ruling family have become more interested and involved in business themselves, the traditional separation of al-Thani-dominated government and merchant class-dominated business has begun to disintegrate. The dynasty and the business community, by symbiotic process, have increased their cooperation and collaboration in a great many areas pertaining to the emirate's economic growth.

Foreign Policy

The emirate's foreign policy has been consistently conservative, pro-Arab and pro-Western in the process of being, above all, dedicated to the pursuit of Qatari national interests. The focus of its policy has been primarily on gulf affairs with the exception of its broader oil interests. On many external policy matters, Qatar has been prone to follow the lead of Saudi Arabia while trying to maintain friendly relations with Iran, with respect to which it shares a maritime border that lies astride potential reserves of significant energy resources, and whose nationals constitute a substantial proportion of the overall population of the emirate. The continuation of traditional forms of rule in the gulf area is of no less concern to Qatar's dynasty than it is to other ruling households in the region, and for this reason, if no other, Qatar has sought to remain on friendly terms with all the littoral states of the gulf.

Qatar has managed to maintain remarkably good relations with most other Arab states. Although it has consistently supported the Arab cause on the Palestinian issue, Qatar fully realizes, as does its neighbors, the threat to its own interests from the radical proclivities of various elements within the Palestine liberation movement. Qatar has also been generous with financial aid, in keeping with the traditional Arabian ethos of those with bountiful resources feeling an obligation to extend a helping hand to their less fortunate neighbors. Foreign aid programs are also a means of maintaining good relations with possible domestic and Arab critics.

On oil matters, Qatar is an active member of both OPEC and OAPEC. Considered a moderate in contrast with some of the more militant OPEC members, the emirate has nevertheless pursued a considerably more activist role on oil price rises than either its Saudi or UAE neighbors.

UNITED ARAB EMIRATES

Historical Background

In 1820, in an attempt to protect maritime trading routes from privateers operating from ports along the lower gulf, Great Britain devised and in rapid succession imposed by force on the littoral emirates the first of what were to become a series of truces designed to put an end to what had previously been practically incessant naval warfare. As a result, the area, formerly known as the Pirate Coast, became known in time as the Trucial Coast and the seven small principalities that dotted its shores as the Trucial States.

The international status of these principalities as British-protected states continued until 1971, when Great Britain terminated its special treaty relationships with Bahrain, Qatar, and the Trucial States. For the previous three years, following the announcement of its intention to withdraw from the gulf, Britain tried to create a federation that would have included all seven of the Trucial States plus Qatar and Bahrain. Until 1970, Iran's territorial claim over Bahrain prohibited these efforts from being realized. Thereafter, Bahrain took the initiative and lobbied for representation in the new federation in accordance with population (it had the largest number of inhabitants). When refused, it elected to withdraw. Qatar, which not only contested Bahrain's drive to dominate the new state politically but also remained in conflict with Bahrain over the latter's claim to both the Hawar Islands and the village site of Zubarah on the Qatar peninsula, then also decided to withdraw, leaving only the Trucial States to form the new UAE. On December 1, 1971, Abu

Dhabi, Dubai, Sharjah, Ajman, Umm al-Qaywayn, and Fujayrah joined the union. Ras al-Khaymah joined in early 1972.

At the outset, the UAE faced numerous difficulties. Abu Dhabi had an unresolved dispute with Saudi Arabia and Oman over the Buraymi Oasis, which lay in the eastern region of the emirate. There were, moreover, strong traditional rivalries among the rulers, which served to dampen an otherwise more favorable atmosphere conducive to achieving a measure of functional integration among the member states. Finally, on the eve of independence, Iran, resurrecting a claim to the Greater and Lesser Tunbs islands claimed by Ras al-Khaymah, and Abu Musa, which was claimed by Sharjah, occupied all three islands. Iran's occupation of Abu Musa was in accordance with an eleventh-hour agreement arrived at between the shah and the ruler of Sharjah but no such understanding had been reached with Ras al-Khaymah regarding the Tunbs. As a result, Ras al-Khaymah's troops forcibly resisted the Iranian invasion and there was loss of life on both sides. The islands problem contributed directly to a coup attempt in February 1972 that cost the life of the ruler of Sharjah. Another long-standing territorial dispute involved a number of villages in the Buraymi Oasis region, which were claimed by Saudi Arabia. In 1974, an agreement between Abu Dhabi and Saudi Arabia ended this long-standing dispute and paved the way for the establishment of Saudi-UAE diplomatic relations.

Political Environment

Population and Social Conditions

The UAE is a federation of seven emirates extending for some 1,200 kilometers (746 mi.) along the southern coast of the Persian Gulf and another 250 kilometers (155 mi.) on the Gulf of Oman. Consisting of approximately 83,650 square kilometers (32,300 sq. mi.), the country has a population of nearly three quarters of a million. Abu Dhabi is almost as large as the rest of the shaykhdoms combined and contains more than half the total population. Six of the emirates—Abu Dhabi, Dubai, Sharjah, Ajman, Umm al-Qaywayn, and Ras al-Khaymah—have territory on the Persian (Arabian) Gulf, with Sharjah having additional, noncontiguous territory along the coast of the Gulf of Oman. Only Fujayrah is located wholly in the latter portion of the federation.

The indigenous inhabitants account for only about one-quarter to one-third of the union's total population. The UAE citizenry is in many ways similar to its counterparts in other countries, which, like it, are caught up in the throes of administrative, social, and economic modernization. Basically tribal and familial in terms of social organization, the native population ranges from an ever-dwindling number of bedouins, who remain basically illiterate and traditional in outlook, to a largely Western-educated, and well-traveled elite.

One of the most distinguishing characteristics of the various shaykhdoms is not so much geography as tribal affiliation. Six principal tribal groups inhabit the country: the Bani Yas, a confederation of nearly a dozen different tribes, two branches of which (the Al Bu Falah and the Al Bu Falasah, respectively) provide the ruling families of Abu Dhabi and Dubai; the Manasir (singular: Mansuri), who range from the western reaches of the UAE to Saudi Arabia and Qatar; the Qawasim (singular: Qasimi); the Al Bu Ali in Umm al-Qaywayn; the Sharqiyin in Fujayrah; and the Nu'aym in Ajman. All the native tribes are Arab and Sunni Muslims. In the nineteenth century, many of them espoused the teachings of the Wahhabi revival that spread from Saudi Arabia.

Of all the tribal groupings, those that can still be classified as bedouins comprise no more than 15 percent of the local population. They usually live around oases and for some years now have been migrating to and settling in urban areas. Numerous UAE citizens of bedouin stock are to be found in the police and military forces, upon whose loyalty the government heavily depends.

A highly sophisticated merchant class has developed, particularly in Dubai. It has maintained and, where possible, expanded, what for several decades now has been a rather extensive trading relationship with Iran and the Indian subcontinent. Most of the merchant families are Sunni Arabs, but allied with them are a substantial number of Persians and Indians who have been resident in the lower gulf for generations. For much of the period following World War II and prior to the emergence of oil as the dominant factor in the region's economies, among the most colorful merchants were those "free traders" in gold and other luxury items whose picturesque dhows concealed powerful engines capable of outrunning curious coast guard vessels of half a dozen countries.

The period of the 1960s and 1970s brought a new kind of entrepreneur: Western contractors and bankers who have played an important role in the oil-revenue-financed development boom. Because of the long-standing ties between the emirates and Great Britain, UK firms have remained in an especially strong position. In addition to Europeans, thousands of Indians, Pakistanis, Persians, Baluchis, and third-country Arabs have flocked to the gulf as clerks, accountants, and manual laborers.

Economic Conditions

Before the discovery of oil in Abu Dhabi in 1958, only Dubai and Sharjah had developed an extensive entrepôt trade. The oft-reported rivalry between these two shaykhdoms stems in part from the fact that Dubai began to eclipse Sharjah both politically and commercially when Sharjah's harbor began to silt up in the 1940s. The conditions for perpetuating the former's economic edge over the latter were practically assured in the 1950s, when Dubai succeeded in dredging its own estuary or "creek" as they are called locally.

Abu Dhabi Town, by contrast, was situated on an island and was little more than a mud-brick village prior to the petroleum discovery. Today, however, it is a major city, by far the most advanced in terms of administrative and social welfare services of any in the UAE. Dubai and Sharjah, which possess oil in lesser amounts than Abu Dhabi, have also undertaken extensive development projects. The contrast between these three affluent shaykhdoms and the other four remains substantial, although the gap has been lessened somewhat in recent years by the fact that the federal government, using largely Abu Dhabi money, has funded numerous development projects in the poorer states. The abundance of new income, the lack, to date, of a strong, centralized planning authority with power to veto or modify individual emirate developmental ventures, and, more importantly, the continuation of intense competition among the various rulers for prestige and preeminence in the area, inevitably have resulted in the duplication of many facilities, such as "international" airports and harbors in Abu Dhabi, Dubai, Sharjah, and Ras al-Khaymah.

Dubai, because of its long-standing position as the major trading center of the lower gulf, and the commitment of its ruler to developing the maritime sector of its economy, has by far the largest port facilities in the region. Attempts have been made to diversify the economies of the individual emirates in order to lessen their dependence on the petroleum industry. Toward this end, a huge drydock is under construction in Dubai, an aluminum plant has been proposed, several cement plants have been constructed, tourism in encouraged, the local fishing industry has been modernized and expanded, and agricultural improvements and experimentation continues to be encouraged in Abu Dhabi and Ras al-Khaymah. In addition, ongoing consideration is given to the establishment of various kinds of light to intermediate industries, for which the principal energy source would be gas that has traditionally been flared.

Political Structure

The UAE's provisional constitution, which dates from 1971, provides for federal legislative, executive, and judicial bodies. The legislature, called the Federal National Council (FNC), is, in reality and in keeping with the norms of traditional tribal and Islamic rule in this part of Arabia, more nearly akin to a consultative assembly. The FNC is composed of forty members nominated by the president and approved by the rulers of the seven member states who constitute the Federal Supreme Council. In accordance with the relative size of their constituent populations, eight of the seats are apportioned to Abu Dhabi and Dubai, respectively; six each to Ras al-Khaymah and Sharjah; and four each to the remaining three members. The FNC's duties are limited mainly to its discussion and approval of the budget, its authority to draft legislation to be presented for action by the Council of Ministers, and, of no small significance owing to the absence of political parties, trade unions, and various other kinds of voluntary associations familiar to Westerners, to its role as forum for discussion and debate of policies and programs under consideration by the government.

The Council of Ministers was composed of twenty-six ministers in early 1980. Although together with the Federal Supreme Council (FSC) and the presidency it forms a key part of the executive branch, two of its primary responsibilities are to draft laws and to act as a legislative body when the FNC is not in session.

The greatest concentration of authority within the federal structure is in the FSC. The seven-member council is charged with formulating and supervising all federal policies, ratifying UAE laws, approving the union's annual budget, ratifying international treaties, and approving the prime minister, the president and the members of the supreme court. In procedural matters, a simple majority vote is sufficient for passage of any resolution. However, in substantive concerns, Abu Dhabi and Dubai have a veto power. Thus, on any substantive vote, five members, including the two veto powers, must approve a resolution in order for the motion to have the force of law. This constitutional allocation of a preponderance of political power to Abu Dhabi and Dubai has been a major point of contention among most of the other emirates.

Since independence, Shaykh Zayid of Abu Dhabi has been president of the UAE, a post to which he was reappointed for a second five-year term in 1976. Shaykh Rashid of Dubai has been the union's vice-president for the same period of time and, in 1979, became its prime minister as well. Although the powers of the presidency are in theory subordinate to the

FSC, Shaykh Zayid has been relatively successful in keeping together what has become in this century the Arab world's foremost example of regional political integration. This has been due in part to Abu Dhabi's preeminence as the most profederation state in the union and Zayid's own strong personal dedication to the UAE's development. Many of the federation's operations are almost completely funded by Abu Dhabi.

Foreign policy decision making is vested in the federal executive branch. However, although articles 120 and 121 of the constitution stipulate that foreign affairs decisions are the responsibility of the union, article 123 states that the individual shaykhdoms may conclude limited agreements concerning local matters, as, for example, in the granting of concessions—including the right to explore for, produce, refine, and export oil—to foreign economic interests. Thus, to some extent, the individual shaykhdoms have considerable latitude and power in the conduct of foreign affairs.

A federal judicial system established by the constitution has both a supreme and lower court. The judges are appointed by the president with the approval of the FSC. To date, however, the function of administering and applying UAE laws through the union's court procedures has remained one of the least developed of UAE government activities owing to the scarcity of local citizens who have received legal training and to the as yet relatively small accumulation of a body of federal laws that the courts might apply.

Consequently, the bulk of cases submitted for adjudication in the UAE are dealt with by the lower courts in each of the shaykhdoms.

The powers reserved to the shaykhdoms, as stated in article 122, imply that the individual emirates remain responsible for all matters that do not fall under the domain of the federal authorities. Additionally, the emirates retain a few expressed powers.

Political Dynamics

Since the inception of the federation, the strongest cohesive force within it has been Shaykh Zayid of Abu Dhabi followed by Shaykh Sultan of Sharjah. Shaykh Rashid of Dubai has always been in a position to play a role in federal affairs. However, in the eyes of his critics he did not seriously begin to perform such a function until he accepted the post of prime minister, having previously concentrated most of his attention and energies on Dubai.

Within the shaykhdoms, politics traditionally have been tribally based and autocratic, even if tempered by such age-old concepts as social democracy, consultation, consensus, and adherence to the principles and norms as enshrined in Islamic law. The ruler, or shaykh, is usually the oldest son of the immediately preceding ruler, although there are instances where his uncle, a brother, a nephew, or a cousin has been the one to accede to power. To remain in power, the shaykh must maintain the support of the inner circles of the ruling family and numerous other groups (e.g., religious leaders, merchants, et al.) within the emirate.

The past history of internal politics of the ruling families has been replete with intrigue and jockeying among real and potential contenders for the limited number of positions of official power. Prior to the establishment of the UAE, numerous local rulers were assassinated, in many cases by their brothers, cousins, or sons. As recently as 1966, a palace coup in Abu Dhabi brought a new ruler to power; and in February 1972, the UAE's Minister of Education, Shaykh Sultan bin Muhammad al-Qassimi, of Sharjah, assumed the rulership in his home emirate following the abortive palace coup in which his predecessor was murdered.

Popular participation in local government along lines or in accordance with organizational forms familiar to Westerners is limited. In the early 1980s there were no trade unions, political parties, or popularly elected bodies through which local demands could be articulated. Neither was there, again as defined by Western standards, the existence of a free press. Political power continued to be maintained and effectively wielded at the top by cousins, sons, brothers, and uncles of semihereditary tribal rulers although an increasing number of foreign-trained technocrats were to be found in such sensitive areas as national defense, internal security, foreign relations, developmental planning, and communications.

Delegation of responsibility between the federal and local level, like that in the United States for decades after its establishment, is not in every instance as well defined as modern practitioners of public administration would prefer. Theoretically, the federal government has control over defense, finance, and foreign affairs. In practice, however, the dual capacity exercised by the rulers as both members of the federal government and rulers of member states, yields additional opportunities for control to the various shaykhdoms. The integration of the shaykhdoms into a federation, therefore, has been no simple or easy task and, for the reasons delineated herein, remains a challenge fraught with myriad difficulties for the members of UAE officialdom.

In 1976, continued dissension among the various members of the federation prompted a crisis when Shaykh Zayid refused election for another five-year term as president unless fundamental changes were made. After considerable negotiation and accommodation, he finally changed his stand, was reelected, and the temporary constitution was extended for five more years.

Undoubtedly one of the most important steps taken toward integration occurred in May 1976, when all external and internal military forces were united and placed under the single command of the Union Defense Force. Previously there had been a separate and independent army for nearly every emirate, plus the union force. Although constitutional in formulation each emirate competed to have its local contingent form an important component of the larger and more modern military force. Abu Dhabi's oil revenues—at more than $5 billion annually, somewhat prodigious in comparison with the income of the other emirates—gave Shaykh Zayid an obvious advantage in pressing for unification of the UAE's armies. Even so, as with most administrative reforms, total integration of the military was evidenced sooner on paper than in practice into the 1980s. The logic behind the process, however, remained unassailable: its major internal task of preventing or pacifying local, tribal disputes would have remained an infinitely more difficult task had the armed forces themselves, as had been the case for the first four years of the union's existence, remained organized along tribal lines.

Foreign Policy

Conduct of UAE commercial and economic relations is shared by the federal government and the member shaykhdoms. One fact of cardinal importance in terms of the outside world's interest in the UAE cannot be overstressed: namely, that the economy of Abu Dhabi is predominant among the concerns of foreign investors and exporters who would seek to increase their share of the UAE's two most important exports—petroleum and capital. Abu Dhabi ranks second, after Saudi Arabia, in terms of exports from the oil-producing states of the Arabian peninsula to the United States. In financial terms, it is the sole member of the UAE, and along with Kuwait and Saudi Arabia one of only three states in the entire Arab and OPEC world, which produced annually a capital surplus during the latter half of the 1970s.

In its external political relations, the UAE is conservative, anticommunist and strives to maintain friendly relations with all its neighbors. In addition to being a fervent supporter of the Palestinians' right to self-determination as a sine qua non for bringing an end to the Arab-Israeli conflict, the UAE has also contributed funds plus a battalion of troops to the Arab Defense Force in Lebanon. Because the occasional divergences between Arab and Iranian nationalist aspirations (such as the Abu Musa and Tunbs islands dispute) have been an element in UAE issues, maintaining a balance between Iran and Saudi Arabia has been a major goal of UAE foreign relations. UAE President Shaykh Zayid has long enjoyed an almost fabled reputation as a skilled mediator in inter-Arab affairs. More than any other head of state in the Arabian peninsula he has succeeded in delineating successfully nearly all of his emirate's internal and international frontiers.

OMAN

Historical Background

Oman has a proud history dating back many centuries. It has maintained its independence since the expulsion of Portuguese garrisons from its coastal towns in the seventeenth century. A Persian occupation in the mid-eighteenth century was ended under the leadership of Ahmad bin Sa'id Al Bu Sa'id, who was subsequently elected imam. The imamate was a combination of religious and political leadership uniquely developed by the Ibadi Muslims of Oman. The Ibadi are part of the Kharijite schism, dating from the earliest days of Islam, and broke with the main body of Muslims over their insistence that the caliph should not be determined in accordance with genealogical considerations but be elected on the basis of merit. Ahmad's successors, however, abandoned this procedure and, in time, became purely secular rulers with the title of sultan. This development created a political schism between the coastal areas administered from Muscat and the more conservative interior ruled by the imam. The sultans in Muscat, as a security measure, developed a close association with Great Britain that has continued to the present. Assisted by British forces, the country was reunified during the 1950s after the military defeat of the imam of Oman at his interior stronghold, Nizwa. Unification was completed under sultan Qabus, who in a nearly bloodless coup d'etat in 1970 replaced his father, Sa'id bin Taymur (ruler since 1932), and changed the name of the country from the Sultanate of Muscat and Oman to, simply, the Sultanate of Oman.

The southernmost province of Dhufar, annexed in the late nineteenth century after years of quasi-autonomous existence, became the site of another insurrection in the early 1960s. By 1968, leadership of the rebellion had been seized by the Marxist-oriented Popular Front for the Liberation of the Occupied Arabian Gulf (PFLOAG), the same group that subsequently changed its name, first to the Popular Front for the Liberation of Oman and the Arab Gulf (also PFLOAG) in 1971, and, in 1974, to the Popular Front for the Liberation of Oman (PFLO). Supported by Soviet and Chinese aid channeled through South Yemen, the PFLO had occupied large areas of the province by the early 1970s. Ideological affinity existed with South Yemen. Both had espoused the radical doctrines of the Arab Nationalists Movement, whose leaders also included George Habbash of the Popular Front for the Liberation of Palestine. The rebellion was finally put down in late 1975 through the combined efforts of mainly British advisors and Iranian combat troops. Under Sultan Qabus the heretofore isolated country has been opened to the outside world on a scale unprecedented in its history while the government has simultaneously embarked on an equally unprecedented ambitious program of socioeconomic development. For the first time, an impressive array of modern government services has been extended to even the most remote regions of the interior of the country.

Political Environment

Located on the eastern reaches of the Arabian peninsula, the Sultanate of Oman is a country of some 212,000 square kilometers (82,000 sq. mi.). The estimated population is around 550,000. The capital, Muscat, has a population of 20,000 and is neighbored by the somewhat larger commercial center of Matrah. The largest single town is Salalah, capital of the southern province of Dhufar. This province consists of three ranges of low mountains surrounding a small coastal plain and is separated from the rest of Oman by several hundred miles of desert. Oman proper consists of inner Oman and the coastal plain known as the Batinah. Inner Oman contains a fertile plateau and the oldest towns in Oman, including the religious center of Nizwa. Separating this region from the Batinah is the Hajar mountain range, which stretches in an arc from northwest to southeast and reaches nearly 3,000 meters (9,800 ft.) at Jabal al-Akhdar (Green Mountain). The majority of Oman's population is found along the Batinah coast, which has the greatest agricultural potential in the country. An important fishing center and traditional port is at Sur, southeast of Muscat.

Population and Social Structure

Most Omanis are Arab, although many Baluchis who were originally from the coastal area of Iran and Pakistan live along the Batinah coast. Many of the merchants of the capital region and the coast are Indians, either Hindu or Khoja (a community of Shi'ite Muslims). There are also Persians and other groups of Shi'ite Muslims, including some originally from either Iran or Iraq. Dhufar and the surrounding desert is the home of several peoples whose primary language is South Arabian. In the

Musandam peninsula to the north, wild Shihuh tribesmen, legendary descendants of the Biblical Shuhites, speak their own language. In recent years, Oman has experience an influx of migrant labor, principally from other Arab states and the subcontinent.

With the change in government in 1970, Oman entered a new era. The accumulation of oil revenues over several years of production (exports began in 1967) was quickly put to work in an effort to modernize the country. Within a few years, the number of schools increased from three to sixty-eight and the number of government employees from several hundred to over nine thousand. Fortunately, the country was able to rely on the manpower and expertise of a number of Omanis who had migrated to Saudi Arabia and various gulf countries for work and education in the years prior to 1970. Another important source of manpower were the "Zanzibaris"—Arabs of Omani origin whose ancestors had migrated to the former Omani dominion of Zanzibar over the last two centuries. With the Africanization of Zanzibar, many of them returned to Oman.

Before 1970, the population was fairly evenly distributed throughout the country. With the rapid pace of development in the past few years, however, urbanization is beginning to occur, particularly in the capital area.

Economic Conditions

Oil is undoubtedly the most important natural resource. However, Omani production has been modest by gulf terms and it likely to decrease in the future unless further exploration by the major producer, Petroleum Development (Oman) Limited, and other concessionary firms is successful. The limited water supply in most areas prevents wide-scale agriculture. Traditionally, Omani cultivation has been of a subsistence nature, with the only significant cash crops being dates and limes. In Dhufar, where monsoon rains fall, coconuts are also grown.

Oman was known as an exporter of copper in prehistoric times and plans are underway to produce copper from a mountain valley in the north. Plans have also been laid for a natural gas pipeline paralleling the oil pipeline from the interior to the coast just north of Muscat. A cement plant and a number of import-substitution schemes are also planned to complement the traditional metalworking industry.

A new six-berth port is in operation at Matrah and a smaller port has been opened near Salalah in Dhufar. A number of major airlines make use of the new international airport at al-Sib (50 kilometers northwest of Muscat) and Gulf Air operates regular flights between al-Sib and Salalah. The government has embarked on a major program of road construction. All-weather routes now link Muscat to Dubai in the gulf and to Nizwa in the interior. Radio and color television stations operate from both Muscat and Salalah.

Although government revenues reached approximately $1 billion by 1975, the sultanate underwent a cash-flow crisis during this period, partially due to overcommitment on various development projects, and partially because of the heavy military and civilian pacification expenditure in Dhufar.

Political Structure

The sultan's father maintained a basically traditional, personalized rule. Modern political institutions in Oman are therefore new and still in a relatively embryonic stage. There is no constitution or modern judicial system and there are no political parties or elections. Islamic law is still the law of the land and is administered through traditional Islamic courts. Judges are appointed by the sultan. In the most remote regions, tribal law still functions in a rough-and-ready manner.

Final legal and administrative power in the country is vested in the sultan. Sultan Qabus is head of state and all authority emanates from him. Since coming to power, however, he has created a formal council of ministers to carry out the administrative and legislative operations of the government. The Council of Ministers is headed by the prime minister, who is appointed by the sultan. Although all important decisions must have the approval of the sultan, the ministers have a great deal of latitude in formulating day-to-day policy.

In 1976, the sultan reorganized regional and local government by establishing thirty-seven divisions (*wilayats*), one province, and a municipality of the capital. The *wilayats* are administered by governors appointed by the sultan, who collect taxes, provide local security, settle disputes, and advise the sultan. The province, Dhufar, was historically a separate sultanate and still has more local autonomy than other regions. The municipality of Muscat was also considered important enough to warrant special status.

Political Dynamics

There are four politically important groups in Oman: the royal family, the tribes, the expatriate advisors, and the merchant class. In many respects the royal family is still the most important group. Among the sultan's most influential advisors are his cousins and uncles. They occupy a number of key ministerial and governorial posts. The importance of the royal family can be illustrated by the fact that Sultan Qabus married the daughter of his uncle, Tariq bin Sa'id, and any male offspring from this marriage will most probably be named heir apparent.

Traditionally the tribes have also played a key role in the Omani political process. Under Qabus' father, Sultan Sa'id bin Taymur, manipulating tribal rivalries was a major element in ruling the country. Qabus, on the other hand, has made attempts to decrease the power of the tribes by decentralizing the government through political reforms such as the establishment of local government councils.

Because of long, close relations with Great Britain, many of the expatriate advisors are British. In the past, Britons held key posts in the government and especially in the military. Today they still direct and train the army, but Qabus has made moves to bring more Omanis and other expatriates into other governmental positions. The process of Omanization is accelerating as the Omani educational system turns out more qualified personnel. Nevertheless, for some time to come, Oman will have to rely on foreigners to assist in developing the country.

The merchant community has traditionally been the sultan's link to the outside world. In addition to old Omani trading families, there is still a sizeable number of non-Omani merchant families from India and Pakistan, reflecting Oman's traditionally stronger ties with the Indian Ocean countries. In recent years, however, there has been a more Westward orientation. Oman has participated in both Arab and world politics. It has strengthened ties with the Western industrial world to gain goods and services for Oman's development programs. As a result of oil revenues, many less-established Omanis are being induced to enter into commerce, a position once monopolized by the merchant families. This process is beginning to dilute the power of the traditional merchant families.

Foreign Policy

Prior to the reign of Sultan Qabus, Oman was one of the most isolated countries on earth. It relied on the British for protection and in return granted the British air and naval bases in Salalah and on the southern island of al-Masirah. Qabus altered the policy of isolation by both design and necessity. He was forced to seek outside support against the Dhufar insurgency, and he also moved to gain international and Arab acceptance of the Omani regime. On both counts he has been successful. By forging strong bonds with Iran, which sent three thousand troops to help in the suppression of the Dhufar rebellion, and by gaining the support of the conservative regimes of the Arab world, the sultanate neutralized the rebels' outside support. Iraq, one of the primary supporters of the rebels, effectively stopped aiding the Dhufaris in 1975, in the wake of its treaty with Iran. Relations with South Yemen have remained hostile, even though its support of the Dhufar rebels ended with the collapse of the insurgency in late 1975.

Relations with the Arab world have centered on the conservative states. Improved relations with Saudi Arabia and other Arab countries were reflected in Arab acceptance of Oman into the Arab League in 1971. Oman has also maintained good relations with the West. In 1975, Sultan Qabus made an historic first state visit by an Omani monarch to the United States.

Bibliography

Literature on the contemporary Persian Gulf states is very scarce especially in the social sciences. There have been a number of more topical studies on the political stability of the gulf and on its role in international politics. David Long's *The Persian Gulf: An Introduction to its Peoples, Politics, and Economy*, rev. ed. (Boulder, Colo.: Westview Press, 1978) is one of the few to cover the entire area. Long analyzes the political dynamics of each gulf state, the regional politics and economics of the gulf, and the international politics of the gulf. There is an especially good account of the U.S. relations and interests in the gulf states. One can also find valuable contributions to scholarly literature in such works as: Mohammed Mughisuddin (ed.), *Conflict and Cooperation in the Persian Gulf* (1977); Abbas Amiri (ed.), *The Persian Gulf and Indian Ocean in International Politics* (1976); and R. M. Burrell, *The Persian Gulf* (New York: Library Press, 1972).

The author's (Anthony) *Arab States of the Lower Gulf: People, Politics, Petroleum* (Washington, D.C.: Middle East Institute, 1975) discusses the internal politics of the United Arab Emirates, Qatar, and Bahrain. There is a section on each of these countries exploring the history, constitutional structure, and political dynamics. The economics of the United Arab Emirates is examined by K. G. Fenelon, *The United Arab Emirates* (London: Longman, 1976) and a comprehensive study on its recent history is discussed in Donald Hawley's *The Trucial States* (New York: Twayne Publishers, 1971), and Muhammed Sadik and William Snavely's *Bahrain, Qatar and the United Arab Emirates: Colonial, Present Problems and Future Prospects* (Lexington: Lexington Books, 1972). A recent book by Emile Nakhleh, *Bahrain: Political Development in a Changing Society* (1976), presents a straightforward account of the political problems Bahrain is encountering and how the leadership is attempting to resolve them.

Robert Landon's *Oman in the Late Nineteenth Century and After* (Princeton: Princeton University Press, 1967) offers an informative guide to Omani politics. In addition, Anthony has written the *Political Dynamics of the Sultanate of Oman* (Washington, D.C.: U.S. Department of State, Office of External Research, Foreign Affairs Research Paper, No. FAR 21070, 1974). Finally a book that deals with Omani society is Michael Darlow and Richard Fawkis' *The Last Corner of Arabia* (London: Namara Publishers, 1976).

There is no comprehensive work on Kuwait. One can refer to Zahra French and Victor Winestone, *Kuwait: Prospect on Reality* (New York: Crane and Russak and Co., 1972) for a more general historical survey of Kuwaiti politics, and Soliman Demir, *The Kuwait Fund and the Political Economy of Arab Regional Development* (New York: Praeger, 1976) for Kuwait's role in regional and international politics. Robert Stevens, *The Arab's New Frontier* (London: Temple Smith, 1973, and Boulder, Colo.: Westview Press, 1977) discusses the Kuwait Fund for Arab Economic Development. John B. Kelly's *Eastern Arabian Frontiers* (New York: Frederick A. Praeger Publishers, 1964) offers a general history of the Persian Gulf shaykhdoms, focusing on Kuwait. One will also find the recently updated American University's *Area Handbook for the Persian Gulf States* (1977) valuable as a resource not only on Kuwait but also on the other gulf shaykhdoms.

8

The Yemen Arab Republic

David McClintock

Historical Background

The Yemen Arab Republic (YAR), sometimes called Yemen, North Yemen, or Yemen (San'a), is situated on the southern Red Sea coast of Arabia and extends eastward, encompassing most of the south Arabian highlands. To the south is the People's Democratic Republic of Yemen (PDRY) and to the east is the vast Rub' al-Khali (Empty Quarter) of Saudi Arabia.

The YAR's strategic location at the southern end of the Red Sea has been the main source of its regional political importance for more than two millenia. In the present day, the YAR, while lacking oil resources itself, has also played a significant but little-publicized role in the development of its oil-rich neighbors in the Arabian peninsula. It has provided a work force that now totals more than one million—a major segment of the regional manpower base. The Yemeni civil war of the 1960s and the resultant foreign intervention brought notoriety of a different kind. Even earlier, in the 1930s, Britain and Italy vied for support of the xenophobic imam of Yemen in a quest for control of the Strait of Bab al-Mandab. Similar strategic interests prompted Turkish military and political control from the sixteenth century up to World War I.

The fact that Yemen has made so little impact on the Western world for a period of many centuries and yet was so famous in antiquity as the home of the Queen of Sheba provides a fitting commentary on the long decline in its political and economic fortunes. If there has been any single dominant influence shaping the events of these three millenia of recorded history, it is that of comparative physical isolation. Significantly, however, Yemen has enjoyed a surprisingly high degree of civilization from ancient times to the present despite geographic and other handicaps.

The beginning of southwestern Arabian civilization occurred some

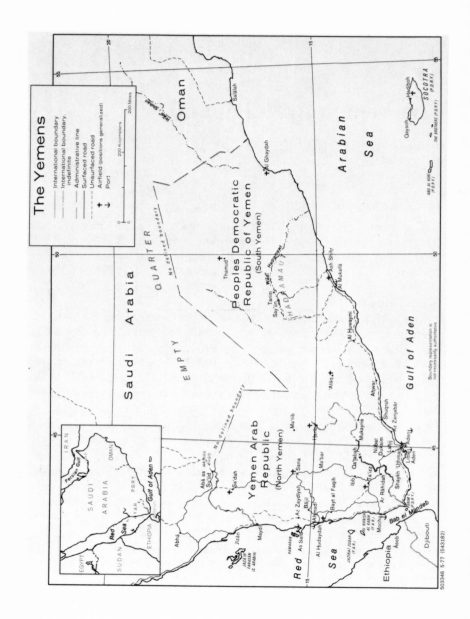

The Yemens

International boundary
International boundary, indefinite
Administrative line
Surfaced road
Unsurfaced road (positions generalized)
Airfield
Port

200 Miles
200 Kilometers

Oman

SOCOTRA (P.D.R.Y.)

Arabian Sea

Saudi Arabia

EMPTY QUARTER

No defined boundary

Peoples Democratic Republic of Yemen (South Yemen)

HADRAMAUT

Al Ghaydah

Ash Shihr
Al Mukalla

Al Huwaymi

Gulf of Aden

Yemen Arab Republic (North Yemen)

Red Sea

Ethiopia

Bab el Mandeb

Djibouti

503346 5-77 (543182)

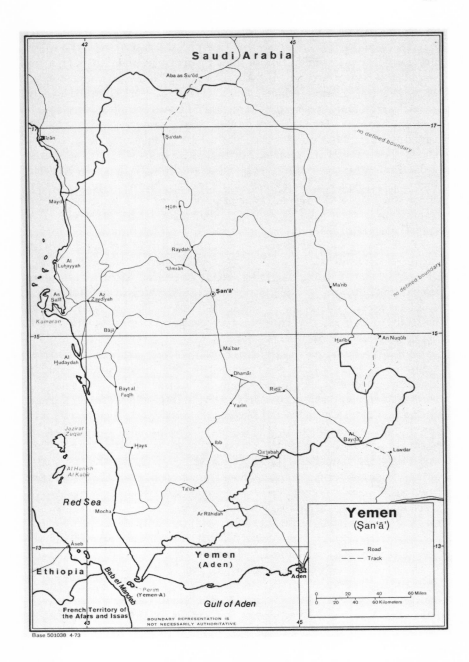

Saudi Arabia

Aba as Su'ūd

43

45

17

no defined boundary

Jīzān

Ṣa'dah

Mayd̄

Hūth

Raydah

no defined boundary

Al
Luḥayyah

'Umrān

As
Salīf

Az
Zaydīyah

Ṣan'ā'

Ma'rib

Kamaran

Bājil

15

Ḥarīb

An Nuqūb

15

Al
Ḥudaydah

Ma'bar

Dhamār

Bayt al
Faqīh

Ridā'

Jazīrat
Zuqar

Yarīm

Hays

Ibb

Al
Baydā'

Lawdar

Al Hanīsh
Al Kabīr

Qaʻtabah

Ta'izz

Yemen
(Ṣan'ā')

Red Sea

Mocha

Ar Rāhidah

Road

Track

Āseb

13

13

Ethiopia

Yemen
(Aden)

Perim
(Yemen-A)

Aden

0   20   40   60 Miles

0   20   40   60 Kilometers

Gulf of Aden

French Territory of
the Afars and Issas

43

45

BOUNDARY REPRESENTATION IS
NOT NECESSARILY AUTHORITATIVE

Base 501038 4-73

time prior to 1200 B.C. with the influx of Semitic peoples from the Fertile Crescent—perhaps from the area of Palestine and east of the Jordan. It is unclear whether this migration resulted from displacement through over-population or warfare, or whether frankincense and myrrh served as an economic lure. These products, which were greatly prized in the ancient world, are actually resin from rare thorn bushes found only in south-western Arabia and the adjacent Somali coast. Frankincense had a ritual-istic use in cremations and myrrh was used in cosmetics. These valuable substances could be transported northward either by sea, with attendant risks from storms or piracy, or by caravan through the south Arabian highlands. It was the latter trade that enriched the small kingdoms that successively rose and fell in regional importance. The most significant among them were Saba (Sheba), Qataban, and Ma'in, with respective capitals at Ma'rib, Timna, and Qarnaw.

In addition to foreign trade, these ministates also developed a high degree of agricultural self-sufficiency based on terracing and irrigation. Near Sheba's capital of Ma'rib, a great stone-faced earthen dam func-tioned until the fifth century A.D., irrigating an area of approximately 2,000 hectares (4,942 acres). While local tribal rivalries persisted then as now, the region enjoyed comparative peace and benign isolation until approximately the fourth century A.D.

Ironically, the formal adoption of Christianity by the Roman Emperor Constantine in A.D. 323 dealt a telling blow to the south Arabian kingdoms. Economically, it destroyed the frankincense trade, since the custom of cremation soon gave way to burial. Ethiopia became Christian within a matter of decades and began a series of regional conquests. Be-tween this time and the advent of Islam in the seventh century, control of various portions of the south Arabian highlands shifted among Coptic and Nestorian Christians, local Jewish rulers, and Sassanid Persians. Since the latter occupiers brought with them Zoroastrian worship, the previously pagan population was exposed almost simultaneously to three major foreign religions. Disruptions emanating from military con-quest and religious upheaval, coupled with the collapse of the valuable caravan trade, set the stage for the Muslim conquest in A.D. 631 that linked Yemen to the neighboring Arab world.

The first Muslim adherents followed Shafa'i teachings and carved a permanent niche for themselves in the southern area of the highlands as well as in the coastal lowlands. In A.D. 893, however, a group of Shi'a or heterodox Muslims arrived under the leadership of Hadi Yahya, who claimed descent from the Prophet's daughter Fatima. Specifically, this group embraced Zaydism, a Shi'ite sect that originated in Persia and paid homage in name to Zayd, the great-grandson of Fatima's husband, Ali.

Settling in the more northerly mountainous areas, the Zaydis soon came into conflict with their Shafa'i (Sunni) neighbors. Their rivalry, which has lasted to this day, has been based not so much on mutual religious intolerance as on political competition. More tribally oriented and warlike, the Zaydis have tended to predominate politically over the more sedentary and agriculturally oriented Shafa'is.

The Muslim conquest brought about a significant change in the role of the monarch. Whereas earlier rulers had been the equivalent of tribal paramount chiefs, the Zaydi imams were spiritual as well as political leaders who ruled over a larger and more politically unified Yemen. Successful imams were adept at capitalizing on both the religious power derived from their title (prayer leader) as well as the tactical advantage of being able to play off one tribe or tribal confederation against the other. While the principle of "divide and rule" normally worked, the tribes periodically would have the opportunity of deposing a weak or unwise imam by temporarily banding together. This historical phenomenon should be remembered by any observer who wishes to understand the political dynamics of the postrevolutionary era.

If Yemen had suffered geographical remoteness since its earliest times, it sank even further into oblivion between the tenth and sixteenth centuries. In 1568 the Ottoman Turks arrived as conquerers. Under Ottoman occupation, Yemen derived a marginal importance from Turkish rivalry with the European powers and Turkish interest in acquiring secure trade routes to the East. With European circumnavigation of Africa and the later development of Indian Ocean commerce, control of the lower Red Sea became more important to the Turks. They ruled Yemen directly only from 1568 to 1630 and again from 1849 to 1904, but here as elsewhere in the Arab world the Turks' impact on legal and governmental institutions was significant. Ironically, the Ottomans were isolated, if not prisoners, within their own satrapy, since their military control tended to be confined to the fortress towns and the few communications routes that their armies could hold. From the sixteenth through nineteenth centuries religious and tribal authority of the imamate ebbed and flowed in opposition to alien Turkish rule. These unique circumstances in effect molded the nation that was to undergo violent revolution and civil war in the mid-twentieth century. The popular description of contemporary Yemen as a medieval state that has run headlong into the modern era ignores this important evolutionary process.

The fluctuating struggle between the Ottomans and the indigenous Yemeni rulers did not occur in isolation. In fact, it influenced the course of events in Aden and adjacent south Arabian territories that came under

British rule in 1839. Britain's arrival not only checked the southern expansion of the Turks but, more importantly in terms of local political history, set the stage for mistrust and periodic conflict between Yemeni imams and a goodly number of sultans in the Aden Protectorates whose authority and territorial claims were supported by the British. While the southern border of modern Yemen thus became a dividing line between two nominally hostile imperial states, it also came to symbolize indigenous rivalries that have persisted to the present day.

Finally rid of the Turks as a result of their defeat and consequent withdrawal at the end of World War I, Yemen's Imam Yahya not only faced potentially hostile petty rulers to the south but also came into conflict with the Saudis and the then-independent ruler of Asir to the north. This eventually precipitated a war with Saudi Arabia in 1934. The Saudis won handily but made few territorial demands, and a large part of the present Yemeni-Saudi border was thus definitively demarcated. An agreement with the British in 1935 fixed the southern border with somewhat less certainty.

His status as an absolute monarch impelled Yahya probably as much as the foregoing external conflicts to maintain his kingdom in virtual isolation. He implemented this policy in part by restricting his subjects' travel abroad. He also attempted to prevent the introduction of outside influences, even by restricting the ownership of radios. This resistance to modernization succeeded temporarily, but physical isolation proved to be an increasingly difficult objective in the interwar years. France, Britain, and Italy occupied key colonial territories around the strategic Strait of Bab al-Mandab at the southern entrance to the Red Sea. The British and Italians in particular became anxious to win the imam's favor at the other's expense so as to expand their geographical foothold. Neither fully succeeded, and Yemen thus survived World War II in its traditional isolation. However, dissident exiles sowed the seeds of change with the creation of a free Yemeni movement in Aden in 1944. Imam Yahya was assassinated in a coup attempt in 1948, but his son Ahmad managed to retain control on behalf of the Mutawakkilite dynasty. Nonetheless, he remained so fearful of the intrigues in the traditional capital of San'a that he moved the seat of his own government to the southern (Shafa'i) town of Ta'iz.

In 1958, Yemen joined with Egypt and Syria in the ill-fated United Arab States, largely through the influence of the imam's son, Crown Prince Badr. This produced no significant political or economic advantages for Yemen, but it managed to intensify the natural suspicions of the neighboring south Arabian sultans who, along with Britain, were fearful of the intentions of Egypt's Nasser. At the same time, the crown prince also initiated a more active Yemeni foreign policy—primarily in an Eastward direction. He brought in development aid from China and East Germany and military assistance from the USSR and Czechoslovakia, which further compounded the concerns of the pro-British sultans. The United Arab States dissolved in 1961 with the rift between Egypt and Syria, but Nasser remained interested in Yemen, in large part because of its proximity to British Aden.

Imam Ahmad died—rather surprisingly of natural causes after surviving many assassination attempts—in September 1962. On 26 September only days after he had assumed power, the new Imam Badr (Ahmad's son) was driven from San'a in a military revolt. The insurgents, led by a heretofore obscure colonel, Abdallah al-Sallal, abolished the monarchy and established the Yemen Arab Republic. Badr fled San'a and mustered tribal warriors loyal to the royal family. The ensuing civil war lasted eight years.

Ironically, the imam—who shortly before had engineered Yemen's entry into Nasser's United Arab States and had established relations with Eastern Europe and China—received his principal support from Saudi Arabia and Britain, both of which were strongly opposed to Nasserist adventures in the Arabian peninsula. Al-Sallal on the other hand received his principal support from Nasser, who ultimately sent an Egyptian military force in support of the republic.

As time went on, the Yemen adventure became increasingly disastrous for Nasser, whose military and political problems in this remote corner of Arabia were roughly analagous to those that later confronted the United States in Viet Nam. Egyptian problems were further compounded by the deficient leadership of President al-Sallal.

The United States recognized the revolutionary republic on the tacit understanding that the Egyptian force would soon be withdrawn. The United States attempted, through a special diplomatic mission led by Ambassador Ellsworth Bunker, to bring an early end to hostilities. This effort, along with those of a United Nations peacekeeping mission, failed in the face of increasingly bitter fighting. As the situation reached an impasse, republican Lieutenant General Hassan al-Amri usurped the authority of al-Sallal during the latter's absence in Cairo in 1965. Al-Amri's move laid the original groundwork for an eventual republican rift with the Egyptians. Nasser was able to reinstate al-Sallal in mid-1966, but the regime collapsed again when the June 1967 Arab-Israeli War necessitated withdrawal of the Egyptian troops from Yemen.

During 1968 and 1969 the republican-royalist conflict was complicated further by intrarepublican fighting in which the more moderate General al-Amri solidified his control within the army. Muhsin al-Ayni, a former

Baathist, became prime minister in February 1970 and skillfully negotiated with exiled royalists in Saudi Arabia for their return to republican Yemen. Since the returnees were accorded a place in the government as well as restoration of their property rights, the assimilation proceeded with extraordinary ease considering the bitterness engendered by the just-concluded civil war.

Although the republic had at last achieved peace, chronic problems remained. General al-Amri's involvement in a bizarre shooting incident in 1971 and his resultant exile indirectly provided a suitable climate for a series of civilian governments whose tenure was determined more by economic than ideological challenges. Under the constitution of 30 December 1970, political power was neatly balanced between a three-man republican council chaired by the nominal chief of state, Abd al-Rahman al-Iryani, and the prime minister and his council of ministers. While the flow of development aid from both Eastern and Western donors and the United Nations gradually increased, the most politically significant assistance began to arrive from Saudi Arabia, which previously had backed the royalist counterinsurgency. However, as relations with the Saudis became more normal, relations deteriorated with the Peoples' Democratic Republic of Yemen—the Marxist-oriented state that replaced the British protectorate (including the crown colony of Aden) in 1967. The conflict with Aden soon degenerated into border raids and alleged PDRY-staged terrorist attacks on prominent Yemenis living abroad. The PDRY was perceived both in San'a and Riyadh as a mutual threat, and this mutual perception tended to hasten the process whereby the revolutionary republic became a moderate one, and by which traditionally conservative Saudi Arabia could cooperate with its former Yemeni republican adversaries.

Notwithstanding the civilian role in the post-civil-war normalization process, army Colonel Ibrahim al-Hamdi successfully challenged the leadership of President al-Iryani and assumed power in 1976. His revolutionary command council replaced the troika-style republican council. Al-Hamdi was a strong and popular leader and went far in healing old sectional, religious, and tribal cleavages. For motives that are still somewhat unclear, al-Hamdi was assassinated in October 1977, and was replaced by Ahmad al-Ghashmi. In June 1978, al-Ghashmi was himself assassinated by a PDRY agent ostensibly bringing a message from PDRY President Salim Ruba'i Ali, who was himself killed in Aden two days later when the resultant binational crisis degenerated into a domestic coup. Lieutenant Colonel Ali Abdallah Salih was chosen to succeed al-Ghashmi. While these recent events underscore the volatility of the YAR leadership struggle, they should not obscure the growth in political sophistication that the republic attained in the first half of the 1970s.

Political Environment

The Zaydi-Shafa'i dichotomy that has pervaded Yemen's Islamic history continues to be a significant factor in the political environment. While the two groups constitute roughly equal halves of Yemen's estimated population of 7.5 million, approximately two-thirds of the nation's tribes are Zaydi. The latter are concentrated in the central and northern highlands and the eastern interior region. They are composed of clans and in turn are sometimes grouped into confederations. The most prominent tribal confederations are the Hashid and Bakil. Not surprisingly, these mountain tribes have warred periodically for centuries, usually as a result of internal leadership challenges or external shifts in alliances. Adroit imams would pit one Zaydi tribe or confederation against another under the time-honored concept of divide-and-rule; however, when tribal adversaries temporarily united, they could overthrow an imam.

Despite the tribal orientation of the Zaydis, they have not followed the nomadic existence so common in similar mountainous terrain elsewhere in the Middle East. On the contrary, Zaydi culture is rooted in permanent villages composed of fortresslike stone buildings. These are frequently situated on hilltops, cliffs, or other defensible sites. The title of shaykh is given to the tribal headman. Theoretically it should pass down through the male line of the same family, but a shaykh can be deposed if deemed incompetent or weak by the members of the tribe.

On an economic as well as social plane, Yemeni society continues to be semifeudal. Despite the nominal socialist orientation of the early republican regime, central government authority within the tribal hinterland has never been sufficiently strong to alter landlord-tenant relationships on the land or traditional intratribe allegiances. What the government has not been able to do, however, might ultimately be accomplished by the large-scale emigration of adult males to the oil-rich countries of the Arabian peninsula. These workers are sending large remittances to Yemen which, in turn, are underwriting new economic and social patterns. Meanwhile, the government is gradually extending its control into the hinterlands.

The Zaydis have tended to dominate Yemeni government both in republican as well as monarchial times. This is due partly to the aggressiveness and military prowess of their tribes, and partly to their dispersion throughout the strategic central and northern highland regions. This political preeminence, rather than religious intolerance, is the primary irritant in Zaydi-Shafa'i relations.

Although village-oriented culture also predominates in the Shafa'i areas of southern highlands, clan and tribal affiliations are less pronounced. Rainfall is generally more abundant here, and agriculture thus is more rewarding. The more outgoing Shafa'is have nurtured not only a farming mentality but also a greater penchant for trading than the Zaydis of the north. Prior to the development of the port of Hodayda in republican times, imports traditionally passed overland from Aden through the Shafa'i city of Ta'iz and on to the Zaydi north. Their contact with the outside world also encouraged the Shafa'is to emigrate to more distant lands long before petroleum wealth in nearby Arabian peninsula states served as a more universal lure. As a consequence of earlier twentieth century Shafa'i emigration, there are small Yemeni colonies even in the United States—for example in Brooklyn and Buffalo, New York, in Lodi, California, and in Dearborn, Michigan.

The inhabitants of Tihama, the coastal plain, comprise Yemen's third population group. Primarily Shafa'is, many of these people are of African origin and construct rounded thatch houses and wattle fences reminiscent of the East African coast. While not discriminated against on racial grounds, they tend to occupy lower economic and social strata than the two major highland groups. Ironically, their land has the greatest agricultural potential, subject to mechanization and development of group water resources.

A small but highly distinctive Ismaili (Shi'ite) community is situated in mountainous regions around Manakha, about halfway between San'a and the port city of Hodayda. The Ismailis follow a variation of Shi'ite doctrines and regard the Aga Khan as their spiritual leader. Favorable relations with their Shafa'i and Zaydi neighbors presumably have been aided by their isolation in what amounts to a semiarid Shangri-La.

A few hundred Jews remain in and around the northern town of Saada, all that is left after the departure of approximately fifty thousand Yemeni Jews to Israel in 1949 by means of the then-famous "Operation Magic Carpet." The Jewish community, which had resided in Yemen for millenia, not only left a considerable architectural and handicraft heritage to their homeland but also injected a unique Oriental note into Israeli culture.

Yemen's population mosaic thus is the product of both religion and geography. Not surprisingly, long isolation from foreign influences and tenuous internal communications have tended to reinforce particularism and a certain degree of xenophobia. The latter is especially characteristic of the Zaydi highlanders. Significantly, the Shi'ite-Sunni dichotomy has not posed the same obstacle to national unity as it has elsewhere in the Muslim world. Likewise cultural and attitudinal differences among the four major population groups have proved less divisive than might have been expected during the brief but traumatic transition from imamate to republic.

Social Conditions

Despite the turbulent nature of Yemeni politics, political change on balance has been more evolutionary than revolutionary. The pace of economic change has likewise been restrained, primarily because of limited resources and massive developmental problems. It is not surprising, therefore, that social change is not occurring in Yemen as abruptly as elsewhere in the Arab world. This is further explained by the fact that Yemen is predominantly rural. Considering that the total national population is probably between seven and eight million, it is significant that San'a has a population of only 150,000, Hodayda less than 100,000, and Ta'iz about 50,000. The emigrant work force, situated mainly in the oil-producing Arabian peninsula states, is estimated at one million or more. As a result, the bulk of the population is scattered in hundreds of isolated villages and consists of a disproportionate number of women, children, and elderly. While there is some urban movement, the attraction of the cities is offset by higher prices, scarce housing, and minimal job opportunities. For the villagers, life is neither wretched nor especially comfortable. The stone and mud-brick housing is good if an outside observer were to consider that per capita income is only in the area of $100–$200 per annum. Likewise, food supplies in most years are adequate and reasonably varied. On the other hand, health facilities are almost nonexistent outside the three urban centers. Annual population growth, estimated at between 2 and 3 percent, occurs in the face of a staggeringly high infant mortality rate in the neighborhood of 50 percent. Schools exist mainly in urban areas, so it is not surprising that the overall literacy level is extremely low—probably around 10 percent. In Tihama, rural life is similar, differing only in terms of the hot, humid climate of the coastal plain and African cultural influences.

Hodayda, Ta'iz and San'a have amenities that are approximately on a par with provincial towns in, for example, Syria or Egypt. Here there is a high demand for consumer goods, fueled by emigrant remittances that could be running as high as $1 billion annually. The economic significance of these remittances can be misleading, since rising living standards are being financed by an exported human resource rather than through comparable expansion in domestic agriculture or industrial productivity. Emigrants work at the sufferance of host nations.

Prior to the recent upsurge in emigrant remittances, income disparity was not pronounced. The majority of the populace was poor (and still is) and few individuals could be considered wealthy by virtue of land ownership or profitable trading ventures. To a Western observer, the life-style of a rich family was not markedly different from that of a poor one. A middle class was nonexistent during the imamate; however, there existed a class of feudal bureaucrats known as *sayyids*—literally, descendants of the Prophet but, more importantly, with connections more royal than religious. Almost universally detested for their role as tax collectors and extortionists, many of these *sayyids* were killed in the early days of the revolution.

In the current republican era there is a small but growing middle class of government bureaucrats and an expanding merchant community living from the import trade. Qualified college graduates still number only in the dozens, but externally funded scholarship programs eventually will bring a few hundred more professionals into the economy. Nevertheless, shortages of trained personnel in the essential public-service areas will remain chronic for the indefinite future. The gap can be filled only through the imported expertise of international organizations and foreign aid missions.

Economic Conditions

Discounting momentarily the peculiar economic relief afforded by emigrant remittances, Yemen has been and remains a poor agricultural country. Repeated attempts to find petroleum have failed, and minerals surveys have failed to locate deposits that would be economically feasible to develop. In the minerals sector, copper might offer limited export possibilities, but extraction and transportation costs presently would be too great. In the eighteenth and nineteenth centuries Yemeni coffee found lucrative markets in Europe and even in America. There are nineteenth-century accounts of New England merchant ships setting sail for the Yemeni port of Mocha as a primary destination, and of British and Dutch complaints that the Americans had outbid their resident buyers. Unfortunately, the middle-elevation coffee slopes proved equally suitable for the cultivation of qat, a leafy plant with high tannin content that the Yemenis chew for its mildly narcotic effects. Today, while premium grades of Yemeni coffee could be earning needed foreign exchange, the substitute crop of qat is being consumed in-country with deleterious effects not only on its users but also on the agricultural economy. Because qat must be chewed while fresh, the distribution process places unnecessary demands on the fledgling truck transport system that is needed for the distribution of market crops. Qat in effect represents an economic opportunity lost since it is not exported and diverts labor and land resources from crops that either could be exported or consumed domestically.

The geographical determinants of Yemen's population zones also differentiate roughtly analogous agricultural zones. The Tihama coastal desert runs north and south along the Red Sea and is physically separated from the interior by an abrupt curtain of mountains situated approximately thirty miles inland and parallel to the coast. Rising in a series of ridges separated by deep valleys, these mountains cradle a high interior plain that slopes gently eastward to the undemarcated portion of the border with Saudi Arabia's Empty Quarter. Intermittent ranges longitudinally intercept this plain, and on the south provide a natural frontier with the PDRY. The moisture-laden monsoon winds blowing from the Indian Ocean strike these successive ranges and normally produce a fairly heavy precipitation for this otherwise arid region. The soil is especially fertile in the central highland plain of Yarim, and in the rainy season this plain is checkerboarded with green fields. Rainfall there ranges from 400 to 1,000 millimeters (16–40 ins.).

In many highland areas terraces have been developed over the centuries to hold soil that otherwise would be washed by the 400- to 600-millimeter annual rains through deep wadis (dry river beds) to the Red Sea. All of the highland areas are cool for these latitudes by virtue of the elevation ranging from 750 to 3,500 meters (approximately 2,500 to 12,000 feet). The somewhat warmer and more moist valleys and mountainsides in the Hujarriyah region south and west of Ta'iz are especially fertile. Rainfall in the mountains provides ample groundwater for the Tihama Desert, which itself receives only about 150 millimeters per year. This is supplemented by periodic flooding of the wadis that bisect the plain.

As might be expected, each geographic region poses special agricultural problems. In Tihama, the flat terrain favors mechanization, and the water resources may be fully exploited only with mechanical pumping or elaborate catchment schemes. By contrast the mountain terraces efficiently capture the rainfall but are poorly suited to mechanical cultivation. The northern and eastern highlands are semiarid and will require irrigation development. The fertile topsoil is a fragile resource in most areas and in some instances has been damaged by too-heavy plowing with oversized tractors.

While Yemeni statistics are of doubtful accuracy and in any event often fail to describe this uniquely underdeveloped economy, it is reasonable to assume that less than 10 percent of the approximately

195,000 square kilometers (75,000 square miles) of national territory is under tillage. Nonetheless, agriculture provides roughly three-quarters of the gross domestic product. Only about 20 percent of the cultivable lands are irrigated, leaving the remaining majority dependent on monsoon rainfall. As the Sahel drought revealed in Africa, these monsoons may be becoming less dependable as a result of increasing fluctuations in the global climate.

Yemen's agricultural production is surprisingly diversified. In addition to the primary crops of millet and sorghum, there is also production of wheat, maize, potatoes, dates, and grapes. Coffee could be reintroduced in quantity at medium elevations, and long-staple cotton acreage in Tihama could be increased. Ironically, however, Yemeni imports are running at a level almost ten times as high as exports; food and beverages constitute approximately half of these imports and probably total more than $30 million annually. Even if agricultural development failed to stimulate a more favorable export trade, at least import requirements could be reduced.

The present trade imbalance is compounded by the rising expectations of the new urban classes who are now living within a new cash economy. Whereas sorghum and millet provide about 70 percent of the food requirements of the village inhabitant, city dwellers are no longer satisfied with this diet. Demand for domestically produced raw foods is low by comparison, and the resultant low market prices offer little incentive for the farmers to produce more. It is apparent, therefore, that international development aid will have to be meshed with government incentives, and that import policies will have to be developed to discourage the squandering of remittance income in this direction. Likewise, the government will have to develop an adequate system of rural credit, discourage qat production by taxation or other penalties, and generally insure that the fledgling cash economy is not confined to the three urban centers. This is a large order, but Yemen cannot live indefinitely on the earnings of its expatriate labor force.

The task of developing Yemeni agriculture and the broader economic infrastructure thus far has fallen to external aid programs operating on both grant and loan bases. Unfortunately, bilateral foreign aid has tended to reflect the political motivations of the donor nations. Consequently, there has been a lack of coordination and attention to specific Yemeni priorities. International aid, primarily through the United Nations, was inefficiently administered in the civil war years but in the 1970s has increased in quality and quantity. Even a partial list of development schemes indicates the mixed results of what has been a massive external financial effort to raise Yemen from its position near the bottom on the world development scale.

As noted earlier, China and East Germany were among the earliest bilateral aid donors. In contrast to rather lackluster East German agricultural and telecommunications projects, the Chinese projects involved successful construction of a high-quality paved highway between the port of Hodayda and the capital at San'a, a cotton textile mill and a technical school in San'a, and extension of the Hodayda-San'a road northward to the Saudi frontier. While the textile mill at first appearances was uneconomical by virtue of its high water consumption in the semiarid capital, it may have represented a deft politicoeconomic maneuver to disrupt East German plans for development of Tihama cotton for a bilateral barter trade. Most foreign observers have given the Chinese high marks for efficiency, good local relations, and programs that have been free of visible "strings."

The United States embarked on its aid programs shortly before the revolution with two major projects: a municipal water system in Ta'iz and a road between Ta'iz and San'a. Work continued after the revolution until 1967, when diplomatic relations were broken as a result of the Arab-Israeli War. The opening of an American Interest Section in the Italian Embassy in 1970 permitted U.S. food donations in the famine of 1970, and the resumption of full relations in 1973 enabled the U.S. Agency for International Development (AID), formerly based in Ta'iz, to initiate new projects—for example in water supply and sanitation—from new headquarters in San'a. The Americans in their turn have received high marks for their water projects but were previously criticized for not paving the Ta'iz-San'a road. Ironically, this project was taken over by West Germany, and the road has since become in Yemeni eyes a "German" one. West Germany also reconstructed the airport at San'a.

The USSR's very diverse aid efforts have had mixed results. The San'a airport actually was first constructed by the Soviets, but the runways proved inadequate for heavy commercial aircraft operations. Like the U.S.-built road, this became a "German" airport. A more successful effort involved the construction of a trans-Tihama road south from Hodayda to the east-west U.S.-built road from Mocha to Ta'iz. Other projects included a hospital at San'a, a cement plant at Bajil in Tihama, and the dredging of a new port at Hodayda. The USSR also has extended a series of large trade credits and has provided a full range of military equipment including tanks, jet aircraft, weapons, and spares. Soviet aid has carried more obvious "strings" than the Chinese aid, with which it apparently has been competing. While Soviet economic development

projects no doubt have been fairly well received, considerable resentment was incurred in the mid-1970s as a result of withholding ammuni-
tion and military spares for purposes of political leverage at a time when
Yemen was strengthening its Saudi ties and clashing with the radical
Aden regime.

Other bilateral aid has come from such diverse sources as Britain,
Hungary, Italy, Kuwait, and Saudi Arabia. Kuwaiti aid has been funneled in large quantities through the Kuwait Fund for Arab Economic
Development, and has been especially helpful in terms of rural development and the educational infrastructure. Even more massive Saudi aid
has assisted the central government in San'a in meeting its budgetary
deficits, and (more recently) in acquiring Western arms to replace the ob-
solescent Soviet inventory. Considering that Yemen now relies extensively on Saudi loans as well as on indirect support through tolerant
foreign labor and remittance policies, political relations have come
almost full circle since the civil war days when the Saudis supported the
royalists gainst the Egyptian-backed republican regime.

International organization aid has changed both qualitatively and
quantitatively since the United Nations began its peacekeeping operations shortly after the outbreak of the civil war. While the peacekeeping
effort failed, subsequent development projects by various U.N. agencies
touched many areas neglected by individual foreign aid missions. Most
importantly, the United Nations has served to focus international attention on Yemen by listing it among those nations most in need of development aid.

The most significant current international development assistance is
being extended by the World Bank. Spanning such project areas as textiles, irrigation, and road building, this financial assistance is accompanied by more careful planning than heretofore available.

Political Structure

The formal structure of Yemen's government has changed greatly since
the revolution. Form, however, has been altered more than substance.

The imamate was thoroughly autocratic and feudal. While in theory
any male citizen of good character was eligible to become imam, the office actually was the preserve of a few aristocratic families and clans. The
accession of one or another of these families would depend on the shifting allegiance of the key highland Zaydi tribes. Provided the imam could
manipulate correctly this tribal support, military, legal, spiritual, and
fiscal power could be concentrated in his own hands. Mention already
has been made of the *sayyid* class, which filled in the entire pyramid of

civilian authority. Military power on the other hand was exercised by Zaydi tribal levies answerable to the imam through a separate hierarchy of shaykhs. To ensure this military support, imams frequently would resort to the medieval practice of holding hostages from the principal tribes. The prison system also could be used to eliminate challenges from within the imam's own family. The legal system represented a combination of Islamic structures and Ottoman legal forms. Administration tended to be divided according to the provincial governorates established by the Ottomans.

Not surprisingly, in creating the Yemen Arab Republic the revolutionaries substituted a modern Arab socialist governmental structure not unlike that of Egypt, the major source of external political and military support. Exercising authority through the revolutionary command council, President al-Sallal placed military officers in many key ministerial posts. Each ministry in turn had an Egyptian adviser, and thus received guidance not only from the presidential palace but also from Egypt's military headquarters and embassy. A presidential council was created by the provisional constitution of April 1964. A subordinate executive council was composed of cabinet ministers, who functioned in this second capacity as substitute legislators. With the departure of al-Sallal in 1967, Abd al-Rahman al-Iryani became chief of state, functioning as head of a three-man republican council. In 1969, a forty-five-member national council was created to function as a legislature. Its membership was drawn primarily from the tribes. With the return of the royalist exiles following the agreement negotiated by Premier Muhsin al-Ayni in 1970, the republican council was expanded to five seats and the national council to sixty-three. However, the national council exercised only token legislative authority as real political power remained with the republican council, the council of ministers, and the army.

Further systemic changes occurred with the introduction of a new constitution in December 1970. The republican council was allowed to fluctuate between three and five members, with the chairman still functioning as a chief of state. However, the national council was abolished in favor of a consultative council of 159 members. Significantly, one-fifth of the council seats could be filled by presidential appointment, while the remaining four-fifths remained elective. Both the national and consultative councils exercised only marginal political influence, representing a proportionately small electorate unused to participatory government.

In 1976 the eight-year process by which Yemen's political structure had evolved following the departure of President al-Sallal changed abruptly with the accession of Lieutenant Colonel Ibrahim al-Hamdi. By creating a revolutionary command council he reversed the process by which power was gradually shifting from the presidency to the prime minister and cabinet and—to a very limited extent—the variously named legislative councils. Even more significantly, he reforged the linkage between the army and the central government that had weakened in the early 1970s. This trend has been maintained by his successors.

Political Dynamics

Under Colonel al-Sallal's military coup in 1962, Yemen became nominally another revolutionary Arab socialist republic. While this formal title might be appropriate if applied to the formal political structure or to proclamations of official policy, an examination of the nation's political dynamics suggests that the revolution has been a limited one and that socialism relates more to tribal egalitarianism than to actual economic practice.

Yemen's political structure has been highly centralized in both pre- and postrevolutionary times, but central authority in power terms actually has diminished during the republican era. The leadership in both eras has relied heavily on sanctions or threatened sanctions in the exercise of power. Control over urban centers has always been relatively easier in Yemeni history, but the significance of this has been diminished by the fact that the population is predominantly rural. Therefore, the tribes have held—and continue to hold—the key to control of the hinterland areas. This control is crucial because, with the exception of the remittance factor, rural agriculture is the prime contributor to the national economy. Both the imams and the republicans have depended on favorable tribal alignments for critical support, but in this endeavor the republicans have proved weaker than the imams. The tribes have been relatively immune to military control due to the difficulty of the terrain, and have been less than fully supportive of the republican central government as a result of their belief that funding for development and social services has favored the few urban areas.

It remains to be seen whether the tribal areas will continue to play the same dynamic political role that transcended imamic times and the early republican years. In terms of simple population statistics, the countryside holds—and most likely will continue to hold—the larger constituency. The key unknown, however, is the extent to which burgeoning employment in the adjacent oil-rich areas of the Arabian peninsula will continue to siphon off working-age males and thus indirectly shift a significant portion of the remaining population to the cities and into more urban life-styles based primarily on remittances. The new economic realities cannot be overlooked, but it would be premature to write off the fundamental tribal conservatism that pervades Yemeni political culture and that, to date, has made the Yemeni revolution a very cautious one by Third World standards.

While population and wealth may shift, leadership patterns in the tribal areas most likely will remain relatively stable. At this late date in the twentieth century, authority is still vested in the tribal shaykh ("old man"). As noted previously, a shaykh who lacks leadership abilities can be replaced with the connivance of various elders and the passive consent of the tribe as a whole. Yemeni tribal politics are complicated, especially in the pivotal Zaydi areas, because the principal tribes are affiliated with either the Hashid or Bakil confederations, headed by paramount shaykhs. Rivalries exist among the tribes and between the two confederations, but these are balanced by shifting alliances. While temporary alliances could topple a universally unpopular or incapable imam, postrevolutionary regimes are more likely to stand or fall on the basis of San'a politics and/or the disposition of the more secular republican army.

Leadership patterns in the republican era have been remarkably varied. Former President al-Iryani and many senior officials occupying republican council and cabinet posts have been traditionalists both in physical appearance and political outlook. Either simultaneously or alternately, modernist civilian intellectuals and military officers have rotated in and out of the prime ministry and key cabinet posts. Personal affiliations and political philosophies have counted, whereas party affiliations have not. With the advent of al-Hamdi and his successors Lieutenant Colonel al-Ghashmi and Ali Abdallah Salih, the pendulum appears to have swung back to the military side. In comparison with the intrigues and violence that characterized the imamate, the postrevolutionary era has been much calmer, despite the violent overthrow of two presidents in less than a year in 1977–1978. This was especially true in the early and mid-1970s, when civilian prime ministers held sway. Political opposition was a riskier business in the preceding regime of Lieutenant General al-Amri and again appears to be so in the new military era.

In the absence of meaningful electoral processes, power tends to accrue through a coalition-building process involving—in various degrees—key military officers, youthful technocrats, a few key tribal leaders, and urban traditionalists with acceptable republican credentials. The leverage of the military is obvious in view of its potential for forceful action. However, the civil war proved that even tanks and jet aircraft cannot control an uncooperative hinterland. The youthful, educated technocrats have no comparable power base but are an increasingly essential human resource in the irreversible process of political modernization. Tribal leaders represent the other side of the political coin—they control remote areas that the military cannot.

Finally, the traditionalist politicians provide something of a human link between the old and new political cultures, neither of which yet predominates. Political change can occur (and has occurred) by violent means such as assassination or military coup, but it is just as likely to occur through a shifting consensus among these power-sharing coalitions. For example, civilian prime ministers until recently rotated in and out of power according to their relative success or failure in dealing with omnipresent economic problems. The mood of the power-wielding constituencies cannot be quantified in the absence of a legitimate electoral process, but the number of governments that have come and gone since September 1962 attests to the efficiency of this system. Now that the pendulum has swung again to the military side, outside observers should not look to the constituent assembly for signs of confidence but within the officer constituency that is now ascendent.

Foreign Policy

As indicated earlier, Yemeni foreign policy during many centuries of the Zaydi imamate was xenophobic in the extreme. The only successful foreign intruder was Ottoman Turkey, and success is a quite relative term if the costs of conquest and two periods of military dominance are compared with the negligible commerce and dubious political benefits that accrued from this remote imperial outpost. In the nineteenth century Britain became the potential intruder through its alliances with the sultans of South Arabia, and in the early twentieth century the nascent Saudi state constituted a disturbing presence to the north. Ironically, the more worrisome British threat never materialized whereas the Saudi one escalated into war and temporary military occupation in 1934. Although King ibn Saud's peace terms were magnanimous, this overt conflict and the earlier, more deeply seated cultural differences fostered a Yemeni mistrust that has lasted into the late 1970s. Equally ironically, the Arab revolutionaries who eventually drove Britain from South Arabia quickly became republican Yemen's principal adversaries. During all but the final years of the imamate, a successful foreign policy meant being left alone. Since the revolution of 1962, foreign policy priorities have been aimed—reasonably enough—at obtaining foreign aid for massive development needs with the minimum of political strings.

Considering the history of Arab nationalism in the late 1950s and early 1960s in the context of East-West regional posturing, it is hardly surprising that Yemen—as an admitted client of Nasser's United Arab

Republic—depended heavily on direct and indirect Soviet military support and simultaneously entered into extensive economic aid agreements
with the USSR, its Eastern European allies, and China. Unlike Britain,
the United States and West Germany recognized the republican regime.
However, their aid programs earned only minimal influence in the face
of Nasserist distrust. Relations with West Germany were severed in
1965 when previously secret German military aid to Israel became public
knowledge, and U.S. ties were severed equally abruptly as a result of the
1967 Arab-Israeli War. By this time, however, the republic had become a
restive client of Nasser; the withdrawal of Egyptian forces in late 1967
amid growing local hostility marked a new period of what might be
termed "political introspection."

After two years of quasi-isolation, there emerged a republican Yemen
free of the Egyptian-client image and ready for a rapprochement with
Saudi Arabia and the royalist exiles. Relations with West Germany not
only resumed but also blossomed into a large-scale aid program. Ties
with the United States partially resumed with the opening of an
American Interests Section in the Italian Embassy in 1970 and expanded
with the establishment of a full-fledged U.S. embassy in 1973. Almost
concurrently, relations with the USSR deteriorated—not as the result of
overt Western moves but rather because of Yemeni dissatisfaction with
what was perceived as Soviet favoritism toward South Yemen in the area
of arms transfers. Prime Minister Muhsin al-Ayni's 1970 agreement,
which permitted the peaceful return of the royalist exiles, paved the way
for a gradual improvement in Yemeni-Saudi relations. By the mid-1970s,
successor regimes had begun to depend so heavily on Saudi economic aid
that this wealthy northern neighbor became the most influential foreign
actor on the local political scene. Ironically, while Yemeni foreign policy
became so dramatically reoriented in terms of friends and adversaries
over this short span of years, relations with China continued in the same
positive vein. No doubt the Soviets were extremely frustrated to witness
a succession of successful Chinese aid projects dispensed without discern-
ible political strings at a time when many of their own projects were falling short of Yemeni expectations. Relations with the United States have
followed an upward course since 1970, undoubtedly boosted by a residue
of goodwill engendered by the favorable interpersonal relations that
have accrued with a series of aid projects that began in the final years of
the imamate. Unlike the Soviets, Americans have been personally
popular even when their government's policies have been unpopular.

Yemeni external relations in the 1980s most likely will be conditioned
by the economic reality of being situated next to incomparably rich oil-
producing neighbors, and by the seemingly perpetual hostility of South

Yemen. The massive development problem already has engendered extensive relationships with international entities—the United Nations from the first days of the republic and more recently the World Bank. Saudi Arabia remains, of course, the most important external factor in Yemeni political and economic affairs. Budgetary support, emigrant remittances, and subsidies for military weapons are all vital to the YAR government, and this northern neighbor is a unique source for all three. However, cultural differences and political sensitivities on both sides probably will continue to complicate this otherwise symbiotic bilateral relationship.

YAR-PDRY relations cannot help but be perplexing to the outside observer. Even since the emergence of the latter as an Arab nationalist state in the late 1960s, the two neighbors have engaged in propaganda battles, periodic border confrontations, and perpetual mistrust. However, unity talks aimed at eventual political merger occur almost as regularly as border warfare. These intermittent negotiations represent a peculiar sort of political safety valve, since actual unification on terms acceptable to one clearly would be unacceptable to the other.

Tensions between San'a and Aden reached an all-time high in early 1979 when an escalating border fight prompted the Saudis to consider active military intervention on the YAR side. This in turn involved the United States, the Soviet Union, and the Arab League in a complex set of maneuvers. Perceiving the evolving pattern of PDRY infiltration, subversion, and—finally—military probes as an element of Soviet adventurism in the area as well as a simultaneous test of Saudi confidence, the United States agreed to sell the YAR modern weapons worth $390 million (underwritten by Saudi Arabia) and to dispatch a naval task force to the area. While the immediate crisis subsided when PDRY forces withdrew from the frontier, the potential for even greater future crises increased by mid-year as peninsula oil soared in political and economic value in step with the latest events in the global energy crisis. Once-remote Yemen is now situated near the focal point of world rivalry for a critical resource.

Bibliography

The most comprehensive recent work on Yemen is Robert W. Stookey's *Yemen: The Politics of the Yemen Arab Republic* (Boulder, Colo.: Westview Press, 1978). Two journalistic treatments of the civil war period are Edgar O'Ballance, *The War in the Yemen* (Hamden, Conn.: Archon Books, 1971); and Dana Adams Schmidt, *Yemen: The Unknown War* (New York: Holt, Reinhart and Winston, 1968). A more scholarly treatment of the latter days of the imamate and advent of the republic is found in Manfred Wenner, *Modern Yemen: 1918–1966* (Baltimore: Johns Hopkins University Press, 1967). Roughly the same period, with a helpful explanation of the complex relations between imamate Yemen and British South Arabia is found in Harold Ingrams, *The Yemen: Imams, Rulers and Revolutions* (London: John Murray, 1963). Eric Marco treats Yemen's earlier history in his *Yemen and the Western World Since 1571* (New York: Frederick A. Praeger Publishers, 1968). There is also a chapter on the Yemen by the author in Abid Al-Marayati, et al., *The Middle East: Its Government and Politics* (Belmont, Calif.: Duxbury Press, 1972). Finally, a useful study aid is the American University's *Area Handbook for the Yemens* (Washington, D.C.: Government Printing Office, 1977).

9

The People's Democratic Republic of Yemen

David McClintock

The People's Democratic Republic of Yemen (PDRY), which is also known as South (or Southern) Yemen or Yemen (Aden), extends along the southern coast of Arabia from the Strait of Bab al-Mandab at the lower entrance of the Red Sea to the Sultanate of Oman in the northeast. To the north is the Yemen Arab Republic. The two countries have antithetical regimes ideologically, but both claim a common south Arabian cultural heritage. The peoples of western PDRY are ethnically Yemenis, although some of the eastern tribes are not.

In recent times, the two Yemens have had many common experiences, though not concurrently. North Yemeni exiles from the imam resided in Aden, where much of the plotting of the 1962 coup took place; many South Yemeni exiles resided in the YAR during British control of Aden and a new generation of antiregime exiles has moved there since PDRY's independence in 1967. Under the imamate, North Yemen was one of the most isolated countries in the region; and in recent years, South Yemen has slipped into comparable obscurity. For over a decade, it has had the only avowedly Marxist regime in the entire Arab world without exciting more than a small fraction of international interest. Despite its isolation, it is situated astride an important international sea-lane. Accordingly, it deserves more attention in the West than it has received in the past decade.

Historical Background

There has been a symbiotic relationship between the two Yemens culturally, politically, and economically that has prevailed since ancient times. Frankincense and myrrh, the export of which made the highland domains of the Queen of Sheba and neighboring ministates rich, actually grew in the coastal areas of south Arabia and the nearby African coast. Both highlanders and lowlanders in much of the area occupied by the present-day YAR and PDRY claimed descent from one of the two great ethnic divisions of Arabian peoples, the Qahtanis. The other division, the Adnani Arabians, were mainly found further north. In pre-Islamic times, these distinctions often had great political significance. While perennial feuds among the petty states throughout the region prevented the development of a larger Qahtani polity, the Zaydi conquest of the Yemen highlands in the ninth century A.D. installed a Shi'ite ruling elite in an otherwise Sunni Muslim area. Henceforth the isolation of the highlands was to a great extent a self-imposed political one.

South Arabia, which was roughly coterminous with the present PDRY, was susceptible to the intrusions of foreign powers pursuing their maritime strategies. The Turks were sufficiently interested in Aden to fortify it in the 1500s as a check on the European powers who were beginning to use the Indian Ocean as a new route to the East.

In 1839 the British seized Aden and the nearby hinterland in order to secure the now highly developed Indian Ocean "lifeline." By that time Turkish power in the region had declined, but Muhammad Ali's Egypt was rapidly becoming a new threat. At the turn of the nineteenth century, Britain had entered into a protective treaty with the sultan of Lahej; after the annexation of nearby Aden, this set the pattern for a succession of similar agreements with other sultans in the south Arabian hinterland. The city of Aden itself was governed from British India as a dependency of the Bombay presidency.

The strategic importance of Aden increased markedly with the opening of the Suez Canal in 1869, since the excellent natural harbor offered ideal naval basing facilities. A short distance to the west, fortifications on Perim Island in the Strait of Bab al-Mandab allowed effective control of the southern end of the Red Sea. The development of large steam vessels also favored the development of Aden as a principal coaling station between Europe, South Asia, and the Far East, and this in turn necessitated the eventual construction of one of the world's largest bunkering facilities. Cable and Wireless Ltd. constructed here a relay station for its undersea cable from India, thus adding another facility of strategic value.

The importance of this British foothold in Arabia was not lost on other European powers. Rival French and Italian colonial ventures in the nearby Horn of Africa underscored the importance of Bab al-Mandab in the later nineteenth century; however, the Somali colonies and Eritrea never matched British Aden in military value. The deeply ingrained consciousness of Aden's strategic importance influenced British policies and

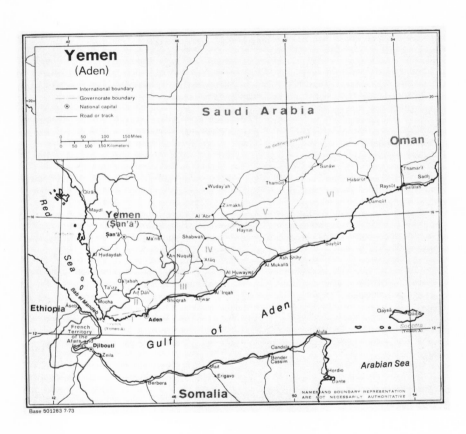

Base 501283 7-73

actions in the difficult preindependence era almost a century later. Similarly, Mussolini's efforts to win the allegiance of the Yemeni imam in the 1930s reflected Italian preoccupation with the southern Red Sea.

The history of British Aden in the first half of the twentieth century is a complex one, but the principal themes were the further development of Aden as a port and dominant urban economic center within the region; the simultaneous struggle to impose uniform political authority over the backward and potentially rebellious hinterland sultanates; and the growth of mutual suspicion on the part of northern Yemen's imam and the pro-British sultans in the south. Four years before their departure from Yemen at the end of World War I, the Turks had demarcated the frontier between the two regions by means of a convention with Britain. The line as drawn was unacceptable to Imam Yahya, but his disastrous encounter with the Saudis in 1934 compelled him to agree to a partial settlement with Great Britain the same year.

For Britain, the principal problem was not the latent hostility of Yemen's imam, but the dubious loyalty of the disunited sultans who provided a territorial buffer on three sides. Significantly, aerial bombardment of tribal villages in the 1930s proved to be the most effective means of eliminating dissidence.

The colonial development of Aden increased the cultural and political differences between this urban area and the remote sultanates. Certain changes in administrative philosophy occurred in 1937 with the transfer of Aden to Colonial Office control. The port city became Aden Colony and the sultanates were divided into the Western and Eastern Aden Protectorates. Wisely, the Yemeni imam resisted Italian overtures on the eve of World War II, and his neutrality afforded Britain a more comfortable position in this strategic location.

Not surprisingly, Aden figured early and prominently in the postwar debate about a British withdrawal east of Suez. In the early 1950s the British political agent Kennedy Trevaskis submitted a plan favored by Conservatives in Parliament to link the sultanates in a federation that could serve as a vehicle for eventual independence. This failed to attract enthusiastic support from the sultans but succeeded in arousing further suspicions on the part of the Yemen's Imam Ahmad. (Imam Yahya had been assassinated in 1948 and his son and successor Ahmad felt so insecure that he moved his capital from San'a to the southern town of Ta'iz.)

Reciprocal misunderstandings were compounded by other regional developments in the mid-1950s. Britain became increasingly unpopular in most Arab eyes as a result of the 1956 Suez fiasco, which in turn paved the way for Yemen's bizarre affiliation with Nasser's United Arab

Republic (UAR) (Egypt and Syria) in the short-lived United Arab States (UAS). During this time, Imam Ahmad's son Crown Prince Muhammad al-Badr pressed successfully for expanded foreign relations. The first foreigners through this slightly opened door were the Soviets, East Germans, and Chinese, who promptly initiated military and economic aid projects. (U.S. aid also began at this time, but on a less visible level.)

If these Yemeni actions were a defensive reaction to a perceived threat from the British and their sultan clients, they produced a mirror-image reaction in the south. Heretofore, the sultans had been indifferent toward the federation scheme, but by 1959 six leaders in the Western Protectorate agreed to join an entity called "The Federation of the Amirates of the South." For the time being, no formula could be found to bring in Aden Colony and the eastern protectorates. The latter area contained the exotic Wadi Hadhramaut, an ethnically distinct region that for centuries had close contact with the East Indies. The Hadhrami merchants were not anxious to dissipate their wealth in this federation scheme, nor were the eastern protectorate sultans anxious to risk the loss of any petroleum wealth that might result from the then-active exploration effort on the part of the Pan American Petroleum Company.

The republicans who overthrew the Mutawakkilite dynasty in Yemen in September 1962 were more actively negative toward the British. With the prompt arrival of a massive Egyptian expeditionary force, the stage was set for Yemen-based subversion of the new south Arabian federation. At the same time the British on the southern border and the Saudis on the north welcomed the formerly hostile royalists in their forced exile and provided two bases for countersubversive action against the republic. After the failure of the Bunker peace mission to obtain early withdrawal of Egyptian troops from Yemen, the United States found itself in the unenviable position of maintaining its close relationship with Saudi Arabia, recognizing the Yemen Arab Republic, and wishing success to British efforts to create a viable preindependence state in south Arabia.

If the British had found the situation of the 1950s less than propitious for building a viable south Arabian political entity, the Yemen civil war made the task infinitely more difficult in the 1960s. Nevertheless, a formula finally was found to allow the merger of Aden with the sultanates, and in January 1963 the South Arabian Federation was born.

While the British and their sultan clients were understandably fearful of the course of events in the YAR, it is fair to assume that similar fears and suspicions motivated the Egyptians and their republican Yemeni clients when the conservative federation came into being. Suspicion soon escalated into overt hostility; the Egyptians and Yemenis began to experience difficulty in maintaining the allegiance of many conservative tribal leaders. None could be permanently "bought" with the newly printed YAR paper riyals, and it proved difficult to impose military control because tanks and jet aircraft were ill-suited to the craggy highland terrain. Thus, the British and Saudi-backed royalist tribesmen in the YAR had a tactical advantage in the countryside. By contrast, the British were highly vulnerable in urban Aden where there was significant anticolonial sentiment. The Egyptians took full advantage of the dissident, antifederation political forces on hand. By 1965, bombings, grenade throwings, and sabotage operations were almost daily occurrences. While the British presumably had hoped that the federation would enable Britain to exercise its influence in economic and defense matters while promoting gradual self-rule, the demand for complete and immediate independence spread from these militant opposition factions to the more conservative ones.

Political coalitions in south Arabia had become well defined by the 1950s. These groups articulated their political demands with a surprising degree of sophistication, considering the lack of experience with anything except colonial rule. The spawning ground for many of these aspiring politicians was the well-developed Aden Trade Union Congress (ATUC). Under the leadership of Abdallah al Asnaj, the ATUC formed the Peoples Socialist Party (PSP). Sharing its anti-British sentiments were the South Arabian League (SAL), and National Liberation Front (NLF). The SAL drew its strength primarily from the Lahej area. The NLF was essentially an Egyptian creation operating from across the Yemen frontier, though its ideology was closely akin to the Arab Nationalists Movement (ANM), which included such leaders as George Habbash of the Palestinian resistance movement. The most conservative group was the United National Party (UNP), which represented pro-British business interests.

The NLF struck the first serious blow to the new federation scheme in 1964 by inciting tribesmen in the Radfan district to revolt. The NLF not only solidified its position through this operation but also gained strength through the defection of Qahtan al-Sha'bi and some of his followers from the SAL. Al-Sha'bi was to become the future nation's first president.

All but the most conservative factions competed among themselves in efforts to undermine the federation. They not only attempted the mobilization of public support (primarily in Aden) but also resorted to paramilitary and terrorist actions in both the port and the hinterland. In the meantime, a shift in British policy doomed the original federation plan. The British Labour government, which came to power in 1964, was inclined to reduce (or eliminate where possible) British commitments east of Suez. Accordingly, it favored the establishment of a unitary state in south Arabia that could serve as vehicle for an early and complete independence. This set the stage for markedly increased infighting among the local political factions.

The British Labour party's resolve to rid itself of the troublesome south Arabia problem was strengthened by anticolonialist pressure in the United Nations. The latter had actually begun as early as 1948 and had been reiterated at the 1955 Bandung Conference of Afro-Asian states. In 1963 a U.N. committee focused on the "Aden problem," and did so again in 1964 as the new Labour government was attempting to develop a constitution for a postindependence entity. Even the Security Council became involved in the spring of 1964 when Yemen charged that the Aden-based Royal Air Force had bombed the border town of Harib. Throughout 1965 the British were frustrated both by escalating terrorism and the resultant need to respond with greater military force, and by the refusal of the competing factions to agree on a constitutional design for a new state. Having lost patience with the continuing impasse, the British announced in February 1966 that all military forces would be withdrawn by December 1968.

During the next two years the already chaotic situation deteriorated even more as the anti-British factions competed for dominance. The NLF continued to grow in strength but at the same time found its Arab opposition more virulent. At about the time that the British set their withdrawal date, the NLF merged with a rival group, the Organization for the Liberation of the Occupied South (OLOS), to form the Front for the Liberation of the Occupied South (FLOSY). Internal rivalries were too keen, however, and the NLF withdrew to become the chief rival of the remnant FLOSY, which then fielded a commando unit called the People's Organization of Revolutionary Forces (PORF). Terrorism became even more pervasive than in the preceding years when the several factions had been loosely united against the British. United Nations mediation efforts failed completely since neither the NLF nor FLOSY was interested in a compromise or in sharing control of the postindependence state.

Britain now moved the departure date to the end of 1967 and in essence marked time while the NLF and FLOSY struggled for domination. Both organizations were perceived by London as unpalatable, but FLOSY's now closer ties to the UAR were probably a factor in the British tilt toward the NLF, given Britain's antipathy toward Nasser. However, considering the years of debate that had taken place on the subject of how to minimize the impact of a reduced British presence east of Suez, it is ironic that the south Arabian struggle was won by the faction that was fundamentally the most anti-Western. During the final military showdown in November 1967, the British-equipped and trained south Arabian Army—which had been attempting to maintain a modicum of public safety—also threw its weight to the NLF, allowing this group to inherit formal authority from the departing British on the last day of the month. On November 30, the independent People's Republic of Southern Yemen came into existence under its new president, Qahtan al-Sha'bi.

After independence, the ruling NLF was renamed the National Front (NF) and many FLOSY supporters went into exile in Yemen. There was no doubt by this time that the NF was leftist, but the more extreme aspects of its ideology appear to have been muted to accommodate negotiations with London over the terms of its promised budgetary support. Despite this ploy, the NF was disappointed on this score. The economy was dealt a worse blow, however, by the closure of the Suez Canal during the June 1967 Arab-Israeli War and by the resultant diversion of world shipping around southern Africa. This maritime traffic and the related profits from bunkering and local trade had made preindependence Aden a mini–Hong Kong.

Through perceived necessity and no doubt political inclination as well, President al-Sha'bi attempted to strengthen ties with the USSR, Eastern Europe, China, and the more radical Arab nationalist regimes. These sources did provide various types of aid, ranging from developmental to military.

South Yemen's relations with its conservative neighbors were predictably poor. The Saudis were distressed by the increase in both communist and Arab nationalist influence on its southern border. Yemeni republican leaders had similar qualms. Resentful of their treatment by Nasser between the 1962 revolution and the withdrawal of the UAR expeditionary force in December 1967, they had become more conservative. They also were disenchanted with Soviet economic and military support. To the east, the conservative Sultanate of Muscat and Oman (redesignated the Sultanate of Oman in 1970) shared Saudi and Yemeni antipathy toward the political philosophies of the National Front regime in Aden.

The South Yemeni regime began to turn progressively more radical. Al-Sha'bi was severely criticized by the militants under the secretary-general of the National Front. At the first party congress in Zinjibar in 1968, an aspiring leader named Abd al-Fattah Ismail framed the Zinjibar Resolutions for leading the country to Marxism. In June 1969, al-Sha'bi was overthrown and replaced by Salim Ruba'i Ali, a militant but also an archrival of Ismail.

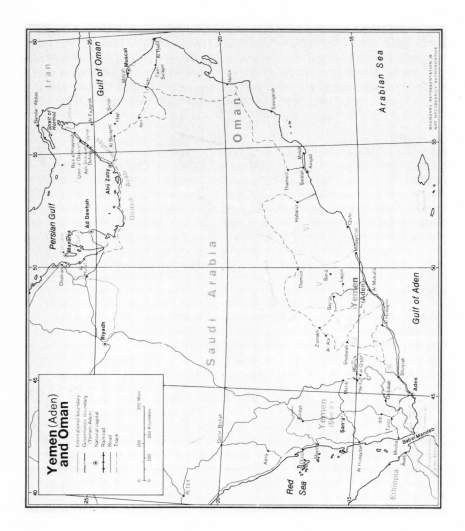

Yemen (Aden) and Oman

- —————— International boundary
- —·—·—·—·— Governorate boundary (Yemen Aden)
- ⊙ National capital
- ＋＋＋＋ Railroad
- ————— Road
- - - - - - Track

0   100   200 Kilometers
0   200 Miles

As a reflection of this further shift to the left, the country was renamed the People's Democratic Republic of Yemen in 1970.

Differences between San'a and Aden were exacerbated when Yemeni Premier Muhsin al-Ayni reached accommodation with the Saudis in 1970 and subsequently readmitted those exiled Yemeni royalists who were willing to accept the republic. Although both Yemens officially espoused some form of political unification of the two countries, attitudes in the north were becoming increasingly more conservative while in the south they remained doctrinaire and radical. Accordingly, during the 1970s the two nations have presented the curious spectacle of calling periodically for unity and equally as often hurling invectives at each other.

Relations with San'a have approached a crisis stage on several occasions during subsequent years. In October 1972, YAR forces seized Kamaran Island, which formerly was a British dependency linked to Aden and thus claimed by the postindependence PDRY despite its remote location north of the midcoastal port of Hodayda in the YAR. In 1972, border skirmishes in the south led to a state of near-warfare that necessitated an Arab League peacekeeping mission. The most bizarre event in this saga of conflict occurred on 30 June 1978, when emissaries from President Salim Ruba'i Ali and from YAR President al-Ghashmi were both killed in San'a by a bomb hidden in the PDRY envoy's briefcase.

Domestic politics throughout most of the 1970s reflected not only a shift to the left but also the rivalry between Ismail and Ali. Early on, Ismail, who was more pro-Soviet, was labeled by outsiders as more pragmatic than Ali, who was called a Maoist. In fact, Ali was much more pragmatic, as seen in his dialogue with the Saudis in 1976–1977. The rivalry, however, was less ideological in nature than personal and culminated in the overthrow and execution of Ali in June 1978. While Ismail appears to have engineered the plot against YAR President al-Ghashmi, he convened the National Front's politburo on July 1, apparently to implicate Ali in the assassination. Ali refused to attend and, in a showdown that night, shooting broke out, Ali was captured and executed, and Ismail seized virtual control of the government. The following day he had Prime Minister Ali Nasir Muhammad al-Hasani also appointed president, but in the fall took over the presidency again in a major party reorganization. Ismail, with the help of Soviet advisors, reorganized the National Front into the Yemeni Socialist Party. Since that time, however, Ali Nasir, using resentment over Ismail's North Yemen origins, appears to have rekindled the political rivalry that for so long has been a major feature of South Yemeni politics.

Political Environment

The People

With a population estimated at only 1.5 million, the PDRY presents a strikingly different demographic picture from the neighboring YAR. On the other hand, Aden, with a population of approximately 250,000, provides an urban focus that is missing in the north. In the considerably more prosperous preindependence era, Adenites were more cosmopolitan than their isolated geographic situation would have suggested. Ship chandlering, bunkering, the oil refinery, and other large-scale economic operations generated a certain affluence that in turn favored a better education by regional standards and the development of a skilled labor force. The next largest towns, Mukalla and Sayun, have populations only a fifth and a tenth as large, respectively, as Aden's, and were never so sophisticated as the capital.

Outside the cities, the PDRY is sparsely populated, with a tribal social structure not markedly different from that in North Yemen. However, since they are predominantly Shafa'i Muslims, the Sunni-Shi'ite dichotomy found in Yemen is missing. The sultans formerly represented a rural aristocracy but of course disappeared with the advent of the radical Marxist regime. The inhabitants of the Wadi Hadhramaut in the former Eastern Aden Protectorate developed a relatively advanced town and village culture based partly on local agriculture and partly on emigration to (and trade with) the East Indies. Intermarriage with Javanese and other Indonesian peoples has given many Hadhrami families a distinctive physical appearance. At the other end of the rural social scale, some tribes remain purely nomadic. At the eastern end of the country, wild Mahra tribesmen predominate. Closely related to Mahras in neighboring Oman, they speak a non-Arabic language.

With the advent of the National Front and its collectivist economic policies coupled with the virtual collapse of the preindependence economy most of the foreigners who gave Aden its polyglot character have fled. Somalis previously were the principal foreign laborers; Indians and Pakistanis worked as merchants and clerks; and Europeans, primarily British, filled managerial and high-technology positions. Many indigenous south Arabians have departed as well, for both economic and political reasons. The tens of thousands of northern Yemenis who once found employment in bustling Aden also are gone. By a perverse twist of economic history, many southerners found sanctuary in the YAR, where their managerial skills have been put to good use. Several have even been appointed to cabinet positions in the YAR. The combined exodus may have approached one-half million. The PDRY thus is demographically weak in terms of population size as well as in a diminished, trained adult work force.

Social Conditions

Social patterns in the PDRY roughly approximate those of the preindependence era insofar as the dichotomy between Aden and the hinterland is concerned. However, there is little doubt that living standards have declined in both areas as a result of collectivization and other governmental incursions into the socioeconomic sphere. The tribal elements reportedly have been resistant in many instances to these policies. Nomads here as elsewhere have found it difficult to adapt to a sedentary agricultural life, and the sedentary tribes with established agricultural traditions have been resistant to collectivization. The regime made early efforts at land redistribution, but this did not lead to the erection of a radically different rural society since poverty prevailed both before and afterwards. In both the rural and urban spheres, employment opportunities have diminished. On the other hand, the PDRY appears to have accelerated women's liberation, primarily through the General Union of Yemeni Women, which has operating branches in all governorates. Since the union is an appendage of the Yemeni Socialist Party, its vigorous activities reflect government interest in this aspect of modernization. Similar efforts have been made to mobilize the country's youth.

Health conditions were never adequate in the countryside and remain substandard. Although adequate statistics are lacking, disease rates and infant mortality are believed to be high. Severe nutritional problems complicate the health picture. There have been intermittent reports of famines, food shortages, and rationing.

By regional as well as world standards, the PDRY society is in a peculiar state of transition. Living conditions both before and after the revolution naturally have been driven by economic realities. However, the National Front appears to have gone out of its way to stifle any vestige of political opposition and to impose a doctrinaire economic system where there were insufficient resources to make it work. As a result, a basically traditional people continues to live in traditional poverty with new, contrived societal norms. Its youth eventually can be acculturated, but for its adults, the effects cannot help but be stifling.

Economic Conditions

Mention already has been made of the coincidence of the closure of the Suez Canal with the advent of independence. The concurrent British military pullout also eliminated large quantities of hard currency, previously funneled into the local economy through the air and naval bases. Whereas the Yemen Arab Republic received developmental aid from both East and West as well as international organizations, National Front leaders in Aden found only token aid in the West and less help from the radical Arab nationalist camp and communist world than they had hoped. Indeed, the major Soviet aid effort has been a military one, which has exacerbated relations between the two Yemens. This Soviet tie also raised the apprehensions of the moderate, oil-rich Arab regimes that could have granted many times as much developmental aid in exchange for a less-menacing external posture.

Postindependence emigration, proportionately heavy in relation to the small total population, could be considered both a product of the politicoeconomic situation and a negative influence on the economy. In the latter instance, the fledgling nation lost its principal entrepreneurial talent with the departure of key Adeni business leaders. Some relocated in the Yemeni port city of Hodayda and continued operations on a small scale commensurate with post-Suez Red Sea trade, while others—particularly the Indian merchant families—went farther afield. Some business even shifted to Djibouti, which subsequently became independent of France under considerably more stable economic and political conditions. The economic impact on South Yemen was inordinately great, because most trading firms were extremely diversified in their business operations.

Steadily deteriorating political relations between San'a and Aden also worked to the economic disadvantage of the PDRY, since frequent border closures effectively served to redirect the Yemen trade through Hodayda. While this trade was comparatively less important in preindependence times, the implied loss was considerably greater with the cessation of the Suez traffic and the benefits derived from it: bunkering, tourism, and general brokerage. Ironically, when Suez reopened in 1975, considerable bulk transport had shifted to wider, deeper-draft supervessels unable to transit the canal. Aden has thus been unable to recapture the entrepôt trade it once enjoyed and has no immediate prospects of doing so. It must be remembered that Aden developed a complex economic infrastructure as a result of unique advantages accruing from the British military presence, port activity, and east-west communications. With the removal of not just one but all three underpinnings, along with the Marxist policies of the government, disaster was inevitable. The once-great entrepôt is now on more even economic terms with its impoverished agricultural hinterland.

Even with official encouragement, the agricultural sector has a limited potential due to the low percentage of fertile land, water shortages, and poor transport facilities. Nonetheless, the area around Lahej retains some potential for cotton production, and fertile but remote noncontiguous wadi areas such as the Hadhramaut could produce more in the way of grains and garden crops. In the absence of even more ambitious foreign aid projects, it is unlikely that productivity can be increased to a significant degree. On the other hand, the development potential for fisheries could be more encouraging in view of the PDRY's extensive coastal waters and established port and handling facilities. Petroleum remains a question mark. Prior to independence, the Pan American Oil Company was engaged in extensive exploration in the interior. New concessions with sufficient financial incentives and investment guarantees would make a renewed search feasible. At present, the great irony confronting both Yemens is that while the rest of the Arabian peninsula virtually "floats" on oil, both countries must import all of their fuel requirements.

Political Structure

Political structures not directly related to the ruling Yemen Socialist Party have little practical significance in the PDRY. Government functions are therefore essentially party functions. Understanding these, however, is a difficult task in view of the secretive, totalitarian character of the party.

The party system was designed with the help of Soviet technical advisors, presumably according to the principles of "democratic centralism" that have been applied in the communist world. The emphasis, of course, is on centralism and vertical control. Notwithstanding the existence of a pro-Chinese faction, the party has never embraced a "hundred flowers" philosophy that might offer opportunities for innovation.

Until the dramatic events of June 1978, real power was divided between the president, Salim Ruba'i Ali, who controlled the armed forces as commander-in-chief, chaired the Presidential Council, and served simultaneously as assistant secretary-general of the National Front. The secretary-general of the National Front, Abd al-Fattah Ismail, was in a constitutional sense subordinate to the president. As events proved, he was able to muster critical military support when the showdown came. In the pre–June 1978 period, the prime minister clearly occupied third place.

Under the new party structure, there has been talk of creating a politburo and presidium form of party-government structure but thus far this has not occurred. The president, Ali Nasir Muhammad, is still technically chairman of the five-member Presidential Council and is also prime minister. He thus stands at the head of the functional side of government, and operational responsibilities are carried out by the various ministries. Likewise, the two leaders control the supreme councils encompassing the regional governorates and their political subdivisions. Officials in the latter realm have been appointed and are generally subservient to Aden authority. By contrast, the party secretary-general wields potentially more ideological authority through his control of the Central Committee, Political Bureau, and the subordinate women's, youth's and laborers' organizations and, most importantly, the independent People's Militia.

The People's Supreme Council, based on the 1970 constitution, is an appointed legislature. However, actual authority at this level is wielded by the Executive Committee of the Yemen Socialist Party. Before the party was reorganized, this body reported to the secretary-general command, which was the pluralistic decision-making body in the initial days before and after the takeover from Britain.

In the PDRY, as elsewhere in the Arab world, the gap between formal governmental authority and personality-oriented sources of power is fairly great. As the events of June 1978 demonstrated, control of the military establishment is the decisive element of power. The only thing that distinguishes the PDRY from other, more typical Middle Eastern examples, is that political-military power is divided between the regular armed forces and the People's Militia.

Political Dynamics

In the absence of normal electoral processes, participation in national political life obviously can occur only through participation in some activity sanctioned by the Yemen Socialist Party. While the party has resorted to the familiar expedient of "mobilizing" women, youths, "workers," and farmers, it must be remembered that these groups were not as readily distinguishable as their counterparts in other more truly revolutionary societies, such as the Soviet or Chinese. Aden became modern in late British times only in an economic sense. Here and in the hinterland, society remained traditionalist and conservative until (and into) the postindependence period. It has not been possible to dismantle this traditionalist society to the extent that the National Front leadership presumably would have desired because the regime has continually lacked the material resources to make the new order function. Consequently, it has found it easier to invoke sanctions against nonconformism than to offer political or economic rewards for supportive behavior. In this latter sense, political rewards can be defined as influential jobs, and economic rewards as pay or perquisites. As a result, political processes necessarily are elitist despite the egalitarian philosophy of the ultra-leftist regime. This situation can remain viable over the relatively short term—that is, measured in years rather than decades. Sanctions have worked during the first decade of National Front rule, but rewards will become increasingly necessary if the regime is to achieve political participation on a scale that will assure its own survival.

In theory, economic and political demands are articulated in pyramidal fashion by local people's councils, operating at a local level and reporting through the regional governorates. Assuming council members are elected by popular will, this offers one democratic element in an otherwise totalitarian governmental process. However, it is questionable whether the councils have exercised any real influence to date, or whether a meaningful electoral process has occurred even at this grassroots level. Since the front leadership reportedly has taken pains to place party members at all levels for purposes both of surveillance and control, it is also questionable whether the people's councils can either articulate popular demands or provide meaningful feedback to what the central government has initiated. Considering the extent to which even the more traditionalist Arab societies are participatory through their ability to extend or withhold confidence in shaykhs at the local level, or in monarchs at the national level, the system espoused by the Yemen Socialist Party and the National Front before it is very alien to the region. Likewise, it is somewhat alien even to other nations in the Arab nationalist world, where old and established societies have continued to function with only minor adaptations to new—primarily military— governing elites and rather permissive socialist economic rules. Considering societal realities, the PDRY's political system is running greater risks in the political sphere than it has incurred in its rigid economic planning.

Foreign Policy

As indicated in the preceding historical sketch, the National Front did not immediately turn away from Britain and the West after inheriting its governing authority. Nevertheless, circumstances prompted the establishment of early links with the Soviet Union, Eastern Europe, and China. While this was politically logical as well as economically necessary, the results—as evidenced by the PDRY's situation vis-à-vis the YAR—must have been disappointing to the National Front. While it is true that the USSR openly favored the PDRY by granting it military hardware and withholding the same from the YAR during various phases of the Yemeni conflict, developmental aid has failed to restore even a portion of preindependence prosperity. Chinese aid, oriented more to the hinterland through such means as medical teams, probably scored more comparative success in terms of grassroots goodwill. In recent years, however, and particularly with the ascendency of Ismail, Chinese influence has waned.

These primary alignments with the two major powers in the communist world have had interesting repercussions in other areas of PDRY foreign relations. During the late 1960s and early 1970s, Western nations periodically suspected that the PDRY had offered the Soviets Indian Ocean base facilities—perhaps on the offshore island of Socotra. While reports of actual base construction thus far have proved unfounded, the fact remains that Aden itself has become a useful Indian Ocean haven for the Soviet fleet. Thus there are new strategic implications for the area of Bab al-Mandab.

During this period, the PDRY was actively involved in efforts to overthrow the sultan of Oman through guerrilla forces of the Popular Front for the Liberation of the Occupied Arab Gulf and the earlier Dhufar Liberation Front. The political affinity of Aden and the Dhufar rebels lies in the fact that both espouse radical doctrines of the Arab Nationalists Front. By the mid-1970s South Yemen support for the Dhufar rebels tapered off for the dual reasons that the guerrillas were gradually being defeated by Oman with the help of Iranian, Jordanian, and British military aid, and that cessation of active PDRY support was the price asked for financial support from the oil-rich peninsula regimes, particularly Saudi Arabia.

The PDRY also actively supported the Eritrean dissidents in their struggle against the conservative regime of Haile Selassie and against the non-Eritrean military leaders who overthrew the emperor. Ironically, this traditional support for the Eritreans became an issue in the final struggle between Ali and Ismail in 1978, since the president reportedly favored its continuation whereas the secretary-general preferred to support the Soviets, who by then had switched support to the new Marxist Ethiopian central government.

In 1976, the Saudis made quiet overtures to Ali, offering financial aid if the PDRY would moderate its militant foreign policies. Some progress appeared to have been made; but as the PDRY gave whole-hearted cooperation to the Soviet-Cuban military effort by Ethiopia against Somalia the Saudis began rethinking their strategy. Nevertheless, Ali was deemed far more reasonable by the conservative Arabs than Ismail. This, coupled with the long-standing personal rivalry and the crisis conditions brought on by the assassination of the YAR president, led to the confrontation in which Ruba'i Ali perished and Ismail emerged triumphant. In retaliation, the Arab League declared an economic boycott of the PDRY in July 1978. It was, however, only marginally successful.

It had been previously popular to interpret PDRY foreign policy in terms of Ali's alleged preferences for China and Ismail's support for the USSR. To the outside world, both leaders were long considered radical ideologues. Ironically, as the dramatic events of June 1968 unfolded, the world press began to portray Ali as the "moderate" and Ismail as the extremist. This was accurate in the context of recent antecedent events, but it overlooked the extent to which the rival leaders had pursued radical foreign policies that had made the PDRY a pariah insofar as other Arab neighbors were concerned. Ali apparently had moderated in his last years and might well have won passive if not active Saudi support as well as improved relations with the West had not events in the Horn of Africa dictated a show of support for the Soviet Union. This in turn might have brightened the foreign-aid picture. The economic imperatives remain the same. Therefore, Ismail has the same options: either to solicit more Eastern—primarily Soviet—aid, or to follow the recently conciliatory line of his former rival. Whichever option is selected, the fact remains that relations with the Yemen Arab Republic reached a low ebb at the time of this internal leadership struggle.

The PDRY's foreign policies may appear relatively inconsequential to much of the rest of the outside world, but they will remain critical to the YAR. This in turn will continue to preoccupy Saudi Arabia, whose policies and concerns are of inordinate economic and political interest to other nations.

Bibliography

There has yet to be written a definitive book on independent South Yemen. The best recent treatment is in the American University's *Area Handbook for the Yemens* (Washington, D.C.: Government Printing Office, 1977). My chapter in Abid Al-Marayati, *The Middle East: Its Governments and Politics* (Belmont, Calif.: Duxbury Press, 1972) gives an overview of its first few years. For the British and earlier periods, a number of works exist. Harold Ingrams, author of *Arabia and the Isles*, 3rd ed. (New York: Frederick A. Praeger Publishers, 1966) is one of the leading authorities on south Arabia's tribes and the problems of pacifying them. Ingrams is the man who engineered peace in the Hadhramout. Three books on the period of transition from British rule to independence are Tom Little, *South Arabia: Arena of Conflict* (London: Pall Mall Press, 1968); Sir Kennedy Trevaskis' authoritative *Shades of Amber: A South Arabian Episode* (London: Hutchinson, 1968); and Gordon Waterfield, *Sultans of Oden* (London: John Murray, 1968). Additionally, the Yemen bibliography in the previous chapter should be consulted.

10

Republic of Lebanon

M. Graeme Bannerman

Historical Background

Though the modern state of Lebanon is a creation of the twentieth century, the people of Lebanon have had a long and distinctive history. The coastal plain was the home of Phoenician merchants whose ships sailed throughout the Mediterranean world more than a millenium before Christ. While the Lebanese of today have only an indirect connection with the ancient Phoenicians, many Lebanese who wish to emphasize their uniqueness as a people reach back to the past and stress their "Phoenician heritage."

In the seventh century A.D., when the Muslim armies swept out of the Arabian peninsula, the rugged Lebanon mountains gradually became a refuge for Levantine Christians, predominantly Maronites, and other dissident groups who opposed the Islamic establishment. Under both the Umayyad (660–750) and the Abbasid (750–1258) caliphates, the Lebanese mountaineers retained a degree of political autonomy. While the Muslim rulers easily controlled the coastal cities, total domination of the mountain was never fully achieved.

The Muslim Arabs who surrounded the mountain, nevertheless, had considerable impact on its inhabitants. Many customs and social values of the surrounding region penetrated the mountain fastness. Symbolic of these changes was the slow growth in the use of Arabic. By the thirteenth century, Arabic had replaced Aramaic as the dominant language, although Syriac, a branch of Aramaic, was spoken in some villages well into the seventeenth century and remains the liturgical language of the Syrian (Syrian Orthodox) church until the present.

By the end of the eleventh century three groups of dissidents— Maronites, Shi'ites and Druze—dominated in the Lebanese mountains. The Maronites were predominant in the northern region of Jubayl, Batrun, and Bsharri. Shi'ite Muslims formed the majority in the re-

mainder of Lebanon. During the eleventh century, however, the
followers of Egyptian Fatimid Caliph al-Hakim (985–1021) entered
Lebanon. Led by the disciple Darazi, the followers joined with local
Lebanese to form their distinctive community, which is widely known as
the Druze.

The crusaders overran Lebanon in the early twelfth century, capturing
Tripoli in 1109, and Beirut and Sidon in 1110. Tyre held out until 1124.
The crusades had a profound effect on the Maronites, for it was at that
time that they were brought into union with the Roman church,
establishing a link that still endures. In addition, the large French component among the crusaders established ties with the Maronites that later
generations would view as the basis of a special relationship between
France and Lebanon. Moreover, Maronite assistance to the crusaders
further alienated their Muslim neighbors.

The crusades also had a devastating impact on Lebanese Shi'ites.
Before the crusades, Muslim Lebanon was predominately Shi'ite rather
than Sunni. The growth of Shi'ite influence was due to a large extent to
the Shi'ite Fatimid caliphate in Cairo, which had successfully competed
for control of Syria with the faltering Abbasid (Sunni) caliphate in
Baghdad. The failure of the Fatimids to adequately protect Muslims from
the Christian invaders, however, contributed to the decline of Fatimid
power and influence in Syria. Without the protection of the powerful
Shi'ites in Cairo, the fortunes of Lebanese Shi'ites also declined. In the
absence of effective Shi'ite leadership, a succession of Sunni dynasties
initiated the countercrusade that ultimately led to the defeat of the
crusaders and to the decline of Shi'ite influence in Lebanon and Syria.

In Egypt, the Fatimids were succeeded by the Sunni Ayubids. They in
turn were replaced by Sunni Mamluk dynasties, which dominated Egypt,
Syria, and Lebanon until the sixteenth century. The Mamluks were
originally slaves and descendants of slaves who had been brought from
the Caucasus region to support the sultans in Egypt whom they eventually overthrew. Under Mamluk domination, Sunni Islam became firmly
entrenched along the eastern shore of the Mediterranean. Less tolerant
than their predecessors, who allowed other religious communities to live
in peace, the Mamluks pressed their subjects to convert to Sunni Islam.
In Lebanon, the Shi'ites and the Druze suffered most. An abortive Shi'ite
rebellion in the late thirteenth century brought widespread devastation
to central Lebanon. For the most part, however, the Mamluks were not
intent on dominating Mount Lebanon directly but were content to rule
indirectly through local leaders. Thus, Lebanese autonomy continued to
be preserved.

In 1516 the Ottomans defeated the Mamluks in northern Syria,

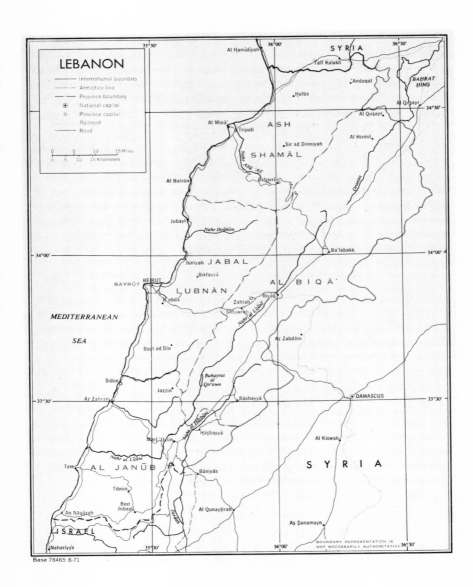

LEBANON

International boundary
Armistice line
Province boundary
National capital
Province capital
Railroad
Road

0   5   10   15 Miles
0   5   10   15 Kilometers

SYRIA

Al Ḥamīdīyah

Tall Kalakh

Andaqat

BAḤRAT
ḤIMṢ

Ḥalbā

Al Qusayr

Al Qusayr

ASH

Al Mīnā'

Tripoli

Sir aḍ Ḍinnīyah

Al Hirmil

SHAMĀL

Nahr Abū 'Alī

Bsharrī

Al Batrūn

Orontes

Jubayl

Nahr Ibrāhīm

Ba'labakk

34°00'   34°00'

Juniyah   JABAL

Bikfayyā

BAYRŪT   BEIRUT   LUBNĀN   AL   BIQĀ'

B'abdā

Zahlah   Riyāq

Shtawrah   Nahr al Līţānī

MEDITERRANEAN

SEA

Az Zabdānī

Bayt ad Dīn

Buḥayrat
al
Qir'awn

Sidon

Jazzīn   Rāshayyā

Az Zahrān   DAMASCUS

33°30'   33°30'

Nahr al Ḥāṣbānī

Ḥāṣbayyā

Marj 'Uyūn   Al Kiswah

Nahr al Līţānī

Tyre   AL   JANŪB   SYRIA

Bāniyās

Tibnīn

Bint
Jubayl   Jordan

An Nāqūrah   Al Qunayṭirah

ISRAEL   Aş Şanamayn

BOUNDARY REPRESENTATION IS
NOT NECESSARILY AUTHORITATIVE

Naharīyya

35°30'   36°00'   36°30'

Base 78465 6-71

establishing Ottoman control over the Arab Levant. The Ottomans dominated this area for the next four centuries. The Ottomans continued the Mamluk policy of recognizing a local Lebanese notable to rule a semiautonomous state. Two great dynasties reigned in the mountains of Lebanon until 1843. The Druze house of Ma'an was paramount until 1697, reaching its zenith under Fakhr al-Din II (1586–1635). His efforts to obtain total independence for Lebanon led ultimately to his defeat and execution. Nevertheless, this Druze leader did much for Lebanon by reopening the country to the West as it had not been since the crusades.

A one-time exile in Tuscany, Fakhr al-Din II later allied with the rulers of that Italian state. These ties extended beyond the political realm. The Druze leader emulated his allies in attempting to create a modern army. He also imported engineers and agricultural experts to promote better land use. These efforts, however, had only a minimal long-term impact on Lebanon. Of greater significance was Fakhr al-Din's encouragement of the Maronite peasantry to move south. Over the subsequent centuries the Maronites spread from their northern Lebanese strongholds and slowly expanded their numbers and influence throughout the Lebanon mountains.

In 1697 the Ma'an family was replaced by the Shihabs as the amirs (princes) of Mount Lebanon. Under Bashir II (1788–1840), the Shihabs pressed for full independence. The early nineteenth century was a time when the Ottoman state was being torn apart by many local rulers who, playing upon the weakness of the central government, strove to break away from the authorities in Istanbul. Bashir made an unfortunate miscalculation, however, by supporting Muhammad Ali of Egypt against the Ottomans who, in turn, were supported by the British. As a result, when the Egyptian leader was obliged to give up his claims to sovereignty in the Levant, his ally Bashir was forced into exile in 1840.

The next twenty years were marked by strife and turmoil. Internal Lebanese rivalries were exacerbated by Ottoman weakness and European intervention. During the preceding two centuries the fundamental economic and political balance of Mount Lebanon had been upset by the growth in the Maronite population and their gradual migration southward from traditional strongholds in North Lebanon. Druze preponderance had been seriously eroded. The Ottomans, in an attempt to ward off potential intercommunal difficulties, in 1843 divided Lebanon into two districts (*qaim maqaimyyah*). A northern district was placed under a Christian subgovernor and a southern district under a Druze.

This system proved unsatisfactory. The Druze and Christian populations were already too intermingled and antagonistic to permit such a simple solution. Despite Ottoman efforts, tensions between the communities increased. These tensions were made worse by French protection of the Maronites and British protection of the Druze. Moreover, the Ottomans were not satisfied with the status quo. Istanbul desired to limit the traditional autonomous status of the inhabitants of Mount Lebanon and resented European interference in Ottoman internal affairs. Another problem was the growing resentment of the industrious Maronite peasantry toward their oppressive feudal aristocracy. In 1858 a peasant revolt broke out. In the northern district, the Maronite peasantry turned against Maronite shaykhs; in the southern district, the Maronite peasantry rose against the Druze aristocracy. Because the Druze peasantry in the south felt closer bonds with their co-religionists than with the Maronite peasants, the hostilities south and east of Beirut became more a religious war than a peasant revolt. Thousands of Maronites were massacred by Druze and other Muslims. These massacres have contributed to Christian and Muslim suspicions and animosities that have yet to be assuaged.

Following direct European intervention, Mount Lebanon was reunited and made a semiautonomous governorship (*mutasarrifiyyah*). The governor was a non-Lebanese Ottoman Christian who was appointed by the Ottoman sultan with the consent of the five great European powers. He was aided by an elected administrative council, which ensured representation to each of the major sects, and a locally recruited police force. This system remained in force until World War I.

The 1860–1914 period was marked by increasing contacts between the Lebanese and the West. Intellectual activity increased, largely through the efforts of foreign missionaries. Presbyterians from the United States founded the American University of Beirut in 1866, and French missionaries founded Saint Joseph University in 1875. Economically, however, Lebanon held little prospect of supporting its own growing population. The Maronites, who had been expanding their area of settlement for over two centuries as a way of providing for their growing population, found further expansion of their community in Lebanon limited. Late-nineteenth-century Ottoman attempts at reviving their state often were colored with Islamic overtones and were politically repressive. At the same time, many nations appeared to offer greater opportunities. Consequently, thousands of Maronites and other Christians emigrated, seeking their fortunes in the United States, South America, and elsewhere. While some Muslims and Druze also went to these areas, many more traveled to other areas of the Ottoman state or Egypt.

Four centuries of Ottoman rule came to an end in Lebanon with World War I. Through wartime agreements, Lebanon was mandated to the

French, who created Greater Lebanon, which included not only Mount Lebanon but also Beirut, Sidon, Tyre, southern Lebanon, the Biqa valley, and the Akkar plain in the north. The French hoped that a larger Lebanon would make Lebanon economically viable and a more influential friend. This expansion, however, altered the demographic balance by including large numbers of Sunnis and Shi'ites in the new state and diluting the Christian preponderance.

Under the French mandate the Lebanese made slow progress toward full independence. The Lebanese nationalists kept pressure upon the French, gaining greater and greater independence. In 1926 a constitution was promulgated. The Lebanese nationalists were not satisfied with this document, however, for the French high commissioner retained final authority. For example, in 1932 and again in 1939 the French suspended the constitution. Despite the French hold, the Lebanese were permitted to choose their first presidents and to assume greater responsibility for their own political destiny. Differences with the French led many Lebanese to examine alternate political philosophies including Arab and Syrian nationalism, socialism, and others. Nevertheless, the French continued to receive significant support from large numbers of Lebanese, particularly the Maronites.

The French mandate authorities were also instrumental in building the economic and governing infrastructure of modern Lebanon. Roads were constructed, electricity was brought to numerous villages, and the Beirut harbor was enlarged and repaired. A bureaucratic structure that continues to be the foundation of Lebanese public administration was established. In 1943, during World War II, the mandate came to an end, and Lebanon was granted its independence.

Political Environment

The Land

Lebanon has a total area of 10,400 square kilometers (4,015 sq. mi.) and is divided into four major geographical regions: a coastal plain, the Lebanon mountain range, the Biqa valley, and the Anti-Lebanon Mountains. The coastal plain varies in width from more than a dozen kilometers (ca. 7.5 mi.) in the north to almost nothing at some points. Most of the major towns and cities of Lebanon are situated on this plain including the three largest—Beirut, Tripoli, and Sidon. Rising abruptly from the plain are the Lebanon Mountains. Their highest peaks are within 20 kilometers (12 mi.) of the coast, creating a situation where one can be skiing on the slopes and still see the Mediterranean below. The mountains are highest in the north, where the tallest peak is more than 3,000 meters (9,842 ft.), and lower to the south, although Jabal Sanin, which is east of Beirut, is still more than 2,600 meters (8,530 ft.).

To the east, the fertile Biqa valley lies between the Lebanon Mountains on the west and the Anti-Lebanon range on the east. It is the breadbasket for the country. To the north of Baalbek, where the valley is widest, it is watered by the Orontes River, which flows north into Syria. For most of the valley, however, the Litani River provides the main source of water. The Litani flows north to south for most of its length, but about 20 kilometers north of the Israeli border it makes a 90-degree turn and flows westward to the Mediterranean.

The Anti-Lebanon Mountains form the eastern frontier with Syria. They are not as high as the Lebanon Mountains and receive considerably less rainfall. At more than 2,000 meters (6,561 ft.), Mount Hermon, on the Syrian, Lebanon, and Israeli border, is the highest peak. In south Lebanon, the geographical regions are less distinct as the Lebanon mountain range degenerates into the undulating hills of northern Galilee. A small line of hills divides the Biqa valley from the northern drainage of the Jordan River.

The People

The mountains of Lebanon have provided refuge for threatened minorities throughout history. Fleeing from conquering invaders or religious persecution, minority communities have found relative security in the isolated valleys and mountain hillsides of Lebanon, making it a patchwork nation with a mosaic of various groups. Almost all Lebanese now speak Arabic, though some speak another language in the home. The distinctions between numerous factions within Lebanon, however, remain great. The focus of these differences is religion. Religion in Lebanon, however, is more than solely a belief system. It represents a major element of self- and family identity and of communal values as well.

The approximately three million Lebanese are divided into two major communities—Christian and Muslim. Each constitutes about half the population. The Christians are further fragmented into more than a dozen sects. The largest of these are the Maronites, a Catholic sect that comprises more than half the total Christian community and has dominated Lebanon since the modern state was founded.

For the past four centuries, the Maronite population has been growing faster than the ability of this mountainous area to provide a living for the people. As a result there has been migration. During the eighteenth and the first half of the nineteenth century the Maronites moved southward through the mountains until their movement was blocked by the hostile reaction from the Druze community. With this avenue closed many Maronites began emigrating. With independence in 1943, however, the majority of those who previously might have left the country congregated in Lebanon's urban centers. Beirut and its eastern suburbs soon had the largest concentration of Maronites in Lebanon.

The Greek Orthodox community forms the second largest Christian sect. Unlike the Maronites, who retired to the mountains for security after the Muslim conquest of the Levant, the Orthodox remained in urban centers in Syria, Jordan, Israel, and Lebanon where they lived under benevolent Muslim rule. The largest rural concentrations of the Orthodox in Lebanon are in the Koura district southeast of Tripoli, where they form the majority of the population, in the Marjayoun area in southern Lebanon, and in several villages in the upper Metn. The Orthodox generally have more contact with the Muslims than do the Maronites. This stems not only from daily commercial exchanges in urban centers, but also from the wider distribution of the Orthodox throughout the Levant.

These differing approaches to minority status have greatly influenced the political outlook of both communities. The Orthodox rarely deny their Arabness, as do many Maronites. On the contrary, the Orthodox have been in the forefront of those who assert that being an Arab is quite different from being a Muslim. Many of the late-nineteenth-century Arab nationalists were Orthodox Christians. By asserting and stressing the non-Islamic cultural and political heritage of being an Arab, these Orthodox were establishing a basis for giving their community equal standing with their Muslim neighbors. For most Arabs, however, Islam is a vital element of Arab nationalism; therefore, early Orthodox hopes of fostering Arab nationalism without a strong Islamic emphasis have proven fruitless. For similar reasons, Orthodox have been active in ideological movements that transcend national and Islamic borders. The Syrian Nationalist party, which promotes a greater Syrian state including Syria, Lebanon, Jordan, and Israel, has always been predominantly Orthodox. Similarly, intellectually active individuals who were drawn to Western ideologies such as socialism and communism were often from the Orthodox community.

In Lebanon, while many Orthodox have been active in such organizations, a majority appear to have been politically quiescent or have chosen to ally themselves with the larger Maronite community. Even in the latter case, however, the Orthodox generally have exhibited greater willingness to reach an accommodation with the Muslims than have the Maronites.

The Greek Catholics are the third largest Christian community in Lebanon. They generally are inclined to follow the Maronite lead, but as a community do so with less zeal. Greek Catholic villages are more often found in areas that are considerably less defensible than are those of the Maronites. Moreover, they do not dominate any areas, such as Mount Lebanon. Their villages are scattered from the Syrian border in the north to the Israeli border in the south. The only rural area with a concentrated Catholic population is in the hills southeast of Sidon. With the urbanization of Lebanon since World War II, the Catholics have increasingly congregated in Maronite-dominated areas of East Beirut.

The most recent Christian immigrants to Lebanon have been the Armenians. Fleeing the Turks during and after the First World War, they were welcomed into Lebanon, mainly Beirut. Of all the non-Arab groups the Armenians have most ferociously maintained their cultural identity. At the same time, they have been active participants in the Lebanese political scene. Six of the ninety-nine members of Lebanon's last parliament were Armenian. The Armenians have generally avoided becoming overly identified with one political faction or another and have usually supported the forces in power. In this manner, they have assured maximum freedom to run community affairs with a minimum of government interference. In recent years, however, because their community is concentrated in Christian Beirut and its suburbs, the Armenians have been under increasing pressure from various Christian political factions to take a more active role in Christian Lebanese affairs. In addition to the major Christian groups, there are numerous other identifiable sects, but none has a large impact on the Lebanese political system.

On the Muslim side of the political ledger, there are three major groups, the Sunnis, Shi'ites, and the Druze. The Sunni community has tended to predominate to a greater degree than their numbers would merit. The Sunnis are highly urban, probably the most urbanized of any major Christian or Muslim sect. They are concentrated in the large coastal cities of Beirut, Tripoli, and Sidon. There are scattered Sunni villages elsewhere in Lebanon—near Sidon, in the Biqa valley, and northwest of Tripoli toward the Syrian border—but most Sunnis are urban dwellers and as a result they have been more politically active than other Muslims.

The Sunnis also have closer ties to the Arab world at large than do other Lebanese groups. They have been more aware of and in tune with trends in the Sunni Arab world. The Sunnis traditionally have desired Lebanon to play a greater role in Arab affairs, which has resulted in sharp differences with the Christians.

The Shi'ites, who according to some estimates may now be the single largest religious group in Lebanon, are economically and politically the most backward of all the major religious sects in Lebanon. They are predominantly rural and are concentrated in the Lebanese hinterland—south Lebanon and the Biqa valley. They lack the European connections of the Maronites and the Arab ties of the Sunnis. They have generally lacked the political influence necessary to get their opinions heard. Their villages are isolated and poor and those who have migrated to Beirut tend to be poor laborers. Moreover, the Shi'ites have been generally ill-served by their traditional leaders. In recent years, some young Shi'ites have turned to radical ideology to solve their problems.

While Druze are historically an offshoot of Shi'ite Islam, their beliefs have evolved to the point where they neither consider themselves Muslims nor are so considered by other Muslims. Nevertheless, in the political spectrum of Lebanon the Druze are generally placed on the Muslim side of the equation. Despite their relatively small number—something less than 6 percent of the population—the Druze have political influence. They are the Maronites' neighbors in Mount Lebanon, mainly living in scattered villages in the mountains to the east and southeast of Beirut. As a well-organized, tightly knit community and by dint of their reputation as fierce fighters, the Druze have been able to retain considerable political influence despite the relative decline in their numbers.

In addition to his religion, each Lebanese traditionally considers his extended family and his village as the other principal sources of self-identity. Because one rarely marries outside one's religion, family and religious identification are mutually reinforcing. The extended family in Lebanon imposes a sense of mutual obligation and commitment that extends to distant cousins. The family is vital to the success of the individual, giving protection and support to its members in return for their loyalty. The success of one member reflects well on the family as a whole, just as disgrace reflects poorly.

The family has traditionally been the vehicle for political advancement. In order to achieve success, one must have the full backing of his family, and the family that can best muster its total resources is likely to be the most successful in the political arena. The family has also retained many of the welfare functions that in the more advanced nations have been taken over by the state.

Economic Conditions

The Lebanese have a long tradition of being clever merchants and craftsmen. This entrepreneurial spirit, which some date back to the Phoenecians, continues to thrive in the towns of Lebanon. Small shopkeepers, artisans, and the service industries have flourished under Lebanon's free enterprise economy. Although the number of large firms is increasing, the self-employed, family enterprise, or small business continues to be the rule.

Since independence, Lebanon's regional economic role has been enhanced by the ability of the Lebanese to benefit from economic and political developments elsewhere in the area. The independence of Israel and the hostile Arab reaction resulted in the cutting of economic ties between the Arab East and most of the former British mandate of Palestine. The break left a large gap that the Lebanese filled. For instance, the terminal for the Iraq Petroleum Pipeline was transferred from Haifa to Tripoli. More importantly, overland transport and communications that might have traversed mandated Palestine were funneled into Beirut. Avoidance of the Israeli ports in combination with the natural advantages of Lebanon created a boom in the Lebanese economy. Scores of international corporations and banks established regional headquarters in the Lebanese capital.

The Lebanese were also able to take advantage of the growing wealth of the Arab oil states. Beirut supplied a source of entertainment and investment as well as a transit point for good services. Arabs from the Persian Gulf states, Syria, Iraq, and Jordan flocked to Beirut and the neighboring mountain villages each summer to escape the heat. The Lebanese provided these visitors with entertainment and European shopping in an Arab environment. Many of these Arabs purchased homes in the mountains or invested in Beirut.

In the decade prior to the 1975 civil war, Lebanon experienced a rapid growth of the industrial sector. The large oil refineries at Zahiani and Tripoli had been the primary industry for years. In the sixties, an industrial belt began to grow in the poor suburbs that surrounded the city. Most of the enterprises were small and engaged in the production of light consumer goods or textiles, and in food processing. Nearly 10 percent of the population was engaged in such industry in 1975.

The agricultural sector of the economy remains very important. The distinction between rural and urban living is, however, diminishing. Most Lebanese have easy access to a large town or city. Nevertheless, nearly half of the Lebanese earn part or all of their income from the land. Apples, citrus fruit, olives, olive oil, and grapes remain major items of export. The Biqa valley is a breadbasket that supplies the cities with much of the agricultural needs. Most Lebanese farmers are small landholders, although there is a large element of tenant farming in some areas.

One of the more interesting aspects of the Lebanese economy is its perenially large trade deficit. Year after year imports are five times as great as exports. This deficit has been offset in a variety of ways. Lebanese emigrants—both long-time emigrants to the West and temporary residents in the oil-producing states—continue to remit money. The large number of tourists and foreign residents also contributes substantially to the flow of capital to Lebanon.

The industrial and commercial sectors of the economy have been devastated by the civil war. Many of the new industries were destroyed in the fighting. Communications facilities were also damaged. The real loss, however, has been the loss of confidence in the state. Lebanon formerly provided a safe haven of freedom and abundance in a sometimes inhospitable region. This has been lost. Rebuilding the economic structure of Lebanon has begun, but a complete economic revival is impossible until the political issues that plunged the nation into civil war are solved.

Political Structure

The system of government bequeathed to the Lebanese by the French at the time Lebanon gained its independence was modeled after that of France but took into account the peculiarities of the Lebanese situation. The two principal pillars on which the Lebanese governing system is based are the constitution and the informal National Covenant. While the constitution generally establishes a three-branch governmental system, Article 95 gives it a peculiarly Lebanese flavor by providing that religious communities shall be equitably represented in government, employment, and key ruling bodies including the cabinet and the Chamber of Deputies.

The unwritten National Covenant of 1943, however, is the vehicle through which this idea has been elaborated and the unique political system fashioned. The system was one in which each of Lebanon's independent-minded religious communities felt its interests were adequately defended and a fair share of government largesse—bureaucratic positions, public works projects, scholarships, etc.—was received. The impact of this confessional system was felt throughout society.

The unicameral legislature, the Chamber of Deputies, is the primary vehicle used for preserving communal interests. There are ninety-nine deputies in the chamber. The seats are distributed on both a confessional and a geographical basis. They are allocated to the various religious communities on the basis of the 1932 census. A new census has not been taken primarily because several groups fear that their influence might be reduced by the redistribution of power that would follow a new census.

There are currently fifty-four Christian seats to forty-five Muslim and Druze. The Christian seats are allocated as follows: thirty to the Maronites, eleven to the Greek Orthodox, six to the Greek Catholics, five to the Armenians, and the remaining two seats to other Christians. Among the Muslims, the Sunnis have twenty, the Shi'ites nineteen, and the Druze six.

The deputies who are elected to fill these seats are chosen from each of twenty-six geographical districts. Each district has a specified number of seats allocated by religion. For instance, from the district of Jubayl north of Beirut, two Maronite and one Shi'ite deputy are elected. All citizens in the district vote for candidates for all three seats. In some districts, however, a religious confession may not have representation. For example, in Bint Jubayl in south Lebanon, the two representatives are Shi'ites, despite the existence of a significant Christian minority. In other districts, Muslim minorities are similarly not represented by a co-religionist.

The question of minority representation has not been a serious problem because, as a rule, the various religious sects tend to be concentrated in specific areas. Tripoli, Sidon, and Akkar are overwhelmingly Sunni; Batrun, Bsharri, Zghorta, Kasrawan, Jubayl, Metn, and Jezzine are predominantly Maronite. Tyre, Bint Jubayl, Nabatiya, and Baalbek have Sh'ite majorities; and the Koura is predominantly Greek Orthodox. Even in areas of mixed population, villages tend to be almost exclusively a single religious group. In towns, mixed villages, and the cities where more than one religious sect is present, each group tends to live in its own neighborhood or quarter. The representative system that was established under the departing French was thus an attempt to adapt democracy to Lebanese demography.

Higher offices in the government and much of the bureaucracy were also distributed to reflect the religious balance. The presidency, the most powerful office in the land, became the preserve of the Maronites. The president is chosen by the Chamber of Deputies for a six-year term. He, in turn, selects a Sunni Muslim prime minister who then forms a cabinet. The ministerial portfolios also are allocated along confessional lines. Both senior as well as many minor governmental positions in the executive, legislative, and judicial are also distributed on a sectarian basis. Even judges and teachers in schools and universities are recruited with an eye on quotas for each sect.

In addition to confessionalism, the National Covenant also dealt with the issue of the conflicting political, economic, and social orientation of the diverse religious groups. On the whole, the Christians, particularly the Maronites, looked toward the Western nations as their protectors.

They often considered themselves to be a part of the Mediterranean community rather than the Arab world. This attitude was expressed in a virulent form of "Lebanese" nationalism in sharp contrast to "Arab" nationalism. The Muslims, on the other hand, considered this Western orientation unnatural and viewed "Lebanese" nationalism as a denial of Lebanese Arabness and Lebanon's rightful position in the Arab world. The Christian desire to be something other than Arab appeared to the Muslims to be harmful to long-term Lebanese interests. To the Christians, on the other hand, the pan-Arab orientation of the Muslims seemed to sacrifice Lebanon's, and particularly Lebanese Christian, interests to broader Islamic and Arab goals.

The National Covenant thus was designed to reach a compromise between the "Lebanese" and the "Arab" nationalists. In the unwritten agreement the Christians committed themselves not to attempt to alienate Lebanon from the Arab world or to draw Lebanon too close to the West. At the same time, the Muslims recognized Lebanon's uniqueness and agreed not to pressure the government to become overly involved in the affairs of the Arab states.

On top of this peculiarly Lebanese system, the constitution provided the framework for the freest democracy in the Arab world. All Lebanese were guaranteed basic rights that included equality before the law, equal aid, and political rights. Personal liberty and freedom from arbitrary arrest were provided. Freedoms of press, association, speech, and assembly were also guaranteed.

The Lebanese central government was given only limited powers. The system of checks and balances whereby each of the religious communities was secure in the belief that its interests were protected also guaranteed a very weak central government. The central Lebanese government in contrast to most modern states provided only a minimum of services. It was truly laissez-faire. Private organizations, mainly religious, were permitted to provide a wide range of functions such as education, welfare, health services, and when one considers the paramilitary forces of semifeudal regional leaders, even internal security.

Political Dynamics

The Lebanese constitutional system was designed to preserve the existing social order, and this it did very effectively. Political control was concentrated in the hands of traditional leaders of the various religious communities. The replacement of the mandatory regime by the Lebanese government reinforced the position of these traditional leaders. The electoral districts were generally small, permitting traditional leaders to call upon village and family loyalties to win elections. Local and personal ties thus far outweighed national or foreign commitments. The key elements of a traditional leader's political strength were his ability to form a coalition with other traditional leaders that could draw the widest popular support and his ability to provide services to his constituency.

In each electoral district, parliamentary seats were divided by religious sects that in a general way approximated the religious makeup of the district's population. The district of Zahlah in the Biqa valley provides an example.[1] The population of the Zahlah district is one of the most mixed in Lebanon and therefore so was its parliamentary representation. The population is approximately as follows: 23 percent Greek Catholic, 19 percent Maronite, 10 percent Greek Orthodox, 8 percent Armenian Orthodox, 5 percent other Christian minorities, 24 percent Sunni, 10 percent Shi'ite, and 1 percent Druze. The district's parliamentary seats were thus distributed one each to the five largest religious groups—Greek Catholic, Maronite, Greek Orthodox, Sunni, and Shi'ite.

During an election, competing lists were formed by traditional leaders. Each list was composed of one candidate for each seat; thus, in Zahlah, each list had both Christians and Muslims. Other districts were either all Muslim or all Christian, so this multiconfessional listing was not necessary. Nevertheless, in most cases, competition for political influence in a district was between co-religionists. In Zahlah, for example, the dominant local leaders have been two Greek Catholics—Joseph Skaff and Joseph Abu Khatir. Each of these men heads competing lists pitting Maronite against Maronite and Sunni against Sunni.

If the system had been designed so that Christian competed against Muslim, a district such as Zahlah would probably have elected five Christians. In several other districts a large Muslim minority would also likely have been disenfranchised. Conversely, Christian minorities would also probably have been unrepresented.

Another consequence of the list system is that a minority candidate tended to reflect the views of his fellow list members more than those of his co-religionists. For example, a Christian elected from a predominantly Muslim district was more likely to support Muslim pan-Arab aspirations than Christian aspirations for close ties with the West. On the other hand, Muslims elected from preponderantly Christian districts would be Lebanese nationalists. As a result, votes in Parliament rarely broke purely along religious lines.

While support for a candidate was in part due to political, religious, and historical considerations, another important factor was the services he could render. Because the central government has been weak, the parliamentary deputy often became the vehicle through which public services were distributed. The local leader also provided direct assistance in the form of loans and subsidies to his constituents from his own personal funds. In this way, he could build up a solid base of support.

Deputies and party lists also maintained support by the direct distribution of funds at election time. Expenditures include payments to political agents, general expenses, buying bloc votes, occasional bribes, and the transportation to the polling places of supporters residing outside the district. The greatest single expense, however, was the purchase of individual votes. Since most of this money went to those who in all probability would have voted for the list in any case, these payments were more in the nature of a subsidy. Few voters actually searched for the highest bidder.

Independent candidates rarely did well. An independent usually had neither the family ties nor the financial backing to challenge established lists. Another important result of the political system was the failure of truly national parties to take root. Politics remained local, not national. Those few parties with a truly national following, as a rule, were not so much national political parties as nationwide lists led by a prominent politician. For instance, the National Liberal party, founded by Camille Chamoun, tends to be a coalition of local leaders who are personally loyal to Chamoun. Rank-and-file members have often had little contact with one another. Thus, a Shi'ite supporting the party from Tyre is probably a follower of Shi'ite leader Kazim Khalil, who is allied with Chamoun. The individual Shi'ite would have little in common with a National Liberal from the Maronite area in the Chouf and even less contact with him.

A few parties are based on a definite political ideology. These include the Lebanese Communist party, the Syrian Nationalist party, and the pro-Iraqi and the pro-Syrian factions of the Arab Baath Socialist party. These parties have had little electoral success. On the whole, traditional Lebanese leaders have been successful in preventing ideological parties from establishing a strong regional base. The very few members of Parliament who represent these parties were often elected because of family ties rather than party affiliation.

Some parties combine traditional leaders with a party organization. For instance, the Progressive Socialist party has two very distinct elements: those who are moderate leftist in outlook and the traditional Druze following of party leader Walid Jumblatt. While the former tend to dominate the party hierarchy and are certainly the most articulate spokesmen, the latter form the backbone of support for the party. Similarly, the Phalange party combines traditional loyalty to the

Gemayel family with a virulent form of Lebanese nationalism. The Phalange is probably the most successful of all parties at gaining a truly national following. However, while membership is more than the personal following of the Gemayels, the Phalange remains largely a Christian party.

Even most successful alignments and political parties could not come close to dominating the Parliament. A bloc of fifteen members was considered very large. Perhaps a third of the deputies consider themselves as not committed to any coalition or bloc affiliation whatsoever. Alliances are made and broken; a one-time ally can easily become a political foe.

For the most part, the Lebanese political system worked. Most Lebanese were reasonably satisfied that their basic concerns—security and a fair share of government largesse—were provided. Many of the younger Lebanese grumbled about the anachronistic system and felt they were held back by the rigid quota system, but when time came to vote or to seriously alter the system most preferred the status quo.

The one great crisis of the first twenty years of Lebanese independence occurred in 1958. In that year, Camille Chamoun was to relinquish the presidency of the republic, because the constitution prohibits an individual from serving more than one term. Chamoun, however, attempted to force a change in the constitution so that he could succeed himself. He appears to have been motivated mainly by personal ambition. Nevertheless, he also was greatly concerned over the growing influence of Nasserism throughout the Arab world and the strong influence of the Egyptian leader on Lebanese Sunni Muslims; and he therefore wished to move Lebanon closer to the West in order to protect it from regional trends.

Despite Chamoun's attempt to focus on these latter concerns, the key issue in the 1958 crisis became his violation of the National Covenant in which the Christians had agreed not to disassociate Lebanon from the Arab world in favor of the West. In 1958, each community believed the other was breaking the agreement and intercommunal conflict erupted.

By the compromise that ended the fighting, Chamoun agreed to step down when his term expired. The new president was General Chehab, Maronite commander-in-chief of the army. Chehab and his chosen successor, Charles Helou, governed Lebanon for the next twelve years by reestablishing the principles embodied in the National Covenant. Despite the relative political calm and the economic prosperity of this period, however, the fatal flaw in the system began to be uncovered. Though carefully balancing the country's many factions in order to ensure security for all, the designers of the system made it too inflexible. Modification was nearly impossible. As a consequence, over time the political system became less and less responsive to changing political needs of the country.

The 1960s were marked by a rapid acceleration of social change in Lebanon. This change occurred in three areas—population growth, urbanization, and the political awakening of the resident Palestinians. Lebanon's population was growing rapidly with some sects increasing faster than others. Nevertheless, political representation was still based on the 1932 census. Fearing that the delicate sectarian balance would be upset, no agreement on how to conduct a new census could be reached. The Christians insisted that overseas (emigrant) Lebanese be included, since they were mostly Christians, and the Muslims naturally opposed the idea. Even excluding emigrants, some Muslims had doubts as to how their own community would fare. Thus, although nearly everyone agreed that a census was necessary, no one was too anxious to press for one, and as a result, parliamentary representation become less and less representative.

Urbanization and all of its related problems brought major changes to Lebanon during the 1960s as Muslim and Christian villagers flocked to Beirut. The capital's metropolitan area expanded to include between one-third and one-half the country's population. A belt of poor suburbs soon ringed the prosperous core. In each suburb, one religious confession tended to predominate. For example, Ayn Rummanah, Hadath, and Furn al-Shebak were Christian strongholds. Others such as Shiyah and Naba were predominantly Shi'ite.

As elsewhere in the Third World, the poor workers and unemployed of these areas were courted by the ideologues—socialists, communists, and rightists. Most, nevertheless, retained traditional loyalties. They still returned to their villages whenever possible. Families remained an important source of support, and communal identification remained strong. Finally, what little influence these people had on the government depended on the traditional deputy who represented their home village. A person, even a second- or third-generation resident in Beirut, by law, voted in the village of his family's origin.

With growing economic prosperity in Lebanon in the early 1960s, disparity in the distribution of income became noticeable, resulting in the alienation of many of the urban poor. The Shi'ites, who had fled from the south to Beirut fearing Israeli raids and looking for work, in particular became disaffected. The Shi'ites were greatly influenced by Palestinian neighbors in the crowded districts where they lived. Indeed, the Palestinian community proved to be a catalyst for social change in Lebanese society. The more ideologically oriented and militarily powerful Palestinian commando groups provided an umbrella under which Lebanese leftist organizations received direct financial assistance and training.

The transformation of the Palestinian community in Lebanon was another development with which the Lebanese system was incapable of coping. Following the 1948 Arab-Israeli War, more than 100,000 Palestinian refugees fled to Lebanon. Relatively less constrained in Lebanon than in other Arab states, this community grew and to a large extent prospered. The poorer Palestinians, however, never escaped the squalid refugee camps.

Even most of the well-off Palestinians were never fully integrated into Lebanese society. Some took Lebanese citizenship, but these were a distinct minority. Most did not want to be Lebanese; nor did the Lebanese want the Palestinians to remain. While they were welcome guests with whose plight the Lebanese sympathized, most Lebanese considered them aliens. Moreover, a wholesale granting of citizenship would have upset the delicate confessional balance and created severe economic strains. In addition, the absorption of the Palestinians into the Lebanese political system would permit the international community to forget its obligation to the Palestinians, leaving the burden of providing for them totally on the Lebanese.

For the most part, the Palestinian community in Lebanon caused little difficulty until the 1960s. Hope of returning to their homeland rested with the Arab states. The Palestinians were politically docile. In the early 1960s, the realization began to grow among the Palestinians that the Arab states were not fully committed to assisting the Palestinians return to their homeland. Increasingly, young Palestinians believed that if they were ever to see their homeland they must rely on themselves and not the Arab states. These young men formed the backbone of the nascent commando groups. The form of Palestinian nationalism espoused by the commandos, however, did not attract large numbers of active supporters until after the 1967 Arab-Israeli War. The humiliation of the Arab armies at that time convinced even the doubters that the Palestinians had no one to rely on but themselves.

This transformation of attitudes radically changed the Lebanese-Palestinian relationship. The Palestinians armed themselves and exerted pressure on all Arabs for more active support. For the Palestinians, the liberation of Palestine became the central aim of the "Arab struggle." According to their view, all Arabs must direct their energies to this struggle, and any act designed to reach this goal was justifiable.

For many Lebanese, particularly the Christians and rightists, the Palestinians became overbearing. Armed Palestinians on the streets of Beirut became the symbol of Palestinian arrogance. The weak Lebanese government and undermanned army, itself made impotent by sectarian politics, were incapable of dealing with the Palestinian militants. The inability of the government to cope with the situation was underlined by a growing cycle of Palestinian attacks on Israel followed by Israeli retaliation on Lebanon.

The Palestinians were able to use the inflexible Lebanese political system to gain allies among the Lebanese. For many Muslim Lebanese, a political alliance with the Palestinians gave them not only the mantle of Arab nationalism but also the military support of the commandos. For the Palestinians, an alliance with the Lebanese left gave them a foot in the Lebanese political system without becoming part of it. Even a small Palestinian foothold was sufficient to prevent a concerted Lebanese effort to limit Palestinian autonomy in Lebanon. Following a series of inconclusive clashes between the small Lebanese army and the Palestinians, an agreement was reached in Cairo in 1969 between the Lebanese government and the Palestinians that regulated Palestinian-Lebanese relations. The Cairo Accord, in fact, recognized Palestinian rights to operate outside Lebanese sovereignty in some areas of Lebanon.

Because of the failure of the government to assert Lebanon's interests over those of the Palestinians, Lebanese rightists built or expanded their own militias. Of all the Lebanese parties, the Phalangists were most determined to provide sufficient military force to counter the Palestinians. The rightists also moved to strengthen their influence in the parliament in order to force the government to take a firmer stand against the Palestinians. In August 1970, by a fifty to forty-nine vote, a hard-line Christian rightist, Sulayman Franjiyah, was elected president. This election was generally regarded as a victory for the pro-Western "little Lebanon" supporters of former President Chamoun and as a defeat for the coalition of General Chehab that had run Lebanon for the previous twelve years. The rightists counted on Franjiyah, who had the reputation of being very tough, to use the Lebanese army to control the Palestinians.

The Jordanian army crackdown on the Palestine Liberation Organization (PLO) in 1970–1971 had a tremendous psychological impact on all Palestinians. Lebanon had become the only Arab state in which the commandos could still organize and operate freely. Moreover, thousands of armed Palestinians fled from Jordan to the relative security of Lebanon. This influx of armed Palestinians further upset the military and political balance in Lebanon.

Thus, by the early 1970s the stage was set for the Lebanese civil war. The rigid political structure that had proved so effective at preserving the status quo was incapable of adjusting to the changes that had been caused by maldistribution of wealth, uneven population growth, rapid urbanization, and the growing militancy of the Palestinians. Attempts to reconcile the differences failed because the consensus that had been embodied in the constitution and the National Covenant was no longer accepted by a sufficient number of Lebanese and Palestinians.

The years of fighting that have devastated Lebanon since the spring of 1975 have further exacerbated political differences. Moreover, some of the old restraints that had at least prevented the society from disintegrating were ignored. Palestinian commandos became intimately involved in Lebanese politics and fought for one faction against another. Leftist Muslims openly demanded that the National Covenant be dropped. The Lebanese army became involved in sectarian struggles and disintegrated. The Syrians, who many believed wanted to absorb Lebanon into Syria, were invited into the country to bring order. Finally, many Lebanese Christians and rightists allied themselves with the Arabs' primary foe, the Israelis.

Just as significantly, the years of civil strife have done much to accelerate the undermining of the traditional sectarian political and social leadership in favor of those who better represent the popular will. This change will make political reconciliation more difficult. Traditional leaders, Muslim and Christian, generally have enjoyed fairly good relations. Their followers, embittered by years of bloody war, have become hardened against compromise. The new sectarian leaders, therefore, also have come to reflect this hostility. The new leaders, moreover, are increasingly outside the framework of the old parliamentary leadership, who last stood for election in 1972. With virtually no prospect for new elections, few Lebanese believe that the elected government represents their views, and they are increasingly unwilling to follow its unrepresentative and discredited leadership. Thus, before the Lebanese can rebuild their shattered political system, they must build a new political consensus, based on the common interests that link the various communities.

Foreign Policy

The formulation of Lebanese foreign policy has been hindered by the same disagreements that have marked Lebanese domestic affairs. The Christian community has tended to stress the non-Arab Lebanese ties and Lebanon's long-established relations with the West. Moreover, they emphasize the enduring links Lebanon maintains with its large emigrant communities in the United States, Canada, Australia, and Latin America. The Christians have usually preferred to emphasize the differ-

ences between Lebanon and its Arab neighbors rather than similarities. In contrast, the Muslims preferred to enhance theirs and Lebanon's
role in the Arab world. Lebanese foreign policy was therefore a compromise between these two trends as embodied in the 1943 National
Covenant.

The first great crisis in Lebanese international relations occurred in the
late 1950s when elements of both communities broke faith with the covenant. Many Muslims, greatly influenced by Arab nationalism as espoused by Egypt's President Nasser, agitated to move Lebanon closer to
the Arab world. Some even advocated joining with Egypt and Syria in
the United Arab Republic. At the same time, many Christians led by
then-President Chamoun attempted to move Lebanon into the Western
camp, possibly even joining the Baghdad Pact. The clashes of these two
trends were a primary cause of the 1958 Lebanese civil war. Only when a
more moderate coalition of Muslims and Christians took control of the
government and agreed to the reestablishment of the former accord was
peace restored.

Neither the Christians nor the Muslims have yet abandoned the hope
of someday prevailing. During the current civil war the same issue came
to the fore. Unable to prevail on their own, many Muslims have looked
for outside assistance from the Arab states, and some Christians have
turned to the international community, the West, and, as a last resort, to
Israel.

Lebanon's foreign policy has also been determined by geography.
Bordering the Mediterranean, it has been a meeting place for the East and
the West. To play this role successfully the Lebanese have had to maintain their neutrality. They have avoided taking sides in Soviet-Western
disputes or in intra-Arab politics. As much as possible, they attempted to
avoid becoming involved directly in the Israeli-Arab dispute. The
Lebanese realized that to maintain their neutrality they either had to be a
powerful regional state, thereby discouraging neighbors from interfering
in Lebanese neutrality, or they must be so weak so as to make any move
against them a blatant act of aggression. The Lebanese chose the latter
course.

Despite the difficulties in reaching a domestic consensus on foreign
policy, Lebanon has played an active role in international affairs. It was
a founding member of the Arab League and generally placed itself in the
moderate range of the Arab political spectrum. The Lebanese have supported anti-Israel measures by the Arab states in the past but not quite so
virulently as some of their neighbors. As Palestinian influence within
Lebanon has increased, however, the Lebanese attitude has hardened. In
the early 1960s it was often said that Lebanon would be the second Arab

state to recognize Israel; this is no longer the case.

Lebanon has also provided a key regional center for educational institutions, international organizations, and diplomatic activity. Having good relations with the Soviet bloc states, the West, the Third World states, and the Arabs, Beirut provided a center of international communication. The Lebanese took their international role very seriously. They are founding members of the United Nations and have viewed themselves as a bridge between East and West.

Notes

1. See Peter Gubser, "The Zu'ama of Zahlah," *The Middle East Journal,* Spring 1973, pp. 173–189.

Bibliography

Of all the Arab Middle Eastern states none has received more attention than Lebanon. There are dozens of excellent works on Lebanon. A few representative samples are mentioned here. For an understanding of Lebanese history Kamal S. Salibi's *The Modern History of Lebanon* (New York: Frederick A. Praeger Publishers, 1965) should be the starting point. His modern history is concise, well written, and not overwhelming in detail. Salibi is perhaps the finest historian of Lebanon. Since the first publication of *The Precarious Republic* (New York: Random House, 1968) by Michael C. Hudson, it has become the measure by which other works are judged.

Lebanon's political and social development are analyzed in a series of more specialized works. Samir G. Khalaf in "Premordial Ties and Politics in Lebanon" (*Middle Eastern Studies*, vol. 4, April 1968, pp. 243–269) discusses the basic personal family, village, and religious identification of Lebanese and how this self-perception affects politics. Khalaf's work is based on years of experience analyzing Lebanese society while he was a professor at the American University in Beirut. A most sympathetic explanation of the traditional Lebanese political system is found in Elie Adib Salem, *Modernization Without Revolution: Lebanon's Experience* (Bloomington: Indiana University Press, 1973). While this work has obviously been overtaken by events of the last several years, it provides a rare glimpse at the positive aspects of the traditional system. Halim Barakat offers the best short study of the Lebanese political and social systems in "Social and Political Integration in Lebanon: A Case Study" (*The Middle East Journal*, vol. 27, no. 3, 1973, pp. 301–318). Barakat's analysis of the Lebanese society provides an excellent framework for better understanding of the former Lebanese political system and the difficulties in creating a new one. A fine study of the functioning of the Lebanese political system on the village and district level is presented by Peter Gubser in "The Zu'ama' of Zahlah: The Current Situation in a Lebanese Town" (*The Middle East Journal*, vol. 27, no. 2, 1973, pp. 173–189). The author analyzes the function of local political leadership in pre–civil war Lebanon. John P. Entelis discusses the formation and growth of the Phalange (Al-Kata'ib) in *Pluralism and Party Transformation in Lebanon: Al-Kata'ib, 1936–1970* (Leiden: E. J. Brill, 1974). This work offers insights into how the Phalange has managed in recent years to begin the transformation from a traditional personality-oriented organization to a more Western political party.

The Lebanese civil war has already generated considerable literature. Completed in the middle of the conflict, Kamal Salibi's *Crossroads to Civil War, Lebanon 1958–1976* (Delmar, N. Y.: Caravan Books, 1976) provides an excellent study of the trends and events that led to the crisis. In Michael Hudson's short article "The Palestinian Factor in the Lebanese Civil War" (*The Middle East Journal*, vol. 32, no. 3, 1978, pp. 261–278, is presented a concise and well-developed analysis of the Palestinian role in the civil war. Hudson is sympathetic to the Palestinian dilemma in Lebanon. In P. Edward Haley and Lewis W. Snider's *Lebanon in Crisis* (Syracuse, N. Y.: Syracuse University Press, 1979), a series of participants discuss the Lebanese crisis from a variety of perspectives. The book emphasizes the international aspect of the conflict.

11

The Syrian Arab Republic

M. Graeme Bannerman

Historical Background

Syria's history is long and varied. Its capital, Damascus, is one of the oldest continuously inhabited cities in the world. The country has been ruled during different periods by Assyrians, Babylonians, Persians, Greeks, Romans, and, more recently, Ottomans and the French. Modern Syria traces its unique heritage as an independent state to the seventh century Umayyad caliphate. Two years after the death of the Prophet Muhammad in A.D. 632, his followers captured what is now Syria from the Byzantine Empire. The Christian majority apparently welcomed the conquering Muslims. Little pressure was placed on them to convert. In fact, from the perspective of government revenue, it was preferred that they did not.

Following the Muslim civil war of the 660s, Muawiyah, the governor of Damascus, was recognized as the fifth caliph, or leader, of the Islamic community. He transferred the capital of the expanding empire from Arabia to Damascus. Syria thus became the hub of an empire stretching from Spain to India. It achieved a glory hitherto unknown. The regime, however, remained a military elite superimposed on the Christian majority. The rulers lived aloof from the general population. Islamic law applied only to the Muslims while the Christians, as long as they paid taxes, were allowed to follow their own customs and laws.

In theory, Syria could have remained indefinitely a Christian state with an Islamic ruling elite. In reality, there were great economic and political advantages in converting. However, the *mawala*, as converts were called, were not treated as equals by the Arab Muslim conquerors. The failure of the *mawala* to achieve parity with their fellow Muslims was a primary cause for the overthrow of the Umayyad dynasty and its replacement by the Abbasids, who moved the capital to Baghdad. Damascus, once the proud center of the empire, became a provincial capital, a status it continued to hold until modern times.

Following the Abbasid revolution, Syria became a political pawn of more powerful neighboring states. Invading armies entered from Mesopotamia, Anatolia, and Egypt. All left their imprint, but none more than the Shi'ite Fatimid dynasty of Egypt. Conquering the eastern Mediterranean shore in the tenth century, the Fatimids, more than any other Muslim rulers over Syria, propagated Islam by forcing conversion and persecuting Christians. Many Levantine Christians contributed to confessional strife by assisting the invading European crusaders. This tactical error further harmed their relations with the Muslim majority. Thus, in the mid-twelfth century, when Saladin (Salah ad-Din) reconquered the area held by the crusaders, the indigenous Christians were considered traitors and suffered greatly.

Relative stability returned to Syria when it was conquered by the Ottomans in 1516. During the four centuries of rule from Istanbul the foundations of modern Syria were laid. The Ottomans ruled not only Syria but most of the Arab world. The Syrians thus were part of the greater Islamic and Arab arena. The Ottomans gave autonomy to local governors and the various religious groups. Under the millet system personal law and certain civil functions were placed under the purview of a hierarchy of each recognized religious community. In addition, governors of major provinces had great latitude of action as long as taxes were paid regularly to the Sublime Porte in Istanbul. Syria was not one province but several. Aleppo and Damascus were usually competing regional centers. This fostering of regional and communal autonomy has plagued the Syrians throughout their modern history.

As the Ottoman state declined, Western economic, political, and military penetration increased throughout the state. The growth of Western interests in Syria exacerbated divisions. Christians and other minorities developed close associations with the Europeans and benefited greatly. The French established particularly close ties with the Catholics, while the Russians took a protective interest in the Orthodox. The British, for their part, were the protectors of Protestant converts and the Druze. By the middle of the nineteenth century, European interference in Ottoman affairs was direct and persistent. French troops, for instance, landed in Lebanon in 1860 to protect the Maronites. The European powers compelled the Ottomans to establish an autonomous region in Mount Lebanon in order to guarantee Maronite security.

The Arab Muslim majority in Syria supported the Ottoman sultans and resented the advantages enjoyed by Christian minorities. When in the last decades of the nineteenth century Sultan Abdul Hamid II called upon Muslim Ottomans to support the revitalization of the Ottoman

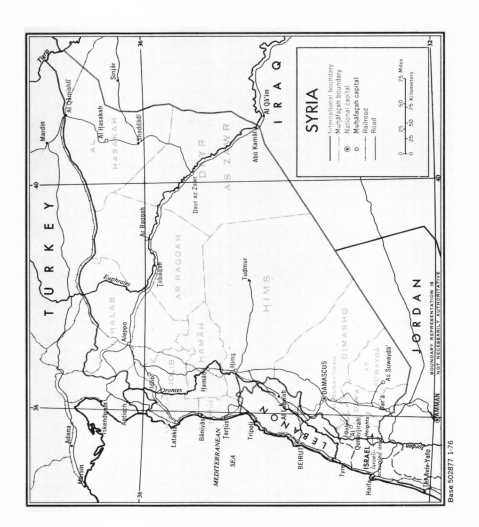

SYRIA

International boundary
Muḥāfaẓah boundary
⊚ National capital
○ Muḥāfaẓah capital
Railroad
Road

| 0 | 25 | 50 | 75 Miles |
| 0 | 25 | 50 | 75 Kilometers |

BOUNDARY REPRESENTATION IS
NOT NECESSARILY AUTHORITATIVE

Base 502877 1-76

state, most Syrians readily gave him their support. As Ottoman territories were lost in Europe, Syria became increasingly important to the Ottoman rulers. Thus, by the end of the nineteenth century much attention was paid to developing Syria's commerce and agricultural wealth. This interest offered added reasons for Syrians to remain loyal to Istanbul.

The key to Ottoman success at that time was the sultan's appeal for pan-Islamic solidarity. However, Islam as a force that captured Syrian minds was soon challenged by the emergence of Arab nationalism. During the last decades of the century, a few Arab intellectuals began to discuss what they called their Arab heritage. They did not deny the importance of Islam to the Arabs or the Arabs to Islam, but they emphasized that being an Arab was something more. Among this group were a considerable number of Christian Arabs who either consciously or subconsciously were striving to find a common identity with their fellow Arabs that transcended religious differences. Despite the fanfare given to this early Syrian pan-Arabism by subsequent historians, most Syrians remained loyal Ottomans, hoping to gain a greater role for themselves and the Arab provinces within the Ottoman state.

The Arab nationalists did not begin to gain widespread support until after the 1908 revolution, when the Young Turks began to implement policies that discriminated against Arabs in favor of Turks. Wider acceptance of Arab nationalism to a great degree was a reaction to the overzealous advocates of Turkish nationalism. Many Arabs, however, still clung to the hope that the Young Turk regime would be based upon Turkish and Arab cooperation. Despite their continued support in the Arab provinces, the Ottoman authorities feared that Arab nationalism in Syria, Lebanon, and Palestine might lead to a revolt. The Christians were notoriously pro-French. Thus, when World War I broke out, Jamal Pasha, a member of the ruling Ottoman triumvirate, was sent to Damascus to strengthen Ottoman control over Syria. His harsh policies, however, drove the population further into the anti-Ottoman camp. In the spring of 1916 the Syrian people were receptive to Sharif Husayn of the Hijaz proclaiming himself king of the Arabs as a means to end Ottoman rule in Arab lands. Few would have supported him several years earlier.

Both the Arab nationalists in Syria and the Hashimites believed that if they rose against the Turks, the British would support the establishment of an independent Arab kingdom. When Amir Faysal, son of Sharif Husayn, led the triumphant Arab army into Damascus in 1918, he was greeted as the liberator of Syria. With the assistance of Syrian nationalists, many of whom had served in the Ottoman bureaucracy,

Faysal established an Arab administration in the interior cities of Damascus, Homs, Hamah, and Aleppo. A French force controlled the coast and the British were in Palestine.

There followed a bitter disappointment that few Syrians have forgotten to this day. The Arab nationalists believed that when the Western nations spoke of freedom, self-determination, and the will of the people, these ideas were meant for all people—including Arabs. Therefore, after the war, when wartime secret agreements dividing the Arab east into British and French spheres of influence were revealed, the Arabs felt betrayed. In a futile attempt to thwart the European plan, Faysal called a general Syrian congress in July 1919. The assembled delegation expressed their wish for a sovereign and free Syria with Faysal as king. In April 1920 at the San Remo Conference, however, the European powers, ignoring the wishes of the Syrians, placed Syria under French control, and in July, after limited Arab resistance, French troops entered Damascus. Faysal and many Syrian pan-Arabists fled. Two years later the League of Nations recognized France as the mandatory power over Syria.

The hostility of the Syrian Sunni Muslim population to French rule led the mandatory authorities to adopt a policy that played upon the divisions within Syrian society. Of all the groups in the Syrian mandate, the Maronites in Lebanon were most friendly. Therefore, the French expanded the border of the Ottoman district of Mount Lebanon and administered the area as a separate entity, although the first three Syrian governors-general simultaneously held the same office for Lebanon. The remainder of French-mandated Syria was then divided into five zones. Each division was chosen to play upon traditional rivalries. Latakia was carved out for the Alawites, Alexandretta for the Turks, and Jabal Druze for the Druze. The Sunni Muslims were divided between Aleppo and Damascus. Moreover, many Circassians were used in the local military force. Thus the Arab nationalists, who were primarily members of the urban educated classes, were isolated from much of the country.

French rule was generally regarded as oppressive. Many of the early administrators had previous experience in either North Africa or the sub-Saharan colonies and drew heavily on this background, which proved inappropriate in Syria. French was introduced in the schools at the expense of Arabic. Singing the French national anthem, the "Marseillaise," was required, and the French franc became legal tender. Embittered Syrian nationalists played upon these obvious symbols of the French presence and won widespread support in their opposition to French rule.

It was not the nationalists, however, who caused the most difficulty for the French. Traditional leaders led a series of minor rebellions. Shaykh Salih ibn Ali led the Alawites, Shaykh Ismail Harir rose in

Hawran, Mulhim Qasim led a dissident movement near Baalbeck, and
the Druze appeared to be in constant revolt. The most serious rebellion
began in the summer of 1925, when rebel Druze tribesmen drove the
French out of the towns and villages in Jabal Druze. The Druze ironically
were not motivated by Arab nationalism but were opposed to the efficiency of French administration in governing their community. Under
the Ottomans they had managed to maintain their communal autonomy.
The Arab nationalists in Damascus, seeing an opportunity to rid
themselves of the French, called upon the Druze to liberate Damascus,
and initiated their own demonstrations in the capital. Despite the alliance
between the nationalists and the Druze, overwhelming French military
superiority symbolized by a bombardment of Damascus extinguished the
revolt by the end of the year.

Thereafter, Franco-Syrian relations remained tense, but differences
were generally played out in the political arena rather than on the battlefield. The next decade and a half were marked by slow progress in attempting to establish a political framework under which Syria could
move toward full independence. A constituent assembly was elected in
1928, but efforts to draft a constitution foundered over the French high
commissioner's refusal to accept several proposals and the assembly's
refusal to compromise. One area of controversy was the Syrians' insistence that all the territories that the French controlled were part of
Syria. This denied the autonomy of Lebanon, Alexandretta, and Jabal
Druze. In 1930 the high commissioner dissolved the assembly and promulgated a constitution based on that of the constituent assembly's draft
but without the offending articles.

The evolution of Franco-Syrian relations took another major step in
1936 when a Treaty of Alliance was worked out. This agreement followed considerable unrest in 1935 and a general strike the next year. The
assumption of power in France of Leon Blum's liberal-socialist government also facilitated obtaining the agreement. Although the French
Parliament never ratified the treaty, it served as a basis from which
future ties evolved.

Nevertheless, Franco-Syrian relations were continually soured by the
issue of autonomous government in Lebanon. A series of weak French
governments also created difficulties. The cession of the province of
Hatay (the Syrian province of Alexandretta) to Turkey in 1939 further
incensed the Syrians. Nearly all Syrians believed Turkish neutrality in
World War II was bought at Syrian expense.

The turmoil of World War II, however, provided the opportunity for
the Syrians to gain full independence. Some progress toward independence was made by the Vichy government, which established par-

tial self-government in 1941 after riots in Damascus. When the free French arrived in the summer of 1941, full independence was promised in order to win popular support. De jure independence was in fact granted that September, but the French still acted as a mandatory power. Although an elected nationalist government came to power in 1943 under President Shukri al-Kuwatly, full independence was not achieved until 1946 when the last French soldiers withdrew. Even then, the British had to prevail upon France to leave gracefully.

Political Environment

The Land

Syria in a geographical sense includes all the states of the eastern Mediterranean shore. Jordan, Lebanon, Israel, and the Turkish province of Hatay (Alexandretta) are part of geographic Syria. To the Syrians, the modern state of Syria is the remnant of the geographical area that the European nation builders left after carving out special-interest areas. Palestine and Jordan were first separated in order to form a British mandate. Lebanon was taken to protect its Christian minorities, and Hatay was turned over to the Turkish minority because of French political considerations.

The boundaries of the modern Syrian state, therefore, have been determined more by political expedience than by geographic realities or by the wishes of the local people. Syria's southern and eastern borders for the most part are arbitrary lines in the desert. In the west, the Syrian frontier with Lebanon generally follows the Anti-Lebanon Mountains northward until it turns west to the sea. Syria's coastline marks its only true natural border. Most of the historical Syrian coast, however, has been given to Lebanon or to Turkey. Syria's northern border with Turkey was drawn at the end of the First World War. A key consideration of the great powers at that time was that the only east-west railroad in the region was located mostly in Turkey.

The Syrian republic is 185,180 square kilometers (ca. 71,000 sq. mi.). Syria can be subdivided into five geographic zones: a narrow coastal plain, a high mountain range, a deep flat-bottomed valley, another range of hills, and the eastward-sloping plain. The eastern four-fifths of Syria is a large plain that gradually declines from west to east. The Euphrates River valley, which diagonally crosses the plain from the northwest to southeast, and the line of occasional mountain peaks running from the southwest to the northeast are the only distinguishing features of the plain.

The key element in the economic development of Syria has been the supply of water. Sixty percent of the country is desert or a semiarid steppe receiving less than 20 centimeters (8 ins.) of rain a year. Heavier rainfall is concentrated in the west and north. This rain is seasonal, with nearly all falling in the winter. Nevertheless, Syria, by Middle Eastern standards, has an abundant supply of arable land and a considerable potential for dry-land and irrigated farming. This land is in the west and to a lesser extent in the Euphrates and Tigris river basins to the north and east. Nearly 80 percent of all Syrians live in the western 20 percent of the country, creating the situation in which western districts are over-populated while manpower is needed in the east. The Syrians are engaged in a constant struggle to push back the edge of the desert.

All of Syria's largest cities—Damascus, Homs, Hamah, and Aleppo—are on the inland side of the two coastal mountain ranges. They have been both regional agricultural centers and entrepôts. They are on the traditional east-west and north-south trading routes. In a sense they are like coastal ports but on the edge of the large Arabian desert instead of the sea. Historically, each has a special relationship with a Mediterranean coastal city. Each could reach the coast through passes in the two coastal mountain ranges. However, political divisions in the twentieth century have created problems for the two largest Syrian cities. Aleppo has been cut off from its principal port, Alexandretta, now Iskenderun, Turkey; and Damascus, to a lesser extent, has been cut off from Beirut in Lebanon and Haifa in Palestine.

The People

In spite of numerous ethnic, religious, social, and geographic divisions, Syria's culture is fairly homogeneous. Ninety percent of all Syrians are Arabs and most of them are Sunnis. The Sunni Arabs have generally been most conscious of their Islamic-Arabic cultural heritage and are the dominant cultural group in Syria.

The Alawites, an offshoot of Shi'ite Islam, constitute between 11 and 15 percent of the Syrian population. They form a majority in the coastal Syrian province of Latakia and have vigorously maintained their religiocultural identity. Some Muslims believe that the Alawites have strayed so far from Sunni (Orthodox) Islam that they are no longer truly Muslims. The Alawites have the reputation of being rugged mountaineers and as such have maintained, through much of history, a high degree of regional autonomy. In recent years, however, the Alawites have played a role in Syrian politics and the armed forces that far outweighs their number.

The Druze, a sect that may have strayed even further than the

Alawites from Sunni Islam, are perhaps 3 percent of the Syrian population. They make up a majority in the area in southwestern Syria known as Jabal Druze, on the Golan, and in Damascus. They too have maintained their autonomy and independent outlook. In addition to the Druze and Alawites there are other schismatic Muslim sects including Shi'ites, Ismailis, and Yezidis, but their influence is limited.

Christian Arabs, who compose about 8 percent of the population, are themselves divided into several groups. Most are Greek Orthodox, but there are also Syrian Orthodox, Greek Catholics, Maronites, Syrian Catholics, and others. The Christians generally live in the urban centers of Damascus, Homs, Hamah, Aleppo, and the coastal area near Tartus. The Greek Orthodox have been active in the development of Arab nationalism and have contributed much to the ideological development of several political parties including the Baath.

The non-Arab portion of the population includes Kurds, Armenians, and less significant numbers of Turkomens, Circassians, Assyrians, and Jews. Perhaps 5 percent of all Syrians are Kurds, who mainly inhabit the mountainous regions along the Turkish border. A significant number, however, live in the Kurdish quarter of Damascus. Like most Syrians, the Kurds are Sunni Muslims. They have, to a limited extent, involved Syria in Kurdish problems with Iraq and Turkey. Tribal identity remains relatively high among the Kurds although most are settled and live in small villages and towns.

The Armenians are the next largest ethnic group but are less than 3 percent of the population, and their number appears to be static or declining. Most arrived in Syria in the early part of the twentieth century fleeing from maltreatment at the hands of the Turks. They had lived in neighboring Anatolia for centuries. Nearly all the Armenians have settled in Syrian cities, with nearly three-fourths of their number residing in Aleppo. The rest are scattered throughout Syria—many in the small towns along the Turkish border. They are Christians, primarily Armenian Orthodox, but perhaps 15 percent of them are Catholics. The Armenians generally are merchants and craftsmen. They have resisted assimilation, clinging to their families and Armenian identity. The failure to identify with Syria and their role as merchants has often strained the community's relations with the Arab majority. Many Armenians have emigrated, often going to Beirut's large Armenian quarter. The Armenian community in Syria is divided, as elsewhere, into two primary political groupings—Hunchaks and Tashnaks.

The Turkomens, who number less than one hundred thousand, originally migrated to Syria from central Asia. They speak a Turkic language and are Sunni Muslims. The Turkomens live primarily in the eastern region of Syria, though some live in and around Aleppo.

The Circassians are Sunni Muslims who fled from the nineteenth-century Russian invasion of their traditional homeland in the Caucasus Mountains. The Ottomans offered them asylum in the Arab provinces. In Syria, most Circassians settled in the vicinity of Qunaytrah in the Hawran region, occupied in large part by the Israelis in 1967. In recent years, the Circassians have increasingly assimilated into Syrian Arab Sunni society.

The Assyrian Christians and the Jews are two additional minority communities in Syria, each of which has a declining population primarily due to emigration. The Assyrians are Nestorian Christians from extreme eastern Syria. They were settled there by the French in 1933 to help them escape persecution in Iraq. Since then many have emigrated to Lebanon. Most of the Jewish community in Syria emigrated after 1948. The once-prosperous community of perhaps forty thousand has been reduced by emigration to roughly three thousand.

The Syrians are also divided by social cleavages—urban dwellers, villagers, and bedouin. The urban dwellers consider themselves the true purveyors of Arab civilization. The cities are the seats of economic and political power. The city dweller believes himself superior to villagers and to the bedouin. The bedouin, nevertheless, are widely considered to embody traditional Arab virtues. Their number and influence are small. In the view of most urban Syrians, the villagers have few redeeming characteristics. They toil on land that they may own but that is more often owned by a leading figure in the village or an absentee landlord. Recent Syrian governments have given more land to the peasants.

Syria has also been plagued with competitive regionalism. The major cities of the interior are centers of regional activities. Homs, Hamah, Damascus, and Aleppo have their own hinterland for which they are the market. Aleppo and Damascus, moreover, have had an intense rivalry for centuries. At one time, Aleppo was the second most important city of the Ottoman state. In recent years, with Damascus assuming an increasing prominence as the capital of all of Syria, Aleppo has been losing ground and is now definitely Syria's second city. Damascus is also drawing away from other regional centers. The Jazira area of eastern Syria, Jabal Druze, and the Alawite mountains of the coastal range are also becoming integrated into the Syrian state.

Despite the fragmented nature of Syrian society there are a growing number of bonds that tie the Syrian people together. To most Syrians the family forms a central place in social organizations. Duty to family overrides nearly all other obligations. Kinship ties are somewhat less in the city than in either the village or tribe; nevertheless, relations among most individuals continue to be governed by family ties.

Since the period of the French mandate, pressure has grown on most Syrians to raise their national identity above traditional particularisms. Family, ethnic, religious, and regional loyalties have been challenged by a wider identity. The concepts of Arabism, Islamism, Syrian nationalism, Baathism, and socialism have forced many Syrians to reevaluate their loyalties. Even more important than these ideological movements in breaking down the barriers between Syrians has been the functioning of a state government centered in Damascus. As greater numbers of Syrians are touched by the central government through conscription, taxes, the provision of services, or through better communications, a sense of loyalty to Syria has begun to take root. Many Syrians are now focusing on their Syrian nationality more than they have previously.

The growth of Syrian national identity, however, has created strains within society. All Syrians feel this new pressure, but the minorities seem to be under the greatest strain because the Syrian national identity has developed a strong Arab-Islamic tone. The emphasis on Islam is natural and has occurred throughout the Arab world. Defense of one's minority status has become increasingly difficult. Some groups, such as the Circassians, the Kurds, and Alawites, have found it easier than have some of the Christian minorities. Many Armenians, Assyrians, and some of the Catholic groups have emigrated, in many cases to Arab but Christian Lebanon. Among the Christians, the Greek Orthodox as a group have had the least difficulty in adjusting.

The process of identifying oneself as a Syrian first is by no means complete. Even among some of the most fervent nationalists traditional ties remain very strong. Many continue to fear that someday Syria could be torn apart by the traditional cleavages. Many were concerned that sectarian tensions in Lebanon could have spilled over into Syria. Others predict that the Sunni majority will someday turn against the ruling Alawite minority. There have been few signs, however, that the Alawite presidents have favored their sect. In fact, they usually have performed well as nationalists with Syrian national interests as their guideposts.

Economic Conditions

With a population of roughly seven million and slightly less than half of its 185,000 square kilometers arable, Syria is fortunate among Middle Eastern states to have a strong agricultural sector. The greatest boon to agriculture in recent years was the completion of the dam on the Euphrates in 1975, which may lead to the eventual irrigation of some 650,000 sq. km. of land. Most of Syria's labor force is in agriculture, although agriculture accounts for only about one-fifth of the gross domestic product. Cereal grains are the major crop, and bread is the staple of the Syrian diet. Cotton, however, has replaced grains as the largest export earner. Syria also produces fruits, vegetables, meat, and wool for export.

Despite years of internal political strife, the Syrian industrial sector has grown significantly though not at a steady pace. The first industry to take hold was textiles, right after World War II. Since then, there has been considerable diversification, including agribusiness, food processing, and tobacco. Syria produces a very small amount of petroleum but collects royalties for the transit of oil from Iraq and Saudi Arabia through a pipeline.

Perhaps the greatest blow to the industrial sector occurred with the massive Israeli bombing attacks during the 1973 war, in which damage was estimated at $1.8 billion. The economy has bounced back, however. With the period of political tranquility under President Hafiz al-Assad, Syria has experienced something of an economic boom. This boom is due to a large extent to the pragmatic policies of the current regime and to luck. In the past, philosophical commitments to the socialist ideologies or economic warfare with other states seriously harmed the economy. While Syria's economy remains a state-directed one, al-Assad has shown greater flexibility in his policies. Syria has moved to open new links to the Western states despite political differences. The vast increase in subsidy payments from the oil-rich Arab states has also helped.

Political Structure

Syria has been marked by considerable political turmoil that has resulted in frequent changes in the Syrian system of government. Nevertheless, since the collapse of the Ottoman state, the Syrians have appeared determined to create for themselves a Western-style republic. At times they have strayed off course and have had a long series of easily replaceable constitutions, but their overall search for a responsive, representative government has not ceased. During the brief rule of King Faysal the Arab nationalists made the first attempt. They wrestled with the same problems that Syrian leaders still face: the need to blend Western and Islamic legal systems in a manner in which minorities are protected but the majority is not harmed; and the problem of the proper balance of an executive with sufficient authority to maintain order without creating a dictatorship. These problems and others have yet to be fully solved.

In 1919 the first Syrian constitution created a limited monarchy.

Because of the almost immediate collapse of the Arab kingdom, however, it was never fully implemented. The next constitution was promulgated in 1930 by the French high commissioner. It created a form of government modeled on the French republic that remained in force with modifications until 1950. In that year, Syria elected a constituent assembly, which studied numerous Asian and European constitutions and drafted Syria's first indigenous constitution. It protected the rights of all citizens, although the president was required to be a Muslim and Islamic law was established as the law of the land. In the 1950s and 1960s, the rapid succession of governments in Damascus promulgated a series of new constitutions and sometimes revived former ones. Typically, when a coup first occurred the new rulers would suspend the constitution for ostensible "security reasons." In all cases, however, they expressed an underlying need to return to constitutional government.

In January 1973 a draft constitution was approved by the People's Council and confirmed by a referendum in March. Many Sunnis, however, objected to the exclusion of the traditional article making Islam the state religion. After some agitation, the critics were satisfied by an amendment that declared that the president must be a Muslim. Islamic jurisprudence was retained as the primary source of legislation and the Arabic character of the state was confirmed. Freedom of religion was confirmed for all groups, however.

The Arab socialist orientation of Syria is retained in the current constitution. The state maintains a great role in the economic sector, as has been the case under previous constitutions. Nevertheless, in response to traditional Syrian reliance on the family and the individual, a non-socialist tradition has been maintained by securing inheritance rights, patents, and copyrights.

The role of the president remained dominant. The president appoints the People's Council on the basis of the will of the Baath party. The members of the Baath party Regional Command (i.e., Syria) are elected. The president also appoints the prime minister and the cabinet, who are responsible to him and not to the People's Council.

The People's Council, which serves as the national legislature, has limited powers. It is at best a watchdog that monitors the actions of the prime minister and his government. It can in theory withdraw its confidence from a minister or the entire cabinet. In practice, however, this is not done, for the president may dismiss the People's Council at any time and then appoint a new one.

The constitution also established an independent judiciary. The appointment, transfer, and dismissal of judges are all determined by a higher judiciary council, that is composed of senior career civil judges.

There are three tiers of courts, the highest being the supreme court in Damascus. On the whole, legislation passed by the various regimes since independence remains in effect. No attempt has been made to restructure the entire legal system. Therefore, law in Syria is based on a combination of Western (mostly French) and Islamic concepts. Many personal cases are still handled by the Shari'a (Islamic courts).

The Syrian civil service for the most part has remained outside politics, and no regime has specifically attempted to politicize it. While nepotism is not uncommon, the general practice has been to employ and advance the most professionally qualified. Repeated government changes and the transition in leadership from the traditional leaders to the Baath has caused some exodus of qualified personnel, however. There are recent indications that after fifteen years of Baathi rule, loyalty to the party has become a key to advancement.

At the local government level, Syria is divided into twelve provinces. Damascus is an independent city that is the equivalent of a province in status. The provinces are divided into districts that in turn are subdivided into localities. In Syria's highly centralized system of government, appointment to the subdistrict level or even to village positions must be approved by the Baath Regional Command Council. Local administration, therefore, has become an instrument for the Baath party to maintain its control at the grass-roots level. In the village, the headman (*mukhtar*), is usually the leading figure or is approved by the village leaders personally. In either case, the Baath must approve the choice.

Political Dynamics

Syria has undergone a major political transformation since independence. The rapid turnover in regimes has led to fundamental changes in the Syrian ruling elite. The clubby traditional leadership has been replaced by the Baath party structure and the military. At independence, political power was monopolized by the traditional Sunni leaders of the major interior cities—Aleppo, Hamah, Homs, and particularly Damascus. They were generally from traditional landholding or mercantile families. Many had reached political maturity at the time of King Faysal, and nearly all had been active in the struggle for independence.

These leaders were divided into two principal groups representing different wings of the elite. The National party was heavily Damascene with a substantial representation of lawyers and industrialists. This party traced its origins to the National bloc that formed a majority in the constitutional convention of 1928. In inter-Arab politics it favored maintaining Syrian autonomy and allied itself with more distant Egypt and Saudi

Arabia. The People's party (originally the Constitutional bloc) formed the opposition. It represented the landed class and merchants of Aleppo. Because of trade ties with Iraq, its members favored a union with Hashimite Jordan and Iraq. Neither group was sufficiently concerned with the Syrian masses, being more concerned with regional and international events, particularly the leadership of the Arab world.

In the nine years following the first Syrian coup in 1949, when Colonel Husni Zaim established a military dictatorship, the National and People's parties were totally eroded. Zaim began the process by disbanding parliament and banning political parties. Zaim's was the first in a long series of military coups that thoroughly enmeshed the Syrian armed forces in politics. A military career became a primary means for political advancement. This has had several significant consequences for Syria. First, the Syrian armed forces have been torn by competing political factions. This has reduced its ability to be an effective force by sending many qualified officers into exile and by promoting on the basis of political loyalty rather than competence. Second, the minorities have been heavily represented in the military. Consequently, minority groups—Alawites, Druze, and Christians—have had a disproportionate influence on government policy. Zaim's coup was welcomed by most Syrians and he was cheered in the streets of Damascus. Syria's poor showing in the Palestine war, quarreling among the political leaders, rising prices, and a general feeling of discontent all contributed to the popularity of the coup. The weakness of the military government, however, was that the army reflected all the divisiveness of Syrian society. After only four and one-half months, Zaim was overthrown by Colonel Sami Hinnawi, who appeared to be a proponent of the old order. Hinnawi, however, was quickly overthrown by another colonel, Adib Shishakli.

Shishakli managed to be either the head of state or the power behind the government for the next four years. His relative success was due in part to his association with one element of the old order—Akram Hourani and his Republican bloc, an offshoot of the old National bloc. Hourani not only gave legitimacy to the regime but he induced Shishakli to introduce a number of social reforms. Moreover, it was under Hourani's guidance that the relatively liberal constitution of 1950 was promulgated. The parliament created by the new constitution, however, gave the old-line politicians a forum from which they could undermine the colonel's authority. Sensing the rising tide of opposition, Shishakli staged a second coup in November 1951 and struck at his opponents. He dissolved parliament and outlawed all sources of opposition, including political parties, student organizations, and trade unions.

Even then, Shishakli felt a need to maintain at least a veneer of traditional legitimacy. He replaced the political parties with his own Arab Liberation Movement, replaced the liberal constitution with one putting more power in the hands of the president, and had himself elected president for a five-year term. Shishakli's heavy-handed rule, however, solidified all factions of Syrian society against him. A coalition of dissidents overthrew him in February 1954.

Although the coalition was dominated by the old-line politicians, a new element had emerged on the Syrian political scene in the form of ideological political parties. Three were of particular note—the Baath, the Syrian Nationalist party, and the Syrian Communist party. Over the longer term, the most important was the Arab Socialist Resurrection party, or the Baath, which was established in 1953 from the merger of Akram Hourani's Arab Socialist party and the Arab Renaissance (Baath) party, led by Michel Aflaq and Salah Bitar. Hourani's party began as a youth group in Hamah and most of its members were personally loyal to Hourani. During the early 1950s, however, Hourani began to espouse more socialist beliefs. He thus brought to the Baath a socialist commitment, experience as a political leader, and a committed following, particularly among the Sunnis in Hamah. Aflaq, the founder of the Baath, was stongly influenced by French leftist philosophy to which he had been exposed as a student in Paris. He rejected Marxism, however, but hoped to adapt his leftist social doctrine to an Arab society.

Aflaq, a Greek Orthodox, became close friends with Salah Bitar, a Sunni Muslim from Damascus. Together they had founded the Arab Resurrection party in 1940. The Baath ideology was not geared solely to the intellectual elite. Three key elements had much broader appeal. First of all, its program of social reform and economic justice appealed to a wide spectrum of the lower classes. Secondly, the Baathis stressed the idea of a greater Arab unity by pressing for political merger. They opposed any form of regional unity that did not have as its ultimate goal a union of all Arabs. Finally, the Greek Orthodox Aflaq recognized the unique relationship between Islam and Arabism. Aflaq structured his ideas upon the common memory of all Arabs of the glory of the golden age of Islam. Nevertheless, the Baathis asserted that discrimination against other religions was unacceptable and thereby promoted tolerance.

The Baathis did not consider their party merely a Syrian party, but rather a pan-Arab party. Much of the leadership's effort was spent winning support elsewhere in the Arab world. They had large followings in Iraq, Jordan, and Lebanon. The strength of the Baath rested in its organization. Bitar was the specialist in administration. The party in each Arab state was designated a regional command. Regional meant the individual states within the Arab nation. The supreme body was the National Command.

In Syria, the Baathis took particular care to organize young military officers. They promoted revolution rather than evolution and in Syria the army remained the key to power.

The chief Syrian rival of the Baathis in the early 1950s was the Syrian National party (PPS). This party, founded in the 1930s by Antun Saadah, a Lebanese Greek Orthodox, favored unity of all geographical Syria, meaning Lebanon, Palestine, Syria, and Jordan. Later, Iraq, Kuwait, and Cyprus were added as part of their scheme to unite the entire Fertile Crescent. The party was tightly organized and conspiratorial in nature but never gained power. The PPS failed for several reasons. First of all, on a practical level the execution of Saadah by the Lebanese government in 1949 deprived the party of his leadership at a crucial moment. Second, the concept of Syrian nationalism was not as strong as Arab nationalism. Moreover, the PPS favored close relations with the West at a time when the Arab world genuinely was attracted to Nasser's policy of leading Egypt and the rest of the Arab world away from the West. Finally, the PPS made serious tactical errors. In April 1955 a PPS army sergeant assassinated Major Adanan Makki, deputy chief of staff and a prominent Baathi. Swift Baathi retribution overwhelmed their rivals. The PPS was accused of plotting a coup d'etat and its influence in the officer corps was eradicated. The PPS never again was an effective force in Syria.

In their attack on the PPS, the Baath was aided by the Syrian Communist party. Founded in 1933, the Communist party had, like the PPS and the Baath, attracted most of its adherents from the minorities—Druze, Kurds, Alawites, and Christians. Also, like the other two ideological parties, it was well organized and in 1955 was probably the preeminent Communist party in the Middle East. Party leader Khalid Bakdash, a Kurd, was elected to parliament in 1954 and became one of its most powerful members. The Communists, however, were handicapped in several ways. First of all, they were considered anti-Islamic atheists by most Syrians. Second, their loyalty to Syrian and Arab nationalism was placed in doubt by ties to Moscow and international communism. Because of these liabilities, Communist fortunes became dependent upon the party's ties to the left wing of the Baath and how that wing fared in intraparty squabbles. The Communist role was also a function of Syrian-Soviet relations.

In 1956, the Baath entered the government for the first time. Shortly thereafter, Akram Hourani became speaker of the house. For the next several years, the Baathis, though outnumbered by the traditional Sunni ruling elite, dominated the government through party discipline and ideological commitment. The Baathis and the traditional leaders were united in their opposition to a shift in Syrian policy toward the Soviet Union and away from Arab nationalism. When, under the growing influence of the Communist and other leftist elements, Syrian policy moved sharply to the left, the Baathis and their allies among the traditional leadership appealed to Nasser to merge Syria with Egypt to forestall what they believed was a possible takeover by pro-Soviet elements. Reluctantly Nasser agreed. In January 1958, Syria and Egypt formed the United Arab Republic (UAR).

The merger of the two states was very unpleasant for Syria, and both the Baathis and the Arab nationalists soon regretted it. The Baathis, who had been riding a wave of success, found their activities increasingly restricted. Political parties were replaced by the National Union, an instrument designed to promote the interests of Nasser. When elections were held in 1959 for ten thousand local committee officers, the Baath received less than 2.5 percent of the votes. In protest over Egyptian control of Syrian affairs, the five Baathi ministers resigned in December 1959. The traditional Arab nationalists of the ruling elite, who had been losing ground to the rising middle class, found the last remnants of its power base destroyed by Egyptian-sponsored policies, which included land reforms.

Elements of the traditional elite, however, managed to foster a coup in 1961 that threw out the Egyptians. In the Syrian nationalist fervor that followed, the traditional parties—the People's party and the Nationalist party—won the two largest blocs in parliament. The election, however, was an aberration. The leadership represented only a small element of society that was of decreasing importance. As the anti-Egyptian feeling waned, political squabbling and governmental paralysis led to popular discontent. This brief interlude was the last hurrah for the traditional Syrian Sunni leadership.

In 1963, a Baathi-supported junta seized control, and the Baath party has dominated Syrian politics ever since. However, the present Baath differs from the Baath of the 1950s in several important aspects. First of all, it is much more broadly based than Aflaq ever desired. Within the party there is a wide spectrum of political opinion and ideology. Moreover, competing loci of power exist: the National Command and the army. The National Command lost some influence, which became apparent in 1966 when Aflaq and Bitar were forced to flee. Nevertheless, the new Baath party encompassed a political spectrum wide enough to include a majority of politically active Syrians.

One aspect of the Baath party that did not change was the disproportionate number of minority members. As a result, Baathi leadership and consequently Syrian leadership has been dominated by the minorities who have been drawn to ideological parties and have been active in the military. The Alawites have been particularly influential.

The struggle for power within Syria has become a struggle for control of the Baath party and the army. This struggle has been both personal and ideological. At times, it has not been possible to separate the two. Generally speaking, there are two wings of the party, a "progressive" wing and a "moderate" wing. When in power, the progressives have pressed for closer ties with the Soviets and greater socialization of society. Their domestic policy has at times precipitated violent antigovernment demonstrations by the conservative Sunni community. The moderates have been more pan-Arabian in outlook and have a more cautious approach to social reform.

Since November 1970 Hafiz al-Assad, currently president of the Syrian Arab Republic, has dominated the Baath regime, bringing a high degree of political stability to Syria. He has ruled with the pragmatism of the moderate wing, dominating the Baathi Regional Command and the army. In order to broaden his political base, he established a National Front within the People's Council with a range of moderate leftist Syrians represented, including such organizations as the Arab Socialists, the Communists, trade unions, and others. In this way, al-Assad appears to have made his potential opponents on the left responsible for government actions without sacrificing Baathi dominance. His policies have done much to transform the Baath from the small, ideological, and closely knit party of the 1950s to an instrument of mass political mobilization.

Foreign Policy

Syrian foreign policy has been largely influenced by two philosophies—pan-Arabism and Syrian nationalism. At times these two doctrines have been mutually supporting, at others conflicting. Neither has been able to dominate totally.

Pan-Arabism was the dominant philosophical force in the Syrian approach to foreign relations in the early years of independent Syria. It appeals for the natural union of all Arabs, emphasizing cultural affinity, opposition to the Zionist expansion in Israel, and resistance to Western imperialism. Syrian pan-Arabism developed along two lines—Islamic Arab nationalism as envisioned by the Sunni urban majority who dominated Syria at independence and Baathi ideological Arab socialism. These two forces dominated Syria until the late 1950s. They carried Syria into the union with Egypt and rejected formal alliances with non-Arab states, whether the Soviet Union or the West. Nevertheless, the Baathis felt philosophically more at ease with the socialist states than with the West.

Like Arab nationalism there were two trends in Syrian nationalism. The first was exemplified by those who believed in the union of geographical Syria. This tendency was best expressed by the PPS, but that party's fortunes have faded. The other strain of Syrian nationalism identified with the Syrian Arab Republic. As the Syrian people have become increasingly accustomed to thinking of Syria existing within its current geographical limits, loyalty to the Syrian Arab Republic has grown and this perception of Syrian nationalism has increasingly gained favor. These "little Syria" nationalists began to gain dominance during the union with Egypt. Few Syrians had realized the extent to which they identified with their own government in Damascus until it became evident that Egyptian policy was not necessarily in the Syrian interest. Syrian nationalism was the banner around which antiunion forces rallied, leading to the breakup of Nasser's United Arab Republic.

The revolution of 1963, which brought the Baathis to power, was in effect a turning away from narrow Syrian nationalism in favor of broader Arab national goals. By this time, however, Syrian nationalism was firmly rooted even within the Baath party. The 1966 Baathi coup was a victory for the Syrian nationalists within the party and led to the exile of the old-line Arab nationalist Baathis, including Aflaq and Bitar. When al-Assad took power in 1970, he moved Syria even further away from Arab nationalism in favor of Syrian self-interest.

The ascendency of either Syrian national views or Arab national views did not mean that the other philosophy was totally disregarded. The difference was in emphasis. Each continued to influence Syrian policy and the Syrian people. For instance, in 1976, despite the outcry from the other Arabs, al-Assad could send his troops into Lebanon and fight pitched battles with the Palestinians because Syria's basic national interests were threatened by events in Lebanon. Nevertheless, this policy of ignoring the other Arabs could not be sustained over time; therefore, Damascus welcomed the opportunity to return to the Arab fold under the standard of Arab unity and Arab nationalism following the October 1976 Riyadh Summit.

No matter which philosophical tendency took precedence at a specific time, Syrian foreign policy has been dominated by two related issues—Israel's and Syria's roles in Arab politics. The question of the fate of the Palestinians and the future of Israel is of greater importance to the Syrians than to other Arabs for several reasons. First, the peoples of

Palestine and Syria share a common ancestry. Palestinian Arabs and Syrian Arabs have been buffeted throughout history by the same forces. Therefore, the plight of the Palestinians is deeply felt. Second, the Syrian people have the feeling that they are in competition for geographical Syria. Israeli occupation of Palestine, which was cut out of Syria by the Europeans, was only a first step in Israeli expansion. Israeli occupation of Golan in 1967 and Israel's actions in south Lebanon have more recently confirmed most Syrians' fears of sinister Israeli intentions.

After the Israel issue, the most serious foreign policy question is that of Syria's role in the Arab world. Since independence the Syrians have been committed to pan-Arabism. The Syrians perceive that Damascus must play a leading role in effecting Arab unity. This view has brought them into sharp conflict with all of their Arab neighbors at one time or another. Although these differences have been intense, they can be put aside very quickly if necessary.

Syria's relations with the great powers have been colored by the Arab-Israeli conflict, Syrian antiimperialism, and the political philosophy of their leaders. As a result, the Damascus regime continues to find more in common with the socialist countries than with the West. Nevertheless, under al-Assad, Syria has attempted to improve relations with the United States and Europe. This action has provided a Western balance against Soviet attempts to dominate Syria as well as providing economic balance.

Bibliography

A good place to begin looking more deeply into the politics and government of Syria is in one of several general studies. Tabitha Petran's *Syria* (New York: Praeger Publishers, 1972) is one of the general survey books in the Nations of the Modern World Series. It is an excellent introduction with some very good sections. Other works that provide a good introduction to the history of Syria include A. L. Tibawi, *A Modern History of Syria Including Lebanon and Palestine* (New York: St. Martin's Press, 1969) and Anne Sinai and Allen Pollack's *The Syrian Arab Republic* (New York: The American Academic Association for Peace in the Middle East, 1976). The latter is a collection of essays on Syrian history, government, ideology, the economy, and population that provide a wealth of information. The essays are uneven, however.

Several more scholarly specialized works delve into particular aspects of the Syrian experience. In *The Struggle for Syria* (New York: Oxford University Press, 1965), Patrick Seale analyzes the regional and internal factors leading to the union with Egypt in 1958. At times the wealth of detail is overwhelming, however. Gordon H. Torrey, in *Syrian Politics and the Military: 1945–1958*

(Columbus: Ohio State University Press, 1964) looks at the same period but with an eye more keenly focused on competition within the Syrian military and between the military and traditional landowning and commercial elites. In *Syria Under the Ba'th, 1963–66: The Army-Party Symbiosis* (New York: Halsted Press, 1972), Itamar Rabinovich analyzes the crucial period of Baathi rule following the 1963 coup and the very special relationship between the party organization and the military.

Two of the many articles on Syria are worth special note. Moshe Maoz's "Attempts at Creating a Political Community in Modern Syria" (*The Middle East Journal*, vol. 26, no. 4, 1972, pp. 384–404) is an excellent place to begin to understand the ebb and flow of independent Syria. Michael H. Van Dusen in "Political Integration and Regionalism in Syria" (*The Middle East Journal*, vol. 26, no. 2, 1972 pp. 123–136) provides the best short study on the problem of regionalism and how it affects the Syrian nation. At the same time, the author analyzes how national leaders have used their position to enhance personal influence in their traditional regional power base.

12

The Hashimite Kingdom of Jordan

M. Graeme Bannerman

Historical Background

The kingdom of Jordan is another of the successor states of the Ottoman state. The territory east of the Jordan River, however, has a reputation dating back several millennia of being the crossroads between the Mediterranean to the west, the Orient to the east, and Arabia to the south. The ancient biblical kingdoms of Gilead, Amman, Moab, and Edom were largely located in present-day Jordan. Because of its relatively remote though strategically important location, the area was usually the last conquered and the first abandoned as the great ancient empires ebbed and flowed. Egyptian, Hittite, Assyrian, Persian, Greek, Roman, and Byzantine soldiers all occupied the region.

Of all the states of antiquity, the Nabataean Arabs were probably the most direct ancestors of modern Jordanians. Shortly after 800 B.C., the Aramaic-speaking inhabitants of Petra, southeast of the Dead Sea, created their kingdom along the key north-south trading routes, maintaining their independence until conquered by the Romans under Pompey in 64 B.C.

The Islamic conquest of the area has had the greatest impact in sociological terms. The battle of Yarmuk in northern Jordan in A.D. 636 expelled the Christian Byzantines and laid the groundwork for the establishment of Islam as the religion of a majority of Jordanians. At various times, the area was ruled from Damascus, Baghdad, Cairo, Jerusalem, and Istanbul. Under Ottoman rule, southern Jordan was governed as part of the Hijaz while the north was included in the province of the Damascus governorate.

Like the countries of the rest of the Levant, the modern Jordanian state emerged as a result of collapse of the Ottoman state in World War II. Arab tribesmen under Amir Faysal, son of Sharif Husayn (al-Hashim) of the Hijaz and advised by the famous Lawrence of Arabia, marched northward against the retreating Ottoman forces. When Faysal's army defeated the Ottomans and conquered Aqabah and Amman, the tribes east of the Jordan quickly joined the Arab revolt against Istanbul. By the end of the war nearly all of current Jordan was in Hashimite hands. Nevertheless, Jordan's destiny was determined by other forces. By the terms of the Sykes-Picot Agreement of May 1916 the Levant had already been divided into British and French spheres. What is now Lebanon and Syria came under French control while Palestine eastward to Iraq was to be under the British. At that time, few considered the area east of Jordan a separate entity. To the Arabs, it was part of greater Syria that included the present states of Israel, Jordan, Lebanon, and Syria; to the British and the European Zionists, it was an integral part of Palestine.

Amir Faysal, who attended the 1919 Paris Peace Conference, pressed for the complete independence of the Levantine Arabs, basing his arguments on President Woodrow Wilson's Fourteen Points promoting self-determination for all people. Arab independence was also promised in the wartime correspondence between Sharif Husayn and the British government (the McMahon correspondence). Faysal failed to win his point against British and French imperial aspirations and Zionist demands for a homeland. Nevertheless, the Arabs were prepared to assert their independence without European acquiescence. In March 1920, a group of Arab nationalists convened the General Syrian Congress in Damascus and declared the independence of Syria (including Jordan and Palestine) and Iraq. The decision was opposed by Britain and France, and in the following month at the San Remo Conference the Levant was divided in accordance with the Sykes-Picot framework while ignoring the Arab declarations and British promises. Palestine and what is now Jordan were effectively separated from Syria. In July 1920, an Arab force was defeated by the French, thus destroying Arab hopes for political independence in the Levant.

The status of Jordan remained unclear at that time. The British position was not fully defined, and in the next several years Jordan was at times administered as part of the Palestine mandate and at other times treated separately. The British felt some obligation to the Hashimites for unkept wartime promises and feared a possible worsening of Anglo-French relations if Arab attacks on Syria were launched from Jordan. Amir Abdallah, the brother of King Faysal of Syria, was in Jordan organizing the tribes to strike at the French in Syria. The British, realizing such an attack was not in their interest, offered Abdallah (who was very popular with the Jordanian tribes) the opportunity to be the amir of Transjordan. In this way, Anglo-French difficulties were limited and British promises to the Hashimites were partially met. Abdallah ac-

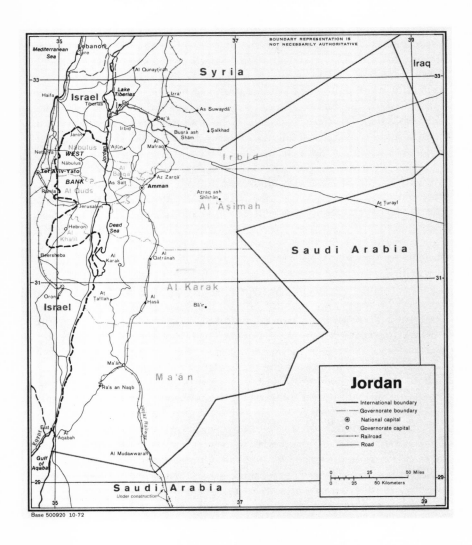

BOUNDARY REPRESENTATION IS
NOT NECESSARILY AUTHORITATIVE

Mediterranean
Sea

Lebanon
Tyre

Al Qunaytirah

Syria

Iraq

Haifa

Israel

Lake
Tiberias
Tiberias

Izra'

As Suwaydā'

Dar'ā

Irbid

Buṣrá ash
Shām

Ṣalkhad

Janin

Nablus
WEST
Nablus

Ajlūn

Al
Mafraq

Netanya

Irbid

Tel Aviv-Yafo
BANK
Ramla
Al Quds

Al
Balqa'
As Salt

Amman

Az Zarqā'

Jerusalem

Azraq ash
Shishān

At Ṭurayf

Hebron
Al
Khalil

Dead
Sea

Al 'Āṣimah

Saudi Arabia

Beersheba

Al
Karak

Al
Qaṭrānah

Al Karak

Oron
At
Tafilah

Al
Ḥasā

Bā'ir

Israel

Ma'ān

Ma'ān

Ra's an Naqb

Jordan

——— International boundary
--------- Governorate boundary
⊙ National capital
○ Governorate capital
·–·–·–· Railroad
——— Road

Elat
Al
Aqabah

Al Mudawwarah

Gulf
of
Aqaba

Saudi Arabia

Under construction

0   25   50 Miles

0   25   50 Kilometers

cepted because an emirate in Jordan was a tangible gain and he had little chance of displacing the French from Syria.

The establishment of a governmental system for the new emirate took much time and effort on the part of the British. Being politically cut off from Syria, with whose government its people had been traditionally associated, Transjordan lacked a national identity and had practically no economic base. The few Arab administrators who were in Jordan were those who had fled from the French invasion of Damascus and were generally more concerned with reasserting Arab control in Syria than with making Jordan an independent self-sufficient state. On the economic side, less than 3 percent of the land was under cultivation and with virtually no other economic assets in the country, the new government was heavily dependent on British economic support.

Thus, when Britain recognized Transjordan as a self-governing state on May 15, 1923, Amir Abdallah was in no position to run a country. National borders were ill-defined. His father's kingdom of the Hijaz to the south was collapsing before the followers of Ibn Saud, and he lacked the resources to assist his father or to protect his own interests. His nation, moreover, was totally dependent on a British subsidy. Therefore, though recognized as self-governing, Jordan was, in fact, governed by the British.

The British were primarily interested in maintaining stability. The prospect of chaos and anarchy—or worse, some rival power assuming control of Transjordan—forced London to take a more active interest in the fledgling country than it might otherwise have done. The British goal was to establish an effective local administration and thus reduce what was considered a drain that the British treasury could ill-afford. British policy, therefore, was to provide British officials to train a pro-British local administration and military force that would become financially and politically independent while remaining friendly to London.

With the assistance of a small but devoted group of British officials, Transjordan under Amir Abdallah made slow but steady progress toward true independence. At first the administration was simple. Abdallah ruled with the advice of a small executive council. British officials handled defense, foreign affairs, and finance.

A major step toward real independence was a new treaty in 1928 between the British and Abdallah. Under the agreement, however, London retained the right to oversee finance and foreign policy and British officers still controlled the Arab Legion. In the same year, the Organic Law of 1928 was promulgated. This law took the first steps toward a representative government by providing for a legislative council to replace the old executive council.

In the early 1930s the progress toward independence continued as Transjordan gained the right to send consular representatives to other Arab countries. In May 1939 the legislative council was converted to a council of ministers or a cabinet. Although actual rule continued to rest with the amir and the British, a loyal opposition composed of Arab nationalists evolved during the 1930s. Their most prominent vehicle for dissent was the Istiqlal (Independence) party, which was also active in Palestine and Syria.

Throughout the period, Amir Abdallah demonstrated ambitions greater than just ruling a small desert kingdom. He envisaged a broader role for his dynasty, possibly even the reestablishment of the caliphate. His immediate ambitions were directed at regaining the Hijaz from the Saudis and at reestablishing the Arab kingdom of his brother Faysal in Syria. During World War II, Transjordan played an influential role in inter-Arab affairs. The Arab Legion, as Transjordan's army was called, helped suppress the pro-German revolt of Rashid Ali in Iraq, and Abdallah also was instrumental in the formation of the Arab League. The Arab League was the first concrete step toward Arab unity, and Abdallah envisioned the reunification of the Arabs under the Hashimites. His wholehearted cooperation with the British stemmed in part from a belief that as a result of his cooperation he could become ruler of an independent Arab state composed of Syria, Lebanon, Palestine, and Transjordan—and subsequently of Iraq as well.

Abdallah's ambitions proved unrealistic, for opponents to such a scheme included the Zionists, the Syrian nationalists, the Lebanese Christians, the Saudis, the Egyptians, and the French. Thus, Abdallah had to be satisfied with achieving total independence for Transjordan and his recognition as king. In 1946, Transjordan and the United Kingdom reached a new agreement whereby the Organic Law of 1928 was replaced by a constitution and Abdallah was recognized as king of Transjordan. Two years later, London agreed to continue paying a subsidy in return for British access rights to two military bases.

The rising crisis in Palestine became the dominant concern of the fledgling state. Abdallah's policy toward Palestine differed from that of the other Arab states. His position appears to have been based on a sense of realism and on a deep commitment to Transjordan's vital links with Palestine. Nevertheless, he complied with the will of the Arab League and sent his forces into Palestine when war broke out in 1948. Of all the Arab armies, Abdallah's forces were the most successful. When the fighting halted, the Arab Legion held perhaps 20 percent of Palestine including the old city of Jerusalem.

On April 24, 1950, Abdallah unilaterally annexed the portion of

Palestine held by his forces and changed the name of his nation to the
Kingdom of Jordan. This action unequivocally altered the history of the
country, and its political, social, and economic structure as well. The
total number of Palestinians, including refugees from Israeli-held areas,
and the inhabitants of Jordan's newly-acquired West Bank (annexed
Palestine) outnumbered the Transjordanians. More importantly, most
other Arabs joined the Palestinians in believing that Abdallah had
betrayed them. Jordan became a pariah among the Arab states with only
the fellow Hashimite regime in Iraq offering support.

The annexation of the West Bank was for Abdallah the natural
outgrowth of his greater Syrian policy. In the same vein, he alone among
the Arab rulers extended full citizenship rights to the Palestinians.
However, he was detested by the Palestinians for what they perceived to
be his self-serving action and his betrayal of their Palestinian national
rights. The other Arabs opposed him as much for his greater-Syrian ambitions as for his role in Palestine. The Arab League so vehemently opposed the annexation that Jordan was nearly expelled. An agreement was
reached with the Arab League when Jordan agreed that it was merely
holding the West Bank in trust and Abdallah promised that he would
forego any separate nonaggression pact with Israel. The Palestinians,
however, never forgave him. While he was praying in Jerusalem on 20
July 1951, he was assassinated by a vengeful Palestinian nationalist.

The smooth transition of power from Abdallah to his oldest son,
Talal, was a reflection of the stability of the Hashimite state, primarily
based on the loyalty of the British officers and Arab Legion. Under Talal,
a new constitution was promulgated in January 1952. Talal, however,
had a long history of mental illness and under doctor's advice abdicated
in favor of his son Hussein, who was still a minor. A regency council of
three was formed to govern for several months until the young Hussein
reached maturity and assumed the throne in May 1953.

Political Environment

The Land

The 95,594 square kilometers (ca. 36,900 sq. mi.) of the Hashimite
Kingdom of Jordan form part of the north Arabian plateau that Jordan
shares with its neighbors: Syria to the north, Iraq to the east, and Saudi
Arabia to the south. There are no natural frontiers between Jordan and
its Arab neighbors. The western border of Jordan is the Rift Valley
through which the Jordan River flows. From an average of 600–900
meters (2,000–3,000 ft.) on the plateau, the landscape plummets to well

below sea level in the valley. The Great Rift Valley also includes the Dead Sea and the Gulf of Aqaba to the south. Jordan's only coastline is a 19-kilometer (12-mi.) stretch on the gulf including the port of Aqaba. Beyond the Great Rift Valley lie Israel and the West Bank highlands.

Rainfall is the most important climatic determinant. More than four-fifths of Jordan is desert or semidesert receiving less than 10 centimeters (ca. 4 in.) of rain annually. Prevailing westerly winds draw winter rains to the northern areas of the country; but in the south, dry winds from the Sahara are the rule. Consequently, Jordan's population is concentrated in the northwestern corner of the East Bank and on the West Bank where rainfall, averaging about 30 to 41 centimeters (12–16 in.) annually permits some farming. All of Jordan's major cities—Amman, Irbid, Zarqah, and the West Bank towns—are concentrated in this area. Some attempt has been made to expand the area of settlement and cultivation. Of particular note are the reforestation projects north of Amman and the East Ghor irrigation canal project in the Jordan River valley. Moreover, plans are being developed to dam the Yarmuk River, which forms a portion of the borders between Jordan and Israel, and Jordan and Syria. This project could enhance the supply of water available for irrigation. Already, the smaller Zarqah River is being used to provide water for the lower Jordan valley. In both cases, however, available water is limited.

Jordan is also poor in minerals and fuels. It has no commercially exploitable oil. There are small manganese ore and copper deposits near the Dead Sea. Phosphates, located at Wadi al-Hasa, are the only large earners of foreign currency other than tourism.

The People

Although most Jordanians are of Arab heritage, they may be roughly divided into two principal groups: Palestinians and East Bank Jordanians. Palestinians are those who lived in the British mandate of Palestine and who have been under Jordanian sovereignty since 1948. These include both the refugees who fled from the Israelis and the inhabitants of the West Bank. By 1967, these Palestinians constituted perhaps two-thirds of the entire population of Jordan. Throughout the period of Jordanian sovereignty over the West Bank, a continuous migration from the West Bank to the east occurred. Amman's population grew from 250,000 in 1961 to 350,000 just prior to the 1967 war. At the same time, the West Bank proportion of the total Jordanian population declined from 62 percent in the late 1940s to 47 percent in 1961. As a result of the 1967 war another 200,000 to 250,000 Palestinian refugees entered the East Bank. The Palestinians now constitute more than half of the total East Bank Jordanian population. Forty percent still live in the

United Nations Relief and Works Agency (UNRWA) camps. The remaining 60 percent are more assimilated into the general population.

Since 1948, Jordan alone among the Arab states has given full citizenship to all Palestinians. No official distinction was made between Palestinians and East Bank Jordanians. Palestinians were afforded the same political and economic opportunities as were all Jordanians. Because of their industry and generally higher level of education, the Palestinians have played a preponderant role in many aspects of Jordanian society despite their traditional antipathy for the monarchy. For example, they have dominated the fields of education, medicine, and the civil service.

Between 1948 and 1967 there was a gradual assimilation of the Palestinians into the rest of Jordanian society. Even the Jordan Arab Army (as the Arab Legion was renamed), the backbone of support for the monarchy, witnessed a growing number of Palestinians in the officer corps. The 1967 Arab-Israeli War, resulting in Israeli occupation of the West Bank, slowed the trend, but did not stop it entirely. Many of the present business and government leaders on the East Bank are of Palestinian origin.

The East Bank Jordanians are, nevertheless, the rock upon which the Hashimite monarchy is built. Unlike the Palestinians, who include a sizable number of Christians, most East Bankers are Sunni Muslims. Most are also members of several hundred Arab tribes. Although today a majority of East Bankers have settled and live in Amman or in the agricultural regions to the northwest of the capital, the bedouin tradition is still strong. Bedouin values and virtues continue to have an important influence on society. Those who continue to live a nomadic life and those who have settled maintain these values. In Jordan, more than any other state of the Fertile Crescent, the tribal elements, who provide a disproportionate number of recruits for the military and are guaranteed representation in government, influence government policy.

Two minority elements on the East Bank—the Christians and Circassians—have also provided backing for the Hashimites. Jordan's Christian population is urban and has lived in the area for centuries. Some are the descendants of early converts to Christianity while others allegedly descend from the crusaders. They are predominantly Greek Orthodox and Greek Catholic.

The Circassians settled in Jordan in the last decade of the nineteenth century. They were part of about one million Muslims who fled the Caucasus when the Russians captured it from the Ottomans, and were given land by the Ottoman sultan in what is now Jordan and Syria. The Circassians are Sunni Muslims and generally have been accepted by their

Arab neighbors. Although they did come into conflict with unruly bedouins from time to time, they have been traditionally loyal to the monarchy and have held very senior positions in the government. They are particularly numerous in the armed forces as well as in the police force in Amman. The Circassians are divided into groups, the Adigah and the Chechen. Both are guaranteed representation in Parliament.

While rivalries have existed between bedouin tribes, between the bedouin and the Circassians, and between the nomads and villagers, the East Bank Jordanians are united in their support for the monarchy and resistance to Palestinian domination of Jordan. In recent years, many East Bankers have welcomed the loss of the West Bank. These elements stress their belief that political benefits to Jordan from the loss of the West Bank outweigh the economic liabilities.

Economic Conditions

Despite the harsh climatic conditions, Jordan remains primarily an agricultural country. About 40 percent of the work force engages in agriculture, forestry, and herding. They contribute perhaps a quarter of the gross domestic product (GDP) and 50 percent of the exports. Agricultural production, however, is very erratic due to political events and to the unreliability of rainfall. For instance, since 1967 cereal production has varied from 56,000 tons in 1973 to 297,000 tons in 1967. Several dams have been constructed and several more are planned in order to better utilize scarce water.

Prior to 1967, the country appeared to be well on its way to becoming economically self-sufficient. The loss of the West Bank was a harsh blow to Jordan's economy, however. Before 1967, the West Bank accounted for 60 to 80 percent of the country's agricultural land, 75 percent of the GNP, 40 percent of the government's revenue, and nearly one-third of its foreign currency income. The hope for self-sufficiency has all but vanished.

Jordan's small industrial and mining sector was not severely hurt by the loss of the West Bank. The nation's oil refinery, the national power plant, and the important phosphate mines are on the East Bank. In addition, most of the larger manufacturing facilities are located between Amman and Zarqah. These include textiles, leather, batteries, food processing, brewing and bottling, and cigarette manufacturing. While progress is being made in developing resources, Jordan's potential remains modest.

In order to maintain its standard of living, Jordan has become increasingly dependent on foreign subsidies and remittances from Jordanian workers who are employed abroad, primarily in the Persian Gulf states. The lure of the work outside Jordan, however, has drawn a sufficient number of men away so as to create a labor shortage in some fields.

Political Structure

Jordan is a constitutional monarchy. The current constitution, promulgated in 1952 during the brief reign of King Talal, gave increased authority to Parliament. Nevertheless, ultimate authority over the legislative, executive, and judicial branches was retained by the monarch.

Executive power is primarily vested in the king. He appoints the prime minister and members of the cabinet and has the power to dismiss members of the cabinet. Power to dismiss the prime minister is vested in the Parliament. When the Parliament is suspended, the king assumes this responsibility. The king's considerable powers include the right to sign and promulgate laws, veto legislation, issue royal decrees (with the consent of the prime minister and four cabinet members), approve amendments to the constitution, command the armed forces, and declare war. He also appoints and dismisses judges.

The question of royal succession is also addressed in the constitution. The throne is guaranteed through the eldest male in direct line from King Abdallah. Should there be no direct male heir, the eldest brother becomes king. On occasion, the king has altered this formula by decree. In 1965, Hussein changed the order of succession by removing from the line of succession his two sons from marriage with an English woman. He also placed his more competent brother Hassan ahead of Muhammad, the second eldest brother. If a king is either a minor or incapacitated for more than four months, a regent or regency council is established.

The council of ministers is empowered to perform necessary operational matters in the absence of a royal decree. The council, which consists of the prime minister and a variable number of ministers, shares executive responsibilities with the monarch. The cabinet's area of responsibility includes all affairs of state in implementing the policies of the king and prime minister. Its members can be appointed and dismissed by the king, but the entire cabinet can be brought down by a vote of no confidence in the lower house of the legislature.

Under the constitution, Jordan has a bicameral national assembly. The lower house, known as the House of Representatives, is elected by popular vote. Since 1973 women have had the right to vote. Representatives are elected for four-year terms. Minority rights are protected. Since the 1928 constitution, Circassians have been guaranteed representation. The current constitution not only provides for Circassian, but also Christian and bedouin representation. The sixty members of the lower house are elected from three bedouin districts and fourteen regular districts. Each bedouin district selects one representative from the local tribes. The other fifty-seven representatives are elected from the fourteen regular districts—seven on the West Bank and seven on the East Bank. Seats are distributed within these districts in order to guarantee representation by Christians and Circassians. In Amman, for instance, there are eight representatives—two Christians, one Circassian, and five Arab Muslims.

The upper house is called the Senate. This body is appointed by the king and cannot be more than one-half the size of the lower house. The prime minister originates legislation and submits proposals to the lower house. Only if the lower house accepts a proposal is the approval of the Senate necessary. Should only one of the houses of Parliament pass a bill, the two meet together to resolve their differences.

Jordan is also divided into eight regional provinces, each administered by a governor who is appointed by the king. Loyalty to the monarch is the key element in each appointment. Five of the governorates—Amman, al-Balqa, Maan, Irbid, and Karak—are on the East Bank, and three are on the West Bank—Jerusalem, Nablus, and Hebron. The governors have extensive local powers, including the right to void the election of a village mayor. This is important, for despite the extensive power of the central government and the governors, the village is the basic political unit for most Jordanians, or in the case of the bedouin, the tribe. Since independence, a major goal of the central government has been to enable the king to enhance his direct contact with the villagers. It has had some success on the East Bank. On the West Bank, where much of the Jordanian bureaucracy was removed following the 1967 Arab-Israeli War and the remainder became associated with the Israeli military government, contact with the king has once again become the prerogative of the mayors, or *mukhtars* (headmen). The former Jordanian members of Parliament, governors, and officials on the West Bank have lost much influence. The mayors, in contrast, make visits to Amman and have direct contact with King Hussein and his ministers. Moreover, the mayors are recognized by the Israelis and other Arabs as the effective leaders of the West Bank.

There are three sources of law: Shari'a (Islamic law), European codes, and tradition. The Jordanian constitution and the Court Establishment Act of 1951 created a judiciary to reflect these sources of law. Three categories of courts were outlined in the constitution—regular civil courts, religious courts, and the special courts. The civil courts system, which is heavily based on Western law, has jurisdiction in all cases not specifically granted to the others. The religious court system has responsibility for personal status and communal endowment. Shari'a courts have responsibility for the Muslims, while the various Christian sects have their own councils. The special courts have responsibility for tribal questions and land issues. The king retains the right to appoint and dismiss judges and to pardon offenders.

Political Dynamics

Despite the trappings of constitutional democracy, true political power in Jordan rests with the king, and his primary support is the army. The legislature is as powerful as the monarch allows it to be. While there is little doubt that Hussein, as Abdallah before him, believes in the benefits of a more representative government, he continues to concentrate power in his own hands.

The Army

The role performed by the Jordanian army in the political arena is difficult to overemphasize. Some authors have stated that Jordan was created by the army.[1] It has been recruited primarily from the East Bank Jordanian population, whose loyalty to the king has been beyond question. Only twice—in the mid-1950s confrontation with the Arab nationalists and in the 1970 clashes with the Palestinians—has the throne been seriously threatened. On each occasion, new and less-reliable elements had increased their influence within the army. The alteration in the composition of the armed forces made it more susceptible to political pressures, which permitted antiregime elements to attempt to undermine the military's support for the king. Every attempt failed.

The Arab Legion, as created by the British, was a small elite corps composed primarily of tribal elements. These tribesmen were loyal to the king and supported Jordan's traditional close ties with the British. With the coming of the Palestine War of 1948, the narrowly recruited elite force had to be rapidly expanded. Increasingly large numbers of East Bank townspeople were brought into the army. Most prominent of these was the anti-Hussein conspirator, Ali Abu Nuwar.

The changing composition of the armed forces resulted in regional political influences having a significant impact on elements within the army. By the early 1950s, British power and influence were receding throughout the Middle East in the face of a rising tide of Arab nationalism. This nationalist sentiment, which developed a decidedly anti-European cast following the overthrow of the Egyptian monarchy, found many sympathetic ears in the Jordanian army. Some even blamed the Hashimite's close ties with the West as a key factor behind Jordanian and Arab military setbacks. As relations soured between the United States and Egypt over Egypt's purchase of Czechoslovakian arms and the U.S. failure to build the Aswan Dam, President Nasser's brand of Arab nationalism gained influence in Jordan at the expense of the British and Hashimite loyalists.

Pressure on Hussein to join the pro-Western, anticommunist Baghdad Pact came from London, Washington, and from his cousin, King Faysal, in Baghdad. Hussein was forced to determine if his primary interest lay in allying more closely with the West or with the Arab nationalists and Nasser. Although the Baghdad Pact was widely denounced as a "tool of the West" and a form of "neocolonialism," Hussein, in late 1955, decided to maintain his ties with Britain and Iraq. Flying in the face of popular wishes and growing Arab nationalist influence in the army, his prime minister, Hazza al-Majali, announced in early December that Jordan intended to enter the alliance. Riots broke out in Amman. After three days, order was restored by the Jordanian army, but the incident drove the young Hussein into the arms of the nationalists.

Jordan did not join the Baghdad Pact, al-Majali was replaced as prime minister, and, on 1 March 1956, General John Bagot Glubb (Glubb Pasha), commander of the Arab Legion, and his British staff were dismissed. The king attempted to ameliorate a hostile British reaction by emphasizing that he had made the decision on his own without pressure from the other Arab states, but such assertions were not convincing. Al-Majali had visited Syria, Saudi Arabia, and Egypt in the month prior to the dismissals and these governments had encouraged Jordan to stay out of the Baghdad Pact.

The king, for his part, had made a daring move by aligning himself with the Arab nationalists. He was greatly influenced by the rising tide of Arab nationalistic sentiment in the armed forces. When Hussein dismissed the British, his popularity at home and throughout the Arab world was never higher. His move also appears to have been calculated to use this popularity in order to solidify his political position. To draw on this strength within the army, he appointed a nationalist officer, Abu Nuwar, to command the army and officially changed its name to the Jordan Arab Army.

While the Arab nationalists both at home and abroad were supportive of the king's action, they were never loyal to him. The tenuous nature of his alliances became evident the following year. Believing that his destiny was more closely tied with the other Arabs than the West, Hussein attended an Arab solidarity conference in January 1957. By an agreement signed at the conference, Egypt, Syria, and Saudi Arabia guaranteed the payment of a subsidy if Jordan terminated its relations with the British. In March the Jordanians abrogated their treaty with Britain, resulting in the withdrawal of the last British garrisons from Jordan and the termination of the British subsidy. Hussein's Arab allies, however, failed to replace his losses. (Saudi Arabia made one quarterly payment; Syria and Egypt contributed nothing.)

By cutting his ties with the British, Hussein had left the monarchy open to a direct challenge from the Arab nationalists. In April 1957, Abu Nuwar and a group of nationalist officers attempted to control the political process by vetoing the king's choice of prime minister. Some have termed Abu Nuwar's action an attempted coup. Hussein met the challenge by addressing his bedouin troops directly. They sided with him against the nationalists, forcing Abu Nuwar into exile. Henceforth, the influence of the Arab nationalists in the army was diminished.

With the army loyalty assured, the only internal group that could threaten the monarchy was the Palestinians. Until the mid-1960s, however, the Palestinians had almost no effective organization and little in the way of a political program. Convinced that they were powerless to regain their lost homeland by themselves, they were compelled to look to the Arab states as the only force capable of confronting Israel. As time went on without any apparent success, a few Palestinians began to assert the idea that they must rely on themselves and that the struggle was theirs rather than that of the Arab states. In the early 1960s, some Palestinians began to organize into commando groups, such as al-Fatah and the Popular Front for the Liberation of Palestine (PFLP). While the commandos launched a few generally ineffective raids into Israel, they failed to persuade the majority of Palestinians that the Palestinian people could achieve their goals without relying on the Arab states.

This attitude changed dramatically with the June 1967 Arab-Israeli War. Israel's humiliation of the Egyptian, Syrian, and Jordanian armies proved to most Palestinians that the Arab states not only were inept but did not care about the Palestinians. The popularity of the commandos soared and groups like al-Fatah had to turn away recruits. This growth in commando strength provided the Palestinians with a military force capable of challenging the army. In addition, the loyalty of some elements of the army was questioned. After twenty years of Jordanian citizenship, many Palestinians had entered the military. While the Palestinian percentage in the military did not equal their majority in the general population and they were not in key positions, the Palestinians, nevertheless, played a significant role.

As a result of the new Palestinian influence, combined with the devastating economic impact created by the loss of the West Bank, King Hussein faced the most serious crisis of his reign. More than half the population of the truncated Jordanian state was Palestinian. The army was discredited. In contrast, at the end of the 1960s the prestige of the commandos was high: They were the heroes of the Palestinians. The commandos from the Jordanian territory made terrorist attacks, each raid enhancing the popular mystique of the guerrillas while leaving the Jordanian army to absorb the retaliatory blows of the Israeli Defense Forces. The Palestinians adopted a no-compromise attitude toward the Israelis and the Jordanians. They demanded that Jordan not interfere in their raids. When Jordanian authorities arrested a group of terrorists who had launched rockets against the Israeli port of Eilat, a threatened confrontation with the commandos forced their release.

More than any other incident, the battle of Karameh illustrated the rising tide of fedayeen popularity. In March 1968, the Israelis struck at the Karameh refugee camp on the East Bank of the Jordan, a key center for cross-river Palestinian raids. The Israelis severely damaged the village, but were not able to intimidate the fedayeen. With Jordanian army assistance, they stood and fought, inflicting numerous casualties upon the Israeli troops. Despite the crucial role of Jordanian artillery, the battle was widely viewed as a great victory for the commandos, in contrast to the previous failures of the army.

The overwhelming popularity of the fedayeen, particularly al-Fatah, enabled the guerrilla organizations to assume de facto control of Palestinian camps and neighborhoods throughout Jordan. With military assistance and training provided by other Arab states, they virtually became a state within a state, challenging the sovereignty of the king. In November 1968, a three-day battle between the fedayeen and the army was the first in a series of clashes. Each concluded with some Jordanian concession to the Palestinians, for Hussein's greatest fear was that continued fighting could lead to civil war.

By the summer of 1970, an all-out confrontation between the monarchy (supported by the East Bank Jordanians) and the Palestinians became inevitable. The fedayeen appear to have made two serious tactical errors. The first was the alienation of the Jordan Arab Army by criticizing the ability of its soldiers and their moral fiber. The disciplined Jordanian troops were subjected to taunts and insults, creating a large reservoir of ill-will. These actions weakened support for the commandos even among the Palestinians in the military. Second, the Palestinians ignored the differences between Palestinian interests and those of the East Bank Jordanians. As a result, King Hussein had the large East Bank Jordanian population and the army clamoring for him to suppress the "arrogant" fedayeen.

The conflict came to a head in September 1970 (called "Black September" by Palestinian groups). For the next ten months the Jordanian army chipped away at Palestinian strongholds, ultimately destroying them. At times, such as late September 1970, the fighting was very intense. Jordan's action alienated most of the other Arab states. Syria sent two hundred tanks across the Jordanian border, but heavy losses, logistical difficulties, and a threat of Israeli intervention forced the Syrians to withdraw. Interestingly, although Baghdad strongly condemned Hussein, Iraqi forces in Jordan did not intervene. Libya broke relations and transferred its annual subsidy from the Hashimite government to the commandos. Kuwait ended its economic assistance. The bitterness toward the Jordanians led Palestinian nationalists to sever their ties to the Hashimites, who were widely considered, next to the Israelis, the greatest enemies of Palestinian nationalism. Despite the criticism of the other Arabs, Hussein's confrontation with the commandos was a tremendous victory for the monarchy. Thousands of Palestinian fighters were killed, captured, or fled. The authority of the king, supported by the Jordanian army, was unchallengeable.

Political Parties

Political parties currently have little influence on the decision-making process. They have been officially banned since 1957. Prior to that time, King Hussein had allowed parties to function freely, with the hope that Jordan's government could develop into a constitutional monarchy. The Baath, Nationalist, Liberal, Communist, Muslim Brotherhood, and other parties were all active in the mid-1950s. The majority of these were ideological or sectarian, without a wide popular base. Many were antimonarchy.

As tensions rose in Jordan with the increasing influence of the Arab nationalists, the political parties criticized Jordan's pro-Western policies and, sometimes, the king. In 1956, the Arab nationalists won the parliamentary election. Their leader, Sulayman Nabulsi, a West Bank Palestinian, became prime minister. Nabulsi, who was closely associated with Abu Nuwar, pushed for greater ties with Nasser and other Arab nationalist states. When the nationalists overstepped the bounds of loyal opposition in 1957, conspiring with Abu Nuwar against the monarchy, the king exercised his power. He not only removed Nabulsi from power but banned all political parties.

The king has attempted to maintain popular representation despite the ban on political parties. Elections have been held periodically. Candidates are chosen by the government; therefore, popular representation is limited. Several other mechanisms have been created to make the government more responsive to the people. In 1971, the Jordanian National Union was established as the nation's sole authorized political organization. It failed to win widespread support. Democracy has not taken root and Jordan remains a monarchy with only the thinnest veneer of a representational government. Influence on the political process in Jordan, therefore, remains with those who can influence the king. Members of the ruling family, close advisors, traditional leaders, and, of course, the military continue to fill this role.

Foreign Policy

In the more than thirty years since independence, Jordan's relative influence in regional affairs has diminished. Whereas in 1950 Jordan was a regional power that could thwart the will of its fellow Arab states by annexing the West Bank, and the Hashimite monarchy could rival the Saudi monarchy, this is no longer the case. The decline has been the result of the diminution of the relative military strength of the Jordanian armed forces and of Jordan's economic base with the loss of the West Bank. Consequently, Jordan's regional influence is less, and its foreign-policy objectives have become increasingly limited.

In formulating its foreign policy, Jordan now finds itself more and more watchful of the policies of others. The preservation of the monarchy and the status of East Bank Jordanians appear to be its primary goals. Until the 1974 Rabat summit meeting, in which the Arab states recognized the Palestine Liberation Organization (PLO) as the sole representative of the Palestinians, regaining the West Bank was of great importance. Since then, the Amman government has adopted a more ambivalent attitude. To achieve even its limited goals, Jordan necessarily seeks outside support from two principal sources—the West and other moderate Arabs.

Jordan's eastern connection originates in the mandate era and the close treaty ties between Britain and the kingdom following independence. As the British influence and ability to intercede in support of the monarchy declined, the United States replaced the United Kingdom as the principal Western ally. In spite of some differences with Washington and considerable criticism from other Arabs, King Hussein has maintained this relationship because it was in Jordan's interest. The West provided a needed subsidy, arms, and some political support. Finding another source of assistance appeared to require unacceptable changes in the Jordanian government.

The Jordanians have also had to seek support from the moderate Arabs. Whereas in the early 1950s the Jordanians were rivals of the Saudis, Amman has now become increasingly dependent on Saudi economic and political support. The economic support keeps the Jordanian economy afloat and helps purchase needed military equipment. The political support helps provide an umbrella from Jordan's sometimes tumultuous relations with its neighboring Baathi regimes in Syria and Iraq. Jordan, in some ways, has become a buffer for the Saudis that protects the Arabian peninsula monarchy from the turmoil of the Fertile Crescent.

Despite the loss of influence and the decline in the military prowess of the Hashimite kingdom, the monarch and his East Bank supporters have displayed a remarkable willingness to tolerate abuse from fellow Arabs when basic Jordanian interests are involved. In 1970, for instance, the Jordanian army crushed the Palestinians and thwarted a Syrian invasion while ignoring the cries of fellow Arabs. Amman has also had to establish a working relationship with the Israelis because economic ties between East and West Bank Arabs have continued and the Jordanian Arab Army is no longer a match for the Israelis.

Notes

1. P. J. Vatikiotis, *Politics and The Military in Jordan*, London: Frank Cass & Co., 1967.

Bibliography

There are several good books on Jordan that offer a general understanding of history and government while providing a background for further study. Raphael Patai's *The Kingdom of Jordan* (Princeton: Princeton University Press, 1958) and Ann Dearden's *Jordan* (London: Robert Hale, 1958) are now somewhat out of date, but remain important doorways to an understanding of Jordan. Anne Sinai and Allen Pollack present a series of informative articles in *The Hashemite Kingdom of Jordan and the West Bank*, (New York: American Academic Association for Peace in the Middle East, 1977). Due to the wide range of topics and authors, coverage is uneven. Nevertheless, many of the articles are excellent and a great amount of information is available here.

Important sources of information about Jordan are the autobiographies and studies by British and Jordanian people who have contributed to the development of Jordan. Most notable are the memoirs of King Abdallah, *Memories of King Abdullah of Transjordan* (London: Jonathan Cape, 1950). Former commander of the armed forces Glubb Pasha has written several books on Jordan. All contribute to a better understanding of Jordan. *A Soldier with the Arabs*, (New York: Harper, 1958) is a necessity in order to truly appreciate the Jordanian army and its traditions. Former Arab Legion Commander Frederick G. Peake's (Peake Pasha) *A History of Jordan and Its Tribes* (Coral Gables: University of Miami Press, 1958) remains a classic discussion of the Jordanian tribes.

Scholars have also provided several excellent works on aspects of Jordanian history, politics, and society. In *Politics and the Military in Jordan: A Study of the Arab Legion, 1921-1957* (New York: Praeger Publishers, 1977), P. J. Vatikiotis analyzes the role of the military in creating and supporting the Hashimite regime. Reeva S. Simon, in his well-documented "The Hashemite Conspiracy: Hashemite Unity Attempts, 1921-1958," (*International Journal of Middle East Studies*, vol. 5, no. 3, 1974 pp. 314-327), discusses the aspirations of the Hashimite regimes of Iraq and Jordan to establish a larger Arab state under their leadership. Detailed studies of social and political structure on the local level can be found in Richard T. Antown's *Arab Village: A Social Structural Study of a Transjordanian Peasant Community* (Bloomington: Indiana University Press, 1972) and Peter Gubser's *Politics and Change in al-Karak* (London: Oxford University Press, 1973). Gubser presents an excellent study of the function of political power at the local level. The author is a keen observer and offers detailed insight into the Jordanian political system.

13

The State of Israel

Bernard Reich

Israel is a product of Zionism (the Jewish national movement). Since biblical days, Jews of the Diaspora (Jewish communities outside Israel) have hoped that they would return to Zion, the "Promised Land." Over the centuries Zionism developed spiritual, religious, cultural, social, and historical concepts linking Jews to the land of the historical Jewish states in Israel. The political variant of Zionism that saw the establishment of a Jewish state as a logical consequence of Zionism developed in the nineteenth century partly as a result of political currents then prevalent in Europe, especially nationalism and anti-Semitism. There was also a revival of Zionism in Eastern Europe and Russia. Groups such as the "Return to Zion" movement, whose goal was immigration and settlement, were established to alleviate the problems of the Jewish communities in Europe through the development of settlements in Palestine.

Historical Background

In 1897 Theodor Herzl, a Viennese journalist who had proposed establishing a self-governing community for the Jewish people in his book *Der Judenstaat* (The Jewish State), organized a conference at Basle, Switzerland, to assemble prominent leaders from the major Jewish communities and organizations throughout the world. This assembly shaped a Zionist political movement and established the World Zionist Organization (WZO). The Basle Program, which became the cornerstone of Zionist ideology, enunciated the basic aim of Zionism: "to create for the Jewish people a home in Palestine secured by public law."

World War I enabled the Zionist movement to make important gains. The WZO had developed into an organized and worldwide movement. With the aid of Dr. Chaim Weizmann, a prominent Zionist leader and chemist who contributed to the British war effort, the Zionist organization secured the Balfour Declaration (1917) from the British government, stating that "his Majesty's Government view with favour the establishment in Palestine of a national home for the Jewish people." By the end of the war British control had replaced Ottoman rule in Palestine. The Palestine mandate was allocated to Great Britain by the Allied Supreme Council on 25 April 1920, and was confirmed by the Council of the League of Nations on 22 July 1922. Between 1920 and the termination of the mandate in May 1948, British control of Palestine was exercised by a high commissioner and an executive council composed of senior British officials. Autonomous Arab and Jewish communal groups were established and each was granted powers of self-government within the framework created by British Orders-in-Council and the regulations of the mandate system.

During the mandate period, the Jewish community in Palestine (Yishuv) established institutions for self-government and procedures for implementing political decisions. All significant Jewish groups belonged to the organized Jewish community with the exception of the ultraorthodox Agudat Israel, which refused to participate. Agudat Israel opposed Zionist policies because of its belief that only by the hand of God, not man, could Israel be properly reestablished. By secret ballot the organized Jewish community chose the Assembly of the Elected (Asefat Hanevcharim) as its representative body. It met at least once a year, and between sessions its powers were exercised by the National Council (Vaad Leumi), which was elected by the assembly.

The mandatory government entrusted the National Council with the responsibility for Jewish communal affairs and granted it considerable autonomy. The executive committee of the National Council—through a number of self-created departments concerned with education, culture, health, social welfare, and religious affairs—acted as the administering power for the Jewish community. The council also controlled the clandestine recruitment and military training of Jewish youth in the defense force (Hagana), which after independence formed the core of Israel's defense forces. The General Federation of Labor (Histadrut), founded in 1920, coordinated labor-related matters and engaged in social welfare and economic endeavors. Political parties were established and they contested the elections for the various political posts. The political elite filled several roles in the Zionist movement, the Hagana, and the Histadrut, and in other political institutions; and it was also involved in relations with the British as the mandatory power and the promotion of Jewish immigration and settlement in Palestine.

Prototypical political institutions, founded and developed by and for the Jewish community, laid the foundation for many of Israel's public

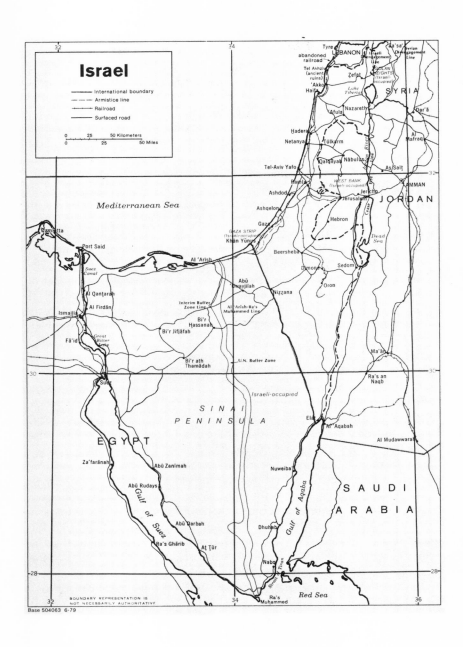

International boundary
Armistice line
Railroad
Surfaced road

0   25   50 Kilometers
0   25   50 Miles

Mediterranean Sea

LEBANON
Tyre
abandoned railroad
Tel Akhzi (ancient ruins)
'Akko
Haifa
Zefat
Lake Tiberias
GOLAN HEIGHTS (Israeli-occupied)
SYRIA
Ra's al 'Ayn
Syrian Disengagement Line
Israeli Disengagement Line
Nazareth
Afula
Dar'ā
Al Mafraq
Hadera
Netanya
Ṭūlkarm
Qalqīlyah
Nābulus
As Salṭ
Tel-Aviv Yafo
Ramla
WEST BANK (Israeli occupied)
AMMAN
Ashdod
Jericho
Jerusalem
JORDAN
Ashqelon
Gaza
Hebron
GAZA STRIP (Israeli occupied)
Khān Yūnus
Dead Sea
Beersheba
Damietta
Port Said
Al 'Arīsh
Dimona
Sedom
Suez Canal
Al Qanṭarah
Abū 'Uwayqilah
Nizzana
Oron
Al Firdān
Ismailia
Interim Buffer Zone Line
Al 'Arīsh-Ra's Muhammed Line
Bi'r Hassanah
Fā'id
Great Bitter Lake
Bi'r Jifjāfah
Ma'ān
Bi'r ath Thamādah
U.N. Buffer Zone
Suez
Ra's an Naqb
Israeli-occupied
SINAI PENINSULA
Elat
Al 'Aqabah
EGYPT
Al Mudawwara
Za'farānah
Abū Zanīmah
Nuweiba'
SAUDI
Abū Rudays
ARABIA
Gulf of Suez
Abū Darbah
Dhuhab
Gulf of Aqaba
Ra's Ghārib
Aṭ Ṭūr
Nabq
Strait of Tiran
Ra's Muhammad
Red Sea

BOUNDARY REPRESENTATION IS NOT NECESSARILY AUTHORITATIVE
Base 504063 6-79

bodies and political processes. The party system was initiated and proportional representation was instituted. Not only were procedures established and tried, but, more importantly, the masses and the elite gained experience in the functioning of political institutions. Several of the semigovernmental organizations that were created (most notably the Histadrut and the Jewish Agency) continued to play important roles after Israel's independence. These have contributed to the growth of a highly developed system of Zionist political parties and the consequential prevalence of coalition executive bodies in the Zionist movement and the local organs of Palestine Jewry.

The National Council functioned concurrently with the internationally recognized executive of the Jewish Agency for Palestine.[1] Weizmann, as president of the WZO, negotiated with leading representatives of Jewish organizations and communities throughout the world for their participation in the work of the Jewish Agency. In August 1929 these negotiations culminated in the establishment of a new body, the Jewish Agency for Palestine, popularly referred to as "the Expanded Jewish Agency." The agency included Jews and Jewish organizations sympathetic to the idea of a Jewish national home but not ideologically committed to Zionism. It took over the activities—such as fundraising and maintaining liaison with foreign governments—designed to build a national home in which concerned Jews everywhere could participate. The agency conducted negotiations with the Palestine mandatory government, the United Kingdom, and the League of Nations. It also sought accommodation with the Arabs but was unsuccessful.

Throughout much of the mandate period the Jewish and Arab communities of Palestine were in conflict over the future of the territory. Unable to find a solution to satisfy these conflicting views, and because of the heavy cost in men and money, the British conceded that the mandate was unworkable and turned the problem over to the United Nations, which placed the Palestine issue before its General Assembly in April 1947. The United Nations Special Committee on Palestine (UNSCOP) was created to examine the issues and to submit proposals for the solution to the problem. The committee recommended that the mandate be terminated and that the independence of Palestine be achieved without delay; however, it was divided over the future of the territory. The majority recommended partition into a Jewish state and an Arab state linked in an economic union, with Jerusalem and its environs established as an international enclave. The minority recommended that Palestine become a single federal state, with Jerusalem the capital, and with Jews and Arabs enjoying autonomy in their respective areas. On 29 November 1947, the United Nations General Assembly adopted the majority recommendation (the Partition Plan) over Arab opposition (they favored the minority report) by 33 votes to 13, with 10 abstentions.

The situation in Palestine deteriorated rapidly. Disorders reminiscent of those of the 1920s and 1930s broke out in all parts of the country. As the end of the mandate approached, these degenerated into a virtual civil war. Israel declared its independence on 14 May 1948, and General Sir Alan Gordon Cunningham, the last British high commissioner, departed. Armies of the Arab states entered Palestine and engaged in open warfare with the defense forces of the new state. The United Nations secured a truce and the military situation was stabilized in 1949 by a series of armistice agreements between Israel and the neighboring Arab states. The United Nations Truce Supervision Organization (UNTSO) was established to oversee the armistice. No general peace settlement was achieved.

The provisional government of Israel, which was formed at the time of independence and which was recognized by the major powers, was new in name only. It had begun to function de facto following adoption of the partition resolution and it drew on the experience gained by the Jewish community in Palestine during the mandatory period. Shortly after the partition vote, the United Nations established a Palestine commission to effect a transfer from the mandatory power to the proposed Arab and Jewish states. That commission had to work exclusively with the Jewish community because neither the Arabs nor the British would cooperate. As early as March 1948 a temporary National Council of State, chosen from the National Council and Jewish Agency Executive, assumed control in many area. On 14 May the new provisional government proclaimed Israel's independence, repealed the British mandatory restrictions on immigration and the sale of land, and converted the Hagana into the Israel Defense Forces (IDF).

The provisional government had three elements: a state council that acted as parliament; a cabinet elected by the state council from among its members; and a president elected by the state council. David Ben Gurion, chairman of the Jewish Agency and leader of the dominant political party, the Mapai (Israel Labor party), was elected prime minister and minister of defense and Chaim Weizmann was elected president. The National Council of the mandate period formed the basis of the state council; the executive of the National Council became the cabinet; and the presidency was entirely new. The provisional government directed the war against the Arab states, levied taxes, established administrative agencies, and conducted essential public services. It functioned from 14 May 1948, until early 1949. At its session just prior to the national elections of 25 January 1949, the state council adopted a transition ordinance transferring its authority to a constituent assembly and convened on 14 February 1949. That assembly, which later declared itself the First Knesset (parliament), was a unicameral chamber composed of 120 members representing 12 of the 24 parties that contested the January 1949 elections.

Political Environment

Israel's special role as the world's only Jewish state has had a manifold impact on its political system. Israel is concerned that all Jews who wish to immigrate are free to do so and is interested in the well-being of Jews everywhere. The encouragement of Jewish immigration has left its mark on every aspect of Israeli life. The commitment to unfettered Jewish immigration was articulated initially in Israel's Declaration of Independence, which proclaimed that "the State of Israel will be open to the immigration of Jews from all countries of their dispersion." It was reaffirmed in the Law of Return of 5 July 1950 (which provided that "every Jew has the right to come to this country as an 'oleh' [Jew immigrating to Israel]") and has been reinforced by the programs and actions of successive Israeli governments. Encouraging the ingathering of exiles has received overwhelming support in parliament and from the Jewish population, and it has been implemented almost without regard to the economic costs and social dislocations caused by the rapid and massive influx of people.

Israel's commitment to immigration results from its view of its mission as the emissary of the exiled and scattered Jewish people—it is an outward expression of a bond of faith between Israel and world Jewry. It removes Jews from areas of distress and thus serves to meet the needs of world Jewry. Immigration serves Israel's needs by providing manpower necessary for Israel's security and development.

Several problems, some of them highly significant, have resulted from this policy. Unlike the period of the mandate when immigration was selective and severely limited by British-imposed restrictions, Israel has admitted whole communities virtually without regard to their economic usefulness or its own absorptive capacity. Initially the immigrants were the remnants of European Jewry; but during the nascent years of Israel's independence, the Jewish communities of Muslim states of the Middle East and North Africa arrived in large numbers. The Jews of Yemen (about 45,000) and Iraq (about 123,000) were brought to Israel by airlifts, popularly known as "Operation Magic Carpet" and "Operation Ali Baba." Between 1919 and 1948, about 90 percent of the Jewish immigrants came from Europe or other Western countries. Since 1948, immigration has been overwhelmingly non-Western (see Table 13.1).

After the Six-Day War in 1967, immigrants again came mainly from the West and the Soviet Union. But after the October War in 1973, immigration diminished and there was increasing emigration to Western Europe and the United States. Israeli government statistics reported that, in 1975, emigration nearly matched immigration: 18,500 Israelis had emigrated and 20,000 newcomers had arrived, about 8,500 of whom were from the Soviet Union (compared to 31,970 immigrants in 1974 and 58,886 in 1973).

Geographically Israel is an Oriental country; culturally and socially, it is Western-oriented. The early Zionists laid the foundations for an essentially European culture in Palestine and subsequent immigration accelerated the trend of Westernizing Palestine. The Occidental immigrants developed the Yishuv structure of land settlement, trade unions, political parties, and education in preparation for a Jewish national state that was clearly Western in orientation. Future immigrants had to adapt themselves to a society that had formed these institutions, and this presented a problem for those who were part of the immigration from non-Western countries.

Massive immigration of Jews from the states of the Middle East and other parts of Asia and Africa has resulted in an influx of large numbers of people whose societal and cultural traditions are akin to the Oriental populations among whom they lived for generations, and different from those of their Western co-religionists. Their customs, practices, and attitudes are those of the East rather than the West. Family loyalty is strong; concepts of responsibility very often do not transcend the family. Suspicion of government and all of its ramifications is great; resistance to taxation, rationing, and other controls is prevalent. Partially because of their lack of education and experience, relatively few members of the Oriental community have succeeded in achieving responsible government posts. Their living conditions and standards are generally lower than those of the Occidental community and a relatively small proportion attend Israel's universities. In the 1970s a wave of immigration from the Soviet Union brought sizable numbers of Western immigrants, but they had their own particular problems, requiring different approaches to integration.

Numerous difficulties have beset efforts to settle and absorb the masses of immigrants. Economic, social, and cultural assimilation of the immigrants in a short span of time would have been a formidable undertaking for a small country even under the most favorable conditions. In Israel, this has been attempted despite the obstacles posed by limited resources, defense needs, and the composition and character of the new

TABLE 13.1

Jewish Immigration to Israel

IMMIGRATION 1919-1977 ACCORDING TO PERIOD OF IMMIGRATION AND COUNTRY OF ORIGIN

Period	Total	Yearly Average	Asia and Africa		Europe and America		Not Known
			Numbers	%	Numbers	%	
1919-1948*	452,158	15,396	44,809	10.4	385,066	89.6	22,283
1948-1951	686,739	189,028	330,086	41.6	336,623	50.4	19,130
1952-1954	54,065	18,022	41,051	76.0	12,982	24.0	31
1955-1957	164,936	54,975	112,185	68.3	52,138	31.7	613
1958-1960	75,487	25,162	27,369	36.3	48,106	63.7	12
1961-1964	228,046	57,012	136,570	69.9	91,462	40.1	14
1965-1968	81,337	20,334	43,805	53.9	37,526	46.1	6
1969-1974	259,219	43,028	56,722	22.0	201,446	78.0	1,081
1975-1977	61,238	20,513	6,019	9.8	55,348	90.2	51
TOTAL:	2,063,255	34,970	799,337	39.6	1,220,697	60.4	43,221

*up to May 1948

SOURCE: Israel Information Center, Jerusalem, 1978

immigration. Israel has been obliged to undertake the training or retraining of the immigrants for gainful employment and to provide housing, schooling, and medical facilities. While the material problems have not yet been fully solved, they are well defined, and manifold activities are directed toward their solution. These include systematic establishment of new agricultural communities in which newcomers are settled soon after their arrival and where they are provided with training and work, medical treatment, a well-developed system of national insurance, and housing.

The nonmaterial problems, which are essentially those of cultural and social acclimation, are more complex and their resolution will require time. Although the basic religious tradition of the Jewish population is an asset because it provides a common core of values and ideals, there are major differences in outlook, values, frames of reference, levels of aspiration, and various other social and cultural components. Army service, which emphasizes education as well as the experience of common living and working and learning the Hebrew language, facilitates acculturation and encourages evolution in the direction of a unified, multicultural society. Despite these efforts, the full integration of immigrants into Israel's society remains the state's greatest social problem.

The Arabs of Israel (i.e., those who have lived in Israel since its independence, or their offspring, and who are Israeli citizens and not the Arabs in those areas occupied by Israel during the June War) are confronted by problems qualitatively different from those facing Jewish immigrants. Following Israel's independence, and as a result of the ensuing war between Israel and the Arab states, a large number of Arabs who had lived in the part of Palestine that is now Israel fled and took up residence in Arab states, either as refugees or members of their permanent populations. The Arabs who chose to remain in Israel—and who numbered about 600,000 in 1979—form Israel's Arab community.

After the 1949 armistice agreements, activities of the Arab community were regarded primarily as concerns of Israel's security system, and most of the areas inhabited by the Arabs were placed under military control. A military government was established in these districts and special defense and security zones were created. Israel's Arabs were granted citizenship with full legal equality but were forbidden to travel into or out of security areas without permission from the military. Military courts were established in which trials could be held in closed session. With the consent of the minister of defense, the military commanders could limit individual movements, impose restrictions on employment and business, issue deportation orders, search and seize, and detain a person if it were deemed necessary for security purposes.

Those who argued in support of the military administration saw it as a means of controlling the Arab population and preventing infiltration, sabotage, and espionage. Furthermore, it was contended that the very existence of the military administration was an important deterrent measure. As evidence developed that the Israeli Arabs were not disloyal, pressure for relaxation and then for total abolition of military restrictions grew in the Knesset and in public debate. The restrictions were gradually modified, and on 1 December 1966, military government was abolished. Functions that had been exercised by the military government were transferred to relevant civilian authorities.

The major long-term problem for Israel's Arab minority is its social integration. Although Israeli Arabs vote, sit in the Knesset, serve in government offices, have their own schools and courts, and prosper materially, they face difficulties in adjusting to Israel's modern Jewish- and Western-oriented society. Most of the major factors facilitating Jewish integration are not operative with regard to the Arab minority. The Arabs tend to live in separate villages and in separate sections of the major cities. They speak Arabic, attend a separate school system, and do not serve in the army. Centuries of foreign control have left their impact on the basic political attitudes of the Arabs—despotic rule, violence, and extortion have engendered an attitude of suspicion and mistrust toward government. There is also an emotional strain because of Israel's conflict with the Arab states and the dual identification of those who are both Arabs and citizens of Israel.

Successive Israeli governments have sought to bring about a more complete integration of its Arab citizens into the life of the country and foster their economic, social, and cultural advancement. However, the problem is complex and continuing efforts are needed.

Over time the Arab community has become increasingly politicized. Israel's Arab population has long enjoyed legal equality, has participated in parliamentary elections and in local government, and has had its own state-supported educational and religious institutions. But below the surface equanimity, Israeli Arabs were discontented with a perceived second-class status resulting from various forms of unofficial discrimination. In the wake of the October War and with the increased international standing of the Palestine Liberation Organization (PLO) and the emphasis on Palestinian participation in the efforts to resolve the Arab-Israeli conflict, the Arabs of Israel seemed to become more restive and more politically aware. In the spring of 1976, Israel's Arabs participated in their first general protest and staged the most violent demonstrations in Israel's history. The riots, whose extent and ferocity surprised both Israeli Arabs and Jews, grew out of a general strike, centered in

Nazareth, that was organized to protest land expropriations in Israel's northern section. The government had adopted a five-year plan to increase the number of Jewish settlers in Galilee and had expropriated lands, some of which were Arab-owned. The Arabs protested that, despite compensation, their land should not be expropriated to provide land for Jewish settlers. The expropriation served as a catalyst; the initial demonstrations escalated and eventually became broader and more general in their focus, incorporating complaints about Arab second-class status and adding other issues to the list of grievances. Although the immediate problems have receded, the basic questions concerning the status of Israel's Arab citizens remain.

Religion and the State

Israel's Jewishness is a basic element underlying its political system. However, the overwhelmingly Jewish character of the state does not ensure agreement on the appropriate relationship between religion and the state, between the religious and secular authorities, nor on the methods and techniques to be employed by religious authorities. The poles of the debate are theocracy and secularism; one segment of the population seeks to turn Israel into a theocratic state and the other wishes to make it fully secular. A large group remains uncommitted. The extreme positions have had to compromise, thereby coexisting under middle-of-the-road arrangements.

Although Israel's government is secular, it takes into account the requisites of that segment of the population that observes religious tradition. The Israel Ministry of Religious Affairs is concerned with meeting Jewish religious requirements, such as the supply of ritually killed (kosher) meat, rabbinical courts, and religious schools (Yeshivot), as well as with meeting religious needs of the non-Jewish communities that enjoy religious autonomy. These functions are noncontroversial; few dispute the duty of the government to meet the religious requirements of the people. Nevertheless, there is sharp and recurrent controversy concerning the extent to which religious observance or restriction is directly or indirectly imposed on the entire Jewish population. The observant community, through its own political parties and through its membership in government coalitions, has been able to secure government agreement to establish separate school systems, to exempt their young women from army service, and to curtail almost all business and public activity on the Sabbath. Thus, the less observant Jews of Israel often argue that they do not possess religious freedom because of governmental acquiescence to demands of the observant Jewish groups, such as restriction of public services on the Sabbath and the limitations placed on the role of non-Orthodox Judaism in Israel.

The religious parties have been able to secure concessions because the need for coalition governments has given them a larger voice in politics than is dictated by their numerical strength. In its search for coalition partners, Mapai found that the demands of the religious parties were in areas of least concern to Mapai's leadership and thus such parties were often attractive coalition members. Whereas the demands of other parties were in the realm of foreign policy, security, or economics—all central to Mapai's thinking—the concerns of the religious parties were generally limited to matters impinging on religion and personal status, and these were generally of less concern. Nevertheless, there were government crises over religious questions. The disagreement on incorporation of principles of religion in a constitutional document marked the Knesset debate on the preparation of a written constitution and suggested that a crisis of major proportions was imminent. There have been disagreements over the religious education of children in immigration camps, compulsory military service for women, the question of uniform national education, and even on the criteria that determine if a given individual is to be considered a Jew according to Israel's laws. After the Israeli occupation of Jerusalem in 1967, a major controversy developed with regard to the status of the Western (or Wailing) Wall and the surrounding areas where the Temple of Solomon once stood. Those of different religious orientations viewed the treatment of the area in different ways, although they all agreed that it was among the holiest of Jewish sites. In 1976 a religious issue, a no-confidence motion in the Knesset based on the charge that a government-organized ceremony violated the Sabbath, since those attending would be forced to travel on the Sabbath, led to the resignation of the Rabin government and a demand for new elections. Clearly, the role of religion in Israel's everyday life remains a major social and political issue.

Economic Conditions

The policy of unrestricted immigration, the scarcity of natural resources, and the security requirements imposed by the continuing hostility of its Arab neighbors affect Israel's economic development efforts.

Israel is a small country (about 20,700 square kilometers [8,000 sq. mi.] in its pre–1967 war frontiers) and poor in natural resources. It has substantial deposits of potash in the Dead Sea and some phosphates and copper but no large amounts of other mineral resources. Domestic sources of energy—other than solar—are minimal. Agricultural land is a prime asset, and although there is some fertile soil in places, much of it requires irrigation. The scarcity of water is a major obstacle to increasing agricultural production. The Jordan River, which plays an important role in Israel's National Water Plan, is utilized to improve agricultural production for both the increasing population and for export. Israel is well located for land and sea trade with neighboring states, but the continuing Arab-Israeli conflict and the Arab boycott forces Israel to trade at greater distances, to its disadvantage.

Israel seeks to produce goods and to generate sufficient revenues to balance its budget and achieve a stable balance of payments. In Israel's earlier years this was achieved through income from several outside sources. This included substantial amounts of foreign capital, a large portion of which came from private sources in the United States through the efforts of the United Jewish Appeal, Hadassah, and other agencies and organizations. German reparations and restitution payments to individuals were an important source in the late fifties and early sixties. United States grant aid, Public Law 480 Food-for-Peace programs, and loans extended by the Export-Import Bank have all made a contribution. Much of the foreign currency income is directed toward Israel's industrial program and has resulted in increased exports.

Israel's overall economic position has improved over the years. It has confronted the problems of material shortages and much of the task of settling a million immigrants while substantially increasing its per-capita gross national product (GNP). Having achieved relative self-sufficiency in agriculture, Israel aims at expanding the industrial sector, particularly those industries with export potential that can be developed to offset the country's large imbalance of commodity trade. Israel seeks the participation of foreign financial activity to supplement its own investments. To this end it has offered tax benefits, guarantees of convertibility, and repatriation of profits and capital. At the same time, Israel's objectives include a reduction in its reliance on foreign financial assistance. The recession that had characterized Israel's economy before the 1967 war became an economic boom, with full employment, shortly thereafter. Building construction developed rapidly and exports grew. Immigration increased. There was a tourist influx and increased contributions from world Jewry, but defense expenditures also increased, amounting to about one-third of the annual state budget after the October War.

Israel's economic situation deteriorated after the October War. The prewar economic boom was replaced by increasingly stringent conditions. Taxes were increased and other war-related levies were introduced and a high rate of inflation (exceeding 40 percent) began to have its impact. Initially, agricultural and industrial production was dislocated by the mobilization of much of the able-bodied manpower, not only during the war but for increased reserve duty in the period that followed, and this slowed the economy. Earnings from tourism and other sources of foreign exchange fell during the war and the port of Eilat was cut off by the blockade at Bab al-Mandab. The replacement of military equipment lost in battle, the servicing of the prewar debt, and the acquisition of new materiel to meet current and future defense needs added to the burden. The cost of the war approximated the annual GNP. In the immediate postwar period defense expenditure reached an all-time high of about 40 percent of the GNP. There was also the realization that Israel could not readily reduce nondefense expenditure for there was the requirement of immigrant absorption and the need to continue development programs and to deal with existing social and economic gaps. In a partial effort to improve the situation, Israel instituted a broad-scale austerity program and the Israeli pound was devalued by 43 percent. The announcement, on 10 November 1974, was accompanied by public opposition and a wave of demonstrations.

Israel continued to face severe economic pressures. The October War had been costly and austerity budgets were adopted. A program of continuous small devaluations (minidevaluations) of the Israeli pound was established to make imports more expensive and, it was hoped, less attractive in an effort to reduce foreign-currency drains and an unfavorable balance of payments. Taxes were raised and restructured to increase government revenues and maintain individual initiative. At the same time, the government reduced subsidies on such basic foodstuffs as bread, milk, and eggs, which led to increased costs of goods and services for most consumers and an increased cost of living. Inflation continued at a high rate although unemployment remained low (about 3 percent).

From independence until 1977 the Israeli government played a decisive role in the economy, aided by semigovernmental institutions such as the Jewish Agency, the United Israel Appeal, the Jewish National Fund, and the Histadrut. In 1977 the system was altered. For the Menahem Begin government, which came to office in 1977, the overriding domestic issue was that of the economy. By October of that year, the government was ready to inaugurate its new economic plan seeking to end the socialist system that had been created under successive Labor governments and to replace it with a free enterprise approach. Finance Minister Simcha Ehrlich declared that the program would check inflation, cut the foreign trade deficit, raise the growth rate, and promote foreign investment. The new economic policy would also remove some of the vast bureaucratic holds on the economy. It eliminated most government-imposed economic controls instituted over the three decades of Labor party administration. Arbitrary exchange rates for the pound were abandoned, and the pound was left to float to its own level on international exchanges. Virtually all foreign-currency regulations were also eliminated. The devaluation of the pound was expected to promote a flow of dollars and other foreign currency into the country. A new value-added tax of 12 percent was imposed. It was hoped that this new policy would increase exports by making Israeli products less expensive and would decrease imports (and consumption generally) by leaving less money in the hands of the Israeli consumer and by encouraging greater productivity. The administration's overall goal was to eliminate the government from the economy and to apply free-market principles.

Political Structure

Constitutional Consensus

Israel's system of government is based on an unwritten constitution. The first act of the Constituent Assembly in February 1949 was to enact a "Transition Law" (Small Constitution) that became the basis of constitutional life in the state. Administrative and executive procedures were based on a combination of past experience in self-government, elements adapted from the former mandatory structure, and new legislation. According to the Small Constitution, Israel was established as a republic with a weak president and a strong cabinet and parliament. It was anticipated that this document would be replaced in due course by a more extensive one.

The First Knesset devoted much time to a profound discussion of the constitutional issue. The major debate was between those who favored a written constitution and those who believed that the time was not appropriate for imposing rigid constitutional limitations. The latter group argued that a written constitution could not be framed because of constantly changing social conditions resulting from mass immigration and a lack of experience with independent governmental institutions. There was also concern about the relationship between state and religion and the method of incorporating the precepts and ideals of Judaism into the proposed document.

The discussion of these issues continued for over a year. On 13 June 1950, the Knesset adopted a compromise that has indefinitely postponed the real issue. It was decided in principle that a written constitution would ultimately be adopted, but that for the time being there would not be a formal and comprehensive document. Instead, a number of fundamental or basic laws would be passed dealing with specific subjects, which may in time form chapters in a consolidated constitution. These basic laws are no different from any other legislation in the hierarchy of

legal norms; they may be amended by the normal legislative process and
do not constitute yardsticks by which to determine the constitutionality
of other legislation. Thus, they have some psychological impact but no
preemptive legal role.

Although a formal written constitution has not yet been constructed,
there are several areas of general consensus which, together with the extant fundamental laws, form the parameters of the Israeli political
system. Israel's "Jewishness" is perhaps the most significant area of agreement, although there is a divergence of views on some of its tenets and
their interpretation. This general agreement centers on what are
sometimes termed the goals or purposes of Israel, such as the "ingathering of the exiles"—the return of the Jewish people from the Diaspora to
their ancient homeland, *Eretz Israel* (the Land of Israel)—and the
establishment of a state based on "Jewish" principles. Those disavowing
allegiance to these Jewish-Zionist ideals, or at least those dissociating
themselves from their immediate manifestations (such as the Communist
and the ultraorthodox Neturei Karta sect), are regarded as outsiders in
Israel's politics and are little more than protest groups. There is also consensus on the view that Israel should be a social-welfare state, in which
all share in the benefits of society and have access to essential social,
health, and similar services, although there are conflicting views regarding the specific scope and method of implementation of this principle.
Foreign and security policy constitutes another area enjoying wide consensus because of its overriding importance in light of continuing Arab
hostility and the resultant conflict. The Israel Defense Forces (Zahal)
(IDF) enjoy an enviable military reputation that was enhanced by the
1967 war and strengthened following the initial reverses in the 1973 war.
The IDF remain outside politics and under civilian control and are identified with the state rather than with any particular group or party.

Political Institutions

The president, the government (cabinet), and the Knesset perform the
basic political functions of the state within the framework provided by
Israel's constitutional consensus.

The president is elected by the Knesset for a five-year term and may be
reelected. He is head of state and his powers and functions are essentially
of a representative character. In the sphere of foreign affairs these include
signing instruments that relate to treaties ratified by the Knesset, appointing diplomatic and consular representatives, receiving foreign
diplomatic representatives, and issuing consular *exequaturs*. In the
domestic sphere, he has the power to grant pardons and reprieves and to
commute sentences. Subsequent to nomination by the appropriate body,

he appoints judges, *dayanim* (judges of Jewish religious courts), *qadis* (judges of Muslim religious courts), the state comptroller, the president of the Magen David Adom Association (Red Shield of David—Israel's Red Cross), and the governor of the Bank of Israel, as well as other officials as determined by law. He signs all laws passed by the Knesset, with the exception of those relating to presidential powers, and all documents to which the state seal is affixed. Official documents signed by the president require the countersignature of the prime minister or other duly authorized minister with the exception of those where another procedure is laid down, as in the case of the judges.

The president's powers and functions relating to the formation of the government fall into a different category. After consultation with representatives of the parties in parliament, the president selects a member of the Knesset to form a government. Until now this formal discretion has not been accompanied by any real choice because the political composition of the Knesset has clearly determined the selection. Nevertheless, situations are conceivable in which different party combinations might gain the support of the Knesset. Were this to occur, the president would fulfill a crucial political role in determining the person chosen to form a cabinet. The president also receives the resignation of the government. Another aspect of the presidential role that could have considerable political significance is his public position—his visits throughout the country, his speeches, and his formal opening of the first session of each Knesset.

The member of parliament entrusted by the president with the task of forming the government establishes a cabinet, generally with himself as prime minister and a number of ministers who are usually, but not necessarily, members of the Knesset. The government is constitutionally instituted upon obtaining a vote of confidence from the parliament. The cabinet is collectively responsible to the Knesset, reports to it, and remains in office as long as it enjoys the confidence of that body. A government's tenure may also be terminated by ending the Knesset's tenure, by the resignation of the government on its own initiative, or by the resignation of the prime minister.

The Knesset is the supreme authority in the state. It is a unicameral body of 120 members elected by national, general, secret, direct, equal, and proportional suffrage for a term not to exceed four years. Voters cast their ballots for parties, rather than individual candidates, although each party presents the voter with a list of up to 120 names—its choices for Knesset seats. After ballots are cast, seats in the Knesset are determined. Those party lists that have received at least 1 percent of the total number of valid votes cast can be represented in the Knesset. Any list failing to obtain this minimum of 1 percent does not share in the distribution of mandates, and its votes are not taken into account when determining the composition of the Knesset. The distribution of seats among the party lists is determined by dividing the number of votes given to all the lists that obtained the minimum percentage (1 percent) by the number of Knesset members (120), and the result is set as the quota for each Knesset seat. Each list receives the nearest whole number of seats thus determined, and the remaining seats are allocated to lists having the largest number of seats (under the terms of the Bader-Ofer Amendment of 1973).

The main functions of the Knesset are similar to those of most modern parliaments. They include expressing a vote of confidence or no-confidence in the government, legislating, participating in the formation of national policy, and supervising the activities of the governmental administration. The Knesset must also approve the budget and taxation, elect the president of the state, recommend the appointment of the state comptroller, and participate in the appointment of judges. It is divided into a number of committees, each responsible for a specific area of legislation. Many of the Knesset's activities are performed in these committees. With some minor exceptions the ratio of committee memberships is generally proportional to that of the party's representation in the Knesset as a whole.

Judicial authority is vested in religious as well as civil courts. The latter include municipal and magistrates' courts for civil and criminal actions, district courts for appeals from the lower tribunals and matters beyond the jurisdiction of a magistrate, and a supreme court. The Supreme Court cannot review legislation passed by the Knesset, but it has the power to invalidate administrative actions and interpret statutes it regards contrary to the law. Each major community has its own religious courts that deal with matters of personal status. Rabbinical courts have exclusive jurisdiction over Jews in marriage and divorce, and they may act on alimony, probate, succession, and other similar questions with the parties' consent. The Christian ecclesiastical courts have exclusive authority over marriage, divorce, alimony, and confirmation of wills, and they may judge other similar matters if the parties agree. The Muslim courts have exclusive jurisdiction in all matters of personal status. The judicial appointment procedure seeks to discourage political influence and judges enjoy tenure subject only to good behavior.

Two other institutions unique to the Israeli system are significant elements of the political structure. The Histadrut and the Jewish Agency, although technically extragovernmental, perform governmental functions and their personnel often attain positions of responsibility within the government. The Histadrut is of greater significance than the usual trade union organization and is unique in that it combines trade unionism, economic enterprise, cultural and social activities, and social welfare. It is one of the largest employers in Israel and has engaged in overseas projects in support of Israel's foreign policy. The Jewish Agency for Israel represents the World Zionist Organization and acts on behalf of Jews throughout the world who are concerned with Israel's development, Jewish immigration and settlement, and the cultural and spiritual ties and cooperation among the Jewish people. The agency has been responsible for the organization of Jewish immigration to Israel; the reception, assistance, and settlement of these immigrants; care of children; and aid to cultural projects and institutions of higher learning. It fosters Hebrew education and culture in the Diaspora, guides and assists Zionist youth movements, and organizes the work of the Jewish people in support of Israel.

Political Dynamics

Political parties have played an overwhelming role in the political, social, and economic life of the country. They publish newspapers, sponsor social and athletic events, and operate medical facilities. Israel's political system is also characterized by a wide range of political and social viewpoints that are expressed not only by political parties, but also by newspapers and a host of social, religious, cultural, and other organizations. Numerous minority and splinter factions freely criticize the government. This diversity has been most apparent in the multiple parties contesting parliamentary elections and in the various coalition governments that have been characteristic of Israel since its inception (see Table 13.2). The Knesset is elected by a countrywide proportional representation (PR) system that allows political fragmentation to continue. However, the profusion of parties basically results from the strongly ideological character of most of these parties and reflects the variety and intensity of views held by various segments of the population on economic, religious, and other matters. The principle of proportional representation is a historical precedent utilized by the Tel Aviv municipality between the two world wars, by the National Council in the period of the mandate, and by the Histadrut and the Zionist congresses. Historical developments, mostly during the preindependence period, and personal differences among the political elite are also important elements in fostering party proliferation. Despite this proliferation, political life has been shaped by the views of a few leading parties and individuals.

Mapai, organized in 1930, and the Labor party into which it merged,

TABLE 13.2

Political Parties and Knesset Election Results

	1949 %	1949 Seats	1951 %	1951 Seats	1955 %	1955 Seats	1959 %	1959 Seats
Mapai	35.7	46	37.3	45	32.2	40	38.2	47
Mapam	14.7	19	12.5	15	7.3	9	7.2	9
Ahdut Avodah[a]	-	-	-	-	8.2	10	6.0	7
Alignment of Mapai and Ahdut Avodah	-	-	-	-	-	-	-	-
Rafi[b]	-	-	-	-	-	-	-	-
Israel Labor[c]	-	-	-	-	-	-	-	-
Alignment of Israel Labor and Mapam (Maarach)	-	-	-	-	-	-	-	-
State List[d]	-	-	-	-	-	-	-	-
Herut	11.5	14	6.6	8	12.6	15	13.6	17
General Zionists	5.2	7	16.2	20	10.2	13	6.2	8
Progressives	4.1	5	3.2	4	4.4	5	4.6	6
Liberal[e]	-	-	-	-	-	-	-	-
Gahal[f]	-	-	-	-	-	-	-	-
Independent Liberals[g]	-	-	-	-	-	-	-	-
Shlomzion[q]	-	-	-	-	-	-	-	-
Free Center[h]	-	-	-	-	-	-	-	-
Likud[n]	-	-	-	-	-	-	-	-
United Religious Front	12.2	16[i]	-	-	-	-	-	-
Mizrahi	-	-	1.5	2	-	-	-	-
Hapoel Hamizrahi	-	-	6.7	8	-	-	-	-
National Religious	-	-	-	-	9.1	11	9.9	12
Agudat Israel[k]	-	-	-	-	-	-	-	-
Poalei Agudat Israel[k]	-	-	-	-	-	-	-	-
Torah Religious Front[l]	-	-	3.6	5	4.7	6	4.7	6
Arab Democratic list	1.7	2	2.4	3	1.8	2	-	-
Arab Progress and Work	-	-	1.2	1	1.5	2	1.3	2
Arab Farmers and Development	-	-	1.1	1	1.2	1	1.1	1
Arab Cooperation and Brotherhood	-	-	-	-	-	-	1.2	2
Alignment - affiliated Arab and Druse lists	-	-	-	-	-	-	-	-
United Arab List	-	-	-	-	-	-	-	-
Communist[m]	3.5	4	4.0	5	4.5	6	2.8	3
New Communists (Rakah)[m]	-	-	-	-	-	-	-	-
Israel Communists (Maki)[m]	-	-	-	-	-	-	-	-
Democratic Front for Peace and Equality[o]	-	-	-	-	-	-	-	-
Sephardim	3.5	4	1.8	2	-	-	-	-
Fighters list	1.2	1	-	-	-	-	-	-
Women's International Zionist Organization (WIZO)	1.2	1	-	-	-	-	-	-
Yemenites	1.0	1	1.2	1	-	-	-	-
Haolam Hazeh	-	-	-	-	-	-	-	-
Civil (Citizens) Rights Movement	-	-	-	-	-	-	-	-
Democratic Movement for Change	-	-	-	-	-	-	-	-
Moked	-	-	-	-	-	-	-	-
Shelli[p]	-	-	-	-	-	-	-	-
Flatto-Sharon	-	-	-	-	-	-	-	-

a   Included in Mapam 1949 and 1951.
b   Formed 1965 - Ben Gurion splinter group from Mapai.
c   Formed 1968 - merger of Mapai, Rafi, Ahdut Avodah.
d   Ben Gurion splinter group from Israel Labor.
e   Formed 1961 - merger of General Zionists and
      Progressives.
f   Formed 1965 - merger of Herut and majority of
      Liberal party.
g   Minority of Liberal party not joining in merger
      with Herut.
h   Formed 1968 - splinter group from Herut.
i   Elected as follows: Hapoel Hamizrahi, 6; Mizrahi,
      4; Agudat Israel, 3; Poalei Agudat Israel, 3.

TABLE 13.2 (continued)

1961 %	1961 Seats	1965 %	1965 Seats	1969 %	1969 Seats	1973 %	1973 Seats	1977 %	1977 Seats
34.7	42	In Alignment		In Alignment		In Alignment		In Alignment	
7.5	9	6.6	8	In Alignment		In Alignment		In Alignment	
6.6	8	In Alignment		In Alignment		In Alignment		In Alignment	
-	-	36.7	45	-	-	-	-	-	-
-	-	7.9	10	In Alignment		In Alignment		In Alignment	
-	-	-	-	In Alignment		In Alignment		In Alignment	
-	-	-	-	46.2	56	39.7	51	24.6	32
-	-	-	-	3.1	4	-	-	-	-
13.8	17	-	-	-	-	-	-	-	-
-	-	-	-	-	-	-	-	-	-
-	-	-	-	-	-	-	-	-	-
13.6	17	-	-	-	-	-	-	-	-
-	-	21.3	26	21.7	26	-	-	-	-
-	-	3.8	5	3.2	4	3.6	4	1.2	1
-	-	-	-	-	-	-	-	1.9	2
-	-	-	-	1.2	2	-	-	-	-
-	-	-	-	-	-	30.2	39	33.4	43
-	-	-	-	-	-	-	-	-	-
-	-	-	-	-	-	-	-	-	-
9.8	12	9.0	11	9.7	12	8.3	10	9.2	12
3.7	4	3.3	4	3.2	4	-	-	3.4	4
1.9	2	1.8	2	1.8	2	-	-	1.4	1
-	-	-	-	-	-	3.8	5	-	-
1.6	2	2.0	2	-	-	-	-	-	-
-	-	-	-	-	-	-	-	-	-
1.9	2	1.4	2	-	-	-	-	-	-
-	-	-	-	3.5	4	2.4	3	-	-
-	-	-	-	-	-	-	-	1.4	1
4.2	5	-	-	-	-	-	-	-	-
-	-	2.3	3	2.8	3	3.4	4	-	-
-	-	1.1	1	1.2	1	-	-	-	-
-	-	-	-	-	-	-	-	4.6	5
-	-	-	-	-	-	-	-	-	-
-	-	-	-	-	-	-	-	-	-
-	-	-	-	-	-	-	-	-	-
-	-	-	-	-	-	-	-	-	-
-	-	1.2	1	1.2	2	-	-	-	-
-	-	-	-	-	-	2.2	3	1.2	1
-	-	-	-	-	-	-	-	11.6	15
-	-	-	-	-	-	1.4	1	-	-
-	-	-	-	-	-	-	-	1.6	2
-	-	-	-	-	-	-	-	2.0	1

j Merger - Mizrahi and Hapoel Mizrahi.
k In Torah Religious Front until 1961 elections and
    again in 1973 elections.
l Joint list of Agudat Israel and Poalei Agudat Israel.
m Split of Communist party in 1965 resulted in
    formation of Rakah and Maki.
n Formed 1973 - merger of Gahal, State List, Free Center,
    Greater Israel Movement.
o Formed 1977 - Rakah and some Israel Black Panthers.
p Formed 1977 - merger of Moked, Haolam Hazeh and
    independent socialists.
q Joined Likud after 1977 election.

was the dominant party in Israel until 1977, when it was supplanted by Likud. Prior to statehood its role was virtually unchallenged. Mapai controlled the Assembly of the Elected and the National Council in the semiautonomous Jewish government in Palestine. In the 1931 elections it received 43.7 percent of the vote for the Assembly of the Elected and gained control of the National Council, which it maintained until 1948. Mapai continued its dominant role after statehood and in elections for the Knesset it consistently obtained the largest single percentage of votes, usually about one-third of the total. It was the major member of all government coalitions and ordinarily held the portfolios of prime minister, minister of defense, foreign minister, and finance minister. Its role in the Jewish Agency was also significant. Although the agency was governed by a coalition of all Israeli parties, Mapai has had the largest representation on the executive board and has usually held the chairmanship and other major posts. Mapai also frequently won the largest bloc of representation in the Histadrut (often a majority), and was the controlling party on the executive board. The continuing role of Mapai as the most important member of the parliament and of the cabinet, and its status in the Jewish Agency and Histadrut, were the basis for its unique position of influence and control in the Israeli system. The party was one of the political institutions of the country and was identified with the state in the minds of many voters. Also, because of its long tenure of office it permeated the governmental, administrative, economic, and other institutions of Israel.

On 21 January 1968, Mapai merged with two other labor parties, Ahdut Ha'avoda-Poale Zion (Unity of Labor Workers of Zion) and Rafi (Israel Labor List), to form Mifleget Ha'avoda Ha-Israelit (Israel Labor party). Together with the Mapai-affiliated Arab parties, the new party held 59 out of the 120 votes in the Knesset, only 2 short of a majority. The June War was the turning point that precipitated the trend toward the merger of the labor parties. The Arab threat led to the establishment of a broadly based government of National Unity. When the termination of the war did not bring peace and the continuation of the conflict with an accelerated tempo became evident, prudence dictated the maintenance of the broader coalition to present a solid front in international negotiations. The need for cooperation for reasons of security and defense contributed greatly to the creation of a climate suitable to the consummation of the merger.

The Labor party remained the single most important factor in Israeli politics until the 1977 parliamentary elections. The merger of the labor parties did not eliminate the differences between the coalition's components but rather shifted the quarrels from the interparty to the intraparty sphere. It was within the Israel Labor party that the problems of leadership and succession were resolved. However, the Labor party began to lose support in the 1970s. Disillusionment with its leadership, particularly at the time of the October War of 1973 and in subsequent negotiations for an Arab-Israeli settlement, combined with scandals and economic and social problems to raise significant doubts about the efficacy of its governmental role. Many of these elements contributed to the emergence of Likud (under Menahem Begin) as Israel's leading party after the 1977 election. But, like the Labor party, Likud did not capture a majority of seats in parliament; therefore, a coalition government was required.

The multiplicity of parties and the failure of any one party to win a majority of Knesset seats has necessitated coalition cabinets, which nonetheless have proved quite stable. Only twice have the coalitions been truly broad-based—the provisional government formed on independence and the government of National Unity formed during the crisis preceding the 1967 war and maintained following the 1969 elections. Both were unusual in that they were coalitions established in times of national stress.

Israel has had only six prime ministers during its first three decades of independence. Although there have been numerous cabinet changes, most have been essentially formal. These changes occurred following the election of a new Knesset, the choice of a president, the retirement of David Ben Gurion, his return to public life, his second retirement, the 1967 crisis and war, the death of Levi Eshkol, the retirement of Golda Meir, and so forth. The stability of Israel's cabinets has been due to several factors. The most important are the stabilizing personal influences of David Ben Gurion, Moshe Sharett, Levi Eshkol, and Golda Meir during their respective tenures as prime minister and the preponderant strength of Mapai and the Labor party. The rigorous discipline of Israel's parties has curbed irresponsible action by individual Knesset members. Finally, continuity of policy has been enhanced by the reappointment of many ministers in reorganized cabinets and the continuity of bureaucratic officeholders.

The coalition system has resulted in the acceptance of bargaining as a procedure for the allocation of portfolios and the distribution of power, both in the government and at high levels of administration. This has permitted the religious parties—National Religious, Agudat Israel, and Poale Agudat Israel—to play strong roles in government decision making because they were essential to secure a majority in the Knesset. The inevitable clash of interests and the persistence of partisan loyalties implicit in this procedure have limited governmental flexibility, and, to an extent, have reduced the efficiency of the administrative machinery. Since members of the Knesset do not represent any specific constituency and since they depend on party backing for election and reelection, their attitude and actions have more frequently been motivated by party considerations than by the general will. Although there have been various suggestions for electoral reform, the basic PR system, which helps perpetuate political diversity and multiplicity of parties, persists.

Despite this party proliferation and general political diversity, Israel's political life has been dominated by a relatively small and cohesive elite. Since prior to independence this group has maintained its position in the major state institutions, especially the cabinet and the Knesset. The members have substantial political experience and are generally older. The elite group is Jewish, and despite ideological diversity, tends to be homogeneous in background. Many of the leaders are European (especially Eastern European) in origin and most are personally acquainted, if not intimate.

The elite group has been predominantly civilian in background. The military is generally not regarded as part of the political elite, although it is consulted on matters relating to national defense and plays a role in the decision-making process on security-related issues. The armed forces are generally excluded from politics. Retired senior military officers (including generals and chiefs of staff) have been coopted into the political elite and included in the cabinet and other key posts. Their involvement has not been the result of military action or influence but rather the decision of the political parties to include highly visible and publicly acclaimed figures in their ranks.

Religious elements have held a somewhat similar position. Although the religious parties have exerted strong influence in the cabinet and Knesset due to their role in coalition formation, it has been in their role as *political* parties. The rabbinate is not considered part of the political elite and the religious establishment generally does not intervene in politics.

The Political Earthquake

The political process and political life of Israel underwent substantial turmoil at the time of the October War of 1973, which set in motion forces that subsequently affected the political process.

Israel's dramatic victory in the 1967 war and the resulting situation including the accompanying economic boom contributed to a nationwide euphoria that permeated thinking on many of the central political, security, and foreign-policy issues. Israelis were confident and sanguine about the situation and the future. The October War stunned Israel. The failure of Israeli military intelligence, initial battlefield reverses, and the "wars of the generals" raised questions concerning Israel's military capability. Questions concerning war-associated political decisions and deteriorating economic conditions also contributed to the political uncertainty. The October War accelerated the momentum for political change and facilitated the change of both personalities and policies in the Israeli political system.

In a society where political participation has always been widespread and where views are intense and diversified, the war heightened the interest, concern, and participation in politics of the younger, better-educated, and native-born generation. In the postwar period there was a greater realism, but also more caution, more questioning of attitudes and policy, and more criticism of both the system and the people who ran it—a direct result of the crisis of confidence created by the errors associated with the conflict, some of which were detailed in the Agranat Commission Report (1974). The impact was only partially reflected in the election for the Eighth Knesset and local authorities that were held at the end of December 1973. Golda Meir was empowered to create a new government and did so in early 1974, only to resign a month later primarily because of dissension within the Labor party that centered on the question of political responsibility for lapses at the outset of the war. This set the stage for the selection of a new prime minister and the formation of a new coalition. After considerable maneuvering within the Labor party, Yitzhak Rabin, former chief of staff and former ambassador to Washington, was chosen prime minister. The choice of Rabin was important in that he was relatively young (in his fifties) and of a new generation—not of the group of pioneers who came to Israel at the beginning of the twentieth century and who had controlled the situation since.

Rabin's government represented a departure from the past and ushered in something of a new era. Some of Israel's most well-known names and personalities faded from power. The coalition was initially constructed with a different structure because the National Religious party did not join and was replaced by the Civil Rights party (although the situation was reversed within a matter of months). Leadership had begun to be transferred from the immigrant-founder generation to the native-born sons. The policy process also underwent some change. The kitchen cabinet of Golda Meir and her strength of leadership was replaced by a cabinet of more diverse views and increased role in the policy process. Golda Meir's single role gave way to the representation of diverse views in Israel's three-man shuttle-diplomacy negotiating team (Rabin, Allon, and Peres) and in their coterie of advisors.

The October War also spawned protest movements and, eventually, new political parties that have attained various degrees of success in establishing themselves in the political structure. Initially, they developed in response to perceived mismanagement during the war and focused on the need for political reform. Among the resultant parties was the Democratic Movement for Change (DMC), which secured sizable representation in the Knesset in the 1977 elections and joined the Likud-led coalition in the fall of that year. It later split into several small groups.

Many of the forces set in motion by the October War and its aftermath seemed to come together to affect the situation in a tangible way in the 1977 elections.

In May 1977 Israel's electorate went to the polls and awarded the largest number of votes to the Likud, led by Menahem Begin. Thus, Israel chose a new regime and the Likud and Begin emerged as the leading political force. To a substantial degree, the results suggest that Labor lost more than Likud won. Voters were concerned with the lack of leadership and the weakness of the government in dealing with a wide variety of issues ranging from labor unrest to broader social problems. The vacillation of the government in response to challenges seemed to confirm general impressions of government weakness. Several major scandals prior to the election contributed to the negative image. In addition there was a somewhat similar and respected new alternative in the form of the DMC that allowed for voting shifts.

Israel's 1977 elections were a political earthquake reflecting and foreshadowing substantial change, with a new group, formerly in opposition, now in control. The parties constituting the Likud bloc had been serving as an opposition group, joining the government only during the 1967 crisis for a three-year period to form the "wall-to-wall" government of National Unity. It withdrew from the coalition in 1970 in a dispute over U.S. Secretary of State William Rogers's June 1970 peace initiative. Thereafter, the parties (especially Begin's Gahal), vocally opposed the government, criticizing its programs, policies, efforts, and leadership. As a result of the 1977 election, Likud became the ruling coalition responsible for establishing and implementing programs for the government.

Foreign Policy

There are three primary elements in Israel's political life and in its foreign and security policy: the pursuit of peace through negotiations with the Arab states; the assurance of security in a region of hostility through an effective defense capability; and the attainment of international support. These goals of peace and security derive from the continuing conflict with the Arab states that remains the preeminent problem confronting Israel; it affects all of Israel's policies and activities—both domestic and foreign. Israel's foreign relations have been influenced by this dispute in every area of concern and application since independence.

The dispute between Israel and the Arab states is essentially a conflict between the goals of political Zionism and Arab nationalism. Zionism or Jewish nationalism sought to create a Jewish national home and to achieve the ingathering of the exiles to preserve world Jewry. This Jewish home could be established only in Palestine—its historic location. Arab nationalists sought the independence and unity of all Arab states and declared Palestine an integral part of the Arab world.

World War I provided the setting for the conflict of these opposing views. During the war, the British entered into arrangements with the French, the Arabs, and the Zionists that laid the basis for the division of the Ottoman Empire and provided the foundation for the claims of both Arab and Jewish nationalists in their dispute for control of Palestine. These included an exchange of correspondence between Sharif Husayn of Mecca and Sir Henry McMahon, the British high commissioner for Egypt; the Sykes-Picot Agreement; and the Balfour Declaration. The British chose to retain control of Palestine following the war and thus the mandate period provided the context for the development of the conflict between the Jewish and Arab communities of Palestine. The Zionists adopted a program designed to secure the establishment of a Jewish homeland in Palestine. In an effort to achieve Arab self-government and independence the Arabs decided on noncooperation with the mandatory regime. They protested Jewish immigration and land purchases in an effort to limit the number and influence of Jews in Palestine to ensure an Arab majority and Arab control when self-determination was implemented.

The submission of the Palestine problem to the United Nations in 1947 provided an opportunity for the antagonists to present their positions. The resultant Partition Plan was generally favored by the Jewish Agency while the Arab delegates strongly opposed it.

Increased hostility between the Arab and Jewish communities in Palestine followed the adoption of the partition resolution and led to conflict in late 1947. Upon Israel's declaration of independence in May 1948, the scope of the conflict was enlarged. The Arab League notified the United Nations that it was intervening in Palestine in order to restore the territory to the Palestine Arabs. The league hoped to thwart the partition resolution and to prevent the establishment of Israel as an independent country. The ensuing war was halted by armistice agreements between Israel and the four contiguous Arab states (Egypt, Syria, Lebanon, and Transjordan), which were signed between February and July 1949, thereby setting the stage for peace negotiations. However, none of the ensuing efforts yielded any substantial positive result in the period prior to the October War of 1973. Instead, major wars in 1956, 1967, and 1973 (as well as the Egypt-Israel War of Attrition of 1969–1970) and continuing small-scale conflict established a negative pattern of relations that has dominated Israeli foreign and security policy.

Prior to the establishment of Israel, and especially since 1948, Israel has continued to recognize that peace and cooperation with the neighboring Arab states is vital for the survival and development of the Jewish state over an extended period. This acknowledgement has remained a cornerstone of Israel's policy. Successive governments have included these concepts in their official programs and have sought their attainment.

Israel's general foreign policy approach began to take shape once it became clear that peace would not follow the armistice accords. Israel directed its major attention beyond the circle of neighboring Arab states and its Middle Eastern region to the broader international community. The effort to establish friendly relations with the states of the developing world and Europe, as well as with the superpowers, was conceived as having a positive impact on the Arab-Israeli conflict, in addition to its strictly bilateral political and economic advantages. The bilateral relationships were also viewed as mechanisms to ensure Israel's deterrent strength through national armed power and through increased international support for its position. Israel has seen Europe and the developing world (especially Africa and Latin America) as important components of its overall policy. It has sought to maintain positive relations with Europe based on the commonality of the Judeo-Christian heritage and the memories of the Holocaust. Its approach to the developing world has been based on Israel's ability to provide technical assistance in the development process. Despite substantial effort in these sectors, the centrality of the Arab-Israeli conflict has enlarged the role of the superpowers.

Israel's leaders early recognized the crucial role that the great powers would play in ensuring the country's defense and integrity. In the euphoric days following independence it was believed that neutrality in the Cold War was possible and that Israel could establish and maintain friendly relations with both East and West (i.e., the Soviet Union and the United States). This was in accord with Israel's perception of its national interest and seemed to be a realistic assessment in light of the policies and activities of both powers in the period immediately following World War II. However, Israel's position increasingly became Western- and especially United States–oriented. The West provided Israel with the political and moral support and arms and economic assistance essential for its survival and defense, while the Soviet Union increasingly identified itself with the Arab cause. The relationship with the United States became the more significant because of U.S. political and moral support, because of extensive economic and technical assistance, and because of the arms aid and central position of the United States in the effort to achieve an Arab-Israeli peace. The U.S. Jewish community also helped to create a special linkage between Israel and the United States.

The June War of 1967 substantially modified the content of the issues central to the dispute and generated change in the Israeli system and Israeli perceptions. The realities of Arab hostility, the nature of the Arab threat, and the difficulties of achieving a settlement became more obvious. However, the issues of the conflict changed with the extent of the Israeli victory: Israel occupied the Sinai peninsula, the Gaza Strip, the West Bank of the Jordan River, the eastern sector of the city of Jerusalem, and the Golan Heights. Israel adopted the position that it would not withdraw from those territories until there were negotiations with the Arab states leading to peace agreements that recognized Israel's right to exist and accepted Israel's permanent position and borders. Throughout the period between the June War (1967) and the October War (1973) the focal point in the Middle East was the effort to achieve a settlement of the Arab-Israeli conflict and to secure a just and lasting peace. In these attempts, based on United Nations Security Council Resolution 242 of 22 November 1967, the regional states, the superpowers (and lesser powers), and the main instrumentalities of the international system were engaged. Israel focused its attention on peace and security objectives and developed positions concerning the occupied territories, the Palestinians, and related questions. This provided the base for the post–October War policy. Although some of the interwar efforts were promising, peace was not achieved and there was little movement in that direction. Instead, the October War erupted and created a new environment for the quest for peace and the development of Israeli foreign policy. Israel's position in the international community deteriorated with the outbreak of the fighting. Israel was condemned by some states and some severed diplomatic relations.

Prior to the war Israel's international position had been declining. The propaganda war had been turning in favor of the Arabs, and Israel had been losing world sympathy. In most instances, this could be traced to Israel's continued refusal to withdraw from occupied Arab territories and her responses to Arab terrorism, which increasingly came under international condemnation. After the break in relations with Uganda in the spring of 1972, several states in Africa severed relations and in September 1973, Cuba took similar action. Immediately prior to the outbreak of the war, Israel had come into sharp dispute with Austria over the latter's refusal to continue to provide facilities for Russian emigrants on their way to Israel—a matter on which the Austrians had refused to relent. There was increasing international sentiment for withdrawal, and resolutions of various international and regional organizations called on Israel to retreat from the occupied territories.

During the course of the war and immediately afterward, Israel's ties with most of the remaining states of Black Africa were broken. Many of them linked the rupture of relations with Israel's refusal to withdraw from the occupied territories. Except for South Africa, no major African state publicly backed Israel or offered assistance. To most Israelis this not only symbolized the injustice of the international community but also the success of Arab oil blackmail and the failure of Israel's program of international cooperation. Israel had provided many of these African states with technical assistance, which the Africans had lauded publicly for promoting African development. Israel retained relations with only five African states: South Africa and four black states—Malawi, Lesotho, Botswana, and Swaziland. Then, later in November 1973, the Organization of African Unity Ministerial Council noted the "expansionist designs of belligerent Israel" and denounced her.

The ruptures with Africa were a disappointment, but a shift in the attitudes and policies of the European states was perhaps more significant. Israel's international isolation was compounded by the unwillingness of the European allies of the United States to allow the use of their facilities and/or airspace for the shipment and transfer of supplies to Israel during the war. Portugal was an exception and allowed the use of the Azores, thereby forcing the United States to establish special systems for the resupply of Israel. The Europeans were reluctant to be associated with the United States effort and were concerned with the reduction of Arab oil shipments to them. On 6 November the nine members of the European Economic Community adopted a joint communiqué on the Middle East clearly aimed at placating the Arabs. It called on Israel to withdraw from occupied Arab territories and recognize the rights of the Palestinians.

Japan, which receives from 80 to 90 percent of her oil from the Middle East and much of that from the Arab states, also began to modify her policy. The Japanese, who had hitherto adopted and maintained a posture of neutrality in the Arab-Israeli conflict, now seemed to shift to a more pronounced pro-Arab position. They called for implementation of

United Nations Resolution 242 (1967) and stressed the Arab interpretation of the resolution, calling on Israel to withdraw from all Arab territories. They also increased their contributions to the United Nations for aid to Palestinian refugees and offered development loans to several Arab states.

The war thus increased Israeli dependence on the United States. No other country could or was prepared to provide Israel with the vast quantities of modern and sophisticated arms required for war or for the political and moral support necessary to negotiate peace.

During the war the United States resupplied Israel with a substantial amount of military equipment, including conventional munitions of many types, air-to-air and air-to-ground missiles, artillery, crew-served and individual weapons, and a standard range of fighter aircraft ordnance, tanks, aircraft, radios, and other military equipment that had been lost in action. Many members of Congress supported the Israeli position and the U.S. resupply effort. On 19 October President Richard Nixon asked Congress to authorize $2.2 billion in emergency security assistance for Israel in order "to prevent the emergence of a substantial imbalance resulting from a large-scale resupply of Syria and Egypt by the Soviet Union." The United States also alerted its armed forces when there was an indication that the Soviet Union might become militarily involved in the area. The United States reacted to the Arab embargo on oil shipments by stressing that it would seek to become independent of Arab oil and that U.S. energy requirements would not lead to a shift in its policies in the Middle East. Despite these reassuring signs Israel was concerned that the United States might withdraw its support from Israel and that it might utilize its leverage to effect changes in Israel's position.

There were questions about the U.S. role on such matters as the ceasefire, the peace negotiations, and the terms of a Middle East settlement. Apparently there were U.S. pressures on Israel to accept the initial ceasefire and to permit a relief convoy to resupply the Egyptian Third Army on the east bank of the Suez Canal. Some Israelis were concerned about an apparent U.S. courting of the Arabs including the restoration of formal diplomatic relations between the United States and Egypt, and the visits by Secretary of State Henry Kissinger to Arab capitals (Rabat, Tunis, Cairo, Amman, and Riyadh). Some elements in Israel expressed concern that Israel might be sacrificed by the United States in an effort to further détente. The oil factor and its potential impact on the United States and the latter's relationship with Israel also became a matter of Israeli concern.

The important role assumed by the United States in the effort to achieve a settlement, the growing energy crisis in the United States, and the increased dependence of Israel on the United States combined to stress the importance of the U.S. relationship with Israel and suggested that this would be the major focus of Israeli foreign policy during the postwar period.

In the wake of the October War, modifications of Israel's policy were relatively minor and there were no dramatic shifts in objectives and content. The primary goals remained: the achievement of an Arab-Israeli settlement and the assurance of security in the interim. This constancy resulted, in part, from Israel's collective conception of its fundamental international position—and the limited policy options that flow therefrom—which was not substantially altered. Israel's view of itself as geographically isolated and without dependable allies, its geographical vulnerability, and its need to acquire and produce arms for self-defense were reaffirmed by the October War. Israel believed that it won a military victory and that its strategic concepts were vindicated.

Israel recognized the dangers inherent in its increased isolation in the international community and in its increased dependence on the United States. In the wake of the war it attempted to reaffirm and reestablish the ties that had been disrupted as a result of the conflict and attendant use of the Arab oil weapon. Israel launched an intensive effort to restore its traditionally close relations with the states of Europe; yet with Israel's increased economic and military needs and diplomatic isolation, the relationship with the United States became more central. After the October War, as before, the United States remained critical to Israel's security, to the search for peace in the Arab-Israeli zone of the Middle East, and to the continued prosperity of the Jewish state. However, there was an ambivalence and an uneasiness in Israel's postwar policy, which sought to solidify the support and aid of the United States while reducing its dependence on that nation.

Within this general framework, Israel continued to focus on the central issue: the Arab-Israeli conflict and its impact on Israel's quest for peace and security.

The policies adopted by the Rabin government after the October War to achieve peace were similar to those of its predecessor Labor governments. The 1977 elections, which brought Begin and Likud to power, also effected changes in certain areas of foreign policy and reconfirmed others.

The primary focus of Begin's foreign policy was peace, which Likud, like its predecessors, defined as the end of war, full reconciliation and normalization, and open borders across which people and goods could cross without hindrance. The question of occupied territory revolved around the national consensus, which opposed return to the lines that existed prior to the June War and which sought instead alterations to create defensible borders for Israel. Jerusalem was seen as the capital of Israel, which could not be redivided; but it was felt that the religious concerns of other faiths could be accommodated. The division in Israeli positions focused on the extent of withdrawal and the extent of territorial compromise in the event of a settlement. Begin and others argued that Israel had a religious-ideological link to the West Bank that militated against withdrawal, while others saw security as the factor that should determine the final Israeli position. On the Palestinian issue, Israel accepted the fact that there had to be Palestinian participation in a settlement but opposed dealing with the PLO, since that organization did not recognize the existence of Israel and was committed to its destruction. Israel also opposed the establishment of an independent Palestinian state on the West Bank and in the Gaza Strip. The national consensus focused on the need for an accommodation. The main obstacle appeared to be the Arab unwillingness to accept Israel as a negotiating partner and to deal directly with it. This position underwent some modification with the Sadat initiative of November 1977, when he visited Israel and inaugurated direct negotiations between Israel and Egypt. Afterward, negotiations began and the issues were considered directly by the parties at the Cairo Conference and Ismailia Summit of December 1977 and in lower-level contacts over the ensuing months. Then, in September 1978, Prime Minister Begin met with President Carter and Egyptian President Sadat at the Camp David Summit and developed a framework for peace between Egypt and Israel, and, ultimately, for a broader arrangement between Israel and the other Arab states. In this process the U.S.-Israeli special relationship took on added significance.

Over the months following the Camp David Summit, the United States worked to achieve the formal peace treaty between Egypt and Israel envisioned in the summit documents. Finally, after substantial effort, a peace treaty between Israel and Egypt was signed in Washington in March 1979. It not only ended the conflict between these two states and provided for Israeli withdrawal from all of the Sinai peninsula but it also established a framework for negotiations concerning the status of the other territories occupied in June 1967 and for ultimate resolution of the conflict. But, despite the developments concerning Israel and Egypt, the Arab-Israeli conflict remains central to Israel more than three decades after its independence, for without resolution of that issue Israel's very existence is at stake. All other issues, both domestic and foreign, continue to revolve around this concern.

Notes

1. The term "Jewish Agency" first appeared in international usage in the mandate entrusting the administration of Palestine to the British government. In Article 4 the WZO was recognized as "an appropriate Jewish Agency . . . for the purpose of advising and cooperating with the administration of Palestine in such economic, social, and other matters as may affect the establishment of the Jewish National Home and the interests of the Jewish population in Palestine, and, subject always to the control of the administration, to assist and take part in the development of the country." The agency was expected to "take steps in consultation with His Britannic Majesty's Government to secure the cooperation of all Jews who are willing to assist in the establishment of the Jewish National Home."

Bibliography

Howard M. Sachar, *A History of Israel: From the Rise of Zionism to Our Time* (New York: Alfred A. Knopf, 1976) and Noah Lucas, *The Modern History of Israel* (New York and Washington, D.C.: Praeger Publishers, 1975) provide histories of Israel that antedate independence. The Mandate Period is discussed in greater detail in J. C. Hurewitz's *The Struggle for Palestine* (New York: W. W. Norton, 1950) and Christopher Syke's *Crossroads to Israel* (Cleveland, Ohio, and New York: World Publishing, 1965).

A brief introduction to various aspects of Israeli society and to Jewish history and values may be found in the Israel Pocket Library (Jerusalem: Keter Books, 1973 and 1974), a series of fifteen paperback volumes containing material from the *Encyclopaedia Judaica*. The titles are *Anti-Semitism, Archaeology, Democracy, Economy, Education and Science, Geography, History From 1880, History Until 1880, Holocaust, Immigration and Settlement, Jerusalem, Jewish Values, Religious Life and Communities, Society,* and *Zionism*. The series also has a *Cumulative Index*. Efraim Orni and Elisha Efrat, in *Geography of Israel*, 3rd rev. ed. (Jerusalem: Israel Universities Press, 1971), provide a detailed examination of all facets of Israel's geography.

The constitutional and legal parameters of the political system are considered in several volumes. Emanuel Rackman's *Israel's Emerging Constitution, 1948–51* (New York: Columbia University Press, 1955) deals with the problems involved in the development of a constitution. Henry E. Baker, in *The Legal System of Israel* (Jerusalem: Israel Universities Press, 1968) and Joseph Badi, ed., in *Fundamental Laws of the State of Israel* (New York: Twayne Publishers, Inc., 1961) discuss the legal system and basic legislation. An important study of the parliament is Asher Zidon, *Knesset: The Parliament of Israel* (New York: Herzl Press, 1967), which is complemented by Eliahu S. Likhovski, *Israel's Parliament: The Law of the Knesset* (Oxford: Oxford University Press, 1971).

The basic features and early issues of the political system are described and analyzed in Joseph Badi, *The Government of the State of Israel: A Critical Ac-*

count of Its Parliament, Executive, and Judiciary (New York: Twayne Publishers, Inc., 1963); Marver H. Bernstein, *The Politics of Israel: The First Decade of Statehood* (Princeton, N.J.: Princeton University Press, 1957); Leonard J. Fein, *Israel: Politics and People* (Boston: Little, Brown & Co., 1968); Yehoshua Freudenheim, *Government in Israel* (Dobbs Ferry, N.Y.: Oceana Publications, Inc., 1967); and Oscar Kraines, *Government and Politics in Israel* (Boston: Houghton Mifflin Co., 1961).

Various aspects of the political system and political process are considered in the following more specialized studies: Alan Arian, *The Choosing People: Voting Behavior in Israel* (Cleveland, Ohio, and London: Case Western Reserve University Press, 1973); Alan Arian, ed., *The Elections in Israel—1969* (Israel: Jerusalem Academic Press, 1972); Yuval Elizur and Eliahu Salpeter, *Who Rules Israel?* (New York: Harper & Row, 1973); Eva Etzioni-Halevy, *Political Culture in Israel: Cleavage and Integration Among Israeli Jews* (New York and London: Praeger Publishers, 1977); Peter Y. Medding, *Mapai in Israel: Political Organisation and Government in a New Society* (Cambridge: Cambridge University Press, 1972); Lester G. Seligman, *Leadership in a New Nation: Political Development in Israel* (New York: Atherton Press, 1964); and David M. Zohar, *Political Parties in Israel: The Evolution of Israeli Democracy* (New York, Washington, D.C., and London: Praeger Publishers, 1974).

Studies of the salient domestic political issues tend to be relatively few in number. Among the more reliable are the following: S. N. Eisenstadt's *Israeli Society* (New York: Basic Books, Inc., 1967) is a compendium containing numerous social statistics not easily available elsewhere. Immigrant absorption is the topic of Judith T. Shuval's *Immigrants on the Threshold* (New York: Atherton Press, 1963). Alex Weingrod, in *Israel: Group Relations in a New Society* (New York: Frederick A. Praeger Publishers for the Institute of Race Relations, 1965), discusses problems of social integration and the attempt to create a multiethnic society. Israel's economy is discussed by David Horowitz, governor of the Bank of Israel, in *The Economics of Israel* (Oxford: Pergamon Press, 1967). The problem of religion's relationship to the state is discussed by Joseph Badi in *Religion in Israel Today: The Relationship Between State and Religion* (New York: Bookman Associates, 1959) and Gary S. Schiff, *Tradition and Politics: The Religious Parties of Israel* (Detroit: Wayne State University Press, 1977). Yigal Allon, *The Making of Israel's Army* (New York: Bantam Books, 1971) and Amos Perlmutter, *Military and Politics in Israel: Nation-Building and Role Expansion* (London: Frank Cass and Co., 1969) consider the role of the military. Jacob M. Landau, in *The Arabs in Israel: A Political Study* (London: Oxford University Press, 1969), presents a comprehensive survey and analysis of the role of the Arabs in Israel. An alternate perspective is provided by Sabri Jiryis, *The Arabs in Israel* (New York and London: Monthly Review Press, 1976).

Israel's international relations are discussed in Theodore Draper, *Israel and World Politics: Roots of the Third Arab-Israeli War* (New York: The Viking Press, 1968) and in *Israel and the United Nations*, report of a study group set up by The Hebrew University of Jerusalem (New York: Manhattan Publishing Company, 1956). Ernest Stock's *Israel on the Road to Sinai, 1949–1956* (Ithaca, N.Y.: Cornell University Press, 1967) is an incisive study of Israel's foreign policy from 1948 to the Sinai campaign, with a sequel on the June 1967 War. Walter Eytan, a ranking Israeli diplomat, has written *The First Ten Years: A Diplomatic History of Israel* (New York: Simon and Schuster, 1958). Israel's international cooperation program is discussed in Leopold Laufer, *Israel and the Developing Countries: New Approaches to Cooperation* (New York: The Twentieth Century Fund, 1967), Shimeon Amir, *Israel's Development Cooperation with Africa, Asia, and Latin America* (New York: Praeger Publishers, 1974), and Michael Curtis and Susan Aurelia Gitelson, eds., *Israel in the Third World* (New Brunswick, N.J.: Transaction Books, 1974). Michael Brecher, in *Decisions in Israel's Foreign Policy* (New Haven: Yale University Press, 1975) and *The Foreign Policy System of Israel: Setting, Images, Processes* (New Haven: Yale University Press, 1972) provide a comprehensive approach to Israel's foreign-policy process and examine some major decisions. Meron Medzini, in *Israel's Foreign Relations: Selected Documents, 1947–1974*, 2 vols. (Jerusalem: Ministry for Foreign Affairs, 1976), provides the major documents of Israel's foreign policy from its inception through the October 1973 War and its aftermath. Nadav Safran, in *Israel: The Embattled Ally* (Cambridge, Mass: Harvard University Press, Belknap Press, 1978), provides coverage of Israel's domestic scene as it affects foreign policy. Yehoshafat Harkabi, in *Arab Strategies and Israel's Response* (New York: The Free Press, 1977), and Gabriel Sheffer, ed., in *Dynamics of a Conflict: A Re-examination of the Arab-Israeli Conflict* (Atlantic Highlands, N.J.: Humanities Press, 1975), deal with aspects of the Arab-Israeli conflict and Israel's position and perspective. Bernard Reich's *Israel and Occupied Territories* (Washington, D.C.: Department of State, 1973) focuses on the problem of the territories occupied by Israel in the 1967 war. Bernard Reich, in *Quest for Peace: United States–Israel Relations and the Arab-Israeli Conflict* (New Brunswick, N.J.: Transaction Books, 1977), deals with Israel's relations with the United States in the context of the efforts to resolve the Arab-Israeli conflict.

14

Arab Republic of Egypt

Bernard Reich

Historical Background

Throughout recorded history the civilization of the Nile Valley has flourished as a result of a combination of plentiful water, good soil, and climatic conditions contributing to a long growing season. The Nile River also provided swift, efficient, and cheap transportation and became the focal point of both ancient and modern civilizations. In ancient days a series of great kingdoms, ruled by pharaohs, developed in the valley and made important and long-lasting contributions to civilization in the fields of science, architecture, politics, and economics. These ancient kingdoms provided a base for the development of the modern Egyptian political system. Throughout its history Egypt has remained essentially a united entity, ruled by a single government, in part because of the need for overall planning for irrigation and agricultural production.

After the sixth century B.C., Egypt fell under the influence of Persia, Greece, Rome, and the Byzantine Empire. Beginning with the Persian conquest in 525 B.C., Egypt was ruled for nearly twenty-five hundred years by alien dynasties or as a part of a foreign empire. This foreign domination left its imprint. Christianity was brought to the Nile Valley and, in A.D. 639 Arab invaders from the east entered Egypt. They converted Egypt into the Arab and Islamic society that it has remained ever since. The period of Arab political domination, however, was broken at various times by other powers, notably the Mamelukes (1252–1517) and the Ottomans (1517–1882). This legacy of foreign control has been a matter of concern to Egyptian nationalists and has been a significant factor in the Egyptian political culture and world outlook.

In some respects, the most significant external influence came after the Ottoman Turks gained control of Egypt and made it a province of the empire in 1517. That initial Ottoman influence was modified by the

Napoleonic invasion of 1798 and the developments that followed. They introduced an unrest and assisted the transition from the military feudalism of the past to a new system. The Western impact, the important reforms of Muhammad Ali (1805–1849), known as the founder of modern Egypt, and the construction of the Suez Canal in the mid-nineteenth century all contributed to the development of the modern Egyptian state.

Muhammad Ali was neither an Egyptian nor an Arab, but an Albanian who came to Egypt from Kavalla (Macedonia) as an army commander in charge of a unit of the Ottoman army sent to deal with Napoleon. In 1805, the Ottoman sultan appointed him governor of Egypt with the title of pasha. Muhammad Ali brought significant change to the country, and, to a large degree, established its independence from the Ottoman sultan. Under the former's control, Egypt began to develop the elements of a modern state and a more European cultural orientation. Muhammad Ali launched an ambitious series of domestic projects designed to improve the economy and general condition of the state. Agricultural production was improved and reorganized and a program of industrialization was inaugurated. He forced Egyptian products into the European market and encouraged the production of cotton. Turks were replaced with Egyptians in the administration. He stressed education and sought to improve its quality. He created a modern national army, organized on European lines, that gained substantial experience in various areas of the Middle East during his reign. He created the base for a modern political system and the conditions for the rise of Egyptian nationalism.

Although European powers had been interested in Egypt for some time, the opening of the Suez Canal to world navigation and commerce in 1869 vastly increased great-power interest in Egypt. England, the greatest sea power of the time, was particularly concerned with the canal because it provided a shorter and more efficient link in its lifeline of the British Empire, which stretched from London to the Far East and included east Africa and the Persian Gulf. Problems associated with the canal's operation and Egypt's financial mismanagement provided the framework for the British occupation in 1882, although other European powers had also been concerned about the financial situation of Egypt. Foreign creditors, anxious about their funds entrusted to Khedive Ismail, pressed their respective governments for relief and assistance. As a result, Egyptian finances were controlled by foreign creditors and Ismail was deposed in 1879. Popular opposition formed against the khedive, his court, and the foreign powers. Khedive Tawfiq, who succeeded Ismail, ruled a country that was heavily taxed and was under British and French

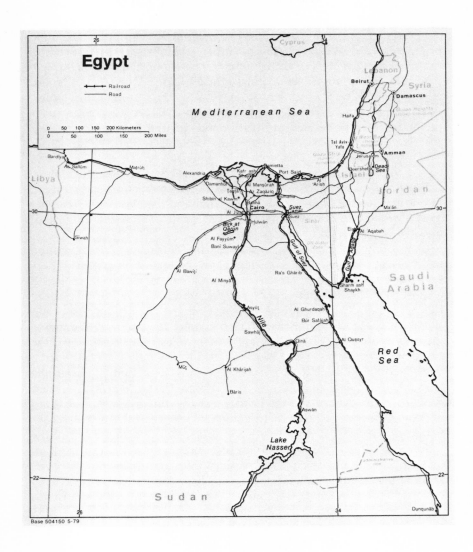

Egypt

▲—▲—▲ Railroad
——— Road

0   50   100   150   200 Kilometers
0   50   100   150   200 Miles

Cyprus

Mediterranean Sea

Lebanon
Beirut
Damascus
Syria

Haifa

Tel Aviv
Yafa

Amman

Jerusalem

Israel

Dead
Sea

Bardiya
As Sallūm
Matrūh
Libya

Alexandria
Kafr ash
Damietta
Port Said
Damanhūr
Al Manşūrah
Tanta
Shibīn al Kawm
Az Zaqāzīq
Binhā
Al
Cairo
Suez
Canal
Suez

Al ʿArīsh

Sīnāʾ

Jordan

Maʿān

30

Birk at
Qārūn
Hulwān

Al Fayyūm
Banī Suwayf

Siwah

Al Bawīṭī

Al Minyā

Raʾs Ghārib

Ela
Al ʿAqabah

Sharm ash
Shaykh

Saudi
Arabia

Asyūṭ

Al Ghurdaqah
Būr Safājah

Sawhāj

Qinā
Al Quşayr

Mūṭ
Al Khārijah

Red
Sea

Bāris

Aswān

Lake
Nasser

22

Sudan

Dunqunāb

financial supervision and political control.

In response to this situation, Colonel Ahmed Arabi led a group of Egyptian nationalists who protested British and French interference in the sovereignty of Egypt and opposed the lack of indigenous political participation in Egypt. They sought constitutional reform, liberalization of Egyptian political participation, and an end to foreign interference in the affairs of Egypt. The British and French supported the khedive. In July 1882 British forces landed in Egypt and crushed the Arabi revolt. Although they were originally to leave after the restoration of order, British forces remained in Egypt until the mid-1950s and real control over the affairs of state resided in British hands for the next seven decades, thereby giving Britain control over the canal. The khedive (and later king) remained the titular authority, but the British representatives (under various titles) were the final authorities on the affairs of state.

World War I added a new dimension to the commercial and strategic importance of the Suez Canal for England and the West. In December 1914, Britain proclaimed Egypt a British protectorate and the title of khedive was changed to that of sultan.

Opposition to the British intensified during World War I. Exasperation and frustration characterized the Egyptian nationalist movement. There had been some hope engendered by such events as the Arab revolt against the Ottoman sultan and such declarations as Wilson's Fourteen Points. Within Egyptian society there emerged the beginnings of nationalistic ideas of a political nature that were to spearhead the movement to remove British control and establish Egyptian control over the country. In this post–World War I context a new political organization developed, al-Wafd al-Misri ("the Egyptian Delegation"). Under the leadership of Saad Zaghlul and later Nahas Pasha, al-Wafd al-Misri sought independence from the British and self-rule in Egypt. The Wafd hoped to present its position to the great powers at the postwar conferences, especially at the Paris Peace Conference, where the fate of the Ottoman territories was to be determined. British opposition to Egyptian independence effectively prevented the Wafd from achieving its goal, and the period until 1952 is replete with Egyptian nationalist efforts to end British domination of the country. The Wafd remained the most important political party in Egypt until its abolition following the 1952 revolution. Throughout the period it opposed British imperialism and sought Nile unity with the Sudan as a part of Egypt.

In the aftermath of World War I Egyptian opposition to British rule became increasingly hostile. In the face of such pressure, the protectorate was terminated and in February 1922 the British unilaterally proclaimed Egypt a constitutional monarchy. However, the British reserved their freedom of action on four matters: the Sudan, the defense of Egypt against foreign intervention, the security of the canal (i.e., the communications line of the British Empire), and the protection of foreign interests and minorities. In March, Sultan Fuad became the king of Egypt. Thus, by 1922 Egypt became technically an independent country with its own king and in alliance with England (which provided assistance in defense and related matters). A constitution was developed and promulgated in April 1923, launching a new experiment in government and politics. A parliament was elected and a government was formed. Domestic politics began to operate and rivalries between power blocs and political institutions began to develop. Local politics reflected a good deal of the rivalry between the king on the one hand and the government and parliament on the other (both of the latter generally dominated by the Wafd, which opposed both the king and the British). Many of the concerns of Egyptian society were not effectively dealt with because the main political forces were in conflict with each other. Fortunately, there was more agreement on the question of the British position in Egypt. All elements of Egyptian society generally agreed that the British should leave and that full control should be vested in Egyptian authorities.

British influence, however, remained paramount. British troops and officials were stationed in Egypt, mostly but not solely concerned with the canal and the security of the imperial communications system. Through them, the British were able to influence political activity and policy decisions. British-Egyptian negotiations continued, on a somewhat sporadic basis, during much of the period until 1936. At that time a new Anglo-Egyptian treaty was written that altered but did not terminate the British role. On many of the key issues little changed and British influence remained significant although its formal trappings were modified.

World War II provided an important milestone in the political development of Egypt. Its territory was used as a base of Allied operations but local sentiment was generally against England as the hated occupier. The war, however, sapped British strength and financial resources and Britain was soon forced to reconsider its position throughout the Middle East, setting the stage for a major political realignment throughout the area, especially in Egypt and Palestine.

After World War II Egypt became involved in two related matters that laid the foundation for the Egyptian revolution. The first was the creation of Israel following the British withdrawal from the Palestine mandate in 1948, which Egypt opposed and which, in turn, led to the Arab-Israeli War of 1948-1949 in which the armed forces of Egypt performed poorly. The corruption and inefficiency of the government of King Farouk, (whose rule began in 1936) was later cited as a major cause for the poor performance of Egyptian military forces against the new state of Israel. The war was probably the most important single event in Egypt's political development prior to the 1952 revolution. It helped to complete the rupture between the army and the king, and increasingly ruthless police actions were instituted by the government in response to the political disorganization and turmoil that followed the war. Egypt's economic crisis also worsened as mismanagement and corruption became rampant.

The second issue was the continuing opposition to the British role in Egypt and the desire of the nationalists, often led by the Wafd, to reduce or eliminate the British position and control. Negotiations to revise the 1936 treaty, especially relating to the questions of the Sudan and the canal, were unsuccessful. Clashes between the British and Egyptian nationalists became increasingly frequent. On 15 October 1951, the government of Egypt under Prime Minister Nahas Pasha abrogated the 1936 treaty and proclaimed Farouk king of Egypt and the Sudan.

An impasse had been reached in the relations between King Farouk and politicians (especially the Wafd) that deadlocked the processes of government and made ruling impossible. Political chaos and the breakdown of public order were indications of the problems. Deterioration in relations with England exacerbated the situation and led to a military overthrow of the alien dynasty.

This provided the backdrop to the Egyptian Revolution of 1952. Disturbances broke out and mobs attacked foreign establishments in Cairo. The British objected, and clashes between British troops and Egyptians soon intensified. 26 January 1952, a day of violence, came to be known as "Black Saturday" and was followed by the ouster of Nahas Pasha and the proclamation of martial law.

The Egyptian Revolution (1952)

By 1952, King Farouk's government was viewed by Egyptian nationalists as incompetent, corrupt, and unable to deal effectively with either the British or the problem of Israel. The obvious solution in the minds of many younger military officers (and like-minded civilians) was to change the country's leadership in order to improve Egypt's ability to respond to these threats.

On 23 July 1952, members of a small clandestine military organization known as the Free Officers launched a coup d'etat that established a new system of government. Farouk was forced to abdicate and left the country on 26 July 1952.

The 1952 coup was swiftly and efficiently executed. The military controlled the major instruments of force and there was no significant opposition to their actions. The guiding hand of the new system was the Revolutionary Command Council (RCC) whose titular head was a senior military officer, General Muhammad Naguib, one of the few successful Egyptian officers in the 1948 war.

The immediate concern of the RCC was to dismantle the corrupt structures of the monarchy and to create a new political order that would institute major social change. The Free Officers, however, were somewhat naïve in their approach to government. Since the ouster of Farouk was the major objective of the coup, the Free Officers did not have a careful and articulated plan for the ordering and functioning of Egyptian life after the coup. Their basic goal was to end political corruption and inefficiency and to prevent further humiliations such as the Arab-Israeli War of 1948–1949 and the British control of Egypt. Moreover, the Free Officers had not sufficiently determined how to achieve the long-term goals of ousting the British from Egypt (especially the canal zone) and securing the linkage with the Sudan. No formal ideological position was articulated although a brief six-point statement of position and goals was advocated. The regime declared its opposition to colonialism, imperialism, and monopolies; and also asserted its support for social justice, a strong military, and a democratic way of life. Theirs was a program that any Egyptian nationalist could endorse.

Immediate decisions were essential to ensure the functioning of the system and to provide an overall perspective. It was agreed that Farouk would abdicate and would be permitted to leave Egypt and live in exile. The constitutional monarchy was preserved at first, and a regency council was established to preside in the name of Farouk's infant son, Fuad II; a general purge of corrupt officials was instituted; and land reform was to be a major program of the RCC. At this time, the RCC intended to return Egypt to a civilian government as soon as possible.

After a period of some uncertainty concerning the organization and structure of the government, the RCC decided that changes they envisaged were simply not possible within the existing political system. In December 1952 the 1923 constitution and the parliamentary form of government were suspended. The following January General Naguib announced that all political parties had been banned and their funds confiscated, and that constitutional government would not operate for a three-year transition period. In February, an interim constitution was proclaimed that provided the terms for the operation of the government during this time. This constitution noted that the people were the source of all authority but all power was clearly vested in the RCC, which would act in all crucial capacities throughout the transition period. With the abolition of political parties the RCC created a new political organization called the National Liberation Rally to replace the banned political parties.

In June 1953 the RCC moved to the next step in the conversion of the political scene. The monarchy was abolished. A republic, with Naguib as both president and prime minister, was declared. The main structural changes were now in place, permitting the processes of government to function within a new framework.

The most crucial factor in this period was the emergence of Gamal Abdul Nasser as the primary force of Egyptian national life. Nasser appeared in the public view rather slowly. When the Free Officers overthrew Farouk, attention was focused on General Naguib as the titular and apparent head of the new regime; therefore, Nasser appeared to be little more than another colonel in the RCC. Slowly his role as the guiding force behind the revolution began to clarify and Nasser emerged as the victor of a power struggle within the RCC, making his primary role apparent to the outside observer. The struggle for control between Nasser and Naguib went through several stages, culminating in the ouster of Naguib on 14 November 1954, and his being placed under house arrest. This secured Nasser's dominant position within the system, allowing him to become the undisputed leader of Egypt, and later, of the Arab world.

Political Environment

Egypt's social and economic structure is closely linked to the Nile River, which has traditionally been an important source of revenue and a central factor in daily life. Traditionally and currently, wealth is most often measured in land ownership and control of agricultural production. Egyptian society has been based to a significant degree on the peasants, the fellahin, who constitute the vast majority of the Egyptian population. The fellahin are the backbone of the Egyptian system, even if they are relatively deprived economically and educationally, and in terms of life expectancy, wealth, health, literacy, and most of the other measures of achievement in society. Both Nasser and Sadat have traced their roots and publicized their connection to this group. In addition to the fellahin there are also the traditional, wealthy, upper-class landowners and the middle-class city-dwellers. The traditional supporters of the king and members of the court came from the upper class. Since the 1952 revolution, however, the growing bureaucracy and the military officer corps have increasingly improved their status and power within the system.

At the time of the revolution Egypt was a poor country facing a host of social and economic problems: low per-capita income, unequal income distribution, disease, early death, low life expectancy, and a low literacy rate. Agriculture was the dominant sector of the economy and this required the use of Nile water for irrigation. Industry was a minor factor and was significantly limited by poor natural and mineral resources and by the lack of sufficiently trained workers.

The Egyptian Revolution of 1952 was launched to deal with a political issue but almost as crucial were the substantial economic and social problems of Egypt, which were among the earliest problems tackled by the regime. There was a two-class system—a very rich upper class and a very poor lower class, with the latter vastly larger than the former. The upper class of bankers, businessmen, merchants, and landlords controlled the wealth of the country and dominated its political institutions. It could and did prevent the adoption of reform measures that would diminish its economic and/or political control. Much of Egypt's land was concentrated in the hands of relatively few absentee landowners. The poor were mostly landless peasants who constituted more than 75 percent of the population. Furthermore, they were illiterate and had little opportunity to improve their situation. Their health standards were deplorable and they had no political influence. Education and employment were severely limited. This disparity between the landowning rich and the poor peasantry was further compounded by overpopulation, exacerbated by the high birth rates of the poor. The population growth rate surpassed that of agricultural production increases. Moreover, the possibility of food production keeping pace with population growth was limited by lack of control of the water resources of the Nile.

One of the goals of the revolution, announced shortly after the takeover by the Free Officers, was the achievement of social and economic justice by eliminating the corrupt system and the monopoly of wealth. Although lacking a specific ideology and well-developed programs for implementing these goals, the new government attempted to raise the standard of living of the average Egyptian, especially of the fellahin of the Nile Valley, and to reduce the poverty and disease that had permeated Egyptian society for so long.

Agriculture

Egypt is the gift of the Nile and has been dependent on that single main source of fresh water for the thousands of years of its recorded existence. There is a narrow strip of poor land along the Mediterranean coast where some crops can be grown on land when there is minimal rainfall. Except for this area, virtually all agriculture is dependent on irrigation from the Nile. The land made inhabitable and cultivable by the river constitutes a small portion of Egypt's overall landmass (about 4 percent); therefore, agricultural production, despite the rich soil and the favorable climate, has been limited, although it is the main occupation of, and provides the livelihood for, most Egyptians.

The limited agricultural production does not provide sufficient food for Egypt's increasingly large population. Despite efforts to control it, Egypt's population growth rate has hovered at about 3 percent per year since the revolution. At this rate of portending growth, Egypt's population will number approximately sixty to seventy million by the year 2000—a population beyond Egypt's projected capacity to feed, clothe, house, and employ.

Agrarian reform became the first and most significant domestic effort of the regime, demonstrated by the Agrarian Reform Law of September 1952. It limited individual landholdings to less than two hundred feddans (approximately two hundred acres) and reduced the rents paid for lands while increasing agricultural wages. In an effort to redistribute existing agricultural land and to divide the wealth of the country more equitably, some lands were expropriated (with compensation) and redistributed. Because land redistribution diminished the power of the major landowners, it was also a partially political act. As a result of shifting wealth from the upper class to the lower class, the technocrats and army officers became part of the new upper class of Egypt.

Related to the Agrarian Reform Law were other measures of considerable importance, of which the Aswan High Dam was among the most significant. The purpose of the dam was to improve Egypt's economic system by increasing the already high productivity levels of the Nile Valley lands through an improved irrigation system. The dam was designed to increase water storage capacity, to prevent devastating floods, to add cultivable land, and to create substantial additional hydroelectric capacity. The dam also had symbolic value as an achievement of the revolution.

The completion of the Aswan High Dam has had mixed results. Many of the anticipated benefits have been realized. There has been a significant increase in the cultivated area of Egypt and in net agricultural output; flood control has also helped to lead to productivity gains; additional electrical power, primarily for industrial use, has been made available; and navigation along the Nile, which is utilized as a major transportation artery in Egypt, has been improved and a fishing industry has been developed in Lake Nasser. However, there are some problems. For example, silt has been trapped behind the dam in Lake Nasser. More chemical fertilizer is thus needed because the soil is no longer replenished in the flooding process. Salinity has increased in the northern portion of the river and in some of the land formerly flood-drained. Other chemical and biological changes have also affected the river and its role in Egyptian life.

Other Economic Sectors

The 1952 revolution was of little immediate consequence to the Egyptian economy. The land reforms resulted in some redistribution of land and wealth, but the economy continued to be based on private enterprise. Some restrictions were placed on the economy but these were directed mainly toward foreign trade and payments. By the end of the 1950s government attitudes had shifted to favor public participation in, and direct regulation of, the economy; and in 1961 a series of decrees nationalized all large-scale industry, business, finance, and virtually all foreign trade. Private enterprise and free trade were replaced by Arab socialism, which was proclaimed the basis of the economic sytem. In practice, this meant establishing a mixed economy with a large public sector (including all foreign trade) and with the remaining private economic activities subject to various kinds of direct controls. Prices were regulated and resource allocation was determined by administrative action and decision.

The system derived its socialist character mainly from the fact that all big business was controlled by the government. Modern manufacturing, mining, electricity and other public utilities, construction, transport and communication, finance, and wholesale trade were primarily owned by the government while most retail trade, handicrafts and repair, housing, professional services, and agriculture were privately owned. The government imposed some control on agricultural production through its control of the irrigation system and through the compulsory participation in government-sponsored agricultural cooperatives. Control was also exercised over the distribution of capital goods, raw materials, and semimanufactures as well as over prices and wages.

By 1962 the Egyptian economy and the context in which it functioned had changed considerably. Ownership of the main branches of the economy had been transferred to the government. The wealth remaining in private hands was essentially real estate and that, too, was carefully controlled. Government budgets accounted for about 60 percent of the GNP. Inequality of wealth and income had been greatly reduced, largely through a process of agrarian reform, higher taxation, the extension of social services, and by a series of nationalizations and sequestrations. The role of foreigners in the economy had been substantially reduced, and, in some sectors, terminated. Industry had made substantial progress—accounting for more than 20 percent of the GNP—and continued to increase its proportion.

Efforts to improve the economic system were severely hampered by the losses suffered in the 1967 Arab-Israeli War. As a consequence of that conflict Egypt lost substantial revenues from the closure of the Suez Canal, the loss of the oil fields in the occupied Sinai Peninsula, and loss of tourism. All three elements had been important to Egypt's earning of foreign exchange for its development and for the purchase of needed imports. The lost revenues would have helped to reduce Egypt's foreign debt.

In the wake of the 1973 October War the situation began to change. The canal was reopened (1975) and the Sinai oil fields were later returned to Egyptian control. The improved tranquillity resulting from the Sinai disengagement agreements (1974 and 1975) and the peace treaty (1979) with Israel also helped to improve tourism and commercial investment in Egypt. Increased donations and contributions to Egypt, especially from the oil-rich Arab states of the peninsula and gulf (who have been contributing huge amounts of money per year since 1967) enlarged Egypt's economic potential for development. The October War tended to have positive results for the Egyptian economy. The war involved the oil-rich Arabs in the process of a settlement and created an aura of stability and tranquillity that fostered domestic, regional, and international involvement in the Egyptian economy.

The war also gave way to the announcement of a new approach to economic matters generally referred to in Egypt as the "opening"—the economic open-door policy. In a 1974 working paper, President Anwar Sadat set forth a statement of Egypt's long-term economic and social objectives. He discussed the successes of the revolution, including the emancipation of women, the establishment of many public sector enterprises, the Agrarian Reform Law, and advances in education and other social services. He also identified some of the shortcomings in Egypt's existing economic employment in the public sector and excessive interference by government ministries in the operation of the economy; moreover, he called for a change in the philosophy of planning and in the implementation of government policy. Decentralization was deemed essential, as were efforts to make Egypt's administrative machinery responsive to innovation and to interested foreign investors. In general the opening sought to unite Arab and Western (especially U.S.) capital, technology, and expertise with Egyptian labor and Egyptian and Arab markets to help rejuvenate the Egyptian economy. To a great extent, this depended on regional and domestic stability and represented a shift from the previous situation in which there was a heavy reliance on Soviet-bloc technology and markets, and on isolation from Western technology, markets, and hard currency.

Poverty and ignorance remain important problems for Egypt. The heavy dependence on agriculture has made the Nile and its control a major interest of the government and a focal point of many of its programs. The government has worked to develop sources of revenue other than agriculture and has also attempted to increase the land area under cultivation. Economic problems, and especially the availability of food, are often exacerbated by the population growth rate. Egypt's main dilemma is population, whose density is one of the highest in the world. In part this results from the fact that only a very small portion of the country's total landmass is inhabited due to the lack of water and cultivable land in the broad desert regions that constitute much of the landmass of the country. Improved health conditions and reduced death rates only add to the increasing population burden.

From World War II until 1961 Egypt held substantial foreign exchange reserves. In 1962 the foreign exchange reserves were exhausted and Egypt entered a period of severe foreign-exchange crises that still exists.

Egypt continues to have an underdeveloped, labor-surplus economy, a high annual import bill, and increasing labor pools owing to the high birth rate. The country still suffers from high defense expenditures that, in the late 1960s and early 1970s, were often between 20 and 25 percent of the GNP. These expenditures increased the need for external financial support in the form of loans, grants, and subsidies.

Twenty-five years after the Egyptian Revolution many of the socioeconomic problems facing the country were quite similar to those that had prevailed at the time of the coup: Egypt remained a poor and developing country; it was densely populated; and its birth and population growth rates continued to be high. A very high, though declining, proportion of the population continued to work in agriculture. Unemployment and disguised unemployment remained problems facing the government. Migration to the cities, for employment and housing, tended to create problems for the major cities while the increasing numbers working abroad constituted a brain drain that adversely affected economic development. Despite the considerable expansion of educational and health facilities, endemic diseases were widespread and illiteracy remained at a relatively high level. Clearly, Egypt was faced with the need to develop new approaches and to achieve new accomplishments in the socioeconomic area.

Political Structure

Egypt's political system has experimented with several variations in the search for a permanent structure. With Nasser at its head, the RCC exercised primary responsibility for the functioning of the system and the establishment of government policy. During the transition period a number of outstanding problems, including the position of England in Egypt and the canal zone, were finally resolved. Then, in 1956, Nasser formally inaugurated a new system that consolidated power in his own hands.

On 16 January 1956, a new constitution was proclaimed in which extensive powers were concentrated in the hands of the president. The constitution also established a single political party, the National Union, which replaced the Liberation Rally. A National Assembly was to perform the legislative function. The political party and the Parliament, as well as most other instruments of government, remained under the control of Nasser, who was elected president by more than 99 percent of the vote in 1956. In the same year martial law was terminated, political prisoners were released, and other changes occurred. The RCC members became civilians (with the exception of General Abdul Hakim Amer, who was minister of defense) and joined various agencies of the government. A plebiscite formally approved a new constitution. A National Assembly election awaited the termination of the Suez crisis (i.e., until 1957). The new system created a strong presidency and seemed to ensure that, with all members of Parliament belonging to a single political party, Parliament would be docile and subservient, while the president exercised virtually all significant powers in the system. But the new system was short-lived.

In February 1958 Egypt joined Syria to form the United Arab Republic (UAR). The union of these two dissimilar and geographically noncontinguous political units into a single state called for the creation of a new political structure. A strong president was to be assisted by ministers appointed by and responsible to him. A single legislative house was to be created. The provisional constitution of the new UAR was proclaimed and Nasser became president. Nasser received nearly all the votes cast in the presidential election on 21 February 1958. The president was assisted by vice-presidents, a cabinet of ministers, the National Assembly, and regional councils. Both Egyptians and Syrians were represented in the institutions of government but much of the actual governing was by decree of Nasser and his chief advisors and aides, especially General Amer, who held much of the responsibility for and control of the Syrian region. In September 1961, Syria, disenchanted with Egyptian domination and Nasser's growing socialism, severed ties with the UAR and reestablished its independence. Egypt continued to be known by the name "United Arab Republic" until it became the Arab Republic of Egypt (ARE) in 1971.

With the termination of the United Arab Republic of Egypt and Syria in 1961 there was an intensification of Nasser's socialist programs in Egypt. A new governmental system was again devised and implemented soon thereafter, with a clear socialistic focus. Socialistic measures adopted in the early 1960s included further agrarian reform, progressive tax measures, nationalization of business enterprises, and, in general, increased governmental control over the economy. A new charter and constitution were created and a new political organization, the Arab Socialist Union (ASU), was formed. Elections for Parliament took place. A new constitution was adopted in 1964 that provided the framework for the remainder of the Nasser tenure.

A new phase in Egyptian politics began with the death of Nasser on 29 September 1970, and his replacement by Anwar Sadat.

Sadat's consolidation of control was followed by changes in the political structures and processes of politics. On 11 September 1971, Egypt's permanent constitution was approved by general referendum. It was designed to embody the goals and principles of the revolution and to form the basis of the government's policy. It is similar to its predecessor in continuing the strong presidential system extant in Egypt since the revolution. According to the constitution, the president of the republic is head of state. He is empowered to declare a state of emergency in the case of national danger, subject to a referendum within sixty days. Legislative power is vested in the National Assembly, composed of at least 350 members, at least half of which must be workers and farmers. The president may appoint up to 10 members. The president may object to laws passed by the National Assembly within thirty days of their passage but the assembly has the right to override his objection by a two-thirds vote. The president has the power to appoint vice-presidents and the prime minister and his cabinet, and is supreme commander of the armed forces. Although the constitution increased the powers of the National Assembly, dominant authority remained with the president, who has the right of temporary rule by decree. The constitution includes guarantees of freedom of expression, as well as assurance of freedom from arbitrary arrest, seizure of property, and mail censorship. Press censorship is banned except for periods of war or emergency. The Arab Socialist Union was declared the only authorized political party, although this was subsequently modified by legislation. Islam was declared the state religion, although freedom of religion is guaranteed.

Political Dynamics

Nasser ruled Egypt from 1954 until his death in 1970. He was the first Egyptian since the pharaohs to control Egypt for any long period. During his tenure he captured the attention and imagination not only of the

Egyptian people but also of the Arab world, as well as of much of the developing and nonaligned Third World, and other portions of the international community. Egypt ended British control and established a republican form of government, and began extensive political change. In an effort to alter and ameliorate the centuries-old Egyptian social and economic systems, reforms were inaugurated.

Nasser succeeded in nationalizing the Suez Canal. He was able to thwart the objectives of Israel, England, and France in the 1956 Sinai War and was able to turn defeat into achievement—if not victory—with the aid of the United States and the Soviet Union. He secured arms and aid for the Aswan High Dam from the Soviet Union and its bloc allies after the United States proved unwilling to provide the military, technical, and economic aid essential to these projects. In the realm of Arab unity Nasser realized achievements (and failures) but he tended to symbolize Arab accomplishment for many of the ordinary citizens of the Arab world.

Nasser's accomplishments in the 1950s were soon followed by difficulties. The United Arab Republic dissolved in 1961, Egypt became unsuccessfully involved in the civil war in Yemen in the early 1960s, and there were feuds with other Arab states and challenges to Nasser's role as Arab world leader. The 1967 Arab-Israeli War proved disastrous and resulted in the loss of the Sinai Peninsula, the closure of the Suez Canal, and the loss of a substantial portion of Egypt's military capability.

Despite these reverses Nasser was still the preeminent Egyptian and Arab, the most influential figure in the Middle East, and a focal point of regional and international attention. Nasser's role extended beyond that designated in the constitution. He exercised unwritten powers by virtue of his unique standing in the system, his accomplishments, and his charismatic appeal to the peasantry that formed the backbone of Egypt. He controlled all the main instruments of violence and of power—including the army, the secret police and intelligence agencies, and the Arab Socialist Union—and dominated the cabinet and the National Assembly. At the time of his death, Nasser's central role and his charismatic appeal to the overwhelming majority of Egyptians raised doubts about a successor's ability to replace Nasser as the undisputed leader of Egypt and the Arab world. Nasser's death in September 1970 marked the end of an era in modern Egyptian history and no figure was clearly identified as his successor. Anwar Sadat became president and was later formally elected to that position, securing approximately 90 percent support in a national referendum.

The problem of succession foreshadowed a power struggle, for the clear and unopposed succession by any one individual was not ordained.

Nasser had not prepared an elaborate institutional legacy that would assure orderly succession. Under the terms of the constitution, and by the terms of Nasser's legacy, Sadat was to succeed as president. But virtually all observers regarded him as little more than an interim leader to be followed by a powerful successor once the behind-the-scenes struggles had been played out among the contenders. Among the possible successors were Ali Sabri (apparently favored by Moscow because of his pro-Soviet leanings and who had headed the ASU) and various other high ranking officials of the Nasser state. The struggle began as soon as Sadat formally succeeded to the presidency.

Sadat sought to consolidate his position, but did not make a major overt move until May 1971, when he purged the government of senior officials who opposed him. This group included Ali Sabri, then vice-president, as well as the minister of war, the head of intelligence, and various other senior officials. These officials were later tried for high treason.

Sadat proclaimed 1971 as a year of decision that was to result in war or peace in the Arab-Israeli conflict, but the year ended with no substantial movement toward achievement of this objective. By 1972 Sadat had become an object of ridicule and cruel jokes, which raised doubts about his leadership. It was in partial response to domestic criticism and to the concerns and complaints of the military that he decided to terminate the role of the Soviet advisers in Egypt in 1972. Sadat soon began to prepare for the October War because he saw little progress toward a political settlement of the conflict with Israel. The beginning of the war in October 1973 and its successes (despite the final outcome and the potential for military disaster) strengthened Sadat's position and enhanced his prestige in Egypt and in the broader regional and international systems. The world's attention was once again drawn to the Arab-Israeli conflict and Sadat began to press the United States for assistance in resolving the issue. Further, he secured support for his position from the more moderate Arab states. This took the immediate form of the Arab "oil weapon" during the 1973 war and of financial assistance afterward. Sadat was able to place Israel on the defensive internationally and to secure further international support for the Egyptian and Arab positions.

In April 1974 Sadat produced a document called the October Working Paper, which discussed the new era ushered in by the October War. It called for extensive reform and change in Egypt and suggested that the lot of the average Egyptian would improve. It embodied his concept of the philosophy and guidelines appropriate to the new era Egypt had entered. The October Working Paper sought to provide a framework for Egypt's economic and social development in light of the significant impact of the October War. Sadat hoped to revitalize the revolution by providing confidence and programs to achieve the goals of modernization.

Clearly the political system under Sadat has been molded according to his conception and functions in keeping with his policies. He has reinvigorated a strong presidential system in which the president determines the general policy of the state and ensures its execution. Crucial political decisions are made by the president with the aid of his closest advisors; they are then implemented by Egypt's senior officials and the bureaucracy that supports them. The president, through his formal powers and functions, and through his informal molding of the system in accordance with his views, has control of or dominates all institutions of politics and all state functions and policies.

Party Politics

In the wake of the 1952 revolution Egypt created a system in which a substantial amount of authority was concentrated in the hands of relatively few individuals, all of whom were associated with the president. Popular participation was enhanced, however, through two mechanisms—the National Assembly and the single political party. In the assembly it was assured that various elements, and not only the upper class, would participate in the political decision-making process, and through the party (especially after the creation of the ASU) all Egyptians could participate in the discussion of problems and policies. Although both institutions allowed for substantial popular participation in the policy process, much of it was informational rather than decisional in nature. To a significant degree the institutions (especially the ASU) were used by the central authority to communicate information and inculcate ideology rather than to seek legitimate, mass expression of ideas, concerns, and grievances.

The Arab Socialist Union attempted to avoid the mistakes of its predecessors (the Liberation Rally and the National Union) and to create a popular mass membership party involving as many of the people as possible. Membership was estimated to exceed seven million, or about 20 percent of the population, in the mid-1970s.

In the National Charter of 1962 the ASU was declared the nation's single political organization. It did not differ drastically from its predecessor, the National Union, insofar as its pyramidally structured organization were concerned. There were, however, two innovations. First, 50 percent of all seats in ASU structures were to be filled by farmers and workers. The second provides for elected ASU basic units in factories, business firms, ministries, and state-controlled industrial enterprises.

Starting with the basic unit, each level was composed of a conference and a committee. At the lowest level the conference consisted of all the ASU members of the basic unit, who in turn elected the committee. Basic units were established in villages, city wards, provincial districts, and factories. Above the basic units were the city, rural district, rural town, the large public organization units, each comprised of two or more basic units and composed of key members plus others designated by higher authority. Above this level, the governorate unit of the ASU supplemented and complemented the local government structure in the twenty-five governorates. At the national level was the National Congress of the ASU and the Central Committee, which designated the Supreme Executive Committee (SEC) at the summit of the structure. An office of secretary general—and supporting staff divisions—was established for national-level ASU administration. Nasser appointed Ali Sabri secretary general in 1965 but assumed the post himself in June 1967.

The ASU was designed to actualize the ideological premise that there must be popular participation and representation on both the local and national levels, and that it would represent the interests of all "popular forces." These were identified in the charter as consisting of farmers (fellahin), workers, intellectuals, national capitalists (independent shop keepers, etc.), members of organized professions (lawyers, doctors, etc.), and soldiers. It was felt that participation by these forces in revolutionary activity must be in a single mass organization of the state in order to avoid social conflict. This approach was designed to prevent the emergence of political parties (and thus social conflict, as the parties presumably represent classes). Thus, the task of the ASU membership was to inculcate in the masses a sense of participation in the leader's implementation of the revolutionary program.

The ASU assisted the smooth functioning of the political system. It helped to recruit lower-level political leadership, attempted to provide political socialization, and ensured that government policies were known (and hopefully understood and supported). It was also a medium of the government for communication to the people, and occasionally of the people to the government. The ASU was a democratic centralist model party where views and ideas tended to move upward but where policies and decisions were communicated down the structure.

In 1976 a new approach to party politics was attempted. Although the ban on political parties other than the ASU was maintained, it was decided that groupings representing specific political views and positions could be established within the ASU. Specifically, three positions, representing the right, the center, and the left, were permitted. Each could lobby for its ideas, disseminate its views through the media, and prepare a program and a slate of candidates for election. All were to function under the legitimizing umbrella of the ASU. The three positions represented different sectors of the Egyptian government spectrum. The leftist group—the National Progressive Unionist Rally—was headed by Khalid Muhyi al-Din, long associated with Marxist-oriented and "progressive" elements of the old Nasser establishment. Among other policies, the left advocated closer ties with the Soviet Union and an emphasis on public-sector investment. The center group—the Egyptian Arab Socialist Organization—included the prime minister, most members of the cabinet, key civil service officials, and the governors of the country's twenty-six provinces. The center supported current government policy, and its theme was gradualism and guided democracy. Its adherents favored a mixed economy and close ties to the West. The rightist group—the Socialist Liberals—favored a return to capitalism, a greater emphasis on private enterprise, and a heavy reliance on market forces to solve Egypt's economic problems. The "groupings" competed in the 1976 parliamentary elections for the first time, with the centerist group winning 280 seats, in comparison to 14 for the right and left combined. Many observers felt that the three groups did not truly represent the significant opposing viewpoints of right and left, but were instead a "tame" opposition. In November 1976 Sadat refused the request of some members of the People's Assembly to form their own party and refused the demands of students who declared their opposition to parties "imposed from above." But in June 1977, after the violent January 1977 riots protesting the prices of food and other basic commodities, a Political Parties Law was promulgated that entitled any Egyptian to form a political party and any citizen to join any recognized party—within certain limitations and restrictions. Due to the new legislation the ban on multiple political parties was removed and the groupings of the ASU formed independent political parties. All ASU bodies, except the Central Committee, were abolished, and most ASU members formed the Egyptian Arab Socialist party (EASP), which supported government policy. In addition, the New Wafd party was founded in early 1978, declaring its support of President Sadat's "defense of democracy" and his efforts to achieve peace with Israel. Egypt had its first functioning, legal, multiparty political system since the revolution. The major nongovernment parties began to view their new roles seriously and joined the nonparty critics of the Sadat administration and its policies at home and abroad. In an effort to curb the mounting criticism of his policies, Sadat sought popular approval for a plan to limit such criticism and received overwhelming support in a spring 1978 referendum. New restrictions on political dissent and on the political parties followed as well as investigation and indictment of politicians expressing dissent. The New Wafd and the leftist party suspended activities in protest of the new limitations. Egypt's experiment with a multiple party system was effectively over, and political life was clearly recentered on the ASU in its new guise as the EASP. Opposition political movements were severely circumscribed in power and prospects. Subsequently, the National Democratic party (NDP) was established to replace the previous government party. In June 1979, Egypt held general elections in which Sadat's NDP won an overwhelming victory, securing about 320 of 380 seats contested, while many of the others were won by "positive" opposition candidates. The government-sponsored party remained in clear control of the system.

Foreign Policy

Napoleon once labeled Egypt "the most important country" because of its central location, which provided a key to Africa and the Middle East. In the post–World War II period Egypt has become perhaps more significant. The Suez Canal is a prime artery for oil. Egypt is the leading state in the African, Islamic, Arab, and nonaligned Third World nations. It is also the primary state for the establishment of peace or the waging of war in the Arab-Israeli conflict. It has been courted by both the United States and the Soviet Union, each in pursuit of its own interests in the region and in the broader international community.

Egypt is the leading state of the Arab world in a number of other respects. Its population and military forces are the largest. It has been the leader of the Arab world in communications (publishing, arts, literature, movies) and other spheres. Egypt has been, and remains, influential throughout the Arab world; much of the Arab world's activity focuses on or takes its lead from Egypt.

In the nineteenth century and the early part of the twentieth century Egypt spearheaded Arab contact with the Western world and helped to develop the intellectual bases for Arab, as well as Egyptian, nationalism. It was a leader in the establishment of the Cairo-headquartered Arab League. Further, its Suez Canal was an important strategic-economic asset.

After the 1952 revolution Egypt emerged as an important Third World—neutralist and nonaligned—power and Egypt and Nasser were increasingly looked to for leadership in the Arab world and beyond. Nasser's concept of three circles of foreign policy provided some indication of the spheres in which Egypt was influential: Arab, Africa, and Islamic as well as Third World spheres of policy and activity.

Egypt's foreign policy was virtually nonexistent prior to the 1952 revolution. Major and assertive foreign-policy positions developed only after the revolution and essentially seemed to be reactive—responding to events as they developed. Nasser's foreign policy focused, in the first instance, on the need to eliminate the British colonial presence in the canal zone and in the Sudan. In the second instance there was the problem of Israel. It is in these contexts that relations with the United States and the Soviet Union emerged.

Initial successes were achieved with the agreement on the withdrawal of the British from their positions in Egypt and the resolution of the Sudan problem (although the Sudan eventually chose independence rather than union with Egypt). On 12 February 1953, England and Egypt signed the Agreement on Self-Government and Self-Determination for the Sudan, which provided for the latter's transition to self-government and its choice between linkage with Egypt or full independence. The Suez question was settled in an agreement of 19 October 1954. That agreement declared the 1936 treaty to be terminated and provided for the withdrawal of British forces from Egyptian territory within a period of twenty months.

Relations with the superpowers were different. Although the United States was initially helpful to the new regime and provided technical and economic assistance, and some assistance in the negotiations with the British, there were difficulties concerning the Nasser requests for arms. Further, U.S. Secretary of State John Foster Dulles viewed Egypt's increasingly close ties with Communist China and the Soviet Union with suspicion. The Baghdad Pact, conceived and sponsored by the United States, was not viewed positively by Nasser, who saw it as a threat to Arab independence and autonomy. Raids on Israel by *fedayeen* and counterraids by Israel into Gaza sparked, in Nasser's view, a need for arms for defense, and his quest led him to closer links with the Soviet bloc, thus further straining the ties with the United States. The Dulles decision that the United States would not fund the Aswan High Dam was a major blow to the plans of the new regime and it decided to continue building and to secure the necessary funding and assistance from alternative sources. The Soviet Union was prepared to assist in the construction and provide some financial assistance. But in Nasser's view a more demonstrable act was needed. And so, in July 1956, he nationalized the Suez Canal and stated that the proceeds of the canal revenues would go to the construction of the dam.

The crucial exchanges between Nasser and the United States set the tone for the less-than-cordial relationship that followed. While the U.S.–Egyptian relationship deteriorated, the Soviet role in Egypt (and elsewhere in the Arab world) improved. The Soviet assistance for the Aswan Dam project and the supply of arms essential to the continued stature and satisfaction of the Egyptian military and ostensibly to the defense of Egypt against Israel were elements that helped to ensure the positive Soviet-Egyptian relationship.

Nasser's nationalization of the Suez Canal and the securing of Soviet arms via Czechoslovakia contributed further to the deterioration of the U.S.-Egyptian relationship. On the other hand, Soviet-Egyptian relations improved during this time. Then came the Sinai-Suez War of 1956, when Israel, France, and England joined in an effort to unseat Nasser and restore the canal to Western control while destroying Egypt's military capability (especially the ability to use the newly acquired arms). The United States opposed the effort and exerted considerable pressure on its three friends to withdraw from Egyptian territory. In assisting the Nasser regime the United States won much goodwill in the Arab world, especially Egypt. But this goodwill was soon dissipated when the United States became involved in the 1958 Lebanese crisis, and opposed the Egyptian position.

The Kennedy administration witnessed a minor reversal of this negativism, as the style and sometimes the substance of the new regime began to be welcomed in the Arab world and important gestures by Kennedy were viewed with favor in Cairo. But, with the death of Kennedy and the establishment of President Lyndon Johnson's position on foreign policy, the relationship began to deteriorate once again. By the time of the June 1967 War, relations between the two states were poor and the war was a catalyst that precipitated the break of diplomatic relations. The relationship between the United States and Egypt remained antagonistic until the October War and until the particular policy of President Richard Nixon and Secretary of State Henry Kissinger, which led to a rapprochement between the two states and the growth of a cordial relationship in virtually all bilateral spheres. This involved, for example, state visits by Sadat to the United States in 1975 and 1977 and a 1974 state visit by Nixon to Egypt, and other high-level meetings between responsible officials in both states.

Relations with the Soviet Union were somewhat different. Beginning in the mid-1950s, Soviet economic and technical assistance were important elements in the Aswan Dam project and in Egypt's economic development. Military assistance was another element in the developing relations of the two states. Because Nasser felt that Egypt required arms to maintain the regime and to ensure proper capability in dealing with the problem of Israel, the Soviet Union became a major factor, since it was prepared to provide arms under terms of cost and payment acceptable to the Egyptians. The Egyptian military soon had a Soviet arsenal. Soviet equipment provided the arms essential for the Egyptian armies in the 1956, 1967, 1969–1970, and 1973 wars. But, despite the consummation of a treaty of friendship in 1971, the Soviet role in Egypt proved to be increasingly problematic from the perspective of many of the senior Egyptian military.

The rift between Egypt and the Soviet Union became more obvious after the accession of Sadat and his consolidation of power. The disassociation began when the Soviet Union attempted to influence the choice of Nasser's replacement after his sudden death in 1970. With Sadat's consolidation of his position following the arrest of his major opponents, the relationship with the Soviet Union deteriorated further as the Soviet Union and its Egyptian clients began to differ on various aspects of the situation and the approach to the Arab-Israeli problem. There appeared to be constraints placed on Egyptian military plans and activities. There were disagreements concerning the Soviet refusal to provide Egypt with desired offensive military equipment. There were tensions between Egyptian and Soviet military officers in Egypt, and these events culminated in the expulsion of Soviet advisors in July 1972. After the October War Egypt complained that the Soviets were lax in resupplying the Egyptian military forces. In addition, Egypt increasingly turned to the West, especially the United States, and Sadat articulated the view that Kissinger and the United States held the crucial cards for peace in the region and could also become the source of essential economic and technical assistance for Egypt.

There were increased Soviet limitations on arms supply to Egypt, difficulties over the repayment of the Soviet debt owed by Egypt, and a growing realization that the United States—not the Soviet Union—could aid the quest for peace. Despite improved relations during the months that followed the ouster of Soviet advisors in 1972, the Soviet-Egyptian relationship has not returned to its former levels, especially since the 1973 war, when the improved relationship between Egypt and the United States began to supplant some of the elements of the Soviet-Egyptian dealings of previous times. Egyptian leaders had recognized that their primary concerns of recovering territory captured by Israel during the 1967 war, resolving the Arab-Israeli conflict, and promoting the development of Egypt had not been attained through the Soviet connection; moreover, there was the growing view that a Western (i.e., U.S.) linkage was more appropriate.

At the heart of Egypt's foreign policy lay questions more closely related to developments in the region. Nasser believed that Egypt's destiny was to lead in three circles: the Arab, the Islamic, and the

African. In his *Philosophy of the Revolution,* Nasser argued that Arab unity had to be established, for it would provide strength for the Arab nation to deal with its other problems. Arab unity was a consistent theme during the period of his tenure (after 1954), and a source of some interest in his policy to outsiders. He argued that Egypt led by Nasser should lead to a united Arab world. He saw Egypt as the state that had to fulfill that role, and in his pursuit of foreign policy he sought to achieve the various goals of leadership involved in his three circles. Sadat has retained that general theme but has focused much of his foreign policy attention on the question of the Arab-Israeli conflict and the future of the Palestinians. In the final analysis Egypt continues to be the primary country for resolution of the Arab-Israeli conflict—it must be the leader if war is contemplated and is similarly crucial if there is to be peace.

A main theme of Egyptian policy has continued to be its leadership role in the Arab world. Developed as a pan-Arab or Arab nationalist role in the forties and fifties, it acquired added dimensions with Nasser's increasing interests in the Arabian peninsula and Persian (Arabian) Gulf in the 1960s. Increasingly, Egypt became the Arab leader in the conflict with Israel and the effort to deal with Israel's role in the Middle East. After the ouster of the British from Egypt and the nationalization of the Suez Canal, the first significant issue for Nasser was the tripartite (Israel-England-France) invasion of Egypt in 1956. Subsequent Israeli evacuation of the Sinai (under U.S. pressure and international cajoling) temporarily relegated the issue to the background and permitted Egypt to turn to issues elsewhere, such as the union with Syria—1958–1961—and the Yemen civil war in the early 1960s. But in 1967 the focus of Egypt's attention was again drawn to the Arab-Israeli issue and the June War of 1967 returned this question to the central position it has occupied since. After the June War the main, if not sole, issue of Egypt's foreign policy remained the question of the Arab-Israeli conflict and the effort to accomplish Israeli withdrawal from the territories occupied in that conflict. Guiding the Egyptian position after the June War was the Khartoum summit resolution of September 1967. At that time the Arab states pledged their joint military, political, and diplomatic activity to achieve Israeli withdrawal from occupied Arab territory; and further, they articulated their position that there could be no negotiation, no recognition, and no peace with Israel and that the rights of the Palestinians had to be restored. These commitments and beliefs provided the framework for Egyptian policy until after the October War of 1973, which modified the environment for approaches to the Arab-Israeli conflict.

Following the October War Sadat began to alter his foreign policy approach in an obvious manner. He began with the assumption that the

key to both his domestic and foreign policy problems lay in closer ties
with the United States and a tenuous relationship with the Soviet Union.
He believed that the United States could admonish Israel to relinquish
territories occupied in the 1967 war and could provide technical and
economic assistance for Egypt's economy and social development at
home. The U.S. option seemed to be the logical approach diplomatically
and politically and also would be helpful for economic reasons. Regional
tranquillity seemed to be an essential ingredient in Sadat's approach to
Egypt's problems.

The postwar approach began in the months following the war. In
January 1974, Kissinger achieved a first-stage disengagement agreement
separating Israeli and Egyptian forces along the Suez Canal and in Sinai.
Relations between Egypt and the United States began to improve
dramatically as relations with the Soviet Union continued to deteriorate.
After further and substantial effort, a second-stage disengagement between Israel and Egypt, known as Sinai II, was signed in September 1975
and provided for further Israeli withdrawals and the return to Egypt of
important oil fields in Sinai. Nixon visited Egypt in June 1974, Sadat later
visited the United States (October/November 1975). Sadat saw only
gains in his dealings with Washington.

In the wake of the Sinai II agreement Egyptian policy took on a new
cast. Sadat seemed to be interested in maintaining the role of the United
States as the power to help attain peace by changing Israel's policies. The
situation was slowed, however, by regional developments, such as the
civil war in Lebanon and by the U.S. presidential elections. The conclusion of the elections in November 1976 and the winding down of the
Lebanon conflict set a new process in motion. During the initial months
of President Carter's administration there was substantial movement
toward the establishment of a process to lead toward peace or at least
toward a Geneva Conference designed to maintain the momentum
toward a settlement. But the movement toward a settlement seemed to
slow substantially by October of that year and this led to Sadat's decision to "go to Jerusalem" and present his case and the Arab position
directly to the Israeli Parliament and people. In so doing he set in motion
a new approach to the Arab-Israeli conflict in which direct Egypt-Israel
negotiations became, for the first time, the means to peace in the Middle
East. The direct negotiations were continued at the Cairo Conference and
Ismailia Summit of December 1977 and in lower-level contacts over the
ensuing months. Then, in September 1978, Sadat met with President
Carter and Israeli Prime Minister Begin for the Camp David Summit,
which provided a framework for peace between Egypt and Israel and,

ultimately, for a broader arrangement between Israel and the other Arab states.

Under Anwar Sadat's rule, Egypt has continued to work for the principles of the Egyptian revolution but the methods have taken on new characteristics. Sadat has sought to modify the nation's political life through a process of liberalization, though it has been cautiously and sporadically implemented. He has adopted new approaches to traditional economic and social problems and sought financial aid (mostly from the oil-rich Arab states) and technical assistance (mostly from the United States and Western Europe) to ameliorate conditions for the average Egyptian. In foreign policy he has taken a number of bold steps, such as the launching of the October War, the visit to Jerusalem, signing the Camp David Summit agreements, and concluding the March 1979 peace treaty with Israel, in an effort to achieve what he considers to be an appropriate resolution to the Arab-Israeli conflict. In each of these areas he has reversed the pro-Soviet approach of the Nasser era and has linked Egypt's future with that of the West, and especially the United States.

Bibliography

The background of modern Egypt and the nature of its people is essential to understand its political culture. Two works are particularly important in this regard. Henry A. Ayrout, *The Egyptian Peasant* (Boston: Beacon Press, 1963), focuses on the fellah while William Lane, *Manners and Customs of the Modern Egyptians* (New York: E. P. Dutton, 1923), surveys much of Egyptian society and culture.

The historical background of modern Egypt is considered in Robert O. Collins and Robert L. Tignor, *Egypt and the Sudan* (Englewood Cliffs, N.J.: Prentice-Hall, 1967); Peter Mansfield, *The British in Egypt* (New York: Holt, Rinehart and Winston, 1971); and Nadav Safran, *Egypt in Search of Political Community: An Analysis of the Intellectual and Political Evolution of Egypt, 1804–1952* (Cambridge: Harvard University Press, 1961). David S. Landes, *Bankers and Pashas: International Finance and Economic Imperialism in Egypt* (Cambridge: Harvard University Press, 1958), provides an account of Egyptian-European commercial relations in the nineteenth century, with emphasis on the Suez Canal. Jamal Mohammed Ahmed, *The Intellectual Origins of Egyptian Nationalism* (London: Oxford University Press, 1960) provides an introduction to nationalism as it developed in Egypt.

General studies of Egypt focusing on the period since the revolution include: Anouar Abdel-Malek, *Egypt: Military Society—The Army Regime, The Left, and Social Change Under Nasser* (New York: Random House, 1968) (translated by Charles Lam Markmann); R. Hrair Dekmejian, *Egypt Under*

Nasir: A Study in Political Dynamics (London: University of London Press; Albany: State University of New York Press, 1972); Harry Hopkins, *Egypt: The Crucible—The Unfinished Revolution in the Arab World* (Boston, Mass.: Houghton Mifflin Co., 1969); Jean and Simonne Lacouture, *Egypt in Transition* (New York: Criterion Books, 1958) (translated by Francis Scarfe); Tom Little, *Modern Egypt* (London: Ernest Benn, 1967); Peter Mansfield, *Nasser's Egypt*, rev. ed. (Baltimore, Md.: Penguin Books, 1969); Amos Perlmutter, *Egypt: The Praetorian State* (New Brunswick, N.J.: Transaction Books, 1974); Georgiana G. Stevens, *Egypt: Yesterday and Today* (New York: Holt, Rinehart, and Winston, 1963); P. J. Vatikiotis, ed., *Egypt Since the Revolution* (New York and Washington, D.C.: Frederick A. Praeger Publishers, 1968); Keith Wheelock, *Nasser's New Egypt: A Critical Analysis* (New York: Frederick A. Praeger Publishers, 1960); and Donald N. Wilber, *United Arab Republic: Egypt—Its People, Its Society, Its Culture* (New Haven, Conn.: Human Relations Area Files Press, 1969).

Understanding revolutionary Egypt is facilitated by the works of its three presidents: Mohammed Naguib, *Egypt's Destiny: A Personal Statement* (Garden City, N.Y.: Doubleday, 1955); Gamal Abdul Nasser, *Egypt's Liberation: The Philosophy of the Revolution* (Washington, D.C.: Public Affairs Press, 1955); Anwar el-Sadat, *Revolt on the Nile* (New York: The John Day Co., 1957); and Anwar el-Sadat, *In Search of Identity: An Autobiography* (New York: Harper & Row, 1978).

Anthony Nutting, *Nasser* (New York: E. P. Dutton, 1972), and Robert St. John, *The Boss: The Story of Gamal Abdel Nasser* (New York, Toronto, London: McGraw-Hill, 1960), provide biographical studies of Nasser.

Studies of particular aspects of politics in Egypt include Iliya Harik, *The Political Mobilization of Peasants: A Study of an Egyptian Community* (Bloomington: Indiana University Press, 1974); Christina Phelps Harris, *Nationalism and Revolution in Egypt: The Role of the Muslim Brotherhood* (The Hague: Mouton, for The Hoover Institution on War, Revolution, and Peace, 1964); James B. Mayfield, *Rural Politics in Nasser's Egypt: A Quest for Legitimacy* (Austin: University of Texas Press, 1971); Nissim Rejwan, *Nasserist Ideology: Its Exponents and Critics* (New York: John Wiley and Sons, 1974); P. J. Vatikiotis, *The Egyptian Army in Politics: Pattern for New Nations?* (Bloomington: Indiana University Press, 1961).

Egyptian foreign policy has not engendered many full-length studies. Nevertheless, several works provide a useful beginning: *Egypt and the United Nations*, report of a study group set up by the Egyptian Society of International Law, prepared for the Carnegie Endowment for International Peace (New York: Manhattan Publishing Co., 1957); Charles D. Cremeans, *The Arabs and the World: Nasser's Arab Nationalist Policy* (New York: Frederick A. Praeger Publishers, for the Council on Foreign Relations, 1963); A. I. Dawisha, *Egypt in the Arab World: The Elements of Foreign Policy* (New York: John Wiley & Sons, 1976).

Bent Hansen and Karim Nashashibi, *Foreign Trade Regimes and Economic Development: Egypt* (New York: National Bureau of Economic Research, 1975);

Charles Issawi, *Egypt in Revolution: An Economic Analysis* (London: Oxford University Press, for the Royal Institute of International Affairs, 1963); Robert Mabro, *The Egyptian Economy, 1952–1972* (London: Oxford University Press, 1974); Patrick O'Brien, *The Revolution in Egypt's Economic System: From Private Enterprise to Socialism, 1952–1965* (London: Oxford University Press, 1966) (issued under the auspices of the Royal Institute of International Affairs) provide valuable studies of Egypt's economy and the problems facing economic planners in the coming decades.

15

Democratic Republic of the Sudan

Bernard Reich

The Sudan is the largest country in Africa (consisting of some 2,506,000 sq. km. or 967,500 sq. mi.), bounded on the north by Egypt; on the east by the Red Sea and Ethiopia; on the south by Kenya, Uganda, and Zaire; and on the west by the Central African Empire, Chad, and Libya. For administrative purposes, the Sudan was originally divided into nine provinces,[1] but these were reorganized in the 1970s and the number increased to eighteen. The dominant geographical feature of the Sudan, as in Egypt, is the Nile; the White Nile flows from the great lakes region of Africa and the Blue Nile originates in the highlands of Ethiopia. The two branches join at Khartoum and form the Nile, which winds through desert for the next 1440 kilometers (900 mi.) until it reaches the Egyptian border north of Wadi Halfa.

The Sudan has a population estimated at sixteen million in 1975 and its density varies widely. The population is not of uniform stock. In the 1956 census 572 tribes were registered. However, approximately 40 percent are of Arab stock and mainly centered in Khartoum and the northern provinces of the Sudan. In the south, the people belong to Nilotic and Nilo-Hamitic groups. The more important of the southern tribes are the Dinka, the Shilluk, the Nuer, and the Zande. Tribes of origin similar to many southern Sudanese are found in Ethiopia, Uganda, and the Congo. In the northern provinces the population is almost entirely Muslim, and in the south, tribal religions and Christianity prevail.

Historical Background

Bilad al-Sudan was the name given by medieval Muslim geographers to the region south of the Sahara and Egypt. Since the end of the nineteenth century, the term has been used in a more restricted sense to refer to the territories south of Egypt, which were part of the Anglo-Egyptian condominium from 1899 to 1955.

The history of the modern Sudan begins in the nineteenth century. Muhammad Ali, the Ottoman sultan's viceroy in Egypt, coveted Sudan because of its wealth—especially the precious metals and slaves—as well as for prestige and strategy. Between 1820 and 1822 his expeditionary forces conquered and unified the north-central areas of the country. During the reign of the Khedive Ismail (1863–1879) the provinces of Darfur, Bahr al-Ghazal, and Equatoria, as well as the Red Sea port of Suakin, were brought under Egyptian control. But local leaders challenged the Egyptians and a rebellion grew out of a fanatical Islamic-revivalist movement. Its leader, Muhammad Ahmad ibn-Abdallah, claimed to be the Mahdi ("divine leader" or "Guided One"), chosen by God. He sought to oust the Egyptians and to establish a religious state. In August 1881, the Mahdi's followers, the Ansar, defeated the troops sent against them. Later they took the initiative and, in 1882–1883, conquered most of Kordofan, Darfur, and the Bahr al-Ghazal. In 1885, the Mahdi's troops conquered Khartoum and, after his death later that year, his successor, the Khalifa 'Abdallahi, ruled until the end of the Mahdist state.

In 1896 the British government decided to reconquer the Sudan in order to reimpose Egyptian control over what was described as Egyptian territory temporarily occupied by Mahdist rebels. The expeditionary force of British and Egyptian troops took Khartoum in Egypt's name in 1898 and by the end of that year the remaining Mahdist forces were defeated, the Khalifa Abdallahi was killed, and the Sudan was reconquered.

The foundations of the new regime in the Sudan were laid by an agreement signed by Britain and Egypt in January 1899, establishing their joint rule—the Anglo-Egyptian Condominium—over Sudan. The condominium agreement stressed the position attained by Britain through its participation in the reconquest of the Sudan, and gave Britain de facto control despite official pretense that it was a joint government with Egypt. The British established a colonial regime headed by a governor-general, appointed by the Egyptian khedive on the recommendation of the British government, with full military and civilian control. The governor-general, who held both executive and legislative powers, was always British. He proclaimed, made, altered, or abrogated all laws, orders, and regulations. In 1943, however, the British started a gradual transition to partial autonomy by establishing an Advisory Council for the northern Sudan. In 1948 a Legislative Assembly was established for all of the Sudan. The transfer of power was slow and caused friction with

Sudan

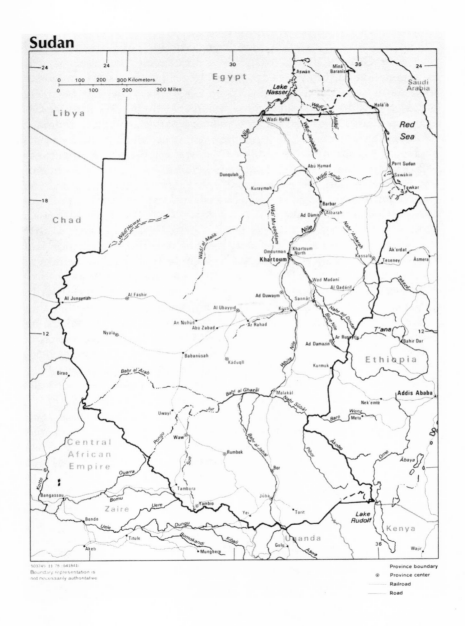

Province boundary
⊕ Province center
Railroad
Road

Egypt, which regarded the Sudan as part of a united Nile Valley whose political future was linked to Egypt, and which objected to any form of Sudanese self-rule under British tutelage.[2]

The 1952 revolution in Egypt marked a turning point for the Sudan. The Free Officers agreed to grant the Sudanese the right of self-determination, as they were eager to secure the British ouster from Sudan as soon as possible. The Free Officers also hoped that the Sudanese would choose to link themselves with Egypt. Late in 1952 the Free Officers concluded an accord with the Sudanese parties, and on 12 February 1953 Egypt and Britain signed an agreement concerning the future of the Sudan. A transition period of three years was established to prepare for self-determination that would allow the Sudanese to decide the future of the Sudan: independence or union with Egypt. During the transition period the administration would be transferred to the Sudanese and elections held under international supervision. British and Egyptian troops would be evacuated as soon as the Sudanese Parliament decided that "Sudanization" was completed and the time for self-determination had come. Two international commissions were to assist in that transition. Elections took place in November 1953, and Ismail al-Azhari's pro-Egyptian National Unionist party (NUP) won an absolute majority. In January 1954, al-Azhari became the first prime minister of the Sudan.

Sudanization of the administration was considered completed in August 1955 and the Sudanese Parliament demanded the evacuation of British and Egyptian troops. This was accomplished by November 1955. Parliament and the government also demanded a simplification of the complicated constitutional procedure originally prescribed for self-determination, and in the end it was agreed that the Sudan's future would be decided by a vote in Parliament. It was now quite clear that al-Azhari and his supporters had changed their minds about a union with Egypt and preferred complete independence. A resolution to that effect was unanimously adopted by Parliament on 19 December 1955, and on 1 January 1956 the Sudan became formally independent.

Political Environment

The Problem of the Southern Sudan

From independence until the early 1970s the Sudan was engulfed in what has been termed "the southern Sudan problem." It often erupted into armed conflict with significant casualties and prevented economic development and the political unity of the country.

Until the increase in the number of provinces, the south was composed of three of the nine provinces of the Sudan: Bahr al-Ghazal, Upper Nile, and Equatoria. The geographical, climatic, and ethnic differences between the south and the rest of the country are considerable, and have given rise to political differences and opposition between the two parts. These political differences are accentuated by a major difference in rainfall and the corresponding agricultural development and potential of the two areas. In the north there is little rainfall and arid agriculture predominates, limited by irrigation potential. The south has a great potential for agricultural development because of its large water resources. Furthermore, the people of the north are generally Arab and Islamic while those of the south are negroid-African and pagan or Christian. Differences between northerners and southerners in cultural identification and ethnic variations added to the separation. The northerners have increasingly oriented themselves toward the Arab world while the southerners have turned toward their neighbors in the states of Black Africa. Communications links between north and south have been sparse. Climatic and geographic factors have also led to different lifestyles. A main complaint of the southern Sudanese has been that the Arabs of the north maintained a complete monopoly over economic, educational, administrative, and military affairs. The Arabs run the Sudan, control the government, and treat the south like a colony.

The history of the conflict predates the immediate causes of incidents in the 1950s. Antagonisms can be traced at least as far back as the slave raids of northerners on the south during the nineteenth century. Southern fears associated with the slave trade and northern ridicule for southerners and their practices helped maintain the tension between the two geographical elements of the country.

Many of the factors promoting separation were further compounded by official policies, first of the British and later of the administrations of the new central Sudan government. Until 1947, British colonial policy was designed to deal with the southern Sudan as a separate entity. Only after the Juba conference (1947) and the determination to establish a united Sudan was the south treated jointly with the north. The initial postindependence Sudanese regimes did not substantially improve the situation.

Southern political consciousness grew perceptibly in the mid-1950s. In August 1955, there were serious disturbances in the south when a local armed insurrection against northern officers at Juba quickly developed into violence against northern officials and northern merchants. The extent of the insurrection indicated a latent southern resistance to all alien administration, which had been evident through the nineteenth century and into the 1920s, as well as a degree of regional and ethnic nationalism that was to spread much more widely in the years that followed. In subsequent years, an open rebellion existed in parts of the south spearheaded by Anya Nya rebels (southern freedom fighters).

Under General Abboud the southern Sudan issue was treated primarily as a military problem. The objectives of the regime were to foster national integration and unity by pursuing a policy of Arabization and Islamization in the southern provinces. A relatively heavy-handed administration and military action against the Anya Nya and their supporters did little to improve the situation. Missionaries were expelled in 1964 because the administration believed that they compounded the problem. Many southerners saw these efforts as confirming their belief that a separate state was the only real solution to the southern Sudan problem.

The inability of the army to pacify the south was only a marginal factor when the Abboud regime was ousted in 1964. But the civilian coalition government that replaced it almost immediately embraced the idea of political reconciliation and stated its wish to seek a political solution to the southern problem. In the south, personal, tribal, and religious divisions soon emerged in disputes over tactics and objectives. The main debate revolved around separatism or federalism. In March 1965 the Round Table Conference on the South was convened in Khartoum to establish a constitutional framework acceptable to all sides—the first genuine effort to resolve the issues involved in the problem of the southern Sudan. The southern leadership and its main political organization, the Sudan African National Union (SANU), split and the position of the northern politicians was fragmented by party politics. The conference itself ended in virtual deadlock. When the Mahjoub government achieved power in June 1965 it was disillusioned by the failure of the Round Table Conference and alarmed by the deteriorating security situation in the south, so it gave the southern army commands a free hand to destroy the Anya Nya. There were a series of bloody reprisals for Anya Nya harassment, numerous civilians lost their lives, suspected Anya Nya villages were burned, and indiscriminate killing in Wau and Juba caused a mass exodus to the bush. The pattern of Anya Nya raids and army reprisals destroyed orderly administration throughout most of the southern provinces, and village life often fell apart as people fled across the borders to refugee camps or scattered into the forests and swamps. Alongside a tribal identity, a "southern" identity was rapidly developing. By January 1971, however, a semblance of order had been restored, as most of the politicians and the majority of the Anya Nya commanders accepted a former Sudan army lieutenant, Joseph Lagu, as leader of both the Anya Nya and of a new Southern Sudan Liberation Movement

(SSLM). It was Lagu's SSLM that, throughout 1971, continued a dialogue with the Sudan government on proposals for "regional autonomy" and that eventually reached agreement on the ending of the rebellion and on a new structure of southern self-government in March 1972.

In June 1969, al-Nimeiri declared his government's policy of solving the southern Sudan problem by granting regional autonomy to the southern provinces, and a ministry for southern affairs was created to implement the policy. Some southerners were appointed to positions of responsibility and some governmental funds were allocated for development and reconstruction in the south. The crucial event occurred in March 1972 with the conclusion of the Addis Ababa Agreement that, *inter alia*, provided for the return and rehabilitation of Sudanese refugees abroad, the reintegration of Anya Nya rebels into the Sudanese armed forces, and the establishment of administratively autonomous institutions for the southern provinces. Hostilities ceased. Then began the difficult task of integrating the south into the political and economic life of the country, while permitting the region to retain a large measure of autonomy. Under the provisions of the 1972 accord, the internal affairs of the southern provinces are administered by an autonomous regional government with its parallel structure of ministries, government agencies, and civil servants. Both the annual and the development budgets of the southern region are subsidized by the national government. The theme of national unity also stresses the reduction and regulation of the ethnic, sectarian, and political cleavages that characterized public life in the Sudan in the past. Elections for the Regional People's Assembly were held in November 1973. Subsequently the assembly elected Abel Aleir as president of the High Executive Council (on the nomination of President al-Nimeiri), and other members of that council were appointed. In 1978 elections General Joseph Lagu was elected president of the High Executive Council.

Economic Issues

The major economic problem of the Sudan is its heavy dependence on a single cash crop, cotton, which is its main source of income and its primary export. The Sudan is primarily an agricultural and pastoral country. Agriculture is a significant element in the country's gross domestic product (GDP) and employs a substantial segment of the population but manufacturing industries and minerals contribute very little to the GDP. No important minerals have yet been found in significant enough quantities to be exploited economically, although oil exploration has identified some promising possibilities in western Sudan. The share of extra-long staple cotton in the exports of the Sudan reaches more than 70 percent in some years. Such dependence on one major export crop, with wide fluctuations in price and quantity exported, has caused political as well as economic instability.

The Sudan has a low per-capita income. The average population density is low and there is no significant population pressure on available resources. Open unemployment is insignificant. There is a shortage of labor, particularly during the cotton-picking season. This has been aggravated by the departure of skilled laborers to the Persian Gulf states and Saudi Arabia. Transportation and other infrastructural elements are inadequate and are among the important problems in the economy, which were worsened by seventeen years of civil war prior to 1972. Perhaps one of the most striking features of the Sudanese economy is the dominant role that is played by the public sector in all important economic activities. The government owns the majority of modern capital establishments in the economy.

The availability of water is the governing factor for agriculture in the Sudan. The cultivable land is estimated to be about 200 million feddans (one feddan = 0.4152 hectare or 1.038 acres) but only about 8 percent of this cultivable land is being utilized in agriculture, and less than 4 million feddans are under irrigation. Half of this area is in the Gezira scheme, the large irrigated agricultural project located in the triangle area south of the confluence of the White and Blue Niles at Khartoum.

Prior to the Nile Waters agreement of 1959 distribution of water between the Sudan and the UAR was governed by the Nile Waters agreement of 1929, which allocated 4 billion cubic meters (5.2 billion cu. yds.) to the Sudan. However, with the 1959 agreement and the construction of new dams, the problem of securing sufficient water to extend the area under irrigation in the Gezira scheme has been solved. The Sudan is now entitled to draw 18.5 billion cubic meters (24.2 billion cu. yds.) at the Aswan High Dam or the equivalent of about 20.5 billion cubic meters (26.8 billion cu. yds.) in the Sudan, and the way has been opened for considerable expansion and diversification of irrigated agriculture, in part because of other projects designed to achieve more efficient use of the Nile waters. In spite of the significant role played by irrigation, the rainlands are more important. With the exception of cotton and some other less important crops, the Sudan's foodstuffs and most exported agricultural products come from the rainlands and the nation is self-sufficient in the essential foods. The agricultural sector does not face any serious land tenure problems.

The main cereal crop is sorghum (durra). It is the most important staple food and is mainly grown in the rainlands. The Sudan produces about 1,500,000 tons (1,360,800 tonnes) of durra annually, which is usually sufficient for domestic consumption.

The ginning of cotton encouraged the beginning of industry in the Sudan early in the twentieth century. With the exception of soap, soft drinks, and oil pressing, large industries that manufacture import substitutes began operation only after 1960. The government has encouraged industrialization by various means. The Approved Enterprises (Concessions) Act of 1959 gave generous concessions to infant industries. The Organization and Promotion of Industrial Investment Act of 1967 has been even more generous to industry. In addition to this, the Industrial Bank, which was established in 1961, assists in the financing of private industrial enterprises, providing nearly two-thirds of the capital required. In 1972 the Ministry of Industry introduced new legislation to encourage industrial investment. The 1972 industrial act was amended in 1974 and an agricultural act was promulgated in 1976 to encourage foreign investment in the agricultural sector.

The Sudan's main exports are primary agricultural products, and since the establishment of the Gezira scheme in 1925, cotton has dominated the Sudan's exports, although groundnuts and gum arabic have become increasingly important export products. The major imports are vehicles, transport equipment, machinery, appliances, and textiles. Perhaps a more striking change that has occurred is in the pattern of suppliers and buyers. The United Kingdom used to be the largest seller and buyer from the Sudan (30–40 percent before independence). In 1973 only 3.4 percent of the Sudan's exports went to the United Kingdom, and only 10 percent of imports were bought from the United Kingdom. Trade with socialist countries increased between independence and the communist-supported coup attempt in 1971 as a result of several bilateral agreements. But their share in the Sudan's trade has, with the exception of the People's Republic of China, drastically declined since that 1971 effort. Trade with the Arab countries has been expanding in recent years and exports to them have reached about 10 percent, but imports from these countries form a smaller percentage. The Arab countries are a good market for the Sudan's animal exports.

Continued agricultural and industrial expansion and further exploration to uncover mineral wealth are the central economic efforts of the government of General Ja'far al-Nimeiri.

Political Structure

Under General al-Nimeiri, a single-party presidential system was instituted with the Sudanese Socialist Union (SSU), a mass political party that held its inaugural meeting in January 1972, as the sole political organization in the state. The permanent constitution became law in the spring of 1973, following a six-month debate by a constituent People's Assembly. The two central institutions defined in the constitution were the presidency and the People's Assembly. The president was nominated by the SSU and approved by popular referendum for a term of six years. He is head of state, exercises the executive powers of government, and is supreme commander of the armed forces. The president may appoint vice-presidents, a prime minister, and other ministers, who are responsible to him, as well as most other senior government officials. He has the authority to declare a state of emergency and to suspend portions of the constitution. Legislative power is shared by the president and the People's Assembly. The assembly consists of 250 members, 25 of whom may be appointed by the president, 125 are elected directly from geographical constituencies, 70 are selected by functional and occupational associations, and 30 are selected by provincial People's Councils. The term is four years and all candidates must be approved by the SSU. Major legislative proposals are initiated by the president after having been approved by the Political Bureau of the SSU and are referred to functional committees before consideration by the full assembly. Legislation may be enacted over a presidential veto by a two-thirds majority of the assembly.

Though the government has been highly centralized, under the provisions of the People's Local Government Act of 1971, government operations in all areas other than foreign affairs, national defense, and justice are to be decentralized and become functions of the provinces. Among the delegated functions are education, public health, agriculture, community development, livestock, minor public works, housing, and social welfare.

A provincial commissioner, appointed by the president, is responsible for planning, integrating, and directing the public services that are being devolved to the provinces. Civil servants from the national ministries are sent to the provinces and are administratively responsible to the provincial commissioner. In each province there is a People's Executive Council, composed of representatives selected by local councils and occupational groups and of senior civil servants in the provincial government. The council has a broad range of legislative powers over provincial and local administration. It reviews the consolidated provincial budget before it is submitted to Khartoum and approves the budgets of local authorities. It is empowered to propose major developmental projects and to recommend national policies to the president, the relevant ministries, and the People's Assembly. The People's Executive Council of each province is enjoined to delegate powers to local social and economic services and to authorize taxing powers to People's Local Councils in towns, rural areas, and villages. Members of the People's Local Councils, a quarter of whom must be women, are chosen by popular election. Civil servants have been posted in growing numbers by the provincial commissioners to serve the local councils.

The SSU has been assigned a major role in promoting the government's developmental programs, mobilizing popular participation, and assisting and controlling public administration. The president of the republic is chairman of the SSU and is assisted by the Executive Bureau of the Central Committee. The Central Committee meets annually to debate and determine party policy. National party congresses meet every three years. SSU headquarters maintains a large general secretariat, which manages the SSU's day-to-day activities and is concerned with dissemination of information, party organization, and the development and evaluation of public policy. It also operates the Institute of Socialist Studies, which trains party cadres.

At the provincial level, the provincial commissioner is secretary-general of the SSU, assisted by a provincial committee. The hierarchy of the SSU structures extends down to the village, neighborhood, and enterprise levels. These units are expected to carry the government's message to the grass roots and to reflect and convey local opinion to senior party officials. The basic units of the SSU in the rural and urban areas are elected by the active members. Higher echelons of the party congresses and committees are filled by indirect election.

The parallel structures of the SSU and the government are intended to ensure a close and continuous link between politics and administration. The party is superordinate to the government. Major policies of the government are to be shaped by the SSU, which is also responsible for guiding the administration at all levels in the execution of these policies. Civil servants are required to demonstrate a positive commitment to the objectives and policies of the SSU. At the local level, SSU cadres and members are expected to counteract the influence of traditional sectarian, ethnic, and political groups—wherever these are not inclined to support the political and administrative authorities.

Political Dynamics

The Sudan after Independence—Political Evolution

Soon after the Sudan achieved independence, Premier al-Azhari lost his parliamentary majority as his NUP split and lost the support of the pro-Egyptian Khatmiyya—a semireligious group almost as large as the opposing sect, the Ansar. He then formed a coalition government that included Abdullah Khalil's Umma party, which was associated with the Ansar, the traditional Mahdist supporters. In 1956 a new coalition was formed by the Umma and the People's Democratic party (PDP) (founded by seceding members of the NUP and supported by the Khatmiyya), and Abdullah Khalil became prime minister. The same coalition returned to power following the elections of February 1958, but its stability was threatened by disagreements between its partners over both domestic and foreign affairs. Thus the suggested appointment of the Mahdist leader Abd al-Rahman al-Mahdi as president of the republic was strongly opposed by the PDP and had to be shelved. The pro-British Umma party clashed with the PDP's pro-Egyptian and neutralist orientation. The threat of an economic crisis, caused mainly by a poor cotton crop, induced Premier Khalil to appeal for U.S. economic aid. He was opposed by his coalition partners. To maintain his parliamentary majority, Khalil had to win the support of the representatives of the south in exchange for a pledge to discuss the introduction of a federal constitution. The coalition, and the premier's position, were soon threatened again by feelers put out by some leaders of his own party for a new coalition with the NUP. In October, talks were held in Cairo between President Nasser, former Prime Minister al-Azhari, and PDP leaders, causing further concern to the prime minister and to a number of senior army officers who feared the increase of Egypt's political influence in the Sudan. On 16 November the Umma and the NUP agreed to form a coalition. But their agreement was thwarted by a military coup on 17 November 1958.

The leader of the coup, General Ibrahim Abboud, proclaimed his intention of saving the country from the "degeneration, chaos and instability" into which the rivalries of the parties and the self-seeking intrigues of the politicians had led it. Political parties were abolished, political activity was banned, Parliament was dissolved, and the constitution was suspended. A Supreme Council of the Armed Forces, composed of twelve officers under the leadership of Abboud as president, ruled the country. The council formally delegated to him all legislative, judicial and executive powers, as well as the command of the armed forces. A cabinet of twelve ministers—seven officers and five civilians—was formed, with Abboud as premier.

Abboud's military regime lasted for nearly six years. Several abortive military coups were crushed. There was no progress toward constitutional rule or toward the resumption of political life and there was little economic advance. Unrest in the southern provinces appeared to be growing and no movement toward resolution of the southern Sudan problem (considered in detail above) was achieved.

Trouble in the south, general discontent with the economic situation, inefficiency, and corruption helped precipitate a coup in October 1964. Politicians, university students, and workers campaigned for an end to military government and the restoration of democracy. On 21 October police fired on demonstrators, killing one student. A general strike was called and Abboud was forced to negotiate with a common front of the political parties supported by the heads of the two main religious sects. It was agreed that Abboud would remain the acting president but would hand over executive power to a transitional government composed of all parties and including, for the first time, the Communist party and the Muslim Brotherhood. Within four weeks, however, Abboud dismissed all his officers and the presidency reverted to a five-member council.

The transitional government put much emphasis on the problem of the southern Sudan and tried—unsuccessfully—to solve it with the help of southern leaders. Freedom of the press was restored and the ban on political parties was rescinded. In June 1965, elections were held in which all parties except the PDP participated. Since no party won an absolute majority, a coalition was formed between the Umma party, with seventy-six seats, and the NUP, with fifty-three seats. Muhammad Ahmad Mahjoub (Umma) became prime minister and al-Azhari (NUP) permanent chairman of the Presidential Council. However, the new regime was split between right- and left-wing factions.

In the meantime, the Umma party was divided again. A right wing (under the leader of the Mahdiyya Order, the Imam al-Hadi al-Mahdi) supported Premier Mahjoub, while younger elements followed the imam's nephew, Sadeq al-Mahdi. Sadeq al-Mahdi became prime minister after a vote of no-confidence forced Mahjoub to resign in July 1966. The new government, also a coalition of the Umma and the NUP, was able to improve the economic situation and promised to deal with the question of southern Sudan by providing a degree of regional autonomy. The drafting of a permanent constitution was expedited. However, as the NUP withdrew its support the government was defeated in the assembly. Mahjoub again became premier, supported by a coalition of the NUP, the Imam al-Hadi al-Mahdi faction of the Umma and the PDP. In December 1967 the PDP and the NUP merged to form the Democratic Unionist party (DUP). The coalition was unstable; the presidency was claimed by both al-Azhari and al-Hadi al-Mahdi; the southern problem remained unsolved; and the drafting of the constitution caused considerable controversy. In January 1968, the government decided to dissolve the assembly.

Elections took place in April 1968. The Democratic Unionist party won 101 seats, Imam al-Hadi al-Mahdi's faction of the Umma 36 seats, and Sadeq al-Mahdi's faction 30. The two former groups formed a government under Mahjoub. Its position was undermined by disputes between the coalition partners and by reports that the two wings of the Umma had reunited and were about to reestablish their conservative rule.

On 25 May 1969 a group of army officers under Colonel Ja'far al-Nimeiri staged a bloodless coup converting the state to the Democratic Republic of the Sudan. The Constituent Assembly, the Presidential Council, and the transitional constitution were abolished. All political parties and organizations were abolished and their leaders were arrested. The new regime proclaimed a policy of Sudanese socialism. The state would participate in the economy to a greater extent, while maintaining full freedom for foreign aid and local capital. Absolute powers were vested in a National Revolutionary Council. A former chief justice, Babikir 'Awadallah, was appointed prime minister. In October 1969, al-Nimeiri took over as premier, and 'Awadallah became foreign minister and minister of justice.

The central role of the president in the system is clear. General al-Nimeiri exercises the formal and informal powers at his disposal to control the politics of the Sudan. He is the dominant figure in the system, seconded by a small group of fellow officers who have been with him since before the coup. Politics in the Sudan take the form al-Nimeiri wishes. His control extends to both the system and the individuals who assist him in managing its activities, although he must, of course, take care that critical elements such as the army are content and under control.

General al-Nimeiri's regime is closely molded to his wishes. Since the coup he has continued to consolidate his position and to increase his control of the Sudan's politics and its major policies. The central role of the president in the formal structures created under the constitution has been enhanced by al-Nimeiri's exercise of the informal powers at his disposal. He has worked diligently to improve the national economy and to solve social and political problems dividing the people and hindering the development of the state. The southern Sudan issue is perhaps the most significant in this regard but there has also been an effort at reconciliation with political opposition and rivals. Despite this and his success in dealing with some of the state's major problems, there have been a number of attempts to oust him from office.

Opposition to al-Nimeiri has come from various sources and a number of abortive coups have been attempted. In 1970 a right-wing, conservative rebellion led by the Imam al-Hadi al-Mahdi was crushed by the government. Subsequently, in July 1971, a portion of the army under communist leadership overthrew the regime. But al-Nimeiri regained power in a countercoup three days later. Al-Nimeiri's position was strengthened in a referendum in October 1971 in which he received over-whelming popular support. Despite this, attempted coups and/or plots were announced by the government in 1974, 1975, 1976, and 1977. Opposition from the left and from conservative Islamic leaders continues and is periodically manifested through violent means, in part because of the frustration attendant upon the lack of significant legal and political alternatives. However, in 1977 al-Nimeiri launched an effort to deal with his political opponents through a process of "national reconciliation." Basically the regime suggested that if its opponents were prepared to forego violence and subversion they would be free to return to the Sudan (from political exile) and, with their followers, compete for political influence within the parameters of the political system. Amnesty was granted to political opponents, political prisoners were released, and security measures were relaxed. Efforts were made to encourage political and religious refugees to return from neighboring states. Some opposition leaders accepted the initiative while others remained more skeptical. Whether this experiment will end the periodic violent efforts to unseat al-Nimeiri is uncertain. Clearly, for the time being, the opposition, whether participating in the system or not, continues to have little impact on the politics and policies of the Democratic Republic of the Sudan under the leadership of General Ja'far al-Nimeiri.

Foreign Policy

The Sudan's traditional foreign policy evolved under the influence of Egypt and Britain. Its relations with Egypt are essentially geopolitical—the Nile Valley links the two states in a geographic unit uninterrupted by physical barriers. There has been constant interaction within the valley and the history of the Sudan is inseparably bound to that of Egypt. The Arabization and Islamization of Egypt extended Arab/Islamic language and culture within the Nile Valley into the northern part of the Sudan. In the twentieth century the key to the relationship between Egypt and the Sudan has been the Nile River—the dual problems of controlling and of allocating the Nile waters. Any power in control of the Sudan could exert considerable pressure upon Egypt and since the Sudan's independence Egypt has attempted to maintain a dominant influence in the Sudan through diplomatic, cultural, and economic relations. The 1959 agreement provided for the allocation of Nile water and compensation to the Sudanese displaced by the projected Aswan High Dam.

Britain's substantial influence in the Sudan dates from the establishment of the Anglo-Egyptian Condominium in 1899. From 1899 until the Sudan's preindependence elections of 1953 British administrators ran the country, and the Sudan's internal and external policies were effectively dictated from London. Direct British influence ceased with the Sudan's emergence as an independent state in 1956. But the British imprint upon the Sudan is evident in the country's political and economic institutions and in the heritage of Western social and political ideals.

With independence the Sudan proclaimed a policy of nonalignment, hoping to remain free of military or political commitments in the Cold War. Although commercial relations with the communist states expanded following independence, the Sudan's primary economic ties remained with the West. Trade and arms acquisition were Westerndominated (United States, United Kingdom, and West Germany).

In relations with the Arab world, the Sudan remained somewhat aloof, largely as a consequence of geographic location. The Sudan is on the periphery of the Arab world and while the northern Sudan is oriented toward the Middle East, the southern Sudan has more affinity with Black Africa. Its interests were divided between the Arab world (it joined the Arab League in 1956) and Black Africa (it also joined the Organization for African Unity—OAU). The emergence of the states of Africa in the 1960s focused more Sudanese attention on Black Africa.

By the time of the 1967 June War between Israel and the Arab states the Sudan had established a foreign-policy pattern of strong ties with the West and a nominal role in Arab politics. At the outbreak of hostilities the Sudan mobilized its armed forces, expressed full support for the Arab cause, and broke diplomatic relations with the United States and Britain. At first these reactions appeared to be a demonstration of emotional support. Later, however, the Sudan began to develop closer relations with the communist states and increased participation in Arab affairs. There was a growing independence from the West and an increasing reliance upon the Soviet bloc. The growth of Soviet-Sudanese friendship was rapid. Soviet arms and technicians were the primary and most effective tools of the Soviet Union's policy in the Sudan. By the end of 1968 the Sudan's former relationship with the United States and its allies had been substantially replaced by a relationship with the Soviet Union and the bloc states.

The Sudan also moved more into the mainstream of Arab politics and further strengthened its ties with the Arab world. A unit of Sudanese troops joined those of Egypt along the Suez Canal and the Sudan was active in arranging the important Arab summit conference at Khartoum in August 1967.

The military coup of May 1969 changed the personalities formulating foreign policy but did not, initially, alter the substance and direction of that policy. The new government of al-Nimeiri followed the trends that had been developing but gave these elements new emphasis. From the first day, the regime emphasized the Sudan's special relations with Egypt and seemed to accept the guidance of Nasser's principles of freedom, socialism, and unity. The regime tilted sharply toward the Soviet Union and the Eastern bloc; it soon recognized East Germany. The new regime reaffirmed its desire to retain and enlarge upon existing commercial and military aid ties and to forge closer diplomatic and trade relations with Soviet-bloc states. By 1970 an estimated two thousand Soviet and East European technical advisors were in the Sudan. Such important areas as military assistance and economic planning were mostly provided by Soviet specialists, while internal security affairs were partly in East German hands. This was accompanied by a substantial increase in trade with these countries, with the effect that Soviet bloc nations become purchasers of about one-fourth of the country's exports and supplied about one-fifth of all imports.

Concomitant with these developments was the further deterioration of political and trade relations with the West. The al-Nimeiri regime identified itself with progressive Arab and African states and took public stances against "Western imperialism" and "Zionist intrigues." The continuing rebellion in the southern Sudan further complicated the Sudan's deteriorating relations with its African neighbors. This was especially true for Uganda, Zaire, and Ethiopia, which sheltered the largest contingents of refugees and were accused of aiding Sudanese insurgents.

Sudan's relations with its Arab neighbors (Egypt and Libya) were unusually cordial during the first years of the new regime. Their sense of common identity resulted in the signing of the Tripoli Charter on 27 December 1969 by presidents Nasser, al-Nimeiri, and Qaddafi. The original purpose of the charter was to commit the three leaders to "cooperation and coordination" of their respective foreign policies, but in the end it proposed the formation of the Federation of Arab Republics (FAR). The FAR never materialized due to deteriorating relations among the three states.

Initially al-Nimeiri was indebted to his Libyan and Egyptian colleagues but he soon recognized the need to reorder his priorities from a Sudanese rather than Arab perspective. There developed an estrangement from Libya, and a strain in ties with Egypt ensued. As the formerly close ties with Egypt and Libya began to fade, other Arab states on the Arabian peninsula came more and more into play. Not surprisingly, the most complete reversal of relations after the 1971 attempted coup occurred with the major East-West powers. The Soviet Union, East Germany, and Bulgaria were all accused of complicity in the abortive scheme, and President al-Nimeiri at one point threatened, but did not execute, a diplomatic break with the USSR. The Khartoum regime resented attacks by the Soviet press and the deterioration in trade terms and temporary unavailability of spare parts for military equipment. The Sudan followed up on the estrangement with socialist nations by rapprochement with Western states, and resumed official ties with the United Kingdom (soon after the 1967 Arab-Israeli War), West Germany (23 December 1971), and finally the United States in July 1972. Relations with Egypt improved in 1973 and the October War further linked the two states. In February 1974 a new Sudanese-Egyptian agreement was proclaimed, aiming at greater "political, economic, and cultural integration," and setting up appropriate committees for that purpose. Continuing improvement in the relations of the two states was characteristic of the post–October War period.[3] Sudan's foreign policy was increasingly oriented toward Egypt, the states of the Arabian peninsula, and the West (especially the United States).

Notes

1. The provinces were: Northern, Kassala, Khartoum, Blue Nile, Kordofan, Darfur, Upper Nile, Bahr al-Ghazal, and Equatoria.
2. For further details see Chapter 14.
3. The Sudan was one of the few Arab states to support Egyptian President Sadat's initiative in going to Jerusalem in 1977.

Bibliography

The Sudan's history is considered in Mekki Abbas, *The Sudan Question: The Dispute over the Anglo-Egyptian Condominium, 1884–1951* (New York: Frederick A. Praeger Publishers, 1952); Robert O. Collins and Robert L. Tignor, *Egypt and the Sudan* (Englewood Cliffs, N.J.: Prentice-Hall, 1967); Richard Hill, *Egypt in the Sudan 1820–1881* (London: Oxford University Press, 1959); P. M. Holt, *The Mahdist State in the Sudan, 1881–1898: A Study of Its Origins, Development, and Overthrow* (London: Oxford University Press, 1958); P. M. Holt, *A Modern History of the Sudan: From the Funj Sultanate to the Present Day* (New York: Grove Press, 1961); Mekki Shibeika, *The Independent Sudan* (New York: Robert Speller, 1959); A. B. Theobald, *The Mahdiya: A History of the Anglo-Egyptian Sudan, 1881–1899* (London: Longmans, Green, 1951); and Gabriel Warburg, *The Sudan Under Wingate: Administration in the Anglo-Egyptian Sudan 1899–1916* (London: Frank Cass, 1971). Also useful is *Documents on the Sudan, 1899–1953* ([n.p.] Egyptian Society of International Law, 1953).

K. M. Barbour, *The Republic of the Sudan: A Regional Geography* (London: University of London Press, 1961) provides a discussion of the geography of the Sudan.

H. C. Jackson, *Behind the Modern Sudan* (London: Macmillan & Co.; New York: St. Martin's Press, 1955) focuses on the problems of administration of the Sudan during the condominium period.

Muddathir 'Abd al-Rahim, *Imperialism and Nationalism in the Sudan: A Study in Constitutional and Political Development, 1899-1956* (London: Oxford University Press, 1969) provides an overview of the preparations for Sudan's political independence.

Peter K. Bechtold, *Politics in the Sudan: Parliamentary and Military Rule in an Emerging African Nation* (New York: Praeger Publishers, 1976) provides an excellent study of Sudanese politics and policy since independence.

General surveys of all aspects of Sudan include Harold MacMichael, *The Sudan* (New York: Frederick A. Praeger Publishers, 1955), which covers the period to 1953, and Harold D. Nelson et al., *Area Handbook for the Democratic Republic of Sudan* (Washington, D.C.: U.S. Government Printing Office, 1973), which focuses on the postindependence era.

The southern Sudan problem is considered from different perspectives in Oliver Albino, *The Sudan: A Southern Viewpoint* (London: Oxford University Press, for the Institute of Race Relations, 1970); Joseph Oduho and William Deng, *The Problem of the Southern Sudan* (London: Oxford University Press, for the Institute of Race Relations, 1963); Cecil Eprile, *War and Peace in the Sudan, 1955-1972* (London: David & Charles, 1974); Robert O. Collins, *The Southern Sudan, 1883-1898: A Struggle for Control* (New Haven: Yale University Press, 1962); and Dunstan M. Wai, ed., *The Southern Sudan: The Problem of National Integration* (London: Frank Cass, 1973). Former Prime Minister and Foreign Minister Mohamed Ahmed Maghoub has written *Democracy on Trial: Reflections on Arab and African Politics* (London: Andre Deutsch, 1974).

16

Socialist People's Libyan Arab Jamahiriya

Bernard Reich

Libya is situated in North Africa, bordered by the Mediterranean Sea in the north, by the Arab Republic of Egypt and the Sudan in the east, by Niger and Chad in the south, and by Tunisia and Algeria in the west. It has an area of about 1,774,150 sq. km. (685,000 sq. mi.), more than 90 percent of which is desert. Libya is comprised of three distinct geographical units: Tripolitania in the west with an area of about 248,640 sq. km. (96,000 sq. mi.); Cyrenaica in the east with an area of about 699,300 sq. km. (270,000 sq. mi.); and Fezzan in the south and southwest with an area of about 826,210 sq. km. (319,000 sq. mi.).

Libya's small population of approximately 2.45 million (1975 estimate) contrasts with its large land area. Overall population density is only about 3.5 persons per square mile, but 90 percent of the people live in less than 10 percent of the total area, primarily along the Mediterranean coast. More than a quarter of the population is urban, mostly concentrated in the two largest cities, Benghazi and Tripoli. The majority of the population is of Arab origin, descending from the two great bedouin tribes of Beni Hilal and Beni Suleim, who came originally from the Arabian peninsula and entered Libya in the eleventh century. Berbers are descendants of the original inhabitants of North Africa and are now found only in the oases of Jalo and Auguila and in the mountain regions of Tripolitania. The Tuaregs live in the southern oases of Fezzan. Virtually all Libyans are Sunni Muslims, predominantly Senussi.[1]

Historical Background

In the earliest days the area that is now Libya was visited by Phoenician sailors who established trading posts along the coastline. Later the Greeks landed. Subsequently, the control of part of the area fell to Alexander the Great and later to the Egyptian kingdom of the Ptolemies. Rome annexed Cyrenaica and Tripolitania, both becoming part of the Roman Empire. Eventually Pax Romana prevailed, and Libya enjoyed a long period of prosperity and peace. A period of decline began in the middle of the fourth century. In the seventh century Arab invaders arrived from Egypt, and most of the Berber tribes embraced Islam. The Arabs who swept across North Africa in the seventh century ruled for 900 years, interrupted by the Normans, the Spaniards, and the Knights of St. John. They were finally replaced in 1551 by the Ottoman Turks, who ruled until 1911. Italy declared war on the Ottoman Empire in September 1911; Italian troops landed in Tripoli in early October and later that month in Benghazi.

The Italian conquest was not accomplished without difficulty, despite a Turkish-Italian treaty in October 1912 by which sovereignty was conceded. In World War I, the Senussis, who had opposed Turkish rule, were led against Italy by the movement-founder's grandson (Muhammad Idris el-Mahdi el-Senussi) with Turkish support. Senussi strength was centered in Cyrenaica. Resistance against Italian control continued until 1931 although, by 1932, Fascist rule had subdued all opposition. In 1934 Italy adopted the name "Libya" (used by the Greeks for North Africa west of Egypt) as the official name of its colony consisting of Cyrenaica, Tripolitania, and Fezzan. Colonization along the coast included the settlement of the Italian peasants and consolidation of Italian control. World War II interrupted Italy's plans, and by the end of 1942 British and French forces had swept the Italians out of the country. In 1947 Idris returned to Cyrenaica from exile in Egypt. The Italian legacy was of little value. Education had been neglected before the war and stopped after 1940; Libyan participation in the colonial government had been discouraged, and training for self-rule had been ignored. However, Idris and his supporters had sided with the British and were promised, at minimum, freedom from Italy. The form this freedom should take, however, became the subject of great-power rivalry. A British military administration was installed in Tripolitania and Cyrenaica, while the French governed Fezzan.

The machinery for settling the country's future was contained in the Italian Peace Treaty of 1947, which provided that the future of Italy's former colonies should be decided by Britain, France, the Soviet Union, and the United States, with the stipulation that if no agreement was reached the question would be taken to the United Nations. Each of the powers proposed alternative plans for the area, and it was decided that a four-power commission should ascertain the wishes of the Libyans. In 1948, after visiting Libya, the commission ended in disagreement on

Libya

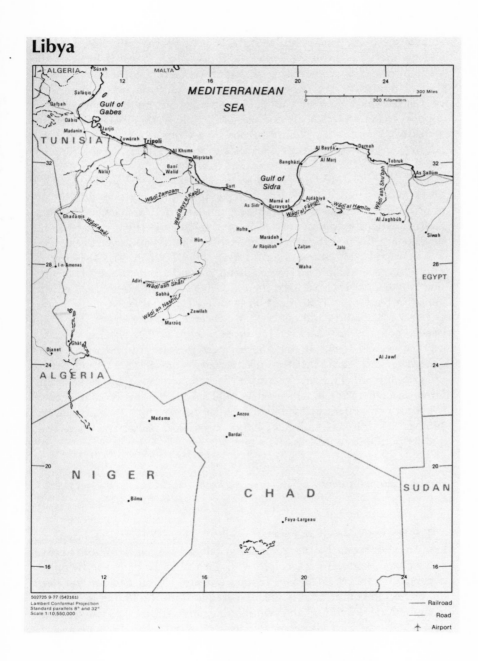

MALTA

MEDITERRANEAN
SEA

300 Miles
300 Kilometers

Súsah

12

16

20

24

Ṣafāqis

Gafṣah

Gulf of
Gabes

Qābis

Madanin

Jarjis

Zuwārah

Tripoli

TUNISIA

Al Khums

Miṣrātah

Banghāzī

Al Bayḍā

Al Marj

Darnah

Tobruk

As Sallūm

32

Banī
Walid

Nālūt

Surt

Gulf of
Sidra

Wādī Zamzam

Wādī Bayy al Kabīr

As Sidr

Marsá al
Burayqah

Ajdābiyā

Wādī al Fārigh

Wādī ash Shuʿbah

Wādī al Hamīm

Al Jaghbūb

32

Ghadāmis

Wādī Awāl

Hūn

Hofra

Marādah

Ar Rāqūbah

Zaltan

Jālū

Al Jawf

Siwah

28

I-n-Amenas

Adiri

Wādī ash Shāṭi

Sabhā

Wādī an Nashū

Zawilah

Marzūq

Waha

28

EGYPT

Djanet

Ghāt

24

Al Jawf

24

ALGERIA

Madama

Aozou

Bardai

20

NIGER

20

SUDAN

Bilma

CHAD

Faya-Largeau

16

12

16

20

24

16

502725 9-77 (542161)
Lambert Conformal Projection
Standard parallels 8° and 32°
Scale 1:10,550,000

——— Railroad
——— Road
✈ Airport

many of the specifics but reached accord on the view that the Libyans wanted independence but were not yet ready to rule themselves. By the summer of 1948, it was clear that the four powers were unable to agree and the matter went to the United Nations, where it was debated in the General Assembly in the spring of 1949. Initial sentiment seemed to favor the postponement of independence and the establishment of some form of trusteeship. But agreement could not be reached on this approach and support for independence increased. On 21 November 1949 the General Assembly adopted a resolution that Libya (composed of the three territories) should become an independent state no later than 1 January 1952.

The assembly resolution allowed approximately two years in which Libya was to be prepared for independence. British and French administration continued during much of the period as Adrian Pelt, the United Nations commissioner appointed to assist in the transition to independence, helped to prepare the institutions of self-government. Pelt was assisted by an international advisory council composed of representatives of several United Nations members and a committee of twenty-one Libyans (seven from each region). A constituent assembly was convened in December 1950, but it encountered difficulties in its efforts to devise a constitution and establish institutions of government. The main issue was the rivalry between the three provinces. Tripolitania sought a unitary system, since it had the greatest population and area, while Cyrenaica and Fezzan insisted on status and representation equal to that of Tripolitania. The matter was eventually resolved by establishing Libya as a federation in which substantial autonomy was given to each of the three component units. Libya became independent on 24 December 1951 as the United Kingdom of Libya, composed of Fezzan, Cyrenaica, and Tripolitania, with Idris I as its monarch.

Political Environment

Economic and Social Issues

The main economic and social problems facing Libya are related and tend to reinforce each other. Primarily, Libya faces a lack of both human and natural resources (except for oil). In the early days following independence, the problem was far more acute, for oil had not yet been discovered in commercial quantities. In addition, the Italian legacy was of limited value and had an essentially negative effect. At the time of independence, at least 90 percent of the population was illiterate and no significant educated elite existed. The best agricultural land was held by

Italian settlers and there was no indigenous economic infrastructure. Furthermore, the substantial amounts of capital required for development were not internally available. These deficiencies were partially overcome by outside assistance. The need for capital was partially met by grants from the United States and the United Kingdom, while large-scale technical aid was made available by the United States and the United Nations. Other countries, notably Italy, also provided some assistance. Although petroleum revenues became available as a source of development financing, and foreign capital assistance became less necessary, the need for outside technical services continued because of the lack of sufficient numbers of Libyans with the education or skills essential to the management of the expanding economy. To overcome the shortage of qualified personnel, Libya recruited foreign experts in industry, aviation, agriculture, and planning and development through the United Nations and its specialized agencies and from various governments. Libyans also studied abroad on government fellowships to acquire and refine their knowledge in technical and administrative fields.

Libya's natural-resource base remains weak, despite abundant petroleum. Mineral resources—other than petroleum and gas—are either nonexistent or not yet proven. Libya is essentially an immense desert with scattered settlements—coastal strips, oases, and the northern plateaus. This factor limits the country's economic development, since the cost of the infrastructure needed to link these various areas is considerable.

The Libyan economic predicament can be better understood in relation to the following background. Before the oil era, economic development appeared to be an almost impossible task: the paucity of both human and natural resources, the constraints on agricultural progress, and the peculiarities of the geography all seemed to pose insuperable obstacles. Petroleum has eliminated a single, although important, constraint on Libya's economic development—the availability of finance. All other constraints still operate today and are likely to restrict the pace of economic development for many years. Since petroleum is a depletable resource, it may not, according to some estimates, sustain for more than two decades the level, or the rate of growth, of income to which Libya has become accustomed. The old predicament was how to break away from the vicious cycles of poverty and backwardness. The present predicament is how to use petroleum wealth in ways that will achieve the old objective, a decisive escape from the constraints of backwardness. Through this achievement the government hopes to prevent economic and developmental stagnation, a fall in incomes, or even the recurrence of poverty after the oil era.

Libya's major resource before the discovery of petroleum at the end of the 1950s was agriculture. This sector still retains its importance, not as a major source of income or of exports but as a large employer. However, water supply is scarce, and in areas where the main source of water is rainfall, the supply is very irregular. Irrigation projects have not achieved levels necessary for agricultural self-sufficiency.

The nature and prospects of the Libyan economy changed drastically with the discovery of important petroleum reserves about 1960. Libya distinguished itself in the history of the petroleum industry as the country in which exploration, development, and production proceeded at very fast rates. Indeed, the first major petroleum discovery was made by ESSO on 10 June 1958 (the Zelten field) less than four years after the granting of the concessions; and the first exports left Libya's shores on 12 September 1961, little more than two years later. The discovery of the Zelten field was rapidly followed by others. The discoveries in 1959–1960 further revealed that Libya had important petroleum reserves and that very large supplies would soon become available. Libya's position was strengthened further after the June 1967 Middle East War because, with the closing of the Suez Canal, Libyan petroleum exports to Europe had a significant comparative advantage over petroleum from the Persian Gulf that either had to be transshipped or routed around Africa. Production and exports continued to increase at a fast rate. In the late 1960s, Libya became increasingly concerned with conservation, partly because it began to realize that the life of its reserves at the current rates of production might prove to be too short in relation to the span of time desired for economic development. Thus, in 1972 and 1973 Libya's petroleum production dipped below the level attained in 1968 and was one-third less than the 1970 peak. These lower rates of production—some 2–2.5 million barrels a day—are close to the optimum rate for Libya, given the nature of her petroleum reserves, the characteristics of the country's petroleum fields, world petroleum prices, Libyan domestic revenue needs, and the time horizon of economic development. Petroleum, Libya's greatest mineral resource, is also its major industry and has become the dominant commodity in its foreign trade.

Apart from petroleum, Libya's exports are chiefly agricultural products, although such exports have decreased by almost 50 percent since 1960, partly because of increased local consumption and partly because migration to the cities has decreased production. About 30 percent of Libya's farm products are exported: agricultural exports include peanuts, citrus fruits, castor beans, almonds, and some wine. Before the discovery and exploitation of petroleum, the agricultural sector employed 70 percent of the labor force and constituted 30 percent of the gross domestic product (GDP).

Other than agriculture and petroleum, Libya's few industries consist largely of government-owned facilities, services, and processing plants, which mostly produce for the Libyan market. The most important government-owned facilities are the public utilities, public works departments, and port and harbor services.

After the 1969 revolution, the Revolutionary Command Council (RCC) redirected the economy toward rapid economic development, a more equal distribution of income and services, greater government economic control, and independence from foreign influence. Among the most important policies of the regime have been those designed to manage and deal with the problems attendant upon a lack of natural and human resources. Managing the petroleum resources of the state and the revenues to be derived therefrom became a major government policy. The revenues, in turn, were to be used to effect some improvement in the human-resource base. An improvement in the literacy of the population was sought through compulsory and free elementary education. Secondary schools, universities, and adult and technical education have also become more widely available. Improvement in health standards and other elements designed to improve the personal situation of the population also contribute to this improved resource base.

The government has made large investments in roads, ports, airports, and communications designed to tie the dispersed population together and to connect Libya to the outside world. It has also embarked upon an ambitious program in health, education, and welfare services designed to reach the villages. In addition, the government has provided generous loans for the development of low-cost housing, small businesses, and industry. Responding to a shortage of private capital, the new regime has set up a variety of government corporations and agencies designed to meet a wide range of needs. Because of a shortage of skilled Libyan manpower, a significant number of foreigners have necessarily been brought into the government bureaucracy, schools, hospitals, irrigation and agricultural management, construction projects, and oil production.

The RCC generally intensified the government's role in the economy. There was progressive assertion by the government of its right to determine prices and quantities of petroleum exports. This was accompanied by eviction of the remaining Jews and Italians; by nationalization of the country's banking, insurance, and petroleum-marketing companies; and by expansion of the participation and control of industry and commerce by Libyans and Libyan-owned firms. On 21 July 1970, all remaining

Italians (about twenty thousand) were expelled after their assets were confiscated. Also, the properties of nonresident Jews were confiscated. In December 1971 the government nationalized the production and exporting facilities of the British Petroleum Company, and in the spring of 1972 it nationalized the pharmaceutical trade. The government's role in the economy is overwhelmingly predominant. Mineral rights are vested in the state, as are water rights. The basic infrastructural facilities—highways, communications, ports, major airlines, major airports, and electric power capacity—are directly or indirectly owned and operated by the government. After expulsion of the Italians the government became a major landowner. It directly controlled the money market and, through its exchange control mechanism, it controlled the movements of foreign trade (except in the petroleum industry) and that part of domestic trade that had its origins or its destination in foreign trade.

Libyan government expenditures have not kept pace with the rapid rise in petroleum revenues. The resulting surplus has led to the growth of large Central Bank reserves of foreign exchange and gold. From mid-1973 to 1976 these reserves were in excess of $3 billion.

The government has a budget for ordinary expenditures and a separate development-plan budget. In addition, there are special allocations for subsidies, foreign aid, and much of the country's military outlays, which also come from petroleum revenues. By law, 15 percent of petroleum revenues must be set aside as reserves each year, and 70 percent of the remainder must be devoted to development.

The first Libyan five-year plan, in which communications and public works were given priority, was ratified in 1965 and extended in 1968. A revised five-year plan was instituted in 1969 by the Idris regime, which placed more emphasis on agriculture, transport, and housing as well as on local government. The second plan was replaced by a three-year development plan (1972–1975) following the 1969 revolution and economic policy shift. The revised plan was modified again in 1973 to allow yearly allocations to be added. The five-year plan for 1976–1980 envisaged a total expenditure of about $24 billion. It stressed the development of agriculture, educational facilities, transportation, housing, electrification, and industrial projects outside the petroleum sector.

Industrialization has been limited because of small domestic markets, uneven distribution of population, lack of skilled manpower, and few natural resources other than petroleum. The largest industrial projects are directly connected with the petroleum sector, including refining and liquefaction of natural gas. A growing number of small manufacturing establishments produce a variety of consumer goods, including food products. Increasing amounts have been allocated for industrial products in the development budgets. There are plans for a petrochemical industry based on natural gas, a resource that is currently underused.

Political Structure and Dynamics

The Kingdom of Libya

The constitution of the United Kingdom of Libya remained in effect and guided the government of the state until 1963, when it was replaced by a revised document establishing a unitary system.

The 1951 constitution established the United Kingdom of Libya as a constitutional monarchy under Muhammad Idris el-Mahdi el-Senussi. Sovereignty was vested in the nation but entrusted to Idris and to his male heirs by the people. Islam was declared the religion of the state and Arabic its official language. Executive power was granted to the king while legislative power was shared by the king and Parliament. King Idris was to exercise his executive power through an appointed prime minister and cabinet or council of ministers, while legislative power was vested in a parliament, which he convened and could adjourn (for up to thirty days) or dissolve. The king sanctioned and promulgated all laws and made the necessary regulations through relevant ministries for their implementation. In "exceptional and urgent circumstances" when Parliament was not in session, the king was permitted to issue decrees, subject to confirmation by Parliament when it convened. He could veto legislation and his veto could only be overridden by a two-thirds vote of both the Senate and the House of Representatives. The king was supreme commander of the armed forces; he could proclaim a state of emergency and martial law, declare war, and conclude peace, with the approval of Parliament. In addition, he appointed senators, judges, and senior public servants. The king was supreme head of state, "inviolable" and "exempt from all responsibility."

The cabinet was appointed and dismissed by royal decrees on the prime minister's recommendation. Although the cabinet was selected by the king, under Article 86 the cabinet members were collectively responsible to the lower house of Parliament, and each was individually responsible for the activities of the ministry that he headed. A vote of no-confidence by Parliament could force the resignation of any or all ministers. The cabinet was responsible for the direction of all of the internal and external affairs of the state.

Parliament consisted of two chambers. The Senate had twenty-four members (eight from each province), one-half of whom were appointed by the king. The others were elected by the legislative councils of the provinces. Each served for eight years and could be reappointed or reelected. The House of Representatives consisted of deputies elected by popular suffrage on the basis of one deputy for every twenty thousand inhabitants or any fraction of that number exceeding half (although each province was required to have at least five members.) The deputies served for a maximum of four years. Parliamentary sessions were called by the king in November. During sessions, a bill could be introduced by the king or by one of the chambers; it had to be adopted by both chambers and ratified by the king before becoming law. However, only the king and the House of Representatives could initiate bills involving the budget.

The federal government exercised legislative and executive powers as described in article 36 of the constitution, which provided a detailed listing of areas for the exercise of its power. In other areas there were provisions for joint powers between the federal and provincial governments. The provinces were to exercise all powers not assigned to the federal government by the constitution. Each province was to have a governor (*wali*) appointed and removed by the king and representing the king in the province. An executive council and a legislative council would be established in each province.

The state was essentially an artificial creation of the United Nations following the failure of the four great powers to agree on the disposition of the Italian colonies of Tripolitania, Cyrenaica, and Fezzan. The three areas of Libya had been separate ones with no common historical tradition. They were geographically separated until Italy formally combined them as Libya in 1934. Population was concentrated in several areas, widely separated, and had no significant transportation links or other elements to tie the regions together or provide a sense of identity or unity. Although the years of Italian rule and settlement generated a strong animosity toward the invader, Libyan society was unable to produce a well-organized nationalist movement. Italian occupation was terminated by the Allied armies, not by armed Libyan resistance or the activities of a Libyan nationalist movement. After the Axis armies were driven out during World War II, the areas under British and French military control were separately administered. The federal system established at the time of independence was a device to hold the disparate areas together.

The original adoption of the federal system was a necessary compromise in the drafting of the constitution and was expensive and cumbersome. Scarce human resources were divided into four governments rather than concentrated in the central government, whose control of the country and its policies was thereby weakened. The system also presented obstacles to the national economic development effort as each of the provinces approached many of the economic issues independently, with varying requirements and regulations governing trade and related economic factors.

Friction between Tripolitania and Cyrenaica plagued Libya from the beginning of the federal system. Tripolitania had strongly favored a unitary state, whereas Cyrenaica and Fezzan advocated federalism. Rivalries between Tripolitania and Cyrenaica frequently developed into conflicts between provincial and federal authorities, but the king and his government were in firm control. Nationalist elements, mainly in Tripolitania, disagreed with the king's conservative regime and his pro-Western policy.

The federal structure was abolished in 1963 and replaced by a unitary system that established the authority of a unitary government with jurisdiction over all matters within the state. The country's name was changed to the Kingdom of Libya, with Idris I remaining the monarch. The provinces surrendered administrative and financial decision making to the national government, whose authority was exercised through ten administrative districts, each headed by a *wali*.

The shift from the federal to a unitary system in 1963 did not alter the government greatly because much of the structure established in 1951 remained intact at the national level. The major changes in the constitution related to the federal elements contained in the 1951 document. The division of powers between the federal governments was replaced by ten administrative districts, for each of which a *wali* was appointed, dismissed, or transferred by the council of ministers and empowered to execute the policies of the government in his district. The powers of the *walis* were more limited than those of the governors under the 1951 constitution. All matters except those dealing exclusively with local affairs were under the direction of the national government. One of the more significant changes in the federal government occurred in the provisions relating to Parliament. As a result of the 1963 constitution the king was empowered to appoint all of the senators and could increase their number. Elections for members of the House were opened to universal suffrage. Before this change was instituted, the system had been based on the fragmentation of power among the palace, the organs of the federal government, the organs of the provincial governments, and other centrifugal powers, including certain religious institutions. However, King Idris I and his loyal supporters remained the focal points of power.

King Idris was the strongest single source of power in the Libyan political system. He determined the policies, which were implemented by his ministers, whom he appointed and dismissed at will. The will of the king prevailed when it was expressed. Often he did not appear to be involved in the daily activity of the government and allowed the prime minister and cabinet to implement policies as they deemed appropriate so long as they retained the confidence of Parliament and stayed within the broad policy outlines established by the king. The king's dominant position in the political system was the result of many factors: his role in Libyan history as leader of the resistance against Italian domination; his personality; the respect he commanded from Libyans in general; his role as a quasi-religious leader of the Senussi sect; his constitutional powers; and the nature of the system itself. Because the system was torn by centrifugal forces, he was able to maintain the balance between these forces, thereby preserving internal stability and order as well as his own special position and role.

Idris's long experience as the head of the Senussi gave him a position of veneration throughout the nation, and he was particularly adept at manipulating Libyan politics. The political circle he led was centered in the palace and in the special ties to Cyrenaica, and not in the populace. Political expression was limited and political parties were prohibited. The ministers were closely linked to and dependent on the monarchy, despite the provisions of the constitution that stated that they were collectively and individually responsible to the lower house of Parliament. In fact, their positions and policies were determined by the king. In the governmental structure the only significant potential alternative power center was the House of Representatives. It consisted of elected members, and its vote of confidence was essential to the continuation of a cabinet in power. It was the only place in which policies were publicly discussed, evaluated, and frequently criticized, and it provided a forum for the opposition to express its views. But its power was limited by constitutional and political restrictions. In theory, the king shared the right of legislation with the House and the Senate and he was the ultimate arbiter in any dispute between the House and the cabinet. Moreover, elections were often controlled to ensure smooth relations between the House and the cabinet.

The king gradually consolidated his power, playing people against each other, maneuvering disparate factions and cliques to suit his purposes, and imposing limitations on various organs of the state. He often trespassed in areas beyond his constitutional limits and even meddled in purely administrative matters. He carefully sought to have the cabinet subordinated to the palace, and the Parliament to the cabinet. The provinces gradually weakened and became subordinated to the cabinet. Despite opposition to his policies and programs, the king controlled the Libyan political system with a firm hand and political development was stifled.

The Revolution of 1969

On 1 September 1969 a bloodless military coup d'etat overthrew the government of King Idris (who was out of the country at the time). There was little resistance, even by elements thought to be loyal to the king (such as the police and the tribes). Although the king made an attempt to secure British assistance to restore his position, he was unsuccessful and eventually renounced the throne. The monarchy was abolished, and a Revolutionary Command Council of twelve young military officers proclaimed a Libyan Arab Republic and vested supreme authority for all government and public affairs in itself. All legislative functions were to be executed by the RCC. The constitution and Parliament were abolished, the government dismissed, and the ban on political parties was continued.

The RCC proclaimed a republic opposing imperialism and favoring the establishment of a revolutionary, socialist, and progressive Libyan state. The basic tenor and approach of the new regime became clear in the RCC's proclamation of 1 September 1969:

> In the name of God, the Compassionate, the Merciful, O great Libyan people: . . . your armed forces have destroyed the reactionary, backward, and decadent regime. . . . In one terrible moment of fate, the darkness of ages—from the rule of the Turks to the tyranny of the Italians and the era of reaction, bribery, intercession, favoritism, treason, and treachery—was dispersed. Thus, from now on, Libya is deemed a free, sovereign republic under the name of the Libyan Arab Republic—ascending with God's help to exalted heights, proceeding in the path of freedom, unity and social justice, guaranteeing the right of equality to its citizens, and opening before them the doors of honorable work—with none terrorized, none cheated, none oppressed, no master and no servant, but free brothers in the shadow of a society over which flutters, God willing, the banner of prosperity and equality. . . . Stand together against the enemy of the Arab nation, the enemy of Islam, the enemy of humanity, who burned our holy places and shattered our honor. Thus will we build glory, revive our heritage, and revenge an honor wounded and a right usurped.[2]

The regime that came to power had certain clear objectives and developed an ideology, albeit often unfocused and confused. Their immediate problem was to create a functioning political system. Much of the period since the revolution has reflected this dual effort—formulating a coherent ideology and constructing a functioning political structure to promote the ideology. Both have undergone substantial evolution.

The RCC sought to move Libya in new directions after the revolution.

Its motto became "freedom, socialism and unity," and it sought to take strong measures to achieve these ends. The definition and meaning of these three concepts and the policies designed to achieve them were increasingly provided by Muammar Qaddafi, who emerged as the main power of the new regime shortly after the revolution. He has continued to exercise authority despite numerous modifications in the structures and procedures of government.

Qaddafi articulated a world view known as the third theory, a philosophy in which he advanced an alternative to Marxist socialism and Western capitalism. In his view, the Quran, in which all wisdom is to be found, provides for an egalitarianism that is the basis of socialism and provides the Islamic content of Qaddafi's socialism. A recurring theme in public statements has been a comparison between capitalism and communism and exhortations that Libyan socialism is not akin to that of Lenin or Marx. Rather, according to Qaddafi, "it is the socialism of the true faith. It is the socialism which springs from the heritage and beliefs of this people."[3] Socialism will thus provide for social justice within the system and all will be able to share in the benefits of society. He sought to free Libya from poverty and backwardness, from injustice and oppression, and from foreign elements and influences. He also strove to build Arab unity by linking Libya with other Arab states. In the final analysis he saw these elements as mutually supportive and increasingly leading to the attainment of the designated goal of unity.

In support of the regime's ideology a series of measures aimed at Arabization and Islamization of Libya were instituted. As early as September 1969, the RCC ordered the use of Arabic for all signs, tickets, and other documents. Subsequently, Libya insisted on passports being written in Arabic rather than the internationally accepted English or French. Efforts were made to increase the use of Arabic in regional and international forms. Libya's Italian community was warned about its colonialist past soon after the revolution. In July 1970, the property of the Italian and Jewish communities in Libya was confiscated.

While the basic elements of the ideology were identified soon after the revolution took place, the machinery and policy necessary to achieve the goals were more difficult to develop. At first the RCC—the group of officers who staged the revolution and continued to run it—was the supreme governing body. Muammar Qaddafi soon emerged as the leading figure of the council, its chief spokesman and ideologist.

Qaddafi was born in 1942 in a bedouin tent in the Libyan desert of a not well-to-do family belonging to a small tribe, originally of Berber origin. He attended local elementary and secondary schools, where his education was Arabic and Islamic and many of his teachers were Egyptian. He focused on the study of history and apparently was influenced by the major historical events of the time: the creation of Israel, the Egyptian Revolution of 1952, and the invasion of Egypt by Israel, England, and France in 1956. His education and his family background provided the basis for his strong and devout Muslim beliefs and his austere and simple life-style and puritanical code of personal conduct and morals. He maintained much of his bedouin ethics and code of action. During his formative years he was influenced not only by events but by the needs of his people. He saw the monarchy as reactionary and under foreign influence, and Libyan society as backward. He viewed the changes in Egypt as beneficial and adopted Nasser as his hero and the Egyptian Revolution as a model for change in Libya. The military academy and a military career appeared to be a logical avenue for upward mobility, political activity, and revolution that would change the system. Qaddafi entered the academy in 1961 and prior to his graduation met many of his future colleagues in the RCC. After graduation he served in the army, rising to the rank of captain (at age twenty-seven) at the time of the 1969 overthrow of Idris. He was made commander-in-chief of the armed forces in October 1969 and became chairman of the RCC.

Initially, the RCC formed a government under Dr. Mahmud S. al-Maghrebi, who was not an RCC member. But, in January 1970, Qaddafi became prime minister with his chief aide, 'Abd-ul-Salam Jallud, as second in command. Internal strife within the junta was suppressed and, in December 1969, a conspiracy led by the ministers of defense and the interior, which attempted to overthrow the regime, was foiled.

Government activities were managed by a cabinet appointed by the RCC, chiefly comprised of civilian technocrats but with RCC members holding such critical cabinet posts as prime minister, minister of defense, and minister of the interior. From the beginning, the RCC functioned as a closed system of authority with supreme power. Power was concentrated in the hands of the RCC, and it was strongly supported by the armed forces and by the general population. Within the RCC the decision-making process was informal and appeared to be in accord with traditional Arab approaches to decision making (rather than Western-style formal and institutionalized procedure), which involved elite consensus rather than formal votes. The consensus resulting from discussion and debate also helped to reinforce unity rather than accentuate division within the ruling group. Within the RCC, loyalty to Qaddafi seemed to be maintained because of the strong agreement among its members concerning the goals of the revolution—Arab nationalism and the improvement of the condition of the average Libyan.

Control over the government has increasingly resided in Qaddafi although, in contrast to the monarchy, he has attempted to promote greater popular participation in government. An early effort was undertaken in June 1971 with the establishment of the first significant post-independence political party—the Arab Socialist Union (ASU)—its character clearly patterned after the model of the Egyptian ASU, developed under Nasser. The Libyan ASU was to be the vehicle of Arab nationalism and would facilitate political socialization and participation. The party was to be based on an alliance of the "active popular forces," which included peasants, workers, soldiers, intellectuals, and nonexploiting capitalists; and peasants and workers were to constitute not less than 50 percent of the members of any branch of the party. The structure provided for provincial congresses, which would elect committees from which the RCC would appoint a national congress. The ASU provided a rudimentary political organization, which took root although, in general, the results were disappointing to the RCC leadership.

In a speech at Zouara in April 1973, Qaddafi launched an attack on the shortcomings of the revolution's domestic progress and the reluctance of the people to contribute to national development. He proclaimed as a new stage in the revolution a program of five principles: the suspension of all laws then in force and their replacement by Shari'a (Islamic law); repression of all adversaries of the revolution (especially communists); the arming of the masses so that they could attain the objectives of the revolution; the purging of the administration and administrative reform; and a cultural revolution directed against everything contrary to the Quran and the promotion of pure Islamic thought. Popular committees came into existence in schools, businesses, industrial enterprises, and public institutions. They were ostensibly created to oversee the administration of those bodies in the public interest. Much of this program remained a dead letter. The Zouara speech was followed by an upheaval that failed to produce any important structural results.

Qaddafi moved ahead with the attempt to construct a political system. In January 1976 a "Green Book" appeared in which he elaborated the principles of popular government, expounded his political ideas, voiced criticism of political parties and parliamentary assemblies, and stressed the necessity for popular participation in government. The publication of the Green Book coincided with the meeting of an elected national congress in Tripoli in January 1976 that considered establishing a new political system in Libya.

On 3 March 1977, a General People's Congress of elected representatives changed the country's name to the Socialist People's Libyan Arab Jamahiriya (state), proclaimed the establishment of people's power, and vested all power in the General People's Congress. Colonel Qaddafi, as secretary general of the General Secretariat of the General People's Congress, continued to be chief of state. The People's Congress replaced the Revolutionary Command Council, which was abolished as the supreme authority, but former RCC officers were named members of the secretariat and served in an advisory capacity. The General People's Congress Committee, which replaced the Council of Ministers, was comprised of cabinet officers appointed by the secretariat and was headed by Abdulati Ubaydi (Obeidi) who was thus de facto head of government. The cabinet ministers were made responsible for day-to-day operations of their ministries. There were local congresses at the village or neighborhood level, labor syndicates, unions, and professional associations. The Arab Socialist Union (ASU) remained the sole political party. The March 1977 Congress decreed that the country's legal codes would henceforth be based upon the Quran.

Despite the new names and structures and the formal end of the RCC, the political system continued to be dominated by the officers who joined with Qaddafi to overthrow the king in 1969. Among them, Qaddafi clearly remained the most prominent and central figure.

Foreign Policy

King Idris followed a pro-Western foreign policy. Treaties signed with Britain (July 1953) and the United States (September 1954) provided for the maintenance of military bases and forces in Libya, in exchange for development grants and budgetary subventions. An agreement with France (August 1955) provided for communications facilities in the southwestern desert areas. Close ties were also maintained with Turkey and Greece. Within the Arab League, which Libya joined in 1953, Libya supported the conservative bloc despite internal pressures for closer ties with Egypt. After the 1967 Arab-Israeli War, Libya committed itself, along with Saudi Arabia and Kuwait, to provide subsidies to Egypt and Jordan as compensation for war losses.

Under internal and external pressure for the liquidation of foreign bases, the government publicly supported the early evacuation of these bases but took few practical steps in that direction. In June 1967 the government officially requested Britain and the United States to liquidate their bases as soon as possible and the process of liquidation was begun. But the matter only became urgent after the revolution.

In the African arena, Libya was a founding member of the Organization for African Unity (1963) and generally supported its anticolonialist resolutions and policies. There were also efforts for closer economic cooperation among the Maghrib states. Discussions concerning this cooperation were held with Tunisia, Algeria, and Morocco.

Qaddafi regarded the coup of September 1969 as the starting point of Libyan independence. The RCC gave priority to removing the foreign bases, to eliminating the vestiges of imperialism, and to supporting the Arab cause. Shortly after the overthrow of Idris, the regime approached the United States and England to secure the removal of their bases. Agreement was soon reached, and the British bases at Tobruk and al-Adam and the U.S. base, Wheelus Field, were evacuated in the spring of 1970. The new government vigorously sought to unite with other Arab states in a pan-Arab federation as a means of achieving Arab unity. The obvious first partner was Egypt, for geographical and ideological reasons as well as the prestige of Nasser, and Qaddafi's efforts to emulate his idol. While Nasser was wary of such a union, Sadat was less cautious and saw it as a means of strengthening Egypt's domestic and regional position.

After the Arab summit conference of December 1969, Qaddafi, President Nasser of Egypt, and President Ja'far al-Nimeiri of the Sudan met in Tripoli for discussions that resulted in the Tripoli Charter of 27 December 1969. The three leaders reaffirmed faith in the objective of Arab unity, announced their intention to work toward some form of unity, and agreed to meet at periodic intervals for planning. Following Nasser's death in September 1970, Qaddafi, Sadat, and al-Nimeiri announced on 8 November 1970 that a tripartite federal union would be formed. Syria, under al-Assad, was accepted into the federal plan and, after further meetings, Qaddafi, Sadat, and al-Assad simultaneously announced from their respective capitals on 17 April 1971 the formation of a federation by Libya, Egypt, and Syria. The Sudan did not formally accede. The three heads of state signed the draft constitution of the new federation in Damascus on 20 August 1971 and the document received overwhelming approval by the electorate of the three countries in the referendum of 1 September 1971. To Qaddafi and the RCC, formation of the federation was a major step toward the goal of unity of the Arab nation.

In 1972 Qaddafi suggested fusion of Egypt and Libya, and, on 2 August 1972, the Benghazi Declaration was issued over the signatures of Qaddafi and Sadat. Libya and Egypt were to be merged subject to approval by popular referendums of both countries by 1 September 1973. There was to be a single capital, Cairo, and one president elected by universal suffrage, who in the first instance would be Sadat. In order to give detailed shape to the union, some three hundred Egyptians and Libyans, in equal numbers, spent months in a series of committee meetings. But the differences between Egypt and Libya presented thorny problems.

Reservations from the Egyptian side grew stronger, and eventually some Libyans also became concerned. The referendums of 1 September 1973 never occurred and union with Egypt was not established. Following the October 1973 war, relations between the two countries deteriorated rapidly with accusations and counteraccusations often voiced—including Egyptian accusations that Qaddafi was plotting to overthrow the Sadat regime and was financing the assassination of Sadat.

The failure to unite with Egypt was followed by an effort to link Libya and Tunisia into a single "Islamic Arab Republic." In January 1974, Tunisia and Libya announced the formation of a union after talks between President Bourguiba and Qaddafi. The plan called for a single state, the Islamic Arab Republic, with a single constitution, a flag, president, and army, and legislative, judicial, and executive authorities. A referendum would be held in Tunisia and in Libya to verify popular approval. But opposition within Tunisia emerged and the plans were aborted.

Under Qaddafi, the Libyan government has been uncompromising in its stance toward Israel and has become a major support of the Palestinians. Qaddafi has condemned Zionism as an aggressive nationalism, has sought Israel's elimination from the Middle East, and opposes all forms of Arab-Israeli negotiations. Despite his rhetoric and support for the Palestinians, Qaddafi has not played a practical role in the Arab confrontation with Israel. He has provided financial, moral, and political support to the PLO, but during the October 1973 war Libya sent no troops to the battle area and its military contribution was essentially confined to the transfer of aircraft to Egypt. It also played a minor role in the use of the oil weapon in 1973–1974, following the lead of Saudi Arabia. Libya has worked to counter Israeli influence in Black Africa by offering aid and assistance in the expectation that relations with Israel would deteriorate.

The volatility of foreign policy under Qaddafi has prevented the development of close and stable relations with other Arab states, and relations with most of the major powers have also been turbulent. Relations with the United States have deteriorated while military and economic ties with the Soviet Union, once anathema to the regime, have increased. The United States has been the object of verbal attack, and there have been few important areas of cooperation between the Libyan and U.S. governments. The October War was followed by increased contacts between the Libyan and Soviet governments and the development of military supply links. This relationship continued to expand as closer military and political links were established.

The described patterns of established Libyan policy have been further intensified over time. Qaddafi's primary attention remains focused on the need to assure "justice for the Palestinians" and to acquire a credible political-diplomatic and military capability for Libya.

Notes

1. The Senussi are a religious order or brotherhood intent on practicing a purified Islam. They have a strong inclination toward Sufism, and the tenets of their sect (*tariqa*) include work, unity, and organization. The order was founded by Sayid Muhammad Ben Ali al-Senussi, the grandfather of King Idris, in 1843.
2. Text as published in *Middle East Journal*, spring 1970, p. 203.
3. Text in *Middle East Journal*, spring 1970, p. 207.

Bibliography

John Wright, *Libya* (New York: Praeger Publishers, 1969) provides a general history of Libya, especially of the period from 1911 to 1951. E. E. Evans-Pritchard, *The Sanusi of Cyrenaica* (London: Oxford University Press, 1949) provides an important study of Libya's main religious order and its role in the country's development. Henry Serrano Villard, the first U.S. minister to Libya after independence, gives a general overview in *Libya: The New Arab Kingdom of North Africa* (Ithaca, N.Y.: Cornell University Press, 1956). The United Nations commissioner in Libya, Adrian Pelt, describes the transformation of Libya from an Italian colony to an independent state in *Libyan Independence and the United Nations: A Case of Planned Decolonization* (New Haven: Yale University Press, for the Carnegie Endowment for International Peace, 1970). Majid Khadduri, *Modern Libya: A Study in Political Development* (Baltimore: The Johns Hopkins University Press, 1963) considers the monarchy in detail, and Ruth First, *Libya: The Elusive Revolution* (Middlesex, England: Penguin Books, 1974) and Henri Habib, *Politics and Government of Revolutionary Libya* (Montreal: Le Cercle du Livre de France, 1975) assess the revolutionary regime of Qaddafi. Salaheddin Hassan's, "The Genesis of the Political Leadership of Libya 1952–1969: Historical Origins and Development of Its Component Elements" (Ph.D. dissertation, The George Washington University, 1973) is a study of Libya's political elite in the period of the monarchy.

Libya's economy is surveyed in the *The Economic Development of Libya*, the report of a mission organized by the International Bank for Reconstruction and Development at the request of the government of Libya (Baltimore: The Johns Hopkins University Press, for The International Bank for Reconstruction and Development, 1960), and in Rawle Farley's *Planning for Development in Libya: The Exceptional Economy in the Developing World* (New York: Praeger Publishers, 1971). A plan for the economic and social development of Libya is detailed in Benjamin Higgins, *The Economic and Social Development of Libya* (New York: United Nations Technical Assistance Programme, 1953).

Biographical data on Qaddafi are available in Mirella Bianco, *Gadafi: Voice from the Desert* (London: Longman Group, 1975), and Frederick Muscat, *My President, My Son* (Malta: Adam Publishers, 1974). *Thus Spoke Colonel Moammar Kazzafi* (Beirut: Dar Al Awda, 1974) contains the texts of interviews with Qaddafi in which his views are clarified.

17

The Maghrib: An Overview

John P. Entelis

North Africa constitutes a unique world of its own, however much it may share in culture, religion, language, and history with the rest of the Middle East. This chapter provides an introduction to that unique world and to the following three chapters on its constituent countries. The distinctiveness is in great part related to its relative geographical isolation. The Arab invaders in the seventh century A.D. named it *jazirat al-maghrib* (island of the west). It is a virtually self-contained region bounded by the Mediterranean Sea on the north, the Atlantic Ocean on the west, the Sahara on the south, and by the three hundred miles of desert running to the Mediterranean between Tripolitania and Cyrenaica on the east. The term North Africa came into being during the 130 years of European colonial rule and today is used by the peoples of the Maghrib themselves in referring to Morocco, Algeria, and Tunisia. Despite the existence of three separate, independent political entities, the cultural unity and ethnic and religious homogeneity of the entire region link them closely.

Historical Background

The indigenous Berber society has been subjected to five major foreign invasions and influences. The first conquest occurred around 1200 B.C. and lasted nearly a thousand years, bringing the Phoenicians and Carthaginians. Roman domination followed next, becoming firmly established with the destruction of Carthage in 146 B.C. and lasting for 650 years. There followed the brief interlude (A.D. 429–642) of the Vandal and Byzantine restoration. This was succeeded by 1,200 years of Arab-Islamic predominance in Morocco. The whole of the Maghrib was brought under Arab control by A.D. 710. However, direct Arab rule by the Eastern caliphate over the Maghrib was terminated by the end of the eighth century, leaving the three states of North Africa to develop their own autonomous sociopolitical forms, at the local level at least. Turkish hegemony was established over Algeria and Tunisia in the middle of the sixteenth century, when European occupation occurred. None of these successive foreign invasions, however, managed totally to destroy the underlying fabric of Berber culture.

The coming of the Arabs and Islam in the mid-seventh century did affect the Berbers culturally. In the 300 years following the initial conquest of the Maghrib by the forces of the Arab-Islamic world, a confused pattern of political rule, social forms, and religious movements emerged. What emerged of lasting importance in this period was the slow assimilation of Islam by the masses of North Africa who were trying to adapt the religion to the solution of local problems. The formal leadership was almost always external, the causes and slogans were Islamic, but the real issue was the social organization of Berbers and the development of a Maghribi personality.

The eleventh century witnessed the emergence of the first of three indigenous empires in the Maghrib that, during the next four centuries, established the foundation for the three states that were later to emerge with their own identities and histories. The Almoravid Empire (1042–1147) was established by Berber-speaking nomads from Mauritania and the western Sahara. The Almoravids were the first dynasty to unify Morocco, and at one time their rule extended as far as Algiers. They established the historic link between the Maghrib and Muslim Spain that lasted 250 years, bringing enormous benefits to North Africa and extending the life of Muslim Spain. The Almoravids also eliminated all heretical sects and imposed, with a permanent imprint, the Malikite school of Islam, named after an eighth-century religious leader of Medina, Malik ibn Anas.

The second major indigenous empire to be established were the Almohads (1147–1269) who were the direct successors to the Almoravids. They were sedentary Berber mountaineers of the high Atlas Mountains who, in the fashion of their predecessors, were inspired by the visionary leadership of a puritanical religious teacher, ibn Tumar (1076–1130). The most significant political contribution of the Almohads was probably the unification of the Maghrib under a single home rule from Agadir (in Morocco) to Tripoli (in Libya) for the first and only time in history.

The dissolution of the Almohad Empire in 1269 was followed by the emergence of three separate Berber kingdoms, the Hafsids in Tunis, the Zayanids in Tlemcen in what is now Algeria, and the Merinids in Fez in present-day Morocco.

Under the Merinids, Fez prospered, making it equal to any town in the world in civility, culture, and refinement. Tunis under the Hafsids became the uncontested capital of Tunisia, and an important center. It was also one of the foremost centers of learning in the Maghrib. The famous historian ibn Khaldoun studied at the Zitouna Mosque in Tunis.

The Zayanids ruled over a society that was essentially tribal, yet urban and civilized life developed in their realm as well. The Zayanid state, like the Merinid and to a lesser extent the Hafsid, profited from the administrative and artistic skills of Andalusian refugees in creating the rudiments of an administration and embellishing the capital, Tlemcen, with mosques and schools. During the Zayanid period, Tlemcen, the "pearl of the Maghrib," became for the first and only time the capital of an independent state.

The vitality of these separate Berber empires began to decline by 1500. From the north, the Iberian powers began to intervene in North Africa and establish coastal enclaves. From the east, the Ottomans had extended their sovereignty to Algeria and Tunisia by the mid-sixteenth century, although they never fully controlled the countryside and never conquered Morocco. By the end of the eighteenth century, political and social stagnation in the Maghrib was so advanced that it set the stage for the full-blown intervention of the European powers beginning with the French conquest of Algeria in 1830.

European colonial rule in the Maghrib varied according to the metropole—France or Spain, the time the occupation took place, and the nature of the country or the portion of the country occupied. Nevertheless, the overall process in all three countries was remarkably similar.

French administrators and colonial settlers sought to implant the civilization of the metropolitan country. However, they remained outsiders, and enjoyed a privileged position vis-à-vis the native population.

Over 90 percent of the population of the Maghrib was colonized by France. Only northern Morocco escaped this pattern, having been administered as a Spanish protectorate. French colonization was intense and far-reaching, more so in Algeria than in Morocco, but pervasive throughout nonetheless. French rule lasted 132 years in Algeria (1830–1962), 75 years in Tunisia (1881–1956), and 44 years in Morocco (1912–1956). Algeria suffered the bulk of North Africa's European settler population. At their height (1955), Europeans constituted 13 percent of the total Algerian population and between 6 and 8 percent in Morocco and Tunisia. In terms of colonialism's impact on the land, settlers appropriated 27 percent of Algeria's arable lands (more than 7 million acres), 21 percent of Tunisia's arable lands (2 million acres), and 7 percent of Morocco's (2.5 million acres).

Juridically, Algeria constituted an integral part of France, whereas

Tunisia and Morocco, as protectorates, preserved substantial elements of their indigenous precolonial governments albeit in emasculated form. Protectorate status should not be misunderstood, however, for in both countries, French administrators eventually controlled the all-important policymaking process in internal as well as external affairs. Under the nominal authority of the native head of state (the bey in Tunisia, the sultan in Morocco), French directors, supervised by the resident general, established new administrations that in effect were carbon copies of modern French ministries. The myth of the protectorate was not without its benefits, however, for it did help ensure the survival of traditional elites in both countries.

In terms of administrative practice, the main trend of the colonial experience was the shifting of the basic structures of the society from tribal forms of solidarity to more differentiated social structures. In societal terms, colonialism caused increasing differentiation, tribal erosion, rural exodus, and the immigration of thousands of people to Europe.

It may be helpful to our subsequent analysis of the country-by-country colonial experiences to identify three analytically distinct forms of colonialism in North Africa. Each form is essentially based on economic criteria. Segmented colonialism, best represented by the experience of Morocco, involves a limited yet highly visible economic domination. However, this domination does not destroy the basic political and cultural order. The case of Tunisia represents a form of instrumental colonialism that also involves exclusive economic domination and exploitation but that does not hesitate, when necessary, to intervene in other levels of society. Finally, total colonialism, experienced by Algeria, was characterized by unrestrained domination of the whole society at all levels, based upon the negation of the social, cultural, and economic order of the colonized country.

The period of colonial rule also witnessed the rise of nationalism in North Africa. In fact, Maghribi nationalism began in part as a direct reaction to Western colonial rule. At the same time, it was influenced by and related to the wider revival of Arab nationalist consciousness that made itself felt in the mid-nineteenth century. The particular form of this nationalist expression, however, was decisively European in ideology, terminology, and structural organization, with French leftist political thought being particularly influential. Because of this origin, North African nationalism has continued to display tendencies that sometimes conflict. That is, the traditionalist, religious, Oriental, and purely Arab components vie with the modernist, secular, Occidental, and bilingual elements of Maghribi nationalism, resulting in an ideological cleavage that has yet to be resolved in a manner satisfactory to both masses and elites alike.

In all three states of the Maghrib, the nationalist response to co-lonialism was relatively similar. First, there were the liberal assimila-tionists, sons of the old, traditional elite who admired and imitated the colonial rulers, assimilated some of their styles and values, accepted their rules of the game, and attempted to engage in a dialogue. A second elite group, both older than and contemporaries of the liberal assimilationists, were traditionalists who assumed a nationalistic-scripturalist orienta-tion. This perspective was advocated by the learned, scholarly, and ur-ban families, which had historically constituted a distinctive status group. They called for a reaffirmation of national, cultural, and religious integrity in the face of Western colonial domination. During the period of colonialism this group was also the first to call for the maintenance of a national personality, usually by stressing the use, revision, and celebra-tion of the Islamic heritage (scripturalism), and by emphasizing Arabism as a language, culture, and common history (nationalism).

A third and ultimately decisive group were the populists who, although they were educated and trained in European schools and en-vironments and sought to recreate in their societies the liberal trends formed in the Europe of the bourgeois revolutions, rebelled against the colonial status quo and appealed for mass mobilization against foreign domination. Unlike the traditionalists, the populists had a broader base of support, higher level of education, and a more cosmopolitan outlook. And unlike the assimilationists, the populists were much more deter-mined to attack and oppose the colonial system and foreign domination. In essence the populists were secularists with a modernizing view of political change who, while profoundly marked by a nationalist ideology and political activism, were influenced by Europe, which was a model for their own growth. Therefore, they were committed to a gradualist, evolutionary form of social change. Yet, their commitment to European principles exposed the populists to certain inherent contradictions so that while they were militant in their struggle against France, once in power they tended to be somewhat reconciliatory.

A fourth category of elite types emerged in the postindependence period. Emanating essentially from the radical intelligentsia and workers, this most recent nationalistic group calls for mass mobilization and the radical restructuring of indigenous society. Its members have tended to view the infrastructure of dependency of their societies much more seriously than did their predecessors. This orientation has only recently appeared, however, and even today, its influence is indirect and its specific delineations uncertain. The populists, who were deeply involved in the preindependence nationalist struggle and who successfully overthrew colonial rule, most appropriately deserve the label of "nationalist" elite.

The Land and People

Although the transition from the green vegetation of the Mediterranean to the barren desolation of the desert is nowhere exactly the same, the topography of the Maghrib follows a general pattern: coastal valleys and plains, followed by mountains, high steppes, more mountains, and finally desert. The most noteworthy geographical element is the long and basically continuous chain of the Atlas Mountains, which forms a horizontal backbone extending across the entire length of the three countries from southwest Morocco to northeast Tunisia. Filled with steep valleys and narrow gorges, this mountain chain cuts off the desert to the south from the more fertile areas north of the mountains.

The descendants of the original inhabitants of North Africa are the Berbers, those six million inhabitants found predominantly in Morocco and Algeria. The Berbers' principal distinguishing characteristic is their individualistic language, Berber. The percentages of Berberophones in Algeria and Morocco are estimated as high as 25 and 40 percent, respectively. Tunisia, because of its historic geographical accessibility, is virtually devoid of any non-Arabic speaking Berbers today. For all practical purposes, contemporary Berbers have been thoroughly Islamized and Arabized in their religious and cultural identity.

Aside from the original Berber inhabitants and Arabized Berbers, the Arabs have made the most important contribution to the demography of the Maghrib. They arrived in North Africa beginning in the mid-seventh century, and over a period of several hundred years managed to transform the Berber-populated Maghrib into an integral part of the Arab-Islamic world. In terms of culture, language, and religion, the Arabs profoundly and permanently affected North African society.

A third group that has made significant contributions to and has helped shape the society of North Africa is the Europeans. Despite their relatively brief presence in the Maghrib and their relative isolation from native society, the Europeans induced profound changes in that society. With political independence, the mass exodus of Europeans, the creation of Israel, and the long-term process of Arabization and Islamization, the Maghrib of today is ethnically, culturally, and religiously homogeneous. Virtually all significant numbers of Europeans (French, Spanish, and Italian), indigenous Jews, and other indigenous and nonindigenous non-

Muslim Arabs have departed from North Africa.

Compared to states farther east, the Maghrib is religiously more unified, with the Malikite school of orthodox or Sunni Islam predominating. There are no indigenous Christian minorities and except for the Kharijites of Jerba and the Mzabites of Algeria, no major Islamic sects. Indigenous Jews, once numerous, now constitute an insignificant and steadily diminishing minority. Because of religious uniformity, Islam is an important common denominator throughout North Africa, mitigating the differences of tribe, language, and life-style. Notwithstanding the different policies toward religion and religious practice adopted by the various political leaders of the Maghrib, Islam is designated as the state religion in each of the three constitutions. The Algerian and Tunisian presidents must be Muslims, and in the Moroccan constitution, the king is given the title "commander of the faithful."

Despite the predominance of Islam as a social, cultural, and ideological force, traditional Islamic institutions have declined significantly in importance. This decline can be attributed to modernization and the increased power of the central state apparatus. It was also related to the Islamic reformist movements that influenced the Maghrib in the late nineteenth century.

Modernization has also resulted in the decline of the old religious elite (the ulama). Even when reformist ulama were directly involved in the preindependence nationalist struggle, as in Algeria, this was not enough to salvage their prestige or retrieve their position.

The high degree of ethnoreligious uniformity does not rule out internal diversities. For example, the Maghrib is geographically fragmented into distinct demographic areas that do not complement each other. Important linguistic and cultural divisions also persist. These disharmonies are reflected in the principal patterns of life that the region supports. Several distinct rural patterns can be identified in the Maghrib, including the pure nomad of the desert; the seminomad of the steppe-desert; the sedentary Berberophone mountaineers who cover all of the Rif and most of the high Atlas Mountains in Morocco and the Kabylia Mountains in Algeria; a large bloc of tribes and loosely organized groups found in the coastal plains and hills of Morocco and eastern Algeria, which is only now settling on the land; and lastly the authentic village life of North Africa, found in the old, settled areas of northeast Tunisia and along the *sahel* of the country's eastern shore. It is here that one finds the highest degree of rural sophistication in the Maghrib.

Those living on the land have been affected by demographic and population forces that have shifted populations away from the land and into the towns and cities; in so doing, these forces often caused the economies to change from wheat-exporting to wheat-importing ones. The overall impact of increased population is accelerated as the delicate balance of a rural economy, trading the products of the pasture with those of the town and village, is broken down.

North African urban life, like its rural partner, is diverse. First, there are the traditional Islamic cities like Fez, Tunis, Tetuan, and Tlemcen. These are old cities whose inhabitants are indigenous bourgeoisie. The best tradition of eastern Arab-Islamic culture is to be found in these cities. A second group of cities is the coastal port towns like Algiers, Tangier, Oran, and Bejaia (Bougie), which possess no distinctive quality but simply reflect the pattern found among most Mediterranean port cities. They are normally separated from their own culture and society and stand out as incongruously populated peninsulas detached from the heartland in a physical and spiritual sense. A third urban type, quite distinct from the two above, is the strategic regional centers that were founded for economic or political purposes. Marrakesh in southwest Morocco and Constantinople in eastern Algeria are two good examples of such cities. Finally, many new towns like Kenitra (formerly Port Lyautey), Annaba (formerly Bone), Skikda (formerly Philippeville), and Casablanca were created to serve European markets. Smaller cities, like Setif in Algeria, were established for security reasons or to exploit natural resources.

Urbanization in North Africa must be distinguished from urbanism. The growth of population in the countryside has resulted in large-scale internal migrations to towns and cities. Thus, the movement into urban conglomerations owes more to demographic pressures in the rural areas than to rapid economic growth in the towns. Such population concentrations, however, do not become transformed into "modern" people exhibiting all the traits associated with urbanism, such as "sophistication," tolerance of change, universalism, and impersonal relations. They are simply relocated from one physical space to another without necessarily undergoing a qualitative change in outlook or behavioral patterns. This overurbanization and underurbanism in the Maghrib represents but one part of a larger phenomenon occurring throughout the Middle East.

Bibliography

For obvious historical reasons research and writing on the three North African states of Algeria, Morocco, and Tunisia have been dominated by French scholarship and French-language literature. In recent years, however, more and more first-rate publications on the Maghrib have appeared in English to such a degree that beginning students can now adequately resort to the English-language literature for an introductory understanding of North African society and politics. This select bibliography concentrates exclusively on English-language materials of either original works or translations. In addition, many useful bibliographical citations may be found in the books listed.

The history of the preindependence period with concentrations on precolonial and colonial North Africa is well provided in Jamil M. Abun-Nasr, *A History of the Maghrib* (Cambridge: Cambridge University Press, 1975), Charles-André Julien, *History of North Africa—Tunisia, Algeria, and Morocco: From the Arab Conquest to 1830* (New York: Praeger Publishers, 1970), and Abdallah Laroui, *The History of the Maghrib: An Interpretive Essay* (Princeton, N.J.: Princeton University Press, 1977), the latter two being English translations of original French works. The colonial Maghrib and the period of the national independence struggles involving both general as well as country-specific analyses can be found in Jacques Berque, *French North Africa: The Maghrib Between Two World Wars* (London: Faber and Faber, 1967), John K. Cooley, *Baal, Christ and Mohamed: Religion and Revolution in North Africa* (New York: Holt, Rinehart & Winston, 1965), Alal al-Fassi, *The Independence Movements in Arab North Africa* (New York: Octagon Books, 1970), Charles F. Gallagher, *The United States and North Africa: Morocco, Algeria, and Tunisia* (Cambridge, Mass.: Harvard University Press, 1963), David C. Gordon, *North Africa's French Legacy, 1954–1962* (Cambridge, Mass.: Harvard University Press, 1964), and Lorna Hahn, *North Africa: Nationalism to Nationhood* (Washington, D.C.: Public Affairs Press, 1960).

Studies devoted to comparative analyses of the three North African political systems include Richard M. Brace, *Morocco, Algeria, Tunisia* (Englewood Cliffs, N..J.: Prentice-Hall, 1964), Manfred Halpern, *The Politics of Social Change in the Middle East and North Africa* (Princeton, N.J.: Princeton University Press, 1963), Elbaki Hermassi, *Leadership and National Development in North Africa: A Comparative Study* (Berkeley and Los Angeles: University of California Press, 1972), Clement Henry Moore, *Politics in North Africa: Algeria, Morocco, and Tunisia* (Boston: Little, Brown, 1970), and I. William Zartman, *Government and Politics in Northern Africa* (New York: Frederick A. Praeger Publishers, 1963). Samir Amin, *The Maghrib in the Modern World: Algeria, Tunisia, Morocco* (Baltimore: Penguin Books, 1970) is explicitly leftist in orientation with a focus on the political economy of North African development. Sizable portions of Michael C. Hudson, *Arab Politics: The Search for Legitimacy* (New Haven, Conn.: Yale University Press, 1977) and James A. Bill and Carl Leiden, *Politics in the Middle East* (Boston: Little, Brown, 1979) deal with the North African political systems in a comparative way.

Diverse social, economic, political, and anthropological themes are treated in several excellent anthologies and edited books on North Africa: Leon Carl Brown, ed., *State and Society in Independent North Africa* (Washington, D.C.: The Middle East Institute, 1966), Michael Brett, ed., *Northern Africa: Islam and Modernization* (London: Frank Case, 1973), Ernest Gellner and Charles Micaud, eds., *Arabs and Berbers: From Tribe to Nation in North Africa*

(Lexington, Mass.: Lexington Books, 1972), Ernest Gellner and John Waterbury, eds., *Patrons and Clients in Mediterranean Societies* (London: Duckworth, 1977), and I. William Zartman, ed.., *Man, State,and Society in the Contemporary Maghrib* (New York: Praeger Publishers, 1973).

Two reference works in English are particularly useful. They are Wilfrid Knapp, *North West Africa: A Political and Economic Survey* (London: Oxford University Press, 1977) and *The Middle East and North Africa, 1978–79* (London: Europa Publications, 1978).

The international politics of North Africa has yet to receive adequate book-length treatment in English. First-rate selective surveys may be found in A. L. Udovitch, ed., *The Middle East: Oil, Conflict and Hope* (Lexington, Mass.: Lexington Books, 1976), John Waterbury and Ragaei El Mallakh, *The Middle East in the Coming Decade: From Wellhead to Well-Being?* (New York: McGraw-Hill, 1978), John Waterbury, "The Soviet Union and North Africa," in Ivo J. Lederer and Wayne S. Vucinich, eds., *The Soviet Union and the Middle East: The Post World War II Era* (Stanford, Calif.: Hoover Institution Press, 1974), Charles F. Gallagher, *The United States and North Africa* (Cambridge, Mass.: Harvard University Press, 1963), Clement Henry Moore, *Politics in North Africa* (Boston: Little, Brown & Co., 1970), and I. William Zartman, *Government and Politics in Northern Africa* (New York: Frederick A. Praeger Publishers, 1963).

The leading English-language scholarly journals treating the Maghrib on a regular basis are the *Middle East Journal*, *The Maghreb Review*, and the *International Journal of Middle East Studies*.

18

Kingdom of Morocco

John P. Entelis

Historical Background

Until 1894, Morocco remained viable under the rule of a strong and effective sultan, Mulay Hassan (1873–1894), who, among other things, maintained internal order and kept the country's finances on a relatively sound footing because of a flourishing export trade. Moreover, Hassan obtained the diplomatic assistance of Britain in his attempt to impede the annexationist ambitions of France and Spain. Relatively immune from outside intervention, the dynamic sultan built up an army, reestablished authority in the Alawi Sharifian Empire, which had been established in 1666, and restored financial order.

After his death, however, the country fell into immediate difficulties, largely because of the mismanagement of Hassan's son and successor, Abd al-Aziz (1894–1908), a young and weak ruler. The monarchy was forced to borrow heavily, and quickly incurred severe debt. No longer able to resist European pressures and creditors, the country's internal sovereignty began to be questioned. The intrigues and maneuvers of foreign agents who ill-advised Abd al-Aziz in economic and financial matters virtually sealed the fate of Moroccan autonomy. By 1908, Morocco was in general revolt against Abd al-Aziz, who was accused of having abandoned the country to foreigners and foreign financial interests.

Abd al-Aziz's successor, Mulay Hafid, further indebted Morocco in a futile attempt to salvage the country from its enormous debts. At the same time, dissident tribes in Fez besieged him and he turned to France for military, political, and economic assistance. The conditions under which France agreed to intervene were exorbitant—nothing less than relinquishing Moroccan political independence. This was formalized by the Treaty of Fez, signed by France and Morocco on 30 March 1912. The treaty formally established Morocco as a French protectorate; moreover, it granted France sole responsibility for all reforms, national defense, foreign affairs, and economic and financial affairs.

It took nearly one-quarter of a century for France to subdue the vigorous opposition in the Anti-Atlas Mountains and to completely pacify the people. Of the three Maghribi states, only Morocco maintained a "continuity of resistance." After the traditional tribal battles and countryside wars terminated, an urbanized version of nationalist resistance immediately emerged, committed to the same goal of eventual freedom.

Under French protection, the basic structure of the sultan's government was retained; indeed, the feudal elements in Moroccan society were encouraged and the great families maintained their powerful positions. Official decrees and legislation were signed by the sultan and promulgated in his name, leaving him at the center of public life and at least the nominal source of authority in the country. Furthermore, extensive European colonization in Morocco came late, since actual pacification of the country was not achieved until the 1930s.

Unlike French colonialism in Algeria, colonialism in Morocco left political and social institutions intact. Therefore, traditionally privileged classes were preserved, especially the commercially and culturally dominant Arab bourgeoisie in the cities of Fez and Rabat and the Berber tribal notables of the countryside. Similarly, internal social evolution was modest and the social elites were neither infused with fresh blood by upwardly mobile lower groups, nor did many of them receive a modern French education nor gain access to modern administrative and professional careers as, for example, some of the Tunisians had.

Although the traditional elite of Morocco—the great bourgeois families from Fez and elsewhere—desired independence and possessed an Islamic-nationalist orientation, they eventually had to capitulate to French demands and reluctantly accepted their status. Between 1925 and 1930, another, younger group of newly educated city dwellers—populists—frustrated and embittered by the French presence, found strong psychological and political support from the traditional elite. This group became increasingly formidable once the sense of national disaffection reached skilled craftsmen in the towns who were beginning to feel the economic pinch caused by the strong competition from manufactured goods introduced by the colonialists. Hence the union of frustrated traditional elite, the radicalized younger elite, and the disaffected lower middle class constituted a powerful nationalist front with an urbanized focus.

The movement toward nationalism gained momentum in 1930 when the Berber *dahir* (decree) of 16 May was issued from Rabat. It established customary tribunals in Berber-populated parts of the country. These

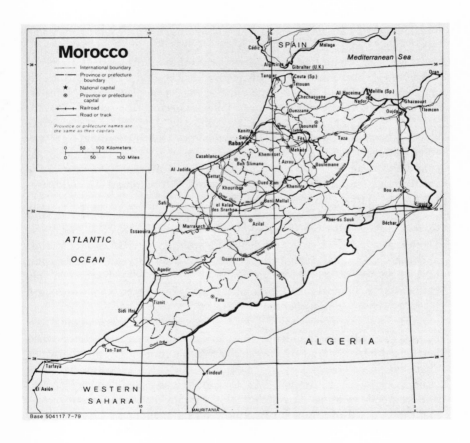

tribunals were empowered to deal with civil cases of the country by creating an artificial division between the Arabs and Berbers.

Incipient nationalist forces representing both traditionalists like Allal al-Fassi and Westernized intellectuals like Ahmad Balafrej immediately and vigorously protested the decree, and they immediately attracted the skilled craftsmen and shopkeepers of the towns to their cause. While French authorities sought to dilute the implications of the *dahir*, the damage had already been done and the sense of nationalist consciousness quickly spread among Morocco's youth.

In May 1934 the basically reformist *Kutlah al-'Amal al-Watani*, or *Comité d'Action Marocaine*, was formed as the first overtly nationalist party in the country. The *comité* worked peacefully, but unsuccessfully, for reforms within the framework of the protectorate.

With the French dissolution of the *comité* in 1937, there was no effective political organization to lead the nationalist movement until the formation of the Istiqlal (Independence) party in 1943. The Istiqlal demanded full freedom for Morocco and a constitutional form of government under Sultan Muhammad Ben Yussuf (Muhammad V), who supported the nationalist movement.

After World War II, the Istiqlal was joined by two other parties who were contenders for the status of "the" nationalist party. They were the Democratic Independence party (PDI), a splinter party from the Istiqlal, and the Communist party, which had very little support. The Istiqlal, with strong support in the towns and tacit alliance with the throne, was challenged by feudal chiefs, some traditionalist elements in the cities, and heads of some religious brotherhoods.

During the late forties the Istiqlal transformed itself from an elite to a mass party, with independence as its primary objective. As the alliance between the Istiqlal and the monarchy became more overt and began to challenge French hegemony in the country, the colonial authorities exercised their power. In August 1953, the sultan was exiled and replaced by a more docile relative. The deportation catalyzed the nationalist movement into an all-out fight for freedom and independence. The reactions at the popular level were totally unanticipated. The king became a martyr and a saint in the eyes of the masses. An incipient guerrilla war broke out, but a relatively quick political settlement was achieved, thereby preventing the occurrence of widespread violence.

The return of Muhammad V from exile in November 1954 marked the virtual end of colonial rule in Morocco. On 2 March 1956, the former French-controlled regions of the west and south were joined with the Spanish-controlled areas of the north and east, and the country was formally declared independent. The Moroccan masses, who had not been politically educated, revered the king for his mystical religious qualities, or *baraka*, while the diverse forces of modern nationalism looked to him to satisfy their demands for a national government. He was the one leader whose right to rule rested on sufficiently diverse modern and traditional grounds to satisfy virtually all sectors of the heterogeneous elite. The monarchy emerged as the major beneficiary of independence at the expense of the national elite, who were relegated to a secondary role. Indeed, Morocco is unique in the Middle East and North Africa in that the struggle for independence centered around the capture, revival, and renovation of a traditional institution, the monarchy.

At the time of independence Morocco enjoyed a sufficient level of national unity, institutional stability, and effective political leadership to give it a moderately promising future. The political parties, with the Istiqlal in the predominant position, provided the necessary cadres for the new government. The urban resistance was incorporated into the police; and the Army of Liberation, which was one of the last groups to recognize the monarchy's independence, was absorbed into the Royal Moroccan Army (FAR). Other civil servants were recruited from among former employees of the ministries under the protectorate or from newly trained Moroccan youth. Over this diverse and heterogeneous group King Muhammad V ruled as arbitrator and symbol of Moroccan unity.

On the surface it appeared that political life in Morocco might move toward a European model of constitutional democracy based on a competitive multiparty system. Political freedom, although circumscribed, was nonetheless real and exercised. Yet, within five years of independence, both the national and the political unity that had existed during the period of the anticolonialist struggle had disappeared. The sharing of power between the king and the Istiqlal and other nationalist leaders soon broke down, for Muhammad V was unwilling to become a constitutional figurehead, and the Istiqlal leadership was unwilling to accept the passive role that the king envisioned for it.

The Istiqlal also quickly began to show signs of internal strain, which hampered its attempts to reduce the political predominance of the monarch. Tension between the conservative and radical wings of the party reached a breaking point in 1959 when Prime Minister Abdallah Ibrahim of the Istiqlal joined a group of young, secular-minded intellectuals and trade union leaders to form a new left-wing party called the National Union of Popular Forces (UNFP). The UNFP charged the more traditional leadership elements of the Istiqlal with undue caution, compliance with the dictates of the royal household, and indifference to meaningful social reform. Moreover, the new party called for more active government direction of social and economic changes and election of a popular assembly to write a democratic monarchical constitution. In its pursuit of social and economic goals, the UNFP worked closely with the large Union of Moroccan Labor (UMT).

Although this disintegration of the nationalist elite was more the result of dissension within the Istiqlal than the result of machinations by the palace, it enabled the palace to manipulate the diverse factions that emerged in the aftermath of the split and explains, in great part, the current king's control of the political elite. In fact, perhaps more than any other political event, the breakup of the Istiqlal determined the course of politics in independent Morocco.

Meantime, the king had been developing the institution of the monarchy. His son, Hassan, was made acting head of state whenever the king was out of the country, and in 1957 Hassan was officially designated the crown prince. This established the principle of primogeniture that was later formally institutionalized in the 1962 constitution. The power of the throne was further consolidated when the police and army, under the direct control of the king, intimidated, harassed, and generally repressed the political activities of an increasingly vocal and oppositional UNFP.

In May 1960 the king, impatient with the partisanship of party politics and resentful of the increasing criticisms being leveled at monarchical institutions, dismissed the government of Abdallah Ibrahim and his cabinet of predominantly UNFP ministers and appointed himself prime minister with the crown prince as his deputy. For all practical purposes, Hassan was given effective executive power, thereby setting in motion a process of continuing direct monarchical involvement in partisan politics.

In February 1961, King Muhammad V died after routine surgery, and, on 3 March, Hassan II ascended the throne. French-educated, with a law degree from Bordeaux, and thoroughly Westernized, Hassan II pursued a policy that consolidated power in his own hands and reduced the political role of the existing parties. The young king, however, lacked Muhammad V's charisma and the advantage of being a nationalist hero. In the absence of genuine popular appeal and personal standing, Hassan's attempts to strengthen and consolidate his authority over national affairs led to serious political schisms.

The new king's first government was constituted essentially of individuals who were chosen more for their personal loyalty to him than for any particular program or policy they represented. This was consistent with Hassan's concept of the role of political parties as one of organizing supplementary support for the monarchy rather than as one of formulating policy and programs based on popular will.

With a minimum of consultation but in keeping with his father's public promise, King Hassan introduced a constitution that was approved in a national referendum in December 1962. Largely inspired by de Gaulle's Fifth Republic, this new national document formally established a constitutional monarchy with guaranteed personal and political freedoms. Yet the constitution's principal provisions solidified the king's own power at the expense of theoretically representative and freely elected legislative organs, the popularly elected House of Representatives and the indirectly elected (and hence more easily controlled) Chamber of Counsellors. The king could also dissolve the legislature and was granted unlimited emergency powers when constitutional institutions were in danger of impairment or dissolution.

The first national elections under the 1962 constitution were held in May 1963. Hassan encouraged the creation of parties unquestionably loyal to the throne, including the Front for the Defense of Constitutional Institutions (FDIC) and a conservative Berber party, the Popular Movement (MP). The FDIC sought to mobilize parties and men who had participated in the nationalist movement from outside, or even in opposition to the Istiqlal, and who would support the monarchy for its own sake or for the sake of personal advantage over the Istiqlal.

According to all accounts the FDIC was a weak and hastily formed coalition and was unable to project a truly nationalist image. It failed to win the majority that the king believed his party would receive to confirm his authority to rule. In the following months, repressive action was taken against both opposition parties—the Istiqlal and the UNFP. Several Istiqlal deputies were arrested for protesting against corruption and mismanagement of the election, and in July 1963, many of the UNFP leaders were arrested in connection with an alleged coup plot.

In this atmosphere, the king was unable to command a loyal and effective government for two years, despite the rise and fall of a succession of cabinets, none of which commanded strong parliamentary support. The FDIC itself underwent an internal split, further diminishing the king's political standing. Finally, on 7 June 1965, following a series of demonstrations, strikes, and bloody riots, Hassan invoked his emergency powers granted under Article 35 of the constitution. Proclaiming a "state of exception," he recessed Parliament indefinitely, dismissed the prime minister, suspended the constitution, and personally assumed full legislative and executive power.

These actions, however, failed to halt the process of political and social unrest that had been set in motion at the death of Muhammad V. The disappearance and alleged assassination of the popular UNFP leader, Mehdi Ben Barka, in Paris in October 1965 by agents of the Moroccan government further accelerated the split between the throne and independent political forces in the country. Other disturbances in Morocco followed, including union demonstrations, and strikes by workers and students. In retaliation, the police seized the newspapers and made mass arrests. For the next five years, 1965–1970, political activity in Morocco virtually disappeared.

In July 1970, the king unexpectedly announced that a new constitution would be submitted for a national popular referendum later that month. While no single event precipitated the return to constitutional government, it had become increasingly apparent that the monarchy, relying solely on the security forces and the army for support, had isolated itself and had jeopardized its legitimacy among the normally supportive mass public. Thus, taking advantage of a period of relative calm, the king hoped to open a new era of cooperation with political parties by reestablishing constitutional authority. Despite general opposition from the main political parties, trade unions, and major student organizations, the new constitution was approved.

Immediately thereafter, in August 1970, elections for a new single-chamber legislature were held. The Istiqlal and UNFP, which had joined together in the National Front (*Kutla Wataniya*) to oppose the ratification of the new constitution, tried to organize a boycott of the parliamentary elections. In both instances, however, the Kutla's efforts were futile in the face of the regime's campaign to arouse popular support. By opposing the constitution and the elections, however, they deprived the regime of a meaningful popular mandate. The regime was forced to continue relying on a motley array of loyal "independent" politicians, the loyalty and effectiveness of the internal security forces, and ultimately, the army.

Yet the throne's orchestrated attempts at power balancing and its elimination of effective opposition failed to prevent two attempts by army and air force officers to assassinate the king (in July 1971 and August 1972). Hassan emerged unscathed in both cases and no less determined to suppress—ruthlessly in some cases—elements that he perceived to be dangerous. In a series of trials in 1973 and 1974, the authorities handed down death sentences and imprisonments in connection with guerrilla operations in the countryside, which were supposedly masterminded by the UNFP leaders with the support of Colonel Qaddafi of Libya. The UNFP itself was officially banned in March 1973.

Between the two assassination attempts, during the spring of 1972, the king announced a third "new" constitution. Executive power was to be vested in the government and an assembly, and two-thirds of the latter's membership was to be elected by universal suffrage as compared to half under the 1970 constitution. The National Front, caught unprepared by the rapid initiative taken by the king to reassert his political authority in the aftermath of the July 1971 coup attempt, urged a boycott of the constitutional referendum. The National Front then accused the government of rigging the referendum, which had approved the constitution by an overwhelming margin. The new cabinet appointed in April was substantially similar to its predecessor. Elections for Parliament, however, were postponed indefinitely.

Following the August 1972 coup attempt, the king approached the opposition parties and asked for their cooperation, but the Istiqlal and UNFP again refused to participate in government unless far-reaching reforms were instituted, including measures to curtail some of the king's powers and to guarantee political freedom.

Once the king felt confident that the military had been brought under his control again, he did not hesitate to ignore the demands of the opposition parties who were themselves in political disarray. By spring of 1972, the old divergences between the Istiqlal and the UNFP gradually reemerged, virtually eliminating the Kutla's already loose coalition. Moreover, within the UNFP itself, tactical and ideological differences that had earlier divided the Ibrahim–Ben Siddiq (Casablanca) and Abderrahim Bouabid (Rabat) wings of the UNFP finally led to a formal rupture in July 1972. The latter reconstituted itself as the Socialist Union of Popular Forces (USFP), while the Casablanca group retained its old name.

All these developments assisted the king in his efforts to retain authority while continuing to project his role as arbiter within Morocco's pluralistic social order. In a manner that has become characteristic of this remarkable monarch, Hassan has combined his skills of manipulating and outmaneuvering the often squabbling opposition parties with liberalization measures that create the impression of change and progress. This combination has helped him monopolize power during his sixteen often-turbulent years as ruler.

In 1973 King Hassan undertook yet another set of programs and policies to maintain political initiative for the throne. Among other things, he announced plans for the "Moroccanization" of parts of the economy over the following two years. He also introduced a new and very ambitious five-year plan (1973–1977) that called for an average economic growth rate of 7.5 percent. At the same time he reinforced his traditional support in the rural areas by ordering the confiscation of foreign-owned (mostly French) lands and their distribution among the peasantry. The king also undertook several foreign policy measures, both substantive and symbolic, that had primarily domestic rather than international objectives. In fact, Hassan has often used external conflict to defuse domestic unrest and to mobilize the population under the banner of national unity. For example, the king derived significant domestic political capital from his strong stand in a fishing dispute with Spain. Moroccan troops were dispatched to the Syrian and Egyptian fronts during the October 1973 Arab-Israeli War, further enhancing the king's image as a supporter of the Palestinian and Arab nationalist causes. He also made several conciliatory gestures in domestic matters. Most importantly, his strong nationalist stand on the Spanish Sahara, an area historically claimed by Morocco, mobilized popular support from all segments of society. The crown's stature was also economically bolstered by the 1974 rise in world phosphate prices (Morocco is the world's leading exporter of phosphates).

While giving no indication that he intended to relinquish any of his powers the king finally permitted legislative elections in June 1977, which marked a sort of return to paliamentary democracy after nearly seven years of royal dictatorship. In a manner reminiscent of previous such "democratic" endeavors the monarchy scored a landslide victory over the opposition and leftist groupings. The independents, who described themselves as "unconditionally monarchist," won 81 of the 176 seats contested for the new Chamber of Representatives. Thirty-three additional seats were won by the three right-wing parties, who declared their intentions of working with the independents. Thus the monarchy was assured of a large and comfortable majority.

The Istiqlal made a surprise showing, winning a respectable 45 seats and reaffirming, in the process, its potential for organizational and electoral strength. The same could not be said of the radical USFP, which suffered a humiliating defeat, gaining only 16 seats in the new chamber. Even the party's popular leader, Abderrahim Bouabid, was unsuccessful in his bid for a parliamentary seat.

In 1979, it appears that the regime is relatively secure. The loyalty of the army and security sources has been reaffirmed and a parliamentary system established in which promonarchical political groups predominate. Several important and symbolically successful foreign-policy initiatives have been taken, including the adoption of a more vigorous position on the Arab-Israeli conflict. Only Morocco's inability to defeat Algerian-backed Polisario guerrillas who seek to establish an independent state in the former Spanish Sahara would appear to pose a major threat to the monarchy. A protracted and costly Saharan campaign could lead to an erosion of Hassan's support within the military as well as within civilian groups.

In addition, persistent and profound social, economic, and political problems threaten the long-term durability of the regime. For example, corruption has spread throughout the society. Nepotism, favoritism, and graft have become increasingly institutionalized in the central administration, notwithstanding Hassan's occasional campaigns against government corruption. The military, although presently loyal, remains unpredictable and therefore a threat to the regime. The party system remains generally moribund, and political apathy runs deep as the futility of participation becomes more evident. Moroccan youth have become increasingly alienated from the regime.

Over the longer term, however, probably the most serious threat to the monarchy lies in the country's economic system. The regime is increasingly unable to meet the rising expectations of an increasingly politicized population that is aware of the growing maldistribution of income between the wealthy elite and the impoverished majority. In a society traditionally apathetic toward politics, economic dissatisfaction will remain King Hassan's most pressing, and potentially most explosive, problem.

Political Environment

One of the outstanding features of Moroccan political culture is the pervasion and intensity of political distrust. Political disputes often degenerate into general vendettas. Power is viewed as a coercive instrument rather than as a cooperative process. The forced imposition of modern, impersonal administration reinforces the native distrust of authority while radically expanding the scope of power and politics. The colonialist repression of Maghribi nationalist movements made the development of a cooperative conception of power even more difficult to achieve.

Conspiratorial politics have also characterized postindependence Morocco. The system lacks accepted rules by which decisions are cooperatively reached. Instead, Moroccan political life is constantly in a state of heightened political tension. However, it rarely develops into open conflict. What keeps the system intact is the overriding desire of its elite members and political participants to defend their positions in a system of stable equilibrium, neither destroying their rivals nor seeking to initiate any great movement of change.

Such a process leads to political stalemate, another salient feature of Moroccan politics today. A group orientation has always existed and continues to play an important role in Morocco's political culture and behavior. It is within this group framework that one can best understand the almost continuous process of alliance building and alliance maintenance that involves both elites and nonelites. Since the Moroccan believes that everyone else is involved in this alliance-formation process, he must always be alert to those that might outmaneuver or trick him.

The peculiar irony of this system of cleavages, with its high degree of tension and conflict, is that it has inhibited the creation of nationwide consensus. The primary loyalty is to a smaller political grouping. Except for political beliefs predicated upon Islamic fundamentalist principles, which still have meaning among many of the tradition-bound masses, it seems doubtful that a broadly based nationalist ideology can be established in such a fluid milieu. The various political groupings display no commitment to a comprehensive political program, focusing almost entirely on short-term tactical objectives. Thus, it is almost meaningless to talk about political ideology in Morocco today, despite the extensive ideological sloganeering and rhetorical posturing that occurs among the relatively small groups of alienated intellectuals, dissident university students, or disaffected opposition politicians.

Economic Conditions

Moroccan plans for development have focused on agriculture as the key to the economic well-being of a large proportion of its citizens. Nearly 70 percent of the population derives their living directly or indirectly from the soil, and in 1975 the agricultural sector contributed 30 percent to the gross national product.

Despite the country's congenial climate and varied soils, Morocco's agriculture is confronted with a number of serious problems. Predominant among these is the increasing lack of water as one moves from northwest to southeast and the year-to-year unpredictability of rainfall. Primitive methods of cultivation, a lack of understanding of the use of fertilizers, and insecticides, and the absence of a means to acquire them contribute to low yields on the vast majority of farms. Fragmentation of land holdings resulting from the traditional Muslim inheritance laws has created large numbers of minute, irregularly shaped, and often widely scattered plots that are inefficient to cultivate.

This traditional agriculture accounts for about 85 to 90 percent of the total land under cultivation. Much of the agricultural land in the traditional sector is devoted to grazing, and the average yields per acre of cultivated land are less than half those in the modern sector. The traditional sector supports over one million families which, even in good years, consume nearly all that they produce. Only about 10 to 15 percent of total agricultural land is farmed by modern methods but that includes some of the most fertile land in the country and accounts for over 85 percent of commercial agricultural production, including almost all of the citrus fruit, fresh vegetables, wine, soft wheat, and other export crops.

The development of Moroccan agriculture since 1956 has been characterized by conservatism, coupled with an emphasis on technical progress, rather than on social change. Despite occasional imaginative projects and certain public-works programs, the government has been unable either to restructure the agricultural sector or overcome the obvious problems of poverty and unemployment in the rural farming areas.

Mineral resources are also important. Morocco's most promising source of overall economic growth is its phosphate industry, especially since its acquisition of major deposits in the former Spanish Sahara. Major investments in the expansion of production were undertaken during the 1975–1977 project (roughly 10 percent of the total national investment), and further development is projected into the 1980s. A windfall from higher world phosphate prices in the midseventies, however, was somewhat offset by the quadrupling of petroleum prices, a resource that Morocco must import.

In addition to phosphates, industry (particularly manufacturing) plays a minor part in the Moroccan economy. Yet there appears to be great determination to increase industrial productivity. Official government figures for the 1968–1972 period, for example, report that the gross domestic product increased at an average annual rate of 5.7 percent, well above the rate of 4.3 percent targeted in the plan for the same period. The 1973–1977 plan, which projected an overly optimistic 7.5 percent growth rate, foresaw a significant increase in the role of the state. Public-sector investment was to be 42 percent of the total, double that in the previous plan. In addition, the public sector was to play a leading role in the "Moroccanization" of foreign business, first introduced in 1973. A new code of investments was designed to increase Moroccan participation in share capital and in the direction of private industry by a strict definition of what constituted a Moroccan company (commercial enterprises had to be at least 50 percent Moroccan-owned).

Foreign-owned agricultural land was finally expropriated by the state under the same March 1973 "Moroccanization" decrees, paving the way for the distribution of 400,000 hectares (988,400 acres) to small farmers and the expansion of a program for cooperatives. The political importance of this land distribution has been obvious. For example, the rate of distribution increased rapidly (19,000 hectares in 1971 and over 90,000 in 1972) between the years of the two attempts on the king's life. In the same period, the king even made available 6,000 hectares of his own land during ceremonies accompanied by colorful celebrations in the countryside.

Economic growth in Morocco is continuously hampered by a high birth rate (over 3 percent) that continues to erase the short-term improvements occurring in the agricultural and industrial sectors. In addition, the job market is expanding more slowly than the available manpower is growing or skills are developing. Unemployment ranges from 20 to 30 percent in the cities and probably averages 40 percent in the rural areas. Including underemployment, the figure could be as high as 50 percent and will probably become higher in the future.

An aspect of Morocco's economic development and planning that has serious implications for social and political stability is the ever-widening discrepancy between society's wealthy few and impoverished many. At present consumption levels, it is estimated that 10 percent of the Moroccan population absorbs 45 percent of the nation's wealth. Despite the call of the five-year plan for a more equitable distribution of wealth, the gap continues to widen. The government's agrarian reform program, for example, has been able to distribute only half of the projected million acres of farmland. Concurrently, economic expectations continue to rise among all sectors of the population, causing increased frustration and a growing potential for political unrest.

Political Structure

According to the provisions of the 1972 constitution, Morocco is a constitutional, democratic, and social monarchy, and Islam is the official state religion. The constitution provides for equality under the law and guarantees freedom of movement, speech, opinion, and assembly. Amendments to the constitution may be initiated by either the king or the legislature, but such initiatives require approval by a popular referendum.

The power and authority of the state are highly centralized in the hands of the king. He is the supreme civil and religious authority, the "Commander of the Faithful," and the commander-in-chief of the armed forces. The crown is inherited and usually transmitted to the eldest son, but another son may be designated should the king so desire. The king appoints all important officials, including the premier and the cabinet. He promulgates legislation passed by the legislature and has the authority to dissolve the legislature, to submit legislation for popular referendum, to declare a state of emergency during which he may rule by decree, and to sign and ratify treaties. He presides over the cabinet, the Council for National Development and Planning, and the Supreme Judicial Council.

The 1972 constitution vests legislative authority in a unicameral House of Representatives elected for a four-year term. The legislature's constitutional powers include the right to initiate constitutional amendments, authorize declarations of war, and approve extensions of a state of emergency beyond thirty days. The king may request that the legislature reconsider legislation before giving his assent. He may also dissolve the House by decree and call for new elections, but he cannot dissolve the succeeding House for a year.

The Moroccan judicial and administrative institutions reflect both French and Spanish influences. The country is administratively divided into nineteen provinces and two urban prefectures, Casablanca and Rabat. The provinces are further divided into seventy-two administrative areas and communes. Each of the administrative regions is headed by a governor, appointed by the king and responsible to him. On 12 April 1976, the king appointed governors to three administrative provinces in Morocco's sector of the former Spanish Sahara.

The judicial system is headed by a Supreme Court comprised of four chambers: civil, criminal, administrative, and social. In 1965, a special court was established to deal with corruption among public officials. All judges are appointed by the king with the advice of the Supreme Judicial Council. Moroccan courts administer a system based on Islamic law but strongly influenced by the French and Spanish legal systems.

Political Dynamics

Morocco's constitutional system, like that of her neighbors to the east, provides only a glimpse of the actual configuration of power in the state. Morocco's King Hassan has, to date, successfully consolidated power by manipulating competing groups and rival factions and, if need be, by eliminating them altogether if they threaten his personal power. While systems of consultation and advice exist within the broader power structures, including constitutional ones, there are no formal systematic procedures to force the ruler to accept advice.

Moroccan political processes are dominated by a group of approximately 1,000 men who constitute the country's political elite. Leaders of the various political parties and other formal and informal groups and associations, including chief representatives of labor unions, economic organizations, and agricultural interests, speak for and control most of those who are politically active and who hold specific political attitudes. All these political parties, pressure groups, and regional interests are in fierce competition for power and patronage. Although political pluralism seems to prevail, political life is monopolized by the monarchy, whose authority and prestige—despite serious social and political buffeting in recent years—remain unequaled in the country. While the other sources of power, including the political parties, labor unions, and rural interests, compete with and attempt to limit the king's freedom of action, he remains at the center of politics in Morocco. The king relies on his traditional legitimacy to balance and dominate the segmented political elite; indeed, monarchical supremacy has depended upon existing social pluralism and divisions among the elite.

The sources of the monarchy's power and prestige are diverse yet interdependent. The king's authority is primarily based on his role as spiritual leader, or imam, of the Islamic community—the "commander of the faithful." Concurrently, he is the member of the Alawite dynasty formally accepted as ruler by the same Islamic community in Morocco. Because of his noble religious ancestry and the attendant supernatural qualities ascribed to him, the Moroccan king satisfies the aspirations of rural Muslims who primarily seek the miraculous qualities inherent in the monarch's personal charisma, or *baraka*. Regardless of what the more modernized sectors of society may personally think of the monarch, he is deeply venerated by the rural masses, who view him as the sharif (descendant of the Prophet), and as a dispenser of *baraka*. In short, Islamic tradition remains an important source of legitimacy for the throne.

The monarchy also represents the symbolic leadership of the nationalist struggle. In the minds of the masses, national independence and political unification are intimately associated with monarchical authority, however marginal the king's actual political contribution may have been in the preindependence nationalist movement.

The king's power and prestige is further enhanced by the fact that he is the nation's most prominent dispenser of patronage and the ultimate source of spoils in the system. The palace has a very real command over Moroccan commercial activities as well as over the distribution of patronage, both of which it uses to sustain the king's secular clientele and to build his secular alliances. Indeed, these commercial and patronage resources are the king's two most effective levers of political control.

As we have seen, Moroccan society consists of numerous segments that have historically related to one another by tension and conflict. Thus, one of the most important political roles in the country has been that of arbiter among conflicting groups. This has made the monarch the pivotal center of Morocco's disparate and factionalized political arena. The king has used his role as arbiter in two ways: by continuing to recognize and encourage the allegiance shown him by the various parties and by developing ways of strengthening his own resources of support at the expense of those very same parties. Thus, the king seeks to preserve the system of factionalism but will move against any party or faction that appears to be growing too strong. His success in maintaining such a balance lies in his ability to reaffirm the direct ties between himself and the people.

If all else fails, power and control can be maintained by the king's loyal lieutenants. An executive staff, the intelligence and security branches of the Ministry of the Interior and the Ministry of National Defense, including a once-again loyal army and officer corps, all assist in the maintenance of royal authority throughout the kingdom.

The past and current success of royal control has therefore centered around the ability of the king to manipulate the elite while maintaining broad political support from the rural masses. As long as the elite remains small, socially and educationally homogeneous, and politically fragmented, the system has fairly good prospects for maintaining power. However, the size of the elite and the balance of its component parts cannot be guaranteed in the future; moreover, rapid population and educational growth will inevitably threaten the equilibrium at all social levels, including that of the elite. The implication of this long-term demographic process on the monarchy's hegemonic role in the system are, of course, obvious. Over time, Morocco will have to broaden the base of participation in the political process if it is to maintain political stability.

Morocco has developed a multiparty system. Yet, since the early 1960s and particularly under the reign of Hassan II, the outcome of party competition either at the polls or in Parliament has not decisively affected the composition or policies of the king's government. The centralized role of the monarchy, the king's tactic of playing one party against the other, and the pervasive infighting that occurs within the parties have all combined to severely undermine the party system, notwithstanding the revival of party activity in the 1977 legislative elections and the reentry of party figures into the government.

Apart from the monarchy, the Istiqlal remains the most influential political force in the country. Its complex internal divisions faithfully reflect the social forces and psychological tensions of Morocco's pluralist society. The Istiqlal was instrumental in achieving Moroccan independence but was unable to capitalize on its national stature and popularity in the immediate postindependence period and was unable to transform itself, before or after independence, into an effective mass-based party. It remained an agglomeration of integrated groups with purely parochial objectives.

The Istiqlal subscribes to a form of Islamic socialism that aims to create a radical progressive image. It firmly adheres to the principles of Islam and concurrently expresses a commitment to economic independence, land reform ("the land to those who work it"), and economic equality. In practice, however, it represents a traditional, defensive, and status quo segment of small-town and rural population. Its traditional strongholds have been the areas around Fez and Meknes. Its founding father and venerable leader, Allal al-Fassi, died in May 1973 and was succeeded by Muhammad Boucetta.

The UNFP arose as a result of the schism between radical and conservative wings of the Istiqlal in 1959. Today it is a coalition of left-wing nationalists, trade unionists, resistance fighters, and dissident members of minor parties. The party's symbolic hero and political ideologue was Mehdi Ben Barka, an original founder of the splinter group, who represented leftist and radical political trends as reflected by his characteristically Marxist vocabulary and occasionally radical methods. With his disappearance under suspicious circumstances in Paris in 1965, Abdallah Ibrahim assumed the leadership of the party.

Under continuous pressure from and harassment by the throne, and weakened by serious internal factionalism, the UNFP was never able to achieve much popular support even from left-wing students and trade unions, especially the country's largest labor federation, the UMT.

UNFP policies have consistently shown an antimonarchist tendency and its theoreticians subscribe to a Marxist ideology. Its radical posture and revolutionary rhetoric have made it attractive to a very narrow yet outspoken sector of Moroccan urban society. Its status as the foremost radical opposition has been challenged, however, by the breaking away of its Rabat section in 1972; the latter reconstituted itself as the USFP in 1974.

The newer USFP calls for thorough reform of the nation's social, economic, and administrative structures, nationalization of the principal means of production, and a general amnesty for all political prisoners. Its participation in the 1977 national elections proved disappointing. Party leader Abderrahim Bouabid was defeated and the party managed to obtain a mere 16 of the 176 seats being contested. Hard liners within the party had warned against participation in elections that were subsequently described by Bouabid as "rigged and manipulated" by the authorities. In addition, the USFP's ideological extremism probably intimidated a generally conservative electorate that apparently heeded the Istiqlal's warning of the "yellow threat" (the USFP's color) during the electoral campaign.

The Party of Progress and Socialism the (PPS) was formed in 1968 to replace the banned Moroccan Communist party and is headed by its long-time secretary-general, Ali Yata. Although the PPS was banned itself in 1969, it was resurrected in late 1974 and participated in the June 1977 elections, in which Ali Yata successfully gained a seat in the new House of Representatives. This development placed Morocco in the rare position of having a legitimately elected communist representative in its parliament.

A number of minor, weakly organized, independent and promonarchy parties of dubious political significance round out the political party system in Morocco.

As evinced by the July 1971 and the August 1972 coup attempts, the Moroccan military, once viewed as a staunch pillar of the monarchy, evolved into the most serious threat to it. Though King Hassan has apparently been able to reestablish control of the armed forces, it can never again be certain that they will remain indifferent to the profound social dislocations occurring in the society. To this must be added the changing social background and educational levels of new army recruits who are less committed to patrimonial attachments and the power of local and national patrons, including the king. As guardian of the state's coercive power, the army will remain politically significant simply because it exists.

University students in Morocco, as elsewhere in the developing world, constitute an outspoken element in the country's political life, both as incipient, aspiring members of the elite and as current elements of support or opposition to existing political arrangements. Given the relatively small numbers that achieve university status and, because a university degree is a virtual prerequisite for entry into elite-level positions, the political orientation of students is significant.

The National Union of Moroccan Students (UNEM), formerly a wing of the UNFP, remains the major student organization. Since the 1960s the UNEM has been extensively involved in extralegal and radical activities directed against the regime and its incumbents, most of whom are viewed with hostility, contempt, or indifference. Either through this and other organizations or simply as individual interest groups, students have demonstrated against a wide range of political, social, economic, and educational grievances. Their grievances are usually articulated in the highly ideological language of Arab politics: Arab nationalism, revolutionism, imperialism, and neocolonialism.

In recent years, students have also been affected by an increasing alienation from, and disenchantment with, political and social life. As job opportunities after graduation continue to diminish, social injustice and economic inequality become more pronounced and manipulative palace politics proceed unhampered. Increased student discontent with the existing state of political affairs has led the more radical youths to outflank even the leftist opposition. In early 1972, for example, UNEM, whose executive committee was dominated by radical students, became independent of UNFP.

The students suffer from the same factional and parochial weaknesses as the political parties; therefore, it has been relatively easy for the regime to keep them fragmented and disunited. However, given the burgeoning birth rate, the majority of young people in the total population, the stagnant economy, and the political stalemate evident among the system's status-quo elites, it seems unlikely that students can be neutralized indefinitely as a political force. With the passage of time their frustrations are likely to give way to increasingly militant radicalization.

The Moroccan trade-union movement acquired skill, conviction, and solidarity as a result of struggling against colonial repression and communist control of unions during the decade preceding national independence. Given greater freedom to organize and strike after 1956, the Union of Moroccan Labor increased its membership and became the largest and strongest trade union in all of the Middle East. From its inception, the UMT was nationalist, not communist, and allied to the Istiqlal. With the split in the Istiqlal the UMT allied with the UNFP camp and provided the main popular and organized support.

Until 1960, the UMT was Morocco's sole labor and trade-union confederation. In that year, the Istiqlal organized a rival union, the General Union of Moroccan Workers (UGTM), but the UGTM has remained weak and unable to compete with the UMT in numerical terms. Since 1960 all other Moroccan political parties have followed the UGTM's example but with meager success. The UMT still commands the allegiance of the majority of workers and is by far the best organized.

Despite the UMT's historically significant role in cooperating with and opposing the regime, the general political and economic climate in Morocco remains hostile to the development of a vigorous and independent labor movement. Three particular factors inhibit such development. First, the high level of unemployment makes the unions insecure and vulnerable to sudden, unplanned changes in membership, recruitment, financial support, and organizational solidarity. Second, the unions are subject to harsh pressure and blandishments from the government. Finally, very serious differences exist between trade-union interests and those of the politicians. In addition, the constant factor of monarchical manipulation accentuates divisions instead of fostering unity in the labor movement, just as it has with the opposition political parties.

Foreign Policy

Foreign policy decisions in Morocco are made by the narrow strata of incumbent political elites that revolve around the authority of the monarch. While pluralistic tendencies are evident in certain sectors of Moroccan domestic life, no such pluralism exists in the articulation, deliberation, and implementation of foreign policy. From this perspective, Morocco's continued strong ties to France are in part a response to geopolitical and economic reality and in part a function of historical conditioning. They are also a reflection of the elites' close affinity with French culture, language, and civilization. These latter characteristics are not shared by the population at large or even by a great portion of its educated classes, thus highlighting the discontinuity between elite and mass political cultures and the incongruous policy decisions resulting from such cultural discontinuity. It is therefore uncertain to what extent the Moroccan people share in their government's strong pro-Western orientation, especially its warm and friendly relations with the United States. France and the United States have rewarded Morocco's "moderation" in world affairs by becoming the predominant suppliers of military aid and substantial contributors of economic assistance to post-independence Morocco. France remains Morocco's closest trading partner and provides the country with extensive technical, financial, and educational aid, for which there is an urgent need. Relations with the Soviet Union are cordial and developing.

Morocco also identifies with the aspirations of the Arab world, including the call for Arab unity, opposition to Zionism, pride in a common cultural, religious, historical, and linguistic heritage, and a desire to assert an authentic Arab identity. However, Morocco is less directly involved in Middle Eastern affairs than the eastern Arab states.

Morocco's relations with its North African neighbors are more ambivalent. The nation continues an ideological and territorial dispute with Algeria, including the most recent conflict concerning the former territory of the Spanish Sahara. This territory was divided between Morocco and Mauritania, much to the chagrin of Algeria, which subsequently began to provide logistical and political support to the so-called Polisario Front, an amorphous tribal group of Saharan residents fighting against Morocco and Mauritania in quest of an independent homeland in the desert. One of the inducements for Morocco's pro-Western policies is the quasi-radical posture of Algerian foreign policy.

Relations with Tunisia are more amicable. Both regimes share similar international orientations and development policies, especially in the crucial area of private foreign investment. As for Libya, the always unpredictable Colonel Qaddafi is distrusted by the Moroccan monarchy, particularly since various plots against the crown in the early seventies have been associated with Libyan-supported agents.

Because the monarchy's legitimacy is questioned by many disenchanted elements of the middle class, foreign-policy issues are often invoked as a means of mobilizing support for the monarchy and distracting attention from the many domestic ills besetting the country. Such was the case with the so-called "Green March" of 350,000 unarmed Moroccan civilians into the Spanish zone of the Sahara in late 1975, which aroused renewed support for the king and his policies. Similarly, in April 1977, Hassan's decision to send paratroop units of Morocco's army to fight in Zaire in support of President Joseph Mobutu's struggle against secessionist forces in the Shaba Province enhanced King Hassan's domestic prestige. Apart from the geopolitical or economic considerations reflected by Morocco's competition with Algeria, Moroccan foreign policy is most often used by the country's elites to maintain their power. The implementation of such policies has focused the cultivation of close economic, technical, and military ties with France and the United States while simultaneously maintaining a symbolic association with the rest of the Afro-Arab world.

Bibliography

The history of preindependence Morocco, including the precolonial, colonial, and nationalist phases, is systematically analyzed by Douglas E. Ashford, *Perspectives of a Moroccan Nationalist* (Totowa, N.J.: The Bedminster Press, 1964), Stephane Bernard, *The Franco-Moroccan Conflict, 1943–1956* (New Haven, Conn.: Yale University Press, 1968), Robin Bidwell, *Morocco Under Colonial Rule: French Administration of Tribal Areas, 1912–1956* (London: Frank Cass, 1973), Edmund Burke, *Prelude to Protectorate in Morocco: Precolonial Protest and Resistance, 1860–1912* (Chicago: University of Chicago Press, 1976), and John P. Halstead, *Rebirth of a Nation: The Origins and Rise of Moroccan Nationalism, 1912–1944* (Cambridge, Mass.: Harvard University Press, 1967).

Islam's importance in Moroccan political and social life receives exceptional scholarly treatment by Clifford Geertz, *Islam Observed: Religious Development in Morocco and Indonesia* (New Haven, Conn.: Yale University Press, 1968), Dale F. Eickelman, *Moroccan Islam: Tradition and Society in a Pilgrimage Center* (Austin, Texas: University of Texas Press, 1976), and Ernest Gellner, *Saints of the Atlas* (Chicago: University of Chicago Press, 1969).

A number of important sociological and anthropological themes in Moroccan life are conscientiously treated in Kenneth Brown, *People of Salé* (Cambridge, Mass.: Harvard University Press, 1976), Daisy Hilse Dwyer, *Image and Self-Image: Male and Female in Morocco* (New York: Columbia University Press, 1978), Vanessa Maher, *Women and Property in Morocco: Their Changing Relation to the Process of Social Stratification in the Middle Atlas* (London: Cambridge University Press, 1974), Paul Rabinow, *Symbolic Domination: Cultural Form and Historical Change in Morocco* (Chicago: University of Chicago Press, 1975), and John Waterbury, *North for the Trade: The Life and Times of a Berber Merchant* (Berkeley and Los Angeles: University of California Press, 1972).

The most reliable analyses of Moroccan political development and institution building are Douglas E. Ashford, *Political Change in Morocco* (Princeton, N.J.: Princeton University Press, 1961), I. William Zartman, *Morocco: Problems of New Power* (New York: Atherton Press, 1964), I. William Zartman, *Destiny of a Dynasty: The Search for Institutions in Morocco's Developing Society* (Columbia: University of South Carolina Press, 1964), and John Waterbury, *The Commander of the Faithful: The Moroccan Political Elite—A Study in Segmented Politics* (New York: Columbia University Press, 1970). The latter is probably the best work in any language on the nature of elite politics in Morocco.

Local government, public administration, planning, and aspects of economic development are the concern of Douglas E. Ashford, *Morocco-Tunisia: Politics and Planning* (Syracuse, N.Y.: Syracuse University Press, 1965), Douglas E. Ashford, *National Development and Local Reform: Political Participation in Morocco, Tunisia, and Pakistan* (Princeton, N.J.: Princeton University Press, 1967), and John W. Behen, *The Economic Development of Morocco* (Baltimore: The Johns Hopkins University Press, 1966).

Rom Landau, *Hassan II: King of Morocco* (London: George Allen and Unwin, 1962) and Rom Landau, *Morocco Independent* (London: George Allen and Unwin, 1961) portray sympathetic accounts of King Hassan II and his regime.

General surveys of Morocco include Nevill Barbour, *Morocco* (New York: Walker, 1965), Lorna Hahn and Mark I. Cohen, *Morocco: Old Land, New Nation* (New York: Frederick A. Praeger Publishers, 1966), and Vincent Monteil, *Morocco* (New York: The Viking Press, 1964).

Indispensable reference works include the *Area Handbook for Morocco* (Washington, D.C.: U.S. Government Printing Office, 1965).

19

Democratic and Popular Republic of Algeria

John P. Entelis

Historical Background

The initial French conquest of Algeria in 1830 was relatively easy, but another four decades passed before all of Algeria was pacified under French control. The French colonial implantation was massive. By the end of the first fifty years of French occupation, the Algerian Muslims had lost not only their freedom but also their land. The French authorities offered French settlers free transportation, land, seed, and livestock, and their products were imported duty-free into France. By 1851, over 150,000 Europeans had settled in Algeria, and after the 1870 Franco-Prussian War, Algeria's political status was closely linked to metropolitan France.

A governor-general was appointed by Paris and empowered to legislate by decree. He was thus able to control the application of, or to withhold altogether, metropolitan legislation. Moreover, as the European settlers gained strength, they were able to exert vast influence on the machinery of government. They could determine policies, influence the enactment and execution of laws, and control the appointment of high officials of the administration.

The political and personal status of native Algerian Muslims was likewise deeply affected. By 1900, Algerian Muslims had been reduced from relative prosperity to economic, social, and cultural inferiority. Three millon inhabitants had died, tribes had been disbanded, and the traditional economy was radically altered during prolonged "civilizing" campaigns. In particular, the production of wine for export replaced the traditional production of cereals for domestic consumption. Virtually the whole of Algeria's traditional economic structure and land-use practices were dislocated as a consequence of French colonial policy with its property laws, sequestrations of land after the early revolts, expropriations, forestry laws, regulations concerning pasture lands, and a host of other measures that were either forced upon the administration or inspired by its policy of giving preferential considerations to the interests of the Europeans.

The intermittent attempts at incremental political and social reforms designed to benefit the native Algerians were inconsequential. As long as the settler population controlled Algeria, Paris-inspired reform legislation was doomed.

In reaction to the policy of total colonialism adopted by the French, an Algerian national movement appeared. It can be divided into four distinct historical periods. From 1830 to about 1870, traditional Algerian nationalists resisted colonial rule. They were typified by Amir Add al-Kadir who led a heroic but futile revolt. By 1870, Algerian society had been so dislocated that an indigenous Algerian political and national identity all but ceased to exist. The period 1920 to 1954 witnessed the rise of a new, urban-based nationalism and the gradual shift from collaboration with the French to radical opposition. The fourth period, 1954 to 1962, marked the Algerian Revolution, which was a time of violence and brutality on both sides that culminated in formal independence in July 1962.

The Algerian Revolution erupted when all hope of an evolutionary settlement was destroyed by blunders of postwar French policy and the opposition of French settlers to any concessions to Muslim nationalist aspirations. For the angry young nationalists who formed the backbone of the revolution, the various reformist efforts of the previous period had become irrelevant. In early 1954 the Revolutionary Committee for Unity and Action (CRUA) was organized by dissidents from the earlier movements, ex-soldiers in the French army who had gained valuable experience in the Indochinese campaigns, and miscellaneous groups of dedicated and desperate men who were unafraid of—indeed, they invited —violence and dangerous risks. The nine so-called historic chiefs who had formed the CRUA shared four basic experiences. All were radical militants of peasant and working-class background; all were ex-French army soldiers; all were members of the Organisation Speciale (OS), the nationalist organization that had been founded in the late 1940s by Ahmad Ben Bella and Hocine Ait Ahmed; and all had served time in French prisons.

After several months of preparation during the summer of 1954, military organization was established and the country divided into six *wilayas*, or districts. On 1 November the National Liberation Front (FLN), with its fighting arm the National Liberation Army (ALN), issued

Algeria

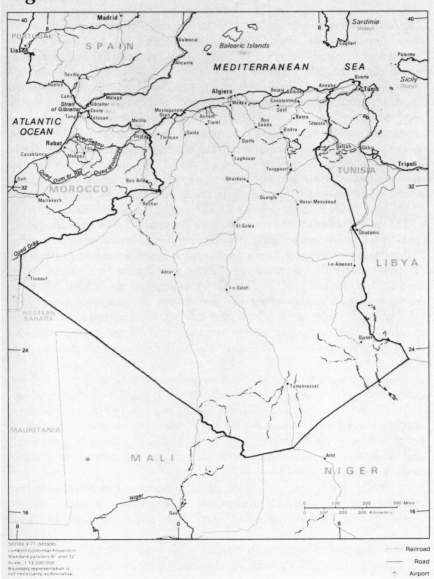

PORTUGAL
Madrid
SPAIN
Valencia
Lisbon
Balearic Islands
(Sp.)
MEDITERRANEAN
SEA
Sardinia
(Italy)
Cagliari
Palermo
Sevilla
Alicante
Sicily
(Italy)
Huelva
Cádiz
Málaga
Algiers
Bejaia
Skikda
Annaba
Bizerte
Tunis
Gibraltar (U.K.)
Ceuta (Sp.)
Tangier
Tétouan
Melilla
Mostaganem
Oran
Medea
Constantine
Setif
ATLANTIC
OCEAN
Strait
of Gibraltar
El
Asnam
Tiaret
Bou
Saâda
Batna
Tébessa
Rabat
Oued Sebou
Oujda
Tlemcen
Saida
Biskra
Casablanca
Meknes
Fes
Djelfa
Qafsah
Qabis
Safi
Oued Oum er Rbi
Oued Moulouya
Bou Arfa
Laghouat
Touggourt
TUNISIA
Tripoli
MOROCCO
Bechar
Ghardaia
Ouargla
Hassi Messaoud
Marrakech
El Golea
Ghadamis
Oued Drâa
Adrar
I-n Amenas
LIBYA
Tindouf
I-n-Salah
WESTERN
SAHARA
Djanet
MAURITANIA
Tamanrasset
MALI
Arlit
NIGER
Niger
Gao

0 100 200 300 Miles
0 100 200 300 Kilometers

502701 9-77 (541900)
Lambert Conformal Projection
Standard parallels 8° and 32°
Scale 1:13,200,000
Boundary representation is
not necessarily authoritative

Railroad
Road
Airport

a proclamation calling on all Algerians to rise and fight for their freedom. The revolution had begun.

In September 1958, the FLN constituted itself into a government, the Provisional Government of the Algerian Republic (GPRA), which negotiated independence after 1958. A final accord on a cease-fire was reached at Evian, France, on 19 March 1962, and formal independence was declared on 3 July 1962.

Independence was achieved despite the military impotence of the revolutionaries and the serious divisions existing within the FLN. These splits were basically caused by the fact that there had been neither an incontestable leader, a political organization, nor an articulated ideology before the revolution. Yet, although the country lay exhausted and prostrate from the draining ordeal of a savage eight-year guerrilla war and the structure of state and society was virtually decimated by the hasty retreat of frightened colons, Algeria finally emerged free and in control of its own political destiny after 130 years of French colonial rule.

The superficial unity that marked the FLN's military and diplomatic efforts broke down immediately after independence, and a vicious struggle for power among contending groups began. The three major contestants for power were the Algerian provisional government, the *wilaya* commands, and the army of the frontier or external army (ALN), based in Morocco and Tunisia during the revolution. At issue were wartime misdemeanors, ideology, ethnic and clan ties, loyalties to specific individuals, and competing perspectives on the nature of postindependence Algerian society. At stake was political predominance in the state.

The first round in the postwar struggle was fought at the Tripoli (Libya) congress of the FLN national council in May 1962. Factionalism and deep-seated antagonism among all the principal nationalist leaders quickly surfaced. The purpose of the Tripoli meeting was to elect a political bureau to assume control of the FLN and to devise a political and economic program, which later became the official policy of independent Algeria.

When the competing factions returned to Algeria, Ben Bella, with the military support of the ALN chief of staff, Colonel Houari Boumedienne, was able to gain the initiative and establish his authority over party and nation.

On 20 September 1962, elections for the National Assembly were held. All powers of the GPRA were transferred to the new assembly and formal proclamation of the Democratic and Popular Republic of Algeria was made. Six days later, the assembly elected Ben Bella premier and empowered him to form a government. He immediately formed a cabinet that included Boumedienne as defense minister. Others were chosen from the Algerian Army (ANP) and Ben Bella's personal and political associates.

Once the new government had consolidated its position, it set about addressing the severe economic plight of the country, caused in great part by the sudden and massive exodus of the Europeans. The latter included virtually all the entrepreneurs, technicians, administrators, teachers, doctors, and skilled workers in the country. After factories and shops closed and farms ceased operations, over 70 percent of the population was left unemployed. In March 1963, overwhelmed by the catastrophic economic situation and unguided by any particular socialist ideology, Ben Bella signed into law several decrees ("the March Decrees") that legalized the takeover of extensive agricultural and industrial properties abandoned in the colon exodus and instituted the system of *autogestion*, or worker's management.

Autogestion was conceived as an economic system based on worker's management of their own affairs through elected officials and cooperation with the state through a director and national agencies. The state's function was to guide, counsel, and coordinate their activities within the framework of an evolving national plan. *Autogestion* was seen as a stage in the transformation from a colonial to a socialist economy. The severe shortage of qualified personnel and the inability of workers and peasants to fully comprehend the principles of self-management made this experiment in socialism more a myth than a reality.

Ben Bella's style of rule did not instill confidence among a war-weary population. He quickly attempted to increase his personal standing and power. In April 1963, he took over the position of general secretary of the FLN. Subsequently, he engineered the passage of a constitution creating a presidential regime with the FLN as the sole political party. In September 1963, he was elected president for a five-year term. He also assumed the title of military commander-in-chief while becoming head of state and head of government.

This consolidation of personal power and apparent move toward dictatorial government aroused opposition and the reemergence of factionalism. Farhat Abbas, the president of the assembly and the leading spokesman for a more liberal policy, resigned from the presidency and was subsequently expelled from the FLN. In the Kabyle, where discontent was accentuated by Berber regionalism, sporadic disturbances broke out and a revolt had to be quashed by police action and political compromise.

In April 1964, the long-awaited First Congress of the FLN was held in Algiers to sort out the ideological differences among various competing groups within the ruling establishment. Toward this end the Algiers Charter, as it came to be called, was formally adopted. The charter defined the relationship between the state, party, and army, and supported traditional Islamic principles as theoretical guidelines for Algerian socialism and the policy of *autogestion*.

The Congress, however, precipitated the feud between Ben Bella and Boumedienne. Ben Bella attempted to strengthen the leftist organizations in the hope that this would help him against the army, while Boumedienne tried to unify the army against Ben Bella by resolving the conflict between the former *wilaya* leaders and the newer officers of the ANP.

Ultimately, Ben Bella lost. Despite his numerous efforts to institutionalize the revolution and its socialist ideology, his popularity among the masses and his status as one of the "historic chiefs" of the revolution, he was never able to overcome the many rivalries, challenges, and controversies that faced his regime. In addition, his ouster of the traditional leaders, his repeated political attacks on the workers union (UGTA), his failure to make the FLN an efficient mass party, his suspicion of plotters behind every door, and his increasingly dictatorial tendencies alienated many political leaders and interest groups. Furthermore, Ben Bella's constant improvisation in policy offended even his closest supporters. Once the army turned against him, he was left virtually powerless and vulnerable, and in June 1965 he was ousted from power.

The military takeover hardly caused a ripple in Algerian society. The constitution was suspended and power was smoothly and efficiently transferred to Boumedienne and a twenty-member Council of Revolution, which was designated as the supreme political body. Boumedienne was named prime minister and minister of defense, and Abdelaziz Bouteflika continued as foreign minister. According to the council, the aims of the new regime were to reestablish the principles of the revolution, to remedy the abuses of personal power associated with Ben Bella, to end internal divisions, and to create an "authentic" socialist society based on a sound economy.

For his base of support, Boumedienne relied on the veterans of the war of independence (*mujahidin*), the ALN officers, and a new class of young technocrats, a reflection of his more somber and low-key style of authority. The shy, introverted Boumedienne was a reformist and organizer who stressed the need for planning and reflection, and was wary of radical change. During the first two years of his rule, he initiated no bold new initiatives. There was little attempt to resuscitate national political life, and the Algerian National Assembly remained in abeyance while the FLN was moribund.

Despite Boumedienne's cautious administration, opposition against him began to crystallize among left-wing ministers, the UGTA, the students, and some sections of the army—notably the former *wilaya* leaders. This group favored the syndicalist approach to socialism embodied in *autogestion* to the more centralized and technocratic system being developed by Boumedienne. They also feared that collegial rule was being supplanted by a dictatorship of Boumedienne and the small group around him.

On 14 December 1967, Colonel Tahar Zbiri, army chief of staff and a prominent former *wilaya* leader, launched an armed uprising in the countryside. It was quickly and efficiently suppressed by forces loyal to Boumedienne, but other groups, especially dissident students, continued to demonstrate their opposition to the new regime by striking and staging street demonstrations. There were reports of guerrilla activity in the Aures and Kabylia regions, and on 25 April 1968, there was an unsuccessful attempt to assassinate Boumedienne.

Between 1968 and 1972, however, the regime managed to consolidate its power, thereby enabling it to initiate bold policies of development in the industrial, agricultural, and political fields. The second stage of the reform of governmental institutions, for example, was put into operation in May 1969 when the government held elections for the *wilaya* popular assembly (APW). Both the earlier February 1967 APC (communal popular assembly) elections and May 1969 APW elections clearly indicated how Boumedienne envisioned the organization of the Algerian state and its political institutions. Specifically, his idea was to implement a system of decentralized local government counterbalanced by a single centralized party, the FLN, and a well-established administration.

It was also during this period that the regime gave priority to the development of heavy industry, particularly of the petroleum and gas industry. At the end of 1971 a major attempt was also made at agrarian reform in order to improve the lagging agricultural sector, which had received only secondary attention in the attempt to boost industrial productivity.

In the political sphere, the lack of political representation and popular participation in the first five years of Boumedienne's rule, despite the creation of local and *wilaya* assemblies, led him to reassess the status of the nation's political institutions, particularly its single party governing structure, the FLN. The regime's successful creation of a stable political environment had been achieved at the expense of public participation in the political process. The FLN had been allowed to become moribund and overly bureaucratized. Thus, on 19 June 1975 (the tenth anniversary of his ascent to power) Boumedienne announced the preparation of a national charter and constitution that would provide for political institutions that were either to be created or reactivated.

In May 1976, Boumedienne submitted the charter to public debate. The extensive and surprisingly candid discussions at party gatherings, trade union meetings, and assemblies of the burgeoning peasants' association reflected widening public participation in political life while reaffirming the power of Boumedienne and his regime.

On 27 June 1976, the new National Charter was overwhelmingly approved by a referendum. The charter represents an ideological inventory of Algeria's socialist history and charts the direction the country intends to pursue. It also delineates the popular and institutional basis of the future Algeria, giving renewed prominence to the FLN as the nation's only authentic representative of the people's will. Emphasis is also placed on the participatory role of citizens in a socialist society.

In November 1976, Algerians again went to the polls and overwhelmingly approved a new constitution that recreated the National Popular Assembly (APN) and restored the country to constitutional rule for the first time since the July 1965 suspension of the 1963 constitution promulgated under Ben Bella. The new constitution was a lengthy document, containing a preamble and 199 articles; it ushered in what has become known as the Second Algerian Republic (the first republic lasted from 1963 to 1965). In theory, the National Charter and the new constitution signaled the return of constitutional government, but since Boumedienne personally led and encouraged the public debate that favored both new documents, the votes approving them were in fact votes of confidence in the man himself and his personal system of rule.

A month after approval of the constitution, Boumedienne, the only candidate on the ballot, was overwhelmingly elected president of the republic. According to the constitution, Boumedienne, as president, officially became head of state, head of government, commander-in-chief of the armed forces, head of national defense, and nominally the head of the FLN—all of which significantly enhanced an institutional power that was already well-fortified by his support from the military.

Finally, as provided for in the new constitution, elections for the new National Popular Assembly were held on 25 February 1977. Although all of the candidates were chosen by the FLN, there was a certain amount of debate over the choices between the grass-roots militants and the party leadership. The representatives elected to a five-year term of the new assembly included six government ministers, diplomats, army officers, peasants, industry and office workers, civil servants, party workers; several of these were women. Emphasizing that the new assembly was composed of a majority of peasants and workers, government officials described in the APN as the final step in the construction of a socialist state that began a decade earlier with local elections.

On 27 April 1977, the assembly formed a new government. The president remained firmly in control, however, since all twenty-four ministers and three secretaries of state were considered to be the "president's men," loyal, obedient, and, for the most part, competent. Since Boumedienne did not designate a prime minister—a constitutional role of his office— he further enhanced the presidential prerogative within Algeria's political system.

In addition to creating the important institutional and participatory bases of Algerian political life, Boumedienne's main accomplishments as leader of Algeria during the years of his tenure included: stabilizing the nation's leadership, consolidating government control over the economy, introducing comprehensive economic planning, capitalizing on petroleum and gas revenues, and generally aiming at rapid industrialization.

Boumedienne's sudden illness in November 1978 and his death a month later from a rare blood disease left Algeria without a designated successor. As stipulated in the constitution, National Assembly President Bitah assumed interim responsibilities as chief of state while a special congress of the FLN was convened to select a candidate. The congress's choice of Colonel Chadli Benjedid—a senior military officer—as presidential candidate and secretary general of the party reflected the preeminence of the military office corps as a predominant political force in Algerian political life.

Political Environment

Political Culture

As elsewhere in the Maghrib, elite political culture markedly differs from mass political culture in Algeria. The masses continue to identify unswervingly with Islam and its religious symbols. It is only in the relatively small "modernized" sector of the population and its even smaller elite component that one finds elements of a more secular political culture and ideology.

Algerian political culture reflects the impact of traditional cultural values, assimilated Western political ideologies, and historical experiences—especially the revolutionary war. A conflictual political culture has emerged in which hostility and mistrust between elite groups predominate. Algerian politicians often behave somewhat like their Moroccan counterparts: as if they are constantly maneuvering and scheming to acquire more power. Further, they expect others to behave in a similar manner.

One immediate consequence of this behavior is the personalization of political differences, where personal rivalries and personal clashes substitute for legitimate political discourse. Another is the distrust of any form of political opposition, which has led Algerian politicians to view any form of public political disagreement as illegitimate and harmful to the political process.

Despite these attitudes, the regime, after ten years under Boumedienne, had apparently begun to encourage and even articulate the need for "legitimate" dissent and a free expression of opposing opinions. The animated debates over the National Charter, for example, were remarkably open and candid.

Paradoxically, another and altogether inconsistent aspect of Algerian political culture is the strong feeling that political relations must be based on equality and reciprocity. This sentiment has its origins in the traditional Islamic concepts of *shura* (consultation) and *ijma'* (consensus), which were central to decision making in the Islamic state. The most noteworthy expression of the Algerian's demand for equality is found in the notion of collegial rule and rejection of the idea of a "cult of personality." This latter was the most damning accusation made against Ben Bella. In contrast, Boumedienne's rule emphasized collegiality and consultation, albeit among a narrow group of political advisers, technocrats, and military men. In his later years Boumedienne personally assumed extensive decision-making authority, but the tendency toward collegiality within the political elite has gained strength since his death.

The mixture of distrust and egalitarianism in political life is often explained by the so-called individualistic nature of Algerians—i.e., the distrust for those who have power and the demand for an equal share of influence. Yet this individualism, manifested at times by a kind of public rebellion and sporadic violence, belies an underlying pressure to conform to rigorous traditional social codes that must be obeyed and to a public opinion that must be respected. As a result, attitudes toward the power role of government are characterized by fundamentally inconsistent behavioral patterns. On the one hand, the colonial and war experiences have exerted a particularly profound impact on the elites' perception of the "proper" role of government. They engendered a belief in the need for a strong centralized state with respect to economic development and organization. On the other hand, Algerian political culture contains a strong current of populism, as reflected by the principles and practices of *autogestion* in the first years of independence.

Algerian populism reflects a belief in the supremacy of the will of the people. It places justice and morality above all other norms and emphasizes the importance of a direct relationship between the people and their leaders, in which intermediary institutions and mediating structures play only a minor role.

Apart from Algerians' perceptions of the role of government in society, their concept of the greatest social and political good is embodied in the concepts of nationalism. Although there appears to be more attachment to the rhetoric and symbolism of these two concepts than to their substance, they have assumed sacrosanct status among the political elite. The statist policies of the Algerian ruling elite are in fact justified by nationalist terms, wherein the state is viewed as having a right to intervene in many areas of national life. Yet there remains a genuine commitment to the welfare of the masses as well as to the idea of socialist mass political participation and administrative decentralization.

Other elements of political culture and ideology in Algeria include belief in a continuing revolution, Arab unity, and the resurrection of an Algerian Arab-Islamic culture through Arabization and under the guidance of a mass-mobilization political party. The Islamic component of socialism remains a salient feature of contemporary ideology. Algerian socialism is linked to the world of Islam, which constitutes the "heart, mind, and soul of the Algerian consciousness." The relationship between socialism and Islam, reflected in earlier ideological documents, is reaffirmed in both the National Charter and the new constitution, which explicitly extol Islamic socialism as the road to political, economic, social, and cultural salvation.

In practical terms, the duality of Islamic and socialist ideological content in Algerian political thought has permitted incumbent leaders to sustain a conservative—indeed puritanical—policy in the areas of personal, religious, and moral affairs while simultaneously pursuing a radical modernization policy involving rapid and sweeping economic growth, the use of advanced technology and scientific know-how, and dependence on Western secularists for administrative, organizational, and financial expertise. Inevitably, the coexistence of Western secular ideas of revolutionary socialism and French republicanism and traditional Islamic political ideology have created unavoidable tensions and contradictions within Algerian political culture.

At the same time, Islamic socialist ideology enables the government not only to reject Western secularism and to identify with other "radical" Arab states, but also to reject certain aspects of local tradition thought to impede social progress. Through numerous government-controlled propaganda organs and the communications media, the regime has continued to advance a socialist program primarily aimed at developing the economic strength of the state, raising the standards of living of its rural and urban populations, and providing a framework for rapid industrialization and agrarian reform.

Economic Conditions

In the decade following independence, Algeria nationalized all major foreign business interests as well as many private Algerian companies. Nationalization ranged from the assumption of a controlling interest in some cases to complete takeover in others. Today the Algerian economy is almost totally government-controlled. State enterprises and government agencies control much of the foreign trade, almost all of the major industries, large parts of the distribution and retail systems, all public utilities, and the entire banking and credit system.

The commitment to what has come to be called state capitalism evolved out of the radical nationalism of the Boumedienne group. They were convinced that true national independence could only be realized through control of natural resources, especially hydrocarbons, and through rapid industrial development—objectives that, in the context of world capitalist domination, could only be achieved through nationalization and state control of the economy.

Since the late 1960s, industrial development has been given priority over agricultural development, and within the industrial sector most investment has gone into basic industries. This strategy has been justified by two arguments. First, continued dependence on the export of raw materials and agricultural products would prevent Algeria from achieving the type of economic independence deemed necessary to make political independence truly meaningful. Second, not only could Algeria's petroleum and gas resources finance industrialization, but they could be used to develop a petrochemical industry that would be the foundation of the entire strategy of industrialization.

It was believed that, over time, industrialization would lead to the creation of numerous jobs, thereby somewhat offsetting the country's chronic unemployment and underemployment problems. In the short run, however, employment generated by the new capital-intensive industries could only marginally alleviate the unemployment problem, especially since Algeria has one of the world's highest population growth rates. Thus, in November 1971 the Charter of the Agrarian Revolution proclaimed the government's intent to profoundly change the economic and political cast of the traditional sector of Algerian agriculture, and there has been a gradual shift in the severe investment imbalance between the industrial and agricultural sectors.

Algeria's emphasis on industrialization was reflected in its first four-year plan (1970–1973), which marked the first real effort at a comprehensive economic policy. The plan allocated 45 percent of total capital investment to the establishment of a capital-intensive industrial sector that was to be the basis of economic growth. Only 15 percent went to agriculture, while 40 percent of investment was allocated to social and economic infrastructure. The investment strategy was called "planting Algeria's oil," thereby using petroleum revenues to create a strong industrial base. At the same time, an agrarian revolution policy, as it was called, aimed at improving efficiency through land reform and a system of cooperatives. The program was not only undercapitalized but owing to resistance from the rural population, it failed to increase agriculture's percentage of the GNP, which in fact declined from 13 percent in 1969 to 9 percent in 1973.

The second four-year plan (1974–1977) attempted to remedy the apparent imbalances and malfunctions of the first plan without jeopardizing the heavy emphasis on rapid industrialization. The new plan, nevertheless, placed more emphasis on developing consumer industries that create jobs, fighting regional economic disparities, encouraging small and medium-sized industries, and promoting land reform. The 1974–1977 plan also placed a major emphasis on housing, an area that was conspicuously neglected in the first plan.

It is still uncertain how much new investment in agriculture will improve the poorest parts of the countryside (in contrast to the state and self-managed farms), and in particular, how much success the authorities will have in coping with the intractable problems associated with rural economic and social development.

Algeria's development strategy of rapid industrialization has been made possible by petroleum and gas revenues. The foreign exchange derived from petroleum exports reached $5 billion in 1974, thanks to the fourfold oil price increase of 1973. While Algeria's proved reserves are limited—in 1971 they were estimated to last for only another thirty years' production at current rates—petroleum revenues have already dramatically increased Algeria's investment opportunities for national economic growth. In 1973, before the impact of the price rise had been felt, the petroleum sector accounted for over 75 percent of Algeria's exports, 68 percent of its foreign exchange earnings, and 35 percent of the government's budget revenues. The gross domestic product, which had risen by 10 percent per year from 1969 to 1972, and over 18 percent in 1973 alone, reached $6 billion in the latter year.

As mentioned above, industrialization centered around projects related to petroleum and gas—refining, gas liquefaction plants, pipelines, port facilities, tankers and petrochemicals such as fertilizers, synthetic rubber, artificial fibers, and plastics. Three refineries are currently operating; a fourth and much larger one is planned at Skikda. Gas lique-faction plants are located at Arzew and Skikda and will be supplemented by others. A gas pipeline, at a cost of over $1 billion, is planned; it will extend from the Saharan gas field across Tunisia to the Mediterranean, to Sicily, and finally to northern Italy.

In addition to petroleum-related industry, an iron and steel complex near Annaba, built with Soviet assistance, is in operation and is due to expand rapidly, capitalizing on substantial iron-ore deposits at Quenza in the northeast. Another very large deposit of iron ore, estimated at 2 billion tons, is located at Tindouf near the Moroccan and Mauritanian borders.

What was initially a peasant revolution has ironically culminated in a form of vigorous state capitalism, using modern large-scale techniques and small-scale local plants. The process of industrialization, however, has tended to bifurcate society into isolated poles of growth and stagna-tion that will require more than money or goodwill to overcome. Finally, Algeria's state capitalism has created and sustained a new elite. This eco-nomic system has put a premium on centralized control of the whole economy and on nationalization of the means of production. Thus, eco-nomic power has come to be concentrated in the hands of the state of-ficials who control the national enterprises.

Political Structure

The 1965 coup suspended the National Assembly and constitution established under Ahmad Ben Bella. During the next ten years, Algerian political life was strongly centralized under the Council of the Revolution and the council of ministers, both headed by Boumedienne. In the absence of a constitution, the council of ministers became responsible for the day-to-day administration of the government and thus became the ef-fective executive and legislative body. The FLN Algeria's only party organization) and other national-level institutions were allowed to atrophy so that Boumedienne's vision of a strong, secure, centralized government could evolve without the challenge that such organizations could present. Boumedienne believed that institutional development could only emerge via a systematic process of political education.

In accordance with this strategy, local assembly elections were held in 1967 and 1971, and *wilaya* (regional) assembly elections were held in 1969 and 1974. However, these local and regional assemblies remain largely administrative in nature and have no significant political authority.

Despite the regime's claim that the assemblies were created with the objective of instituting a greater measure of self-government at the local level, they actually strengthened national political control. For example, although the elections permit choice between candidates—there are, according to the system, twice as many candidates as seats to be filled—all of the candidates are nominated by the FLN. There is also no party competition nor do candidates engage in an electoral contest, as campaigning is the work of FLN notables and ministers. The result is politically lethargic and administratively marginal local-level associations that depend on the central authorities for guidance and animation.

Either because the system of assemblies had succeeded sufficiently or failed altogether, Boumedienne began, in the early 1970s, to call for greater politicization of the masses by advocating renewed involvement in the FLN as the sole ideological and institutional organ of the socialist revolution. In mid-1976, he personally directed the revival of constitutional politics in the form of public debates that preceded the voting on the National Charter. The nationwide referendums that approved the National Charter and constitution in June and November 1976, respectively, represented the formal reestablishment of constitutional government.

The 1976 constitution states that the republican nature of the state cannot be altered and that the state religion is Islam. It reaffirms the socialist system and the territorial integrity of the country and guarantees freedom of expression and assembly. The document also reaffirms state control of the means of production, land reforms, free medical care, worker participation in industry, and campaigns against corruption and nepotism. It guarantees that so-called nonexploitative private property of artisans, small farmers, and traders who derive their income from their own work will be respected. The constitution also guarantees the "liberation of women and their full participation in the political, economic, social and cultural life of the nation."

Executive powers are vested in the president of the republic, who is elected for a six-year term by direct, adult suffrage and can be reelected for an unlimited number of terms. While the day-to-day administration of government is the responsibility of the council of ministers, the president is empowered to enact laws by decree when the legislature is not in session. A new institution provided for by the constitution is the High Council of Security, charged with advising the president on all questions affecting national security.

The unicameral legislature is entitled the National Popular Assembly, or APN, and its members are elected by secret, direct, and universal suffrage under the banner of the FLN for a period of five years. On 24 February 1977, the first legislative elections in well over a decade took place, with 783 FLN-sponsored candidates vying for the 261 available parliamentary seats. It is still too early to determine whether the new APN will be permitted to act as a forum for serious political debate or whether it will simply serve as the regime's bureaucratic rubber stamp. There are also regional legislatures called *wilaya* popular assemblies, and on the local level there are communal popular assemblies. Both are primarily administrative in nature and have little independent authority.

The judicial system in Algeria is in the process of transition from the French legal system. All civil, criminal, public, and family laws remaining from the preindependence era are being reviewed by the national commission of legislation. The supreme court has been retained under the revised system as the highest judicial authority. A state security court has been created to try individuals for crimes against the state. In addition, a series of tribunals for economic crimes has also been established. Finally, the code dealing with family and personal status continues to be based on Muslim law but is administered by the civil courts.

Political Dynamics

Algerian political dynamics in the postindependence period have been dominated by a small civil-military oligarchy, with very little participation by the masses. However, the regime's policy of deliberate institutionalization and mobilization, begun in earnest in 1976–1977, may foreshadow some political liberalization through revitalized national, regional, and local assemblies and of the national party (the FLN). Effective power can be expected to remain concentrated in the hands of a technocratic elite whose claim to authority is based on the modern skills that they possess and for which there is a high value in the society.

Algeria's technocratic system consists of three major units—the military, the party, and the administrator-technocrats. While they have very different internal characteristics, they are united in an overriding new allegiance to the state and its developmental objectives. Most of them share a common background in the National Liberation Army and its experience in the revolutionary war. Boumedienne depended on this triumvirate to maintain and aggrandize power as well as to erect his socialist state using the crucial technical skills that this group possesses. For nearly a decade, however, these elements were unevenly aligned, with the FLN reduced to a minor, functionary role, in contrast to the military and the administrative elite. If the language of the National Charter and 1976 constitution is a guide and the new parliament is to be taken seriously, then an apparent balancing of forces may be occurring that is to the relative advantage of the hitherto much maligned and often ignored party.

With the ALN firmly in control, the military remains the most decisive force in Algerian politics. The army's claim to privileged status is not limited to the obvious fact that it monopolizes the nation's coercive instruments of force. Nor is it based entirely on the fact that Boumedienne was the wartime chief of staff and later defense minister who provided the critical support that brought Ben Bella to power and later engineered his overthrow in a military coup. Equally important has been the fact that the military continues to possess a revolutionary mystique; that it was instrumental in establishing law and order from the chaos that followed independence; that it possesses the special skills of organization and management that have enabled society to stabilize and develop; that it has become directly involved in local rural affairs, thus gaining popular support at the mass level; and that, finally, it has continued to adhere firmly to the notion that it alone is the guardian of the revolution. In fact, the military has so far played a guardian role, directly involving itself in politics only when the situation required, as it did in 1962 and 1965.

In addition to its explicitly military functions, the army is also heavily involved in a variety of civic-action and educational projects. It is thus directly involved in the state-building process, which further enhances its already wide appeal among the rural masses. Its representation in all elite political institutions, including the council of ministers, the national assembly, and FLN, permits the military to monitor all political activities directly. Finally, the qualitative and quantitative improvement in manpower and equipment since the 1967 Arab-Israeli War, when Soviet military assistance and training accelerated noticeably, has made Algeria a power in regional Arab and North African affairs, and has further increased its domestic standing among elites and masses alike.

The administrative elite constitutes a second important component of the Algerian political system. In fact, with the increasing industrialization and complexity of Algerian society, the administrative elite may eventually replace the military as the paramount voice in policymaking.

This category includes the civil service, whose activities extend beyond the actual administration of the country into the substantive functions of various other ministries and their local networks, as well as a more narrowly defined new class of technocrats who have the authority and responsibility for the planning, development, operation and expansion of the nation's industrial complex, particularly petrochemicals. The largest and most prestigious of all the state-owned industries is SONATRACH, the huge Algerian state petroleum combine.

The administrative elite has expanded so rapidly since the Boume-dienne takeover that it has tended to divide into component groups. In fact, ever since the technocratic revolution began in the late 1960s, bu-reaucratic politics within the ministerial and presidential councils have been conducted primarily among the competing administrators. This ad-minstrative group constitutes an important subelite within the larger rul-ing elite and has been the most noticeable recipient of new class status, including conspicuous wealth and other tangible signs of social advan-tage. Furthermore, unlike the military and the party elites, the adminis-trators manage programs that exert a major influence on the country's development and its political dynamics.

While the role of the FLN in achieving national independence was a decisive one, the party was not able to maintain its power and prestige after independence. Factionalism that had been suppressed in the name of national unity during the revolution quickly reappeared as the party leaders vied with one another for positions of power. The quality of FLN leadership at the local level declined and individual party officials in many cases seemed more intent on personal advancement than in building up the party as an effective peacetime organization. Conse-quently, the influence and role of the FLN has been negligible.

Despite its shortcomings, the party remains the predominant institu-tional medium for the expression of popular will. Moreover, its subordi-nation to the military and administrative elites may soon end if its role as described in the National Charter and constitution is in any way taken seriously. For example, Part 2 of the charter devotes a lengthy section to the avant-garde nature of the party, which is to become the ideological vanguard of the socialist revolution. Moreover, political participation at any level of political organization requires FLN membership. This re-flects Boumedienne's desire to create a viable national political organiza-tion that will permit popular participation in the political life of the state, thereby maintaining the populist quality of his regime. The success of his efforts to revitalize the party, however, is far from assured.

Various other national organizations remain subordinate to the FLN: the workers union (UGTA), the farmers organization (UNPA), the Youth Association (UNJA), the organization of former resistance fighters (ONM), and the women's association (UNFA). None have any signifi-cant power or authority. The student union is the only group that has sought to challenge centralized authority and assert its own view; and it was finally suppressed in the 1970s after a series of student boycotts, strikes, and demonstrations. It has not been revived and is conspicuously absent from the list of national organizations included in the party sec-tion of the National Charter.

Foreign Policy

Algerian foreign policy has been strongly influenced by the revolutionary experience of the nearly eight-year war of independence. The revolution left a legacy of emotional extremism, verbal excess, and diplomatic abrasiveness in the conduct of foreign affairs. To these have been added the Algerian predisposition to suspicion, which is inherent in the political culture and nurtured by a clandestine guerrilla life and the internal rivalries of postindependence politics.

Despite the country's modest natural and human resources and limited military capabilities by global standards, Algeria sees itself playing a major role in world politics. In geopolitical terms the country's leaders have described Algeria as the core state of the Maghrib, on the borders of the Mediterranean, with a dual attachment to the African and Arab worlds and, thus, ideally located at the crossroads of three continents. Using its position as a major petroleum producer, Algeria has also taken a leading role in the so-called north-south dialogue betwen the major Western industrialized countries and the developing countries of the Third World. Algerian nationalization of its own petroleum industry and the policies it has been able to pursue as a member of the Organization of Petroleum Exporting Countries (OPEC) are the most important ways in which Algeria has sought to be an exemplar to the rest of the Third World.

Emotionally and ideologically, Algeria's revolutionary heritage has brought it into a kind of spiritual communion with those nations that had similar experiences, notably Yugoslavia, Cuba, and Viet Nam. One practical consequence of this revolutionary ardor has been the emergence of Algiers as a center for any number of Black African liberation movements, and even of fringe revolutionary groups in Latin America, the Middle East, and other parts of the world, although in recent years it has tended to discourage revolutionary "renegades" such as America's Black Panther party from establishing a political presence in the capital.

Boumedienne, unlike his predecessor, somewhat reduced the verbal encouragement for violent revolutionary activities especially when these may have jeopardized advantageous economic relationships. Yet, given the Arab-oriented background of the Algerian president and the mythology of the success of the revolution—a mythology continually being shaped into a central pillar of the new national tradition, certain predominant principles of foreign policy have remained throughout the postindependence period. These principles are: nonalignment in the global struggle between the USSR and the United States, identification with the Third World, promotion of revolutionary independence movements and wars of national liberation directed against colonialism and imperialism, advocacy of African and Arab unity, and unswerving support of the Palestinians in their struggle against Israel and Zionism.

Such an orientation—although more radical in words than deeds—has brought Algeria into conflict with its ideologically different neighbors. Its geopolitical competition with Morocco, especially, has led to serious disagreements involving direct armed conflict in 1963 and indirect military engagement through the Algerian-supported Saharan independence movement (the Polisario Front) since 1975. Even after the settlement of the dispute in the former Spanish Sahara, serious disagreement will remain, given the fundamental dissonance in attitude, style, and ultimate objectives of the two countries.

Relations with Tunisia are somewhat better. Territorial disputes between the two countries have been resolved in favor of Algeria and its petroleum and gas interests. Tunisia's espousal of Western values and its particularly close relations with France and the United States make it ultimately suspect by Algerian decision makers.

A paradoxical feature of Algerian foreign policy is that, despite its revolutionary rhetoric, austere manner, and radical posturing, Algeria maintains direct and continuing contacts with a wide variety of different regimes. Algeria's wide range of contacts qualifies it as one of the few countries in the Third World to advocate and successfully maintain an independent position in international affairs. For example, it has been able to sustain a close military assistance relationship with the Soviet Union, while simultaneously developing an extensive economic relationship with the United States. In fact, in 1976 the United States became Algeria's main trading partner, supplanting France.

Despite the legacy of bitterness engendered by the revolution, Algeria still maintains close bilateral relations with France, reinforced by economic, cultural, and trading ties. At the same time, Algeria is highly sensitive to any suggestion that its independence is being undermined by its relations with France or any other power. Moreover, foreign policy rhetoric is never allowed to interfere with foreign trade dealings and international business transactions, which Algeria conducts in a highly businesslike and efficient manner, all seemingly designed to enable others to understand that its commerce and its foreign policy rhetoric are distinct matters.

Bibliography

Probably the most comprehensive analysis of the complexities and dynamics of the Algerian revolutionary war fought against France from 1954 to 1962 is that of Alistair Horne, *A Savage War of Peace: Algeria, 1954–1962* (New York: Penguin

Books, 1979). Paul Henissart, *Wolves in the City* (London: Rupert Hart-Davis, 1971) is a fascinating and chilling account of the last destructive, anarchic days of French colonial rule in Algeria. Martha Crenshaw Hutchinson, *Revolutionary Terrorism: The FLN in Algeria, 1954-1962* (Stanford, Calif.: Hoover Institution Press, 1978) formulates an analytical model of terrorism that she then applies to the case of the war-time FLN. More standard accounts of that bloody struggle for independence include Edward Behr, *The Algerian Problem* (London: Hodder and Stoughton, 1961), Michael K. Clark, *Algeria in Turmoil* (New York: Grosset & Dunlap, 1960), Richard M. Brace and Joan Brace, *Algerian Voices* (Princeton, N.J.: D. Van Nostrand, 1965), Richard M. Brace and Joan Brace, *Ordeal in Algeria* (New York: D. Van Nostrand, 1960), Joan Gillespie, *Algeria* (New York: Frederick A. Praeger Publishers, 1960), David Gordon, *The Passing of French Algeria* (New York: Oxford University Press, 1966), and Alf Andrew Heggoy, *Insurgency and Counterinsurgency in Algeria* (Bloomington: Indiana University Press, 1972). Brief analyses of the Algerian Revolution are included in Eric R. Wolf, *Peasant Wars of the Twentieth Century* (New York: Harper and Row, 1969) and John Dunn, *Modern Revolutions* (Cambridge: Cambridge University Press, 1972). Frantz Fanon, *The Wretched of the Earth* (New York: Grove Press, 1963) and Frantz Fanon, *A Dying Colonialism* (New York: Grove Press, 1967) provide philosophical and highly ideological insights into the origins, causes, and consequences of the revolutionary war and its impact on native and colonialist alike. Fanon's credo on the need for the violent transformation of man, state, and society remains a central theme in the writings of many Third World revolutionary leaders. The impact of the Algerian war on French society and politics is competently treated by Tony Smith, *The French Stake in Algeria, 1945-1962* (Ithaca, N.Y.: Cornell University Press, 1978).

Pierre Bourdieu, *The Algerians* (Boston: Beacon Press, 1962) provides an outstanding socioanthropological insight into the colonialist system and the destructive effect it had on Algerian man and society. Thomas L. Blair, *The Land to Those Who Work It: Algeria's Experiment in Workers' Management* (Garden City, N.Y.: Anchor Books-Doubleday, 1970), Ian Clegg, *Workers' Self-Management in Algeria* (New York: Monthly Review Press, 1971), and Marnia Lazreg, *The Emergence of Classes in Algeria: Colonialism and Socio-Political Change* (Boulder, Colo.: Westview Press, 1976) focus on specific socioeconomic themes and issue areas. Sid-Ahmed Baghli, *Aspects of Cultural Policy in Algeria* (Paris: UNESCO, 1977) devotes his study to cultural policy in the Boumedienne period.

Although over a decade old, William B. Quandt, *Revolution and Political Leadership: Algeria, 1954-1968* (Cambridge, Mass.: M.I.T. Press, 1969) remains the most authoritative study of Algerian political development at the elite level. The critical roles being played by military and other elites in independent Algeria are comprehensively analyzed by I. William Zartman, "The Algerian Army in Politics," in Claude E. Welch, Jr., ed., *Soldier and State in Africa* (Evanston, Ill.: Northwestern University Press, 1970) and I. William Zartman, "Algeria: A Post-Revolutionary Elite," in Frank Tachau, ed., *Political Elites and Political Development in the Middle East* (New York: Schenkman, 1975). David Ottaway and Marina Ottaway, *Algeria: The Politics of a Socialist Revolution* (Berkeley:

University of California Press, 1970) and Jean Leca, "Algerian Socialism: Nationalism, Industrialization, and State-Building," in Helen Desfosses and Jacques Levesque, eds., *Socialism in the Third World* (New York: Praeger Publishers, 1975) describe and evaluate Algeria's socialist experiment. Arslan Humbaraci, *Algeria: A Revolution that Failed—A Political History Since 1954* (New York: Frederick A. Praeger Publishers, 1966) provides an informative although at times biased general political history of the country since the early 1950s.

The best reference work on Algeria is the *Area Handbook for Algeria* (Washington, D.C.: U.S. Government Printing Office, 1972).

20

Republic of Tunisia

John P. Entelis

Historical Background

The French colonial experience in Tunisia, while not benign, was nonetheless free from the social disruption that occurred in neighboring Algeria. Indeed, Tunisian society remained relatively immune to French colonial practices. If anything, traditional social and political institutions were supported and strengthened under the French protectorate imposed on the country in the Treaty of Kassar Said, also known as the Treaty of Bardo, signed on 12 May 1881. Under its terms, the bey of Tunis agreed to the "voluntary limitation" of the external sovereignty of Tunisia for a "temporary but indefinite period." France was empowered to act in a sovereign manner in all external Tunisian affairs and in matters relating to the defense of the country. In 1883, under the terms of the Treaty of La Marsa, another one-sided treaty arrangement, the French gained control over Tunisia's domestic affairs. Although the traditional hierarchy of the bey's government was preserved, a separate parallel French administration was established that quickly acquired all effective control in the state. The bey was reduced to a figurehead and all real power passed to the French Resident General.

Although there was no large-scale colonialization as in Algeria, the French administration placed the European settlers' interests first and subjected Tunisia to so-called reforms that were clearly not in the interest of the Muslim population. As land was bought by settlers, the dispossessed rural Muslim population sank into a destitution similar to that experienced by its Algerian counterpart. Though, in theory, administrative offices were open to both Tunisian and European civil servants, all the major posts were occupied solely by the French until after World War I.

However, the French colonial experience in Tunisia was moderately positive. This is explained in great part by the process of modernization that was begun prior to the French arrival. The local government of the Ottoman bey was already modernized and reinvigorated by a reform-minded prime minister, local government was relatively ordered and effective, and the foundations of a modern educational system were already being laid, as exemplified by the Sadiqi College. The French were thus able to rule by discreet and indirect means. French military presence, so pronounced in Algeria and Morocco, was virtually absent in Tunisia. Even the French settler population, which never numbered more than 7 percent of the total Tunisian population, had a limited economic and commercial penetration of the country. For example, the fertile and commercially prosperous area of the Sahel along the central eastern coast of the country was largely left to the Tunisians.

Furthermore, despite certain qualitative limitations, the French-instituted bilingual system of Arabic and French language instruction, which was discouraged in Algeria and never really developed in the brief protectorate period in Morocco, enabled Tunisia's educated elite to learn bilingual cultural and language skills, reinforced by university training in France. These skills were used to great advantage in the nationalist struggle for independence and the subsequent modernization of the country.

Tunisia was the first of the three North African countries to be influenced by modern nationalism. In 1905 the Young Tunisian movement was established by members of the young Europeanized professional middle class of Tunis. Borrowing from the Young Turk movement of the decaying Ottoman Empire, the Young Tunisians represented the reformist and liberal aspirations of the first generation of North African nationalists. The demands they made were for better education, a combination of French and Arabic cultures, and access to government by Tunisians. While the emphasis they placed on Arabic and French cultures varied, they all focused on both to some extent. The Young Tunisians commanded neither national support nor mass following, however, and their demands were framed within the limits of the protectorate that they sought to modify but not to overthrow.

The achievement of at least nominal independence in eastern Arab countries after World War I and the example of the nationalist movement in Egypt inspired Tunisians with a greater national consciousness. In February 1920, a new party called the Liberal Constitutional party was organized, more popularly known by the Arabic word for constitution, the Destour. The party's founder, Shaykh al-Thaalibi, was one of the founders of the prewar Young Tunisians. The rise of the Destour marked a new moment in Tunisian nationalism, that of traditionalistic anticolonialism. The party was essentially comprised of middle-class urbanites. As a bourgeois pressure group, it lacked the force of a mass

Tunisia

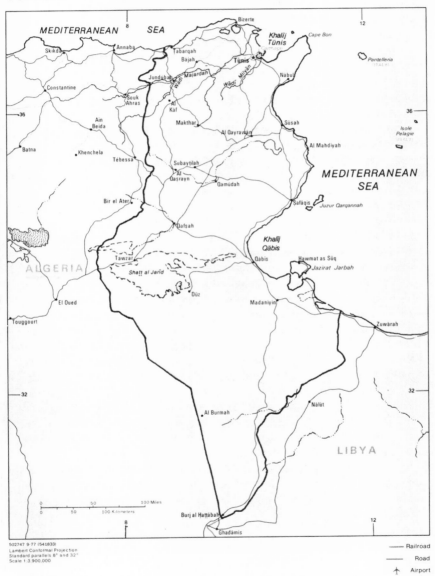

MEDITERRANEAN SEA

Skikda
Annaba
Constantine
Souk Ahras
Ain Beida
Batna
Khenchela
Tébessa
Bir el Ater
Tawzar
El Oued
Touggourt

ALGERIA

Shaṭṭ al Jarīd

Bizerte
Khalīj Tūnis
Cape Bon
Tabarqah
Bajah
Tūnis
Jundubah
Wādī Majardah
Nābul
Al Kāf
Makthar
Al Qayrawān
Sūsah
Al Mahdiyah
Subaytilah
Al Qaṣrayn
Qamūdah
Ṣafāqis
Qafsah
Juzur Qarqannah
Khalīj Qābis
Qābis
Hawmat as Sūq
Jazīrat Jarbah
Dūz
Madanīyīn
Zuwārah

MEDITERRANEAN SEA

Pantelleria (ITALY)
Isole Pelagie (ITALY)

LIBYA

Al Burmah
Nālūt
Burj al Haṭṭābah
Ghadāmis

100 Miles
100 Kilometers

502747 9-77 (541833)
Lambert Conformal Projection
Standard parallels 8° and 32°
Scale 1:3,900,000

—— Railroad
—— Road
✈ Airport

party in its efforts to gain various reforms. However, because the party was the obvious channel of protest, it recruited young men who, in the next decade, took over the nationalist movement. In March 1934, they broke away from the Neo-Destour party.

The principal force behind the new party's creation was a thirty-one-year-old French-educated lawyer, Habib Bourguiba, who eventually led Tunisia to independence and, in the process, earned the label "father of his country." In his socioeconomic background, education, and professional training, Habib Bourguiba exemplified the entire Neo-Destour leadership.

Bourguiba was born in 1903 at Monastir in the Sahel of middle-class parents, and was educated as as lawyer at the Sorbonne. Like many of his generation who were trained in French universities in the twenties, he adopted a populist mode of nationalist consciousness. Bourguiba and his contemporaries inherited a strong faith in liberal France and in its economic and cultural innovations from the Young Tunisians, and from the old Destour they stole the banner of anticolonialism. What they reacted against was not the actual French presence, but rather the relationship of subordination it implied.

Unlike the old Destour, the Neo-Destourians were secular nationalists who were not averse to using religion as a political weapon occasionally. They also turned to the masses throughout the country for support. The Neo-Destour was committed to nationalist independence as well as to the modernization of the country via extensive grass-roots organization and political education and mobilization. The party's efforts were unchallenged by other nationalist groups and occasional French attempts at repression, exile of leaders, and other paralegal means of suppression failed to impede their efforts.

The nationalist movement did not resort to violence in Tunisia until 1954, when groups of guerrillas, or *fellaghas*, began to operate in the countryside, thereby paralyzing nearly seventy thousand French troops. With its hands full in Algeria, Morocco, and Indochina, the French government under the premiership of Pierre Mendès-France finally offered full internal autonomy to Tunisia in June 1955. Less than a year later, on 20 March 1956, Tunisian independence was formally declared.

Postindependence politics in Tunisia have been dominated by two overwhelming forces: the charisma and popular appeal of Habib Bourguiba, the country's only president in twenty-three years of independence, and second, the political supremacy of the Destourian Socialist party (PSD) over all other national organizations and governmental institutions. Despite his regime's increasingly authoritarian cast in recent years, the "Supreme Warrior" has provided national unity and political stability in a country threatened by poverty, military weakness, social, regional, ideological cleavages, and the aftereffects of more than seventy years of French colonial rule. Indeed it is not an exaggeration to credit Bourguiba's authoritarian presence and manipulative skills with the evolution of Tunisia into a relatively stable, effective, and developed polity.

There are five distinct historical phases in postindependence Tunisia. The first period, 1955–1959, saw Bourguiba overcome internal challenges and consolidate his position. On 3 June 1955, he signed a convention with France proclaiming Tunisia's internal autonomy. The secretary general of the party, Salah Ben Youssef, denounced the autonomy convention with France as a "step backward," and openly attacked Bourguiba. Instead, Ben Youssef called for immediate Tunisian independence within the framework of pan-Arabism. Toward this end he had the popular support of strongly religious and conservative groups as well as urban elements that sympathized with his espousal of a radical Arab nationalism drawing ideological inspiration from Nasserism in Egypt. Bourguiba, on the other hand, represented moderation, an attachment to specifically Tunisian (as opposed to broader Arab-Islamic) virtues and possibilities; moreover, he had the support of educated, Gallicized, Western-trained elites from the Sahel and Tunis.

In the bitter and personal confrontation that took place between these two charismatic leaders, Bourguiba prevailed because of the overwhelming support of the party and the crucial backing of the trade union movement, headed by Bourguiba's ally, Ahmed Ben Salah. Ben Youssef organized a guerrilla insurrection in the south, but this was quashed with the help of French troops. He then fled to Libya in 1956, and was later assassinated in 1961 in Frankfurt, Germany. His opposition to Bourguiba, which was related to radical pan-Arabism, Islamic beliefs and practices, socialism and anti-Westernism, constituted the most severe direct political and military domestic challenge that confronted Bourguiba and the Neo-Destour. More important perhaps was the fact that Youssefism and its challenge to Bourguiba's rule had far-reaching effects on the future course of the regime and permanently shifted it to authoritarian ground, thereby fixing the style of Bourguiba's power.

The termination of the Ben Youssef challenge and the granting of political independence in March 1956 did not completely eliminate internal differences. A conflict between Bourguiba and his former supporter, Ben Salah, subsequently emerged. Essentially Bourguiba's political objectives were to unify the party on the broadest possible base, to secure a virtual monopoly for it, and to avoid risking national unity or foreign investment by radical economic change. Ben Salah, on the other hand, envisioned the General Union of Tunisian Workers (UGTT) as the national instrument for social and economic revolution. He also spoke of the nationalization of all resources and proclaimed the need for a socialist plan for development. Ben Salah was removed as head of the union and replaced by Ahmed Tlili, who shared Bourguiba's vision of a liberal, reformist system of social and economic change.

Thus, in the first years of autonomy and independence Bourguiba was able to establish his supremacy not only in the party but also in the formal machinery of the state. In April 1956, he became prime minister leading a government in which sixteen of the seventeen ministers belonged to the Neo-Destour. In July of the following year, Bourguiba became head of state, as well, when the government's first official act unanimously abolished the powerless and unpopular monarchy of the bey, Muhammad al-Amin, and proclaimed Tunisia a republic.

A new constitution, promulgated in June 1959, established Tunisia as an Islamic republic within the Greater Maghrib, with Arabic the official language. In confirming the paramount authority of the president, the constitution declared the government responsible to the president rather than the legislature. In the strong presidential system that emerged, Bourguiba simply replaced the traditional bey as chief of state while at the same time remaining at the head of an effective political party. It is significant that the most important and striking reform legislation enacted during the entire independent period came through presidential decree and was passed without legislative review in the period between 1956 and 1959.

On 8 November 1959, Tunisia held its first elections under the new constitution. President Bourguiba ran unopposed, and all ninety National Assembly candidates were backed by the Neo-Destour. Thus, by 1959, Bourguiba and his Neo-Destour party had placed their indelible imprint on the Tunisian political system.

The second period, 1960–1964, was highlighted by a series of internal and external crises and by the regime's gradual shift from reliance on the private sector to reliance on the public sector as the vanguard of economic development and modernization. In July 1961, fighting broke out between Tunisian and French troops over the Tunisian demand for French evacuation of the large naval base in Tunisia. After nearly two years, the French departed in March 1963. The confrontation enhanced the prestige and popularity of Bourguiba in the eyes of his own people and the world community. Nonetheless, an abortive assassination plot against Bourguiba was discovered in December 1962. Several junior army officers, including former officers in the bey's forces, a member of the presidential guard, and a former commander of the armored forces, were arrested, convicted, and executed. The Communist party was banned. Relations with newly independent Algeria were also strained as a result of charges that the newly independent country had aided Youssefists in the coup attempt.

In the economic realm, Bourguiba's policies seemed noticeably inadequate. In fact, the policies pursued in the first half-decade of independence proved unsuccessful either in attracting significant private investment or preventing a serious decline in the economy. As a result, the government turned to state planning in order to encourage economic growth, to break up the rigidities of social stratification, to equalize opportunities, and to increase social mobility. Toward this end, in May 1964 the Tunisian National Assembly enacted legislation authorizing the expropriation of all foreign-owned lands, mostly French.

The nationalization legislation also signaled a new political commitment to socialism. In October 1964 the Neo-Destour party officially changed its name to the Destourian Socialist Party (PSD) in order to emphasize the party's commitment to socialism. A month later, Bourguiba was again elected—unopposed. The PSD, the only party to present candidates, won all the seats in the National Assembly.

During the 1964–1969 period, the chief issues dominating internal politics was the effort to collectivize agriculture. Agrarian policy was enacted by the minister of finance and planning, Ahmed Ben Salah, who had returned to government in 1961 after a five-year absence. Ben Salah, fully backed by Bourguiba and the party, formulated an ambitious ten-year plan of economic development and reform almost completely based on state control and initiative in industry and agriculture. The core of Ben Salah's scheme was a system of agricultural cooperatives that were to be developed primarily on the large nationalized French estates in the north of the country but were also to involve the Tunisian small landholders as well.

Ben Salah's cooperative scheme was seen as a threat by the larger Tunisian landowners. Since many of them wielded considerable influence in Tunis and the government, opposition to Ben Salah became more directly political. His mismanagement also became an issue as large subsidies were required for an increasingly unproductive agriculture. In September 1969, he was shifted to the ministry of education and his agricultural plans abandoned. He was later arrested, and in May 1970 was sentenced to ten years of hard labor on assorted charges of financial mismanagement and other abuses and irregularities. He escaped to Europe in February 1973 and remains a critic of the regime. More importantly, the socialist orientation he had introduced to the nation's socialistic economic policymaking was abandoned.

The Ben Salah affair and the radical socialist objectives associated with it represented the second most serious challenge that Bourguiba had faced. Bourguiba was indirectly implicated because of the political support and the warm personal encouragement he had given to Ben Salah earlier. Consequently, the president's prestige and popularity suffered from Ben Salah's ouster; this was offset only by public sympathy for Bourguiba's chronic illness and weakened physical state that required prolonged absences abroad for medical treatment. The president's control of the party and government, however, remained unchallenged as reflected by the November 1969 presidential and National Assembly elections.

The period of the early seventies (1970–1974) witnessed a brief reemergence of liberalism as Bourguiba sought to reestablish his public support and stabilize the country's economic and political systems. Several former high government officials were reappointed to important positions in the party and government. These included Ahmed Mestiri, the leader of a Tunis-based liberal faction; Habib Achour, who returned as head of the UGTT; Muhammad Masmoudi, who became minister of foreign affairs; and Bahi Ladgham, who served briefly as prime minister before being replaced by Bourguiba's close ally and a respected economist, Hedi Nouira.

The government's sensitivity to charges of excessive authoritarian tendencies was clearly demonstrated at the 1971 PSD Congress in Monastir. The regime's characteristic balance between authority and liberalism tipped toward liberalism and reconciliation at Monastir. Discussion was free and open, democratic in spirit and practice. Bourguiba, however, chose his own men for the key political positions in the party's political bureau, ignoring the general sentiment at the congress favoring increased liberalism and competitive politics.

Over the next three years, this experiment in liberalism was ended. The September 1974 PSD Congress was held to counter the tendencies of the previous one. The delegates unanimously acclaimed Bourguiba as party president for life and called for a constitutional amendment to make him president for life of the republic. It also established the system by which the president named the members of the party's political bureau. In December 1974 the new National Assembly voted by acclamation to permit Bourguiba to remain president for life "as an exceptional measure and in recognition of services rendered." The measure made the premier, Hedi Nouira at this time, the automatic successor in the event of the president's death or incapacity.

The years 1970–1974 witnessed the rise and rapid decline of a liberal spirit in Tunisian politics. The expectation that a two-party system would eventually emerge reflecting Tunisia's increasing political sophistication and development was rejected by Bourguiba and his party deputies. While basic political order had been maintained and popular support for the regime continued, power was exercised in an increasingly authoritarian manner, especially against students and other outspoken leftist critics of the regime.

The current period, which began in 1975, has seen increasing authoritarian tendencies in the political sphere and greater reliance on capitalist support in the form of accelerated foreign investments and encouragement of private enterprise domestically in the economic sector. Not only have opposition figures and dissident groups been effectively removed from the political process, but the PSD itself has virtually ceased to function as an effective political party. It is no longer a vehicle for accommodating the various factions and tendencies in the national political arena. Rather, it mainly functions to orchestrate the adulation of the leader.

Several currents of opposition have remained active in anticipation of a more flexible political situation in the post-Bourguiba period. The authoritarian nature of the regime has aroused a strong reaction among a relatively small but extremely vocal group of liberal politicians, leftist university students, intellectuals, and activist labor leaders. The primarily Paris-based Movement of Popular Unity (MUP), headed by the former socialist minister Ahmed Ben Salah, represents a diverse group of intellectuals and students. In March 1976 another group, headed by former Interior Minister Mestiri, issued a declaration condemning the one-party system as "no longer adapted to the needs and aspirations of the people" and espousing an organized opposition outside of the PSD. In June 1978, Mestiri's group formally requested the government's permission to establish a social-democratic party. Another critic of the regime is Habib Achour, former head of the labor movement. Until his ouster by the government in the wake of the January 1978 riots in Tunis, he had viewed the country's increasingly independent and active labor confederation as a springboard to power.

In addition, several figures within the current party hierarchy are jockeying for position in anticipation of Bourguiba's death. Meanwhile, Prime Minister Nouira, with Bourguiba's backing, has managed the day-to-day affairs of government since the early 1970s. Though he will probably automatically succeed to the presidency after Bourguiba's death, he appears to lack the charisma, prestige, and political capacity to maintain power.

The present period of political authoritarianism seems destined to continue at least until Bourguiba dies. At that time, the internal dynamics of the country could lead to a gradual liberalization, despite the efforts of those within the regime who argue that Tunisia cannot yet afford the luxury of Western-style political liberalism.

Political Environment

Culture and Ideology

The Bourguiba system has stressed cultural modernity, humanistic transformation, ideological change, and social adaptation according to a Gallicized model of progressive development and modernization. The ruling elite are conscious and proud of what they call Tunisia's Mediterranean heritage, which draws historical inspiration from Carthage and Rome as well as from Arab and European culture. More than their counterparts in Algeria and Morocco, the Tunisian elites deeply identify with the French language, culture, and civilization. Bourguiba has long placed emphasis on Mediterranean Islam and the Franco-Tunisian synthesis as the core from which Tunisia's predominant political culture is to evolve. Despite pressures from traditional elements and supporters of Arabization and Islamization, the dominant elite have continued to pursue a policy of biculturalism and bilingualism. In this way they hope to effect a cultural synthesis that is equally amenable to Arab and Western civilizations.

The dominant influence in the formation of Tunisian political values has been the Destourian Socialist party under the ideological direction of Habib Bourguiba. Three components of the PSD's political belief system directly influence the nature and direction of the modernization process. They are the party's concept of the nature of man, nation, and society, and of the interrelationship of these three in the context of developmental change.

The nature of man is summarized by Bourguiba as "humanistic liberalism," meaning a preoccupation and overwhelming concern with the "promotion of man," which the Tunisian leader regards as the "supreme end and fundamental value" of all political action. Elevating the individual's intellectual and material level should be the ultimate goal of all collective effort.

The relationship between people and modernization is an intimate one for Bourguiba. His objective is to make "a good citizen, capable of initiative, eager to learn and cooperate [so] that the battle against underdevelopment will be won." Hence, there is a need for a "psychological revolution" that will transform people and in the process restructure social and human relationships in a way that will make modernity possible.

In many respects, humanistic liberalism is not relevant to the sociopolitical exigencies of emerging nation states. This fact has contributed to discrepancies between the European ideal and the Arab reality and is particularly evident in the notion of "guided democracy" that constitutes an integral theme in reformist ideology. Given the need to introduce rapid social, economic, and political changes that often involve major social dislocations, it is not surprising that authoritarian political patterns have manifested themselves among the top elite of the PSD. However, the PSD's reformist ideology remains authentically humanistic, with a moral commitment to liberal concepts of democracy and freedom, despite the authoritarian nature of the regime.

The concept of nation in Destourian ideology is somewhat more complex. Tunisia possesses a distinct and historical national tradition. While the country has been conquered by foreign invaders throughout the centuries, it has nonetheless retained its individualism and identity. Despite some vestigial regionalism, Tunisia remains a geographically, ethnically, religiously, and linguistically homogeneous nation-state. Even in the tide of pan-Arabism that has swept the Arab world in this century, Tunisia's elite continue to espouse a local—rather than a regional—nationalism to a degree that distinguishes it from many other Arab states. Recognition and acceptance of local nationalism as the psychocultural core of the nation-state constitutes the second basic component of reformist ideology. Tunisia has a long and distinguished recorded history. The Neo-Destourian leadership shared a collective commitment to an autonomous, independent Tunisian state as a means of gratifying strongly felt psychocultural needs and of establishing the necessary political vehicle for modernizing Tunisia's traditional society. Because Tunisia already had a historical tradition of national consciousness, the process of adapting that consciousness to the country's political ideology was a rather easy one.

The existence of an aggressive pan-Arabist current also manifested itself in the strength of the Youssefist movement in the late 1950s. Determined to keep Tunisian nationalist ideology unencumbered by the overt influences of pan-Arabism, the Destourians emphasized the historical uniqueness of the Tunisian nationalist experience. The centrality of Tunisia in the Mediterranean world constitutes Bourguiba's historical rationalization of his country's cultural duality; hence the "crossroads" theory of history, which states that Tunisia lies at the crossroads of Europe, Africa, and the Arab world, is frequently invoked. Moreover, this juxtaposition has created a synthesis of traditional Tunisian national identity fortified by interaction with and assimilation of secular French civilization.

While the notion of a nationalist ideology based on Tunisia's Mediterranean heritage and the development of a Franco-Tunisian synthesis appeal to many of Tunisia's Westernized elite, the essentially traditional, Islamic masses have not fully accepted it. The public identifies more with Tunisia's Arabic and Islamic heritage than the intellectuals would concede. And even among many of the country's younger educated groups and nongoverning elites there is an increasing affinity to Islamic culture and tradition. More and more, this group appears to be seeking to reaffirm the universal qualities of Islam rather than to ignore, suppress, or amalgamate them within a European-oriented cultural matrix.

In recent years the ruling elite, conscious of the declining popularity of Western-inspired images and symbols among an Islamic-oriented population, has sought to invoke traditional religious symbols as a means of buttressing its rule. For the most part, the Bourguibist system has managed to integrate successfully the Arab-Muslim identity with a secular, although not necessarily Western, notion of Tunisian nationalism. Whatever else may happen to ideology and organization in post-Bourguiba Tunisia, a sense of secular nationalism with which all Tunisians identify—however much they may differ in its interpretation—seems certain to endure.

Likewise, the Destourian concept of society is an amalgam of traditional Arab-Islamic concepts and Western socialist thought that has been filtered through the experience of a colonial past. Destourianism is thus a pragmatic response to the needs of society, reflecting Bourguiba's desire for efficiency and adaptability to new conditions.

As has often been observed, developmental socialism is a reorientation of nationalism to meet the challenge of independence. Therefore, Destourian socialism is an attempt to rationalize Bourguibist ethical concern for humanistic liberalism and then to devise an ideological framework for development involving the rational use of human and natural resources, equitable distribution of wealth, industrial and agricultural growth, social justice, sectorial and regional development, and until 1969, the emphasis on cooperatives as the highest form of economic and social organization.

Destourianism's closest historical counterpart is probably Fabian socialism. The Bourguibist vision stresses socialism's pragmatic and utilitarian, rather than its doctrinaire, qualities. As Bourguiba himself has noted: "The Tunisian plan is socialist, if socialism means the formation of a society that works for the benefit of the majority and is based on an economy whose interest is the respect of man, ensuring balanced development that responds to his needs and possibilities within the framework of justice and equality."

According to the Destourian frame of reference, national citizenship (representing unity), is the critical form of social acceptance, and no other loyalties take precedence over loyalty to the state.

It is noteworthy that in his shift from liberalism to socialism in 1961 Bourguiba retained the coherence and continuity of his original ideology, with its human and nationalistic components. The dignity of man was reinterpreted to facilitate a great effort at production and an insistence on an equitable distribution of wealth, in order to ensure material conditions for moral and intellectual growth. The function of the state was simply one of coordinator, harmonizer, and regulator, for society itself should still generate its own decision-making centers so as to limit the powers of state control. Yet the individual and his personal desires remain subordinate to the interests of the nation at large.

The strategy and tactics employed by the ruling elite to translate the principles of Destourian socialism and humanistic liberalism into concrete policy have come to be known as Bourguibism. The hallmark of Bourguibism is its pragmatism, as revealed in Bourguiba's "policy of stages," which involves the objective appraisal of forces and problems and the realistic setting of objectives. Moreover, this is a policy in which strategy is geared to the realization of what is attainable now, and yet currently contributes to the achievement of long-range objectives. The essence of Bourguibism, with the exception of the disastrous Bizerte conflict in 1961, has been its reliance on methods of persuasion, rationality, and mutual self-interest to achieve desired ends.

The legitimization of Bourguibism in the international arena was easily transferred to the domestic sphere, where the adversaries were defined as underdevelopment, illiteracy, economic backwardness, mismanagement and corruption, and crass self-seeking individualism. Not unlike its manifestation in foreign affairs, Bourguibism's internal objective was to modernize traditional Tunisian society within the framework of stable, evolutionary, and rational planning. Internal Tunisian development required a gradual change in attitudes and behavioral norms to be achieved through education, party, propaganda, and most importantly, Bourguiba's oratory. The predominant role of pedagogy in the struggle to transform man and society is justified in the context of Destourianism's humanistic liberalism.

Until society is elevated to a state of social consciousness (at which time citizens would be permitted to enjoy the full benefits of democracy and individual liberty), a dedicated, competent, and enlightened elite must assume leadership and control of the state. Guided democracy is thus a critical component of Bourguibism. Civic education and encadrement become the means to cultivate good citizenship and, consequently, to achieve democracy. If neither works adequately then other forms of persuasion are invoked, including intimidation and discrimination. While ostensibly no one is forced to accept the dictates of Bourguibism, aspirants to elite status have no other path except violent opposition.

Economic Conditions

Tunisia's economic development strategy has undergone three distinct phases since independence. From 1956 to 1961 the government pursued a liberal economic, laissez-faire policy. However, the results of private investment and initiative were disappointing, largely because of the exodus of the resources Tunisia most needed—capital and skills—as the French departed.

In 1961 the Tunisian leadership, faced with a deteriorating economic situation, assigned Ben Salah the task of developing a planned economy, with strict controls assuring protected internal markets as well as fixed exchange rate and currency regulation. A ten-year developmental perspective (1962–1971) was then drafted, the objectives of which were to implement the objectives of Destourian socialism, especially its development component. The first three-year (1962–1965) and four-year (1966–1970) plans stated four broad objectives of economic and social development: (1) decolonization; (2) reform of economic structures, including industrialization; (3) human development, including education, the training of cadres, and the fight against illiteracy and unemployment; and (4) the generation of internal investment designed to lessen the dependence on foreign assistance. Most of Ben Salah's objectives were unrealistic since they required investment that was disproportionate to the real economic capability of the country.

The most distinctive feature of the Tunisian economic policies in the 1960s was the promotion and imposition of a system of cooperatives. It was intended that cooperatives should play an important political and social role in the development of the country. It was also expected that the system would provide the key to a range of economic problems and would effect a more efficient mobilization of the country's resources. Yet the socialist experiment was eventually discontinued in 1969, mainly because of economic mismanagement and widespread opposition to the agricultural cooperatives among the rural middle class.

Tunisia's experiment in economic socialism was replaced by the reestablishment of a liberal economic policy by Prime Minister Nouira. Nouira has emphasized the need for greater foreign private investment, primarily as a means of creating much-needed employment. An April 1972 law, for example, gave major fiscal advantages to foreign companies producing primarily for export, and a 1974 law gave similar incentives based on the number of jobs created. In its efforts to attract foreign enterprises, Tunisia has emphasized the availability of cheap labor and the relative absence of social conflict.

The program's critics assert that the liberal investment laws will be of marginal use to Tunisia's economic development. Thus far, the policy has generated little revenue for the government, little training and development of management expertise (because the law allows the free entry of alien staff), only marginal creation of local sources of capital (because profits are repatriated), and few employment opportunities for skilled or semiskilled workers (because most new jobs have been for unskilled labor, a category of people for which there is already an abundant supply of jobs). Furthermore, if carried to the extreme, the government's encouragement of foreign industry could create an indigenous proletariat in Tunisia, while the profits leave the country unchecked.

Yet, in the short run at least, the overall shift in economic policy has proved beneficial. The redress of the economic and financial situations enabled the country, in 1971, to attain a rate of growth slightly above 7 percent. Despite the fact that a greater degree of rationality in economic management has been introduced and the long-term prospects for economic growth seem relatively favorable, Tunisia continues to face several difficult economic conditions—substantial unemployment, a massive balance-of-payments deficit, and an increasing foreign-debt burden.

Political Structure

Tunisia's major political institutions—the presidency, the cabinet, the National Assembly, and the single political party, the PSD—all bear the unmistakable imprint of President Bourguiba, who is both head of government and head of the party. The president exercises great power. He is guardian of the constitution and has the authority to appoint his government, which is directly responsible to him. He drafts the general policy of the country and controls its execution. The president is also designated commander-in-chief of the armed forces and makes all military appointments. With the agreement of the National Assembly, the president also has the authority to ratify treaties, declare wars, and make peace.

The president's initiative to draft legislation has priority over that of National Assembly members. He also ratifies legislation and has the power of veto, subject to a two-thirds overriding majority that has never been invoked since the postindependence constitution and assembly have been in effect. According to the constitution, the president may convene special sessions of the parliament, issue orders in council when the assembly is in recess (constitutionally limited to six months of the year), and may take exceptional measures in times of crisis. Though presidential tenure was originally limited by the constitution to three five-year terms, a constitutional amendment passed by the National Assembly in December 1974 named Habib Bourguiba president for life.

In all his functions the president is assisted by a cabinet. The prime minister is appointed by the president and responsible only to him. Since 1970 Hedi Nouira, a long-time Destourian and close friend of the president, has held the premiership. In the event of death or incapacity of the president, the premier succeeds him until new presidential elections are held.

Legislative authority is constitutionally exercised by the people through the unicameral National Assembly, which has 112 members directly elected to five-year terms coinciding with the presidential term. By eliminating all candidates on minority lists in order to favor the majority list, the election rules deliver the assembly to the PSD alone. The party controls individual candidacies through its political bureau, which drafts the lists after consulting with the leaders of the national organizations.

The assembly must meet at least twice a year for sessions of not more than three months, but additional sessions may be called by the president or a majority of the assembly members. The president may dissolve the National Assembly in response to a vote of censure against him and request new elections but if the newly elected assembly confirms the vote of censure, he must resign.

Since independence there have been four elections for the National Assembly; all have been won by PSD candidates. Since the demise of the Communist party in December 1962, no organized political opposition has contested legislative elections. Therefore, the National Assembly has not commanded much respect or attention as a forum for serious political debate or as a source of meaningful legislation.

The Destourian Socialist party is Tunisia's only political party. The president is head of both the party and its top decision-making body, the political bureau. Party and government hierarchies are parallel, with extensive overlapping of personnel. In this symbiotic relationship, both bureaucracies have overlapping staffs, vaguely differentiated functions, and parallel structures. The president, as the head of this "party-government," has at his disposition a hierarchical party organization for mobilizing the nation and a political cabinet for deciding and implementing policy.

The PSD national congress, which meets at irregular intervals (four times since independence: 1959, 1964, 1971, and 1974), is the party body corresponding to the National Assembly and commands slightly more attention since it elects the party's central committee and reviews government and party policies. Yet, like the assembly and despite the apparent openness of the debates and procedures, the national congress follows the broad lines of Bourguiba's wishes.

In terms of local government Tunisia is divided into thirteen governorates, or provinces. Each province is headed by a presidentially appointed governor, who is assisted by either appointed government councils or elected municipal councils. The provinces are subdivided into delegations, communes, and *cheikhats*.

In general, Tunisia's formal party and governmental structures legitimize leaders and policies more than they function as effective mechanisms for representative participation in the political process.

Political Dynamics

The cult of personality that has long dominated Tunisian political life leaves uncertain the degree to which the "party-government" created by Bourguiba and his contemporaries will endure his passing. As we have seen, Tunisian ideology seems committed to a democratic, pluralistic sociopolitical order that Bourguiba has encouraged, indeed initiated, but for which no autonomous or effective institutional structures yet exist. The structures currently operative, including the National Assembly, the PSD and its political bureau and national congress, and the cabinet, are now mere appendages to Bourguiba's system of personal rule. They have been allowed little opportunity to demonstrate independent action or influence. Given the relatively sophisticated level of political awareness and experience extant among many of society's educated elites, both in and out of power, it would not be surprising, in the period following the president's demise, to see either a drastic change in the existing political institutions or the development of ones more representative of Tunisia's increasingly differentiated and pluralistic social order.

Bourguiba's extensive political skills have been effectively employed for more than two decades to establish and maintain Tunisia's strong presidential system. Assisting the leader have been two groups of ruling elites found in both party and government. The old guard is comprised of long-time associates of the president who participated in the preindependence struggle and who attained their positions through long years of party service. There is a second category of younger men brought into government by Bourguiba because of their specialized education, technical skills, and modernist outlook. Neither group has been allowed to achieve an independent base of power strong enough to challenge

Bourguiba's rule. Bourguiba has retained his preeminent role in the political process by deftly manipulating and controlling his political subordinates. Particularly effective has been the way dissidents have been removed from office, even forced into exile, but later rehabilitated and returned to positions of responsibility. Thus, there is an atmosphere of perpetual insecurity among the political elite as they struggle for presidential favor while never really knowing when their political fortunes may turn.

The most prominent recent case of revolving fortunes has been the case of Ahmed Ben Salah, who was dismissed from his position as head of the UGTT in 1956, brought back into government as minister of finance and planning, fired in 1969 after the failure of his cooperativist experiment, and later tried for treason and jailed. Similarly, trade unionist Habib Achour, former Foreign Minister Muhammad Mas̓-moudi, liberal leader Ahmed Mestiri, and former Interior Minister Tahar Belkhodja have been in and out of favor several times.

This system of political "musical chairs" has long been a trademark of Bourguiba's style. The Tunisian leader's ability to engineer these successive purges while maintaining his authority over both the government and the PSD can only be explained in terms of his own enormous charisma, his prestige as the father of his nation, his deftly developed skills as a political tactician, and the continuing availability of talented individuals who have managed the affairs of state and party in effective style.

The ensconcement of patrimonial leadership has been accomplished through the instrument of the PSD. As the ruling party in a strong single-party system, the PSD has come to represent political power itself. While broad and continuous consultation occurs at all levels, all important decisions within the party originate at higher levels and are transmitted down the party hierarchy to the branches. The latter enjoy considerable latitude in expressing local grievances, provided they are not of such a nature as to embarrass, compromise, or threaten the regime; but policy is not discussed at branch level—it is explained and received.

The process of consolidation and centralization of power within the party, despite brief periods of liberalization in 1964 and 1971, has been effective. The upper levels of the party hierarchy have been transformed into docile sounding boards for the government; the party's representative organs, such as the national congress and the national council, were hardly ever convened and, when they met, demonstrated little independence, meeting simply to express solidarity and approval, and the political bureau itself, supposedly constituting the party's executive decision-making body, was reduced under the impact of presidential government to a ceremonial role and, like other party organs, limited to advisory functions. The party's one important element of strength—which may indicate a greater role for the party in the post-Bourguiba period—lies in the fact that Bourguiba sometimes requires the party's corporate consent to a policy in order to legitimize that policy in the eyes of the party faithful. What Bourguiba has accomplished is the extensive concentration of power in his own hands, and the party as a political organization has consequently lost much of its popular support.

The most important role the party has historically played and continues to play today—however imperfectly and notwithstanding Bourguiba's aggrandizement of power—is that of legitimizing the Tunisian political system. It does this in symbolic and, to a lesser extent, substantive terms by providing a unifying national institution, a historical link with the recent preindependence past, a decision-making organ, and a forum for popular participation, however circumscribed.

The PSD's work is partially supplemented by the national organizations, the officially recognized professional bodies, and interest groups that lack an autonomous existence. Most of these groupings (representing businessmen and artisans, farmers, women, youth, and students) exist in part to facilitate communication from the government to interestgroups and, in part, to represent professional interests. They are all strictly subordinated to the PSD and none possess sufficient strength of organization to play an independent role in the system. The labor confederation, for example, after showing signs of independence in the midseventies, saw its leadership purged in the wake of its call for a general strike in January 1978 and has again been brought under party control. The national student organization, for its part, was once an important medium for the articulation of specific student interests and a valuable source for the recruitment of future party elites. The student association is no longer taken very seriously because its autonomy from the middle 1960s on has been virtually eliminated. Moreover, in the opinion of most students, it has become a mere pawn of the party and a neglected appendage to Bourguiba's system of personal rule.

Students probably constitute the regime's greatest sngle internal challenge. The system's increasing authoritarianism has disaffected many independent-minded university students who have responded with regular and intense demonstrations since the middle 1960s. Recent attitudinal surveys of selected student populations representing a cross section of ideological types seem to cast doubt on the previously assumed effectiveness of the Bourguibist socialization process. The studies have reflected mass disaffection with specific leaders and policies but, more fundamentally, with the elite political culture itself and its ethical and ideological underpinnings. The result is that the system's future is not ensured nor is its ideology confirmed among Tunisia's elites-to-be.

The regime's response to student agitation has been harsh and has catalyzed the support of previously apolitical or politically neutral students for leftist demonstrators and their causes. Many dissatisfied students and intellectuals support the Tunis-based Social Democrats and the more radical MUP led by Ben Salah from Paris.

None of these developments signal an imminent threat to the regime, even if one includes disgruntled elements of the traditional religious classes. The country's security forces remain loyal to the regime. Nonetheless, the legitimacy of the regime's leaders, institutions, and ideology may be seriously contested in the immediate post-Bourguiba period, thereby undermining judgments on the wisdom and political efficacy of current authoritarian policies being pursued by president and party.

Foreign Policy

Tunisian foreign policy has thus far been the creation of Habib Bourguiba, whose views on foreign affairs have been greatly influenced by his links to France. As a product of Western liberal thinking, Bourguiba has shunned radical and extremist policies. He has consistently assumed a moderate, pro-Western stance on East-West issues, generally remaining suspicious of the communist bloc and of those Afro-Arab leaders who have sought communist friendship in the form of military aid agreements and tacit military-political alliances.

Tunisia's basic foreign policy since independence has been to maintain its independence and to develop its resource-poor economy. During the Cold War, it was natural for Tunisia to turn to the United States as a countervailing force to the power of the Soviet bloc. When decolonization disputes during the sixties undermined Franco-Tunisian cooperation, the United States also became Tunisia's principal supplier of economic assistance.

Tunisia, however, has consistently demonstrated a close affinity to France, with whom it maintains extensive cultural, educational, and commercial ties. While the United States is perhaps regarded as the world's preeminent military power, Bourguiba and his generation of Gallicized elite consider France the most influential cultural, intellectual, and "spiritual" force. Economic and military ties between the two countries have increased since the mid-seventies.

Bourguiba's basic approach to foreign policy remains the cultivation of close ties with the United States as Tunisia's ultimate security guarantor (though U.S. economic assistance is much less significant now than it was during the sixties) while cultivating "privileged" economic, political, and cultural ties with France. These objectives have been achieved largely through a policy of moderation, pragmatism, and a sense of proportion. Yet Tunisia has sought to avoid compromising its nonaligned status. It continues to maintain proper diplomatic and economic relations with all the major states of the communist world and is a member in good standing of the Third World. The country's receipt of significant economic and technical aid from numerous international organiz-tions, petroleum-exporting Arab states, Soviet bloc countries, China, and most Western industrialized states reflects its general acceptance by the world community.

Tunisia's major foreign-policy problems have arisen from ideological, political, territorial, and economic disputes with its neighbors. Tunisia's pro-Western orientation has brought Tunisia into conflict with both Algeria and Libya. Its failure to implement the hastily announced January 1974 merger with Libya has strained relations between the two countries and led to Libyan economic retaliation, political subversion, and military threats. Tunisia stands in sharp ideological contrast to the puritanical, fundamentalist, and fervently Arabist Libya of Colonel Qaddafi. Given the profound differences in style, temperament, and political orientations, tensions will remain. Relations with Algeria, though less likely to develop into open hostility, will stay correct but cool, as long as Tunisia's foreign policy remains closely aligned with that of France.

Tunisia has worked to reestablish its credentials as a loyal member of the Arab community. During the sixties Bourguiba alienated most of Tunisia's Arab "brothers" by advocating the then unthinkable recognition of, and negotiations with, Israel. Aware of the strong emotional identification of Tunisia's population with the Arab cause, the Tunisian leadership has since then been careful to maintain its solidarity with the Arab world, primarily through consistent—though largely rhetorical— support of the Palestinians.

In conclusion, Tunisian foreign-policy goals have been modest, its techniques eminently practical and realistic, and its results undramatic, though very beneficial to the country in terms of economic assistance. Given Tunisia's small size, limited resources, and military vulnerability, Bourguiba has managed to establish a respectable position for Tunisia in world affairs. This, even more than his considerable accomplishments within the domestic sphere, will probably be Bourguiba's most lasting legacy.

Bibliography

Tunisia's colonialist experience is sensitively treated by a Jewish "native son," Albert Memmi, in *The Colonizer and the Colonized* (Boston: Beacon Press,

1967). Several works deal with Tunisia's political history from the precolonial period through independence, such as Charles F. Gallagher, "Tunisia," in Gwendolyn M. Carter, ed., *African One-Party States* (Ithaca, N.Y.: Cornell University Press, 1962), Wilfrid Knapp, *Tunisia* (London: Thames and Hudson, 1970), Leon Laitman, *Tunisia Today: Crisis in North Africa* (New York: Citadel Press, 1954), Dwight L. Ling, *Tunisia: From Protectorate to Republic* (Bloomington: Indiana University Press, 1967) and Nicola Ziadeh, *Origins of Nationalism in Tunisia* (Beirut: Khayat's, 1962).

As one of the few instances of evolutionary political development in the Third World, Tunisia has received its share of scholarly attention. Themes such as modernization, social change, and political development are intelligently treated by Douglas E. Ashford, *National Development and Local Reform: Political Participation in Morocco, Tunisia, and Pakistan* (Princeton, N.J.: Princeton University Press, 1967), Willard A. Beling, *Modernization and African Labor: A Tunisian Case Study* (New York: Frederick A. Praeger Publishers, 1965), L. Carl Brown, "The Tunisian Path to Modernization," in Menahem Milson, ed., *Society and Political Structure in the Arab World* (New York: Humanities Press, 1973), and Charles Micaud with Leon Carl Brown and Clement Henry Moore, *Tunisia: The Politics of Modernization* (New York: Frederick A. Praeger Publishers, 1964).

Prospects for political institutionalization with special reference to Tunisia's single-party system are the concern of Clement Henry Moore, *Tunisia Since Independence: The Dynamics of One-Party Government* (Berkeley and Los Angeles: University of California Press, 1965), Clement H. Moore: "Tunisia: The Prospects for Institutionalization," in Samuel P. Huntington and Clement H. Moore, eds., *Authoritarian Politics in Modern Society: The Dynamics of Established One-Party Systems* (New York: Basic Books, 1970), and Lars Rudebeck, *Party and People: A Study of Political Change in Tunisia* (New York: Praeger Publishers, 1969).

Sociological, cultural, and psychological studies of Tunisia may be found in Mark A. Tessler, "The Tunisians," in Mark A. Tessler, William M. O'Barr, and David H. Spain, eds., *Tradition and Identity in Changing Africa* (New York: Harper & Row, 1973), Russell Stone and John Simmons, eds., *Change in Tunisia: Essays in the Social Sciences* (Albany: State University of New York Press, 1976), and Rafik Said, *Cultural Policy in Tunisia* (Paris: UNESCO, 1970).

Area Handbook for the Republic of Tunisia (Washington, D.C.: U.S. Government Printing Office, 1970) provides adequate reference material for the country.

Index

Green March, 411–412
Green Mountain. *See* Jabal al-Akhdar
    highlands
Gulbenkian, Calouste, 121
Gulf Air, 143, 159
Gulf of Aden, 10
Gulf of Aqaba, 259
Gulf of Oman, 10, 12
Gulf Oil Company, 82, 135
Gurler, General, 58, 59

Habbash, George, 158, 194
Habubs, 16
Hadassah, 285
Hadith, 21
Hadi Yahya, 168
Hafid, Mulay, 391
Hafsids, 382, 383
Hagana, 274, 277
Haile Selassie, 205
Hajj, 21, 100
Hajjar Mountains, 12, 130, 158
Hakin al- (caliph), 208
Halaqah, 122
Hamah, 238
Hamdi, al-, Ibrahim, 172, 181, 183
Hamitic language group, 20–21
Hanafi school of jurisprudence, 22
Hanbali school of jurisprudence, 22, 90,
    100, 102
Harib, 195
Harir, Ismail, 235
Hasa, al-, 98
Hasani, al-, Ali Nasir Muhammad, 198,
    202–203
Hashid, 173, 183
Hashimite Kingdom of Jordan. *See*
    Jordan
Hashimites, 111, 113, 234
Hassan (brother of Hussein of Jordan),
    262
Hassan, Mulay, 391
Hassan II (king of Morocco), 396–397,
    398, 399–400, 401, 405, 412
Hatay. *See* Alexandretta
Hawalli, 139
Hawar Islands, 149
Hebrew (language), 17, 18
Helou, Charles, 223
Herzl, Theodor, 273

Hijaz, 89, 90, 92, 98, 100, 102
Hijaz Mountains, 12
Hinnawi, Sami, 245
Histadrut. *See* General Federation of
    Labor
Hodayda, 174, 175, 179, 198, 201
Hoggar massif. *See* Ahaggar massif
Holms, Frank, 100
Holy war. *See* Jihad
Homs, 238
Hormuz, 130
Hourani, Akram, 245, 246, 247
Hulagu Khan, 70, 108
Hunchaks, 239
Hungary, 180
Husayn (grandson of Muhammad), 90
Husayn (son of Ali), 107
Husayn, Sharif, 94, 95, 234
Hussein (king of Jordan), 258, 262, 264,
    265, 267–269

Ibn-Abdallah, Muhammad Ahmad, 340
Ibn Abdul Aziz, Nayif, 103
Ibn Abdul Aziz, Sultan, 103
Ibn Ali, Salih, 235
Ibn Anas, Malik, 22, 382
Ibn Hanbal, Ahmad, 22
Ibn Rashid, Muhammad, 93, 94
Ibn Saud, (king of Saudi Arabia), 89,
    93–95, 103, 104, 184
Ibn Taymiyyah, 90
Ibrahim, Abdallah, 395, 396, 399, 408
Ibrahim Pasha, 92
Idea Clubs, 46
IDF. *See* Israel Defense Forces
Idris I, 362, 367, 369–371, 375
Ijma', 424
Ikhwan, 94, 95
Illah, Abdul, 112
Imam, 22
Imperial Bank of Persia, 72
Imports. *See* individual countries,
    political environment of
Independence parties. *See* Istiqlal
    party (Iraq); (Jordan); (Morocco)
Independent Democrats (Iraq), 122
India, 22
Indian Ocean, 10, 12
Indo-European language group, 17, 20
INOC. *See* Iraq National Oil Company